The
BIG
STORE

The

BIG

STORE

Inside the Crisis and
Revolution at Sears

DONALD R.
KATZ

VIKING

VIKING
Viking Penguin Inc., 40 West 23rd Street,
New York, New York 10010, U.S.A.
Penguin Books Ltd, 27 Wrights Lane, London W8 5TZ
(Publishing & Editorial) and Harmondsworth, Middlesex,
England (Distribution & Warehouse)
Penguin Books Australia Ltd, Ringwood,
Victoria, Australia
Penguin Books Canada Limited, 2801 John Street,
Markham, Ontario, Canada L3R 1B4
Penguin Books (N.Z.) Ltd, 182–190 Wairau Road,
Auckland 10, New Zealand

First published in 1987 by Viking Penguin Inc.
Published simultaneously in Canada

Grateful acknowledgment is made for permission to reprint
excerpts from the following copyrighted material:
The Crow Indians by Robert H. Lowie. By permission of
Holt, Rinehart and Winston.
The Prince by Niccolo Machiavelli, translated by W. K. Marriott.
Everyman's Library edition published by J. M. Dent & Sons Ltd.
"The Truly Great" from *Collected Poems 1928–1985* by
Stephen Spender. Copyright 1934, renewed 1962 by Stephen Spender.
Reprinted by permission of Random House, Inc.
Authority and the Individual by Bertrand Russell.
By permission of Allen & Unwin.
"The Gambler" words and music by Don Schlitz.
Writers Night Music (ASCAP) copyright © 1978.
Photos not otherwise credited are courtesy Sears, Roebuck and Co.

LIBRARY OF CONGRESS CATALOGING IN PUBLICATION DATA
Katz, Donald R.
The big store.
Includes index.
1. Sears, Roebuck and Company.   I. Title.
HF5467.S4K38   1987   381'.45'000973   87–40060
ISBN 0–670–80512–2

Printed in the United States of America by
Haddon Craftsmen, Scranton, Pennsylvania
Set in Caledonia
Designed by the Sarabande Press

95793

To my father's generation,
but mostly in loving memory of him.

For all of a century Sears, Roebuck has resided within history's most advanced society of producers and consumers as a central warehouse for the culture. Each year, the current sum of American invention was collected and distributed as material portions of a national dream. Americans rocked in Sears cradles, played with Sears toys, wore the company's plain clothing, lined their homes with its ponderous furniture, learned to enjoy something called leisure by virtue of its time-saving machines, and were eventually buried in its coffins and remembered to eternity by offerings from its special tombstone catalog. Time and again surveys confirmed that Sears was the most trusted economic institution in the country. Even as it grew to become one of the seven or eight largest corporations in the world, Sears continued to command the sort of fealty normally reserved for nations and churches. It was a private enterprise ennobled and made powerful by its perceived dedication to a public purpose.

By 1972, as the Sears Tower began to rise high above Chicago, it seemed that a great number of the institutions and ideals that meant something in America had been severely injured. Patriotism, the military, organized religion, big business—all of them seemed to have been taken down a notch. But Sears remained unhumbled. The Tower rose up into the firmament like a great bar graph, a lasting monument to the invincibility and boundlessness and extreme profitability of a company that now accounted for fully 1 percent of the Gross National Product. Two of every three Americans shopped at Sears within any three months of 1972, and more than half the households in the country contained a Sears credit card. One-third of the families in America—some twenty-five million of them—owed the company an average of $256 for past purchases. There were now almost nine hundred big Sears retail stores, *over twenty-six hundred smaller retail and catalog outlets, and well over one hundred warehouses, catalog plants, and other distribution facilities. A single share of original Sears, Roebuck stock was now worth over $20,000, and because of a generous, half-century-old profit-sharing plan, individuals who worked among the half-million employees of the corporation as secretaries and elevator operators were able to retire with stock valued at upward of $500,000.*

But then, quite suddenly, Sears began to fall apart. Within five years the seemingly invulnerable company would appear so badly injured and so lacking in direction that it verged on paralysis. Corporate profits from retailing had either stagnated or declined each year since 1972. Interest expenses had fully doubled because of the monetary inflation since 1972, and the general cost of running the massive business had plainly run out of control. The Sears stock price, adjusted for an intervening split, had collapsed from a 1972 high of $61 per share to $24—and it was headed much lower. A spate of lawsuits, government investigations, and adverse publicity had shaken the company. Once-loyal customers had begun to stay away from Sears stores and to avoid the company's venerable catalog in such numbers that it appeared the American middle class, which Sears had decorated and lent physical definition over the years, had given up on the floundering company altogether.

Nobody at Sears was able to fathom what had happened, and nobody had any idea what to do. Nothing decided or decreed at the top of the empire of stores inspired direction or even activity at the bottom. For the first time in modern memory there were layoffs at Sears, and the élan that had characterized life inside the company since World War II had turned into despair and fear. An organization that only five years earlier had seemed utterly unstoppable was now a crippled leviathan, and by 1977 many of those who depended upon Sears, who studied it or loved it, had come to believe that if something was not done very quickly, the company was doomed.

This is the story of the crisis and revolution that followed.

Preface

├───────────────┤

M oments after he finally announced the name of his successor, I walked in on the chairman of the board of Sears, Roebuck as he faced the man who would lead the great company into its second century. The legendary chairman's desk, as always, was empty of work. There were no contracts visible, no mantles or crowns or bottles of champagne to be seen, nothing to mark the passage of power but the grip of their right hands.

The younger man said, "Thank you, sir."

The chairman turned away and looked down at the haze covering Lake Michigan, then turned back with a quick nod.

The heir to the chairmanship noticed me standing in the doorway. "Come pick me up tomorrow after lunch," he said. "We'll go out to the West Side and look for ghosts."

Lunch comes early at Sears, so it was just noon when we drove out from under the tallest building in the world and headed five miles west, toward the old Headquarters, a red brick complex so wide and long that the author of the early catalogs claimed it was "The Largest Commercial Building in the World." Seven thousand men came to the forty-acre tract of heartland prairie during the mild winter of 1905, and in just nine months of twenty-four-hour labor, they threw up the company's "great works," a place where for several generations goods representing the sum of American invention and know-how were collected and meted out as spare parts for the way people lived.

For sixty-seven years the old West Side plant served as the plexus of the world's greatest mail-order empire, and then the world's largest network of stores. Since the Headquarters was moved downtown, most of the old plant has remained abandoned. The company still maintains the ornamental gardens across the street from the entrance, just as the French attend to their memory of an old order at the gardens of Versailles.

As we pulled up to the old administration building and climbed out into the August heat, the next leader of the company waved his cigar toward a group of workmen at the edge of the complex who were dismantling Sears, Roebuck's first retail store. "That's where I first saw Santa Claus," he said. Then he looked back through the heat at the gray Sears Tower, the vertical company town where robots deliver the mail.

"O.K.," he said after a moment, turning back to the older buildings, "let's go inside."

I would like to begin this chronicle by thanking Ed Telling for allowing me to enter the private world of Sears, Roebuck, a thing he did against the well-intended advice of some of his close advisers and against much of the conventional wisdom, such as it resides in American corporate management circles.

I have tried to do here what I told the chairman of Sears I would do if he allowed it: to present a monumental business crisis and its resolution within a human context.

Amid the events described in this book, one company executive estimated that twenty million people worked directly for Sears or for a company that depended on the Sears supply line for its livelihood. I once mentioned to Telling that as a Chicagoan I had numerous relatives who'd been associated with Sears as suppliers, buyers, Allstate functionaries, and store employees.

"No big surprise there," Telling said. "One in thirty living Americans has worked for Sears."

At the time this story begins, it was a rare member of the middle or upper ranks of the company who had ever worked anywhere else as an adult. The goods-buying side of Sears, headquartered in Chicago, was fragmented into forty-nine quite discrete businesses possessed of a nearly complete operational autonomy and an umbilical relationship to many thousands of companies that produced the more than two hundred thousand different things Sears sold. The selling side was subdivided into five similarly independent "territories," each of them more populous and lucrative than all but a few American corporations. There was also the subsidiary Allstate Insurance Company, as well as a foreign corporation that ran stores throughout South and Central America, and another company that developed and managed huge shopping centers.

Sears had become an enclosed, private civilization, a place with a "corporate culture" that was so old and densely coded that, by the time the term was conjured up by students of modern management, the Sears culture was already calcifying and drawing violently inward upon itself. The men who rose up and tried to change Sears were not necessarily the ones who would have risen to the top of a large enterprise during better times. The executives who were ready to do whatever they thought necessary to redirect the empire included the most gifted, opinionated, aggressive, driven, unusual, mysterious, and in a few cases plainly the craziest inhabitants of the corporate society. As they were swept up by events, they began to act not like the characters in business journals and management primers, but like the characters in novels and plays, full of will and urgency.

By the time it was over, they had changed the way every single inhabitant of the company lived and viewed the world, and they'd changed just as profoundly the way the outside world viewed Sears. When the dust settled, one era of business and businessmen was gone and another had arrived. The great American corporation of the past, which began one hundred years ago with an orphaned box of pocket watches and a kid with a brilliant scheme, had become a variegated, futuristic corporation. Many observers of the events at Sears during the reign of Ed Telling call what happened then a "corporate turnaround," but those who lived through the firestorm know it was nothing if not a revolution.

When the tendentious reference to radical change first came up during our discussions, the chairman of the board began to tap his huge farm-boy fingertips on his empty desk top; he jingled his pocket-full of keys with his other hand and tapped both of his size-thirteen shoes on the floor. But, then, he always did that when someone was in the room.

"Sorta wish there's another word but revolution," the chairman said in his strained, almost sweet voice. "But I s'pose so. S'pose that's just what it was."

Great mystery still invests the interior life of big businesses. The public mask of the modern corporation is carefully designed to obscure the psychological and political resonances that exist there. Ubiquitous terms like "management," "turnaround," "streamline," "acquisition," and "succession" stand in place of the powerful passions that everywhere inhabit economic life. The meager data the government and its agencies may require of public companies are rarely supplemented at any depth, because of the lack of access granted observers. The information that filters out often comes from a former insider working from a private agenda.

I think that Ed Telling understood all of this, and after thirty-seven years of endeavoring with his colleagues to keep Sears as far from scrutiny as possible, he decided that this too should change. A single nod from Telling opened up meeting rooms, file cabinets, the doors of company jet planes, chairs at numerous meetings, as well as countless stores, warehouses, factories, private homes, and office doors that had been closed to the outside world since the days of Richard Sears. Senior executives who'd been proscribed from discussing their careers with their own children for three and four decades felt free to tell their stories. I was allowed to tread the executive corridors during the late years of the turmoil at Sears and to travel company rivers that flow below Ozark mountaintops, through suburban shopping centers, into urban barrios, and between the office towers of Wall Street. A research process I thought would take several months took several years.

Inside Sears I found brilliant managers, awful managers, great tellers of jokes, selling fools, natural merchants, operators, computer geniuses, wheeler-dealers, hatchet men, martinets, victims, sycophants, patricians, good old boys, and ghosts. And whatever Ed Telling and the others may think of the way I tell the tale of their separate world and how it changed, I want them to know that I tried hard to get it right, and that I like and respect them all.

Contents

PREFACE ix

PART I: THE UPHEAVALS 1

PROLOGUE: A TERMINUS 3

1 *THE GLORY YEARS* 9

2 *THE OUTSIDERS* 26

3 *THE WIND FROM THE EAST* 43

4 *JUMPIN' JOE* 75

5 *THE GENERAL'S GHOST* 89

6 *THE TERROR* 114

7 *THE PUBLIC FRONT* 130

8 *THE GYRE* 146

9 *THE KID* 163

10 *THE CHALLENGE* 186

11 *THE PURGE* 204

PART II: THE CHANGES 221

12 *THE GREAT AMERICAN COMPANY* 223

13 *ED BRENNAN'S THERMIDOR* 252

14 *FISHING WITH ROD AND PHIL* 265

15 *A CHRISTMAS AT HICKSVILLE* 304

16 *DARK TIMES* 324

17 *MAPS* 342

PART III: THE RACE 371

18 *THE RUN FOR THE ROSES* 373

19 *THE STORE OF THE FUTURE* 399

20 *THE FLOW* 423

21 *THE FLIGHT OF THE KILLER BEES* 441

22 *THE GAMBLER* 464

23 *TELLING* 479

24 *THE TOWER* 504

25 *THE RACE EXTENDED* 519

26 *THE STRETCH* 533

27 *THE GREAT WORKS* 559

AFTERWORD 579

CHRONOLOGY 585

AUTHOR'S NOTE 587

Part I

The

UPHEAVALS

Ask an Indian of the old school whether he prefers modern security to the days of his youth: he will brush aside all recent advantages for a whiff of the buffalo-hunting days. If there was starvation then, there were buffalo tongues too—supreme among earthly dishes; if you were likely to be killed, you had a chance to gain glory.

—*Robert H. Lowie*
The Crow Indians

PROLOGUE

A Terminus

|————————————|

John Lowe, the king of the West, boarded his company jet and flew up over the Rocky Mountains toward the far edge of his portion of the empire. The de Havilland required just two hours to travel from Los Angeles to the little airstrip ten miles east of Pueblo, Colorado, and just north of the jagged seam where the Arkansas River stitches the West to the southwestern edge of the Great Plains.

It was Tuesday, the first day of November in 1977, and the sky was clear enough above Pueblo to see ninety miles into the distance over the high country. The cold wind that usually falls off the peaks of the front range with such fury was remarkably calm.

With the early-1970s opening of the Flower Aviation Company's Executive Terminal out at the Pueblo airport, the old fur-trade outpost became a travelers' crossroads again. Pueblo joined other high plains towns like Dalhart, Texas; Salinas, Kansas; and Grand Island, Nebraska, as an elite way station to the citizens of Bechtel, TRW, Atlantic Richfield, Mobil, and many others.

John Lowe had landed to refuel in Pueblo many times during his trips to "Parent" in Chicago, but this bright morning his jet taxied up to the white stucco executive terminal and the engines shut down. Lowe climbed out and turned his gaunt, no-nonsense face into the sun. He searched the horizon for around ten minutes before he spotted the Falcon bearing Ed Telling coming in from the east.

Lowe often observed that he'd done all right for a poor country boy,

———— 3 ————

and by any measure of corporate attainment he really had. He started out at the company during the Great Depression, "pickin' and packin' " catalog orders at the Los Angeles catalog-order plant and rose over time to become one of Sears, Roebuck's five territorial officers—and thus one of the most powerful businessmen in the world. Lowe's Far Western Territory employed over sixty thousand people, as many as entire companies like Boeing, Texaco, Monsanto, and General Mills. The intricate network of stores and catalog outlets in the territory garnered yearly sales equal to those of Coca-Cola, Standard Oil of Ohio, Lockheed, or Gulf and Western. Lowe had become a civic leader in Los Angeles and an active member of the illustrious California Club—a poor boy from Hemet, California, running with the local power-brokers over at the California Club. Sears did that for people, and it was one of the many reasons he loved the company with all his heart.

Ed Telling was another of the Sears poor boys made good. At fifty-eight, Telling was just a few months older than Lowe, and though they'd ascended at opposite edges of the empire, the two men had still "grown up together in the company," as they say at Sears. They'd teamed up on occasion back when Telling was king of the East in order to crush some no-brain initiatives from Chicago that were designed to exert central control. Over a game and a bottle of gin, they used to agree that only a fool in one of their positions would ever want to become president or chairman of Sears, because the head of one of the five territories would be crazy to give up all that power. He and Telling had crossed swords now and again over the years, but they were still both children of the stores and soldiers of the Field, and even though Ed had taken a job in the Tower, everyone knew Telling still believed that the very meaning of Sears, Roebuck was inextricably bound up in the sanctity and everlasting sovereignty of the Field. If Ed Telling remained something of a mystery to Lowe, then at least Lowe knew he was far from alone in that. But Telling had been more mysterious than ever since he'd left the East, and something about the phone call summoning Lowe to an airstrip in the middle of nowhere that autumn day made him jumpy.

After the Falcon from Parent pulled up next to his own jet, Lowe was surprised to see Art Wood, the chairman of the board of Sears, follow Ed Telling onto the top of the metal staircase. The two travelers from Chicago clambered down to join Lowe on the black tarmac, and for a moment the three tall Searsmen stood eye to eye in the noon sun.

Most of the thirty-one officers of Sears, Roebuck in 1977 stood over six feet tall. This was largely the doing of the company's leader for four decades, General Robert E. Wood, though the old man had been dead now for eight years. The General liked his executives tall and lean, and thus for fifty years a Searsman who "looked the part" stood somewhere around six foot two.

John Lowe was of the rangy Western-rancher subgenre of Sears, Roebuck executive. He held himself slack below the chest, but tall and proud up top. Lowe tended to make terse statements and then set his jaw hard in punctuation. So did a lot of the other executives who worked for him in the Far West—the "Pacific Coast Territory," as most of the Westerners of the old school preferred. Lowe was one of the few at the California Club who didn't look like he'd gone to Yale. He looked more like a pioneer than a pilgrim.

Lowe's cowboy version of the post-war Searsman compared subtly to Ed Telling's hayseed model. Telling usually stood with his oversized shoes splayed out to the sides, and he tended to loll back on his heels with his belly protruding prominently from a Sears, Roebuck suit coat he invariably buttoned and unbuttoned all day long. Unlike most corporate executives, Telling looked like he'd been squashing cow patties on the back forty within the previous hour. During the fall of 1977, he was wearing his dark-gray hair cropped close and square, and the recent addition to his huge head of a pair of the streamlined metal-rimmed eyeglass frames that had become fashionable in executive circles a few years earlier made him look almost as stylish as a Sears humidifier salesman working somewhere in southern Illinois.

It was as if he'd carefully designed an outward appearance and personal style in direct counterpoint—almost in parody—of the man who'd ridden out to Pueblo with him in the Falcon. And according to more than a few students of the ways of Edward Riggs Telling, that was exactly what he intended.

Arthur Wood, the chairman of the board of Sears, who was scheduled to retire in February of 1978, was the consummate old-world gentleman-businessman. For almost six years, the soft-spoken patrician with the wild welter of eyebrow had served Sears as a chatterer to presidents, a testifier to public forums, and CEO of the corporation, with all of the grace and high-mindedness of a nineteenth-century diplomat. Wood, who bore no blood relationship to the old General of the same name, was the sort of upper-class executive whom post-war sociologists like David Riesman doubted could ever meld into the middle-class world of the modern corporation. The son of a noted Chicago financier who was president of the local stock exchange, Wood married the daughter and granddaughter of two men named Potter Palmer, the elder of whom was the owner of a significant portion of the land upon which rests Chicago, Illinois.

Art Wood's office in the Tower displayed just a few of the works from

his noted collection of Impressionist paintings, including a particularly
rich pastel by Degas and one of Claude Monet's seasonal masterpieces,
the *Haystacks.* Wood actually was thought by many Sears employees to
own four of the *Haystacks* canvases, and the advent of spring in Chicago
or the coming of another bitter winter was said to be attended by the
rise of the appropriate Monet behind Chairman Wood. If a visitor to his
office commented upon one of his masterpieces, Wood might say, "Oh,
I see you're a person who appreciates fine art," and he would intend the
bon ton in all good faith and with equally good cheer.

John Lowe would never forget how uncomfortable the elegant chairman looked as the three of them entered the small executive terminal,
a building ringed by an Aztec-style frieze and lined with foam-stuffed
furniture that was covered in an eye-watering shade of green. And he
never forgot that it was Arthur Wood who spoke first.

"John," he said. "I've decided that Ed will succeed me as chairman of
the board. I'm going to recommend him at the board meeting next
week."

Lowe offered Telling congratulations without disappointment. The
Californian had been mentioned as a contender for the chairmanship
along with Telling and several others earlier in 1977, but he would be
content to continue to rule his fifth of the company from Los Angeles.

Then Ed Telling began to speak in that strained, almost feminine
voice that startles those who've taken in the size of the man. He said,
"We have to make a change on the Coast, John."

"What do you mean by that?" Lowe said, training his darkest stare
back at Telling.

"You've lost credibility with your people, so we have to make a
change."

"What do you perceive that I've done to lose my credibility, Ed?"

"It's not what I perceive," Telling said, as Arthur Wood shifted and
rocked all over his bright-green chair. "It's what the whole organization
perceives."

Lowe thought, "That's a spongy goddamned answer . . . goddamned
spongy." But he didn't say it out loud.

All three of the men sitting in the Flower Executive Terminal that day
knew that a Sears territorial officer had been questioned rarely in the
past—let alone reproached—and they had each been schooled for all of
their adult lives in the ways of the incontestable system of local rule at
Sears. The tradition was thought to be inviolable.

Lost credibility with his people! His numbers might have slumped a
bit the last few quarters, but John Lowe *was* the West. He owned
California, Oregon, Washington, Arizona, Utah, Nevada, Idaho, Alaska,
and Hawaii, and operated them for Sears from *his* headquarters, which

he'd designed and built with his own capital dollars. He was godfather to several of the children of his senior managers and he'd ushered at their weddings. The idea of tearing John Lowe from atop his great pyramid of authority was an affront to everything Sears, Roebuck had meant for half a century; it was inimical to everything the General had intended for Sears, a blow to that special promise of individual autonomy that made Sears different from all the other big companies—and it was exactly what Ed Telling meant to do. But firing a strong and notably independent territorial officer like John Lowe outright could be too much for the organization to bear, so Telling's strategy called for Lowe to resign.

"In light of your long service, John," Telling continued, "we're going to offer you the chance to run the Midwestern Territory."

Lowe knew instantly what Telling wanted. Telling expected his sense of pride to cause him to quit rather than be torn from the power base he'd spent decades constructing in the West. There was nothing in the world John Lowe wanted more than to do the honorable thing. He wanted to stare into Telling's eyes and damn his treacherous violation of the system left in their trust. He wanted to inform Telling of just what he could do with his offer and the entire Midwestern Territory too. But Lowe couldn't quit his job.

Because he once believed that nothing would ever change for mighty Sears, John Lowe was a million dollars underwater that fall. He'd borrowed so heavily to purchase Sears stock that the stunning drop in the value of those shares recently had taken him well beyond the point where he could repay the loans by selling the stock. All of those forty years of fervent labor in fee to Mother Sears had suddenly winnowed down to a single moment on a God-forsaken stretch of high desert, and he was helpless.

"Fine," Lowe managed. "I'll take it."

From that moment, John Lowe would move away from the territory he'd run, and he'd step away emotionally from the company that had shaped the course of his and so many others' lives. He would bear pained but silent witness as, in a breathtakingly short amount of time, the fortunes of Sears continued to fall into a spiral of decline and failure, as the great company would be questioned in public for the first time in modern memory, and as the two powerful camps that dominated the organization would go to war.

To outside observers of Sears, to the business press, and even to the Wall Street analysts who watched Sears for a living, the announcement of John Lowe's move to the Midwestern Territory at the press conference in Chicago the next week seemed an innocuous lateral adjustment, or possibly a promotion. The Midwest, after all, had been a powerhouse territory for Sears for many years, and it was still responsible for a larger volume of gross sales than the West. Those not of the company couldn't begin to understand the internal violence of the act. Only members of the private society inside Sears realized that the Far Western Territory was known as John Lowe's "separate kingdom." As the news sped between departments, headquarters, and stores along the company grapevine, only the inhabitants of Sears understood that Ed Telling had killed a king.

CHAPTER 1

The Glory Years

T he idea of Sears began in 1886, at a terminal alongside a railway track in the middle of nowhere, when a twenty-three-year-old man came upon a means of selling gold-filled pocket watches to rural folks who previously marked their lives by the movement of the sun. By the time Richard Warren Sears moved his budding business from Minnesota to Chicago and teamed up with a quiet watchmaker named Alvah Curtis Roebuck, it was clear that the kid was possessed of a peculiar strain of genius that rendered him capable of convincing otherwise skeptical individuals to buy things they'd never even heard of from a man in Chicago, Illinois, whom they'd never even seen.

Richard Sears was so adept at describing the shape of a young nation's material dreams that it was said a few years later that he could sell a breath of air. He housed the perfervid prose he composed day and night in big, illustrated catalogs that became for significant segments of the population one of the only two books they ever read. The big books promised "FREE TRIAL OFFERS" and unheard-of "MONEY BACK GUARANTEES." Dick Sears' odes to things taught common people about cream separators, bicycles, and machines that sewed clothes. He also offered to send out sure-fire bottled cures for consumption, drug addiction, stammering, deafness, and stupidity—but, like Huck Finn, mostly he told the truth. "Honesty is the best policy," Richard Sears observed toward the end of his short, fast life. "I know. I've tried it both ways."

Year after year Sears and the people who flocked to join him in Chicago offered up in the name of democracy a new list of objects and devices that were previously attainable only by a privileged few. "Our Stradivarius," he wrote of one popular musical item, "only $1.95."

Within a decade of the company's founding, Sears' inflammatory prose had spawned a breadth of popular desire that could only be served by a carefully organized and disciplined enterprise. The unadorned insertion of himself between a box of goods and people who wanted what was inside was no longer enough; at this point the company was presented with another business wizard, whose particular genius allowed him to envisage massive organizational structures and intricate systems designed to ensure the service of supply.

Sears' new partner (Roebuck sold out for $25,000 in 1895), Julius Rosenwald, became determined to rein in Richard Sears' more tendentious salesmanship. In 1905 he insisted that his partner cease promotion of the popular "Heidelberg Belt," an electrified contraption that when fastened around the waist cured "impotency, emissions, losses," and an affliction the founder called "drains." All of this for $12 ($18 if "a stronger current" was needed). The belt cauterized many an American farmer before Sears yielded to Rosenwald's demand that the item be edited from the catalog, but such was the people's trust in the word of Richard Sears that only three customers ever returned a Heidelberg Belt and invoked their money-back guarantee.

Two years later, when the business panic of 1907 moved Rosenwald to institute the company's first expenditure cutbacks, Sears clashed again with his partner, arguing with all his skill that the slump was nothing a few adjectives and some cash for new advertising wouldn't fix. In late 1908 Sears up and quit. Systems were replacing his literary talents, and it seemed that he was out of place, that his own company had passed him by. He sold his stock in 1913, and during the following autumn Richard Sears—a type-A personality in a type-B world—died.

Under Rosenwald, Sears became a catalog empire. The network of factories selling products to Sears and the means of financing and moving goods became so large and complex that the company became a full-fledged working economy unto itself. By the second decade of the century, Sears arguably encompassed more of the basic functions of a capitalist economy—from extraction, to fabrication, to distribution and consumption, from finance to communications—than any company before it.

Rosenwald decided to pass the business on to yet another visionary executive during the 1920s. "J.R.," as Rosenwald was known at the West Side plant, who once claimed his goal in life was to make $15,000 a year, had by then accumulated one of the largest personal fortunes in the world. He said he wanted to stop running Sears in order to dedicate the rest of his life to what became a legendary effort to give much of his money away. Rosenwald went on to create and support social programs throughout the country that were often adopted later by the government as public policy—the county farm-agent program and decent schooling for black people among them. He was such a conscientious white benefactor to black Americans that some called him the best white friend to blacks since Abraham Lincoln. Photographs of "Cap'n Julius" Rosenwald hung next to those of Lincoln and Rosenwald's close friend Booker T. Washington in many of the 5,347 schools he helped build throughout the South.

At the time Rosenwald passed the management of Sears to General Robert Wood, the Golden Age of the American catalog was already in decline. The big books thrived at a time when over half of the citizens of the Republic lived in rural regions, and as an early student of population and economic trends, Wood realized that farm income levels, which had always mirrored the success of Sears, were bound to fall. Wood arrived at Sears in 1922. He told his new colleagues he saw new markets for Sears in the rise of the American workingman and his family from levels of mere economic subsistence. He said the future could be seen in the Model T's that were burping down the roads, and in the cities of under one hundred thousand people—some of them in parched regions in the middle of nowhere that would eventually be known as the "Sun Belt." Julius Rosenwald envisaged Sears, Roebuck as an institution so central to so many people's day-to-day life that he called the company "the buyer for the American farmer." The General dreamed of a company so deeply entwined in the life of the nation that it could call itself "the purchasing agent for the American people."

Wood decided to use the regional mail-order plants Rosenwald and his catalog men had built as supply bases for a sprawling network of stores. By 1928 there were twenty-seven stores, and by the end of 1929 there were 324 of them. In 1932 the volume of the General's retail store sales surpassed those of the catalog for good.

Eventually Sears retail stores began to rise from cornfields and orange groves outside the towns like great, squat silos. There was considerable amusement in business circles when Sears began to buy up the corner lots at rural crossroads and build huge blockhouse stores surrounded by expanses of cement painted with orthogonal lines. The General called the private pavements "ample free parking space." Soon the big stores were surrounded by clusters of new homes that everyone called "suburbs." Wherever people moved to build new homes it seemed that a well-stocked Sears retail store was located nearby. The General became world-famous for his prescience, and Sears became one of the most powerful economic organizations of all time by virtue of the business system he built upon the franchise of trust and loyalty he'd inherited from the catalog.

Though for fifty-four years he was known throughout the country as "the General," Wood actually quit the Army in 1915 at the age of thirty-six. The son of a Civil War hero, he had graduated from West Point in the class of 1900 and had served for ten years as right-hand man to the famously hard-driving General George Goethals while they built the apparently unbuildable Panama Canal. After he left the service, Wood did agree to come back as acting Quartermaster General during World War I, but in truth he never much cared for the Army. It always seemed such a top-heavy thing, and so restrictive of human will.

The General hated bureaucracies. Aside from his desire to personally raise the standard of living of an entire nation, he dreamed of creating an institution that could accomplish large works without restricting the individuality of the people within it. He said he wanted to make an American corporation that had a soul.

During the latter days of World War II, the observation passed through barracks and officers' clubs that a veteran could do a lot worse back home than to hire on with Sears. It was said that at Sears a fellow didn't have to stop winning battles or even handing out silk stockings to ladies. The place was everywhere now and it apparently had its own sort of *esprit de corps.* It was even run by an old guy called the General.

Former sailors and supply sergeants, bombardiers, noncoms, and dog-faces began to flock to Sears, Roebuck, all of them ready to transfer an indomitable capacity for loyalty they'd learned on battlefields to a great American company.

Leaders of other big corporations were scared of the postwar economic climate, but the General maintained that Sears would soldier on. New stores were thrown up by the week. Sales doubled between 1946 and 1947 alone as consumers satisfied their long-pent-up demand for new goods. By 1949, five of every one hundred dollars spent on merchandise went to the General's peacetime army, which since the end of the war had swollen by fifty thousand employees—twice the number employed in total when Wood came to Sears.

The company was able to grow so quickly, and with such incomparable élan, in part because of the unusual structure of corporate governance Wood had conceived. As early as 1918, Julius Rosenwald declared that the company had "applied the principles of democracy to a commercial enterprise." The General believed so strongly in decentralized management that he'd considered breaking Sears up into six regional corporations during a period of anti-chain-store sentiment before World War II, but he aborted the experiment in the spring of 1932.

"We have deliberately tried to treat you as free, independent merchants and men," the General told some former soldiers a few years later. "We have endeavored in a chain-store system to have a cooperative democracy." Under the headline "Goal for Worker: Democracy," the *Chicago Tribune* quoted one of the General's chief lieutenants and polemicists on the urgency of Wood's concept of corporate order in September 1949: "The enemies of democracy in business enterprise are the same as the enemies of democracy in government. . . . They include centralization of administration, an excessive growth of authority, growing dependence upon formal systems, bureaucracy, and mechanistic or technical solutions to human problems." The people of Sears grew to hate centralized business systems just as they hated the centralized orders they'd defeated in Europe.

The formal decentralization of authority at Sears had begun with the creation of the Pacific Coast Territory in 1940. After the war the job was finished when four more regional administrations were set up. The headquarters of the five territories would reside in Los Angeles, Dallas, Atlanta, Chicago, and Philadelphia. Thus Robert E. Wood "widened Sears, Roebuck's frontiers and spread autonomy to the outposts," as *Fortune* magazine put it in a lengthy study of the "art of industrial management." The decentralized structure of Sears, Roebuck became a model of progressive corporate management, and the General became an American business hero with his face on the cover of *Time* magazine.

By the mid-1950s, during the "management administration" in Washington of Dwight Eisenhower, Sears was widely thought to contain an elite corps made up of the best managers in the world. "One of the most alert management groups in the country," wrote William Whyte in his classic study, *The Organization Man.* "There is no better illustration of what a business is and what managing it means," wrote Peter Drucker at the beginning of *The Practice of Management.*

To its employees, Sears was unlike other big businesses in that it was a place where country boys and infantrymen could speak their minds and still roam free. The loyalty Sears commanded from its people was the envy of other corporations. The young John Lowe was offered a $25,000-a-year job running a major store for the May Company at a time when he was making only $7,000 a year as a minor functionary at Sears. He turned it down.

Why would anyone want to leave Sears? The stores coursed with business, and the catalog that Franklin Delano Roosevelt once suggested should be air-dropped all over the Soviet Union as a testament to capitalism's rewards was still by far the dominant means of buying goods at home. Their sellers were *the* sellers in the business, their buyers were nonpareil, and everyone was free.

Many employees believed the myth that nobody ever left Sears, whereas in fact a huge number of young people filtered through the company ranks. The ones who stayed were true believers. They were soldiers of Sears, and the wind always seemed at their backs. The roads they traveled all seemed to be bordered by schools, post offices, churches, and Sears stores.

They were also sellers, and quite proud of the fact. If the Searsmen inundated the cities and provinces with a new materiality, the boys believed they were doing it so as to make people happier. They'd won a war in the name of liberty, and now they sold things for Sears, Roebuck so that liberty might lead to the finest quality of everyday life in all of history. There was little thought about the possibility that the manly arts of soldiering bore scant resemblance to selling goods for Sears. Somehow—for some strange reason connected to the moral underpinnings of the times and the charged life inside the company—the two jobs felt the same. For these Searsmen, selling was nothing at all like coercion. It was almost an organic activity. They sold to nurture a process of economic expansion that turned work into wealth and wealth into goods and more work, and it all felt as natural as the rains in spring.

A firm policy of promotion from within, and the best profit-sharing and benefit program in the country, so completely enclosed the human ring of the company that by 1954 hardly any of the huge number of people working for Sears had ever worked anywhere else. A "psychological contract" Sears had made with its people was widely understood, and with it came the assurance that you could only be fired for stealing from the company or taking untoward liberties with your secretary— and the latter only applied if you were caught in the act. In exchange for acceptance of the company's elongated time horizons, life-long service was rewarded handsomely, but only at the very end. During an employee's "infancy" in the company—the first twenty-five years or so—the Searsman who worked in the stores and the attendant administrative outposts that made up the Field was expected to move across the American landscape like an inland seafarer, parking the family while he roamed a new territory, or uprooting the family altogether and moving once again—sometimes several times in a year. They moved more often than any other discernible group of people, save plainly unhappy ones. Ed Telling's father never did understand all the "hopping around" his son had to do between the ages of thirty and forty. The elder Telling figured something must have gone wrong.

But this was the life, and most of the Sears soldiers thought it was a hell of a good life too. They had the best of all possible worlds. There was the *éclat* born of drumming out the people's goods and the sort of job security normally vouchsafed only by the civil service. The stores of the Field were their harbors, and they traded homes and hung their plaques and awards and photographs of themselves beside the disheveled figure of General Wood on the same nails in the wall. And if they did just trade and rearrange keys on a ring for a while, there was always the possibility of rising to the administration of one of the several retail "groups" of stores that made up the powerful territories. And if you really soared, you might make it onto a territorial staff.

You could even get rich in the end. The *Reader's Digest* informed thousands of Americans beyond the borders of Sears that the persistent rise in the value of Sears stock over the years had allowed *elevator operators* at the West Side plant in Chicago to retire with several hundred thousand dollars in stock gained through profit sharing. Investors chased the price of Sears stock higher every year during the 1960s, for most large investment portfolios of the time called for a 5-to-10-percent investment in the retail sector—and Sears was the retail sector. A Mr. Austin "Joe" Cushman, the chairman of the board of Sears between 1962 and 1967, was known to have retired with ninety thousand shares of Sears stock he'd bought each year with his bonus, for an average of $2.00 a share. The stock was worth some $5 million when Cushman retired.

By the mid-1960s, Sears, Roebuck was a superpower, as invincible a business as the nation it served. Articles about Sears referred to the company as the "colossus of American retailing" or the "monster of the Midway." Journalists invariably digressed in order to express Sears' sales as a percentage of the Gross National Product. One in five Americans shopped the company with regularity, and the internal populace was fast approaching three hundred thousand residents, many more than lived in ancient Athens during the Golden Age.

"Sears is the paragon of retailers," proclaimed a *Fortune* cover story in 1964, and in a reference to the five awesomely powerful territories it said, "It is number one in the U.S., and also number 2, 3, 4, and 5." It was just that big. *Fortune* noted that the company's sales volume was bigger than that of the entire tobacco or furniture industry. Alone Sears dwarfed the American entertainment and lodging industries. As huge shopping centers began to cover the landscape, entire developments were predicated on the presence of a Sears store, and fundamental alterations in surrounding marketing areas occurred because of corporate advertising that made the sound of Sears part of the background noise of everyday life.

The magic benchmark of $1 billion in sales within a single month was passed in December of 1967, the year when John Lowe took over the Far Western Territory. There was a widely held conviction within the company that Sears could never be stopped or even slowed. If a Sears-man was asked to choose one explanation for why this was true, the answer invariably referred to the internal doctrine of individual free-dom, and the system of local autonomy that had been constructed ac-cordingly. Any good retailer saw his job as something akin to a calling, but the General's dream of institutional liberty had moved a system of buying and selling toward something close to a religion.

A nationwide free market existed inside Sears. The buyers, most of whom were based at the old West Side plant in Chicago, purchased goods from some twenty thousand loyal manufacturers. They bought things without checks or control from above. But they then had to turn around and "sell" the goods to the store runners out in the Field, where items were rejected, bought, displayed, and even priced according to the desires of the local merchants. Favors, advantages, good dinners, good whiskey, bad jokes, compliments, hot company gossip, political favors, and even—due to Sears' singular system of informal accounting—great piles of money were traded in the internal marketplace. A buyer slipping some money to a store or group manager for a big ad in the local paper was considered an example of good politics instead of bad busi-ness. Meanwhile, the territorial officers actually bought goods for their stores privately from local sources. "Buying off the reservation," as it was known, was in direct contravention of corporate policy, but it still oc-curred. The term "decentralization" now described the raw power that rested in each individual store, each administrative "group" of retail stores, and especially in the almighty territories of the Field, and any effort emanating from company Headquarters ("Headquarters" or "Par-ent"—the terms were interchangeable, though the latter was spoken with an ironic, rather derisive inflection in the Field) in Chicago that was designed to tell the soldiers of the Field what to do was resisted as a foreign invasion. Al Davies, the ruler of the Southwest Territory (a former Texas A&M boxer who refused to hire an executive not big enough to "whup" him because, he said, "A small man puts forth the wrong side of his nature"), referred to the merest suggestion of control from the "so-called" Parent—"Parent" housed the buying organization but mainly referred to the corporate staff—as "superimposure," a crime Davies associated with mortal sin.

Sears was so completely dominated by the five separate pyramids of authority by the 1960s that Professor Alfred Chandler stated, in his landmark study of corporate structure at the time, that the territories had gained "complete charge of operations." Homage had to be paid to the sanctity and sovereignty of the Field at all times. A 1967 Harvard Business School case study contains a quote from a senior executive at Headquarters who caught himself in the mere suggestion that the stores sold what the Sears buyers bought: "You should not, however, allow this willingness to follow Parent recommendations [in the Field] mislead you. The important thing about autonomy is that it exists—as a right!" A Parent telephone directory of the time contained a bright-yellow page that described the territorial overlords: "For all practical purposes he's 'president' of the territory. . . . A territory v.p. is a man with really sweeping authority. His word is law."

In the spirit of decentralization, each vice-president in charge of one of the five sovereign territories developed his own administrative procedures. Each had authority to design and "drop" his own new stores. They could take out bank loans at will. They protected the right of local store managers to price the goods and select the things they wanted to carry from the warehouses. They could structure a staff around themselves in whatever way they liked, and even after the territories each employed over fifty thousand people, the territory kings preferred to dole out raises and bonuses personally to even the most junior executives.

The territories had gained so much control over company communications that corporate directives from Chicago were rewritten when they weren't thrown away. Muscle flexing in the form of subverting the slightest hint of administrative control from the Parent organization became a regular Field pastime. A young merchant on the Pacific Coast named Lou Oliver was once fired by a Parent man for writing some bad checks. He was subsequently physically concealed in a far corner of the territory every time the personnel men came out from Chicago. Oliver rose after a time to run the Southern Territory. The young auditor Gordon Metcalf was also fired once by order of the personnel director at Parent. "You're not fired," Murphy of the Midwest told him when he heard about it. "You work for me." Murphy then promoted the future head of the Midwest and eventual chairman of the board of Sears to be an assistant store manager.

When "Gordo" Metcalf (or "Mumbles," as Metcalf was often called because of his peculiar oratorical style) got the call to the big corner office in Chicago during 1967, he was out on the road. A young aide brought a bottle of bourbon up to Metcalf's hotel room and asked him what he planned to do with the corporation as chairman. "Well, I'll let the boys run it," Metcalf said. "I'm not gonna have Headquarters meddling. I'm gonna keep things nice and even 'cause they're goin' real good."

Ever since the mid-1950s, when old General Wood had receded into "retirement" in order to pull the corporate strings from the shadows, a succession of short-term chairmen had come to Chicago from the Field to serve at the behest of the General's dream for a cooperative democracy in a company. If anything, Gordon Metcalf accelerated the process of ceding ever more authority to the territories. Each time a problem arose, he tended to call the territorial officers. "Let's see what the boys say," the chairman would mumble. "What do you boys think?" he'd ask each of the men. After listening for a while, Metcalf would say something like "You boys just work it out."

When the boys heard in 1968 that Gordon was going to build for the largest merchandising company in the world the largest building in the world, several of them looked around at their old offices, still housed in mail-order warehouses built during the 1920s, and decided it was time for them to build something too.

By 1971, John Lowe's twelve-story cubical office block began to rise in Alhambra, California, and Al Davies was just about done building his glass-and-steel tower in Dallas. Davies built himself a suite of offices replete with a library, a private dining chamber, a large administrative assistant's office, a meeting room, and places for his three secretaries to sit. His own office was heavily paneled and adorned with a pair of cattle horns and a great deal of the dark, heavy furniture everyone always thought perfectly characterized the man who ran the Southwest.

When Lowe's Alhambra palace was completed, Ed Telling brought his construction manager, his property manager, and a personnel man out from his bailiwick in the East to check it out. Telling had only taken over the East a year earlier. After his tour in Alhambra he said, "Well, I'm gonna build John Lowe's office building—but I'm gonna put Al Davies' office in it." Soon a new Sears building—filled with natural-wood panels, old lamps, and bathrooms and drinking fountains adorned with the sort of brass fittings Telling enjoyed—was built in a wealthy Main Line Philadelphia suburb.

By the time the sparkling new imperial outposts were in place, the generation of warriors that had managed the glory years was moving well into middle age, and the old soldier whose obsession with individual freedom lay at the bedrock of the structure-building was finally dead.

Just before World War II, the General addressed a banquet hall filled with Sears executives at the old Stevens Hotel in Chicago: "I believed no man is indispensable," Wood proclaimed in that gravelly voice of his, "but just as every rule has exceptions, there is occasionally a remarkable man who retains great mettle and bodily vigor, who is uncanny in his ability to get profits, and who cannot be replaced."

Those present may indeed have understood that the executive so lauded was a good man, but they understood too that there was only one man of great mettle and vigor in whom General Robert E. Wood had consummate faith, and who could not be replaced. The General was supposed to retire once in 1937, but he was "convinced" to remain in residence as chairman instead of president of Sears. "I'll still be interested in everything that goes on," the General promised as he took on his new title. And from that day forward, the real executive power at Sears transferred from the presidency to the chairmanship.

In 1954 the old man said it was time to retire again. Others could be chairman, each of them hand-picked and preordained by Wood to take a turn on the bridge. The General took an office at Parent from which he controlled his packed board of directors, made up of numerous Sears insiders and "dollar-a-year" cronies. He lingered within the last retreat of true democracy as guardian of the order. "If I were dictator," he'd grumble to reporters, "the first thing I'd do would be to outlaw New York and Chicago headquarters and move management back to the factories, where it belongs!"

The General began to wander the endless halls at the West Side Headquarters during the 1950s; a man approaching eighty, who drooled, ate cigarettes whole, forgot to take the wrappers off candy, and often forgot to zip his fly. Between his supposed retirement in 1954 and his death in 1969, five chairmen took a brief turn as CEO. Like the Roman Emperor Hadrian, who chose Antonius Pius to follow him and Marcus Aurelius to come next, the father of the system named and blessed all of the short-term chairmen. As late as 1973, the men the General had personally culled from the pack toward the end of World War II were still coming up and taking their crack—sometimes for as little as two years—because the General, the arbiter of fairness, had said thirty years earlier that it was "the fair thing to do."

Wood had taken particular, almost perverse care in developing a special strain of Sears executive fit to interbreed with the cowboys and shit-kickers of the Field, and eventually to inherit the empire some time in the future. His private stock of Sears Tall Men tended to be quite tall and so handsome that they "looked the part" not only by Sears standards, but by the standards of the people who ran the rest of America. It was as if the General believed Sears had become an institution that could afford a real gentleman at the helm, someone who could operate high above the horse-trading and artifice and unceasing noise of the sale.

The General's special favorites among the peculiar subculture he'd created within Sears had grown up with servants, and gone on to good schools and universities. The Tall Men included people like Charles Meyer, a razor-chinned Yankee with glistening blue eyes. An uncle of

Meyer's, the chairman of the Guarantee Trust Company in New York, had said to young Charles one day in 1939, "You fellows born in Boston and educated at Harvard don't know anything about the real United States of America. If you're willing to take the time, I'd like to send you on a tour of the forty-eight states." So the recent art-history major at Harvard commenced a tour of industrial America. Through his uncle's connections, Meyer was received by the leaders of Campbell's Soup, Chrysler, International Harvester, Anaconda Copper, Owens Illinois Glass, and several others. He decided to cast his lot, however, with the true Americans of Sears, Roebuck, a company he realized had been built and was still populated by people who worked because they had to. But Charlie Meyer settled into Sears close under the wing of the General, and, but for a stint in the State Department, he remained there until his mentor died.

To the zealots of the territories and the buying organization, the coterie of patrician Searsmen hung like some aristocratic barnacle on the side of the company ship. Though only one of this particular strain actually ascended to the chairmanship (and that occurred after the old soldier had transmitted onward), all of the Tall Men got big jobs. People like George Struthers and the film-star-handsome Jim Button ran the powerful buying organization, and several others were farmed out from Headquarters to the territories to gain real-life experience alongside "the boys."

In 1962 the General sent one of his favorites, Arthur Wood, the son of a personal friend, out from Parent to be schooled in the ways of the Field. Art was to serve temporarily as chief officer of the Far West. He'd run a store in Waukegan, Illinois, for a while, but he needed more seasoning. Even in the separate kingdom of the Far Western Territory, the Field men accepted that the General could do whatever he liked.

Just after the end of the war, the General had declared publicly that Arthur Wood and one other of his favorite Tall Men would eventually run Sears. When Arthur Wood was just a young lawyer at Headquarters, the General would embarrass him by saying, "Young Artie Wood is one of our bright young men and he's going to run this company some day." But even the General acknowledged that the system of local sovereignty had grown so powerful that no man could serve as chairman of Sears without having run one of the territories. So, after serving as a Sears lawyer, the corporate secretary, and then the controller, Arthur Wood was sent out to the separate kingdom to be schooled. An old-style merchant out west named Don Craib was convinced to postpone his retirement to keep Wood out of trouble. The big group managers like John Lowe, then head of the powerhouse Los Angeles stores, tended to take their day-to-day administrative problems to Craib, while Arthur Wood distinguished himself at the Los Angeles Chamber of Commerce, the Music Center, and the new visitors' bureau. It was said that if you called Arthur Wood with a question on a Tuesday you could expect to hear back from him a week from the following Monday.

The late General would have been pleased by the article in *Business Week* that attended the announcement of Arthur Wood's ascension to the chairmanship toward the end of 1972. The article called Wood "a sophisticated urbane intellectual with impeccable social credentials" and went on to proclaim that "his appointment reflected the changing nature of retailing and the necessity for having more than a buyer and seller of goods at the top."

The appointment was the triumph of the Tall Men, and though the rank and file accepted that Arthur Wood looked and talked like the people who ran the other great companies, it was still hard to believe that this was the way the General had intended things to go. Most Searsmen had grown up poor and nominally educated by the standards of an Arthur Wood or a Charles Meyer, and part of the ingrained lore of the culture instructed that this was something good. One past president of the company hadn't made it past eighth grade, and that was thought to be all right too. The boys were so adept at understanding what people wanted to buy in America, they all thought, because they'd grown up wanting things themselves. "The chairman has got to be a merchant," the short-term early-1960s chairman, Charlie Kellstadt, said when he was asked about Wood years later. "And a merchant just can't be a sissy."

Despite what anyone said about the changing nature and impending sophistication of American retailing, the foot soldiers never quite got used to the fact that the great American company, a place made invincible by 1972 by virtue of selling millions of things to millions of people who had never had very much, was being run by a guy who looked and talked like an Englishman, who wore funny-looking prep-school suits and was always talking about someone "having his innings."

They all knew that Arthur Wood was going to be chairman for five years, so for five more years, and maybe five years after that, a man retired since 1954 and dead since 1969 would continue to walk the company halls. Sears, Roebuck was singular in the history of enterprise in that in less than a century it had been founded and refounded three times by three charismatic business geniuses, any one of whom could have created a significant corporate empire. By 1972, as Sears reached the apogee of its success, fame, and power, and a great tower rose over Chicago as monument to that success, fame, and power, the faces of the three founders stared down at those who would continue the tradition like the faces atop Mount Rushmore. But, unlike the figures of Richard

Sears and Julius Rosenwald, the one with the imploded face and the pince-nez was still talking. His face still hung on the wall behind most Sears store managers. His system, designed to hang together an army of entrepreneurs and foot soldiers within a noble federation predicated on individual freedom, was stronger than ever. But, like so many other great systems designed by great men, it was not designed to prevail after he was gone.

Since Art Wood wasn't a merchant, a president for Sears was chosen from among the five territorial officers to serve under him, to be a merchant for him as old Don Craib had been when Wood was out in the Far West being groomed. It just so happened that in 1972 the five kings of the territories included two incredibly nice men. Nobody knew for sure how it happened, but Dean Swift, who ran the South, and Cul Kennedy, of the Midwest, were two of the nicest guys around. Swift was chosen as president. But when Arthur Wood declared that the territorial officers would henceforth report to good old Dean instead of to the chairman, the Field took offense. John Lowe of the West and Ed Telling of the East led the delegation of territorial vice-presidents who approached Wood after the announcement to demand a meeting to which Swift would not be invited. The new chairman agreed to exclude Swift, and at the private meeting the next morning, Lowe reminded the new chairman of just what had made the company strong. Lowe and Telling contended that the territorial officers must have direct access to the chairman. Wood countered by saying that running the largest merchandise company in the world and the fifth-largest insurance company as well, plus dealing with shareholders and government regulators, was too much for one man. The boys, Wood declared, would just have to learn to deal with Dean.

So the boys went back to their palatial headquarters and began to figure out how to get around good old Dean.

Meanwhile, the Sears Tower, the stock price, the price/earnings ratio, the profit margins, and the size of the work force all began to top out.

"Being the largest retailer in the world," former chairman Gordon Metcalf had told *Time* magazine, "we thought we should have the largest headquarters in the world." The plan was to rent out the upper floors of the Tower until Sears employees occupied all 110 floors at the end of the century. But as the Parent employees ate their lunches in the ornamental gardens on the West Side, and watched the Tower rise higher over the lake to the east, some of them began, for the first time in their working lives, to feel something akin to doubt. Inside the company, the Tower was named for the vainglorious executive who ordered its construction. It was called "Gordon Metcalf's last erection."

Almost all of the hundreds and thousands of citizens of Sears had grown up and worked in a world of consistent, record-breaking financial success. The vocabulary of decline—talk of "red" profit, "flat growth," or the wonderfully oxymoronic "negative growth"—sounded to the Sears ear like a foreign language. No one was left who remembered the dark hours of 1921, when Julius Rosenwald had bailed out the teetering company with his own money. For most of them, life had been a childhood, the war, and then Sears. Just one battle after another, and all of them won.

Somehow the incredible pride Sears people always talked about had become pridefulness by the early 1970s; the great march of the providers for the American masses had become a strut. By the time the Tower was finished, America seemed to have stepped away from Sears, Roebuck during the few years it took to build the monolith.

There just weren't that many people left in the country who hadn't already acquired their first electric refrigerator, washing machine, freezer, color television, or expanse of wall-to-wall carpeting from Sears. A phenomenon called "market saturation" was occurring in some of the product categories Sears dominated. People were only buying new big items to replace old ones.

And though most people at Sears refused to accept it, there were competitors now. No other company could presume to go head to head with mighty Sears—Montgomery Ward and J. C. Penney lagged so far behind the giant as to be inconsequential—but there were different kinds of threats. The huge regional malls Sears anchored were becoming the scene of the revenge of the small shops. Many decades after Sears raided the Main Street shops and local general stores with a new way of selling, little shops now lined the contrived Main Streets of the malls, swiping customers who previously would have gone directly to Sears.

At the other end of the market were large companies dedicated to selling goods that were even less expensive than the bargains at Sears. The local store runners from Kresge were traditional objects of condescension among the Sears Field people, because they would never fork out for the annual Community Chest drives. Kresge was considered a poor citizen as well as a doomed store, but a fellow named Harry Cunningham had an idea of turning the Kresge stores into emporia designed to house only bargains secured by his opportunistic buyers. Cunningham franchised out half of the old Kresge stores and filled the rest with good deals. Kresge changed its name to K mart, and from the early 1960s the new stores loomed as an obvious threat that Sears chose to ignore.

An agenda cast in the old spirit still called for new stores everywhere and all the time. During the 1960s, the company research department began to point out to senior managers that many of the new stores Sears continued to drop across America were not making good returns. But the leadership had been taught only how to grow, not how to change.

The real volume of retail sales in the United States began to decline during the spring of 1973, just before the quadrupling of the world's oil prices during the Northern winter of that year. The company economist at Sears was warned by a senior officer, toward the end of 1973, that if he disseminated his official forecast of an abrupt and deep recession during 1974, he'd be fired.

Sears, Roebuck was blindsided but good in 1974, and the company took the hit like the tired old veteran it had become. Other national retailers recovered much more quickly from the business slump. Profits at Sears dropped off by $170 million. Sales projections had indicated a 15-percent rise over 1973, and the company didn't even hit 7 percent.

Much more damaging was Arthur Wood's acquiescence to layoffs in response to the slump. Arbitrary staffing cuts that ranged from 1 percent to 10 percent were carried out, many of them up and down the just-completed Tower. As lifelong Sears employees carried their belongings out of the aspiring new Headquarters, it was noted, and passed along the grapevine out to the territories, that the departing members of the family had run into workmen carrying in hundreds of thousands of dollars' worth of house plants to decorate the 110-story testimonial to a company that never failed.

Sears had been warned by the government in the summer of 1973 that it was being watched closely because the corporation was suspected of discriminating against its minority and female employees. The Sears way of allowing well over a thousand people spread all over the country to hire people as they each saw fit—a practice once heralded widely as a brilliant organizational experiment—appeared increasingly anachronistic instead of progressive as public scrutiny of such uncontrolled methods increased. A few months later, the Federal Trade Commission filed a complaint alleging that Sears salesmen in the Field practiced "bait-and-switch" tactics. Bait-and-switch is a venerable maneuver by which a customer arrives in a store in search of an advertised bargain, only to find that only higher-priced items are available. Aside from the adverse publicity, the bait-and-switch and discrimination raps were particularly disturbing to Arthur Wood and some of the other officers, because they all knew the charges were true. They also knew that, despite government threats, they could do little to stop the practices. So much power had been ceded downward from level to level, from territory to group to store, that no officer in Chicago or even the territory kings could make local store managers do much of anything at all. The General could have cut through the localist prerogatives, but the General was dead.

The company was much more than "flat," a word the Searsmen had learned to pronounce by the mid-1970s; it was beginning to writhe in agony. "We know what's going on here," Arthur Wood insisted defensively to *Business Week* but what the kindly gentleman knew was that the sudden economic reversals were straining the delicate tendrils that held Sears, Roebuck together. Two utterly conflicting large-scale institutions within Sears had apparently coalesced around separate histories and ways of life, and now they were moving apart.

On one side were the sellers, the loyal Sears soldiers of the Field, whose ranks now numbered 407,958 workers divided among the five territories. On the other side were the buyers and the corporate staffs. The regulars of the Parent buying and administrative forces included 9,253 strategically situated employees operating out of the monolith in Chicago. Each side had its own leaders, laws, language, and long lists of epigrams and declarations from the General that were regarded as holy writ. Each camp was subdivided into powerful smaller cultures.

Nothing seemed to move easily from top to bottom through the decentralized units anymore, and nothing seemed to move from one side of the map of Sears to another without a fight. Pent-up dissatisfaction with a remote and aging officer corps had been surfacing among younger executives in both Field and Parent camps since the recessional downturn. The place looked to many of the younger men—and they were men, not women, in the middle and upper echelons of the company, just as the government contended—to be run by councils of elders, like some latter-day Indian tribe living in the footsteps of the past.

Arthur Wood may not have been a powerful general executive, and he may not have had an ounce of the thick blood of a merchant in his veins, but he was a student of history and a man with an eye for cultural nuance. The company was such that a chairman couldn't see very deeply into the awesome machinery below him, but as Wood considered the portions of Sears he could see at the beginning of 1975, he perceived the makings of a humiliating business failure and possibly a civil war that could destroy the company.

It was then that Arthur Wood decided to break profoundly with the tradition he'd been elevated to serve. He contracted the services of the Hay Associates of Philadelphia, a consulting firm that specialized in studying corporate staffing and organizational issues. Wood assigned Hay the task of assessing the climate inside Sears in order to help the unsettled chairman decide what was to be done.

CHAPTER 2

The Outsiders

It took a great deal of courage for Arthur Wood to invite professional management consultants into Sears, Roebuck. He knew that the arrival of consultants would indicate his own loss of confidence to uneasy employees, and to the huge community of manufacturers, investment professionals, and competitors who watched Sears as sports fanatics follow a favorite team. "If they say everything is fine," Wood told the Sears board of directors when he was questioned closely about his plans to hire the Hay Associates, "then it still will have been worthwhile and reassuring."

But Wood knew that outsiders of any stripe were simply not welcome inside the company. No one in the world could tell Sears, Roebuck anything about the business it towered over—the assertion had become an irrefutable central tenet of the post-war era. The "bean counters" over at the Allstate Insurance Company had allowed highfalutin consultants from Booz, Allen & Hamilton to poke around the corridors of Allstate since 1949, and this was seen at "the real Sears, Roebuck" as a sign of nothing but Allstate's comparative ineptitude and absence of pride. If the Allstate subsidiary had been the largest and most powerful insurance company in the whole world, instead of just one of the largest, maybe the number crunchers wouldn't need to humiliate themselves by employing hired guns.

It never surprised any member of the old guard that Arthur Wood hired a goddamned Englishman with an M.B.A. from the University of

Pennsylvania's prestigious Wharton School and two last names to snoop around and ask them what they'd been up to for the last thirty or forty years. The Hay partner, Ian Sym-Smith, who set up shop in Chicago during the early spring of 1975 seemed almost decadent by Sears standards. He was as tall and lean as any of the General's patricians, had gray suede eyes, spoke from the side of his carefully comported mouth, and pronounced words like "organ-i-zation" with a long "i." He said "pro-*sit*-till-ize" all the time, and it wasn't too long before that was what Ian Sym-Smith started to do.

He wasted no time in designing a series of the sort of sophisticated questionnaire and interview queries in the spirit of the "Hay method" for which the firm was famous. In order to avoid detection, Sym-Smith managed to slip many of his questions about life and work at Sears into the regular "employee morale and attitude study." The Parent-produced attitude studies had been subverted in the Field for years, because the survey used to arrive with "yes/no" and multiple-choice questions presented on two attached sheets of paper, and it was widely known that you could physically separate the questionnaire to see which answer would produce a carbon impression on the bottom score sheet. Entire stores would submit attitude surveys back to Parent with the "correct" answers checked.

Sym-Smith studied the government and people of Sears via surveys, interviews, and special committee meetings for months before he concluded that without exception the Sears, Roebuck of the mid-1970s was the strangest and most inward-looking private society he'd ever come upon. Sears was a place "frozen in time," he said, "like a train stopped on a steep hill." Sym-Smith could not understand by what guise a sweet fellow like Arthur Wood had been chosen to lead such a politicized system of power-brokers and local kings; and he said he would never understand how a man like Gordon Metcalf had been elected to serve before it became Art Wood's turn. Sym-Smith would go back to his office in Philadelphia and tell his partners tales of the astonishing power wielded by the territories, of an expensive, sprawling series of groups and subgroups replete with assistants serving assistants, all of whom labored at the whim of a usually rough-and-tumble personality. The stores of the Field were operated by warlords who vied for power with the corporate "staff kings" and "buyer kings" and residual culture of "catalogmen" who dominated the Parent organization in Chicago.

It turned out, for instance, that, until his retirement a few months before Sym-Smith arrived, a character named Wally Tudor, the personnel and employee-relations VP, was not only for some reason one of the most highly paid men in all of Sears, but also one of the most decidedly powerful. Tudor had come to Sears just before World War I to work for

$16 a week, rising over time to become a refrigerator salesman. A small man in a big-man's company, Wally kept a box next to his demonstration models from which he would speak down to his customers from above. As a senior executive, Tudor continued his pedagogical ways. He had developed a large personal staff in personnel to whose members he assigned book reports meant to broaden their intellectual horizons. The reports on subjects like "the history of the Jews" ("They've managed to stay around for a hell of a long time," Tudor told the fellow who got the assignment) were presented at men-only dinners. It was Tudor who first uttered the widely heralded epigram "The ideal Sears employee hails from a town of less than ten thousand located somewhere in the Midwest." Tudor figured small-town boys understood authority and hard work. Wally Tudor was still sitting on the board of directors in 1975, along with seventeen other Searsmen or Rosenwald family members, and just six outside directors.

Sym-Smith found that another veteran, named Linden Wheeler, simply *ran* the largest consumer-credit business in the world without any controls over him whatsoever. It turned out that Sears was very late in acquiring computer technology, solely because another Parent king, a vice-president for operations named Paul Brown, wanted no part of the "goddamned newfangled things."

At one point during his investigations, Sym-Smith asked his subjects how controversy was handled at the upper levels of Sears. He was told that there was no controversy. Senior Searsmen were trained from their corporate infancy to participate in a veritable cult of contrived harmony and consensus. General Wood had tempered his promise of individual freedom by declaring that while disagreement was fine, sustained discord was anti-Sears. You were supposed to be independent and free, but also supposed to "go along" with things in line with a tradition begun with the General's admonition that as long as the top executives worked together as a team, and no divisiveness or factionalism developed among them, Sears could be strong forever.

The Hay consultant found that no managers at Sears knew anything about what employees outside their purviews did or were paid. He recommended to Arthur Wood that committees be formed to catalog and analyze all of the tens of thousands of jobs inside Sears. Each territory was to have its own "Hay Committee" to re-evaluate jobs in the localities. At Headquarters there would be a Senior Committee of corporate officers assigned to analyze the officer corps. As Sym-Smith saw it, the most important part of the exercise would be the work of a more junior "Corporate Hay Committee" made up of younger men—for they would essentially coordinate the examination of the swollen organization and offer up reports for discussion and approval.

Sym-Smith told Wood this special Corporate Hay Committee should be drawn from both Field and Parent. He wanted a group of energetic "young Turks" who also "represented the basic values of the organization." He wanted most of them to be representatives of the Sears generation that would serve in the officer corps when the current group retired. Wood approved the concept, and Sym-Smith—aided by the personnel department—began to draw up a list of men working in all corners of the empire. But Arthur Wood became convinced, by later in the spring of 1975, that more outside assistance was required. The first-quarter sales had flagged again, and the profits compared with 1974 were off by 58 percent. The stock price had fallen below $60 from a high of $90 during the previous year. The cost of running Sears was rising rapidly while sales were stagnating. Wood knew that any overall programmatic plan to change the status quo—even if he'd had one—would be subverted below him as a matter of course. Planning systems that included strictures such as annual goals for buyers and sellers were casual at best, because prearranged goals and most other planning initiatives entailed a tacit surrender of local control. The structure of administrative autonomy that the General had sought to imbue with so much political and moral superiority had become the most important thing in the world to most of his half-million heirs, and Arthur Wood knew that powerful assistance would be needed if he was to promote any level of alteration.

Three big management-consulting firms—Booz, Allen & Hamilton; Cressap, McCormick and Paget; and McKinsey & Company—were interviewed by Wood and Charles Meyer, the Sears Tall Man whom Arthur Wood had summoned back from a stint as assistant secretary of state for Inter-American Affairs to serve as his director of corporate planning.

The winner would take on the job of analyzing Sears' corporate superstructure, while the Hay consultants would continue to look at the various jobs within the structure. Representatives from the three other firms competed aggressively for the lucrative Sears assignment. Booz, Allen dominated the consulting field in Chicago during the mid-1970s, but McKinsey & Company was thought to have surpassed Booz's billings in New York and several other cities. McKinsey promised Wood and Meyer the Chicago office's full personal attention for the two months they estimated the study of Sears would last. They would commit 50 percent of the time of the number-two man in the firm, Jack Cardwell, and all the time of a young hotshot managing director based in Chicago named Phillip Purcell.

In December 1975, Meyer and Wood chose McKinsey. Wood told the McKinsey consultants they were to study the structure of Sears and

suggest changes, but they were to respect the extant power centers—
especially those in the Field. Wood also reiterated to the McKinsey team
that it was the corporate structure of Sears he wanted them to think
about changing, not, he instructed, "the people"—a request that coincided with management-consulting-industry gospel of the moment
anyway.

Phil Purcell was a "big stud duck" at McKinsey. A graduate of the
University of Chicago and the London School of Economics, he had
become the firm's youngest principal director at twenty-seven, and by
now, at thirty-two, he had fifteen organizational studies of large corporations under his belt in nine years with the firm.

Purcell was well versed in current business theory, but throughout all
of the studies he'd conducted, he'd never found a single company in
which structure was the real problem. Companies, he'd learned, are run
by people, and personality weighs profoundly on policy. But the observation was something young Phil tended at the time to keep to himself.

So he came to Sears with notebook in hand and, like some latter-day
de Tocqueville, began to travel across the map of Sears. Instead of the
two months originally allocated to his corporate anthropology, he spent
the next year and a half wandering through the disparate fiefdoms of the
Field and dwelling in the bailiwicks of the Parent. He was amazed by
how profoundly the proud company was still tethered to its glorious
past; everywhere he went he felt as if the old General still walked among
his people. As Ian Sym-Smith had already observed, Sears was a world
utterly encased in time.

Purcell was charmed by the grand old soldiers of the Field. By company standards, he wasn't old or rough enough to carry a Searsman's bag,
and when many of the old boys observed the tall, tassel-haired consultant, a child by Sears standards, as he walked into their offices and
presumed to ask what they did all day, it was often taken as a joke. But
sometimes they would condescend to tell him tales of "running the hell"
out of the General's stores for just $6,000 a year during the late 1940s,
only to find a $35,000 bonus in their December envelopes. Purcell
learned about the lifetime of Elks Club and Chamber of Commerce
meetings Sears store managers lived, sometimes in fifteen or sixteen
towns and cities over the course of a single career. He heard of escapades: The peg-legged Westerner Stan Donough, who parked his
helicopter on the roofs of stores; the inebriated Indians who used to
stagger into the plumbing-and-fixtures department of the Klamath Falls,
California, store and use the display toilets. There was the store manager
out in Las Vegas who got his bedding department's customers on the
credit rolls by calling the ladies from the red-light district "entertainers
in boarding houses." This Las Vegas manager gave over an entire level

of his store to box springs and frames and rang up some of the large profits under "sporting goods."

Purcell realized he was wandering through a secret museum containing not only a history of material plenty, but also variations on all-American characters whose roots extended back far beyond World War II, to the days of the Yankee peddlers of the eighteenth century. There were rough diamonds and tough guys; and there were good citizens so solid and square they appeared to go home to sleep in Norman Rockwell paintings at night. There were hundreds of fast, fast talkers, the golden-tongued singers of a jazzy song of the sale that rises in varying degrees from the throats of all true retailers, so full of the boasting promise of something better.

Searsmen who'd worked side by side for decades still addressed one another formally, as "Mr." Johnson or "Mr." Jones, but many of the boys also had or told stories of those who had first names like Corny, Slick, Whiz, Prep, Press, Obie, Finn, Swede, and more than a few Docs. If there was no natural nickname available, popular Christian names were attended by the diminutive "y." There were countless Jimmys and Tommys and Johnnys and Eddies, some of whom were over sixty years old.

Purcell listened to idylls of company glory delivered in a patented Sears, Roebuck store-runners' twang that even a Field man from New Hampshire could adopt in order to utter the word "territory." After a while, Purcell drew on his Utah roots and began to say "turah-tory" too.

From Tower to Field, on both sides of the huge cultural divide between buyers and sellers, he learned that the only thing better than being a "good Sears soldier in the trenches" was being a "good merchant." A "merchant" inside Sears was something different from a merchant on the outside. A merchant was a Sears soldier with wings, a sort of retail mystic, who could see a sale coming a mile off. A great merchant could look at an item and know in a glance how many Americans would want to buy it—and the best of the great ones wouldn't ever be able to tell you why. Purcell learned that the greatest "natural merchants" were born that way, possessed from the earliest days with a special heat rising from the palms of their hands. The material world flowed past the gaze of these gifted merchants as the old Sears mascot Ted Williams used to say a fastball looked to him—like a grapefruit moving in slow motion through the air.

"Operators" were the opposite of "merchants" at Sears. Operators were seen by the merchants as uninspired cost-trimmers, whose main purpose was to take the fun out of life. Even if your job was selling goods, you could still be tagged as an operator. Operators were bottom-line boys, devoid of soul, and the dichotomy between the two strains of being

ran up and down the entire organization like the left and right side of
a brain.

Purcell would smile his big kid's smile as executive after Sears executive echoed the old company adage: "All we want is our 80." This was
the idea that the middle 80 percent of the American people were as
loyal to Sears as they were loyal to America, and, until Sears stores
started opening on Sunday, just as loyal as they were to their churches.
The wealthiest 10 percent of the populace shopped at department
stores, the apocrypha instructed, and the poorest 10 percent were the
responsibility of the government and K mart. The Searsmen called the
network of public fealty their "franchise."

They'd say these things, and Purcell would comport his face into his
best "aw shucks" grin and think, "They don't know what's happening
to them at all. There's competition all around them."

"Son," said Charlie Meyer, the Tall Man who'd helped bring McKinsey inside, "Sears doesn't have competition save ourselves. Sears is Number one, number two, three, and four. Take our sales and divide them
by four, and we're still bigger than the next guy." It was early 1975 when
Meyer made this proclamation. Purcell realized immediately that he
was paraphrasing the lead sentences of the famous *Fortune* magazine
cover story about the paragon of retailers published in 1964.

He would ask them which companies competed with them.

"We don't have any competition, son," even the most senior of executives would say. "We compete internally with each other."

If Field employees believed they sold everything needed by 80 percent
of the populace, then the Sears buyers believed the company "had
everything" by the 1970s because they—the true heirs of the company's
founders—bought everything. The modern buyers were the descen-
dants of Searsmen who'd figured out how to make cream separators,
bicycles, plumbing, refrigerators, washers, dryers, radios, televisions,
and power tools all cheap enough to be owned by average Americans.
In their hearts and minds, Phil Purcell and Ian Sym-Smith learned, they
were more than buyers; they were the creators and translators of the
people's desires, the chief sutlers to the army of the American dream.

Back during the early 1920s, a Sears buyer of children's dolls decided
that the delicate china-faced fairy princesses from Germany that were
the only mass-produced dolls available at the time were simply not
suited to the United States. Kids in America wanted dolls that looked like
real babies—and they didn't much cotton to breakable German princesses, or any other sort of princesses, for that matter. Americans were
like that. So Sears offered them an American baby doll, and a company

buyer helped by another tiny increment to define the look and feel of a young culture. By 1963, nearly half of the thousands of things Sears sold had simply not been for sale a decade earlier. The buyers boasted that 95 percent of all items sold bore some or all of their design details because of the Sears product labs or because of brainstorming between the buyer and a factory.

If there was no factory big and solid enough to assure a constant supply of goods the people wanted, the buyers would create a company. Early on, a buyer approached a small manufacturer named Arnold Schwinn and helped him build a bicycle-making company. After the war, some "white goods" buyers brought together a refrigerator manufacturer called Seeger Corporation with a company other Sears buyers had founded years earlier called Whirlpool. In 1961 the buying organization arranged to merge together sixteen small textile suppliers located in towns from West Virginia and across the South to Arizona under the aegis of the Kellwood Corporation, a name chosen in honor of the then chairman of Sears, Charlie Kellstadt, and General Wood. Sears buyers sought suppliers capable of mass productions that would facilitate low prices, but they tried to search out the sorts of entrepreneurial creators of manufactures who shared their independence and pride.

A buyer for Sears, Roebuck could make a small-time entrepreneur a millionaire with the stroke of a pen; entire backwater factory towns could spring to life because of the size of a single order. It was still acknowledged in hundreds of manufacturing communities around the country—particularly in the South—that the Sears buyer who patronized the local factory was far more powerful than the region's local government. Orders from Sears so affected the economy of manufacturing regions that the buyers made programmatic efforts to direct orders to depressed regions. They called one early program "Dixie Progress," and well into the 1960s Sears kept track of its "balance of payments" with each state in the union in an effort to give out orders at levels commensurate with revenues the stores in the region took in. The postwar buyers were hugely powerful men who didn't flinch at the prospect of buying up the entire production of the corner of a state. When they began to range abroad, they became used to seeing citizens of Third World cities lining the streets with tiny flags in hand to welcome them to town.

From the days of Richard Sears, the buyers were encouraged to be independent of style and direction. Sears referred to the buying organization as "a great college of commercial economies." Rosenwald said the organization was designed to be a "confederation of merchants" in which each individual wielded complete authority over his department or line.

If the store runners of the Field saw themselves as foot soldiers, Phil Purcell discovered, then the Sears buyers were like hunters. Discipline and conformity were subsumed in an appreciation of atavistic instincts, hunches, and tour-de-force gestures. Badges were won less for big dollar profits at the end of the year than for brilliantly conceived buys. You won them for studying *your* industry, for peering out at the culture and seeing that central heating and an easing in the formality of men's fashion had conspired to create a need for a lightweight cotton shirt that looked like a flannel. The idea was of something that didn't exist yet in the world, but as a buyer for Sears, Roebuck, you had the task of bringing it to life. Despite the inherent risk, you then contracted an entire factory to tool up and cut you a few hundred thousand shirts—for nothing was ever done on a small scale—and if it worked, you made a million. If it didn't, you'd still have done your job. In the middle of the Great Depression a Sears buyer bought ten thousand kerosene refrigerators that turned out to heat food rather than cool it. The company took a bath on returns to the tune of $2 million, a considerable figure for the times. When the buyer was called into the General's office, the old man said, "A buyer has to venture. I hope you don't lose such a sum again, but I don't want this experience to inhibit you. You have to venture. A good Sears buyer has to assume the risks."

With the rise of the stores, and the development of a separate way of life in the Field, the buyers' long-independent hunters' and gamblers' club was enhanced by the presence of gifted pitchmen who could handle the securing of merchandise from factories one day and the selling of the local lords of the Field the next. There were legendary buyers who would drink paint in front of a roomful of Field representatives just to demonstrate its purity. Others were known to slip a hand under a lingerie model's brassiere, to give the boys from the Field a wink and a thrill.

The leader of the buyers in 1976 was the rather unlikely, strikingly handsome Tall Man, James W. Button. Under the title "senior executive vice-president, merchandising," Button managed the army of buyers at Parent, as well as the hundreds of buyers and support personnel stationed in buying offices in Los Angeles, Dallas, Atlanta, and in the gigantic outpost of two thousand Sears soldiers based in New York City.

Button had come to Sears as a young man, fresh from the University of Chicago, after he found out that research psychologists didn't make much money. From his earliest days as the General's office boy, Jim Button sensed that there was something terribly interesting about mass retailing.

"With the science of today," Button contended around the time he took over the buying organization during the 1960s, "the frustration of opinions and guessing" might be obviated by sophisticated research.

Science could "make heroes of knuckleheads," he said, and thus relegate the "natural," seat-of-the-pants, rough-diamond style that dominated Sears merchantry to the proverbial ash heap of history.

The Sears research department had conducted pioneering analyses of products since the early part of the century. There had been sophisticated studies of population concentration—the General's special favorite—since the mid-1920s. But the nature of the human desire to buy was tacitly assumed, as Lord Keynes contended in his *General Theory,* to be unquantifiable. If Sears concentrated on quality, price, and convenience, it was thought, everyone would shop at Sears. Jim Button thought this a weak-minded supposition.

In May of 1966, he wrestled the continually ignored research department away from the chairman's office and placed it under his buying organization. He proceeded to turn the group into a mammoth polling agency that by 1969 was making seventeen thousand "consumer research contacts" each day. Button held early panel discussions or "focus" groups for consumers, and he'd even bus in groups of college students to find out what young people in America really thought.

Button came to know, for instance, that a Sears steam iron with some seventy holes in the bottom outsold the competition because customers equated the number of holes (incorrectly) with the amount of steam an iron produced. His staff created weather-forecasting systems, the earliest "lifestyles research," and intricate psychographic profiles of average customers and their habits. Most of all, Button loved to study women, the inevitable "her" by which all retailers refer to the generic customer. He knew the favorite color of the average American woman, based on her hair color and skin tones. He became a renowned student of the retailing science called "marketing," and by the early 1970s had gained considerable respect in academic circles by virtue of the sophisticated research and marketing systems he developed for Sears.

Jim Button was far from your average Sears soldier. His efforts to conceal from the rank and file his privileged education, social status, and intellectual pursuits never really squared with the way his every encounter with the rank and file trumpeted his separateness. It was well known that he had been born of aristocratic Kentucky hill people, that he served on the board of trustees at the elite University of Chicago, that his social world was different from that of more pedestrian Searsmen, and that he was a gifted piano player who broke long periods of isolated, abstract thought at his easel with palette in hand. Button never did understand how Arthur Wood—fellow Tall Man and collector of distinguished modern art—could have kept the original Button pastoral painting he once gave the chairman on the wall of the chairman's executive bathroom. Even *Fortune* had devoted a page to Jim Button's painting in 1971 ("He discovered his talent on a rainy day about eleven years ago when he and his two-year-old daughter were playing with her finger-paints").

It never seemed just or proper to Jim Button that the man in charge of the merchandise at the paragon of retailers, a man known all over the world by virtue of this position as the American "merchant prince," should have to go out and justify his inspired cogitation about markets and microeconomic behavior to the five dullards who ran the Sears Field. But the venerable system dictated that his job was to sell for Sears as well as buy, and this meant convincing the company's sellers to do his bidding. Yet, since Button simply didn't want to deal with the stores, he tended to stay in his office. He believed that his role was to create a market for Sears goods through research and attendant national adver-tising, and that the Field's role was to exploit the markets he made. He knew he was speaking Greek to the Field, and he knew that his personal assistants, young M.B.A.s from good schools, were rejected by the Field at a glance. But he refused to get down and "hee-haw" with the boys. Even Arthur Wood on occasion partook of what that good gentleman referred to as "high jinks with the fellows." Therefore Button's docu-ments went unread, and his requests for data were often ignored. His bell curves were thrown away and his better products just pushed the low-priced items off the shelves in stores, which alienated poorer cus-tomers and distorted the carefully planned curves.

By the time Phil Purcell entered the scene, Jim Button was already giving it up. He'd stopped trying to get his ideas beyond the edge of his ever-overflowing desk-full of documents and studies, and began to spend time alone with his door closed or at his easel. Close friends thought he'd become rather "metaphysical," as the Chinese bureaucrats said of Mao during the later years.

Phil Purcell noted closely Button's apparent impotence, but, then, he had spent enough time inside by now to understand the enormity of what Button had been up against. Button dreamed of exerting authority from above, an act that in any other company would have seemed the very purpose of senior management. But the society of Sears was dedi-cated to a proposition that equated control with tyranny, and changing that particular state of affairs has never been an easy task. Purcell now believed that the guardians of the General's dicta would rather die honorably with the system than sully something pure just to employ economies of scale, fight off competition, and appear up-to-date. Sears was above fashion. Purcell would ask all his subjects what their real purpose was at Sears, Roebuck, and time and again they would say, "To give better value, to sell good goods to good people at better prices." It was such a good culture, the consultant thought; such a fine and noble way of life. But he knew he hadn't been allowed inside Sears, Roebuck to fall under the exotic spell of the old Sears; he was there to ring the tocsin of the new.

During the early weeks of 1976, the young Sears executives chosen to serve on Ian Sym-Smith's Corporate Hay Committee had all been summoned rather mysteriously to a Sunday-night reception at the Stevens Hotel in Chicago. There had been so little contact between the rising stars of the five territories, or between any of the territorial hotshots and the stars of the Parent organization, that many of the young Turks (all but two or three of whom had passed fifty) assembled at the reception knew the best managers from other regions of Sears only by reputation. Powerful urban retail-group managers like Stu Thomas of Miami, Bob Tippet of Dallas, and Charlie Wurmstedt of Cleveland were there. A youthful manager named Eddie Brennan, who was said to have a machine for a mind and an encyclopedic knowledge of the Field organization, was there from the Boston group, and John Lowe's administrative assistant, M. E. "Burk" Burkholder, was in from the separate kingdom. The personnel and operating staffs were represented, as well as the buying organization in the form of two well-known Chicago heavyweights, the star buyers Ira Quint and the colorful former catalog writer called Jumpin' Joe Moran.

From his own people at Hay, Sym-Smith selected a "guru" for the committee of all-stars to act as both mediator and *provocateur.* He sent John Keane, a foul-mouthed, hard-drinking ex-priest from the South Side of Chicago, who'd left the Church several years earlier to marry an ex-nun. Keane was a huge, pugnacious man who took great pleasure in communicating to the committee of Searsmen that they worked for a "goddamned company full of lousy, crappy old farts who called themselves managers." He pointed out that the factor by which inflation was augmenting the prices of the mix of goods Sears sold was around 4 percent in 1976. This compared, Keane claimed, with the factor of 7 percent by which the cost of the goods, services, labor, and distribution facilities Sears bought and paid for were rising each year. The differential called for a methodical attempt to weed people out of the organization by redefining job titles, and setting up new systems for evaluation and compensation. But this meant that committee members would have to trespass on the "psychological contract" that guaranteed job security within the Sears family. More shockingly, it meant that a committee representative from the East would have access via the committee to the files and systems of the West; and that Field men would finally see how things were done in the Parent. The very idea of the exercise was a stab at tradition. But the lists of job titles were divided up and each committee member was assigned a two- or three-page analysis of jobs that existed in his corner of the company.

From the first day there were fireworks. Ian Sym-Smith relished his visits to the Corporate Hay Committee meetings just because of all the brilliant rhetoric loose in the room. He loved the emotional soliloquies delivered by the dazzlingly intelligent New Yorker Ira Quint. Quint was an intellectual street brawler who'd managed to conceal his Harvard education from the other buyers for thirty years behind a Garment District tell-ya-what-I'm-gonna-do style. With his shock of curly gray hair, Quint had come to resemble the writer Norman Mailer. He had a cracking smoker's voice from his habit of inhaling half the length of a cigarette in one mammoth puff, and at the time the Hay Associates began their project, he'd taken to padding around the halls of the Sears Tower in an old pair of bedroom slippers because of a foot problem. But that was just Ira.

Everyone in from the Field already knew Ira, because of his years spent on the road as a master manipulator of the Field. Quint distinguished himself while running the children's-clothing department, and was rewarded eventually with the job of overseeing a variety of hardware buying departments. Quint was one of the five managers of the buying side directly under Jim Button. The loquacious Joe Moran, who was responsible for the home-furnishings departments, was another.

Ira and Joe were often mentioned as a duo in business talk at Sears, because nobody was ever sure who was smarter or crazier. When Phil Purcell decided in 1976 that the successful "merchants" at Sears were in fact "unbalanced people," he had been learning about merchandising from Ira and Joe. Ian Sym-Smith believed that during each Hay Committee meeting thousands of years of scholarly tradition were on display in the fiery conflicts between the worldly, Jewish intellectual's perspective portrayed by Ira Quint, and the Jesuitical and Aristotelian references that were apparent in the conversations of John Keane and Joe Moran.

Behind the walls of what seemed to be one of the most self-satisfied and least vibrant corporations of the world—especially during those flat and drifting days of 1976—the young Turks of the Hay Committee gathered for several days of each week, either in Chicago or in hotels in warmer cities, to conduct titanic battles over the philosophical precepts that dictated what Sears, Roebuck was really supposed to be. With information available from all realms of the company, the participants came to acknowledge that they all labored within the confines of an American subculture that had ruptured into separate spheres as different now from one another as the whole of Sears was from the rest of the business world. Each examination of a seemingly innocuous job title and its true purpose within the organization moved the group toward discussions of principles and metaphors.

Joe Moran was the oldest young Turk on the committee, and all the other Hay Committee members were aware that the disheveled veteran treated them like his young sons. Moran took it upon himself to stop pitched battles between Field and Parent representatives in order to elevate the debate to what he called the "country of the mind." He tried always to "define" a problem in terms of "principles"—pompous principles, to the mind of several of his colleagues. Moran contended that the salient metaphor by which Sears, Roebuck could be understood, and thus resuscitated through reformation, was the hierarchy of the Roman Catholic Church. He felt that the Church, with its history of reliance on decentralized power ceded to the regional dioceses, its use of moral persuasion and irrefutable dogma to sustain the central force of the order, and even its similar genesis from the mass popularity of a very big book, rendered it quite similar to the world of Sears—and the brawny ex-priest Keane was quick to agree.

Beneath this lofty level of discourse the tedious work of labeling and ascribing a numerical value to the thousands of job titles at Sears continued. It was clear from the start that the exercise would run long past the six months Ian Sym-Smith had first allocated. The young Turks were astonished daily by the quantities of dead wood they were turning up. There was a man who thought he was "in charge" of inventory control, and another who thought his job was to report the inventory figures to another man, all within one department. They began to categorize hundreds of job titles as "no-job jobs" because they simply floated in the organization with no apparent purpose.

The committee's work churned up inevitable comparisons between Field jobs and Parent jobs, between staff and line, and between similar functionaries within similar divisions. Was the fellow who bought a quarter-million examples of essentially the same washing machine from the Whirlpool Corporation each year—and was therefore entrusted with the perpetuation of Sears' complete dominance of the American laundry market—more or less valuable than a crack apparel-buyer who knew how to scour Hong Kong and Manila for a profitable clothing line and had to be able to assess a garment in a glance? Ira Quint and John Keane attempted to construct a matrix—the most current organizational tool in management science circles in 1976—designed to break the Sears buyers into a dozen or so "levels" dictated by the difficulty and import of their jobs.

The General had been proud of the arbitrary, personalized, American manner by which the wealth of Sears was shared with its employees, and such an attempt to turn what was essentially a gigantic patronage system into a regulated hierarchy was an act of violence to the established order. As the group explored the mazes and tunnels of the organization, they couldn't help noticing how nervous their superiors were becoming about the amount of time they were spending with the other young Turks in Chicago. Several of the committee members came under direct pressure from their superiors to report to them on what they were up to with the intruders from the Hay Associates.

All the participants agreed that they were involved in the best experience of their working lives. Many of them also began to view their small, energetic band as qualitatively superior to the sorry general state of their company. A feeling like disdain for many of the traditions they'd been taught to respect since their corporate infancy grew more powerful with each new boondoggle they identified and so named. Though a level of dissent was always tolerated in the internal democracy of Sears—as long as it didn't violate the General's admonition against active personal disharmony in the officer corps—there had never been an official grouping of insiders designed to criticize the status quo. The Hay participants were beginning to share emotions born of their sense that the elders were debilitating the company they would inherit. If Phil Purcell, Jack Cardwell, and the other McKinseymen were designing new organizational structures to bring about change, then Ian Sym-Smith and the Hay Associates had created a council of disaffected young colonels, with representatives in every corner of the establishment.

The anxiously awaited McKinsey & Company organizational study proposed only a few changes that would alter the intricate status quo. There was a suggestion that the territorial powers relinquish to a central office their authority over store planning in the spirit of "cooperative implementation." The report also called for a new managerial body in which the viewpoints of both sides of the company might be considered in a spirit of unity. These unified voices, the proposal claimed, should be heard within the confines of a new "office of the chairman," a form that management consultants had been planting atop various other corporate structures around the country for five or six years by late 1976. The Field should have its own representative officer working as a co-equal with the buyers' merchant prince, Jim Button, in a decision-making quartet that should include Arthur Wood and the ever-affable president, Dean Swift.

From his earliest days inside the company, Phil Purcell knew he wouldn't believe in the McKinsey study he was assigned to write. A few aggressive observations and the simple imposition of a new administrative body over all the powerful individuals, offices, and traditions ruling Sears was not going to accomplish real change within the empire. The lifers who ran the divisions of the company still marched to cadences struck by a military man born not long after the Civil War. Almost every one of them still believed in a business system that flourished back when it took half a day to crank a phone call through from Los Angeles to Chicago. Each of them believed that the system to which they'd made so many sacrifices made Sears invincible, and that any faltering of late was a result of not doing well enough what they were supposed to do. "Son," Phil Purcell heard over and over again, "all we need is to do what we do a little better."

The modern professional management consultant ideally offers a corporate insider the sober objectivity of the disinterested outsider. The job is simply to hold up a mirror to a company so that its leaders can take a good look at what others see. But there was something about Sears, Roebuck in 1976 that brought forth from the consummate professionals from Hay and McKinsey a powerful instinct to radical action. None of the consultants had ever encountered such awesome cultural and political impediments to altering an economic organization. They all sensed the richness and religiosity of the contrived family of Sears, and though they believed it continued to be the best of America in so many ways, they believed also that the Sears system was inimical to the survival of a great enterprise.

Arthur Wood had warned the McKinsey consultants to be sensitive to existing power centers—especially those in the Field—so Purcell did what he was told. The officer representing the Field inside the office of the chairman was to be viewed as a king of territorial kings, a Field voice and a set of loyal Field eyes resident at Headquarters (Purcell and Cardwell convinced Arthur Wood to retire the "pejorative" term "Parent" from the official lexicon in July 1976, a change that was ignored by all parties for a long time). But secretly Purcell believed that if a Field man of huge strength got the new title "senior executive vice-president, Field"—"someone capable of killing a couple hundred rogue elephants with his bare hands," as he put it—the new officer would be in a position to force a central will upon the autonomous units of the Field. During the early days of 1976, far from the ears of Arthur Wood, Purcell uttered a metaphor for the sort of fury he believed was required to change the system. The quote leaked out of the meeting and echoed through the company for years: "What's needed here at Sears," Purcell said, "is a two-thousand-pound gorilla."

"Just as it took a Julius Rosenwald 50 years ago to make Sears into a business enterprise, and a General Wood 25 years ago to change its basic nature and thus ensure its growth and success during the depression and World War II," wrote the management expert Peter Drucker in 1955, "it will take somebody—and probably quite a few people—to make the decisions that will determine whether Sears is going to continue to prosper or will decline, whether it will survive or will eventually perish."

But no one capable of providing inspirational new direction had presented himself since 1955, and now that the prophesied decline had begun, Purcell believed that the next leader had to be capable of going beyond the organizational stasis to create a renewal.

Purcell realized too that Sears, Roebuck was much more than a company based upon a means of distributing goods to the people. Sears was less a place to work for the people inside its great heart than a place to live. The residents had been taught to love and protect a corporation in the way people used to be taught to love and protect the land. Years later, when Purcell would retell some of the best stories of the best guys he came to know during his early travels, his voice would still take on the tones of tales told by hunters around campfires.

Purcell loved what he saw inside Sears. It made him think of where he came from, and of things he'd forgotten about "real Americans" during his years of studying and consulting among the elites of management. But he still believed a great deal of what he'd learned about why businesses rise and fall, and he knew that the old ways of Sears had to be destroyed.

CHAPTER 3

The Wind
from the East

The old hands of the New York group never forgot the day Ed Telling stormed into the Eastern Territory from Illinois, because the next day he turned around and stormed back home. Tradition dictated that a Sears manager assigned to a new job arrive in town a few days early to learn the ropes from his predecessor. The ritual act of deference was particularly important on the rare occasions when an executive from another territory was sent in from the outside. But after a few hours at the 31st Street Manhattan headquarters of the New York group of stores that January of 1965, Ed Telling disappeared until someone at the territorial personnel office in Philadelphia eventually found him in Rockford, Illinois. "I can't learn anything from him," Telling explained. "So I'll just wait out here till he leaves."

You weren't supposed to say things like that.

All they knew about him in New York was that he was a great big country boy said to be mighty casual about the serious business of supplying the people. If you asked him about his childhood in Danville, Illinois, he'd say, "It was like most boys'. There was school and then I left." He started out in college attending Duke University, where he'd been granted a full football scholarship. Telling liked Duke, but during the spring of his freshman year, the home-town girl with whom he'd been deeply in love since they met during a high-school play, Nancy Hawkins, finally asked her parents if she could move to North Carolina to attend Duke and be near Ed. Her parents refused, so Ed quit Duke and his scholarship and moved back to a tiny downstate school called Illinois Wesleyan to be near Nancy, who was attending college across the border in Indiana. But Nancy's parents put her on a train to California, where she was to attend UCLA and forget about the young man with such slender prospects, and Telling's father cut him off and never gave him another nickel.

Ed was never able to buy a textbook throughout the rest of his college career. He sold pumpkins in the fall for tuition and made beds and waited tables to support himself during the year. After graduation in 1942, he finally married Nancy Hawkins, in spite of her parents' feelings about her taste in men, but not before Telling had been made to pay for pursuing what he really wanted. He never talked to Sears colleagues about experiences like this, but he never forgot them either.

He'd come to Sears from the Navy in 1946, after running into a fellow named Bailey on the main street of their home town of Danville, Illinois. Bailey said that soon after he left the Marines a colonel, he'd been interviewed in Chicago by a man called the General, who told him he could ship out to South America and build a lot of stores if he joined up with Sears. Telling decided to join the General's army too, though after fifteen subsequent jobs at Sears, Roebuck, ranging over the next nineteen years, he'd never worked farther south than Lexington, Kentucky.

Telling was running a midwestern zone—the rural form of a retail group—on the day in 1965 when he was told to pack a carpetbag and join a veritable invasion of the Eastern Territory as part of a general seeding of Sears' weakest territory from the talent-rich ranks of the other four. When asked why the world's largest retailer was so comparatively weak in the world's largest retail market region, company officials of the mid-1960s would note that Sears stores were built around the automobile and there was more public transportation in the heavily urbanized East. But it was no secret to anyone inside Sears that the Eastern Territory had been kept down purposefully by the hand of General Wood. The General called the territory "the decadent East" in public, and he consistently funneled expansion funds to the other regions. Wood thought the air smelled rotten out east, in part because it contained a place he truly loathed, the "evil city of New York." Sears, Roebuck was a company for "good towns," and New York was as bad as Europe—which he also hated—a moribund place laden with sick markets and a decadent citizenry. It was full of liberal, Harvard-educated ethnics and a host of other, similar types who did things the increasingly reactionary leader of Sears during the post-war expansion never liked—such as controlling the American capital markets and starting World War II. All in all, the East didn't deserve the great gifts of Sears, Roebuck.

Because of its contrived deprivation, the East came in fifth by such a distance in all categories of competition between the territories that it had become a sort of company joke. It never surprised Ed Telling that he found in New York some of the only Sears people in the country during the boom times who seemed depressed, or that they wholly resented the carpetbaggers moving in from other territories.

The New York group of stores was a disaster in 1965. The group administration in Manhattan was so weak that Telling found stores running advertising specifically designed to compete with neighboring Sears stores within the group. The internal financial practices he discovered at group headquarters could have served as confirmation of the General's suspicions of local degeneration. The group was clearly out of control, and as Ed Telling began the job of trying to turn the fortunes of the New York stores, he saw that the rogue group was not unlike the other local bastions of the company. New York was what Sears could be without the palliative of great success. Under the aegis of decentralization, the region had fallen into an ineffectual anarchy that each staff employee or store manager believed he could perpetuate as an inalienable right.

The day after Telling took over the Eastern Territory four years later, in March of 1969, he stunned the employees of the territory by killing off a couple of administrative groups. He also moved on the powerful Baltimore and Washington groups and merged them into one. The number of groups suddenly shrank from nineteen to twelve—seven baronies fell with the stroke of a pen. It was an anti-cultural gesture such as most of the boys had never seen. It was as if a new governor had decreed the dissolution of a few counties, or a new U.S. president had signed an edict summarily doing away with some states.

Telling made it known through the few executives who got to talk to him that he thought a group with just two or three big "A" stores in it was a waste of talent and money.

He was often heard to use the un-Sears-like term "discipline," as he and his increasingly loyal group of lieutenants began to set out organizational guidelines that related the number of employees in a store to the volume of sales. The action was viewed as an audacious and irresponsible shot at the sovereign authority of the stores to manage as free merchants. Shock over the usurpation of local prerogatives persisted until the day Ed Telling began to close Sears stores outright. He said he believed that too many of the stores in the East had been built just to enhance the power of a local group warlord or to flatter the ego of the territorial king, so he closed down the struggling store in Torrington, Connecticut, and did the same in Brockport, New York.

Events in the East were observed with horror as news of the fall of long-time local bosses filtered west. The other territorial executives assured one another that Ed was only able to execute such stunning blows against the status quo because of the sorry state of the East. The other territorial powers knew of Telling's Field loyalties and anti-Parent opinions, so they believed it wasn't out of any disrespect for the larger sanctity of the Field that he acted so strangely. He was simply addressing the problems of a sick and faintly corrupted wing of the business.

Suddenly the East started to rise up from the cellar. The territory had been the lowly "wet shivering dog" of Sears for so long that the Field populace was electrified when the comparative profit chart for 1971 showed the Eastern Territory in third place. Then, during 1972, Telling's Easterners leapfrogged to number one in profit by a considerable distance. Management trainees began to hear that the place a young man looking for action really wanted to be was in Ed Telling's Eastern Territory.

When the oil-price recession of 1973 and 1974 laid into Sears, and the directive for layoffs went out to the territories, Telling ignored the call for staff reductions from Chicago and still managed to show the biggest profit and quickest recovery after the economy picked up. The decision to ignore the Parent-required layoffs caused many of the Eastern soldiers, who could never accept Telling's consolidations from above, to come over to the view that the man was in fact a hero of the Field and the true heir of the General's dream. Some veteran merchants had mistrusted Telling, because his actions were so characteristic of the typical Sears operator, and because some of his tactics—like closing stores—plainly violated company taboos. But when he pretended that he had not heard a call for layoffs that was announced in every metropolitan newspaper, the old boys realized that the mysterious fellow from Danville must be one of them after all.

Telling realized early on that a great many directives from above could be ignored in the Field. The sensibility to do so, as far as he was concerned, had been all but *"in-*grained," as he said it, by the system: "Store managers, zone managers, group managers, territorial vice-presidents—we were all taught not to pay attention to anybody—'less it was me." It was never that layoffs were anathema to Telling as such; he just resented the sloppiness of a 10-percent across-the-board layoff when some areas of the company should have been cut by 40 percent and some built up by half. The East, he felt, was already pared down to a reasonable number of employees.

So Ed Telling became known as an intractable enemy of centralized control from the Parent. He always fought off Jim Button's futile attempts to run marketing programs from Chicago. He managed to keep the Sears shopping-center development group, called Homart, a pet project of the Parent brass, from imposing on store placements in the East, and at one point he even managed to halt the construction of a $67-million catalog facility that he believed was unnecessary.

When the consultants from McKinsey & Company studied the resuscitation of the Eastern Territory, they found that the infamous backwater guardian of the General's way in the East was not really the enemy of rule from above they'd heard about. Phil Purcell interviewed Ed Telling at length about his management of the East, and he found that Telling was indeed dead-set against administrative centralization—but only from himself up. His loyal group of aides would later repeat with irony a description of their local hero's take on the General's sacred system: "Ed Telling believes in home rule, and home is wherever Ed happens to live."

Despite his success in the East, Telling was still considered a maverick. Because of the apotheosis of individualism at the company and the corporate tolerance of colorful characters, a maverick manager could transcend the negative connotations of the image as long as he didn't cause overt dissension among senior officers—and as long as he knew enough about how to "run the hell" out of a store, group, or territory so as to make money. But it still seemed that Ed Telling's personal style was carefully designed to test the limits of the dictum.

It was known, for instance, that he often went home from his territorial office at lunchtime and didn't come back to work. He would even make a point of telling his administrative assistant that he was going home to rake leaves. "And if Gordo calls," he'd often add between 1968 and 1972, when Gordon Metcalf was chairman of the board, "you please tell him that I'm at home raking leaves." The administrative assistant would do just that; and the grapevine would carry the news throughout the East, that Ed was once again sticking it to Gordon Metcalf—"Superchairman," as Telling called the company's Tower-builder in disdain.

Before Telling took over the leadership of the East, his predecessor as Eastern territorial vice-president, Charlie Meyer, had to go into the hospital for some proctological surgery. Meyer asked Telling to help him out by giving a speech for him in Pittsburgh. "I'll do it on one condition," Telling said to his boss, "and that's if I can open the speech by informing the crowd that Charlie Meyer couldn't be here because he's in the hospital being made into an even more perfect asshole."

Telling's career was marked by a long history of acts against the cultural order. Early on he made it clear that he had no time for the powerful cult of the "natural merchant" at Sears, so he was tagged by many veterans as the worst sort of number-crunching, soulless operator. It was always said that your career was effectively over at Sears if you ever turned down a new assignment, but Telling had turned down two of them—one an important Parent job—and lived to tell the tale. He actually walked out of an interview with the legendary Wally Tudor of Parent personnel, and Tudor came close to pulling enough strings to get Telling fired that time.

In the East, Telling made several decisions that flew in the face of powerful Sears traditions concerning rank and promotion. As if the trauma of consolidating the Washington and Baltimore groups hadn't shaken up the territory enough, Telling moved a thirty-five-year-old store manager—a little boy by company standards—into the most powerful store in Baltimore and sent the venerable former lord of Baltimore, the new kid's recently deposed boss, to run the kid's previous store in a withering minority neighborhood. That stuff just wasn't done and Telling knew it.

But the other thirty-five-year-olds in the East decided Ed Telling was nothing short of a genius for doing things like that, and so did the veterans who believed their own careers lay in Ed Telling's wake rather than his path. The king of the East was surrounded by a court made up of men who had both rather large families and a particular ability to tell a good story. The tales of Telling's short work hours were part of the constant flow of Telling lore offered up with great color and flourish by his loyal lieutenants. Many of the stories were odes to the man's iconoclasm and strangeness as much as to Ed Telling's skill. It was known that a chess master's memory made Telling almost unbeatable at gin, but it was known too that he played gin when he was supposed to be inspecting a store or having a meeting. Sometimes a long-awaited store inspection would begin with a two-minute tour and end with a funny story only a few minutes later. "I just don't think there's any correlation at all between the length of time spent on something and its relative productiveness," he'd say. "My most productive conversations occur by roaming the halls."

Every so often Telling would just stop talking and let his mouth fall open, as if he'd been shot in the back of the head. He could remain silent like that for hours, his eyes empty and glazed. From his early days as a senior manager, Telling never tried to mask the fact that he possessed the attention span of a hyperactive toddler. No one who ever attended a baseball game with him ever saw the last inning, and it was known that if you had something to say to Ed Telling, you'd better know how to make it interesting within the first few seconds and finish it up a few seconds after that. Even if he was intrigued by talk, Telling would jingle the keys in his pockets and drum his great fingers on his desk. The general counsel for the Eastern Territory was a bright but garrulous attorney who had developed the affectation of taking off his glasses, tilting his head up toward the ceiling, and squinting his eyes shut as he discoursed upon an issue. The lawyer started such an exposition one day in front of his boss and another executive, and after less than a minute Telling got up and left the room. Five minutes later the lawyer opened his eyes to find Telling gone. He was located in his conference room reading *The Wall Street Journal.*

At times, Telling would return from his daydreams as cold as ice, and then it wasn't funny anymore. Long-time associates had seen him go cold so quickly from another, lighter mood that they appeared to shiver while recounting their memory of the incident. Telling rarely gave a direct order, so the Searsmen near him knew they had to listen hard and learn to read his arcane signals. You had to understand his gnomic comments and apparent throwaway lines, for you would only hear what Telling thought about something twice. The requirement made people scared, because the third time he spoke you were gone. "No need to beat a horse if he's not able to pull," he'd say. "Let's get another horse."

He had a habit he said he couldn't do anything about of judging the utility and character of a man the first time he looked into his eyes. Quick-draw decisions like this were a part of the general managerial ethos at Sears. The practice might have descended from the store master's knack for spotting at fifteen paces a shopper in the mood to spend freely.

The endless list of mysterious personal habits and managerial idiosyncrasies mystified the other officers at Sears, because the stories never really squared with Telling's loyal following or the sudden success of the East. An internal personnel study of the Eastern Territory was commissioned by Parent in 1974. The project was meant to explore the myth of the East under Telling, but the results came back showing that the difference between it and the other territories was that, from the group managers to the clerks in the stores, employees in the East seemed to know exactly what they were supposed to do for Sears and Ed Telling. It seemed that through the haze of all that cool silence and strange behavior a "peculiar alchemy with people," as one officer called it, caused subordinates to run themselves ragged for a man who rarely finished a sentence.

The East had risen high above the other territories in all the competitive financial rankings when it came time for a new president to be chosen to serve as the on-line merchant under Arthur Wood in 1972. When Telling was passed over in favor of Dean Swift, the friendly man from the South, the troops in the East took it quite personally. For all their effort, they were still second-class citizens in the eyes of the Sears establishment, and the slight further solidified the Eastern executive corps's identification with the territory and its maverick leader rather than with the Tower growing taller in Chicago by the day. Telling offered his boys the old Field men's line about how he would never give up the power of a Sears territorial officer to become president of the company. He contended he would have turned down the job if it was offered. But it wasn't offered, and his disciples never quite forgot or forgave.

In May of 1975, Arthur Wood asked Telling to run the then faltering Midwestern Territory upon the sudden death of old Cul Kennedy, the long-time Midwestern territorial VP, so Telling left his Eastern Territory in the hands of a close aide and moved to Chicago. He knew there was an interesting thing going on at the upper layers of Sears with this invasion of management consultants running around in the Tower— which just happened to be ten miles from the home base of the Midwestern Territory in Skokie, Illinois. "We got these damned McKinsey people runnin' out our nose," Al Davies of the Southwest would bark when the territorial officers got together in Chicago for the board-of-directors meetings they dominated. John Lowe and Telling would nod their heads and agree with Davies, but the fact was, Telling was more than a little intrigued by the outsiders he'd met.

Phil Purcell had expected more of the same tired gospel when he first met Ed Telling. He waited for the clichés about invincibility, the paucity of worthy competitors, and the age-old sanctity of the autonomous Field. He assumed the presence of a McKinsey observer would be seen as an incursion by Telling—and it was. But he still got answers from the legendary officer unlike any he'd heard at the company.

Telling admitted that Sears was being slowly humbled by competition—"eaten alive," he said. He said the economic force of Sears had been subsumed within a company that had become two companies, with each side further subdivided into "a whole bunch of little empires."

By 1976, Phil Purcell was by far the best-informed student of Sears not of family blood, but he was still an outsider and thus an innocent. The consultant was unaware that Field executives he interviewed after he met Ed Telling had been hearing Telling's voice in his questions for several months. So involuted was the society that specific terms and ideological lines on business issues could be attributed to one leader or a specific regional school of thought, and everyone knew from listening to him that Purcell had been completely taken in by Telling's opinions. When Arthur Wood told the territorial officers he'd decided to accept the McKinsey organizational study as company policy, the Field intelligence network carried word that Ed Telling would be the one "going inside" to join the new office of the chairman as the Field's man in the Tower.

From the Field perspective, McKinsey had ushered an old-fashioned Field gorilla into a Parent decision-making body run by the chairman. It looked like Ed Telling was supposed to go head to head with the leader of the buyers, the noted snob, Jim Button. Telling would sit in council with the kindly Arthur Wood and the even kindlier Dean Swift, and Ed would straighten out this centralization stuff the company had purchased from McKinsey.

After only six months in control of the Midwestern Territory, during late January 1976, Telling moved into an office on the sixty-eighth floor of the Sears Tower as senior executive vice-president, Field. A few weeks later he called the boys in from the Field for a get-together. Telling informed the five territorial officers that if any of them had it in mind to run a detour around him in order to gain direct access to the chairman, they were bound to encounter a good deal more resistance than they'd had from Dean Swift.

They'd had from Dean Swift? The territorial officers exchanged glances. Hadn't Ed blazed the trail around Dean? "If issues concerning what's to be carried in the stores and at what prices come up in the office of the chairman," Telling continued in the emotionless voice he took on in front of any group of two or more people, "I will speak for the Field—and I'm not necessarily gonna insist that all prerogatives should reside at the grass roots."

John Lowe, speaking for the West, said, "I agree that a certain amount of centralization is in order here, Ed—and *all* of it should occur at the territorial level."

Telling's first year in the Tower was actually quite frustrating to him and less disconcerting to the territorial leadership than his early pronouncements might have indicated. He supported efforts by the office of the chairman to curtail territorial authority over dropping stores at will, and he made numerous though brief trips into the Field to explain the "unified" position of Headquarters on any number of issues, but he complained constantly in private that the McKinsey structural accouterments would never change Sears.

As Telling looked down at the company's sellers, he thought about the metaphor of the creation of the wheel. He would say within earshot of astonished Headquarters people that if the wheel was created at the Tower, the Midwest would say they'd carry it but cancel the order at the last minute, and the Pacific Coast would reject it and invent their own model. The men and the traditions were too strong to bow to a polite consensus-oriented decision-making body like the office of the chairman. "You can't structure around a problem," he'd complain to Phil Purcell. "You really sold us out."

Old-timers at Headquarters were shocked to see Ed Telling show up at the funerals of former buyers. He arrived at the events in his big Mercedes and even stood by the door to shake everyone's hand like some seasoned old pol looking for votes. He made symbolic pilgrimages out to the old West Side Headquarters in the company of Parent executives, and even made some of them believe he was deeply moved by the sight of the shrine. Those who'd worked with him in the Field couldn't believe the whole performance. Telling always hated the old red brick Headquarters. He used to note how appropriate it was that the place resembled a high school.

He was polite to the point of solicitousness to other senior executives in the Tower. He spent a lot of his time hanging out in the corridors wearing his huge country-boy grin, and was spotted regularly lumbering through the hallways and skydecks of the Tower with his arms full of papers. One long-time Parent man from the catalog side of the business asked Telling where he was going with all the papers one day. "Learned this in the Navy," Telling said. "If you don't have anything to do, you get some paper in your hands and you run very fast up and down the deck."

A singular opportunity to exhibit how powerful the Field kingdoms could be if properly directed presented itself to the office of the chairman during discussions of corporate battle plans for 1977. Since sales had begun to shrink a few years earlier, the Sears buyers contended that the fundamental cause lay with the territorial administrators' refusals to cut the sale price of goods in the stores in order to get rid of them, because they didn't want the results of markdowns to show up in their reported store profits. The buyers' intelligence sources in the Field reported to them that the length of sales on their items in the stores was often cut short. When they suggested the store managers take $5.00 off the price of a slow-moving item, the stores would take off $3.00. Prices at Sears therefore remained higher than the competition's, and customers used to getting the best value for money at Sears were becoming disenchanted.

A central bone of contention between Field and Parent concerned control over "the kitty." Every Field man in the company knew that the buyers in Chicago accumulated each year a tremendous pool of extra cash. By the fall of 1977, a billion dollars had been socked away by the buyers at Headquarters. The money was known in the Field as the "Parent slush fund," though the buyers preferred to call the balances "credits" or just "599," a term derived from the column on the balance sheets where the cash was stored, and an accounting demarcation understood and respected in mills, forges, and factories from Maine to Hong Kong as a working symbol of Sears, Roebuck's singular power.

The account existed because for all of this century factories lucky enough to supply the needs of Sears, Roebuck tended to make much more money than ones supplying smaller retailers. By the late 1950s it was estimated that most of the over twenty thousand suppliers garnered around 20 percent more profit because they sold to Sears than they would have made if they didn't. Sears would borrow money for a factory at its elite low interest rates. The company would sometimes buy raw commodities like cotton and rubber for the factory at lower prices. Sears would finance a factory's new machines and retooling, and it saved the supplier much of the cost of advertising, distribution, and a sales force because, once the goods hit the shipping docks, they became the responsibility and property of Sears. Often the goods acquired a Sears brand, such as DieHard automobile batteries, Roadhandler tires, or Toughskins blue jeans before heading out into the world. Suppliers whose research departments had cooperated with Sears technicians to create products like the first radial tires, the miracle of trash compactors, and the fiber products called Fortrell and Perma-Prest were perfectly happy to let the biggest advertiser in the world make their products household words.

There was so much economic advantage in the relationship that after a while Sears asked for an agreement with its larger suppliers that effectively made Sears buyers co-managers of hundreds of large and small businesses. Sears had access to a factory's books. During the late 1960s, Sears could use its economic muscle to help a tool producer like Black and Decker make a normally priced power drill for just $9.00. The Sears buyer knew it cost them $9.00, because he, or, on the rarest of occasions, she, had shepherded the process along from the beginning. The kitty came into being when the Sears buyers deemed it reasonable to cull a bit of the difference between the $9.00, it cost Black and Decker to make a drill and the $29.95 the Sears stores received from consumers when they sold it (for Sears was also able, at the time, to undersell the full-price retailers). Buyers told suppliers to ship the drills directly to the stores and to "overbill" the store managers something on the order of $18 for each drill. The supplier was then instructed to put a portion of the excess profits aside—in this case some of the $9.00 per drill—and mail it to the power-tool buyer in Chicago, who in turn added the sum in his "black book" under column "599."

After a while everyone in a given buying department monitored the 599 account as if it were a box score, and each year they all expected it to be a little bigger. If there was money left in 599 at the end of the year, the buyer, in his benevolence, would distribute the cash to the catalog departments and the Field units as profits. As the scouts and hunters for the largest single private consumer in the world, the buyers believed the takings born of their power should reside in Chicago.

The fund served other purposes: before 599 there had been only a few official means by which a buyer could convince the stores to carry goods, but with the advent of the kitty a buyer could now sit down with a local group manager and offer to pay for an expensive full-page ad in a local newspaper from 599 funds—as long as the Field man would push the buyer's line a bit in the store. The inimitable Ira Quint, now holding forth regularly to the members of the Corporate Hay Committee, made his name by forcing his children's wear into American homes through his constant tours of Field and his brilliant manipulation of the pork-barrel political power of 599.

Conversely, a Field group manager might say to a buyer, "Boy, I'm in a little trouble this quarter. If I had the cash to run a big ad, I'll bet your drills would just clean out here in Detroit." And the next week a check would arrive in the company mail.

Only Sears, Roebuck, a microcosmic working economy by itself, could afford such a freewheeling intermediary financial system. Five ninety-nine worked like a dream as long as the Sears stores were buying their Sears goods from Chicago at a lot less than the going price on the open market. As long as they could sell goods below the competition's prices, nobody complained. But during the 1970s, as sales floundered and production and retail prices rose, the horse-trading had turned ugly. Suddenly Field soldiers openly accused buyers of using 599 funds for their personal use. They refused to run sales out of resentment of 599, which was by now known throughout the Field as "overbilling," an incendiary term that from the Field perspective was an accurate assessment of the process. Buyers contended that the stores were lying to them about their sales figures in order to milk more 599 money out of Chicago to pay for desperate price cuts. Factory executives began to feel bullied by the buyers. The checks the suppliers sent to the Tower looked more like tithes than indications of wealth to be shared. In a smaller company, or one with less emphasis on moral imperatives, traditions, and territories, the accounting issue might have been ironed out over the phone or a couple of drinks, but at Sears the debate caused men to offer to step outside or simply to refuse a direct order from above because it was wrong under their perception of higher company law.

During 1975, Jim Button and his buying staff had directed an experiment with the billion-dollar-a-year business called the Sears, Roebuck paint department. All concerned parties in Parent and Field agreed that the markdowns on the selling price of certain paints in the stores would be charged directly back to the buyer's account in the Tower instead of to the store's balance sheet in the Field. The experiment on the eight lines of paint was judged a great success, not in the least for its political effect. The buyer was pleased because the stores in the Field finally conducted sales for the proper length of time and at the prescribed prices, and the results proved the buyers' point that this had been the problem at Sears all along. The store managers didn't have their balance sheets invaded, and they felt they finally had what they'd wanted and believed was their right to have for years—their fingers in the buyers' till in Chicago.

The idea of basing a massive national promotional program on the successful paint-department experiment was received by the office of the chairman with great interest. The experimental system held the possibility of a tremendous rise in sales after a few years of painful, ahistorical stagnation. The charge-back system could not only fix the numbers, it could serve to condition the Field lords to greater involvement with the Tower. A program of drastic price cuts on specified items might also put a major hit to the irritating upstarts from K mart, who had more than doubled their sales volume in the previous four years. No company anywhere could run the hell out of a sale like Sears, Roebuck when Sears decided to sell, and the decision to plan 1977 around the "ATM system" (for the "Audit Transfer Memoranda," the document by which the Field would send the cost of markdowns back to the Tower) sent a whiff of the old glory throughout the organization.

All the dormant firepower could once again be utilized, and Sears would regain the sort of respect it had always had and still deserved. The buyers could really buy; the sellers could sell like hell without having to worry about the impact of price cuts. Ed Telling could demonstrate what the Field was capable of doing when the kings and barons worked together; Jim Button could show off his rarefied marketing research in choosing the items to be sold; and Chairman Arthur Wood could enter the pantheon of Sears merchants past by virtue of the triumph, for 1977 would be the year the fluffy-browed gentleman would reach his mandatory-retirement age.

If the General's extended plans for Sears were respected, then the next chairman would be Charlie Meyer. General Wood announced in the early 1950s that he wouldn't rest easy until Artie Wood and then Meyer had taken a turn. Another candidate of similarly noble tradition was Jim Button, the former office boy to the chairman and current leader of the buyers. Button had been considered a shoo-in only a few years earlier. By 1976, Button was still considered at the front of the pack, though everyone inside Sears knew that he was tired now.

The man Arthur Wood actually intended to name as his successor during the early days of 1977 was Dean Swift, the reigning president of Sears whose ascension had so enraged the Telling men back in the East. Swift had risen through the territories on a smile. "If you could pick yourself a father," it was said of Swift, "it would be Dean." Through all of the corporate faltering in recent years, Swift had maintained an unswerving faith in the way Sears had been built. Dean was pure Sears.

Though the McKinsey study stated that the reorganization it recommended would "strengthen the role of president," the changes had in fact relieved the presidency of its connection to the territories and left Swift with little more than titular control over the staff functions in the Tower. But Dean Swift still endeavored to conduct himself within the traditions of an heir apparent at Sears, and most observers thought he was rather pleased to hand over the job of dealing with the territory empires to Telling and his new McKinsey-created office, because Swift never really liked to intimidate people.

"So Ed Telling must really beat up on people; he must order everybody around," Swift would say to Charlie Bacon, Telling's old colleague from the East and the current Parent personnel director.

"No, Dean," Bacon would answer the president's constant questioning about Telling. "I've actually never seen him do that at all."

Swift became obsessed with how Ed Telling had gotten where he was. It just didn't figure. He observed Telling leaving the Tower after a half-day in his office, so it was clear that the man's secret was not hard work. Swift was a workaholic who thought that leaving the office before 5:30 was immoral. He subscribed to what a former chairman, Charlie Kellstadt, used to say about a day's work for the company: that you work until you're embarrassed; then you go home.

Swift knew Telling was always taking little personal field trips on company time—often in a company plane. Telling would wander down to the Field Museum of Natural History in Chicago or leave a meeting in another city to visit some monument he'd always wanted to see. One afternoon Telling left a meeting in Boston and knocked on the door of Fenway Park until somebody let him in to look around. He would travel miles to see the campuses of small universities ("I just can't imagine being in Maine and not takin' a look at the University of Maine"), and he'd travel much farther away to catch a few races at a local track he wanted to see. Telling telephoned a few of the boys he liked in the Tower one afternoon in 1977 and told them to meet him in the executive garage. He proceeded to take them all out to the Sears hangar at

Midway Airport and then down to Louisville, Kentucky, to catch a few races . . . and he still got everyone home for dinner.

Except for the airplane, Telling appeared to have no interest in the things most senior corporate executives love about a big job. He hated the public aspects of executive life—speeches and hobnobbing with celebrities and politicians—and he didn't much care for the ceremonial appurtenances of life inside the company either. Charlie Bacon knew about Telling's disdain for such things, so he would try to remind Telling to at least show up at important corporate functions. During the morning Charlie reminded Telling of one major company banquet held to honor prominent suppliers that his attendance was expected, but the chair on the dais between Dean Swift and Arthur Wood remained empty throughout the evening because Ed had gone home for dinner.

Despite his low profile and his friendly smile, it almost seemed as if Ed Telling's presence was designed to inform the other senior officers in the Tower that he had no interest in being anything like them. Nobody as plainly odd and mercurial as Telling had been allowed into the executive ranks of Sears since Julius Rosenwald hired the General, and before that you had to go back to the wild man, Richard Sears.

The company ranks were full of mavericks, strange genius types, goofoffs, and even people with socially marginal personal lives, but they all had a place in out-of-the-way corners of the middle levels, away from the front lines or the public eye. The idea of somebody like Ed Telling having the slightest chance of representing Sears to the outside world was a laugh. His style ruled him out as a successor to Wood just as specifically as Dean Swift's every gesture over the past five years mandated his ascension. The succession of a good, solid soldier of Sears to the chairmanship every few years had become an act of sanctification that assured everyone who believed in the Sears way that the way was still good and right. Most Searsmen outside of the Eastern Territory believed that Dean Swift ought be the next chairman of Sears, and even the Easterners thought he would get the call. And if it hadn't been for the skills of the second-best memo-writer at Sears, Roebuck and the dubious professional conduct of an audacious young outsider, this probably would have been the case.

Charlie Bacon never professed to understand Ed Telling any better than anyone else, though company scuttlebutt had it that Charlie was Telling's Boswell, his best friend, and the most adept translator of the man's obscure signals and signs. As a personnel man, Charlie Bacon also thought it amazing that someone so far from the Sears mold had risen so high in the organization. But he still believed in 1977 that his enigmatic long-time associate should run the company if the previous glory was to return and endure. Bacon had been assessing talent for Sears, Roebuck for twenty years before he came across Ed Telling, and he knew from the start he'd never find another man who was quite the same. Bacon had been the personnel director in the East from 1958 to 1973, so few others had a better view of how Telling had redirected the fortunes and psyche of the weakest territory.

Personnel men at Sears were supposed to operate above the fray of office jockeying in order to assure the fairness and due process of the internal democracy. They were seen as promoters of talent for the larger sake of the corporation, who were always ready with an objective assessment of the available talent pool. In fact, the department had become a political base for would-be kingmakers and backroom deal-makers. The General's version of Sears was conceived so as to exalt the role of talented men, and the personnel department grew powerful by knowing where these men were. Territorial powers like John Lowe and Ed Telling deeply resented the Parent personnel department's arrogation of authority, and the arbitrary refusal to promote people who were too young, short, or eager. Charlie Bacon's imperious predecessor, Wally Tudor, even staged a bald-faced campaign to have himself named chairman in 1969 and 1973. Tudor went so far as to take board members out for dinner as part of his effort, but in the end he settled for retirement as yet another man made wealthy by Sears.

As soon as Charlie Bacon got his job at Parent, he began steering Ed Telling through the labyrinth of natural obstacles toward the chairmanship. Up until 1977, however, Bacon had refrained from making a clear case for Telling as chairman to Arthur Wood. He knew the chairman would have considered it inappropriately partisan as well as unlikely in the extreme. But by the middle of 1977 it was clear to Bacon that Wood still intended to elevate Dean Swift, so Bacon decided to try to dissuade the chairman.

Bacon wrote Wood a long memo questioning Dean Swift's abilities as a manager. He even criticized Swift's purported strong points, such as his ability to work with people. The memo also enumerated Ed Telling's contrasting talents, and evenly beseeched the chairman to have the courage to break with a tradition that had ceased to serve them well.

As in other corporations, the succession of the chairman at Sears had developed the trappings of an electoral process. The nominating-and-proxy committee of the board made the official nomination, and the board of directors convened to make the selection, but the chairman really picked the chairman, and nobody was ever supposed to talk to him about it unless asked.

But this particular chairman was known to like memos, and Charlie Bacon was known to write good ones. As a trained attorney, Wood preferred to have his staff write him briefs he could take home at night to ponder, and usually, after several days, the writer would receive a reasonable response. But Arthur Wood never told Bacon that he'd received or even read the un-Sears-like memorandum of the vice-president for personnel, and Bacon never asked if he got it. One day Bacon told his secretary to pull his copy of the memo from the file and shred it.

During the previous summer, of 1976, the senior McKinsey consultant to Sears, Jack Cardwell, accepted an offer to become CEO at Consolidated Foods, the Chicago-based conglomerate. As he was saying goodbye to Arthur Wood, Cardwell couldn't resist a final violation of the McKinsey & Company rules that proscribe meddling in the internal politics of a client company. Cardwell told Wood that he believed the revival of Sears' fortunes depended upon the next chairman's ability to shake up the status quo. Cardwell said he believed the right man had lately surfaced in Ed Telling.

As soon as Cardwell was gone, and Phil Purcell had officially taken his place, Purcell dedicated himself fully to convincing Arthur Wood to make Telling the successor. While Wood allowed Purcell to speak at length, he offered no response. Wood knew that if he passed over Dean Swift he would be remembered as the first chairman in modern memory to break radically with the natural sequence. Dean Swift had been groomed as Wood had been groomed, and he knew that Swift would be deeply injured by having his turn denied. If he picked Ed Telling, Wood knew he might be saddling the company with a notable embarrassment, a man capable of injuring the delicate spirit that made Sears special.

The decision weighed painfully on the good gentleman. He began to hold numerous off-the-record meetings with the outside directors of the nominating-and-proxy committee of the Sears board, and the encounters made it clear to all of the board members that the chairman's distress was compounded by the great ambivalence with which he was facing his own retirement. Few officers had retired from the company easily during the post-war years. It wasn't so much the loss of authority or of something to do as it was the feeling of having left the family.

The idea of a decision that broke with tradition was also complicated by the fact that the unsettling aura of deterioration that had dominated the business climate in the company for four years was on hold in mid-1977. The office of the chairman's brilliant sales promotion program was working like a charm. The monthly sales statements made the appointment of someone like Ed Telling seem like an act designed for more desperate times. For a short while during 1977, Wood considered a plan whereby he would make the urbane Charlie Meyer chairman of the board and appoint Telling as an on-line, operating-officer-style president. Charlie could be counted on to show up at the White House for dinner. If he was spotted in public, it wouldn't be at museums and racetracks during office hours. Charlie could go to the right clubs and talk to security analysts, and Ed could do whatever it was Ed did that had seemed to work so well for him in the East.

During early fall, the members of the nominating committee became concerned about how Arthur Wood was handling his dilemma. No chairman had ever waited until just a few weeks before the traditional November announcement to pick a successor, and it was clear to them that Arthur Wood was in trouble. *Chain Store Age* came out with its posttime odds, and somehow rated Jim Button at two to one; Dean Swift at five to one; Ed Telling at three to one; Jack Kincannon, the powerful chief financial officer who was, in the manner of Wally Tudor, conducting a personal campaign with board members, at five to one; and John Lowe (described as a "Western innovator, creative runner") at twenty to one.

Early that fall, the Hay Associates team leader, Ian Sym-Smith, asked Ed Telling to step aside after a meeting. During 1975, when Telling still ran the East from Philadelphia, the two men had spent time getting to know each other, sharing many gin rummy games during their flights in the territorial jet to meetings in Chicago. Now, the Englishman informed Telling that the smart money at Hay and among the young Turks of the Corporate Hay Committee was riding on the big runner out of Danville.

"You're crazy," Telling said to Sym-Smith. "There haven't been any signs."

"You'd better come to see me in Philadelphia right away," Sym-Smith said. "If you do get the job, you'll have just a day or two to ask Art Wood to make some changes for you, so you better get your list of requests ready."

When Telling showed up at Hay's Philadelphia headquarters on Rittenhouse Square, Sym-Smith took him into a conference room where he'd set up a large felt board containing an organizational chart representing the top of each of the various Sears pyramids. Sym-Smith approached the board and began to pull off and replace the little cards on the chart in a way that no leader of Sears in his right mind could ever think to do.

．　．　．

The bleak Chicago fall contrasted sharply with the bright Monet behind the straightened back of Arthur Wood by the time he rose and strode down the sixty-eighth-floor hallway to pick up Ed Telling on the way to lunch. They ate under the great chandeliers at the elite Chicago Club. On the way out they stopped off in the reading room, where towering windows opened on the east. The trees in Grant Park, along the southern rim of Lake Michigan, had turned and dropped their leaves by the end of September that year, and Arthur Wood commented briefly upon their absence. Then he told Ed Telling it was him.

The next day, Charles Wurmstedt sat waiting on the stone terrace overlooking the eighteenth green at Onwentsia Country Club in the North Shore suburb of Lake Forest. Wurmstedt had been accepted for membership at the prestigious and legendarily exclusive club after he took over the Midwestern Territory in 1976, when Ed Telling moved into the Tower to take that new job. Wurmstedt bought himself a big house across the street from the club, and he still got a kick out of walking out to sit on the club terrace, with its tittering population of rich, white-haired old ladies and men in white shoes with ducks flying across their trousers—people who didn't know a thing about a day's hard work. Only through the grace of God and Sears, Roebuck could an old Field hand like Charlie Wurmstedt end up sitting on the terrace at Onwentsia Country Club. The company wouldn't pay its officers' membership dues at country clubs, because "Sears, Roebuck sells people in stores, not on golf courses," but it was also assumed by some that if the General had enjoyed golf as much as shooting birds at the Fin and Feather Club, then the golf-club memberships would have been part of the package.

Several of the Tall Men from Parent were also members of Onwentsia, while others belonged to the even more exclusive, all-male bastion that was contiguous to Onwentsia called Old Elm. Arthur Wood belonged to both clubs, and Telling had joined Old Elm when he came back from the East. Some old colleagues were amazed about the Old Elm move, since Telling didn't really know how to play golf and was given to picking up his ball after a few holes and strolling around the fairways with his mouth open and looking up at the sky.

Charlie Wurmstedt was used to waiting for Ed Telling to show up, as much as he always disliked it. The two men had traveled the backroads of the Midwest together when they were young company soldiers during the early 1950s. Telling was supposed to make sure the stores in their zone (a rural form of the retail group, since disbanded) had the proper appliances and hardware, and Wurmstedt checked out their "soft goods," like clothing. The two men were lucky to come off the road for a weekend back then, so all they had was each other, card games, and another store down the road. It was a period Wurmstedt remembered with pleasure, and Telling with a great deal of pain. Charlie Wurmstedt had come to realize that one of the ironic symmetries of life in Sears was that loyal and striving young men moved rootless across America for most of their careers by force of their need for money. Almost every one of them had started out as a poor boy. After a while—a long while—the family was secure and money wasn't a problem anymore. At that very moment it seemed like a switch was thrown, and a man's ego would take over and make him take up his family and move on again. Charlie's wife was familiar with a certain smile he wore when he got home from work. It meant it was time to pack. Wurmstedt had held eight jobs since he and Ed Telling rode the Midwestern zone, all of them in the territory he now ran except the two years when Telling brought him to Philadelphia to be his administrative assistant. It had been a hard life in many ways, Wurmstedt thought, but that certainly made him able to appreciate a bright, Indian-summer afternoon along the edge of the eighteenth green at the Onwentsia Country Club in a way that few other members of the club could ever understand.

Charlie liked to think he was a lot like Ed Telling. They shared a tiny attention span, and they both preferred to get to the point. But his gruff, rather Prussian management style never quite gathered for Wurmstedt the sort of awe and respect Telling inspired in those below him. In fact, people who worked with "Wurmy" often noted his ruddy face and sort of goofy smile by referring to him privately as "Howdy Doody." It was the sort of jocular Sears nicknaming that Telling had never once encountered.

Charlie was used to cooling his heels while waiting for Ed Telling to show up. Telling had just called him on the telephone to say he was about to be named chairman of the board. Ed said that he wanted Charlie to take over the Headquarters job of senior executive vice-president, Field. Wurmstedt never much liked the idea of the SEVP, Field, even if it did free up a territory for him to run—he believed that no man working next to clouds in a Tower could presume to lead merchants who were battling it out day, night, and Sundays on the ground—but the old ego and his loyalty to Ed Telling would help him to accept the job downtown anyway.

Arthur Wood arrived on the terrace along with Ed Telling, and after cursory congratulations were accepted and an order given to a waitress, Telling said one of the things he wanted to do right away was get rid of John Lowe, the powerful leader of the West. Telling said that Lowe had been opposed to every program that had come up recently—including

the brilliant sales strategy and novel accounting experiments of 1977—
and that Lowe was loyally protecting some of his least successful old-line
group managers at the company's expense. Lowe was perceived by
some of the younger executives in the Far West as being too Patton-like
and cocksure, Telling contended, so there wouldn't be a unanimous
protest out west after they moved on the powerful officer. On top of that,
John Lowe's numbers were poor, and, for all the power of a loyal force
of sixty thousand territorial workers, you had to keep your numbers up
to remain above reproach.

Wurmstedt had observed first-hand Telling's history of radical symbolic action upon taking on a new job, and he'd seen what a powerful
agent of change were his dislocations of headquarters, closing of offices,
and figurative assassinations of powerful local lords. It was like Alexander the Great crushing the Thebans upon his father's death, just to let
people know he was there, and in Wurmstedt's estimation those decisions had served Telling pretty well. But Wurmstedt said that he'd
known John Lowe a long time. He mentioned some of the unusual
expense problems, the high real-estate taxes, and the aerospace- and
paper-industry slumps that had conspired to hurt the recent performance of the Pacific Coast operation.

But Telling wanted the king of the West dethroned, and he proposed
to do it within a few days.

Then Arthur Wood spoke up. "I should do it, Ed," he said. Wood had
worked closely with Lowe when he'd been sent to earn his spurs in the
West from 1962 to 1967, and many of the people Telling was now calling
inadequate had reported to Wood for five years before the territory was
given, with his approval, to John Lowe, his best manager. Arthur Wood
had helped make John Lowe a corporate king, and he felt it was only
right that he now take responsibility for Lowe's fate. Still the act of
termination unnerved him. Wood told Telling he favored offering Lowe
Wurmstedt's job as head of the Midwest. He said it was only fair.

So Ed Telling offered the ranking proponent of the sanctity and sovereignty of the field a different territory in the Flower Executive Terminal
at Pueblo four days later, but he never thought John Lowe's pride would
allow him to move.

Telling called the strategist Phil Purcell when he got back from Pueblo. "You ready for this?" he said. "Lowe's actually gonna run the Midwest."

Telling wouldn't take command officially until February 1, 1978, but
tradition called for the chairman to announce his successor after the
November board-of-directors meeting, which was scheduled for No-

vember 7. The last press conference is usually like a funeral for the outgoing chairman of any big company, for few things are as lifeless as a lame-duck chairman of the board of a modern corporation. From the moment the successor's name is mentioned, the focus shifts to the new man. Regular visitors appear only on rare occasions. Memos seem to stop coming through, and when they do come, they've usually passed by the new man first.

Arthur Wood took the elevator down from the board room on the sixty-sixth-floor "skylobby," transferred at the forty-ninth floor to a stainless-steel elevator located in "mega-module I," and descended out of the cloud that enclosed the Tower that day to the level of the Jackson Room in the twenty-seventh-floor Conference Center. There, after the large crowd settled down, he told the assembled reporters that Ed Telling would be the tenth chairman of Sears, Roebuck in its ninety-one-year history.

A stunned-looking Dean Swift sat next to Telling at the table as Wood proclaimed that a "thoughtful process" had preceded the apparently unfathomable decision. As to rumors of a power struggle in the Tower, Wood said, "We don't have turmoil around here. These men," he said, turning to Telling and Swift, "are both so well liked it will be a relief to the company to know who's on first base in 1978."

Swift was asked if he had withdrawn from the competition. "Ed and I are good friends and have been for thirty years," Swift said weakly. "I'm . . . looking forward to working with him."

After Telling mentioned the strong retail sales the new strategy was creating for Sears in 1977, and Arthur Wood proclaimed that "the change in top management will not affect the thrust and direction of the company," Dean Swift and a long-time Sears associate left the Tower and wandered the streets of Chicago in the general direction of the bar at the old Chicago Club.

Swift couldn't believe it. Arthur Wood had waited until the very last moment to break it to him, and that made it even worse. For some reason, the reality of his loss and the full extent of his humiliation only came to Dean Swift as he and the other Sears officer neared Michigan Avenue. Then the president of Sears began kicking a can of Coca-Cola in front of him like a child. The can rattled noisily along the busy street, and people stopped to stare as the pale man in a blue overcoat came up and kicked it hard again.

"For Christ's sake, Dean," the other Searsman said. "The police are gonna stop you if you keep this up."

They stopped in front of 130 South Michigan, an ornate old building with soaring columns, on the first floor of which resides the Chicago

Chamber of Commerce. The president of the Chamber for twenty-three years, Tom Coulter, was just leaving.

"Jesus Christ, Dean," said Coulter. "What in hell happened over there?"

Swift looked back at him and choked. "I honestly don't know," he said. He'd done everything right since June 18, 1937, when he went to work at a Sears service station north of Chicago. Dean Swift didn't understand what had happened.

The New York Times called Telling's appointment "something of a surprise." The *Chicago Sun-Times* ran an analysis of the selection process that led to the elevation of a Sears maverick. The article speculated that something about a "major corporate reorganization in 1976 seems to be the reason."

A Sears chairman of the early 1960s used to say that the company grapevine was faster than the speed of light. It was assumed that major executive decisions on the West Coast were known in the East within thirty minutes, and intraterritorial gossip between groups and stores was even faster.

The Sears grapevine was already in a state of severe overload by midafternoon on the 7th, as the jungle drums beat out word of Ed Telling's coup and the electrifying news—announced at the same press conference—that John Lowe was being ripped from his power base in the West.

The Midwestern Territory newspaper came out with a photo of Arthur Wood, Telling, and Charles Wurmstedt, the new SEVP, Field, all sitting together; and another of John Lowe sitting alone, on the other side of the front page. Lowe was depicted at his desk, with fountain pens and books behind him. His lips were curled under into a grim look that could have been despair.

Some wondered if Telling had sold out on the Field, because he appeared to be doing the dirty work of Parent in lopping off Lowe. If a kingpin like Lowe could be hit, who was safe? No territorial vice-president had ever fallen like this before.

But, then, no one so secretly dedicated to altering systems, institutions, laws, and ways of living within Sears had been elevated to the top since the time of Rosenwald and Robert Wood. Ed Telling thought the company, its people, and its guiding ideas had grown old.

For a very long time the General's experiment had worked like a dream. His system could make you rich and make you free. While most Americans struggled over the choice between the security of one of the efficient industrial enterprises Americans organized so well and a life of liberty and risk in the general marketplace, the Searsmen could have it all. But the old man had been there for what seemed like forever, adjusting the mirrors and carefully blunting an unruly will to independence with his periodic calls to unity. The system worked, in large part, because the General was there running the system . . . and now the General was long gone. His creeds and incantations were called out now as if from a spell, and his once lively organization was in danger of becoming a fossil.

For his part, Telling had come to loathe the contrived departmental and regional localism that dominated the government of the company as much as he resented the self-satisfied protection of that incoherence as if it were writ from God. The company needed new writ. He dreamed of reconnecting the organization—Field to Parent, coast to coast, top to bottom—but he knew as well as anyone at Sears that he would be resisted in this and called a traitor. In order to proceed he would need some long-trusted collaborators, possibly some professional planners of strategic change, and a few insiders willing to batter down the grand old doors. He required men politically adept enough not to coalesce the forces of resistance. And it wouldn't be too bad if the new fellas knew how to play gin and spin a decent yarn either.

Back in the spring of 1972 Ed Telling had stunned the Eastern Territory by taking a slight, heavy-eyed executive named Henry Sunderland from a superintendent's job at the Boston catalog plant and making him the territorial administrative assistant in Philadelphia. Sunderland had begun his career in June of 1952, in the same Los Angeles mail-order plant where John Lowe started out fifteen years earlier, and he had later been among the carpetbaggers sent in by Parent personnel to prop up the East. No catalog man had been given such power over retail stores since the General had built the stores atop the chassis of Rosenwald's catalog business. Sunderland had never even worked in a retail store, let alone run a group, as was usually required of someone moving into such a high-level grooming post. He didn't look the part by any man's standards, and most Field soldiers in the East considered the move a plainly perverse repudiation of the age-old separation between two unrelated business spheres.

When Telling came to work in the Tower as SEVP, Field, he asked Phil Purcell to write a job title for Sunderland into the McKinsey proposal so his long-time lieutenant could come along. They came up with "executive staff assistant for catalog sales," a nonjob title which everyone thought was pretty funny at the time. But bringing Henry to Chicago like that raised numerous eyebrows, because having your "boys" follow you into a big job in the Tower from the Field was en-

visaged traditionally as an act of near-feminine weakness. By the time
Chairman-designate Telling called Sunderland in and told him he was
going to send him back home to subdue the unruly Far West, Sunderland had long since become known not only as a dyed-in-the-wool soldier of the East but as one of Ed Telling's personal commandos.

When Henry Sunderland first left Los Angeles there were twenty-one
powerful Sears stores, no Penneys, no K marts—nothing but Sears. Now
there were twenty-seven Sears stores and twenty-seven Ward's stores.
Penney was in every mall, and K marts seemed to be lurking on every
corner. Things had changed.

Sunderland agreed with Telling's contention that his old territory had
become like a secessionist state. The employees in the Far West had
been told by their maverick king that they were different and special
for so long that they'd come to believe it. Sunderland knew he was going
to have to get rid of the Lowe cronies running the Los Angeles group,
and he knew he was going to have to change a few minds. Being a
comprador in the separate kingdom wasn't going to be easy.

"Henry," Telling said when he called Sunderland in, "I want you to
go out and bring 'em back to the company."

As he sat alone—as he did often that that fall—thinking of what else
needed to be done, Telling reasoned that if he could find someone with
no history of a childhood within the company, no axes to grind, someone
who could operate outside the insidious chains of family, regional, and
departmental loyalties, that individual could serve as a powerful agent
of change. He also didn't mind the idea of beginning his tenure with a
few more gestures that might serve as stentorian announcements of his
presence and his determination to ring in change. He decided that one
way to accomplish both objectives would be to hire Phil Purcell away
from McKinsey and make the now thirty-four-year-old outsider a Sears
officer.

An outsider hadn't ever been hired into the senior ranks of the seventeen thousand executives working at the time for Sears. Not one. The
last outsider was the General. "Sears, Roebuck never goes outside" was
an axiom the most casual student of the larger corporations in America
had heard at one time or another. The dictum was one of the few things
that the Field and Headquarters still agreed was sacrosanct. Most Searsmen believed that one reason Ward's had eaten Sears' dust for seventy-
seven years was that the place was full of disaffected ex-Searsmen they'd
taken on over the years, and that a sense of family and shared fervency
never had a chance to grow properly. Sears was all Sears.

It had become almost as axiomatic that Sears was a venerable institution run by mature, venerable businessmen with gray hair and long-service pocket watches. A punk like Phil Purcell couldn't land a high-level job in most Sears stores, let alone in corporate administration, and that would be as much because he had an M.B.A. and had gone to the London School of Economics and believed the world conformed to theories instead of demonstrated patterns drawn from day-to-day experience as anything else—even if the kid did hail from Utah and say "naw" instead of "no."

Telling went to see Arthur Wood, who was still the chairman of record until February 1. He explained that while he realized Sears had a policy against going outside, Phil Purcell had been granted the rare opportunity to study Sears, Roebuck for almost two years, and his accumulated knowledge shouldn't be wasted. "It's just stupid to let it all just walk off into the night," Telling said.

Telling was aware he couldn't put young Phil in place of one of the powerful staff or Field executives. The ripple effect of usurping an entrenched insider's rightful place might cause demoralization to the point of mass defection, but the job of vice-president for planning was sufficiently devoid of personal traditions or cultural substance at Sears to at least be worth a try.

Purcell had been offered several jobs by McKinsey clients in the past—in fact, the majority of companies he'd worked with over the years had asked him to come aboard—but the offer from Sears was different because it came from Ed Telling, by far the most intriguing and unusual senior executive Phil Purcell had ever observed.

Phil knew that McKinsey & Company had its own myths and private ways. Prime among them was the belief that no "really good" people ever left McKinsey. He'd heard many talented McKinseymen called the worst sorts of names in the revisionist wake of their departure from the firm, and he knew McKinsey shared with Sears the unwritten law that once you leave you can never come back. But he still wanted to accept the job at Sears, Roebuck. He kept thinking about the storybook America he'd discovered inside Sears, encased as if in suspended animation. He'd come to see the thing as more than a company. It was like a romance. Somehow working for McKinsey & Company seemed meaningless and rather academic compared with the real work of building a nation and raising the living standards of an entire people. No matter what he did at McKinsey, nothing could be as important as changing Sears. Telling promised him during their talks that if they could break the spell of the past and cashier the company kings, they would move again and create something new. The institution *had* to change, just because it was Sears, Roebuck. The idea struck something deep inside

Phil Purcell that came from his own past, something he thought he'd forgotten.

He remembered his Utah childhood as being a simple one: "Just playing basketball and chasing Annie," his high-school sweetheart, Anne McNamara, whom he married when they were both twenty. But as a Catholic in Utah he grew up feeling different from his Mormon peers. He knew early on that once he left the West, he would never return. It would be crazy to go home to settle in Utah, if for no other reason than that there were too many people who were smarter than him there. "The whole goddamned place was smart people," Phil said, as if a long effort to prove himself intellectually had begun there. He was only twentieth among the eighty kids in his Salt Lake City high-school class, but from then on he'd always been at the top of the heap. He was first in his class at Notre Dame; first at the University of Chicago when he got his M.B.A.; and third at the London School of Economics, where he picked up a master's degree in economics. He was McKinsey's youngest principal director at twenty-seven, then the firm's youngest managing director soon after that, but through all of it he'd never felt completely at home. With all of his elite credentials, Phil Purcell felt inevitably an outsider. He was as much an anti-mandarin mandarin as Ed Telling was an anti-Sears Searsman.

When word hit the grapevine that Purcell had been adopted into the family, some of the territory boys couldn't help reflecting upon the day a tall, smiling kid with glasses and a rough complexion came to ask them what was wrong with their company just a year or two earlier. A few of them remembered they hadn't much liked the guy; some of them had condescended to the young consultant, and they remembered how Purcell had called them "Sir" anyway. Now they wondered if they'd drawn an X over their own faces the day they presumed to lecture Phil Purcell. Up and down the Tower and throughout the headquarters of the Field, executives reflected in horror upon the recent course of events in Pueblo and Chicago.

During the beginning of 1978, Telling's unsettling new appointments were pushed to the background by the devastating realization that a business debacle of historic proportions had been created by the celebrated 1977 sales strategy.

One week after the news conference where Arthur Wood announced his successor, Sears was still boasting to the business press that the magic was back. An extra stock dividend of thirty cents per share was declared, and the stock price was split, all in the spirit of the corporation's "confidence for growth in the future." They were on their way to nothing short of a "stunning year." Ed Telling noted to the *Chicago Sun-Times* that he had been "fortunate enough" to be a part of the policy decisions made by the office of the chairman. Their aggressive sales plans kept sales roaring along all year at a pace exceeding the previous year by margins Sears hadn't experienced since the end of World War II. September retail sales were up a full 20 percent over September 1976, and October was up 19.9 percent. Every store was reported to be full of "hot items" and "runaways," and the consumer-research department indicated people who'd turned away from Sears over the past few years had all come back home to the store that wrote the book on fair dealing and good bargains. Maybe the managers had overreacted to the slumping sales after all. All they needed to do was do what Searsmen do a little better. The entire organization was geared up for the sort of star-spangled Christmas that would electrify the industry. Arthur Wood was told by his merchants to prepare himself for what would undoubtedly be Sears, Roebuck's greatest year of all time.

For every retailer, the few weeks before Christmas Day provide the meaning for the entire year that preceded them. Christmas opens a tiny blowhole on the retail business year through which vast quantities of goods and money must course at high speed if a retail business is to have a good year. Eleven months of slack sales and profitless labor can be redeemed by the careful management and promotion of the acquisitive orgy called Christmas.

For the Christmas selling season of 1977, goods were shipped to Sears stores in September. It was at the point of shipping the goods, not selling them, that the buyers in Chicago accumulated their "credits" culled from the tremendous variance between the cost of things to Sears and the price at which they were billed to Sears stores, and then put the money into the great "599" fund that in 1977 would pay directly for all the "super values" the stores would offer at Christmas. The kitty was swollen with cash in September. Some $1.5 billion had been accumulated by the buyers, and they were poised to remit the funds to the American consumer as so many dazzling Christmas bargains.

By early November, the stores were already selling the hell out of the goods as they never had before. Two hundred and 300 percent sales increases were registered on items that had been flat for years. The number of items marked down and on sale in the stores was up 75 percent. Giddy shoppers streamed into Sears stores looking for one or two discounted items, only to find many other things lining the aisles that were up to 60 percent off the regular prices. It reminded the Field soldiers of the consumer carnival days of the post-war boom, when the hysterical crowds had to be restrained. The store managers just sold and sold, and every day they'd fill out one of those wonderful "ATM" forms and send the bill covering their price markdowns back to the Tower.

Some time in November, certain individuals in the Tower noticed that the hail of ATM statements waiting to be credited against the great kitty was rather sizable. And by the end of November, several people privy to the numbers were worried. The kitty was being dissipated by the ATMs at a terrifying rate. By the third week in December, it was clear that the kitty would never pay for the markdowns coming in. "We have to stop this," the merchant prince, Jim Button, said in a meeting of the office of the chairman. But they all knew it was too late to do a damned thing about it. The $1.5 billion was soon gone, and the ATMs kept coming in and gobbling up the year's profits.

The customers Sears had made so happy had "cherry-picked" the company to death; they'd bought only the goods on sale. They'd bought all the specials—advertised and unadvertised—but they'd passed over the items on which Sears made big profits. Sears sold things at 50 percent off full price that would have sold just as well at 25 percent off. Sales went on for weeks, when retailing gospel had long dictated carefully limited durations on sales. Almost $100 million worth of goods were trundled out as bargains for the people on each day of that December, but there had been no checks and balances on the system, and the company had run clean out of control. The soldiers had all done what they knew how to do better than anybody else in the world. The buyers bought like demons and the sellers sold like selling fools. What originally appeared to the leadership as the best scheme for transcending the multitude of schisms and unifying the company had turned out to be the worst idea they'd ever had. The bright glow of rebirth that shone down on Arthur Wood's final year was just another stage of disintegration, like a star flaring nova-bright.

If the Field in all of its independence and democratic vigor did what it did best, and the Headquarters did the things it did so well, the combined efforts of the two wings of the company would contrive to destroy Sears. That was the worst of it. All that work; all those hundreds and thousands of things; all that money. The whole thing looked doomed.

The kitty went over $100 million in the hole before it was over, and pre-tax corporate profits were off by $130 million, despite one of the biggest sales increases in Sears' history and a powerful showing by Allstate Insurance Company. The tremendous sales increase had yielded an almost 20-percent decline in profits. Despite Allstate's $417 million contribution to net income (the insurers kicked in only $76 million during 1975), the public humiliation of the paragon of retailers was noted by observers all over the world. The merchants of Sears had sold a year's worth of goods at less than they'd paid for them. They'd committed a cardinal sin of merchantry; they'd "given the store away" in front of the whole business community. The retail industry reacted with obvious pleasure at the faltering of the once-feared monster of the Midway, and K mart, Penney, and even tired old Ward's punctuated the humiliation of Sears by racking up record years.

But in the spectacle of one of the largest organizations in the world's running utterly out of control, Ed Telling was still able to see something worth committing to memory. Through the chaos of the defeat he saw the possibility of gaining control. For the first time, Sears executives in an office in Chicago had done something that translated into specific, simultaneous action everywhere in the far-flung kingdoms and baronies. Millions of private decisions between factories, buyers, truckers, bankers, warehousers, salesmen, and a significant portion of all the active consumers in America had harmonized in response to a system. The same form was filled out in Los Angeles and New York. For a moment the institution moved as one. The "great selloff" or "the debacle," as it was soon known, was a palatable event only if you looked at Sears, Roebuck in a peculiar way, so Telling would not mention this treasonous view of the events of 1977 until much later, but he would not forget what they'd seen.

Telling would also not forget which senior members of the buying organization had, in his estimation, taken advantage of the system. The Field would have its period of investigation ánd recrimination, and Charlie Wurmstedt would eventually fire two store managers for "going crazy" with charge-backs and abusing the privilege of access to the kitty in Chicago. The managers were accused of padding the size of the markdowns they billed back to the Tower to get more money out of 599—not for themselves, of course, but for their store.

But the new chairman blamed the buying side for going out of control and trying to break records at the expense of the company. It was decided informally within Telling's circle that the urbane leader of the buyers, Jim Button, would take the fall for the debacle. Button would never recover from 1977, and he would eventually join John Lowe as a dark symbol of the way things would never again be at Sears. But for two points of profit margin, such was the size of Sears' business, Jim Button would have been the hero of American retailing. Without the 2 percent, it was easy to let Button take the rap.

A widely read mid-1977 article in *Forbes* had already blamed Button for the pre-debacle malaise at Sears. "How could such a smart company be so wrong?" the article asked. "It all started in 1966 when James Button took over as Sears chief merchandiser at the old red-brick corporate headquarters . . ." At the interview that led to the *Forbes* article,

Button had the same difficulty restraining his intellectual contempt that he experienced before the Field warlords. "You don't know a thing about merchandising," Button had said to the young reporter on the story. "And here you question my intelligence and integrity. You should know better."

All Jim Button had ever wanted to do was make Sears the greatest marketing machine in the world. He saw a sludgy, labor-intensive community transformed into a gleaming pipeline to the people, flowing full with material culture, all of it run by science and machines with flashing lights instead of a bunch of guys called Doc. He had a sophisticated vision of what the company should look like, but not an ounce of the political acumen necessary to do anything about it.

Jim Button was fifty-nine years old now. He was much too young to think about retiring on his own, and too much a part of an internal society in which Ed Telling had no allies to be moved aside like John Lowe. Killing off a territorial king was one thing; it was a justice dealt to one of Telling's own. But the Sears buyers were an entirely different breed.

One of the things Ian Sym-Smith had suggested to Ed Telling when they met before the felt board on Rittenhouse Square was that he place a strong executive underneath Jim Button with similar job responsibilities—to go "one on one," as Phil Purcell would later refine it—in order to eventually ease Button out. Button could continue to make scholarly pronouncements for a time, but the man under him would operate the merchandising business and begin to take over the management of the unruly buyers. The buyers had plenty of power to undermine a boss if he wasn't acceptable, so Telling needed an officer in the buying unit who could do much more than just subvert Button's personal authority; he had to be strong enough to crack through the calcified barricades that surrounded each department in the Parent buying organization. The new man would have to be wily enough to operate without obvious assistance from Telling, so his actions would not be interpreted by the politically supersensitive buyers and loyal Parent troops as a portent of the Field's eventually storming the Tower.

When the race to succeed Arthur Wood picked up during mid-1977, several members of the Hay Committee noticed that the loquacious buyers Joe Moran and Ira Quint began to make comments during meetings that they knew would eventually travel to Ed Telling via one of the Eastern Territory boys on the committee. It appeared that both men were suddenly prepared to criticize Jim Button. Button was referred to in code during meetings as "the forty-third floor," where his office was located, or as "733," which was his departmental classification, but both buyers made it clear that the revisionist spirit of the Corporate Hay Committee could under the right circumstances supersede their loyalty to the buying establishment.

It was said that every secretary in Sears, Roebuck saw through the appointment of Joseph T. Moran, Jr., to the new post of "vice-president for merchandise groups." Charlie Wurmstedt's opposite number would not in reality be Jim Button; the real merchant prince would be the notorious Jumpin' Joe Moran.

Charlie Wurmstedt had bulldogged a few too many stores, and seen too many exhibitions of fancy footwork in his time, to be fooled by the Moran appointment. And he was just a bit past being scared by anything that came across his path, so he decided the "Joe Moran move" deserved a comment. Part of it was just for the record, and part of it was because of the way Charlie Wurmstedt was. "If you ever do sumpin' like that to me," he told his old sidekick the chairman just before the new Telling administration took over on February 1, "I'll tell you to shove this job up your ass."

Ian Sym-Smith was walking down a hallway at the Hay Associates head-quarters on February 1 when he ran into one of the men who'd assisted him on a portion of Hay's lengthy study of Sears. "Congratulations, Ian," his associate said. "I see your man's got Sears. Guess we're in there for good now."

Sym-Smith shook his head and smiled. "On the contrary. We're out of Sears. We've done our part, but this man will do the rest alone."

CHAPTER 4

Jumpin' Joe

Everyone in the Chicago buying organization knew Joe Moran, because Joe was kind of crazy. He was the fellow who quoted Aeschylus and Saint Thomas Aquinas with such emotion in the lunchroom; the former catalog-writer who always looked like he'd slept in his suit after reeling home from a messy barroom brawl. Some believed Joe's ravaged appearance was the result of never sleeping at all, staying up as he did to write thousands of words on the long yellow legal sheets he brought to work in the morning. He had ten—some said twelve or thirteen—children at home, whom he marched into stores en masse on a Saturday to clothe in different-sized versions of the same outfit. The in-house "book" on the thirty-one-year career of the man Ed Telling chose to undermine the authority of Jim Button was almost as long as it was colorful.

Moran was the guy who bellowed and threw Sears catalogs at a subordinate during the morning and then lovingly drank the same employee under the table after work. He was always in deep trouble with someone in the company, and he was known to have accomplished the Sears miracle of "coming back from the dead" on at least two occasions. He was handed his pencils and nameplate on the grounds of sheer presumptuousness the first time in 1954, and then again a few years later, but he always bounced back into another decent job—something that just wasn't in the cards for the average employee.

They called him "Jumpin' Joe" because the nearsighted Moran memorized an eye chart in order to qualify to serve with General Joseph Swing's "angels," the 11th Airborne division that dropped on the Asugi Aerodrome during the occupation of Japan in 1945. There were tales told by company storytellers of Joe Moran "ripping the throats" out of enemy soldiers "with one hand." There were other stories of the day Captain Moran misread a map, passed a practice jump zone, and loosed hundreds of paratroopers in full battle regalia on downtown Charlotte, North Carolina.

There was no doubt that at one time Moran was a bull of a man, but by 1978 the nickname Jumpin' Joe had taken on the same patina of irony as calling a bald man Curly. Those sharing a drink or an office chat with him were confronted by a rumpled, abstracted, wheezing and hacking, dissipated-looking, and all-but-toothless executive, who made the old stories about Moran's heroics seem distant at best. Not since the General had walked the halls in crinkled suits covered with slobber and bits of the Styrofoam cigarettes he chewed had there been a senior general executive of Sears, Roebuck who displayed such a slovenly physical aspect. By the time Ed Telling gave him his big job, Joe was overweight by at least fifty pounds. His unpolished shoes, raised always onto his desktop, extended beyond lifeless white socks that nestled around his ankles. Joe Moran didn't look a thing like a normal American business-man—let alone one about to direct the purchase of $10 billion worth of goods in a single year. With his long strands of graying hair falling wildly over one eyeglass stem beside his broad Irish face, he looked more like a symphony conductor or one of the old-school, back-of-the-yard Irish newspaper reporters who still haunted the taverns of Chicago.

Though schooled as he was by the Jesuits in the great books and thoughts, Moran could play up the loquacious West Side Irish kid. He could speak with great charm and insight about the work of Kipling or the strategic deficiencies of the Green Bay Packers. He could talk in Latin. He could argue one side of a political issue—usually the left side—for half a night, then switch over to the opposition for practice. As a skilled debater Joe was said to be a man "many times wrong, but never in doubt." If cornered in dispute, Joe began to emit lengthy verbatim quotations and lists of statistics that were difficult to dispute at the moment and impossible to corroborate upon further investigation. He frustrated easily, and at these times would proclaim that a large percent-age of the people on earth were idiots—the actual figure ranged from 98 to 99.9 percent. A young nephew once endeared himself to Joe when, after hearing his uncle mark 98 percent of all people as idiots, he added, "and the other 2 percent are Morans."

Joe quoted his beloved seventeenth-century Cavalier Poets, such as

Richard Lovelace, with the same passion he lent to "Casey at the Bat." A near-photographic memory allowed him to quote hundreds of lines of poetry at a clip. One night Joe was sitting around with a bunch of Headquarters boys when a phrase brought the poetry of Algernon Swinburne to mind. Moran proceeded to recite the pertinent long passage of "The Garden of Persephone" as the others just stared at him in wonder.

To many in the kingdoms of the Field, Joe Moran was nothing but a frothing eccentric, a pretentious man barely in control of himself, a "maverick," "hair shirt," and "character" of the Parent order, a fellow who wouldn't have made it past a "B" Store in Paducah, Kentucky, if he'd grown up in the Field. Through the early 1960s, only 6 percent of the store managers in Sears had attended college, so it wasn't surprising that much of the scholarly pontificating of Jim Button or the hyperintellectual posturing of a Joe Moran was deeply resented by the employees who believed they served Sears in the far-flung trenches. One of the problems with the Sears of the 1970s, to the Field sensibility, was that the Parent organization had become lousy with rich men and wacky professor types like Jumpin' Joe.

During the late 1960s, Moran stormed the Field with an entourage presenting "clinics" about new products and sales plans. Instructional visits to the territories were acceptable, but Moran's decision to call the trips "Medicare visits" carried an implication that was widely resented. During a meeting in Houston one day, Moran noticed a man sleeping at the far end of a long table. While still talking, Joe took off his shoes and crawled the length of the table top until he could place his mouth under the sleeping man's ear. "Don't you agree, Jack?!" he screamed.

The general consensus was that this just wasn't normal behavior. But just as unbounded affluence and consistent success had allowed Sears the luxury of statesmanlike senior managers during the third decade after the war, a quirk in the popular structuring of corporate managerial and operational processes had made a home in big companies for disputatious wild men like Joe Moran.

By the early 1970s, the burgeoning staff organizations supporting the fewer than a thousand people who actually bought the goods for Sears in Chicago had grown to some eight thousand people. The staff assigned to support the buying of drapes and curtains alone included forty executives. These Headquarters buying staffs became a haven for the intellectually gifted souls capable of transcending the simple transmission of claw hammers to America's tool boxes. Many a Sears line worker of the era referred to the office building at the West Side Headquarters that housed the high-level merchandise staffs as Disneyland, a fantasy world filled with crazy guys like Joe Moran.

The day he was transferred to the work-shirt-department staff early in his career, Moran disappeared to a university library for two weeks to study various case histories, corporate monographs, and technical material until he felt he'd mastered the whys and wherefores of the textile industry. He became well known for his habit, upon taking over a new post, of retiring for one hundred days of study, and then emerging to address his staff with a complete reassessment of the department. In a matter of weeks he learned to spot a bombazine at ten paces. Joe would study each new business he was moved into (like the Field soldiers moved between cities and towns, the buying-organization recruits were moved from tools to sweaters to cosmetics with regularity) until he knew just a bit more than the people he worked with.

Moran eventually decided that his observations about management ought to be recorded. "Unfortunately, the managing of communications in a large enterprise has outstripped our oral abilities," he wrote in a memo that inaugurated Joe Moran's single-handed, voluminous, and often fevered efforts to elevate the latter-day office memorandum to the loftiest realms of what he believed to be art and literature.

Joe had always planned to be a writer. "From the time I was twelve years old," he said, "I would be hard pressed to think of a day when I didn't sit down at a typewriter and turn out two thousand words or so." He published his first piece of pulp fiction when he was fourteen. He wrote a musical comedy as an undergraduate at Chicago's De Paul University and went on to a graduate program in the Medill School of Journalism at Northwestern University before the war. After returning from the Pacific, he did some magazine work and a short stint at a small mail-order house before becoming, like the novelist Edgar Rice Burroughs before him, a catalog writer for Sears, Roebuck. He went out to the West Side to join the other copywriters in the famed "bullpen," where he applied his skills to descriptions of goods that were illustrated by drawings and photos of Sears work clothes that looked like wall posters of the Socialist Realism school.

Joe was always mysterious about his decision to commit his talents to descriptions of the sturdy sofas in the Sears Catalog. He contended to *The New York Times* once that a professor at Northwestern had told him, "You're a literate man who writes well, but you're really a merchant."

In 1969 Moran took to calling his blustering memos about merchantry "white papers." Though he attempted to restrict circulation of the treatises to his own staff and up to twenty selected superiors (whose names

were listed prominently on the first page), the white papers were invariably copied and passed quietly between confidants at Headquarters like
the salon poetry that moved through London in the days of Keats.
Dictionaries appeared on desks in the buying departments in 1969 because nobody wanted to miss a pearl from the resident Irish scribe.

"I believe in dissent and debate, but I insist it remain in the country
of the mind and never sink to the valleys of emotion or personalities,"
Moran wrote to his home-fashions staff in a memorable 1969 white
paper called "The Style of a Staff." *The premium for forbearance and
tolerance is completely on us.* No matter the provocation, no matter the
difficulty, you must listen, you must persuade, you must act as if you are
in the company of angels.

"No organization can afford more than one evil-tempered, opinionated, narrow-thinking, super-demanding, wicked old man! *And, that
is I, not thee.... You constitute a line staff.* That is you speak in my name,
and this suggests certain cautions. . . . *Creative people with ideas are
either evangelists or dictators.* You must be the former . . . and evangelists have a certain priestly humility, not like Uriah Heep, but like Aris-
totle. It is a truism that the more one knows, the more one is bemused
by one's own ignorance. There are nineteen different ways to add up to
ten, and I have generally found that prideful, dogmatic minds are igno-
rant ones. So, to be considered bright, be humble . . . Knowledge is
Power in any institution, and the only real authority that anyone needs."

Now Joe Moran would become the first "vice-president, merchandise
groups"—a title Phil Purcell had written for the new merchant prince-
beneath-a-prince. After so many years of frothing on informally about
the "power vacuums" he perceived within Sears, Joe was now being
given the opportunity to fill a void. During discussions preceding
Moran's appointment, Telling considered briefly the idea of just bringing in a Field man to tame the buyers, but such a putsch was judged too
risky. The changes had to be accomplished by degrees, and since Joe
Moran had so eloquently demonstrated his willingness to break from
historical precedent and the Headquarters ranks during Hay Committee debates, Telling decided the new job would belong to the only Sears
executive who ever sent missives to his subordinates signed "God."

The announcement of Jumpin' Joe's rise was made at the same time
blame was being assessed for the "pissing away" of the $1.5 billion the
buyers had accumulated in the kitty during 1977. "Must be a hell of a
company that can lose track of $400 million in two weeks," Telling
mentioned in passing to Moran just before both men took up residence
in offices on the sixty-eighth floor of the Tower. Joe Moran was well

versed enough in the mythology of the East to know that the comment was an example of the way Ed Telling called for action.

Moran contended that a fairly simple adjustment would return the lost profits to the company during Telling's crucial early months as chairman. The sales debacle of 1977, Joe argued, was a simple case of too many goods on sale too long and at prices that were too low. Moran demonstrated that the number of markdowns had risen from 6 percent in 1976 to 10 percent of total sales in 1977. "If we knock that figure down to just 8 percent in 1978," Joe said, "that 2-percent difference will translate into around $400 million."

The exponential relationship by which the rise or fall of a few pennies in the cost of a Sears wrench translated into a million dollars once the system did its massive work always fascinated Joe. Now he was in a position to direct the buyers to "get back the 2 percent."

Joe Moran told his buyers they were to stop giving the people such good deals. "We will tell them what to buy and at what price," Moran said to a group of buying managers in February of 1978.

"The sky has not fallen," Moran wrote in a memo. "Chicken Little is not dead, and God is still in his heaven," but many of the buyers didn't see it that way when they were told what was expected of them for 1978. The managers of the fifty-one buying departments were presented with a form that required them to sign their names to an agreement to create a portion of the $356 million Moran planned to "get back" for Ed Telling. Ira Quint walked into the office of the chief buyer of Sears' paint department and told him that Joe Moran expected him to manipulate the price at which he bought his paint and the price at which he sold it to the stores so as to garner $25 million more in the departmental kitty in 1978 than he'd collected in 1977. The buyer refused to sign. "I've never been able to put more than $10 million extra into the kitty," he said. "Moran's dreaming."

Worse than the specter of raising prices substantially, or of turning the screws hard on the factories for a better price, was the sight of Joe Moran—one of the buyers' own—dictating a policy that smelled of Field retribution. It was clearly designed to punish the buyers for simply doing in 1977 what they'd been trained to do all their lives.

It began to leak around the lower floors of the Tower, where the buying offices were located, that Jumpin' Joe Moran had told some old colleagues that he was determined to play Attila the Hun. The prima donnas and backroom power-brokers among the buyers were to be reined in, just as Big Ed Telling had once tamed the lords of the decadent East.

·   ·   ·

Phil Purcell felt eyes on his back from the moment he arrived at Sears as the new vice-president for planning, the job that he'd described and titled himself while still a McKinseyman. During his early weeks on board, Phil traveled the Field to chew some fat and hee-haw with the boys, just as he had when he first arrived as Jack Cardwell's bag carrier. During this trip across the company map, nobody called him "son," but he came back aware that his personal survival in the company depended on support and protection from three small but forceful factions: the Telling loyalists from the East; the veterans of the Hay Committee who were open to the most subversive sounding plans for change; and the strata of even younger executives at Sears—Purcell's contemporaries— whose careers were mired in the muddy midsection of the company because of the inviolable tradition of lengthy dues-paying and the sheer weight of the massive World War II generation of General Wood's warriors that held sway above them.

Purcell's new planning group was to be known as "702-P." No Sears insider ever talked about "the luggage department." The luggage department was "614." Joe Moran's old group merchandise office for home fashions was "seven-hundred-dash-two" in Searstalk. Many a random stroller on Manhattan's 34th Street knows that "631" is where the dress buyers at Sears, Roebuck work.

So when word filtered down through the company that Phil Purcell and his hand-picked batch of young planners would be 702-P, the full implication was quite clear: 702 was the "executive office," and the executive office contained the shortest list of employees in the nearly two-hundred-page Sears Headquarters phone book. There were just two secretaries under 702 . . . and Ed Telling.

A personnel man was assigned to help Purcell select a staff for his new planning department. "You make damn sure you get him the brightest, farthest-thinking people we've got," Telling said to the personnel specialist. "I want him to have people who aren't afraid to think about things."

Purcell decided to pick one staff executive to concentrate on planning issues for the Field, one for the buyers, and another for the corporate staff. He chose a long-time Telling lieutenant from the East, named Charley Moran, to be his liaison with the territories, but he decided to pull some "babies" from deep within the structure to complete the group. One was a thirty-nine-year-old buyer named Robert E. Wood II, the General's grandson.

On April 1, 1978, the unlikely grouping called 702-P began to consider some of the dark trends they were supposed to alter through sophisticated state-of-the-art business planning—that Sears had lost more than 5 percent of the general retail market over the last decade, for instance, or that the cost of running Sears was moving inexorably to the point where it would exceed corporate revenues. Purcell knew that it would take much more than a page of bleak figures to convince the citizens of the democracy of merchants that there could be a careful plan drawn up for a business they believed to be unplannable. Retailers lived by the item and by the day, by the vagaries of the weather and by the spirited desire to beat last time. A day in the life of most Sears buyers and sellers had meaning only in relation to that same day last year, and "planning" was just a bureaucratic exercise carried out to humor the operators and maybe to look snappy at bonus time. The Field always sent in their yearly budgets—a store manager would usually pick a 3-percent sales rise out of his hat, send it to Chicago, and then exceed the estimate by two digits for the fun of it. The buyers were similarly scientific. Both sides called the knee-jerk estimations "good planning."

Before the McKinsey invasion, back when it was first suggested that all the slumping giant needed was a bit of planning, Sears prevailed on some of the trendier corporations that depended upon a relationship with them to allow a committee from Sears to come observe their planning mechanism. Next to the government, Sears was the largest customer of both IBM and AT&T, so both were studied, as were NCR and Texas Instruments Corporation. But none of them seemed to be such avid planners either. Everyone thought IBM had been a pre-planned operation for years, but the Sears visitors found they'd only gotten into highly disciplined planning quite recently.

Most insiders believed profits came to Sears by virtue of the confluent skills of talented individuals. Planning was a practice of the faceless organizations to which Sears served as a monument in counterpoint. The deal was between an individual and history, and how a fellow got the profit out was his personal and private business.

McKinsey had already drawn up a "decision tree matrix" for Sears that attempted to define the chain of command. The matrix was a means of forcing a template down onto the organization and attempting to draw physical maps and descriptions of seemingly unchartable terrain by locating the source of decisions. Most employees found the tree an entertaining conceit, but the planning-matrix forms that "the kids in 702-P" (alternatively called the "think tank" by the spring of 1978) circulated to all the buying departments during the early weeks of Telling's new administration were not well received. The form was said to be straight from the elitist Harvard Business School. The buyers were asked, via the form, to reassess each of the eight hundred lines of varied merchandise available through Sears. They were asked to categorize the long-range profit potential of their goods in terms of buzz words ranging from "invest and grow" for the best lines (the upper left-hand corner of the matrix) to "harvest and abandon" for the ones in "mature" product industries (a mark in the lower-right-hand corner of the foursquare chart).

After the paperwork came back up to 702-P, it was discovered that only one buyer in Sears thought he bought a product that ought to be milked for what it was worth and abandoned. Nobody in Headquarters had decided to play along. The buyer with the biggest and most profit-producing item at Sears—washing machines—was apparently hard pressed to accept the fact that the washing-machine business was "saturated" or "mature," and that he should therefore relegate his line to a region of the matrix that might affect his access to development and advertising money, and maybe even money to buy new washers. The washer business had indeed become geared to replacing people's old machines. But it was also a $600-million-a-year business to Sears, and the buyer would be damned if he was going to call that bad in writing, damned if he was going to put a shroud over his own head, and damned to if he was going to assist some suspicious effort from upstairs that seemed designed to usurp elements of his own authority.

Old-timers started calling up Charley Moran, the veteran on 702-P, to ask him what the hell he was doing with these Ivy Leaguers up on the forty-third floor. Charley was a good soldier, so he defended the matrix, though by his lights it was one of the most upsetting and disruptive things ever done at Sears, Roebuck, an exercise so atypical of company history as to be plainly stupid. But Ed Telling had told Charley to blaze a path for Phil Purcell and to watch the new boy's back for him, and for many years Charley Moran had done what Ed Telling told him to.

Joe Moran thought the matrix was a dumb idea too, though he had nothing against planning. He had personally planned and replanned the company's future over coffee for years, but the Harvard B School matrix was far from what he had in mind. Moran believed that, rather than importing exogenous new business systems from the cutting edge of academic management, a fix for Sears could be found in the ways of the past. A simple scientific retracing of steps would lead back to the point where things had gone sour. He knew the buyers were never going to cooperate with some graduate-school methodology, but since Phil Purcell was supporting Moran's plan to get the 2 percent of profit back in 1978 by restricting price cuts, Joe kept his disdain for 702-P's matrix scheme to himself.

But on May 25 Moran issued a short white paper entitled "On Certain Changes to the Third and Fourth Quarter Programs." The memo admitted to a huge shortfall in profit for the first quarter. Moran had promised Telling that the kitty would swell to nearly $59 million by the end of April. At the close of the previous April, the 599 account had contained almost $50 million, so a rise of $9 million during the slowest quarter for all retailers seemed conservative. Moran reported in his May memo, however, that only $18 million had in fact been collected and saved, $41 million short of the goal.

"Unfortunately, the re-awakened earth was not accompanied by an awakened sense of the urgent need for program change," Joe wrote in the spring white paper. The memo demanded the cancellation of over fifty planned promotional programs, a compulsory reduction in the number of days goods could be on sale, and, to the horror of the entire buying organization, an across-the-board restriction on the depth of price cuts offered the stores to 20 percent off the regular price: "I expect the changes I am now directing each of you to make to be the Final Solution for 1978, and I do not expect to require of you any further changes except in the event of fire, brimstone, catastrophe, or the acts of a less than benevolent God. . . . Please, no games. No funny numbers. I am rather used to being stonewalled. But enough is enough."

The "elite corps of Sears buyers," as the business press had called the Parent merchants for decades, had worked around or ignored some fairly absurd dicta from above over the years, but this one from Jumpin' Joe took the cake. For one thing, entire departments at Sears operated day in and day out at 20 percent off the "regular" price, and any change in that tradition would cause the most nominally educated consumer of cosmetics or paint, for instance, to take a walk out of the stores and down the street. Moreover, this "across the board" stuff was simply out of line. Sears buyers hadn't done anything across the board since the day during the late nineteenth century when Richard Sears stopped buying all the goods himself. The freedom to buy, to promote, and to cut prices to the stores at will was an inalienable prerogative of a Sears buyer, akin to his right to establish personal relationships and cut his own deals with the factories.

Setting the price of goods going out to the Field in relation to the cost of those goods from a factory was how the buyer kept control of the kitty, the source and symbol of the Sears buyers' incomparable power. But shortly after Joe Moran sent out his "Final Solution" white paper, Ed Telling told Joe Moran he wanted the slush fund and the entire system that had developed around the billion-dollar institution to be abolished by the end of the year.

The edict would destroy an accounting system that had taken on near-religious as well as political overtones over the years, and nobody knew better than an old manipulator of 599 funds like Joe Moran that

Headquarters would try to "finesse" the destruction of 599 that he scheduled to take place by 1979. Joe could run down the Tower and point out which buyers and senior managers were just politic and smart enough to circumvent the ruling. The buyers now believed their bonuses were based on the size of their 599 kitty, a fact that had confirmed to a Field veteran like Telling that the buyers had been pumping up the slush fund all along out of simple greed.

Phil Purcell knew that Telling had hated 599 as a tool of Parent power and profiteering for fifteen years, so he reasoned that the special 702-P recommendation that called for its destruction would be actively considered. Purcell's early impression of 599 was that it made it impossible to see which items were selling well in the Field or which buyers were buying well, because 599 dusted everyone's tracks. Purcell couldn't locate the real promotional costs of the goods or the cost of markups or markdowns in the way he'd been trained to do at Chicago and McKinsey. He couldn't draw a bead on market share. Every numerical indicator was tainted by politics and history and held close to the vests of guys named Doc and Charlie. All managerial logic, all organizational precedent militated for the destruction of 599, but after Ed Telling called for 599's demise, the internal ramifications of the act made Phil Purcell pause. "What we're about to eliminate," he warned his 702-P colleagues after Telling gave the nod, "is the only system we have that has any meaning for the buyers."

The second-quarter results turned out to be as bad as the first. The double-digit sales increases of 1977 were diminished by two-thirds. In June, Joe Moran killed off the traditional fall sweater-promotional program. Then he canceled most of the back-to-school promotions.

In the wake of the new restrictions, unsettling sales news, and the reverberating trauma of the 599 edict, Joe Moran—though still a titular subordinate to Jim Button—decided to call a meeting of his top executives. He planned to assure the managers of the various groupings of buying departments that he realized it was the Field that was subverting the 1978 turnaround strategy by jacking up prices. He would explain to the buyer-kings that his 20-percent across-the-board restriction in price cuts was not a blow struck in the name of the Field, but a means to assure that the stores cut their prices by at least 20 percent. It was a way for the buying organization to coordinate its muscle and to force a united will on the Field. He would remind them that the spirit of the old retail adage still prevailed. The business still "flowed from the goods," and since the buyers controlled the source of goods, the business was still theirs.

The meeting was scheduled for August 2 at the Château Louise, an old ruin of a resort located fifty miles west of Chicago in Dundee, Illinois.

Moran asked the participants to come prepared to make a presentation on the general theme "what the hell is going wrong."

The participants were shocked at how beaten down the once-popular hotel had become. A few noticed mice racing for the shadows as they were ushered down into a medieval-looking dining room in the basement. Waitresses dressed as serving wenches were putting food out on one very long table. When everyone was seated, the serving wenches began to sing and demand that each embarrassed Searsman sing or perform for his supper.

As great steins of beer and roast pigs came out of the kitchen, it might well have crossed the minds of Jumpin' Joe's long-time colleagues that the evening was called to reassure them, as Moran intended, to convey the sense that good old Joe Moran was still the lovable character they knew and loved. But there were too many differences, and most of the buying-side executives would remember the meeting as a nightmare. For one thing, the attendees couldn't help noticing that the titular number-one executive on the buying side, Jim Button, had not been invited. For another, the interloper Phil Purcell was seated in the baronial throne at Moran's right hand. And for another—and this was the thing the veteran executives would remember long after they'd forgotten Jumpin' Joe's protestations of their continued suzerainty—Joe Moran spent the entire meal seated at the head of the table with a paper crown fitted atop his great square head.

As tension increased beneath him during the early fall of 1978, Jim Button seemed almost as wispy, ethereal, and loosely connected to the true form of things as the suggestions of land and sea in his beloved watercolors. The office door of the senior buying-side executive was often closed now, and his long-time secretary complained that the garrulous characters from the lower floors and the visiting emissaries from the factories who used to drop by the office never appeared anymore. Ira Quint went to see his former mentor to talk about how disturbed he was by recent events at Sears, but all Jim Button could talk about was himself. Quint had trouble making sense of the conversation.

Button had a bad lung now, and his doctors had suggested surgery. The health problems would be offered time and again as the cause of his sudden retirement that fall. Button would later blame the Field for plotting his demise, but it was clear that the focus of the company was shifting to men of action, to students of power rather than abstract observers of the science of satisfying material desires.

Button took two old colleagues over to the Chicago Club for lunch during September and lifted his glass high after the wine was poured.

"Here's to you fellows," he declared. "I'm out." His two friends lifted their glasses back toward him, and that was all there was.

The autumn of 1978 turned out to be a time of soaring sales increases for every big retail chain in the country except Sears. During September, the stores sold 32 percent fewer products at cut-rate, nominally profitable prices than they had during the back-to-school sales of 1977—just as Moran had dictated. More profit was indeed being reaped from each item sold, but the total volume of sales was decreasing at a startling pace. It was a trend that Joe Moran believed could be halted only by an institutional rededication to the true historical purpose of Sears, Roebuck—a role that had been obscured, according to Joe, by the sin of arrogance.

Since April, the buyers had been laboring over planning documents requested by Phil Purcell and his 702-P staff, and by early fall each of the nine managers of the buying department groups had presented Joe Moran with a written projection of each of the fifty-one buying departments' merchandising strategies for the period between 1979 and 1983. Moran considered the documents and decided that he would draw from the welter of planning matrices something more than the "Unified Headquarters Merchandising Strategy" he'd been assigned to collate. He would create instead a treatise for Sears, a tour-de-force description of a new direction. He would write a redeclaration of the company's proper role in America.

It would not be the first time that Joe had labored late into the night in order to apply an intellectual perspective to the day-to-day work of supplying the people. Back in 1972, he applied himself to a sociological and psychological penetration of the changing Sears "target customer": "Above everything else she remains an incurable romantic," he wrote. "She values love, desert islands, and sophisticated soap operas. . . . She has champagne tastes on a beer pocket book. To reach the target customer we must develop the style, the value and the quality that she finds in competition. We can't get her with the downscale chain store image we now have."

But the regime of the man from Danville called for organizational and merchandising changes promulgated under the aegis of a massive rededication to the common man: "We are not a fashion store. We are not a store for the whimsical nor the affluent," Moran wrote that fall. "Sears is a family store for middle class, homeowning Americans. . . . We are not a store that anticipates. We reflect the world of Middle America, and all of its desires and concerns and problems and faults. And we must all look on what we are and pronounce it good! And seek to extend it. And not be swayed from it by the attraction of other markets, no matter how enticing they might be."

For all of the corporate efforts to increase market share through promotional price markdowns, he argued in the "Headquarters Merchandising Plan," Sears had not in fact increased its share of the general
merchandising market *since 1965* and had instead whittled down profit
margins and besmirched its venerable reputation as a place where the
great silent majority got good value for their money.

Moran's "yellow book," as the document became known, proposed
numerous policy reversals, all of them in the spirit of reclaiming the old
verities of a nobler past. He wrote of a return to "discipline"—a term
that was not historical to Headquarters but well understand as a buzz
word from Telling's days in the Eastern Territory. Discipline, Moran
wrote, meant a return to the old Sears "good-better-best" pricing guidelines—this from a Headquarters veteran who ran a drapery-and-bed-
spread department between 1964 and 1969 that offered the largest and
least disciplined assortment of such goods ever assembled. The plan
called for a cut in advertising expenditures to help profit margins—a
proposal that flew in the face of the traditional means of boosting flag-
ging sales. In one section of the planning document, the former cham-
pion of corporate staff operations wrote: "We have simply let these staffs
grow to the point where they're killing us," and went on to recommend
reductions in the size of the Headquarters organization.

The secret planning document was sent under tight controls to the
members of the office of the chairman. But the Tower was alive with
rumors that fall, many of them spawned by the sheer length of time that
Joe Moran was spending behind the usually closed office door of Ed
Telling.

Telling considered the yellow book pretty brilliant stuff. The unkempt
Irishman appeared to have grasped a sense of his own commitment to
cleaning up the creaking machine: to blowing away the smoke of obscu-
rantist devices like 599 and tearing down the walls surrounding the
resilient suborders, camps, coteries, and schools of thought. Jumpin' Joe
was well on his way to making the team.

CHAPTER 5

The General's Ghost

E d Telling didn't want to go to New York City on November 8, 1978. He didn't like New York; he didn't like having to justify his actions to anybody; he didn't like professional securities analysts from fancy Wall Street firms; and he hated appearing in public. In crowds he often seemed to grind to a halt, like an appliance with a failing battery. His massive neck would ease into a posture of almost primordial relaxation, and he could recede so far from the levers of physical action that he appeared to lose his powers of speech. His voice was occasionally mellifluous, a pleasant tenor lofting to long sentences, but in public it fell as flat as a cornfield in the winter. At a briefing of retail analysts, Telling once allowed that he really didn't know too much one way or another because he was "just a small-town banker's son from Danville, Illinois." The statement greatly embarrassed Jack Kincannon, the Sears senior executive vice-president in charge of finance and the man responsible for corporate relations with the investment community. Since becoming chairman, Telling had made himself unavailable to the sort of phone calls powerful analysts were used to making to CEOs, so Kincannon usually fielded the inquiries.

Sears was at one time as much the darling of New York securities analysts as it was a favorite of the New York business press, but the relationship had altered radically since the days when Jim Button could present a brilliant-sounding merchandise plan, hand out eight-button Sears blenders from Department 611 as mementos of the evening, and wait for another rise in the stock price. The price of Sears shares was falling by the day, so Telling acquiesced to an invitation from the New York Society of Financial Analysts to go to New York to assuage the growing sense of concern there.

The meeting was held in a banquet room at Fraunces Tavern, a Lower Manhattan restaurant housed in a two-and-a-half-century-old building run by the American Sons of the Revolution. As soon as the officers from Chicago arrived, they saw they should have booked a larger room. The place was hot and overcrowded, because a large number of journalists had shown up to take a look at the hayseed CEO who was causing so much rumor and fear in financial and manufacturing circles. Word was beginning to circulate among suppliers and competitors about serious problems at Sears. There were rumors that the two great camps within the company were drawing to opposite ramparts behind the unlikely figures of Charlie Wurmstedt and Joe Moran.

Telling lumbered to the lectern at Fraunces Tavern. "I know that one question is uppermost in your minds," he said. "What's going on at Sears? How do we account for the current lag in our monthly sales at a time when the major merchants are registering double-digit in-creases?"

Telling said that "inbred practices" were being changed within Sears. A new merchandising strategy was being implemented that indeed involved change at a pace that made some people uncomfortable.

After he admitted to the sorry state of the sales figures that the company would register in the third quarter, someone in the foul-tempered crowd asked him to comment on rumors that Sears was about to cut off thousands of suppliers. The fortunes of many companies dependent on orders from Sears had suffered along with the retailer's for several months—business at the Singer Company, makers of many Sears power tools, was off by 46 percent; Whirlpool's third-quarter earnings were off more than $20 million.

The General used to warn suppliers to protect themselves from a change in policy at Sears by never selling his boys more than 50 percent of their production—but when business was hot, buyers would not only expect the lion's share of a company's goods, but would lean on suppliers and urge them to expand production capacities. Over the years, buyers for Sears had been accused of building up a factory with huge orders and easy money for new facility construction until the very existence of the concern became dependent on Sears.

The potential for tyrannical control of the factories was mitigated by personal relationships between factory managers and buyers, by the Sears tradition of fair play, by the buyers' access to 599 funds that they would occasionally let suppliers use during rougher times, and by a long-held Jeffersonian allegiance to the sustenance of independent, usually small-time manufacturers that was yet another of Sears' hallowed legacies. It was the little factories of the Republic that had worked together to make great cities rise and powerful dictators fall. The suppliers were family.

So journalists and analysts who monitor Sears in behalf of tens of thousands of businesses, employees, and investors waited anxiously for Ed Telling's answer that fall morning in New York: "I've become a little testy with some suppliers," Telling said with a smile. "There's just nothing in fine print that says we have to keep these guys happy. . . . Some should settle down and start running their business instead of expecting Sears to run it for them."

Within an hour, buyers in the Tower began receiving phone calls. The word on the grapevine was that Telling had said Sears didn't "owe suppliers a living." Buyers turned to their group managers to find out what the hell they were supposed to say. The group managers on the buying side had been listening to Joe Moran's pledges to cut out manufacturers ever since the day he showed up at work with his opus about merchandise planning. Purchases from many of the factories had been revved up almost 35 percent for the big sales of 1977, but with sales killed off and prices higher, orders were being cut. "If they squeal about smaller orders," Moran said to the nine buying-organization managers one afternoon, "tell them to try to find three other customers to replace us."

Telling was upset by the aggressive, disrespectful tone that many of the attendees had adopted in New York, and he was enraged by the way his comments about the suppliers were played up to the exclusion of other remarks. He was told that many of the analysts believed they'd been misled as to Sears' projected results by Jack Kincannon, which the chairman noted for the record, but for weeks after the analysts' meeting he appeared even more withdrawn than usual.

The panic among suppliers after the Fraunces Tavern episode was particularly intense in other parts of New York City, where by the fall of 1978 over fifteen hundred companies were in the process of supplying Sears with some $4.5 million worth of goods every business day. Aside from the added fear that they might be cut off entirely, held up for lower prices, or forced to warehouse goods until the Sears slump subsided, the New York–based suppliers were already in turmoil because of Telling and Moran's plan to close down the lifeline to the Tower, the seventy-six-year-old colony the buying organization maintained in New York.

The Corporate Hay Committee had recommended closing the New

York buying office during a secret presentation to Arthur Wood, and though the young Turks justified the proposal on the basis of cost containment and the movement of major apparel markets away from New York, the closing was actually part of the planned assault upon company tradition. The buying office at 51st Street and Broadway, with its special vice-president and its hundreds of honorary members of the New York rag trade—people who understood Yiddish phrases and were able to consume monstrous 34th Street–style lunches—was as much a symbol of the historical independence of the line buyers as the glass-and-steel headquarters in Alhambra, California, constructed under John Lowe was a symbol of decentralization and territorial sovereignty.

To Joe Moran, the New York office was also a vivid counterpoint to the new spirit of recommitment to the common man. It had been run for years by a fellow with a monstrous ego and a constant suntan, the latter being due, in large part, to the sun lamp located in one of the recessed lamp emplacements above his head. The current leader of the New York buyers worked at the same desk, between furled American flags—like the President of the United States—and the people who worked there with him were so far from the minds of Middle America that they believed they were paid to promote the elitist conception of "fashion."

A few months earlier, Ed Telling had heard that a seven-passenger limousine had been delivered to the 51st Street Manhattan buying headquarters. Within twenty-four hours, the limo was heading west along Highway 80 toward Chicago. In Sharon, Pennsylvania, the New York office chauffeur rendezvoused with a Sears chauffeur from the Tower, who got into the new limousine and drove it back to Chicago. The New York man returned in a broken-down four-door blue Cadillac sedan Telling had selected from the carpool himself.

"Jesus, Ed, didn't take you long to get that new car," one of the officers said to Telling after he'd dispatched the junker.

"Nope," said Telling, "and when I get the goddamned thing back here I'm takin' a pick ax to it."

The plan to relocate some employees and close down the office was received by the New York organization with extreme bitterness and rage. There were rumors of threats to both Joe Moran and Phil Purcell, and some employees held a prayer vigil at a nearby church.

Outside of Sears, from the cutting rooms of 34th Street to the office of the deputy mayor of New York, who received the Sears executive bearing news of the executive exodus, the actions by Sears were seen as those of a historically anti-Semitic institution showing its true colors under the stress of hard times. By mid-November the ugly old joke was again circulating through the garment trade about how "made-up goods and Sears, Roebuck have killed more Jews than Adolf Hitler."

The General would have been nearing his hundredth birthday by the late months of 1978, but the deep personal prejudices he managed to associate with the company were not forgotten. Wood's mid-century anti-Semitism was born publicly, through his association with right-wing groups such as the isolationist America First and later the reactionary American Security Council. The old man believed that the capitalism of free men would survive Adolf Hitler without resorting to a war that would only save the decadent regimes of Western Europe. He also thought that Senator Joe McCarthy would have made a fine president of the United States. In his personal files he collected examples of anti-black and anti-Semitic literature and numerous cartoons displaying the styles favored by Joseph Goebbels.

The General loathed New York, Europe, bureaucracies, communists, and something he thought of as the Harvard University–New York combine. According to his relatives, Wood thought Harvard was an unofficial branch of the Kremlin. He didn't hate Jews per se, it was said, just Jews educated at Harvard. The narrow definition of his anti-Semitism was evidenced, apologists argued, by Wood's close friendship with Goldman, Sachs' senior partner, Sidney Weinberg, by the presence of Jews at Sears—almost exclusively in the buying organization—and by the simple fact that the General had been trusted with control over Sears, Roebuck by none other than Julius Rosenwald, one of the more prominent Jews of the twentieth century.

Wood had had reservations about going to work for Julius Rosenwald and his "Jewish family firm" in 1925. As he wrote to a friend at the time, he didn't want to "find himself hampered by a lot of Jewish relatives. Life is too short to be surrounded by people that you do not like, no matter how much money you may be making." But the Rosenwalds rarely imposed themselves on the General in any way—much to the chagrin and confusion of the Jewish business community. One exception came when the General's friend and associate in isolationist causes, Charles Lindbergh, proclaimed the Nazi war machine "invincible." Julius Rosenwald's son, Lessing, who was then running the catalog plant in Philadelphia, demanded that the General publicly disassociate himself from Lindbergh's statement. The General never did.

During the great expansion after World War II, Sears executives refused to believe that their private democracy was being run by a leading anti-Semite. They noted invariably the presence inside top management of a Harvard-educated, Jewish executive named Eddie Gudeman, who was thought by most observers in Chicago and New York business circles and those throughout all of the retail community to be the heir apparent to the company presidency. But when Gudeman's turn came in 1957, he was passed over, and the murky circumstances of his rejection persisted within a generation of executives as one of the great business mysteries, to resurface at intervals whenever there was a suggestion of an insidious strain of residual anti-Semitism at Sears.

Gudeman joined Sears in 1927 as the chief assistant to the legendary Searsman, Ted Houser, the scholarly executive the General had chosen to run the buying organization. Houser become the first chairman to take a turn at the helm upon the General's "retirement" in 1954, and Gudeman succeeded him as head of the buying organization, the owner of a national reputation as a brilliant student of retailing, and the teacher of merchants like Jim Button and Joe Moran.

When events such as those of 1978 revived the old questions about the passing over of Gudeman, relatives of Julius Rosenwald and Jewish employees of Sears usually contended that, whatever the General's personal prejudices, the old man would never have let his political prejudices influence the leadership of the company. But on February 1, 1957, General Wood, then seventy-eight years old and the honorary chairman of the board of Sears, went into the small office he kept in the Chicago Board of Trade building and wrote a letter to a fellow Sears board member named Russell Stearns, a Boston financier. The letter informed Stearns that Ted Houser indeed intended to appoint Eddie Gudeman to be president of Sears, Roebuck.

However, Wood wrote in confidence to Stearns that, although he had a "brilliant mind" and had done "a brilliant job" in the past, Gudeman had made some serious mistakes during his time as merchant prince. Then there was "the question of his race." "I am not prejudiced against Jews as individuals,"* Wood wrote, "but I think it would be a terrible mistake and do injury to this company if a Jew were in as president, for I am convinced that he would not get the same measure of loyalty and devotion that we have been used to."

The General added that Gudeman was high-strung and given to stomach ulcers, then he asked Stearns to support his position if the issue came to a "showdown" in an upcoming board-of-directors meeting: "I had hoped that Ted [Houser] would revise his opinion, but knowing him as I do, I doubt it as he has an extreme obstinacy. However, if he is outnumbered and finds he cannot put it over, the matter may be adjusted."

Russell Stearns replied four days later from Boston: "I have known that with some of the top management Eddie Gudeman has been looked upon as a crown prince. . . . I have a feeling, however, that the leadership of Sears requires a little different type of person." Stearns then suggested some alternatives, including the young lawyer Arthur Wood.

---

*"It's *not* that he's a Jew," Wood said to his protégé, Charlie Meyer, at the time. "It's just not the right Jew."

. . .

When Eddie Gudeman found out that he was being passed over, he resigned immediately. The General wrote Gudeman to say that "an individual must be the judge of what he wants to do in life" and wished his associate of thirty years the best of luck.

Gudeman moved to New York to become a partner in the Lehman Brothers investment-banking firm. One of his first assignments turned out to be in behalf of Montgomery Ward's. His departure deprived the World War II generation of Sears buyers of a mentor, and it had the added internal effect of passing the chairmanship out of reach of the buyers for good. From the end of Houser's tenure there began the succession of caretaker chief executives from the Field. Gudeman never contended publicly that the end of his stellar career at Sears had been brought upon him by the General's religious prejudices. He died in 1968 an enigma to some, a martyr to others, and the traitor who abandoned the mother company and trundled his sour grapes over to help Montgomery Ward to many more.

The Gudeman incident was discussed once again in 1978, along with rumors that Ed Telling had instructed Joe Moran to "de-ethnicize the buying unit," a remark thought to have been quoted in a magazine in Milwaukee—or was it Detroit? It was noted that Ed Telling was on record as hating New York himself. He was proud of being from a small town. So powerful was the corporation's history that, in trying to dispose of the residue of one aspect of the past, Moran and Telling had conjured up bad memories of another.

During the early winter, Joe Moran began to spend a tremendous amount of time behind closed doors with the nine buying-organization group managers, whom he called his "apostles." "You are my cardinals—my curia—upon whom I will depend," he told the men. Joe had used a papal motif back when he ran the big home-fashions staff ("Our father who art in seventh," his kids used to tease when they found out the floor where his office was located in the Tower), but the terminology surrounding the apostles elevated the metaphor a few notches.

Most of Moran's apostles had worked with Joe for years. The tall appliance man, Bob Thompson, had worked with Joe back in the furniture department, and tough-talking Wayne Holsinger, the apostle of men's wear, served with Moran on one of the many buying-organization staffs. All of the nine had been around long enough to have heard Joe declaim upon all sides of any issue. Most of them knew, for instance, that much of the thinking in the yellow book was reconstructed from the gospel of merchandising according to a hard-bitten old hunter buyer who'd taught them all named Cliff Joy. Joe had simply taken all that rich old stuff about serving the common people down off the shelf and added some polish. But that was just Joe. If Ed Telling wanted to think the stuff was new, that was fine.

But every so often toward the end of 1978, Moran would stop a meeting and let his guard drop. He would sigh and speak to his long-time colleagues of the tremendous pressure he felt to somehow stop the slide in Sears' fortunes. He would commiserate with his managers about the growing resistance to buying-side programs in the territories. He said they all had to figure out how to draw the independent buyers together into a unit strong enough to force the Field powers to do what needed to be done.

But on other occasions Joe became vindictive. He would refer to individuals in the organization by name as people "who've already retired but just haven't told the rest of us yet." He would rail against inept buyers, calling them "mindless morons." Acts by his managers that didn't meet his approval were often called sins or heresies.* Every so often, during an intense philosophical discussion of strategy, Moran would say, "I have no comment on that." He would then stand up and leave the meeting without explanation.

He announced that a series of seminars would begin in early 1979 that every buyer and assistant buyer was expected to attend. The eight days of re-education, he said, were designed to explain new techniques that would allow the new strategies to be achieved. The re-education announcement was as universally resented as was the fact that every meeting seemed to spawn a new task force and another series of meetings at which attendance was closely monitored.

Moran had plucked a young junior executive named Frank Tuma from the obscurity of an amorphous staff-administrator post and named the ex-Marine his personal attaché. Moran told Tuma that his real job was to "cut through the entire building" and to do whatever had to be done to force intransigent buyers to cough up requested documentation and arrive at meetings on time. From the day Joe Moran established Frank Tuma's authority with the veterans—by sending the young staffer into a room full of senior buyers and managers one afternoon with orders to take over the proceedings—Tuma's military haircut, round face, and

---

*The internal nomenclature of crisis at Sears, Roebuck between 1976 and 1984 changed daily from political to managerial to hierarchical. I have attempted not to mix metaphors unnecessarily, but as the desperate desire to find a framework for understanding what was happening to them increased inside Sears, the use of variegated metaphors borrowed from history increased apace.

habitual look of constant amazement appeared everywhere. Tuma was to report heresies against the new spirit of unity or lapses of discipline immediately to Moran, who would sometimes humiliate the negligent executive personally in a subsequent meeting. Because of the manly pride that was deeply bred in the buyers' bones, the petty day-to-day insults were as destabilizing as the thought that 599 would soon die, or that the standing army of irregulars in New York would soon return home, all because of edicts from above.

By the end of the year, Jumpin' Joe's old debating partner, the apostle of hardware, Ira Quint, decided he'd had enough. Quint used to say there were three qualities of action in life: "right, wrong, and Sears-think." But he told his colleagues that he now thought there were "right, wrong, Sears-think, and Moran-think." Quint was of the right age to have a good shot at succeeding Moran as merchant prince in five or six years, but Joe told Ira that Ed Telling believed Quint was one of the chief slush-fund fiddlers who'd caused the company to careen out of control in 1977. Moran advised him to forget running the buying organization. So Ira Quint decided to become the first senior executive of Sears since Eddie Gudeman to quit. He went to run one of Sears' largest suppliers for a time, and then moved over to Montgomery Ward.

Great streams of prose were produced that winter. Occasionally two long white papers would travel from Joe's desk and pass through the photocopy machines of the company in a single day. Much of it was directed at the buyers' continued refusal to cooperate with merchandise planning exercises. Since Frank Tuma had begun to monitor compliance, Moran's requests for data were never ignored anymore: the data sent back were instead rendered inaccurately. "You think this is a mental straitjacket?" he asked in one white paper. "A form to fill out? Wrong! . . . Write your own symphony but use these notes. Develop your own novel, but use my plot."

The Chicago boys would read Joe's memos and put numbers on his forms, but they clung fast to their traditional methods of finessing goods into the stores. They called in well-aged chits and found sample-room items for some Field man's kids, but even the best of the old operators sensed now that the stores were farther away from them than ever before. News was coming back to the buying departments about store managers' unilaterally killing off entire departments, just eliminating divisions out of the stores at will. The leaders of the hundreds of thousands of employees in the Field had also been called upon to unify and learn to plan their business. But response in the territories to the idea of rigid forward planning was no more favorable than it was in the

Tower. "People built this company," complained the manager of the Los Angeles group, "and we damn well better not ignore them in our rush to be great planners and strategists and technicians. If the god-damned people don't do the damned job, the damned job ain't gonna get done." But the soldiers in the territories worked around Charlie Wurmstedt even more easily than the buyers circumvented Joe Moran.

Charlie Wurmstedt was a straight-talking, street-fighting retail man of the old school. He was neither a creative merchant nor an inspired leader, though in the past he'd always known how to do his job. Charlie was a Sears soldier, Field bred, and for all of his working life that had been exactly what was called for. If you asked him what the advertising budget should be, Charlie would give you an answer. He saw the world as it was and was willing to proceed according to plan—but striking the plan was not in his repertoire. He believed in local rule, but he never considered that a matter of power or politics; it was just the way it was supposed to be. He also believed in Ed Telling. And he believed in himself.

But working above it all on the sixty-eighth floor of the Tower gave Charlie the willies. He simply didn't belong up in the clouds, yet, when he went back out to visit the stores as the senior officer for the Field, he sensed that he was somehow no longer one of the boys either. Early in 1978, several groups had been dissolved, leaving fifty administrative offices, and the Field powers openly resented Wurmstedt's association with the acts. They called Charlie a hatchet man.

The territorial leadership had been worried about the policy zigzags from the Tower since long before Headquarters restricted promotions and passed along those higher prices so suddenly to the customers. Prices were so high in some departments in the stores that there were reports of veteran Sears salesmen simply refusing to sell the goods, out of pride. The sellers in the Field were beginning to feel as embarrassed in front of their customers over the state of things at Sears as the buyers were embarrassed to talk to their long-time suppliers.

Meanwhile, sales were terrible and Christmas was coming.

Sometimes a Field manager who knew Charlie Wurmstedt well enough would ask him what the hell was going on in Chicago. Was it the doing of the madman who kept writing all those weird memos they kept reading? Wurmstedt's overbig smile would fade away, and he would recite chapter and verse from the unified strategy derived from the yellow book. His job was to try to create a unified Field. Inside the Tower, Wurmstedt tried to protect the Field's turf and was resented for his efforts. In the Field, he presented the programs negotiated in the office of the chairman as if they were his own, and the boys didn't like it a bit. Charlie was a soldier, but the cross-purposes and his distance from the ground made him ache.

"What are we doing wrong, Charlie?" they would ask him in the stores.

Charlie didn't really know.

At least the Field executives in the populous territory and group offices could divine from events such as the end of 599 and the scheduled fall of the long-resented New York office that the old lion of the East had not forgotten where he came from. But suddenly even that security was taken away.

It had always galled the managers who ran the groups of buying departments that they had to travel into marketplaces they dominated, responsible as they were for billion-dollar merchandise businesses, only to end up at meetings with title-laden officers from the suppliers. It never seemed right that the personnel and public-affairs guys were vice-presidents and had toilets in the corner of their offices when they did nothing at all in the real world of work to move the company.

When Joe Moran was the merchandise group manager over the home-fashion departments, he had clearly felt deprived of the appropriate trappings, so a few days after he convinced Ed Telling to let his apostles become officers of Sears, Moran went to the director of building operations to make sure that each of his new vice-presidents got an executive parking space under the Tower and a symbolic toilet too.

In one fell swoop Moran managed to publicly proclaim his influence upon Telling; separate himself forever from the weak administration of Jim Button; and convey to the beleaguered army of buyers in the Tower that the glory days were not over yet. Even more important, the elevation of the apostles gave him as much titled executive firepower as existed in the Field. The McKinsey structural reorganization had moved the officer in charge of the catalog business, and the vice-president in charge of advertising and sales under the SEVP, Field, and the combination of these two VPs and the five territorial vice-presidents had given Charlie Wurmstedt seven vice-presidents. Now Joe had nine vice-presidents of his own.

After he heard the news, Charlie Wurmstedt demanded to see Telling, who had been much less evident at meetings or in the halls lately. "My man running Detroit isn't a vice-president!" he said. "You wanna have more officers at Sears, that's just fine. Make my group manager, who's doing near a billion dollars of business in Los Angeles, a vice-president. Take my twelve biggest group men and make them vice-presidents or associate vice-presidents or something."

Telling listened patiently. "You did your duty," the chairman said with a dismissive smile Charlie Wurmstedt had known for many years. "But we can't have a few Field group managers be vice-presidents and not the others. So we're jus' not gonna and that's it."

By now Charlie Wurmstedt hated everything he knew about Jumpin' Joe Moran. In Charlie's book Joe was crazy—clean off his rocker; hot one minute and cold the next, he'd say. Executives sat in meetings between the two leaders and watched them grasp for some means of connecting the two sides of the company, but invariably Joe became pedantic and pontifical and Charlie became obtuse and intransigent. Then Joe would froth and rage and Charlie would appear ready for physical violence. Every single time Wurmstedt and Moran sat down together toward the end of 1978, the effort to unify the company was set back again.

Since Phil Purcell was the architect of the structure that vested so much countervailing authority in the two senior executive vice-presidencies, it was ironic that his 702-P staff was now charged by Ed Telling to bridge the gap between the two camps. Purcell had come to Sears to write a new constitution for a company of "real Americans," to be master tactician to a turnaround, not a messenger running proposals and pleas between the leaders of two warring camps. He'd been reduced to little more than a referee in the effort to translate his inexact plans into action.

Joe Batogowski, a thirty-nine-year-old merchant, was the 702-P staff member under Purcell assigned to the buyers after Robert E. Wood II took Ira Quint's place as one of the nine apostles. Every few days Batogowski would take a series of new planning proposals, covered in woodgrain plastic, from one of Joe Moran's many task forces, into Charlie Wurmstedt's office—just next door—and Wurmstedt would immediately begin to scream at him. "I'm not gonna do that! Who the hell says I gotta do that? Who the hell do you think you are, coming in here like that!" One day Wurmstedt jumped to his feet, and screamed, "Goddamn these things!" Then Charlie grabbed three white papers and a woodgrain binder from his desk and threw them across the room.

Batogowski would thereupon go back and report a less incendiary version of Wurmstedt's reactions to Moran, who would simply refuse to discuss it further.

Joe told Phil Purcell that he didn't much care for young Batogowski.

He said he found the curly-haired kid a bit too eager and youthful, but others believed Joe's animosity could have had something to do with the day Batogowski asked Moran if he could read his collected white papers. Moran could hear Batogowski howling with laughter in the next room. When he finally emerged hours later, Moran asked Batogowski what he thought.

"Well, they sort of remind me of a cross between Erma Bombeck and [Chicago tough-guy newspaper columnist] Mike Royko," the young merchant said—which was a mistake.

The comparison to the two newspaper columnists seemed less far-fetched when examples of Joe Moran's lively late-night prose appeared on every newsstand in downtown Chicago that December. An issue of the Chicago business newsweekly *Crain's Chicago Business* ran an eleven-page report on the turmoil inside Chicago's largest corporation that included numerous passages and much detailed information drawn from a "closely guarded internal document" leaked to *Crain's*. The paper noted the report was known inside Sears as the "yellow book."

The front-page introduction to the story, under the headline "Sears Top Secret Plan Revealed," stated that the yellow book contained hints of "massive upheavals at Sears" that "will send extensive tremors through the multi-billion dollar retail industry and will directly affect most Americans."

Telling was handed a copy of the article as he was boarding a company plane for Atlanta on the Sunday before the issue appeared on the stands. Former Chairman Arthur Wood sat across from Telling and watched his eyes narrow. Telling said he couldn't believe a journal would publish a private corporate business plan replete with market strategies and pro-posed advertising ratios. Telling read of proposed cuts in the numbers of suppliers, of plans to shake up an "overgrown and complacent bu-reaucracy," and of "field operations that too often thwart the will of top executives." He turned to page 13 of the issue, which exhibited a sober photo of himself, a very old shot of the youthful Joe Moran, and another of Phil Purcell all lined up along the top of the page. Telling became apoplectic: "It's . . . like publishing a lady's diary you found in the street. A business plan!" he raged. "There's a place in hell for people who do things like this!"*

---

*As enraged as he was, Telling still refused to hire private detectives to find out who had leaked the strategic plan to the press. For months, accusations and conjecture concerning who had betrayed the company dominated casual conversation in executive ranks. Many

. . .

The Christmas season was turning out to be another disappointment. Sales were off around 5 percent, and profits were so flat that it was feared the bean counters of Allstate were going to make more money for the corporation than the merchants. Sears was becoming more expensive to run by the month. Profit margins were still shrinking, sales still declining; customers were confused, and suppliers were scared. Since the reversals had arrived so suddenly, and since none of the inhabitants of Sears had experienced decline, from top to bottom the employees reacted to the descent with an almost neurotic desire to discover what was still good and secure about their world. What they found was history and tradition, particularly the rich tradition of the highly wrought culture that characterized whichever of the two sides of the business they'd been taught to believe in since they'd joined up.

The state of entrepreneurial tension between Parent and Field that had made Sears invincible among other big stores was beginning to turn inward. Many of the executives on both sides had come to believe by early 1979 that the opposite camp had cheated them out of money, and where most of the Sears boys came from, that was the sort of thing that called for a fight. The two forces circled anxiously; the semi-permeable membrane between the two sides had been scarred.

The two men Ed Telling had assigned to unify their organizations and bring them together tried to appear amicable in Telling's presence, but after a while the chairman could see fierce hatred in their eyes. He tried to bring them together in private, tried to get them to let it out, but he just couldn't get the rage out of their eyes. Two months into the new year, Telling realized he was going to have to gather the powers from both sides together and try to cool the fire.

He decided to bring the two factions together in Florida for a few days of golf and a series of informal "sit-downs" during the third week of March. The chairman had called another retreat for October of 1978 at a resort in Colorado Springs, Colorado. There were informal discussions about the business during the day, drinks, jokes, and long games of gin

---

on the buying side believed Ira Quint had passed the documents. In the Field, a consensus developed around the theory that so proud was Joe Moran of his prose that he sought a wider audience by leaking the plan to *Crain's* himself. In fact, the documents were leaked by Wiley Brooks, a twenty-nine-year-old assistant to the corporate national news director. Brooks had been working at Sears less than a year when he began to leak the plan. By the time *Crain's* went to press, young Brooks had left Sears and moved on to a newspaper job. Several years later, when he was approached and asked about his employment at Sears, Brooks spoke of how unnaturally closed the Sears society was when he worked there. He said he hated having to say "no comment" to so many queries about Sears from the press.

in the evening, and a general sense of good cheer throughout—even if that part was largely staged for Telling's benefit. But over the ensuing six months business hadn't improved, and there was a surfeit of bad blood.

Charlie Wurmstedt and his "gang of guys" rendezvoused early at the Cricket Club, a private condominium development located along the sandbar just north of Miami Beach, and proceeded immediately to the golf course to wait for the other side. Wurmstedt knew that Telling planned to mix the hostile factions together into specifically designated golf foursomes, but the chairman's plane was held up in Chicago. Once again Charlie Wurmstedt found himself sitting next to a golf course waiting for Ed Telling, but this time his patience wore thin. Everything seemed to be turning up rotten lately, and he simply wasn't in the mood to cool his heels.

Just a day or two before he left the Tower, Wurmstedt had received a message to call the vice-president in charge of operations, Tom Wands. Nobody liked Wands. He was always fretting about one thing or another—like how to get toilets installed in the corners of certain offices—and he had an irritating habit of getting to the Tower at the crack of dawn and making all his phone calls at around 7:00 A.M. When the calls were returned, Wands would say, "You know, I called you this morning, but I guess you weren't in yet." Wurmstedt had previously marked Wands as a prime example of a Headquarters-style petty bureaucrat, but he returned the call anyway. Wands said he was calling on Mr. Telling's behalf. Charlie Wurmstedt heard him say, "We have to schedule a meeting right away, because we want to discuss the elimination of one of the territories."

"Eliminate a territory!" Wurmstedt raged. "I'm not talking to *you* about eliminating a territory, and if Ed Telling wants to talk to me about eliminating one of *my* territories, he can come to me to talk about it!" Wurmstedt couldn't believe that Ed Telling—of all people—would consider such an act of violence—and even if he was actually pondering such a thing, how could he have discussed it with Tom Wands before he brought it up with the man he'd chosen to manage the territories?

Nothing more had transpired on the issue before Wurmstedt flew down to Florida, but the incident had decidedly diminished Charlie's willingness to wait for Ed. A short while later, Wurmstedt decided to rearrange the preordained foursomes from among the executives who'd already checked in. Charlie told the men to go ahead and tee off, thus making the second of several serious errors. The first mistake was allowing one of his "gang" of vice-presidents to choose the Cricket Club for the peace conference. As soon as the Searsmen entered their purple rooms and saw the mirrors on the ceiling, they knew it wasn't the kind of place Ed Telling was going to like. Some of the rooms had hot tubs, and if you stood and looked out the window toward the entranceway, a number of rather dangerous-looking people emerged at intervals from Rolls-Royces. The lobby was filled with elderly men wearing gold chains who appeared to be in the company of their granddaughters. By the time the first of the scheduled meetings convened in a room on the top floor of the Club the next morning, someone asked Charlie Wurmstedt what significance should be drawn from his taste in lodgings.

Most meetings of senior Sears executives took place in extremely large rooms. It was not unusual for a team of visitors from Headquarters to end up sitting fifty feet away from the Field managers they'd come to see, because the size of projection screens, conference rooms, and especially massive wooden tables had taken on a certain metaphorical association with breadth of authority over the years. But, like the overcrowded room where Telling met the analysts in New York the previous fall, and the smoky private room at the Château where Joe Moran wore his paper crown, the chamber in the Cricket Club was cramped and airless. Telling told someone near the French doors leading to a large balcony to open them up to let in the breeze.

Telling placed a chair against the wall at the back of the room while Joe Moran and his vice-presidents spaced themselves around the room, as good Headquarters executives had been taught to do for years. Back when the buying staff used to bring Field powers in to hear about a Headquarters merchandise plan, buyers were strategically placed throughout the room to lend a sense of spontaneous consensus to a discussion that was in fact as carefully pre-planned as any script. Old friends and those with similar merchandising philosophies would often split up for meetings, because teaming up was considered a manipulative breach of the spirit of Sears individualism and generally in poor taste.

But Wurmstedt and his gang—especially the five territorial officers—weren't used to these sorts of strategic considerations. The Field had only been represented by a coherent staff entity in the Tower since Telling became the senior executive vice-president, Field, and that representational unity existed only on paper. When Wurmstedt sat down in the middle of the room, his territorial officers and staff vice-presidents huddled near him in their armless chairs with notepads on their laps. The Field was surrounded on all sides by apostles.

There was tension from the start. A Field officer led off by reciting the age-old gospel about how the thing that made Sears great was decentralization. The recent noise from the buying organization about controlling advertising and dictating the price of goods to the storekeepers was out of the question. If a man is responsible for the profits and losses of his territory, his group, or his store, then—by God and General Wood—that man *must* have control over the price at which he purveys an item and the manner in which he runs his business.

John Lowe sat near Wurmstedt looking as rigid and set-jawed as he had every day since the incident at Pueblo. As vice-president in charge of the Midwestern Territory, Lowe signed everything that came across his desk, and did so without comment or even thought. His Midwestern Territory was in tatters. The population base in the industrial regions of Michigan, Ohio, Indiana, and Illinois was dwindling, and no matter what you do in a store, the business falters when the people leave. Two years earlier John Lowe would have had a great deal to say about the ways of merchants and markets, but the fire was gone from the old king's eyes now, and when he sat in most meetings or offered a short informational presentation as he did that morning in Florida, he always thought the same thing to himself—"The hell with it."

When Eddie Brennan, the leader of the South, took his turn, he attempted to steer the meeting away from old hobby horses. The word from the South was that Brennan was taking huge numbers of people out of the organization with systematic cost-cutting; and the South had put in a relatively stellar performance in 1978—moving from third to first in net profit. The forty-four-year-old veteran of the Corporate Hay Committee had further distinguished himself by publicly admitting a number of extremely serious problems at Sears—a breach of the Sears tradition of spreading only good news to the rank and file that irritated Charlie Wurmstedt. This morning Brennan avoided the issue of Field sovereignty when he took his turn and spoke instead about the expense of running the business. Between 1973 and the end of 1978, expenses at Sears were up 40 percent, and, despite the changeable business climate, the internal population had swelled over those years to an all-time high of 491,945 company employees during 1978. "Our problem at Sears is that our arithmetic doesn't work," the young officer said. The cost of running the stores is a percentage point and a half *higher* than our gross profit, so it's no surprise our prices are rising. We've got a company that's just too expensive, and that's why the numbers are killing us."

By the time the apostles began to offer a Headquarters view of the problems, Charlie Wurmstedt's back had stiffened noticeably. He'd heard through his contacts on the other side that, just as the buyers used to talk privately before Hay Committee meetings, Joe Moran had held meetings to coach his boys on what each of them was to say in Bal Harbor. The meetings had indeed occurred, but each of the apostles was a full vice-president of Sears now, and several of them weren't about to adhere to Joe Moran's script during their maiden addresses as officers.

Thus the man in charge of the automotive departments stated in all seriousness that what Sears, Roebuck really needed was a $4.99 muffler. "We could really promote the hell out of that and get the automotive business moving again," he said. Then he sat back down.

As the Field officers and half of the apostles grimaced and rolled their eyes, a long-time crony of Moran's, who was running the home-improvement group, got up and called for a "return to basics." Everyone in the room recognized the source of the phrase.

"You know what the problem really is?" asked Wayne Holsinger, the men's-apparel boss. "The problem is, everything's screwed up! The Field won't buy our programs, and they don't even run the programs right that they say they'll run. The only way I get things done is 'cause I know a few guys in the Field from the old neighborhood. But it's a hell of a way to run a candy store."

It fell naturally to Charlie Wurmstedt to defend the Field, reminding Holsinger that the Headquarters programs that attended the goods invariably ignored the realities of life in the Field. The buyers seemed to be on a campaign to centralize both prices and advertising, and that was plainly unacceptable.

"Why's that?"

The question came raspy and crackling from the back of the room, and Charlie Wurmstedt didn't need to look to know who'd said it. Wurmstedt was suddenly the only man in the room unfrozen enough to turn around and look at Ed Telling.

"Why?" Charlie asked incredulously. "Because . . . you wouldn't expect a man in Los Angeles to have to do something the same way it's done in Miami. That's why."

"Why not?" Telling said. "Seems to me a claw hammer looks the same in L.A. or Miami."

Wurmstedt was still the only one in the room who was turned back to face Telling. The others sat electrified, watching Charlie Wurmstedt's hard gaze without turning their heads.

"We still think we can do whatever we want because we're Sears," said another buying-side officer. "Just look at batteries. The whole world is selling D-cell batteries at a dollar forty-nine and my surveys indicate our average price out in the stores is up to a buck ninety-nine. That's arrogant—"

"You guys just provide the damned goods," Wurmstedt interrupted. "We know how to price 'em."

People in the room began to sneak quick looks back at Telling now. For weeks stories had been filtering back to the Tower about how

Charlie Wurmstedt had taken to presenting the "unified Headquarters" program for lists of goods to his troops in the Field, and then rolling his eyes or winking, so as to tell the boys what he really thought of it all. But even the apostles, who referred to Wurmstedt as "Mr. Dumb" or "the Peter Principle Incarnate," doubted that Charlie would do something so destructive. It was clear he didn't know a stick about financing a business or merchandising a line of goods, but Wurmy was still a soldier. In most cases, Charlie really did try to sell the programs with a straight face. But from the way things were transpiring in the sweltering room, it looked like Ed Telling might have heard the stories and believed them.

Al Goldstein, the apostle in charge of the womens'-apparel buyers, the group that dominated the New York office, contended that the cutbacks in promotions and the end of 599 caused costs to rise from factory to store. The stores weren't holding big sales, and advertising was cut back so the demand for goods had fallen, Goldstein argued in his tough rag-trade syntax. Lower orders to the factories meant higher costs, and those costs were now being passed directly to the stores because of the end of 599. It might have seemed reasonable to "get back the 2 percent" by raising the prices to the stores a bit, but that caused less business, which caused smaller orders to the factories, which caused higher prices to Sears buyers, who then passed the higher costs directly onto the stores. It was a spiral that could destroy them.

Joe Moran was less than impressed by Goldstein's analysis. Moran believed that he'd already dealt with the problem of rising prices when he told the apostles to apply their considerable muscle to the factories and simply prevent them from passing along sudden price increases. "If we have a source who cares so little for our business, or are such poor managers of their own that they surprise us with cost increases effective tomorrow," Moran had proclaimed, "then you surprise them with the door."

Various others in the room were perturbed by Goldstein's lecture because of its length. They'd been in the room all morning and the sun was shining. Dean Swift, who considered himself, rather perceptively, to be a "spare" executive these days—though he still held the title of president of Sears, Roebuck—was shifting uncomfortably from side to side in his seat. Several participants were whispering.

The chairman then spoke up again from the back of the room.

"I think we should all listen to what Al has to say. There's some good points here." So everyone sat silent and motionless until lunch.

Some of the executives noticed that Charlie Wurmstedt was hitting his bourbon pretty good at lunch, and when the cards came out afterward he was still drinking. Even though a couple of Moran's people had broken rank in front of the chairman, the time since Charlie came south and teed off with the wrong foursome encompassed a few of the worst hours of the life of the VP for the Field. After a few more bourbons, Charlie watched without fear as his boss and one-time sidekick approached him where he was standing near the French doors. Then Charlie decided to tee off again.

"You know, having Tommy Wands call me like that wasn't right, Ed," Wurmstedt said as Telling approached.

John Lowe was standing a few feet away. Lowe watched Telling turn his massive frame toward the slender Wurmstedt and begin to physically back him up beyond the French doors, onto the balcony. The two men, moving together, their unblinking eyes locked together, passed by Lowe as Ed Telling roared, "I'm the chairman of this goddamned company, Charlie!"

Lowe turned away and led a small group away from the door as word passed through the crowded room that something was happening out on the balcony.

Telling backed Wurmstedt all the way to the railing, next to a sauna located at the far end of the balcony, and the officers inside could see one of Telling's beefy fingers describing intricate swordsman-like patterns close to Wurmstedt's face. He grazed the senior vice-president's tie as his criticism of Wurmstedt's conduct in the morning's meeting grew more passionate.

Wurmstedt contended that he was only doing his job. He was offering his views in the name of the Field. ("Just as *you* always did," he was thinking. "Just like you.")

"When I want your opinion I'll ask for it!" Telling barked.

Wurmstedt came back from the balcony looking crestfallen, and immediately switched over to beer. Charlie would make light of how he'd "gotten in trouble" by drinking too much, but everyone in the room knew that they'd witnessed an incident full of meaning. Ed Telling had worked over the executive who obviously envisaged himself as the Field's guardian—right there in front of everyone—and beyond the fact that they all knew Charlie Wurmstedt could never fully recover from the humiliation and would never again be one of Ed Telling's boys, they all realized that, despite his apparent distance from the fray, Telling was indeed aware of the dangerous storm brewing between Headquarters and the Field. He was clearly prepared to move against the tradition of subsuming conflict in order to bring the whole thing to a head.

Before the conference in Florida broke up, Joe Moran succeeded in getting the five territorial vice-presidents to agree to some minor but centrally coordinated sales programs based around experimental advertising directed from the Tower, but the parties all knew this was but a gesture.

Many of the participants at the Bal Harbor meeting went home on March 23 and told their wives that they'd just attended the worst meeting of their careers. Some of them did something they'd never done before: they told their wives they were scared.

If not for the delicate lines of the Georgian furniture that stood everywhere in the halls and alcoves of the sixty-eighth floor, the ambience of the corporate suite could have been called clubby. But Telling told his designer that he didn't want a "homey" atmosphere when the floor was redesigned and redecorated. He said he wanted some of the formality he'd observed in banks. So the sixty-eighth floor read bank—right down to that oppressive, puritanical silence that pervades the offices of the oldest old-line banks, an aura so powerful that the most boisterous merchandise man up from the buyers' lairs was suddenly reduced to tentative whispers the moment the elevator doors slid open.

Oriental rugs sat on top of plush beige carpets so thick that the bleating robots assigned to deliver the mail on most of the lower floors wouldn't work on sixty-eight. The silicon path sprayed on the floor for the hated machines disappeared into the carpet like the noise, and the robots wouldn't know where to go.

Walnut trim ran along the walls bisecting the nubby woven beige wallpaper, and there were shelves of old, weathered books like *Lives of American Merchants,* and oil paintings, and the sorts of unpretentious American etchings Ed Telling loved.

The executive floor was considered a cold place in a cold office tower by most visitors and inhabitants. Something about all those ornate chairs that will never know a backside lining the long, empty hallways seemed inappropriately representative of hierarchy and isolation. The interiors on sixty-eight were indeed more appropriate to a bank than to an institution run by a country boy that was dedicated to the sorts of real people who did real work with or for real things.

Behind a dark wood door, Ed Telling's office in the northeast corner of the sixty-eighth floor was appointed in the same beige and wood tones that had been his trademark since he redesigned the interior of the Eastern headquarters during the era of territorial palace building. Telling didn't like the usual corporate knickknacks or souvenirs to clutter his vista, and he was happiest when his huge glass-topped Sears, Roebuck desk was empty of everything but a bright reflection of the weird light that emanates when the sun hits the top of the clouds. On the

credenza behind him there was only a photograph of his wife and two
of his daughters, all of them looking inexplicably tired and drawn after
a day of touring in London. There was a small Plexiglas frame containing
an old bubble-gum baseball card of Los Angeles Dodgers manager
Tommy Lasorda during his playing days; and a dollar bill given Telling
by former Sears board member and eventual U.S. Secretary of State
George Shultz.

   To the right of the doorway sat a slender dictionary stand bearing a
copy of *Catalogues and Counters,* the corporate history of Sears' first
half-century, which dwells most voluminously on the exploits of General
Wood. Early in his career, Ed Telling met the General, and his lasting
memory of the imperious old man was that his fly was open. Telling
thought the one element of the General's genius that was too seldom
discussed was the way he'd managed to run an entire empire by himself
while managing to convince everyone around him that they were free
merchants and men. All that perceived heterodoxy belying all that
kingly sway. Sears stayed "chairman-oriented," as Telling used to scoff
when he was in the territories, though its people sang regularly their
anthems about democracy. The General left the company with a goddamned totem pole aspiring above it, and Ed Telling was discovering
every day how deeply the pilings extended under the thing as he tried
to knock the pole down. Telling thought *Catalogues and Counters* was
nothing if not a tedious read, but he tended to keep the observation to
himself. The book came with the office.

   Though the several coffee tables at far corners of the large office bore
ashtrays and a few small sculptures, most of the extraneous artifacts in
the room were housed in a single set of bookshelves set into the wall
about fifteen feet from Telling's desk. The shelves held lovely old books
by Emerson, Byron, the fifteenth-century French poet François Villon,
Samuel Pepys, Irving, and Thackeray—all of them airily spaced between
examples of Telling's fine collection of the sort of Eskimo soapstone
sculpture he had fallen in love with while on a train trip through Canada
once with Nancy.

   In the center of one of the shelves sat one particularly striking example of Eskimo art carved in rich black stone. It was a rendering of a large,
ponderous torso bearing three rather angry-looking heads. In his own
mind, Ed Telling had named the sculpture *The Office of the Chairman.*
The day after Telling returned from the disastrous meeting at the
Cricket Club, he went into his office, closed the door, and spent a long
time staring up at the sculpture with the three dark faces staring out
immutably from one hulking trunk. He thought he saw in the two faces
on either side of the middle one the angry eyes of Charlie Wurmstedt
and Joe Moran.

For much of his career, Telling's penchant for snap judgments about people and his masterful ceding of tremendous responsibility to subordinates had come back to him as great success, but with the company seemingly at the verge of a destructive stalemate, even his closest confidants began to wonder why he didn't act forcefully to stop the drawing apart of the two sides of the company behind two such intransigent men. The two of them were as impenetrable and hardened now as the faces on the shelf, and while Telling knew he'd made a dreadful mistake in expecting so much—especially from old Charlie, whom he observed changing now by the day—he believed that the problems were much deeper than Charlie and Joe and that the time to act hadn't arrived.

A few months earlier the chairman had been invited back to Illinois Wesleyan to give a speech. Though Telling had graduated from the tiny downstate Illinois school in 1942, he'd retained few pleasant memories of the college because he'd ended up there poor and without Nancy. When the president of Illinois Wesleyan asked the chairman of Sears to come back and pick up an honorary doctorate-of-laws degree, Telling reminded him that he'd never given the school money and never would.

"This isn't the loyalty award, Mr. Telling," said the administrator from Wesleyan. "Just come down and give us a speech."

Telling liked the comeback, so he traveled down to the rambling red brick college carved from the cornfields of central Illinois to give some students there an opportunity that hundreds and thousands of others would have paid money to have at the time—a glimpse into what Ed Telling was thinking about things.

Telling rose to the podium in his academic robes and told the audience that from his point of view "a lot of our institutions, our practices, and our ideas need to be grabbed and shaken." He said he perceived a fundamental ideological cleavage within these institutions that bore analogies from history. "American political life has been characterized by the conflict of two powerful and competing liberal traditions," he argued. "On the one hand, there is the largely British tradition of Hume, Adam Smith, and Burke, which held that the basic function of government was simply to provide a framework within which the creative powers of all the people would be free to operate. The good society, they felt, would emerge spontaneously within a government of limited power which simply maintained the rules of the game.

"The continental vision of Voltaire, Rousseau, and Descartes, on the other hand, held that man, by reason and design, could lay out the blueprint of the good society. That being the case, it followed that government could—and should—be used to achieve and implement what pure reason declared to be good.

"In this competition between the two traditions," Ed Telling told the students that day, "my bias, of course, is for the British liberalism. The company I represent, with its thousand of different items of merchandise, epitomizes the richness and diversity which can develop only when a central authority does *not* dictate."

Few people at Sears ever heard that Ed Telling delivered a speech at Wesleyan. The draft of the address was not circulated through the organization or reprinted in the usual manner, and the only copy went back into his files. But the speech was the closest Telling would come to stating his ambivalence over what he and Phil Purcell had set in motion at Sears. The company appeared now locked in stasis, the once-fluid, ever-moving forces of Field and Tower stuck between two fundamental philosophical principles of human organization—centrifugal forces against centripetal ones—and both sides willing to fight. The old cultures were protecting themselves at all costs. You could depose territorial kings, impose new orders of the day, close down power centers, and disarm people by taking weapons like 599 away—but the belief system would remain, and remain to the end, if another didn't appear to replace it.

The irony was that the two internal armies wanted to fight over opposite sides of the General's promise that they would all be forever free and independent. None of the Searsmen, except possibly the interloper Phil Purcell, would speak for the Rousseauian creed of a sovereign indivisible authority from above—not even Telling could imagine turning the General's "last democracy" into that.

It crossed the minds of some observers in early 1979 that what had really happened at Sears was that Ed Telling had lost his nerve. It was recalled now that back in the days when he was taking down some of the entrenched fiefdoms in the East, he never did enjoy watching the battles. Even in the mighty East, Telling loyalists were beginning to wonder now why their man had receded into the oblivion of Headquarters, almost like one of the much weaker men the Field had sent to Chicago after the General. The great fear of just a year earlier over what Ed Telling would do had turned into a great fear of what he wouldn't do. During the early days of 1979, the *Gallagher President's Report* named Telling one of "the worst corporate executives of 1978." The annual list cited Telling for his "failure to give direction to the nation's largest retailer in his first year as CEO resulting in flat earnings and depressed fortunes for the company's major suppliers."

Nobody saw Telling wandering the Tower with a handful of papers anymore. The litany of hokey all-American declamations that used to filter down from his office had ceased. Instead word filtered down all the way to the grass roots that the chairman's inept performance in front of the analysts had taken another couple of dollars off the price of the same

Sears stock that through the profit-sharing and pension plan was supposed to provide most inhabitants of the grass roots with security in
retirement. Though the details of the Moran-Wurmstedt conflict hadn't
really been transmitted below the level of the buying departments in
Chicago, the retail group offices in the Field, or the senior management
of major suppliers, everyone in and around the company knew there
were severe problems at the top.

Ed Telling had spent a career managing by mystery, moving through
seasons of time as if by a secret cause. People assumed for decades to be
his closest friends at Sears didn't, in fact, know much about him at
all—but being thought close to a man as personally powerful as Telling
wasn't such a bad thing, so the supposed friends tended to keep their
true ignorance of the man to themselves. Few of them knew how exten-
sively or deeply he read, for instance, for he purposely obscured the fact
with contrived anti-intellectualism. And nobody knew how intensely
he felt the company's failing, because letting it show had never been
his way.

    Telling was lonely and alone. Every morning the three-headed Es-
kimo stared out from the bookshelf and reminded him that he had to
do something "very radical, something that just had to work." He was
not as empty of ideas as the people around him were beginning to
believe—not by any stretch of the imagination. He had plans. But the
company just wasn't ready to accept them—at least not yet—so until it
was he'd have to withdraw and wait. If nothing else, a life in Sears taught
you how to wait.

CHAPTER 6

The Terror

├────────────────────┤

From the moment he was told of the decision, Henry Sunderland
sensed that 1979 was the wrong year to hold the May annual shareholders' meeting in Los Angeles. It had been only fifteen months since
Ed Telling sent Sunderland out to bring the separate kingdom back to
the company, and although his pacification program was moving along
well enough, Sunderland feared that staging the annual ritual in the
spiritual home town of territorial independence was simply asking for
trouble.

For many years, the Sears annual meeting had been a family affair, a
huge outing usually staged in Chicago for the entertainment of some of
the tens of thousands of Sears retirees, selected employees, and a handful of outside investors. But during the mid-1970s, the meetings were
disrupted by members of the National Organization for Women protesting Sears' hiring practices, and by various local associations protesting
discriminatory insurance practices by Allstate. To return the meeting to
a joyous and insular family conclave again, it was decided in 1977 to
move the event around the country among the "catalog towns." These
were the traditional inland ports of the Sears system, like Dallas, Kansas
City, Atlanta, Memphis, and Philadelphia, where there were still huge
Sears warehouses employing tremendous numbers of long-time company workers who were honored and pleased to have an afternoon off
to be bused to a meeting hall where they'd applaud for two hours.

The May 21, 1979, annual meeting was to be staged in the cube-shaped Los Angeles office complex John Lowe had built. Henry Sunderland had moved quickly to rid the separate kingdom of several of Lowe's managers, the ones who "didn't think they could do any better," but in most cases Sunderland attempted to be sensitive to what he called the local "anti-dictatorial" atmosphere. He'd removed the group manager who ran San Francisco and the veteran running Los Angeles, but, rather than importing another Telling soldier from the East to take over Los Angeles, Sunderland made the politic decision to hand the big group over to "Burk" Burkholder, a Hay Committee "young Turk" and John Lowe's popular administrative assistant before Lowe was transported east.

During 1978, Burkholder brought the L.A. group's profit ranking from seventh in the territory to first in just six months. The performance led a general territorial upswing that had continued into 1979 against the powerful downward trends experienced elsewhere in the company. The rise was due, in part, to the effects of California's Proposition 13 tax breaks and a particularly lucrative contract to install cable-television systems signed under John Lowe, but the comparative numbers had caused the Tower to perceive Henry Sunderland's return to the West as a consummately successful bit of managerial carpetbagging.

Sunderland was not as popular over at the 4.1-million-square-foot catalog order plant where he had begun his career during the summer of 1952. His attempts to deploy the sorts of Eastern Territory "disciplines" that once inspired Ed Telling to call Sunderland's Boston plant "the jewel of the East" had been deeply resented by the largely Hispanic Sears people of the Los Angeles barrio, but at the time of the annual meeting, the territorial personnel specialists believed the labor troubles at the plant could still be controlled.

But there was trouble brewing inside another region of the Far Western Sears family that spring, and Henry Sunderland feared that the annual meeting might turn ugly.

For years, the Los Angeles retirees' club had met periodically to reminisce about the glory days and to agree once more that Sears, Roebuck would have been much better off if the General hadn't died and left them. For a long time, the three hundred or so most active members of the club lobbied to have a representative of the retirees on the corporate board of directors. Retirees at Sears were unlike those from other companies in that retirement was just the final stage of an individual's lifelong relationship with the company, the time when a life of sacrifice and constant movement and unswerving fealty was finally rewarded with financial security and a level of respect that verged on reverence. So involving was the afterlife that many a Sears retiree simply added a stamped "Ret."—for "retired"—on his Sears business card. They were like former ranking officers in the military, still hooked into the grapevine and never fully accepting that they'd left the fold.

Sears retirees believed, with some accuracy, that they owned a piece of the business by virtue of the company's fifty-three-year-old profit-sharing plan. Sears sought to protect the quality of the latter years of its employees' lives two decades before the idea was institutionalized by the government as Social Security. "It's good business to treat people right," Julius Rosenwald used to say, years before the thought crossed the minds of most captains of industry. During the dark October of 1929, the front page of *The New York Times* told how Rosenwald had guaranteed personally the stock-trading accounts of all the employees of Sears on a day when his own fortune was reduced by $100 million in a matter of hours (legend has it that Rosenwald found his personal reversal rather "exciting"). A brass plaque fixed to a wall at the entrance to the old West Side administration building quotes Rosenwald: "Profit sharing is good business. On leaving the company an employee will take something with him for the future."

Accumulating Sears stock through the fund taught the employees about capitalism, and provided "an opportunity to develop an appreciation of the purpose of profit in an enterprise," as one officer later put it. The steady flow of profit-sharing and other employee-invested money from Chicago into Sears stock was also a stabilizing factor that had made the stock so very attractive to others on Wall Street over the years.

During a meeting of the Los Angeles retirees' club in 1969, each of those present wrote down on a piece of paper the number of shares of Sears stock he'd accumulated by virtue of the profit-sharing plan. When they toted it all up, the members realized they controlled $30 million worth of stock.

Nineteen sixty-nine was the same year that Henry Sunderland's longtime secretary retired after forty-three years of service to the company. On her last day at work she asked Sunderland to come along to help her pick out a new Mercedes-Benz. He asked her which model she wanted and she said "a red one." It didn't really matter which model she bought, because the woman was about to cash in her several thousand shares of Sears stock from profit sharing and realize a $500,000 reward for dedicating her life to Sears, Roebuck.

General Wood once declared, "I have had three main interests in life—my own family, our company and its employees, and the Sears Profit Sharing Fund." On another occasion, the General warned his top executives: "You have greater responsibility than the officers of any other corporation in the United States, because the future of thousands of people lies in profit sharing, and if you don't run this company right and [you] destroy their values, you've committed a crime."

The private social-security system was lasting proof that Sears was indeed a company with a soul.

Just as the plan represented the unique humanity of the company the retirees had once served, the ever-soaring stock price was more than a source of financial security, it was a testament to the system the old-timers had worked to serve and protect. Thus by the spring of 1979—as the stock price hovered precariously at just $20 a share—members of the Los Angeles retirees' club like Harry Brown, a former buyer who kept track of the price of Sears stock on his family-room wall, believed that Ed Telling had committed the very crime the General had warned against. Whereas the company contributed $416 million to the profit-sharing plan in 1972, only $72 million had been kicked in during Ed Telling's first year as chairman. The retirees living off the stock remembered a time when Sears shares were called the best performing equity on the list; when it was selling at thirty-two times earnings instead of eight times the sorry earnings Sears was heading for now.

This was humiliating enough, but some of the internal changes promulgated under Ed Telling seemed acts of betrayal. When Henry Sunderland heard about the annual meeting's coming to town he approached Harry Brown and some of the other old soldiers in a spirit of appeasement. Sunderland even held a luncheon for the club members, which descended within forty-five minutes into an unfortunate mass shouting match. Old booklets entitled *Lifetime Income for the Years Ahead* that described the Sears retirement program were waved in Sunderland's face. Promises made to retirees by the General were recounted to the territorial leader like lessons from a text. It turned out that the retirees at the luncheon were well aware of the bitter internal strife between the Field and Parent; they'd heard about Jumpin' Joe Moran and the entrance of the outsider, Phil Purcell, to the inner circle. The retirees maintained strong opinions about any number of recent corporate events—not the least of which involved the removal of John Lowe in favor of the Field turncoat, Sunderland.

Ed Telling had always hated the contrived and archaic choreography of corporate democracy at the annual shareholders' meetings. After the analysts' meeting at Fraunces Tavern, he now had less confidence in his ability to "play the public role" than ever, and though he believed he was paid, in a large part, to serve Sears shareholders as chairman of the board, he didn't see what getting up and performing in front of a thousand or so of the 350,000 holders of Sears stock—most of whom were bused over from the catalog plant—had to do with anything at all. "The retirees are like a bunch of hungry spring robins," Telling said. "They think they oughta make as much money retired as they did working."

Most Sears, Roebuck annual meetings look the same. The board members sit sleepily upon a twin-tiered dais under bright lights. Before them are endless wide rows of card chairs, the first three or four of which are filled with men in sincere gray suits and $18 haircuts.

Behind the gray suits, extending back almost seventy-five rows to within fifty feet of the back wall of whatever great hall had been hired or borrowed, are rows of astonishingly similar-looking elderly people wearing pleasant smiles and bright clothes. The last fifty feet are occupied by hundreds of milling middle-level Sears territorial and group executives, many of whom were still wearing quite long razor-cut sideburns in 1979, and more than a few of whom were wearing loud, B-store neckties and sport coats in shades of red and green that are usually reserved for marching bands.

Up front even the roughest officer-merchant attempts to dress up like a banker for the annual meeting, and in Los Angeles, even Joe Moran was dressed in a gray, albeit rumpled and ill-fitting, suit. If Joe Moran's apostles milled around near their seats in the front row a bit more importantly this year, it was because they knew they were scheduled to be introduced as officers of the corporation right after the territorial kings took their bows, and though the five territory guys were up on the dais as members of the board, this was the closest to the front row any of the apostles had ever been.

Henry Sunderland gazed down from the dais at the horizontal stripes of gray and brightly colored miracle fibers just before the meeting was called to order. He realized that the noisiest members of the Los Angeles retirees' club were spaced strategically throughout the hall. As Telling rose to the podium to welcome the shareholders to the 74th Annual Meeting, Sunderland felt that all hell was about to break loose at his expense.

"Good morning!" Telling crowed. It was the traditional salutation of any large Sears, Roebuck meeting.

"Good morning!" echoed back from the throng.

Then Telling began rocking back and forth and scratching himself unconsciously as he read in his tinny, affectless public voice. When he was done with the opening statement, a man planted in the audience by the corporate secretary moved to nominate the board of directors. Toward the late 1970s this nomination was usually made by either a minority employee or a well-known and beloved local retiree.

Telling then asked the crowd to hold their applause until he was done introducing the entire board of directors. The assemblage was silent until Telling got to John Lowe. As the lanky, sad-eyed vice-president of the Midwestern Territory rose slowly to his feet, the entire room erupted into applause, which grew in slow waves to include cheers and whistles. The demonstration continued for almost two minutes as Telling stood back from the microphone. John Lowe remained stiff and square-jawed as always, but he felt happier and more at peace than he had been since the day he'd stood on the runway in Pueblo.

As soon as the introductions ended, the public airing of family problems began. One after another, speakers moved to the microphones held by security personnel in the aisles and demanded to know in the most vindictive terms what Ed Telling was doing to *their* company.

A woman criticized a new pension plan concocted recently in the Tower and then yielded the microphone to a retiree named John McCue who said he couldn't understand why Telling's own salary had risen, given the state of company affairs.

Telling said nothing.

"We'd like an answer from you regarding that!" screamed a member of the retirees' club, but another man grabbed the microphone from McCue:

"For as long as I can remember, we have had a compensation plan for executives for the obvious reason—to get the best men possible. However, why is our stock down to $19 if we have the best men possible?"

Derisive snickers and verbal agreement accompanied Telling's reply: "If you could draw a correlation between the men and the stock price there would be an answer, but it really has nothing to do with the stock price. . . ." Telling added that all retail-company stock prices were depressed.

A retiree named Yvonne Sylvan took a turn: "Well, what do you propose to do to increase the sales and profits?"

"Madam, that's been pretty well published across the country," Telling replied, referring ironically to the leaked documents first published in *Crain's.* "It's no secret as to our strategy, and if you haven't read it, you're remiss."

George Winters, a well-known Pacific Coast Field retiree, then identified himself and noted that sales had declined 14.4 percent so far in April, when all of the other retailers had gone up during April.

Telling tried to cut him off by asking him to raise his question at the proper point in the meeting, but Winters moved on to address the stock price: "From a high of $61 to its current $19—you, as management, are responsible for this fiasco. *You* have lost your stockholders, your investors, 66 percent of *their* investment. Many of these stockholders, including myself, are retirees who devoted their life to building Sears, and who have now had their retirement benefits nearly wiped out. . . . Mr. Telling, in three years you have given yourself a $367,500 raise plus thousands of option shares, increases in retirement benefits and in pensions. The other officers have also cut themselves generous increases in salaries. Stop feathering your nests and enriching yourselves at the expense of your employers, the stockholders! It doesn't take any great effort to plan for a decrease and get it. I'd like to see you plan for an increase and get it. . . . Thank you."

Telling asked if there were other questions as if he hadn't even heard Winters, and several people jumped to their feet to demand a comment on what had been said.

"Well, I suppose I could comment that whatever percentage he said my salary went up," Telling said softly, "I have a different job than I did before. . . . Occasionally I look back and think how good that job was." He went on to say that Sears must have a competitive compensation package for executives to retain "outstanding men."

"Oh yeah?" said a man from the audience. "If you didn't given them a raise, would they quit?" The sarcasm of the question was evident to all observers. Nobody quit Sears.

When the formal question-and-answer period finally began, a retiree named Harold Pearce rose to ask Telling when he planned to return to "basic philosophies that the General referred to as the three Ms—men, merchandise, and methods." Pearce described for the audience the new executive dining room on the sixty-eighth floor, "complete with sterling silver and expensive china." He juxtaposed the observation with the high prices of Sears goods in the stores.

"The General felt very strongly about decentralization," Pearce continued as the gray suits in front moved back and forth in agitation. "As a result, the first territory was established right here in the Pacific Coast. These feelings proved to be successful. Why, then, the dramatic change to centralization? This move has, probably more than anything else, contributed to the downslide of the company." Pearce called for more authority to be passed back to the Field. "All the brains in the great Sears certainly are *not* in the Chicago Tower. Let's get back to the three Ms and get off this egomania kick!"

Pearce sat down to loud applause and cheers. Even members of the board now looked over at Ed Telling expectantly. Many of them were just as confused about the chairman's opinion of the General's legacy.

"Well, Mr. Pearce," Telling said. "There is certainly no one in Sears who is going to disagree with the three Ms. That is exactly where we are. You mentioned decentralization and giving the Field more authority. We're more decentralized today than we have ever been, and the Field has more authority today than has ever been."

The men in gray all lowered their eyes, as twenty-six more speakers

continued to bear-bait Ed Telling. Most were infuriated retirees like
Harry Brown; one was a customer who couldn't understand the instructions on the automotive kit he'd bought; and several others represented
political groups interested in Telling's position on some of the litigation
Sears was involved in at the time. But the most aggressive pronouncements were those made by Sears' own retirees.

The company had a higher purpose in the life of the nation, to the
mind of the retirees, and in their vision of a legacy being squandered
the family elders were unforgiving. They were accusing Telling and the
other officers of acting as usurpers of a glorious history of other people's
work. The General had told them back in 1939 that at the point where
Sears deviated from its higher purposes—of "raising the standard of
living of the American people"—then the company would "decline and
eventually pass out of the picture." The retirees in Los Angeles believed
the process was well under way.

To the old-timers, the numbers reflected moral chaos. The April
drop in sales of 14.4 percent mentioned during the Los Angeles meeting represented the eighth straight month of decline, and by the time
May was over another comparative decline of 7.1 percent would run
the string to nine. A five-year, $2 billion expansion plan that Phil Pur-
cell had signed despite his ambivalence was still unaltered by April of
1979, though the plan to build 250 new stores and to increase spending by 40 percent by 1983 was beginning to appear to several members of the board of directors as a portent of doom. Several board
members approached Edgar Stern, Julius Rosenwald's grandson and
one of Ed Telling's major supporters during his rise to the chairmanship, and asked him if he too was losing faith in the dark horse they'd
placed in command of Sears. Stern said that he was surprised at how
slowly Telling was moving. "But he's our horse," he said, "and we've
all got to ride him."

The annual meeting was yet another public indication that Sears,
Roebuck was falling from grace with its customers, family, and friends.
The outbursts at the meeting were reported on the front page of
the *Los Angeles Times,* another addition to the spate of articles about
corporate mismanagement that tended to mention Sears in a list that
usually included the withering regimes at International Harvester and
Chrysler.

Several generations of Americans had mailed Sears millions of personal letters over the years, and tradition dictated that they be read and
considered. Late that spring a letter to Ed Telling from a man in New
Jersey was passed among executives in the Tower. "Get out of your
tower," it said. "For God's sake see the writing on the wall and do
something!"

"When processes fail like this," Joe Moran instructed the apostles during one of their many lessons that spring, "management has to act."

Ever since the buyers' apparent triumph at the Cricket Club conference it seemed that all Joe wanted to do was hold forth behind closed doors. He talked endlessly of how the buyers must stop being soloists. They had to be taught that they are like tuba players in a band: there only to march in the background "going boom, boom, boom." Joe said to them that, since only 150 Headquarters people and 150 Field employees really ran the company, the new spirit of percussive, basso management need only be communicated to them. "Below that level," he told the apostles, "the people have less loyalty."

During a Monday meeting in April, Moran outlined principles he called the "Four Myths of Management," as Frank Tuma sat dutifully to his right taking it all down. "It is a myth," Joe lectured the seasoned managers, "that organizations function in practice as they do on paper; that people perform their assigned functions and seek no others; that orders once given are always carried out; and that when managers are asked to direct specific departments, their loyalties always lie with the larger interest of the corporation."

A few days later, the nine group VPs were shocked to find that Moran had written the four cynical myths into a memo. Now the entire organization could see that Joe Moran had begun to ascribe the myriad problems of Sears to insubordination and disloyalty.

Before long the spring maxims echoed through the ranks. Joe said and Frank Tuma wrote:

—"Communicate, Educate, Infiltrate minds, Subjugate rebels."

—"Do not trust anybody."

—"Saying something won't necessarily make it so."

Joe told the apostles that "rumor can be used to management's advantage." Rumors, he said, were simply another form of corporate communication. A related management tool Moran used often that spring was the writing of threatening letters to managers that contained a "cc." to Mr. Telling and other senior executives. But Joe would actually tell Frank Tuma not to send the copy to Telling or anyone other than the individual to whom the letter was addressed. It was just another trick of the trade—the management of "rumors and signals," he called it.

Each Monday there was further instruction of the apostles at a table on the forty-third floor, and each Friday afternoon Moran would collapse into his chair and, between his coughing and wheezing fits, he would review the state of the company with Frank Tuma. After they went though a stack of documents, Tuma would take up his pen and legal pad and write down another hour's worth of excited "philosophy": "Establish a network of people to give feedback," Tuma jotted one afternoon, "but be careful not to be spying."

For his own part, Frank Tuma could hardly avoid identification as Joe Moran's spy, because that was exactly what Moran had made of the eager young executive. Frank had become the symbol of the new "discipline," and he accepted the difficult role because Joe Moran was the first person at Sears who'd ever asked him where he lived, or how he felt.

But the apostles who'd known Joe for years felt their old colleague was slipping away from them. Whether the subject was the superior practice of management, advertising policy, the pricing problems, the catalog's decline, the way of planning a new season, or the ongoing standoff with the Field, Moran would set forth the Sears tradition concerning the subject and then, in the best traditions of the sorts of dialectical political interchanges Joe had participated in as a young man, he would tear the thing to shreds. Many a long meeting would consequently conclude in exasperation. "People can be made to follow," he said on occasion, echoing the Confucian axiom, "but they cannot be made to understand."

Sometimes he would rage; sometimes he would stomp out of the meeting in mid-sentence; sometimes he would openly share his frustration. "We sell ten or eleven *million* units every day," he moaned once. "Do you realize that if we could just reduce the cost of selling each item by one penny, it would translate into ten cents a share in return?"

Every day, Frank Tuma distributed more white papers. One time he sent around letters of complaint from seven- and fifteen-year-old customers, to which Moran expected a personal response. With the mist of 599 gone, Moran wanted to study the details of each buyer's relationship with suppliers and with the Field, but his demands for documentation were often circumvented. The buyers envisaged the privacy of their numbers as one of the last remnants of their former latitude. After the numbers would go the power. "Their history and their numbers are all these people have," Phil Purcell said to Moran. "They won't give them up easily."

But Moran called the resistance to his surveillance "heresy," and as summer approached, he declared that buyers must be resisting his efforts to draw up information out of disloyalty, or possibly in order to cover up a lack of "integrity" in their relationships with suppliers. A few buyers might have been cut in on a deal here and there, and nobody would ever have denied that the boys threw their weight around and cracked whips in the name of the company, but the suggestion of dirty dealing was a shot in the back. Moran even suggested to the apostle of the men's-apparel departments, Wayne Holsinger, that the buyers doing business in the Orient were all on the take. It was as if Joe was turning on his own.

The intimation of dishonesty caused many buyers to back off from what remained of the intimate relationships they had with the factories, for fear of being judged guilty by association—this at a time when the suppliers were suffering so badly from the cutbacks in orders from Sears (down by 22 percent over the slim orders of 1977, that the entire manufacturing industry now spoke of a dire economic phenomenon called "the Sears recession."

One Monday, Moran stormed into a meeting and announced that he wanted to simply drop the Kellwood Corporation as a supplier. Sears still owned 22 percent of the $500-million St. Louis–based corporation it had helped create, and during 1978, 80 percent of Kellwood's output was sold to Sears. Moran and Tuma had gathered statistics demonstrating that a high level of "omissions"—the name given to the problem of orders from catalog customers or Sears stores that went unfilled because a factory hadn't shipped the merchandise—could be traced to Kellwood.

There was a long silence at the meeting before one of the group managers spoke up. "Ah, well, you know, Joe," he said, "Kellwood accounts for 50 percent of the business in my group, and I think it sort of figures they would also account for a high percentage of the omissions."

The idea of punishing Kellwood never came up again.

Every day that summer there was news that another product—once made exclusively for Sears by a supplier—had just shown up at Penney's or Toys-R-Us or K mart, as factory managers scrambled to protect themselves from going down with the ship. As Moran offered long lectures on a "return to quality," the buyers began to worry that the quality of their goods was in decline. "Squeeze a supplier," the General used to say, "and he'll take it out on the goods."

By the middle of June, the studious apostle Al Goldstein decided he'd had enough. Goldstein's New York buyers were due to be relocated in Chicago by August, but he'd been getting precious little support from Moran. Goldstein knew that Moran referred privately to New York as "the blight," and he'd heard that the eleven floors that had been rented for the New York buyers in an office building at Two North La Salle, several blocks from the Tower, was already known in the Chicago buying organization as "the ghetto." Phil Purcell had joined Goldstein in questioning the wisdom of locating the former Sears colonists away from the other buyers and had proposed to Moran that other buyers should be moved out of the Tower if there really wasn't any room. The proposal and several other requests for assistance made to Moran were denied, so during the summer the apostle of women's wear began negotiations that would lead to his becoming a senior vice-president of the American Can Company.

Executives leaving the Tower for a trip to factories or through the Field were specifically warned not to discuss morale problems at the Tower while they were gone, but from line workers in Indiana appliance factories to garment magnates in Seoul, Korea, there was talk of Joe Moran's rampage. Moran told Frank Tuma that he knew the buyers were scared of him. "But let the rabbits bark," he said mysteriously. Every time he spoke of the rabbits barking, Frank Tuma knew Joe Moran was hardening toward another new "discipline," another slashing of the supplier list, another hint of layoffs or office closings, or another public calling down of a long-time employee.

Even Jumpin' Joe's oldest associates at Sears kept their distance now: "I find for some reason that many people apologize for wanting to see me or talk to me on the phone," he wrote at the end of a memo passed around the Tower during the fall of 1979. "They usually preface it with 'I know you're busy, but'—I'm never busy. . . . I write my white papers at 3:00 A.M. and do what passes for thinking while walking my dogs over hill and dale."

There was a time during his hair-shirt days when Joe's small number of rather large obsessions were a source of cafeteria humor. Joe's preoccupation with Sears became so unhealthy at one point that someone suggested he take up gardening. He did, but, after acquiring considerable expertise in his inimitably concentrated manner and then planting a huge garden, he became so obsessively concerned with the care and sustenance of his rosebushes that a doctor made him give up gardening for the sake of his health.

Moran's colleagues were often embarrassed by his constant and frequently quite intimate talk of his family. At work, he talked endlessly about his family; and at home, in the big house in suburban Barrington, he talked endlessly of Sears. Joe Moran and his wife, Margie Lou, a former Sears Catalog copywriter, rarely socialized. Joe tried golf during the late 1950s, but gave it up right away because he missed the family. The clan tried a family vacation as a change of pace, but Joe became convinced that one of his ten kids was going to drown in the lake where they swam and sailed, so he paced the shore the whole time in misery. He was always worried that something awful could happen to one of the kids. Something could occur all of a sudden when his back was turned, like a sudden frost off the lake coming ashore to kill a rose. Some things were impossible to control.

Joe decreed that each of his children attend Notre Dame or one of several small, rigorously academic, Midwestern liberal-arts schools. Sears colleagues were for years intrigued by Moran's intimate knowledge of schools like Knox, Rippon, Oberlin, Kenyon, Lawrence, and Carleton. He even knew professors at each of the colleges. As dire as the business crisis became during 1979, it was rare for Moran to get through a single meeting without at some point mentioning Notre Dame, an institution about which he knew much more than even Phil Purcell, who'd had the privilege of attending the university. The first four kids all went to Notre Dame or the contiguous women's campus, St. Mary's. After Notre Dame or one of the intense small schools he loved, the kids were free to attend Harvard for post-graduate work. Some Sears friends believed Joe was so obsessed with colleges because he always resented the fact that he had had to attend a local school like De Paul.

Joe had spent much of his nonworking life supplementing his early educational experiences through voluminous reading, memorization, the writing of up to five thousand words each night, and countless hours of pure cogitation. The huge family dinner table, rather like the meeting room where the apostles convened each Monday, was a place reserved for instruction. On rare occasions Joe would read Margie Lou and the children a short piece of writing, but more often there were loud political debates that brought forth the various ideological extremes that existed within the family.

Almost every dinner was at some point embellished with a parable about human nature such as it was demonstrated daily at Sears, Roebuck. The Moran kids grew up believing that Sears was a paradigm for life, a fish bowl where all the elements of psychology and politics were played out. They never met many of the fantastic characters with whom their father had generated the physical stuff of everyday life over the years, but the kids knew that, by the middle of 1979, Joe had broken with many of them over the question of what was to be done. By the fall of 1979, the family knew their husband and father believed the company was so riddled by dissension, disloyalty, lack of integrity, ineptitude, and intellectual deficiency that it was up to him and him alone to pull Sears out from the gyre of its decline.

After the dinner discussions were over, Joe would go down to his library in the basement to write about Sears. He would sit for hours amid his collection of seven thousand books, and usually he would rise from bed a few hours later to continue his fevered alchemy at the small desk off the master bedroom.

If only he could delve a bit more deeply into the mystical process of supplying the people, he thought, perhaps he could discover the flaw. Then, through a combination of management technique and internal redefinition, he would help Sears reconstitute as a political and economic whole. If he could just state overarching principles that were true from top to bottom, from past to present, then all authority could be delivered up to Ed Telling, and the empire could be run from the Tower, just as the Parent soldiers had always wanted.

Moran wrote a series of white papers designed to redefine "the character of American consumption that will dominate the rest of this century." He called for the creation of massive task forces and sub-task-forces to help him define the "common personality," the formulary "unity" that might allow the flow of red ink to be stemmed: "Just as all manufacturing is fundamentally the same process," he wrote, "so, too, are the underlying movements in color, shape, pattern the same across all product lines, durable and non-durable. The customer is the same, and the socioeconomic forces that drive style cycles affect all products in pretty much the same way."

A claw hammer looks the same in L.A. or Miami.

The white papers were read by buyers who had been taught to believe that manufacturing processes and products were in no way similar, just as the soldiers of the Field had been taught that the individual integrity of each customer called for a decentralized system dedicated to a celebration of American diversity, with each citizen served according to need and taste. The buyers prided themselves on the part they played in defining the most complex and diverse material culture in history. They were soloists, not tuba players. The sort of people who said that the historical patterns, motivations, modes, and structure of the manufacturing and distribution of commodities are all essentially the same were communists, not Searsmen.

For all the Promethean late-night efforts that fall, for all the breadth and shrewdness of Joe's metaphors and diagrams, all the lessons and revelations of secret tools and myths of manipulating human action in organizations, the company was no better off. Executives were copying his white papers and sending them to friends as if they were entertainments. Even buyers having trouble working deals with the Field would still fire the latest white paper out to Field contacts with notes saying things like "You think you got troubles?"

In November, Joe Moran announced that "ineptitude" had "infected" all of the buying, catalog, and planning functions within the company. A memo about the new surveillance of the buyers and their staffs said that Frank Tuma would be notified of lapses in "on-time performance or lateness" at 9:00 A.M. on the morning following the due date of documentation, and that Tuma would then publish and post a list of offenders in a formal "report of ineptitude."

Moran began now to hector his apostles during the Monday meetings so much that many of them would push their papers away in despair and confess publicly that they had no idea what to do anymore and that the whole company seemed doomed. Only when the admission of hopelessness was spoken would Joe ease up. The group VPs found that only when they'd joined in the spirit of self-immolation and blurted out, "I just . . . I just can't figure it out; we are having such a bad month in my group!" would he sit back. The worse you were able to make everything sound, the more relaxed he'd become, as if the sheer weight and darkness of his burden was the only touchstone that gave him comfort. Moran would sometimes reveal to his managers that the previous night he'd awakened "with a howl" and found himself in a cold sweat. "My health," he'd say to Tuma and the others. "Why am I doing this?"

Joe did appear more jangled and unhealthy all the time now. His hazel eyes looked glazed behind his smudged glasses, and his weight moved up and down erratically. His periods of sulking silence seemed to be lengthening, as did his ragings.

"Ah," he groaned to Tuma one afternoon, " 'a man's reach should exceed his grasp or what's a heaven for!' " It wasn't Frank Tuma's nature to question the aptness of the quotation from Browning's epic poem about a man full of self-doubt and in search of peace, but Frank never forgot the way the man to whom he'd become such a loyal aide groaned when he said it.

For the first time it dawned on Tuma that Moran might not really believe he could think the company back to health.

By November, most senior executives of the buying organization felt exhausted and betrayed. They'd danced nimbly through the mine fields of long careers, building systems of influence, wells full of owed favors, and illustrious reputations as the most knowledgeable, well-liked, and powerful men within hundreds of industries. Now, after some three decades of dancing and spinning toward open field, they'd come upon the edge of an abyss. At any other moment in many of their careers, the idea of "reports of ineptitude" or instructions to subjugate rebels and manage by rumor and threat would have been so absurd as to have been funny. After a lifetime of hunting and venturing and taking chances for the company without fear of recrimination, simple errors were being cast back at individuals as crimes against the company. Offenders were being denounced, their names published in lists. Certain buyers were accused of having "loyalty" problems, sometimes for no more apparent reason than the location of their offices outside of Chicago. Some of the brightest people—other Parent intellectuals who'd grown up with Moran, in fact—had left the fold in disaffection. Meetings had taken on the tone of public inquisitions, and many of the endless white papers were filled with accusations and fulminating hints of treason on the part of those on the same side of the internal conflict.

Personal loyalty had so replaced managerial utility that business policy was subsumed in a swirl of who did what to whom. The white papers read now like latter-day versions of *L'Ami du Peuple,* Marat's radical newspaper during the French Revolution.

If Sears was indeed in the throes of a "revolution," as Phil Purcell took to saying to friends during the fall of 1979, then the Headquarters organization was in the midst of its Great Terror. A freewheeling sort of company life had turned quite suddenly into a nightmare, where nothing of the old glory seemed to be remembered and nothing at all was forgiven.

CHAPTER 7

The Public Front

It was during the third week of November that Ed Telling stalked into the small room on the sixty-eighth floor where corporate officers gathered early in the morning for a cup of coffee. From the moment his frame blocked the entranceway, Telling locked onto the eyes of old Jack Kincannon in a way even the Eastern Territory veterans in the coffee room had never seen before. The chairman lowered himself very slowly into a seat across from the new vice-chairman of Sears, all the while staring hard at the lean Texan he'd referred to for years as "the prick with ears."

Long before the rise of Ed Telling, the advent of Joe Moran's campaign against ineptitude and sedition, or the appearance of institutional emergencies everywhere they looked, the central object of popular fear at the upper levels of Sears was Mr. Jack Kincannon. A forty-year veteran who rose from a job in the accounting department in a backwater town in Louisiana, Kincannon came up through the Dallas headquarters of the Southwestern Territory. By the time he was drafted to Chicago to audit the Parent's books in 1956, he was already known as a hardened, foul-spirited fellow, and by the time he became the company controller in 1968, and then a director in 1972, and then the company's senior vice-president of finance in 1975, Kincannon had made being a first class son-of-a-bitch a veritable art form.

The General believed in accountants and controllers who made "sharp, persistent inquiries" into the merchants' affairs. The numbers watchers were to provide a check-and-balance against the otherwise autonomous employees of Field and Parent. By the 1960s, the fiefdom of bookkeepers had become so powerful that groups of rogue auditors could swoop down upon territorial, group, and Headquarters departmental ledgers without higher sanction. It was never unusual in big corporate hierarchies for auditors to exist in the minds of some employees as a sort of secret police under control of the chairman, but at Sears the policemen worked for Jack.

Kincannon remained, in late 1979, as the most powerful representative of the old Headquarters establishment of staff kings. He sat on the boards of Sears, Allstate, and the insurer's Allstate Life Company subdivision. He'd managed to become the primary liaison between the merchants in the Tower and the executives up in the suburban Northbrook, Illinois, headquarters of the insurance company. He sat on numerous operating and merchandise committees, and as he demanded of the auditor, who sat among the young Turks of the Hay Committee, Kincannon expected full reports from his people on all administrative functions he didn't attend to personally. He had spent the years under the succession of unsophisticated chairmen preceding Art Wood developing an image as the official Sears emissary to Wall Street, to the international business community, and, to a large extent, to the business press.

Amid all the gloom surrounding the business in the spring of 1979, *Institutional Investor* ran a lengthy story about Jack Kincannon and his coup in cracking the Japanese capital markets to issue debt for Sears ("a pin-striped Marlboro-man"; "the kind of chief financial officer who inspires effusive praise from investment bankers"; "low keyed"; "unflappable"), but within a few months the $100 million in creative financing described in the article would appear as a proverbial drop in the bucket. By the fall, Sears would have been losing money no matter what Joe Moran or Charlie Wurmstedt worked out between their warring tribes, because the interest rates charged to Sears had risen to over 11 percent—the point at which every sale was conducted at an effective loss to the company. Sears borrowed around $400 million each business day in order to keep the wheels turning, largely through the vehicle of commercial paper—IOUs from the company—which it sold through the twenty-three-year-old Sears, Roebuck Acceptance Corporation in Wilmington, Delaware. Borrowed money was used to pay for inventory, to pay taxes, to satisfy other credit obligations, and, most important, to finance the massive Sears credit-card system that allowed nearly one-third of the citizenry to purchase goods on time at Sears. The outstanding loan balance required to finance customer installment accounts during the fall was around $10 billion—a figure up from $3.8 billion a decade earlier, and so large and so heavily weighted down with expensive short-term debt that an interest-rate rise of less than 1 percent could do away with a year's profit margin.

The way of channeling cash in and out of the corporation was still dictated by philosophies first articulated during the 1950s, when the General finally allowed Sears to borrow money in credit markets at all. It was thought that Sears should finance its short-term "receivables" (such as items customers bought but hadn't yet paid for) in a manner that reflected the purposes of the debt. Since most people paid for their washing machines within twenty months or so, the conservative theory was that the duration of given vehicles of corporate finance should also extend for a short time, and that dabbling in very long-term commitments like corporate bonds was decadent and risky. It was all on the straight and narrow, and as unlike flashy Wall Street dealings as possible. There was no speculation involved—you got what you paid for—and when the deal was done it was done. People seemed so eager to own a paper commitment from trustworthy Sears that the commercial-paper window in Wilmington was often closed by 11:00 A.M. after a few hundred million dollars' worth of business passed through it.

But with the coming of inflation a credit crunch began to tighten around Sears. By 1979, outside debt analysts had expressed shock over the company's 70-to-30-percent short- to long-term debt ratio, and the Wall Street debt-rating agencies had begun to consider a downgrading of Sears' debt-safety rating, a public humiliation unimaginable only a few years earlier.

Ed Telling blamed Jack Kincannon for the financial crisis that piled into Sears along with the other problems of 1979. Another grand tradition and its particular guardians in the senior ranks had caused a lot of trouble. If Kincannon had protected the company with long-term debt back when the rates were around 4 percent in the 1960s, Telling and his advisers believed, then they wouldn't be in such a mess. Telling thought it obvious that Sears needed to finance an eternal mass of debt "as long-term as life itself" with long-term issues. The ritualistic picture of the debt as a short-term liability was a typically weak-minded example of Parent-style arrogance.

The case for refinancing the receivables with long-term debt had been put to Kincannon for almost two years by Phil Purcell. Purcell would illustrate at length why short-term assets don't necessarily have to be financed by short-term liabilities. As Purcell remembers those interchanges, Kincannon, never a mincer of words or a great fan of young Phil's, would then observe simply, "Why, you're just a stupid son-of-a-bitch." It never crossed Jack Kincannon's mind to be wary of Phil Purcell because of his personal relationship with Ed Telling. The way Kincannon operated you'd think Jack believed if there was a man worth being wary of at Sears, that man was him.

One day in 1979, Kincannon managed to bring Joe Moran and Charlie Wurmstedt together briefly on the same side of an issue. Charlie and Joe both sat on the finance committee of the board of directors, a group Kincannon had dominated for years. Kincannon came into a committee meeting during mid-1979 and told the outside directors present that interest rates had peaked. Accordingly, he said, the three insiders on the committee were "in agreement" that the stock dividend should be augmented. Moran and Wurmstedt both supported the rise, but afterward Wurmstedt confronted Kincannon with the fact that he had just railroaded through a hike in the dividend in the face of Sears' most severe business crisis since 1921.

"You had your chance to disagree in the meeting," Kincannon snarled. Then he walked away.

In Telling's book, Kincannon was much too powerful. He was just another Sears country boy from Waco, Texas, who'd built a career by catching people cheating on expense accounts, climbing the ladder by virtue of nothing but the fear he evoked in others. Kincannon and Charlie Bacon had conducted a feud for years over the time when Telling was running the Eastern Territory and Bacon—then running the personnel operation in the East—learned that Kincannon was having Telling's expense accounts monitored. Kincannon's only motivation, Bacon thought, was his desire to check the rising reputation and authority of someone who might be a threat down the line. Bacon never confronted Kincannon about the audit, though he did warn Telling to watch his back. Kincannon proceeded to audit Bacon's personal expense records, and after that he audited the expense records of Bacon's daughter, who was working as a buyer in the New York office.

Many Tower observers figured Kincannon had hit his open switch when they heard that Telling blamed him for the analysts' and journalists' ire at Fraunces Tavern, but, as much as he didn't like Kincannon, as committed as he was to bringing down the company kings, and as much as he believed old Jack desperately needed cutting down to size, Telling didn't think he could safely remove the chief financial officer, because of his links to Wall Street and the absence of any other financial executive at Sears not raised under Kincannon's tutelage.

Telling finally acted just a few weeks before the November day when he stalked into the officers' coffee hour and trained a withering stare over at Jack. Telling had announced then his intention to "elevate" Jack to the position of vice-chairman on February 1. The financial press hailed the promotion at Sears of the "architect of its recent innovative funding efforts," but in fact Telling was moving Kincannon aside, just as he'd moved Jim Button aside when he placed Joe Moran underneath him in early 1978. Though Kincannon would be vice-chairman, Telling planned to recruit a long-time Eastern Territory man, Richard Jones, to occupy a new financial-officer's position directly beneath Kincannon.

Dick Jones warned Telling that he wasn't at all comfortable about taking over Kincannon's duties. Jones had come up through the ranks running stores and groups, and he wondered about the wisdom of appointing an old store-runner like himself to a finance job in the midst of a credit crisis. But Telling desperately wanted Kincannon moved aside, and he couldn't see anyone else around he could trust, so Jones got down the finance books he'd bought during his weeks of management training at a special Harvard Business School program he once attended and began to reread the sections on corporate finance.

For some reason Jack Kincannon missed the true purpose of his promotion. Shortly after the announcement, an article appeared in the *Chicago Tribune* in which the vice-chairman-elect of Sears waxed on about the future of Sears, Roebuck—such as Jack apparently planned to direct it from his new position of authority. The article by Joseph Winski appeared under the title "Kincannon Plans Sears Changes," and it observed that Kincannon was "well-suited to pump more life and purpose into Sears' diverse non-merchandise operations." Kincannon allowed in the interview that he was aware that Sears was the subject of criticism from securities analysts lately, but he added assuringly, "We will improve our relations with the investment world." There was even a nice picture of Jack looking vice-chairman-like and generally pleased.

Charlie Bacon, Charlie Meyer, and several other officers were already in the small room having coffee when Telling came into the room after reading the article and began to stare into Jack Kincannon's sallow, loose-skinned face.

"I noticed you speaking on our behalf in the newspaper, Jack," Telling said, all cold and determined. Then his eyes lit up and he exploded. "I turn my back for one minute and there you are in the newspaper!"

The room fell into silence. Kincannon tried to form a smile and tend to his coffee. "God*damn* it!" Telling raged on. "I put you up on a shelf and you get right on down off it! Shootin' off your goddamned big mouth in the newspapers!"

The tirade continued for several minutes. Before Kincannon excused himself, he turned to Charlie Bacon and said in his deep drawl, "Just cut me the right deal and I'm out of here."

Telling always claimed that he'd never read a single accurate sentence about Sears, Roebuck, so the fact that the press and financial communities had interpreted his demotion of a senior executive as a promotion indicative of a new strategic direction really didn't surprise him. But lately he'd observed the previously benign vacuity of the press turning into active aggression.

For a variety of reasons, the majority of Sears people of the past didn't take press coverage of the company as seriously as the employees of most corporations. For one thing, almost every article about Sears for the five or six decades preceding the late 1970s was so embarrassingly adulatory that even the truest believer inside saw that much of it was fable. For another, the awesome power of Sears derived from its special franchise with its customers, a relationship that was characterized by a popular perception of Sears as the store down the street. Most company CEOs, and later the public-affairs officers, endeavored to craft an image for Sears that was as decentralized and localist as the company.

Sears was a fat catalog and a store out at the edge of town. It was just a store run by the sort of basic folks who lived by the old rural rules of keeping news about what you have close to your vest. The public focus was so profoundly local that generations of clerks and salespeople joined the general populace in being unaware that the corporation was one of the largest in the world, or even that it was headquartered in Chicago, Illinois. To this day Sears Catalog customers throughout the South think the company offices are in Memphis, Greensboro, Dallas, or one of the other catalog cities.

But as soon as Gordon Metcalf's great Tower began to climb skyward, the low profile began to disappear. From the precise moment Metcalf decreed that the largest merchandising system in the world should be architecturally represented, the company, by degrees, began to receive the sort of scrutiny and legal writs drawn by other big businesses. The Tower became less a monument to invincibility than a lightning rod, and just as the hokey servants-to-the-American-family imagery gave way to Metcalf's mega-corp motif, the business faltered so badly that for the first time Sears employees turned to magazines and newspapers for information, because neither the grapevine nor the official company news systems were explaining what was going wrong. Out in the West, Henry Sunderland was shocked at how deeply injured his employees were by articles about high corporate mismanagement that began to include Sears. The papers said Sears was a loser, a company run by a latter-day Babbitt who hated the sophistication of big business, a man named one of the worst executives in the country.

The Tower was depicted in a hangman's noose in *Chain Store Age* in 1979, and as "The Leaning Tower of Sears" in *Fortune.* At some point during the early months of Telling's reformist regime, another metaphor was uttered to reflect the improbability of a company like Sears' ever changing enough to return to its glory days and by late 1979, everyone had accepted the image of a huge ship mired in a slender stream. No fewer than twenty Sears executives claimed authorship of a version of the phrase "Saving Sears is like turning a battleship in a river." Joe Moran said he coined it as "turning the *Queen Mary* in the Chicago River." There was "turning a battleship on a dime"; "turning a foundering ship 180 degrees in a canal"; and "turning an oil tanker with an outboard motor." The contention from Allstate headquarters in Northbrook was that the simile had its genesis there as "like turning around the U.S.S. *Missouri* in Upper Chesapeake Bay." No articles or public discussions of the troubles at Sears were lacking a version of the image of the great leviathan sitting dead in the water, helpless and adrift, as opportunity and progress and the world of selling Sears had dominated for so long just flowed by all around it.

One article in *Forbes* was simply entitled "Too Big." Soon afterward, Telling was depicted shaking his head and acknowledging in a rare interview given to *Fortune* that Sears' inability to reach its goals did indeed have to do with "the management of size."

Telling—and especially the corporate sophisticate Phil Purcell—had hoped that the decision to let a writer from *Fortune* have unusual access to the management of the company might help divert the investment, journalistic, and governmental communities from their growing sense that the company leaders had no idea what they were doing.

Carol Loomis had collected numerous awards during her twenty-eight years writing about companies for *Fortune*. She was unusual for a *Fortune* writer of the later 1970s in that she approached corporate executives from the vantage point of the company's stockholders, rather in the spirit of the shareholders' democracy envisaged in the writings of Adolf Berle and Gardiner Means during the 1930s.

Loomis sat in Joe Moran's office on the sixty-eighth floor and tried to get Moran to explain to her satisfaction how the end of the 599 account would save money for the company and its stockholders. She went back to his office time after time for another explanation before finally concluding that either Joe Moran didn't fully understand the 599 system he'd killed off or that he wasn't leveling with her about why it had died.

When Loomis' article appeared in *Fortune*, Telling felt he'd been double-crossed. Loomis had concluded that Sears was being woefully mismanaged by a fascinating and likable chairman who would have made a delightful dinner partner in other circumstances, but her feature began with references to the "sloppy management" of the company and quoted Telling as saying that while his pay as chairman was good, the chairmanship was "the worst job I ever had."

"Telling's impatience with the job," Loomis noted, "might raise some questions about his aptitude for it."

Joe Moran was depicted in his office holding forth about the "terrible" performance of the company. Loomis observed Moran consulting one of his lists of figures and explaining that he didn't really believe the numbers he received from his own buyers because "a source and a buyer could always fudge the data."

"It is a myth of management," he told the journalist, "that orders once given are followed. It never happens that way."

The piece included a photograph of Charlie Wurmstedt and Joe Moran standing side by side. "Heading camps traditionally at odds," the caption read, "Charles Wurmstedt (left), the senior sales executive, and Joseph Moran, chief of buying, have determined to cooperate and, says Wurmstedt, 'make this company work.' "

Though the photo caused some ironic snickering in the Tower, the general effect of the piece was devastating. Phil Purcell was infuriated that Loomis had made no attempt to show how large the task of changing Sears really was or how bold had been some of the moves already made. She concentrated instead on quotations from disenchanted suppliers and portrayals of the senior merchandise executives as plainly out of control.

In a memo circulated shortly after the *Fortune* "Leaning Tower of Sears" article appeared, Joe Moran wrote, "All of us managers must show and tell our people of our confidence in our own future. The journalist and the economist together are important examples of the Seven Deadly Crimes that come out of American Lower Education, and have about as good a track record on predicting tomorrow as any other group of friendly neighborhood witches."

It was as if someone had declared open season on Sears, Roebuck. The faltering of the company seemed to trigger an instinct to pile on. Writers, regulators, business experts, and members of the general public all appeared eager to partake of the dark pleasure of unmasking the most trusted company in the world.

During 1979, a U.S District Court judge, George Leighton, ordered Sears to pay a former Sears salesclerk named Peter Roberts up to $60 million for allegedly defrauding Roberts of patent rights to a ratchet wrench he said he invented when he was a teen-ager. The treatment of the case in the press was indicative of how powerfully the public image of the supplier of the American people had suffered. An editorial in *The Washington Post* declared: ". . . raise a glass to Peter M. Roberts, and to justice too—the justice in question being Judge George N. Leighton, who on Thursday ruled that Sears, Roebuck, and Co. had cheated Mr. Roberts out of his quick-release, one-handed socket wrench, which was a poor thing but his own. 'It shows how a small man can receive justice even against an enormous corporation if right is on his side,' said Mr. Roberts. Amen."

The editorial reiterated reports being published and broadcast all over the country: that Sears had paid Roberts' own lawyer for advising them a patent was about to be issued.

"Here's to you Mr. Roberts," the editorial concluded. "You brought back the old dream; you knocked off the villains; you made yourself rich. Only in America."

So the company that had rendered the fruits of American invention available to the citizenry for almost a century was now the usurper of invention, the exploiter of its own suggestion box. A stupid mistake made during the glory days by some misguided middle-level functionary had bubbled up at precisely the wrong time. It was the same thing with the widely publicized casting of Sears as a villainous force against the cause of equal opportunity. It didn't seem fair.

One of the ironies of the discrimination suit filed against Sears by the Equal Employment Opportunity Commission in 1979 was that egalitarian hiring practices had been a programmatic preoccupation of senior managers for well over a decade. Because of decentralization, superimposure from above was resisted whether it came from Chicago or Washington, but the powerful Sears personnel department seized upon the issue of equal opportunity quite early in comparison with other corporations. By the mid-1960s, the company had the beginnings of one of the most sophisticated and progressive corporate affirmative-action programs in the country. Some time before a formal system for injecting minorities into all levels of the Sears system came into force in 1968, the personnel executives, under Wally Tudor, conducted a campaign throughout the company to force managers to change their arbitrary and, if not discriminatory then certainly idiosyncratic, hiring and promotion practices. At one point Tudor addressed a congress of major store managers and Field executives in Detroit. In front of invited managers from major suppliers and local leaders from the Urban League, Wally said, "I would not like to hear from any of you that you can't find qualified blacks. I have spent my life trying to find qualified whites, and some of you don't qualify yet."

Thus equal opportunity at Sears became yet another example of Headquarters elites trying to force a new system down upon the territories and sovereign Parent departments. Not surprisingly—especially in the Field—the incursion was resisted. Memos about affirmative action that came from Chicago were often suppressed in the territories, and though there was eventually some hiring of minorities at the store level, the personnel department found that college-educated black employees were being relegated to the candy department or the shipping docks, without any plans for moving them along.

Group managers "finessed" the program as a matter of course. Though 22 percent of the market area served by the St. Louis group of stores was inhabited by blacks in 1967, there was not a single black employee in any St. Louis Sears store, because the group manager simply didn't want to hire them. The personnel department reasoned that the only way to break such local resistance would be to get each territorial personnel-staff member to work on his boss until the five kings got behind the program. Gordon Metcalf was still running the Midwestern Territory in 1967 when his personnel man, Gene Harmon, gave a formal presentation to Metcalf and his group managers about the importance of equitable hiring practices.

At the end of the discussion, Metcalf mumbled to his boys, "Well, now Harmon's done talkin' about the niggers, let's get back to merchandising."

Ironically, it was Gordon Metcalf who, as chairman in 1968, was talked into issuing the formal decree to Sears managers that one "business watchdog" periodical said included "the most complete disclosure ever made by a corporation on female and minority representation." A goal of 38 percent was set for the concentration of women in all job categories, and full-time staff executives were hired to monitor the program.

Arthur Wood augmented the corporate commitment to equal employment with a program of "mandatory achievement of goals," which essentially called for women or minorities to get half of all future job openings. In February of 1973 Wood convened a huge meeting of his 250 top managers at the Continental Plaza Hotel in Chicago, where the chairman basically warned the Field soldiers that if they didn't like hiring and promoting blacks and women they should leave the company.

But the system wasn't geared to demanding or monitoring such a change. Sears executives knew that as early as 1973 the EEOC was investigating charges by Sears employees that the company discriminated against women and minorities. The commission also studied hiring patterns at General Electric, the Bell system, and General Motors. An administrative complaint against AT&T was settled out of court for $38 million, and eventually GM and GE settled too. But there was no settlement with Sears, and the government constructed a legal case under Title VII of the 1964 Civil Rights Act that formally charged the company with discrimination. A suit that included forty-two separate claims of discrimination was filed amid the nose dive of 1979, and, possibly because he felt Sears was being kicked around enough already, Ed Telling decided that rather than trying to appease the government agency, as the other large corporations had done (all of them had settled by now), he would make a federal case out of the situation.

"Let's not roll over and play dead this time," he said to the Sears lawyers. "Let's stand up." Sears hired the veteran Washington-based civil-rights lawyer Charles Morgan to construct a countersuit against ten federal agencies. The idea was to charge that it was the government itself that created inequities in employment opportunity. Morgan's novel argument alleged that the huge glut of white male veterans of World War II at Sears currently impeding minority advancement was a product of the G.I. Bill and other government programs that encouraged the General's massive hiring and rehiring of ex-soldiers.

Liberal attorneys and civil-rights proponents across the country were shocked that the Birmingham, Alabama-born Morgan would defend a corporation accused of racist practices. But Morgan said it was the government's regulatory laws that were discriminatory in this case.

By April of 1979, the Labor Department's affirmative-action chief had joined Chicago's Reverend Jesse Jackson (who had earlier accused his home town's premier corporation of going "to the jugular of affirmative action") in comparing Sears, Roebuck's action against the government to Southern resistance to desegregation.

In May, a Washington Federal Court judge dismissed the Sears suit, and Telling issued an angry statement declaring that Sears would no longer do any business at all with the federal government. The company wouldn't sell them goods or services, he said, because of its "campaign of harassment, subterfuge, and retaliation" against Sears. This from a company with a long history of loaning executives to the government during time of crisis, of testing government issue in its labs, and finding boots, tents, and sleeping bags for troops during times of war.

Telling believed he could have bought off the wrench-maker Peter Roberts for a lot less than $60 million, and he knew he could have settled the problems with the EEOC quietly—as AT&T had done—but he just wasn't going to acquiesce. He never liked the fact that you had to be wealthy and powerful to protect yourself in America, but he thought that if you did happen to find yourself in control of wealth and power, it was your duty to fight it out. The cost of battling the government ("Finally Sears is taking on something its own size," was heard often in general discussions of the suits) would run beyond $100 million before it was over.

Most editorials concerning the suit by Sears were supportive of Telling's *chutzpah,* but the affirmative-action suits still weighed upon the ongoing governmental crisis inside the company. The heightened scrutiny obviated the possibility of upward movement among young, mostly white executives, at the very time when they were already growing restless because of the business stasis and rumors of massive personnel contractions. The action also crippled the Sears personnel department, just when the talent-rich, comparatively enlightened organization could have been helpful to the delicate diplomacy required to close some of the widening rifts. Lawyers so closely monitored the action of personnel executives that they came to see their roles as reduced to little more than statistics gatherers. Every effort to move new blood into the many places where the system was clotted was met with the same warning: "The trial's coming up."

Almost every week now, the company was in court again to be accused of yet another antisocial act. Days after Telling took office, Allstate had been accused of discriminatory insurance practices in thirteen different urban areas. There were constant product-safety problems, and Telling spent time during 1978 trying to deal with pressure groups protesting Sears advertising accompanying violent television programs. In April of 1979, President Carter's Council on Wages and Price Stability charged that Sears had raised prices beyond the limits set out in Carter's executive order about the matter. Carter even telephoned Sears and asked to talk to Ed Telling about it personally, but Telling wasn't in.

The Federal Trade Commission charged that Sears had used deceptive advertising in promoting dishwashers during the 1970s, and the company was indicted by a federal grand jury in Los Angeles on charges of evading customs duties. Later in 1979, the Federal Trade Commission challenged the way Sears labeled the energy-savings features of its products—that was just after Sears hairdryers were found to contain dangerous asbestos fibers.

The legal and regulatory problems arrived as endlessly as the dismal monthly sales statements. Shattering internal dissension was complemented by public floundering and now long lists of crimes against the people. As Sears had joined Chrysler and International Harvester on the list of American managerial disaster areas, it had now joined ITT and Lockheed in the pantheon of corporate outlaws. This was happening to a company dominated by members of almost every Elks Club and Chamber of Commerce in the Republic, to an institution that financed the Officer Friendly Program in the nation's schools and paid for the daily public-television shows featuring Mister Rogers.

The only positive public association awarded the company during all of 1979 was the induction of General Robert E. Wood into the Junior

Achievement's "Business Leaders Hall of Fame." The General joined Henry Ford, Alfred Sloane, Andrew Carnegie, John D. Rockefeller, and fifty-one others during the year that marked the hundredth anniversary of his birth.

During a bright Indian-summer day that fall, Charlie Bacon was playing golf at the Mission Hills Club, a course about twenty-five miles north of Chicago, not far from Allstate's headquarters in Northbrook. As his foursome approached the twelfth tee, Bacon pointed to a small townhouse just beyond the rough. The drapes were drawn across the windows, and it appeared that the lights were turned off inside. Bacon told his friends that the home belonged to his boss, Ed Telling.

"Guess he's not home," said one of the golfers.

"Oh, he's in there," Bacon said.

"But the house is completely dark."

"Ed's home today," Charlie said.

For months executives at Sears and other acquaintances of Bacon's had taken Charlie aside to ask how Ed Telling was bearing up under all the pressure. It was well known that on most evenings Telling met his tall, easygoing personnel officer after dinner, and the two men would take a stroll around the edge of the golf course for a while. Sometimes they'd walk five miles. For a time, Charlie had joined Telling again the following morning at 6:15 for the drive down to the Tower, but Bacon finally convinced the chairman that their habit of driving through the dark along the same route was dangerous, given what the papers reported was happening to powerful people in other parts of the world, so Telling started to take a train or a Sears limousine to work.

It was assumed that Charlie Bacon was just being loyal when he contended to inquirers that he didn't have a clue about how Ed Telling was shouldering the strain or about what was going on in the chairman's mind. Bacon knew he was thought to be Ed Telling's best friend, and, as far as he could tell, he probably was. But that had never meant he was close to Telling, or that he knew what Telling was thinking or feeling, or that he understood much at all about what made Ed Telling tick.

On more than a few of those five-mile hikes, the fact was that Telling didn't utter a word. They would talk a bit of their mutual interest in sports and books, and occasionally the business would come up in passing, but usually they just walked along in silence. During 1979, Telling's son-in-law was killed in a car crash, and though the walks, the trips downtown, and the time Bacon would spend sitting across from the beleaguered chairman in his office continued without pause in the wake of the tragedy, Telling never mentioned it once.

For all the years they'd worked together, Bacon had also known that, as introverted as Telling usually was, he also hated more than anything having to be alone. But he'd never developed a social life or a circle of more than a few friends, so he was happiest at home with Nancy, or in the company of one of the few people he trusted, just sitting or strolling in silence while his mind reeled far away. There were others who knew about the silences, but each of them kept his experience of the unusual behavior to himself. Each thought that Ed Telling must only share his thoughts with one of those he truly considered his friend.

As every day new events focused unprecedented pressures on Sears and its leadership, those "close" to Ed Telling, like Bacon, Charlie Meyer, Phil Purcell ("like an adopted son," the grapevine instructed), and Henry Sunderland, became so concerned about Telling's penchant for keeping his own counsel that they began to wonder how he was bearing the strain. But the psychological toll of leadership wasn't the sort of thing you waltzed into this particular chairman's office to talk about, any more than the buying-side executives were about to engage in discussions of pathological behavior with Joe Moran.

Charlie Bacon desperately wanted Telling to see that he'd gone too far in delegating authority this time. He wanted to say that he thought Charlie Wurmstedt and Joe Moran were selling the company down the river. But you didn't do those things with Telling. Arthur Wood began to come down to Telling's office from the small suite the former chairman occupied on one of the upper floors of the Tower as director of the Sears savings and profit-sharing fund. Wood tried to speak reassuringly to Telling—who would just smile and nod. One time Wood decided to write an angry letter rebutting yet another negative article in *The Wall Street Journal,* but Charlie Meyer approached the usually placid gentleman and talked him out of sending it.

Telling had a personal secretarial assistant named Pat Jamieson, a blond lady from South Carolina who was known, before Telling discovered her, for having typed Joe Moran's early white papers and for her incomparable ability to make fudge. Jamieson would sit outside Telling's office and shake with frustration as one thing after another went wrong. Occasionally Pat couldn't take it anymore and would storm into the big office to "get something off her chest." She would try to draw Telling into the venting of her own rage as another sales decline came in, or news of another program subverted on the way to the stores, or another suit or derisive article, but he'd just smile at her—just swallow down the hurt of the moment—and at the end of the day he would trundle home for dinner with Nancy and, if the weather was right, for his evening's stroll with Charlie.

Telling continued to dominate the corporation with the power of his distant silence. He still drew authority from the long history of his capacity for action from a standing start, but by the end of the year it was observed that powerful passions had surfaced at the Cricket Club and the morning he had finally exploded after so many years of hating Jack Kincannon.

"What kind of management do we have here?" he growled at Joe Moran one day during 1979.

"Mismanagement," Jumpin' Joe replied.

Telling used to sit silently as constant action occurred all around him. He sat in his office in New York and then Philadelphia, surrounded by business revivals and brilliant performances by those he entrusted with unusual authority. "If you try to please me, you'll be wrong," he used to say before sending someone into action, "but if you do a good job I'll be happy." Somehow the mystery and distance and silence always contained information that made those around him know what to do. They would move swiftly in his behalf, breaking power centers, drawing the power up. He would deliver an enigmatic charge, and then withdraw from sight—"clam up," he called it—intimidating people all the while through silence ("intimidating up and down," as an old Eastern Territory acolyte once put it), until it was time to move hard again.

But now many of those around Ed Telling had been made to wait so long for a bolt from the blue that they wondered if this time the silence contained no plan or hope at all.

Ed Telling said that if he'd ever in his life stopped to give a moment's credence to what other people thought, said, or wrote about him, he would have killed himself. A long time ago he decided that there would forever be at least one person who would never get down on Ed Telling, and that would be him. Telling said he didn't understand why Joe Moran couldn't sleep through the night. The Tellings were always a family of sound sleepers.

But after almost two years of unceasing adversity, he realized that the way he'd always lived and worked made the disintegration of Sears come upon him as a painful, reverberating sort of loneliness—the only way he could describe how badly he felt was that it made him feel lonely. He'd handled adversity by himself for a long time, a lot of it dealt out to him by Sears, Roebuck, and he wasn't about to change his style now. He got out of bed early every morning and stared at his deeply creased face in the mirror while shaving. "You stick up for yourself today," he'd say. "You might be all alone." But by the end of 1979, Telling realized that aspects of his management by mystery were failing him now.

From his observation of others who'd run Sears over the years, Telling decided that one of the things that needed changing was the way the company chairman involved himself in the day-to-day, hands-on operation of the retail chain. He decided, during his time of closer study, during his stint as senior executive vice-president, Field, that one of the reasons Sears had become an island enterprise was that, after the General grew old, there was no one paid to watch the world for Sears, to mull over what was out there, and to make decisions and changes on an institutional level accordingly.

So it was by objective design, as well as by force of a rather unusual personality, that Ed Telling operated from silence, but recent events had conspired to instill nothing but chaos below him. Nineteen seventy-seven was an embarrassment, 1978 a fiasco, and 1979 was turning into a tragedy. The call from the middle ranks of the company—especially from the Field—was for Telling himself to emerge from his office and come down to insinuate his powerful presence into the broad chasm between the two wings of the company. But the chairman believed he couldn't do that. He couldn't make it through an entire tour of a store without having to bolt out the side door.

CHAPTER 8

The Gyre

├──────────────────┤

From the perspective of the big stores, it appeared that the lights were quite literally going out all over the company by the end of 1979. The managers of the stores had drawn back into such a strict "operating mode" that lighting the aisles sparingly was often judged worth the dingy cast it gave the goods. Every extra cent you could find was needed on the profit-and-loss statement. By Christmas, the number of times the stockrooms in the stores didn't contain the goods customers wanted had multiplied far beyond any of the managers' experience. There wasn't a store manager left in the system who hadn't been accosted by a customer waving a fistful of the "rain checks" that were handed out when goods weren't in the store. "No wonder I read that Sears is in serious trouble in the papers," customers said.

In many locales, store managers actively resisted recent orders from above to trim their staffs. When the time came for the traditional profit-sharing meeting for employees in the stores, an event that used to be marked by cheers and handshakes, there was a spontaneous grass-roots move to refuse to read the numbers and to demand that Headquarters send news of the embarrassing state of the veteran employees' nest eggs out on videotape. Just before the Christmas selling season of 1979, several territories informed their store managers there would be no money passed down for the traditional Christmas luncheon for the store staff and their spouses. Many managers held the luncheon anyway, at the expense of their stores' account. "If we have to tell them that we can't even afford a single day of pride anymore," one manager complained to a group administrator, "we might as well just come out and tell 'em we're done for." No true store-runner can live with red numbers day after day. It's just not in the repertoire. By the end of the 1979 Christmas selling season, it appeared that sales would actually be lower than they had been in 1978, despite a fulminating rate of inflation that should have hiked up the numbers considerably with no real improvement at all. It would be the first overt sales decline since the brief slackening of the post–World War II demand boom in 1949. The merchants reported year-end revenues of over $19 billion, but it took every pulley and mirror in the controller's office to show $70 million more in profit than Allstate, a company with just over $5 billion in sales. It was a humiliating performance.

The warring between Joe Moran and Charlie Wurmstedt had by now become more than a conflict between two overworked and obdurate men. It was perceived below them as something strikingly emblematic of two separate visions of how an organization should run and to what moral and political purpose. Wurmstedt was the rock-ribbed, country-boy, don't-tread-on-me traditionalist; a man wary of big words and regulations that encumbered free men. Wurmy represented the landed interests of the territories, the populists of the Field. Joe Moran was the big-city, big-money, machine politician, who had risen through a complex system of patronage and deal-making only to impose a new party line and party disciplines on the precincts through slogans and fear. Many observers in the company began to refer to the two factions as the left (Headquarters) and the right (Field).

News of the battles between Moran and Wurmstedt now filtered down below the level of group administration, and there were rumors at the store level—apocryphal ones—of the two men's punching each other in meetings. There were also rumors that Joe Moran had received death threats: "Better watch your back," Charlie Wurmstedt would say to Moran.

The days of Wurmstedt's arriving in meeting rooms in the Field and honestly attempting to promote a "unified" Headquarters program were over by the winter. He scoffed at the "so-called bannered program" from the Tower to his troops. One day he just tossed his papers away from himself and said, "Oh hell, this is a lot of crap. We're not gonna do this." Since Charlie Bacon happened to be sitting in the room at the time, word went around that Charlie Wurmstedt had either gotten real brave or real stupid since he left the Field to work in Chicago. So the territories resisted Wurmstedt's authority, just as the groups were in some areas resisting the territorial office and the stores were resisting the groups.

Wurmstedt tried to discourage openly rebellious acts in the Field not sanctioned by his office. He was disapproving, for instance, of the unilateral experiments being carried out in the Southern Territory by the young vice-president Eddie Brennan during 1979. Brennan had devised a system of accomplishing deep personnel cuts through attrition at the store level, but since tradition in the Field dictated trimming a long list of other expenses before taking out family members—especially those who served the public on the selling floor—Wurmy didn't approve of Brennan's cuts.

During a meeting in Atlanta, Wurmstedt told Brennan what he thought of his experiments.

"Well, then," the young officer said to his boss, "maybe I should just quit."

Wurmstedt calmly replied that quitting would be a mistake for a young man with a decent future before him at Sears.

Meanwhile, a fellow officer with a considerable Sears past, John Lowe, was looking forward to quitting the company. John Lowe had run the Midwest like a sleepwalker, wishing every day that he could go home. Lowe hated getting up in the morning and going to work for a company he didn't even recognize anymore. Sears had become a dictatorship in John Lowe's estimation, just as the General always warned would happen if proper vigilance was not kept. Before Lowe left, Ed Telling did away with the tradition of having each territorial officer give a formal report to the board of directors once a year. Bit by bit Telling was taking away all the stuff of the days that used to mean something.

Lowe would not regret his decision to hold back and let the gauntlet lie there that day on the airstrip in Pueblo, if only because he'd managed to work his massive debt down to $250,000. He agreed to leave in exchange for two full years in continued compensation, and this last deal meant that he and his wife could retire back to southern California with his head above the water line for the first time since the company went bad.

During the early days of 1980, one of Phil Purcell's six children asked him if Sears was going to go bankrupt. That's what the boy had heard from his friends at school. Some of the same Sears, Roebuck executives who had only a few years ago boasted to Purcell about the endless power of the company now came by his office to ask the plan-maker if there was any hope at all.

Purcell was assumed throughout the executive corps to be Ed Telling's proxy. For much of 1979, when Purcell "monitored" meetings participants were on guard, as wary of what they said as they would have been if Telling himself were in the room. But now some executives began to take a chance and come to Purcell to describe for him another scenario of doom: simply that "Sears is so big."

Purcell understood now that some of the actions taken during 1978 had been too extreme. Every action at Sears implied an exponential reaction because of the surreal scale of the thing. "Until you've been in a huge institution like Sears—or, I suppose, GM, or the Defense Department—you cannot understand how big it is," Phil was quoted as saying in *Chain Store Age*.

The new Sears would have to be something much more sophisticated than a simple repudiation of the old Sears ways. Ending the Balkanization and old artifices of accounting and operations by decree was only one small thing, but the hands of the master strategist from McKinsey were tied now. Purcell spent most of his days trying to alleviate the destructive discord between Field and Parent. He traveled back and forth between the lairs occupied by Charlie Wurmstedt and Joe Moran like a shuttle diplomat, hating every moment of the task.

If a meeting was called to discuss the contentious issue of whether more money should be spent on advertising, and if so whether it should be local (Field) advertising or national (Headquarters), within minutes the battle lines were drawn and Joe would be yelling, "Well, if that's your attitude, then I'm not gonna authorize any more national advertising at all. *None.* Let's just not advertise anymore."

Wurmstedt's face would turn red, and he'd stare back at Joe. Purcell could see the physical effort Charlie made trying hard to keep from striking at the bait, trying to convince himself that Joe was too crazy to fight. But never once would he manage to resist it. "All right," he would scream. "Fine! The Field says that's just fine! No more national advertising for Sears."

"Right, then," Moran would say. "Guess that's it."

"That's it."

The meeting would end there, and, as had happened so many times before, phones were lifted in offices up and down the Tower to report that on this day Charlie and Joe killed off advertising.

Purcell would then find Joe Moran back in his office. His shirt sleeves would already be rolled up high, his legs crossed on top of his desk. "I know. I know," Moran would moan, rubbing his hands over his face. "Now we're really in a mess."

At one point near the turn of the year, Wurmstedt heard that Joe was planning a series of orchestrated "visits" to the stores, in the manner of the old "Medicare" sweeps he used to make back when he ran the furniture group. Rather than responding to the planned invasion verbally or through 702-P, Charlie sat down and wrote a letter for circulation that appeared to ban all Sears buyers henceforth from trespassing in Sears stores.

By the beginning of 1980, Purcell knew that most operational, historical, and emotional links between the two armies were now severed. The simplest proposal to buy, advertise, and send to market throughout the country a simple Craftsman claw hammer was now impossible. Backroom deals by which buyers used to send goods to the Field through traditionally efficient private channels were blocked because the buyers were so scared of Joe Moran and the consequences if they got caught.

A two-day planning meeting was called for January 15 and 16. Purcell was to "monitor" the first of a series of peace and planning meetings, which were to be chaired by a representative from the Field one time and a Headquarters man the next. The first meeting was to be held at the Hyatt Regency O'Hare Hotel, a structure just off the highway between the Tower and O'Hare Airport that looked like twin mylar missile silos rising above the vast industrial park that sprawled to the west. The combatants arrived at the Hyatt during the middle of a Chicago mid-January freeze, and despite a twirling bar atop of one of the silver silos, where travelers can drink watery cocktails and watch the traffic flow in and out of the busy airport below, the feeling of the meeting place seemed cold. Lately, it seemed that no gathering of Searsmen was held in the right sort of place. If it wasn't run-down and rat-infested, they always seemed to end up in places that looked like brothels or airports.

When Joe Moran walked into the meeting room at the Hyatt and fell into a chair at the end of a table, most participants recognized that he was in the midst of one his sulks. He was swaddled in a huge alpine turtleneck sweater, into which he seemed to sink by degrees for much of the next two days, like one of the garment's namesakes. Every so often Joe rose to pace the room with his arms crossed in front of him, talking about deficient advertising and the insufficient lead time the catalog people were giving the buyers to purchase what was needed. Both the catalog and advertising were officially under Charlie Wurmstedt.

The main subject on the agenda was "traffic and transactions," which was Searstalk for why it was that fewer people were coming into the stores, and why, when the ones who did come got in there, they seemed to be buying fewer items each time. Once the cause of the desertion was agreed upon, it was hoped, a solution could be found. Joe Moran eventually descended into his sweater until only a pout was visible, so several of his vice-presidents made the Headquarters-side pleas for some coordinated mass buying, advertising, and pricing of certain items at such obvious value to the customers that the programs would bring back the people.

The apostle and vice-president Bob Wood suggested that a planning program should be constructed around the running of one or two items from each department at the same low price in every store.

"Burk" Burkholder, who had replaced John Lowe in the Midwest, turned to Wood and said, "Bob, what you are suggesting would amount to two or three hundred items a year."

"That's right, Burk," Wood said. "We have eighty thousand different things for sale here at Sears, Roebuck and, yes, I am indeed suggesting that we should coordinate on three hundred of them."

"Well," the leader of the $4.5-billion territory said, "that strikes me as an unwarranted and dangerous amount of control from Headquarters. I mean, three hundred items, that's . . . that's a lot."

"I don't believe what we are trying to do now is going to work," Wood wrote to Purcell after the Hyatt meeting. "We try to keep telling ourselves that if we provide the right product at the right price we can do anything. The problem is that we cannot provide it at the right price, since the gross profit required to overcome our expenses is high enough to preclude offering the right price to the consumer. And as we continue to make decisions forced upon us by this situation, our position becomes ever more precarious. We are victims of a non-strategy for two decades and the unchecked growth of an oppressive bureaucracy."

The next major meeting of the two sides was scheduled for February 13 in the Tower. Joe Moran was to chair the planning session, but when word got around that Joe planned to address "The Catalog Problem" at the meeting, other executives knew the February session might be particularly ugly. Ever since the early fall, Moran had been increasingly vicious about the state of the catalog business. In writing and oratory, he accused the people who created the catalogs of being the company coterie most resistant to his new rules and regulations. "It takes a degree of maturity for all of our people to understand that Freedom can only come out of Discipline, and Planning is a high order of business discipline," he wrote in reference to the catalog. "Who's minding the catalog store?" he asked in one of the white papers published during the campaign. "And where has all the wisdom gone?"

Everyone in Headquarters knew who ran the catalog store in 1979, and one of the reasons the thought of Joe's full-scale assault on the catalog was so unsettling was that it was being managed by Jack Kelly,

Joe Moran's oldest and best friend at Sears, Roebuck. In turning on Jack Kelly, Joe was indicating that there were no boundaries left for him.

The two men had worked together as friends for nearly twenty-five years. Jack was sitting in Joe's office shooting the breeze out at the old West Side when they heard that John Kennedy had been shot, and Kelly had listened to Joe Moran worry aloud for hours about the tragedy. Moran was convinced that the "son-of-a-bitch Lyndon Johnson" was much too far to the right of the political spectrum to run the country properly.

Jack Kelly was the only person at Sears who knew the truth of Jumpin' Joe's legendary disappearances to university libraries after taking over a new job. After Moran disappeared from the men's outer-wear department for his famous weeks of rigorous study of the textile industry, he wandered into Kelly's office and, as always, dropped his battered shoes and stretched-out socks on Jack's desk.

"Joe," Kelly said. "How come you have white paint all over your eyelashes and the tops of your glasses?"

"Oh Christ!" Moran yelled, as he jumped up and hurried off to the men's room.

So only Jack Kelly knew that Joe had really been home painting his house the whole time. But even after Joe had become almost unrecognizable from the strain, and turned on the catalog, Kelly didn't tell anyone about that or any of the other secrets he knew. The slightly built Kelly was universally acknowledged to be a particularly sensitive and gentle man. He was as reserved and low-keyed about his love and knowledge of classical music and literature as Joe was overt and argumentative about things he knew and cared for. Other executives loved to have Jack Kelly around them because he was such a warm, sophisticated, yet unpretentious man, and his presence was edifying to those who liked the idea that such a freewheeling world of rough diamonds and tough guys also had room for a guy like Jack. Ed Telling was forever calling Kelly out of meetings to accompany him on a field trip or a day outing to a racetrack or museum. In Searstalk, Jack was an example of a straight-shooter, Headquarters style.

Joe Moran's and Jack Kelly's mutual mentor in the catalog business, Frank Schell, used to say that the catalog was an American document that demonstrated yearly "what Americans can do in a society based upon free choice." The crafters of the beautiful woodcuts that once adorned the catalog and the writers of the old screes had long been replaced by a production staff that assembled their images of the protean components of daily life in cubicles on the lower floors of the Tower. The days of small-town parades including entire floats piled with Sears big books was over, but the company's dominance of the American catalog business had still persisted and even grown until the 1970s. During the 1960s the size of Sears' business doubled, and though the catalog still accounted for almost three times the sales of its strongest competitor, it had lost its original domination of more than half the markets it served. The constant dollar growth of the business had been flat for some time by 1980, but in eight of the ten years during the 1970s, the big book's percentage sales increase had still outpaced the stores.

Phil Purcell had recommended to Telling during 1978 that the fourteen old catalog plants that serviced catalog customers be converted from "profit centers" to "cost centers." The seemingly innocuous accounting adjustment was one of several others made that year that in fact curtailed numerous traditional prerogatives. The fact that each plant was still a decentralized business responsible for its own profits and losses was the source of a great deal of pride. The mail-order executives in the territories took the loss of their chance to make money as an attempt to whitewash once and for all the fact that they used to make *all* the money at Sears—money that had allowed the experimentation in retail stores to occur in the first place. To Purcell and Telling the change was simply an effort to eliminate another group of unruly fiefdoms, but the catalog boys in the old plants read the change as a final blow to the heart of a venerable system that the noncatalog troops had been out to change for fifty-four years.

Long before the emasculation of the plants, the balance of power in the catalog business was tipped heavily toward Headquarters. Not only were the catalog writers and coordinators of distribution housed in Chicago, but, because of the nature of catalog selling, the buyers had a particularly close relationship to the catalog people. If nobody bought goods on a buyer's page in the book, it was impossible to blame the problem on the Field. The catalog was a pure offering of goods to the public, so the buyers and catalog people at Headquarters tended to know one another. Former buyers became catalog executives—like Jack Kelly—and former catalog writers—like Joe Moran—became part of the buying-staff structure.

Catalog people effectively auctioned off the relative size of spreads and the placement and number of pages displaying the buyers' wares. A buyer would vie for position in the big book by using his 599 money to cover heavy price cuts, and then get the difference back in dealings with stores.

Jack Kelly wasn't surprised when his old friend trained his guns on the catalog. If Joe left just the catalog portion of Wurmstedt's turf alone, he could be accused of favoring the wing of the business everyone knew he loved the most. Besides that, after the demise of the 599 kitty and the promulgation of Joe Moran's managerial terror during

1979, Jack Kelly continued to run the demoralized catalog business like a wily old Chicago ward boss. The persistence of the horse-trading bothered Moran.

Jack Kelly had never called upon his considerable personal authority within the organization to challenge his old sidekick publicly. Kelly had also indulged Joe's irritating habit in recent months of launching a tirade over something in a meeting and then suddenly saying, "I have to go now, so Jack Kelly will take over the chair." Joe would thereupon rush from the room and leave his old buddy to pick up the pieces. Charlie Wurmstedt had asked Kelly, as an ex-buyer, to intercede with Moran, and Kelly had held private peace meetings in his office with the two senior executive VPs that were much more successful than any diplomatic efforts by Phil Purcell or his 702-P team.

But the leaders from the Field came back to Chicago for the next peace-and-planning meeting on February 13 and watched Joe Moran present a two-hour attack on the catalog business. Joe blamed the high prices in the enlarged catalog on Jack Kelly, though all of the apostles in the room knew that Joe had dictated the changes leading to the rising prices himself. "The catalog was once the jewel of Sears," Joe railed, "but now it's full of last year's goods at next year's prices." He claimed there was nothing new in the Sears catalog at all because of the small-mindedness of Jack Kelly's staff, and he argued that his own merchants should seize control of the business from the "silly catalog staff" with its "pedestrian way of thinking."

This was the last straw for Kelly. Maybe Sears no longer could afford a large organization of catalog-staff employees, but since the individual who was largely responsible for the growth of the catalog staff between 1958 and 1965 was none other than Joe Moran, he just wasn't about to let this one slide. When Joe had his heart attack in 1959—something that few people left at Sears knew about—Kelly had taken over the building of the staff for Joe while he recuperated, so he knew what he was talking about.

Back in 1971, when Jack Kelly got the top executive job in the Sears Catalog business, several witnesses to the event told him that Joe Moran bought a bottle of Chivas Regal Scotch when he heard about the promotion and drank it down in one sitting. Kelly knew that Joe had desperately wanted to run the catalog himself, but he'd never before sensed that Moran held it against him—especially after Joe became such a star of various corporate staffs that he was eventually catapulted into the chief merchant's chair. Even when Joe's agitation against the management of the catalog business began, in late 1979, Kelly still figured it was simply because catalog reported to Charlie Wurmstedt, and since Moran was waging an all-out war against everything Wurmstedt did, the catalog was just an item on his hit list. But this latest episode seemed personal, something that had been smoldering for a long time. It almost seemed as if Joe didn't want Jack Kelly around him anymore, as either a friend or a witness.

As Moran finally drew toward the conclusion of his onslaught and Jack Kelly readied himself for the counterattack he'd been waiting to deliver for a long time, Moran suddenly scooped up his papers, lumbered to the door, and announced, "I am leaving on vacation now, so I know you will all excuse me." Then he stomped out of the room and went back down to his office.

Moran threw on his coat and stopped in for a few final words with Frank Tuma. Tuma had gone to visit Jack Kelly several times during the preceding weeks to try to mediate the growing storm between Kelly and his boss. Frank knew a lot about what the combination of pressure and isolation can do to a company man from his own experience at Sears, and for some time he'd feared that if Joe Moran alienated Jack Kelly, one of his last close friends in the organization, the effect on his mentor could be psychologically disastrous.

"Frank," Moran said quickly, "I'm going on vacation now, and I'm going to spend some time thinking about whether I want to continue working here while I'm gone. I just don't know if this is worth it. . . . Why, Frank?" His voice grew sad and slow. "Why is it worth it, Frank?"

Before Tuma answered, Moran was gone.

Jack Kelly was scheduled to take some "personal days" himself (many Sears executives tried to take their vacations during the retail doldrums of January and February), but before Kelly left he wrote a letter addressed to Phil Purcell, which he fully intended to be circulated like one of Moran's white papers. While the acid reply included a point-by-point defense of the catalog, Kelly also went out of his way to comment on Joe's leadership of the buying organization. He decided to remind his readers of the widely forgotten fact that Jumpin' Joe Moran had never really been a Sears buyer. He'd never really cut his teeth on the goods or served the company in the trenches. All he'd ever done was talk and write about it: "Our buying organization, for generations, has lived and breathed merchandise—the goods. It's great merchandise that makes great catalogs, and it alone will cause customers to want Sears catalogs and Sears goods rather than someone else's.

"I worked as a buyer. Grew up with lots of them and talk to them almost daily about Sears and their work. We've got a problem. . . . After years of being under-managed, our buyers have become woefully over-managed. Buried under a blizzard of white papers, pronouncements, and new forms, they dream of the day they'll have a few moments to execute some of the plans they've made.

"They [the buyers] view the MPC [the Merchandise Policy Committee—the official name Moran gave the grouping of apostles and several others like Kelly who met together once a week] as being completely involved in procedures, policy, and as inventors of Task Forces that seldom come to grips with the merchandise—the life blood of the Company."

Kelly signed the letter "Jack."

"Jeez, Mr. Kelly," the 702-P planner Joe Batogowski said when he saw a draft of Kelly's letter. "You can't send that."

Kelly considered young Batogowski to be an "errand boy" for Phil Purcell. "What do you mean, 'I *can't*'?" Kelly said. "If you'd like, when Joe gets back the three of us can go up to Purcell's office and I'll read it out loud to him." Purcell begged Kelly not to commit his attack to paper. He pleaded with him, arguing that Kelly was simply too well respected in the company to let fly like this. It was expected of Moran, but a letter like this from Kelly would further destabilize and demoralize the organization.

On February 17, Kelly made sure the letter was copied and sent before leaving for his own vacation. Joe Moran returned while Kelly was gone, and immediately issued a short public reply designed to trivialize Kelly's break as a minor storm between two old friends: "Dear old Jack, your comments on my management of the buying organization are really so intemperate and outrageous, that they're funny. They're also totally wrong, but you're entitled! I haven't seen you this way in 20 years, when we both used to say the same things about Frank Schell!"

Most of the other executives Moran had called "old friend" when he'd seen them in the hall—"How *are* you, old friend?" he'd say, draping an arm lovingly around his colleague's shoulder—the ones who shared a history with Joe, were gone or under attack now. The apostles were all paralyzed by fear and lack of direction, and their ritual confession of failure in meetings was becoming almost bizarre to behold. Ira Quint was gone. Goldstein was gone. In fact, all the executives who'd seen that Joe Moran was "really a bit of a blodger," in Jack Kelly's words, the ones who still owned copies of early white papers that revealed Moran's recent policy flip-flops, had been moved far away from him now.

In February Moran made it known publicly that Sears planned to "lop off 1200 suppliers." A few weeks later he photocopied an article from *Chain Store Age* that described a Sears apparel executive "enviously" considering J. C. Penney's spring 1980 catalog. Moran had encircled the line "a Sears apparel executive," and in his sloppy hand written in bold letters, "Who?"

He came to the office soon afterward with a long night's work he called "Meditations and Musings on Advertising, Budgets, and Who Gets What." The fifteen-page white paper questioned the masculinity of the ad writers; wondered if Sears had gotten old "like Eisenhower"; paraphrased the playwright Luigi Pirandello; and generally rambled over issues of business, art, and philosophy in a way that utterly obscured the document's call for a huge increase in advertising before it was too late:

"Deus ex machine, ve quid erat latibus, etc.," the white paper concluded mysteriously. "God works in mysterious ways, and is only testing us; get back up on your horse Saul of Tarsus and fight again, for I have armed you with the word of truth and the shield of perseverance."

Through his own injury, Jack Kelly felt sorry for his old friend. Joe was a basket case. Kelly had watched him work like a driven man for much of his life, only to end up with little pleasure and not a bit of peace. He'd worked beside Jumpin' Joe for almost twenty-five years and had witnessed the creation of his original and colorful personae, but he just couldn't buy this latest effort of Joe's to present himself as Sears, Roebuck's saving grace.

So in love with his own words had Joe become that he'd torn Field and Parent further apart than they'd ever been. He seemed bent on destroying Headquarters structures like the buying departments in the name of some ephemeral unity. And now he was driving away the very people who could have been most helpful to him.

One minute Kelly thought he could still discern the warmth in Joe, the Irish bard: the good old Joe, who'd studied with Kelly at the feet of the great catalog-philosopher, Frank Schell. But suddenly there would appear another Joe Moran, who seemed driven by nothing but the paranoid personality of a martinet, a man scenting plots behind every door, publishing lists, and planting rumors.

By the time they crossed swords, Jack Kelly had already come to see Moran's inexorable movement toward the edge of reason as a tragic metaphor. As Joe moved away from hard ground, so moved the company. As he seemed so deeply psychologically severed, so, it now seemed, was all of Sears, Roebuck.

From store to Tower, rumors were now sweeping the company indicating that Sears wouldn't survive 1980. Many executives at Sears heard and believed that the company might default on its next dividend payments and possibly some of its bills. Early data about the first quarter of 1980 indicated earnings would make the dismal first quarter of 1979 look like a sellout. The quarter would eventually show a $432-million loss in the column where a slight $67-million gain resided in 1979.

The amazing speed with which Sears had fallen from grace with the nation had so dizzied employees that the full force of the company's business crisis only acquired a vocabulary with which it could be talked about around the beginning of 1980. Now, like the retirees before them, employees lamented openly the sickening slide in the stock price, which on March 10 touched $15.25 per share. You didn't need an M.B.A. to see that the cost of servicing Sears' massive debt was soaring out of control, or that the cost of paying the bills now dwarfed the shriveling revenues. Most employees believed that it would be only a matter of days before the company—which spent 26 percent of the money it took in from sales on its payroll—announced massive across-the-board layoffs. Controller's office personnel did pirouettes in order to show a measly 4.5-percent increase in merchandise sales since Ed Telling took over, this while the consumer-price-index measure of inflation had appreciated by a factor of 20 percent.

There were rumors that certain members of the board of directors— notably Julius Rosenwald's grandson, Edgar Stern—were garnering support for the replacement of Ed Telling. Some of the younger and most talented executives—including several of the top personnel managers and one territorial officer—were actively thinking of fleeing the disaster and going to work somewhere else, while those who were older and too "Searsized," as they called it, possibly to work anywhere else, were left helpless and afraid.

The trade magazine *Inside Retailing* weighed in at this moment with a benediction upon the sudden humbling of the world's premier selling organization: "The Sears of 1967 was in many ways a microcosm of the America of 1967. It was all powerful, sophisticated, and in comparison with the competition, very adept in the use of marketing. As was the case with the U.S., Sears too believed that the world was its oyster, because at that given moment in time the world was. . . . Now, in 1980, with the country confused about its own future, Sears appears again to be a microcosm for the nation's total economy. . . . The problem with Sears is that the company has just run out of steam."

Maybe there was no more America left for Sears. Maybe the kingdom had an end. Articles in the press now described the destruction of the American mass market Sears once owned and operated as its leaders saw fit. The world outside really did look strange to many members of the generation of soldiers that built the post-war version of the company. Every night that early spring, the evening news showed fanatics thousands of miles away holding Americans hostage, celebrating the act by raising fists that bore wristwatches just like the ones Sears sold in its invincible blockhouse stores.

A terrifying scenario was now visible inside Sears from top to bottom and from sea to sea. The same exponential economies of scale that had so rapidly multiplied Sears' power and triumph for almost a century were now inverted, as if the full weight of the corporate pyramid rested ominously on a pinpoint. Smaller, more rangy retailers encircled Sears on the nation's strips and in the shopping malls Sears "anchored," hanging off the injured leviathan like so many parasites. The sniping from regulators and reporters was more intense all the time, and the customers were defecting in droves. Each tiny incremental rise in interest rates, each tiny fall in the number of items a single customer bought during a shopping trip, each small price rise coming out of the fearful, stricken factories that produced the goods, all came together now as a huge and swirling destructive force.

The merchants of Sears had all seen other big chains enter the spiral of failure. Korvettes had gone down into the whirlpool. So had W. T. Grant. Montgomery Ward seemed to have fallen so hard into a self-perpetuating day-to-day decline that an oil company had to come in to take over the company, and it still looked doubtful that the other Chicago retailer would survive. Perhaps because retail organizations are so peculiarly ruled by their states of mind, so dependent upon a mass elan to make the system work, the numbers of big stores that had ever come back from a sustained, pervasive decline was limited. Only a few had ever pulled out of the hole.

The institution had risen to utter dominance of its economic sphere, only to find that its necessarily bureaucratic order had curtailed innovation and change. Now public humiliations and factional in-fighting had spawned what the brilliant student of economic failure Joseph Schumpeter called a "critical frame of mind," which was destroying the moral authority of the company and turning its intricate culture inward upon itself.

Everywhere there were stains from red ink flowing from the deep lesions in the business—the red of blood and the red of insurrectionary change. It was clear now that the hopelessness and bitterness were so enlaced within the order that any reconstruction of Sears would have to include a new reason to believe. The rude cracking of tradition had conspired with failure and fear to create the sort of milieu from which dictators and madmen rise up, and to which visions of new messiahs come down.

The day before the officers were scheduled to meet for another peace-and-planning meeting at Southern Territory headquarters in Atlanta —on March 12—Ed Telling called a summary meeting of the Headquarters corporate officers. At eleven o'clock Telling shambled into the small gathering and announced that Dean Swift had decided to retire four years before his formal retirement age for "personal reasons." On April 8, Telling continued, the day Swift would leave his office, the current vice-president of the Southern Territory, Eddie Brennan, would become the new president of Sears.

The officers all drove out to the company hangar after the short meeting and flew south. They regrouped a few hours later at the old Capital City Club in downtown Atlanta for 6:30 cocktails, a late start for drinking time by Sears standards. The Southern Territory had jumped from fifth to first in various productive categories of interterritorial competition during recent quarters, but more prominent on the grapevine were descriptions of the formal banquets held in what was once the most informal territory—and in the midst of the company-wide depression. The executives in for the planning meeting from Chicago, Philadelphia, Dallas, and Los Angeles sipped mint juleps and stared nonplussed at the spectacle of hors d'oeuvres being served by black waiters wearing white gloves. They waited in anticipation for a dinner they expected would be unusually sumptuous by usual standards, and they waited for Brennan.

Eddie was still known to many of the officers by the epithet he'd acquired as the junior member of the Corporate Hay Committee: they still called him "the kid." Brennan was known to have missed not a single meeting of the Hay Committee from the time he joined the others as the youngest Turk. Fellow committee members were awed by the enthusiasm with which he would write and read the hundreds of six-page write-ups they were supposed to produce about the various jobs inside Sears. Once Eddie looked into an issue it was hard to move him away. He would fix on a thing with such intensity that he would on occasion forget his junior station and trespass across the old lines. During a Corporate Hay Committee meeting at the Whitehall Club in Chicago one afternoon, Brennan spoke at length about a series of contradictory job titles he'd discovered in the area of the corporate controller—the hallowed turf of one Jack Kincannon. The Hay Committee representative from the controller's office was a fellow named Van Tilburg. "Brennan!" Van Tilburg cut in that day. "Do you think you know everything about everything?"

Brennan's almost Oriental eyes narrowed to a thin line and his ears flamed bright red above his high-clipped sideburns. He slowly rose from his chair and left the meeting room for almost an hour. By the time he got his corner-office job in Atlanta, it was known by those close to him that you should run far away when Eddie Brennan's ears got red. Now Ed Telling had apparently catapulted the kid over the heads of numerous individuals he used to work for. He would replace in Dean Swift a man who'd first come to work for Sears when Ed Brennan was three.

Telling had called upon the symbolic power of his "token youth," as he'd called Brennan in the past. After Telling crushed several of the old baronies of the Eastern Territory in 1969, he demoted one of the now surplus group managers to a bleak ghetto store in downtown Baltimore, Maryland, while transferring that blighted store's thirty-five-year-old manager to one of the biggest and best stores in the territory. The manager Telling promoted then was the energetic newcomer to the Field, Eddie Brennan. Ten months later, Telling moved Brennan up to New York as assistant manager of the group. At the time Telling had spent only an hour in conversation with the young man, and everyone in the New York group knew it. In 1972 Telling aimed Brennan at the Western New York group of Sears stores. The group encompassed the economic disaster area in and surrounding Buffalo and was the worst in the territory, but by the end of 1972 Brennan won a Tower of Achievement award for making it the best.

Five years later, during the Christmas debacle of 1977, Brennan was running the big Boston group, and somehow running it profitably against the tide of profit collapse that visited almost every other sector of Sears that year. Brennan made $31 million in his Boston stores during the year they gave the store away, more than New York or Los Angeles, and the next year he'd been duly rewarded with stewardship of the South.

Most of the boys were well past their first cocktails when Ed Brennan finally swept into the room, looking aggressively youthful—much too young to run a territory, let alone be the president of Sears. He began to walk slowly through the crowd at the Capital City Club, fielding graciously his congratulations and calling men a generation his senior by their first names for the first time.

There was no mention that evening of what this new job of Brennan's really meant. Telling said at the morning meeting that Brennan would "run the merchandise business"—a confusing and ahistorical statement. The merchandise business *was* Sears, Roebuck, and though it had been run officially by a chairman for many years, the arrangement left the other senior executives free and able to do battle over turf and philosophical predisposition. The president of Sears was supposed to be an old hand, as comfortable and stable and ineffectual as the honorific, appointed presidents of some European democracies.

As the veterans sipped their drinks and watched Eddie work the crowd, they all agreed that this latest promotion just didn't figure, even for Telling.

.   .   .

The next morning the planning meeting convened in a room containing a large, U-shaped table. Most of the tables used during previous peace-and-planning conferences were arranged like a U or a horseshoe, and at each of the meetings Joe Moran occupied the center seat of the transverse table, with Charlie Wurmstedt to his left. Phil Purcell and the other Headquarters and Field officers sat in an array that extended out to the ends of the arms of the U.

By the time Joe Moran walked into the meeting room, everyone but Ed Brennan was already sitting down. They all watched Moran go to his chair in the center as Brennan moved toward him purposefully. The two men arrived in back of the center chair at the base of the horseshoe at the same time. Joe paused and looked at the younger man quizzically. "Joe," Brennan said, "I'll sit here today."

Moran gathered up the files and papers he'd placed at the head of the table and slowly moved down to the far end of one side of the horseshoe.

Every man in the room watched Joe trudge away from the chair now occupied by the kid, and every one of them knew that they'd just witnessed a moment floating free between two eras.

CHAPTER 9

The Kid

For all of the first ten years of his life, Ed Brennan had worn only Sears clothes and Sears shoes his father brought back from the "pile" at the West Side plant. He never owned a pair of blue jeans, because his father had stopped working in a Sears store to become a boys' dress-slacks buyer for the company, so Ed painted houses and played baseball in Sears' best. Every so often his father—also named Ed—would tell him to put his foot on a piece of paper on the floor. Then he'd draw an outline of his son's foot in order to pull another pair of Sears shoes out of inventory.

But one snowy weekend day in February of 1944, it was discovered that Ed didn't have any winter boots, so his father took him to a shoe store in downtown Oak Park, the Chicago suburb next to the West Side Irish ghetto. Ed walked up and down in front of the shoes, which were arrayed with such a concentrated sense of order and evidence of care that the shoes themselves seemed to propel his eye from display to display. He was allowed to touch the shoes and even try them on. If he asked a question, the people who worked in the store answered as if they cared about him, as if it meant something that he was alive and standing there. Ed was mystified by the store. The whole place seemed full of icons designed to imbue reverence and awe. Decades later, Ed Brennan would still utter the word "store" with special care. His lips would carefully form the noun and it would be delivered in a voice made a bit more gentle and reflective than it was for the words surrounding it: "store" . . . like a word spoken in a dream.

The good store became over time a paradigm for good thinking and good works, places where "the goods"—which he also mentioned in that special voice—were endowed through order and care with an ultimate integrity before entering the general flow.

Bad stores, on the other hand, were forms of desecration.

Ed Brennan believed that retailing was less a job than a calling. He thought that buying and selling were much less the basic transactions of economic life than they were the stuff of moral drama. He also believed that Sears, Roebuck was something much more than a very sick business: it was the world's most noble institution this side of the Church, and it was his own ancestral home. The sprawling civilization of Sears had enclosed hundreds of thousands of people, but the Brennans ranked among those special families so bred to the romance of the place that it was hard to tell company and family apart. Even by Sears, Roebuck's unusually emotional standards, Eddie Brennan took it all quite personally.

From his new office in the Tower, Brennan could look down to South Michigan Avenue and see the site of the Catholic charity hospital where on a cold day in 1934 he was born to a beautiful young woman with a peculiarly affecting high color in her cheeks and a twenty-three-year-old C-store Sears, Roebuck salesman, who was so tall and handsome that people would stop and stare when he passed by. The new president could squint into the haze beyond the hospital site and see the monumental Museum of Science and Industry, a gift to the city of Chicago from Julius Rosenwald's fortune, and a place where Ed Brennan's mother dragged him and his brother regularly before she left them at the age of thirty-one and went to be a Sears pioneer in Mexico. To the west, beyond the streets where he had lived and the corners where he had delivered papers, a clear day would reveal to him the old Sears Headquarters, where Luke Brennan, his grandfather, worked beside Richard Sears, and where his father, two uncles, and his brother Bernie had all worked as Sears buyers.

The family Marge Brennan left in Chicago reorganized continually after she went to Mexico with Ed's younger sister. For a time, Ed would iron shirts and cook meals for his father and brother. Then there was a housekeeper for a while, and then Ed, Bernie, and their father moved in with an uncle. Bernie, who was four years younger than Ed, was eventually farmed out to another uncle, so the two brothers essentially grew up in different families, but though his brother lived somewhere else, and his mother lived somewhere else, no one in Ed Brennan's family ever managed to leave Sears.

In part because of the sheer weight of the Brennan legacy at Sears, when it came time for Ed to be confirmed as a retailer and enter the fold at the age of fifteen, it was he who first ventured to leave the company. He went to work for a store in Chicago called Benson and Rixon, a fairly successful men's-clothing shop where he could observe the processes of buying and selling from beginning to end. He worked there at the end of high school alongside a gifted buyer of clothing named Moe Freeman and an inspired clothes-seller named Mortie Marx. Business was so good during those post-war years that a fellow practicing the fine art of selling a suit didn't have time to write up the sales check and take down alteration information, so a kid like Ed Brennan was hired to mop up the sales.

Brennan went to Marquette University while working his way through Benson and Rixon. The company owned a store near the Marquette campus in Milwaukee where Ed began working—Saturdays and weekend nights included—the day he started college. He stopped working two days before graduation. Brennan never tired of watching the true craftsmen, like Art Smith, a man who'd been selling suits since 1880. The older salesmen would take him home for dinner, and in some ways they became Ed Brennan's best friends.

When he'd first gone north to college, Brennan had acquiesced to his father's desires and applied for a job at the local Sears. But the Field personnel man had seemed decidedly uninterested in Brennan's special feel for the trade or in his family connections to Parent, so Brennan stayed with his friends at Benson and Rixon. He worked for the company as a salesman, cashier, inventory-control man, in auditing, and as a credit supervisor. By the time he was twenty-one, Ed was the number-five man in the company, though his father urged him continually to come back home to Sears. They would have great debates in which Ed would argue the virtues of a small company and his father would take the side of the large ones. They were still arguing the point when his youthful father died suddenly while at work in his office on the West Side. The elder Ed had recently remarried. He'd fallen in love with a Sears copywriter, married her, and then he died.

Brennan had begun working full-time with Benson and Rixon in Chicago as an assistant buyer a week after graduation from Marquette. He was making almost $9,000 a year in 1956, and he was one of the only twenty-two-year-old apparel-buyers in Chicago who had lunch at the Palmer House or the dining room in Merchandise Mart. But Sears kept pulling him back. He finally explained to his wife that he had to return to the fold. He joined up with Sears for $4,400 a year and took a low-level job in a retail store in Madison, Wisconsin. As he began to fly up through the Field ranks, he realized that his detour outside the world of Sears, and the lessons of Moe, Mortie, and Art, would serve him well.

In 1959 Brennan was moved from Field to Parent; there he labored with the buyers and Headquarters kingpins for seven years. He fired a man when he was twenty-five years old, and was given a miniature buying department to manage at twenty-nine. The golden days of Department 644—men's made-to-measure clothing—had been gone for thirty years by the time Brennan took over, but soon it was making money again. Next, at the beginning of 1966, he was transferred to a staff job, where he stayed for only a year before heading back out to the territories. Because of his unusual and rapid movement across company borders and his significant familial roots in the catalog (where Luke had worked) and the buying organization, as well as in the stores, Brennan was never pegged as a full-fledged member of any one of the clans.

Even among the elite soldiers of the Eastern Territory, Brennan was never invited into Ed Telling's inner circle. Telling had rarely moved anyone as quickly as he moved Brennan, but the token youth was never associated with the grand strategic offensives in which Telling intimates like Charlie Bacon, Henry Sunderland, and later Phil Purcell were involved. He participated in the structural upheavals Telling wrought in the East only as a symbolic presence. He'd worked like a demon to salvage the business performance of the increasingly larger bits of the Field entrusted to him during the recent years of decline. He'd run the hell out of his stores, retail groups, and finally his Southern Territory as he saw fit—just like the willful, independent Searsmen he'd heard about and observed since he was a little boy—but he was always kept just far enough away from the blood-letting so as not to be stained.

If anyone knew that Sears, Roebuck was a way of life, it was Ed Brennan. He knew what it was to be a grandson, son, nephew, brother, and—for a while after his mother left—even a wife of Searsmen. He had roots as streetworthy, urban, and Parent-minded as Joe Moran's, but he'd also done time in the consummate Field environment of Ed Telling's Eastern Territory. He'd been a storekeeper in rustic places like Oshkosh, Wisconsin, and a storekeeper at the Mondawmin store in a blighted section of Baltimore the year the surrounding community burst into flames. He'd been a buyer and a member of a powerful mid-1960s-style Headquarters staff.

Brennan was forty-six years old now, yet, with his sideburns cut away near the tops of his ears and that smooth, somewhat pale Celtic complexion, he still looked at first glance like an altar boy. But most people tended to stare at Brennan's fluid face beyond that first glance, or to look back at him at intervals, because, along with aspects of youthful innocence, there was also something there that made him look very old. Sometimes he seemed a young Turk and sometimes an old soldier. He was young enough to have Vietnam fixed in his consciousness when he spoke of "the war," and old enough to have watched the early mail-order men play cards in the company clubs at the old Headquarters, and to have later helped the old General pick out his topcoat and suits from the pile in inventory. It was as if fate had formed him as a ready-to-wear hero—born low and risen high, and delivered up just when it looked like the empire was beyond fixing.

Ed Telling met with Brennan briefly the day he told him he would soon become the youngest president of Sears since General Wood. The two men pored over computer printouts bearing numbers and trend lines more dispiriting than either of them had ever seen. The raging inflation alone should have been adding 10 percent to the company's sales figures—the consumer price index was leaping full percentage points in a single month—but the numbers all indicated an increase only in the rate of their decline. The first-quarter sales-and-profit picture was matched only by a few quarters Sears had experienced during the Great Depression. Though they all hoped nobody would notice, it was now clear that Sears was about to fall to the position of Chicago's second-largest company, behind Standard Oil of Indiana.

"What are we gonna do?" Telling said. "We can't let it keep goin' like this."

Brennan believed that Joe Moran had urged Telling toward a terrible overreaction to the great selloff of 1977. The restrictive cutbacks on promotions and advertising had crippled the delicate mechanism by which goods are bought with inspiration, quickly distributed, priced within a slender margin of error, powerfully advertised, and gracefully purveyed. The process was held together by thread, trust, hair triggers, and countless egos, and somehow the Draconian policies, as well as they had served to do away with a Byzantine power structure, had also caused the drawing apart of the company into two camps. The sales collapse tore what Brennan called "the fabric of Sears." The company had lost its spirit and its will.

Just as Ed Telling and Phil Purcell intended, great numbers of things that had been true of the company only a few years earlier were no longer so. No one could still believe that a job at Sears included implicit authority over how, when, why, and for whom they did it. Whether the soldiers accepted it or not, the Field subdivisions were no longer sovereign on any official plane, and the Field employees no longer believed they bought goods from the Parent with impunity. It was unclear how goods should leap the gap from Headquarters to store, but it was quite clear that the internal free market was dead. The "federation of independent merchants" that was the powerful army of the buyers and their support staffs was in retreat. The political power of the buyers over the Field was almost gone, as were many of the small suppliers who used to be considered part of the greater corporate family. A long list of hallowed systems and manners were gone—gone, for instance, was the animating belief that Sears, Roebuck was the most powerful distributor of goods in the world—but little had been constructed with which to fill the charged and bitter void.

Even if the old spirit of the sale could be resuscitated, Brennan believed Sears was simply too bloated and ponderous to return to health. He didn't really know how it could be done, but he sensed that the business fortunes of Sears could only be turned if a new spirit of discipline, contraction, and consolidation could somehow join with the ole-time religion to form something new.

Brennan didn't discuss his full analysis of recent history with Ed Telling the day he received his charge. He did say that something radical had to be done immediately to get customers back into the stores, even if it meant taking risks that could sink the enterprise all at once.

"Go ahead and try," Telling said.

"You know," Brennan said before he left Telling's office, "all we really are is a big store. We're nothing but items and lines and departments. We have advertising and operating and credit and service—just like a store."

"So run it like a store," Telling said.

At the meeting in Atlanta a few days later, after he replaced Joe Moran in the center chair, Brennan attempted to maintain a low profile. He realized that his sudden leap over the top of the others must have shocked the veteran officers, and since he was in the unusual position of still officially being the head of the Southern Territory for a few more weeks, until Dean Swift vacated the president's office on the sixty-eighth floor, he announced at the beginning of the Atlanta session that he would refrain from entering the discussion. The meeting began with some of the same old proposals being aggressively offered up by one side and rejected, as always, by the other side. After a short while, several of the participants sitting around the U-shaped table saw the color rise into Ed Brennan's face.

"You know," Brennan finally interrupted, "when I used to run a store for Sears, I had merchants and I had operators. And they worked together and reported to me. The only way I can think of to run this company is to run it like a store. We're a family that has to pull back together as one. The merchants are going to work with the operators, the buyers with the sellers." Brennan's eyes moved from one end of the horseshoe to the other. "That," he said, "is the way it's gonna be."

As soon as Brennan arrived in Chicago, he found that most of the senior merchandise executives believed that the only "quick fix" available to them was a program of massive layoffs. A few months earlier, layoffs had been discussed at a meeting held in Chicago, after which territorial personnel staffs were given the authority to effect dismissals of employees with up to ten years of service. The ensuing layoffs appeared arbitrary to some observers and halfhearted to others, and the amount of money saved was negligible. But by the spring of 1980, many managers who'd resisted terminations earlier now felt the decline was so precipitous that another breach of the General's psychological contract with the people of Sears was necessary.

Brennan had instituted a wave of terminations in the South based on performance rather then longevity of service. Salesmen were to be fired only for not selling. The territorial office reviewed every single case, one group at a time, before the notice of termination was sent out, but mistakes and the improper termination of some employees by Field hands used to ruling by impulse and gut feelings had caused numerous incidents that were passed along the grapevine.

Brennan sensed that one of his only trump cards was the popular hope that his appointment meant that the bloodshed and fear would end, that he had been brought in to close the wounds and ease the pain. He wasn't about to squander that hope at the start. He called his officers together in a conference room on the sixty-eighth floor shortly after taking up residence across from Ed Telling and told them that, although he was aware of the consensus on the subject, there would be no mass layoffs. As bad as it was, he believed layoffs would destroy what was left of the spirit of Sears.

As Ed Brennan mulled over his options during the weeks after his arrival in Chicago, he decided that if he was to have the slightest chance of rapidly mobilizing his forces to a new plan once he decided what to do, he had to do something about the tenuous state of the buying organization. Morale was at a low ebb everywhere in the organization, but the level of fear and confusion at Headquarters was clearly out of control. Brennan called Joe Moran into his office during early April and told him in no uncertain terms that he was to bring his period of management by intimidation, rumor, and literary hyperbole to an end.

Eddie Brennan had first had business dealings with Jumpin' Joe Moran back in 1968, when Joe came to his store in Baltimore to inspect the drapery department. Brennan had heard some of the tales of Moran, and he knew that Joe had worked with his father and one of his uncles back at the West Side. The first visit was cursory, and their paths didn't cross again until the Hay Committee meetings convened, where Brennan was the kid—the pickle-washer—and Joe was chief dialectician and dean of deans.

Out in the Field, Brennan had learned that Chicago-based intellectual posturers like Ira Quint and Joe Moran were considered "idealists," "perception people," or "dreamers" by the guys on the line. They were "good generals from the hill" who "didn't know how to dig a foxhole" from the Field soldier's perspective, but Brennan found during the Hay Committee debates that he could play at being a perception person too. There came a time when Brennan presumed to challenge both Joe and Ira to intellectual duels. Occasionally Brennan was left alone to defend the Field viewpoint against Moran and Quint together, and other committee members became increasingly impressed with the younger man's oratorical skills—especially, several committeemen thought, when a senior officer came into the room to visit.

Brennan already knew Ira Quint fairly well before their Hay Committee days, because Quint was one of the few senior buyers who had visited him regularly when he was running the group out of Buffalo. Quint sensed that Brennan believed he could handle the job of running the Field as early as 1976, and he used to joke with him about the time when Brennan would run the company and Ira would serve as his head merchant. But there was always an edge to Brennan's relationship with Joe.

After one particularly grueling Hay session at the Whitehall Club, Moran and Brennan were sitting in the bar unwinding when they were joined by a tough-talking older woman named Helen Lee, who'd worked for years as a free-lance designer for Sears. After a few drinks, Lee began to reminisce about some of the most gifted Sears merchants she'd worked with over the years, and neither member of her audience could miss the fact that Joe Moran wasn't on the list. "You weren't much of a merchant," the brassy designer scoffed at Moran after a few more drinks. At this, Ed Brennan began to laugh, and he complimented Mrs. Lee on her superior judgment.

Joe turned to young Brennan and said, "Well, shit, *you're* no merchant. In fact, your kid brother works for me and is a better merchant than you are." Moran knew enough about the Brennans to realize that he was treading on a sensitive area. By the time Ira Quint came into the bar, Ed Brennan's ears were bright red and both Irishmen's fists were clenched. Quint eventually convinced Brennan to leave the bar and take a walk around the block.

After Brennan took Joe's chair in Atlanta, there was much conjecture among veterans of the Hay Committee council of colonels about what would transpire from the new relationship. "Hey, Joe," the Hay delegate from personnel, Gene Harmon, said to Moran. "How you gonna like working for the kid?"

"At my age, everybody who gets promoted seems younger than I am," Moran replied.

Joe didn't mention that soon after the appointment of a president above him he went to Brennan and offered his resignation. Charlie Bacon told him he was a damn fool to resign, but Moran said it was the honorable thing to do. He knew he was considered a destructive force in the company, and he believed Brennan's appointment was a repudiation of his efforts.

Brennan said he didn't want Moran's resignation, but he did say he would not abide further implicit accusations by Moran that Sears buyers were dishonest people. For one thing, Brennan didn't think it was true, and for another, he felt that the fear Moran had released within the organization had caused the buyers to stop taking the sorts of risks that kept the lifeblood coursing through a good merchant. Brennan reasoned that one way to curtail the reign of terror would be to still Joe's pen. Thus, at a subsequent "meeting of the minds" in early April, Jumpin' Joe was informed that his open letters and white papers were to cease. He could write memos when appropriate, but he was to excise the lofty turns of phrase that had kept him up night after night in the crafting. He was also to curtail his comments to the press. He was, in effect, declawed and muzzled.

A melancholy and ravaged-looking Joe Moran told Frank Tuma he thought Sears had four months to come up with a short-term fix; six at the most. Ever the historian of the company, Moran talked often now of the near-fatal crisis of the winter of 1921. Joe believed that the central error made by Sears managers in 1921 was that they allowed the independent buyers of the time to build up a huge inventory of goods that the company couldn't sell or afford to finance. Joe contended at length to his apostles (a term heard more infrequently in the days following Brennan's appointment) that shriveling sales would not suddenly kill the ailing company, but that interest cost entailed in carrying too much inventory could. "The banker is your enemy," Moran warned his merchants. The times, he believed, called for discipline.

But Moran and Charlie Wurmstedt were summoned to a meeting in Telling's office during late April at which Ed Brennan declared that the restrictions ("disciplines") on the buyers were to be lifted for a time so that they could go out and find some "opportunistic" goods upon which the company could build an emergency sales program for the fall season of 1980. Having passed on wholesale layoffs, a sales hype of some cast was clearly in order. Brennan knew that these sorts of sales-promotion programs had been proscribed ("b-a-a-anned," he said sarcastically in private) since they were associated with the 1977 debacle—and that Moran, and by association Ed Telling, were closely associated with the proscription. The whole thrust of the twenty-seven-month effort to gain control over the buyers had been to restrict their purchases to a few price points as part of a regular, previously approved, "disciplined" assortment of goods. But Brennan said he believed the state of the crisis called for a temporary reversal of policy. The prices were already too high in the stores, and while Sears continued to hike prices by an annual average of 7 percent, the general cost of the goods they bought was escalating at twice that rate.

Something had to be done.

During early April, Brennan was urged to kill off the Sears credit-card system. Since the beginning of the year, the cost of financing the merchandise business had climbed to $20 million a week in debt service alone. Inflation had rendered money ever more expensive, and the lion's share of the money secured through the Sears Acceptance Corporation window went to pay for installment contracts purchased internally from the credit operation of the merchandise company. The credit card had always made money for Sears—even during the dark year of 1979, the credit division added almost $15 million to the bottom line. But now the rising cost of financing the purchases of the company's twenty-four million credit-card families was alone causing net losses at a rate nearing a million dollars a week, and each territory was still competing through games and contests to get more Sears credit cards into more wallets, because the cards were thought to be engines for growing sales. Less credit spending meant a further deterioration in sales, a consequent further deterioration of morale, smaller orders to the strangling factories, higher prices of goods to Sears, higher prices in the stores . . . and less spending.

But more credit spending meant larger losses because of high interest rates, losses that had to be covered by capital taken out of the merchandise company. Companies that have increasing debts and decreasing equity occasionally can go bankrupt as suddenly as if they'd been struck by lightning, and the "debt-equity" ratio at Sears in early April of 1980 was deteriorating at a terrifying pace.

On the public front, President Jimmy Carter declared to the nation that the "dangerous situation" inflation was causing throughout the Western Hemisphere was due in large part to a bad case of consumption. While the much-criticized federal debt had ballooned by 300 percent over the previous three decades, consumer debt had risen by 1300 percent. During March, Carter called for "the entire American family" to "try harder than ever to live within its means." The President noted that the various forms of consumer installment debt had doubled to $300 billion during the past four years.* In order to assist the national effort to spend more conservatively, Carter planned to invoke his authority under the Credit Control Act of 1969 and authorize the Federal Reserve to establish controls designed to curtail the use of credit cards.

Proponents of calling in the cards argued to Brennan that the debt situation was so precarious that Sears might face the public humiliation of having the safety rating on some of its long-term bonds downgraded. They pointed to the dwindling reserve of funds set aside for paying the dividend, and to the credit operation as the main drain on cash balances. Customers shopped at Sears because of the goods, they contended, not credit, and since Jimmy Carter was trying to convince Americans that spending on credit was unpatriotic, an opening was available by which credit could be killed. After all, K mart had abandoned its credit card during the first wave of oil-price-inspired inflation back in 1974.

But the cake of custom was particularly rich and dense around the issue of credit. Sears was a pioneer of the concept and practice of lending working people enough money to buy things. The company first offered its customers "credit"—a term derived from the Latin verb meaning "to believe"—in 1910, four years before the establishment of the Federal Reserve system ("How long at your present address?" queried the first credit application; and then "How many cows do you milk?"). Sears gave the masses credit because banks would not.† Much of the rise in the standard of living of the American masses was thought within the company to have been promoted by Sears and its credit policies—and many historians of economic development have tended to agree.

The credit business at Sears exploded during the 1920s and then again during the 1950s. The Golden Age of corporate growth during the 1960s was fueled by a 75-percent rise in the number of sales made on credit. "Credit-intensive merchandising" had eventually become profitable as a purely financial enterprise, but the original noble purpose of credit extension was still a powerful source of pride. The company view of the world included the sense that young American families were formed through the combined acts of marriage, birth, and obtaining credit from Sears, Roebuck.

---

*In fact, outstanding consumer debt service now accounted for 29 percent of total disposable income.

†It was actually the Great Depression that opened up consumer credit beyond the realms of Sears and one or two other companies, because it was then that poorer Americans demonstrated that they pay their bills—even when times are tough.

One particular devotee of this age-old proposition from company lore turned out to be Ed Brennan. Brennan thought ordering half the families in the country to open up their wallets and cut up their Sears cards was tantamount to ordering the burning of a flag. Credit customers were the last of the card-carrying believers in everything Sears, Roebuck once stood for; they were the ultimate equity juxtaposing all the debt incurred by a crumbling system, and their good will was essential to the effort to save the business. The $10-billion debt Sears carried represented unsecured loans to average Americans that were indicative of the mutual trust that made the company.

The day Brennan decreed that the credit card would be spared, he declared, "The ability of the American consumer to purchase on credit, in my opinion, is fundamental to the United States free enterprise system. Without that ability, the system we know will crumble."

Though Brennan disapproved of the government's credit controls, Jimmy Carter's programmatic attempts to curtail credit spending would eventually allow Sears to raise the rates it charged customers under the guise of patriotic acquiescence to government policy, and thereby stem some losses. But sales would suffer badly. As smaller retailers all over the country began to curl up and die that spring, Brennan regarded all of them as Jimmy Carter's personal victims. Where Ed Brennan grew up, people just didn't do things like that.

Brennan found an internal ally in his pointed refusal to kill off credit in an unusually verbal Ed Telling: "Nobody would give me or my family a nickel on credit when I was starting out—'cept Sears," Telling said. "Sears, Roebuck has done more than anyone else to increase the standard of living in America, and we're not about to stop now." An article appeared in *Fortune* on April 21 under the title "Protest from an Angry 'Middle American,'" the angry man being Ed Telling. *Fortune* noted that the consumer credit restraints couldn't have come at a worse time for Sears, but quoted Telling as saying that Sears would make a "concession" to Washington by raising its customers' monthly minimum payment. But the company would resist all other efforts to reduce the use of its credit cards.

The day the article appeared, Standard & Poor's, one of the two Wall Street firms that rate the relative safety of corporate debt issues, lowered the rating on $2.5 billion worth of Sears long-term bonds from a "triple A" rating to a "double A." S & P said the action was dictated by Sears' decline in profitability coupled with its ever-more-expensive debt.

Within a few weeks of the imposition of credit restrictions, the trajectory of the trend line in appliance-department sales turned toward the bottom of the page. As was expected, Sears was far more seriously battered by the restrictions than competitors less dependent on selling "big-ticket," credit-intensive goods. Brennan's projections indicated at least a 5-percent decline in sales each month for the rest of the year—a rate of descent that simply could not be sustained for long.

After touring some of the beleaguered Field outposts in April, Brennan asked all his Field and Parent officers to meet him in Tucson, Arizona, during the first week of May. Nobody would leave the Skyline Country Club in Tucson, Brennan said, until they had a new plan.

Spirits were higher than they'd been in ages at the beginning of the meeting in Tucson, but it was soon clear that the Field vice-presidents were less committed to turning back the curve via a sales hype than they were to Ed Brennan's own point of view back at the disastrous meeting at the Cricket Club—that the cost of running the company was just too high, and expenses like advertising and personnel must be cut away immediately.

If profits and sales are down, then expenses must come down too. Since the time when Richard Sears and Julius Rosenwald had fallen out during the world financial panic of 1907 and 1908, this is the way the business had been run. Dick Sears wanted to increase advertising to avert a crisis at the time, and Rosenwald wanted to cut staff and other expenses. Rosenwald prevailed. The General had spent a great deal of money in the face of soft sales, but he spent his money on stores, not an ephemeral luxury like advertising. During the depths of the Depression, when sales were drying up, the General sent the buyers into the New York apparel market to buy liberally, but that gamble was on *goods,* not advertising.

Long after the company had joined Procter and Gamble as one of the two most aggressive advertisers in the world, the internal financing and planning of up to $600 million worth of advertising remained a casual if contentious process, as subject to private agreements and under-the-table transmission of 599 cash as any function of the company. Charlie Wurmstedt, not surprisingly, ascribed to the traditional Field line that advertising should be carried out on the local level by the stores and groups. He thought national advertising was too expensive and too dangerous a tool of potential Headquarters control to use for much more than promoting the general image of Sears.

Joe Moran, on the other hand, would never be convinced that advertising should be anything other then centrally conceived. Joe had been thinking and writing about advertising on a regular basis for thirty years—which he figured was about thirty years more than Charlie had given to the subject. During the early part of Telling's administration, Joe had called for an advertising strategy that directed deep cuts in the advertising budget, but this had coincided specifically with the buying side's loss of authority over advertising to Wurmy.

Now Ed Brennan's request for coordinated programs presented an opportunity to draw advertising back to the buyers' sphere. Joe reasoned that if Brennan bought a powerful new campaign run from his office, the momentum of subsequent sales figures would strike a blow for Headquarters and serve to revive his own fortunes after his censoring and dressing down by young Ed.

When it was his turn to speak, Joe jumped from his chair to offer an emergency plan he'd named "the 80-plus" program. Buttressed by a constant flow of numbers called into the Skyline from Chicago by Frank Tuma at prearranged times during the day, Moran proposed a massive promotional campaign that would cost several hundred million dollars. Field executives and apostles alike looked on in disbelief throughout the presentation. It was Joe who was behind the 7.5-percent cut in advertising expenditure executed during 1979; now he wanted to buy millions of dollars' worth of ads.

The expected Field response never materialized. Charlie Wurmstedt's mother-in-law had become very ill, so Charlie apologized to the group and left for St. Louis in the middle of the meeting. With Wurmstedt gone, the possibility of violent confrontation disappeared, but several of the participants felt that in his absence there was only despair.

At the next morning's session, new ideas seemed hard to come by. Eventually the meeting slowed to a halt, and everyone found himself staring over at Ed Brennan, who looked much paler than usual.

"What do you think we should do, Bill?" Brennan said, turning to Bill Bass, the long-time Telling foot soldier who had been running the Eastern Territory since Dick Jones was drafted to the Tower to deal with Kincannon.

"We can't afford to spend any money," Bass said. "Let's batten down the hatches and operate a little better. We can't promote ourselves into a sales increase, so let's screw the expense down hard."

Burk Burkholder agreed for the Midwest: "It's like the government dealing with its deficit," he said. "I'm not against sales promotions, but if you raise taxes you better cut expenses too."

"You all know I support that, and supported it as policy in the South," Brennan said, "but . . . how are we gonna do it?"

Brennan asked the ever-reasonable Jack Kelly what his experience of spending money as a recession approached had been over his years in the catalog business. As Kelly began to speak, several participants saw a look of utter bewilderment lock onto Brennan's youthful face.

Nothing new was being said. Wurmstedt was gone, and, after presenting his "80-plus" proposal, Joe Moran had lapsed into a strange "What-

ever you say, boss" posture that was as devoid of fire as his recent
memos. In place of the screaming and passion there was nothing, and
the void brought a look to Ed Brennan's face that the others would never
forget. It was as if it suddenly came to Ed Brennan right there, in front
of them, that all of it—past, present, and future—had come down to him.

Though spending toward a recession was against every tenet of conservative retail management held dear by the Field side of the company,
the fabric was too thin to stand the kind of slashing that would turn the
curve. Brennan decided he would have to strike a compromise.

There would be a great promotional drive, he announced before the
Tucson meeting broke up, but it would not cost as much or involve as
many special items as the Headquarters camp suggested. The $35 mil-
lion or so extra he agreed to pump into special advertising was far less
than Moran wanted, and it would be specifically targeted at a narrow
range of items. The program would not be called "80-plus" but "Power
Plus 80," a name the Field preferred only because it was their proposed
title and not Joe Moran's. The traditional name for a one-time special
purchase of an item to be advertised and offered on sale was "Class I,"
but since Moran, Telling, and Purcell had spent over two years making
sure the troops knew that the sort of Class I's a buyer might use his
connections and clout to scare up were no longer worthy of Sears,
Brennan decided to call his Class I's "President's Items."

The items were not to be part of a Headquarters "program" of the sort
the Field had subverted as a matter of course since the early 1960s; the
special goods would be sent to the stores as part of a "placement strategy
designed to increase our everyday business." The buyers and the Field
would have to agree up front on what could be sold and when. The
agreed quantity would be bought, shipped, and sold in a way designed
to unload 90 percent of the goods so there would be no inventory
hanging around.

The "President's Item" program was clearly not the decision that
would save the company, but Brennan said that no other ideas would
stand a chance unless the buyers were once again given "freedom to
breathe."

The buyers flew into the streets. A fellow from Brennan's father's old
turf found a manufacturer willing to tool up and make dress slacks that
Sears could sell that fall for $7.99 a pair or two for $15. A mechanic's tool
set was located that could be had for a song, and some sundresses were
hunted down in Hong Kong that the apparel buyer knew in his guts
would sell like hell in the stores.

The subdued hints of the good old days during the weeks after the
Tucson meeting highlighted the enormity of the political task confront-
ing Ed Brennan. The chance to work the marketplace might brighten

the spirits of the buyers, and a short-term but nominally promotional sales program might intrigue the storekeepers, but Brennan saw that his hopes would be fleeting without new infrastructure and programmatic clarity. He could say no to layoffs, no to killing the credit card, yes to sales hypes, and the company would still be so much less then the sum of its parts that it would fail. He saw now that the path into the future was going to require brand-new tracks.

Brennan had been fascinated by systematic approaches to planning the cost side of the traditionally "unplannable" business of retailing since his earliest days on the floor of Benson and Rixon. He wasn't in a position to experiment with his ideas about containing expenses and bureau-cratic growth on a large scale until he ran the small Sears retail group of stores in Buffalo, New York, during the early 1970s. Brennan bor-rowed a 1969 personnel cost-control program Ed Telling had instituted in the Eastern Territory, and in the tradition of complete Field auton-omy he began to modify Telling's system for the Buffalo group.

Telling's program was ostensibly a census of territorial employees on a store-by-store basis, a seemingly innocuous requirement that was in fact perceived as a radical imposition on the old sovereignty of the store managers. By taking similar census data and running comparative anal-yses of the ratios of store personnel to indices of the store's perfor-mance, Brennan saw a way to direct the psychological force of the system. Though his store managers had been trained to resist goal-setting from above, Brennan found that if reasonable goals were sug-gested to the managers in January, the deadliest month for sales, the managers tended to make tacit expense cuts by not rehiring as many employees when business picked up later in the year. The payroll bur-den in the benighted Western New York group disappeared within two years through the subconscious perception of the cuts as good bottom-line management rather than politically loaded layoffs and pre-planning from above.

At his next post, in Boston, Brennan found that if a gross number of hours instead of employees was proposed as a target, the tradition of protecting good-old-boy salesmen who weren't selling and old-timer warehousemen who couldn't hoist was conveniently ignored by manag-ers. The change from people goals to hours goals allowed the managers to violate sacred traditions without having to articulate the acts as such.

In the South, each store's "miscellaneous expense" category was bro-ken up into ratios of sick days per employee. The cost of janitorial supplies was compared, the number of bad checks written at each store was compared, and the square footage of store space used for selling was compared with sales. They compared unemployment benefits, Social Security contributions, amortization costs, insurance—they even compared the number of wheel-balance jobs per hour that were performed in the territory's automotive departments. The statistics were surrendered because they were rarely thrown back at store managers as disapproval. They were presented as "challenges." While Joe Moran fumed with frustration in Chicago over his inability to draw any numbers at all from the woolly system, and Phil Purcell saw his planning forms come back full of misinformation, Brennan labored quietly down south building an X-ray machine.

As the system of goals was insinuated more deeply within the traditions, Brennan began to cast the young operating wizard who'd been with him since Buffalo, Eric Saunders, in the role of the carpetbagging number cruncher from the North. With Eric running the regression analyses back in Atlanta, Brennan was able to spend most of his twenty-six months in the South barnstorming his thirteen groups and 150 stores, selling his new system of attrition in the traditional language of Sears' past. He worked to convince the good old boys that a new Searsman of his own vintage was just the spirited, independent retailer of old, his soul leavened slightly with a bit of the latter-day efficiency expert. Brennan would settle down in the lunchrooms of the stores to tell stories about helping the General pick out his top coat in that earnest, lilting way that made the old soldiers hear echoes. He'd explain that Sears was so very big that if they just budged the sales up a fraction, and knocked the expenses down a fraction, the company would surely prevail.

None of the Southern store managers had ever seen a man crawl so slowly and methodically through a retail store as the Irish kid Ed Telling sent down from the North, and few of them had experienced a manager who so specifically demanded that attention be paid at all times. It was known that Brennan had stopped early meetings of his group managers when he noticed some of them chatting among themselves. "Can you give this subject the attention it deserves!" Brennan demanded, by which the executives of the Southern Territory soon understood he referred to the attention *he* deserved. If you didn't listen, he'd cut you off at the knees.

Brennan implored his managers to think in terms of "the ideal Sears store," a store operated as if it had just opened, a store unburdened by old loyalties and traditions. But to many of the veterans, stores were supposed to conform only to the personality of the store manager and the collective will of the local populace. If there was an operative "ideal," it was the ideal of internal democracy and family such as it came down from the mind of the General.

Brennan and Eric Saunders developed a goal-setting system that would flow down through the territory. Sales and profit goals would be "suggested" from above, and after a system of negotiation on down the line, commitments would rise up replete with signatures acknowledging that everyone up and down the system knew what was expected. The system fed into the traditional Sears seller's acceptance of games and challenges.

As he pondered his dilemma during the spring of 1980, Brennan knew that the dream of imposing his planning system upon the entire society of the merchants would require the most titanic selling job of his career. He believed that the system of controls had only worked in the past because it was supplemented daily by his personal campaign to build up morale and to portray the goals to each embittered employee as a methodology worthy of Sears. It had taken him well over two years to establish goals for the Western New York group, and all of two years to provide the cushion of visible success that finally sold the system throughout the South.

Brennan needed his hands free, and he needed his own numbers man. He liked Phil Purcell. Ed Telling's other token youth had been gracious about complimenting Brennan on the way he'd adapted Phil's early work to his own purposes. But Phil seemed a bit disorganized by Brennan's rather rigorous standards, and the thought of having to run his rescue plans past an outsider without an ounce of retail blood in his veins was anathema to the new president.

"Eric speaks my language," he explained to Telling at the time. "I'll save six months this way."

So Eric Saunders arrived from Atlanta in early June, with two fat books under his arm containing what was known in the Southern Territory as "the Plan." Eric also arrived with a palpable swagger for a Searsman of his tender age that served to further unsettle Headquarters executives who were still in shock over Brennan's leapfrog to this new sort of presidency.

Saunders had torn up his path through the Field, and by the time he came to Chicago to assume the title of director of planning for the Field, he'd handled twelve jobs while logging only fifteen years of Sears service, including a stint as secretary to the Corporate Hay Committee during the fieriest days of committee debate. In addition to his facility for numbers, Eric was one of the only executives who'd ever worked with Ed Brennan who could physically keep up with him. Saunders had been a passable athlete at Rutgers, a fact that in true Sears fashion had been passed along the grapevine and over time had been so distorted that most people thought the tall ex-jock had been an NCAA basketball star. But, other than serving Ed Brennan well through many eighteen-hour days, Saunders had still done little to earn his wings. He was going to have to show something special if he was going to make it with a Headquarters establishment that was unanimous in its disapproval of this early move by the young president.

Though Eric would work under the title of planning director for only the Field, he would in fact coordinate all the planning functions for the merchandise company from now on. Phil Purcell would continue to direct "overall planning" for the company. Phil said he wouldn't miss his time as an official peacemaker. He'd come to Sears to revolutionize it—not to run stores or settle arguments—and he had a few other projects of his own he wanted to concentrate on anyway.

Ed Brennan moved from territory to territory and store to store during the late spring of 1980, sometimes traveling through ninety-hour weeks. Everywhere he went, he tried to explain the metaphor of the big store. In a store, he would say, a great day in one department simply does not make the day for the store. A single great day in a store doesn't make a good month, and a good month doesn't make a year. Everything has to work together, he would lecture: "The total is nothing but the sum of the parts."

But they couldn't hear him.

The company had broken down completely; it had broken down as a distributive mechanism and it had broken down emotionally. The Field managers believed they'd operated the hell out of their stores and were already scraping bone. It was clear that the first-half retail earnings would fall short of 1979 by a number nine digits long. Short-term sales palliatives and the sort of local drum-beating that had worked in the South were obviously not going to work quickly enough. Brennan had not spent an entire life working and watching, rising up over the greatest selling machine in all of history, in order to preside over its dissolution. He needed to do something else.

"Let's just tell them how bad it really is," Joe Moran said after Brennan once again rejected massive layoffs in June.

"I agree with Joe," said Charlie Wurmstedt, aligning himself, however fleetingly, with the man he hated. "Let's explain to the people where we are, and ask them to do a little more. If we provide good leadership, they'll follow."

"Not anymore," Brennan said.

Sears needed a spectacular event—something that would open the hearts of the employees and bring them back to the company. There had to be an experience that would redirect the collective focus back outward, toward customer and competition, after too many years of looking inside across internal divides. Brennan envisaged something like a great secular revival meeting that would boost morale, end the "finger point-ing" and intramural disharmony, sell the new planning mechanism, and serve as a chronological endpoint of an era of failure and fear. There would be a rally, a clarion call, a last meeting of the assembly, and the first convention of the new dawn.

Brennan believed the aura of such profound despair made people more open to change than ever before. Climbing up above the company to deliver the news about the new store seemed more suitable to the current task then his usual method of climbing down to the grass roots to spread the word "hands on." All he had to do was figure out a way to touch everyone—buyers, store operators, promoters, conceptualizers, efficiency experts. All he had to do was draw forth the varied strains of the company woven within himself. He would try to lead them all through the aisles of the store in his mind, just as his father had once revealed the store to him that day he needed new boots.

When Brennan would return from his barnstormings, he and Joe Moran began to meet and speak at length about the early post–World War II history of the company, a legacy Ed Brennan understood largely as family lore and Joe remembered as participant and chronicler. One day Moran had mentioned that one of the great moments in his own experi-ence of the company was the time in May 1950 when the General had brought hundreds of his boys together for a meeting he called "On to Chicago." In the company archives on the fortieth floor, Brennan read the General's "On to Chicago" address. Wood began by informing his managers that he would probably never see them together again, be-cause of the expense of such an event and the reality of his own life expectancy. He went on to place himself within the flow of history by defining the first period of corporate development as the "Richard Sears era," the second, from 1908 through 1924, as the "Rosenwald era," and the third, from 1925 (the time when General Wood received what he referred to in the speech as "the vision") through 1950—humble man that Robert E. Wood was—he called "the retail era."

The General reminded his executives that the customer was still their employer. "The moment we lose his confidence, that moment marks the beginning of the disintegration of this company." The purpose of the meeting, he said, was to bring "the two great divisions of the company together—the buying force and the selling force," and he echoed again his long-held belief that only three things could ever bring down "the mightiest distributing organization in the world." They were war, gov-ernment interference, or dissension among the senior officers of the company. Toward the end of the speech, the General declared that "the greatest weakness of the modern, large corporation is the fact that too often controls and planning are so centralized that the great mass of employees begin to consider themselves as robots, lose interest in their work, and give only a small measure of their potential efforts to their work. . . . We must always consider our 150,000 employees as 150,000 individual human beings, with personalities of their own."

Brennan took some notes, and went back up to the sixty-eighth floor. It was always a matter of politics for the old man. Those who had served at his side admitted, only after he was gone, that he never really loved the goods like a buyer, and he never really loved the hot jazz of the sale either. He loved the idea and ideal of his own "cooperative democracy," and as long as there was a senior employee of the company who'd been raised under the General still present in the system, anyone who wanted to change that system would have to match political skills and performances with the General's ghost.

The only other major convention of Sears personnel since "On to Chicago" was the meeting in 1973 called by Arthur Wood to talk about affirmative action. Whatever Brennan's feelings about equal opportunity, he felt personally injured by that meeting in Chicago. To have the luxury of all the senior merchants of Sears together for two days and never to discuss merchandise was to him a crime against history. By 1973, Brennan already sensed the company drifting away from its commitment to the goods, and he always associated the affirmative-action meeting with the empire's humbling.

At his meeting, one of the central media for communicating a new beginning would be a "recommitment to the merchandise," and a "platforming of the goods." Brennan decided to take the unifying theme straight from the pages of Norman Vincent Peale's *Power of Positive Thinking.* He would call it all "the Challenge." The items the buyers were out looking for as one-time sellouts designed to hype the fall sales would be called "Challenge Items" instead of "President's Items." The coming year of 1981 would be dubbed "the Challenge Year"; and the three-day meeting he and Joe Moran decided to stage in front of hundreds of company executives in early August of 1980 would be called "the Challenge Meeting."

Joe Moran took his lead from Brennan and began to call the Challenge Meeting a "hymn to the goods." The second week of June, Moran issued one of his most straightforward white papers, called "The Challenge Year," in which he informed his buyers that the big event in August would require "split second timing, detailed preparation and professional coordination." He assigned 126 buyers exactly five minutes each to show off their finest wares to representatives of the Field. Brennan wanted the goods up on a pedestal to remind the warring factions that the company in fact flows from baby cribs, bench power tools, terry-cloth bathrobes, hacksaws, and pantyhose, not from the traditions of one side of the business or the other. The goods, like Brennan's new presi-dency, would reside above the troubles as physical embodiments of the company's unity. The participants in the Challenge Meetings would hear the hymns, be "immersed" in these goods, and made pure.

By the middle of June, the efforts of seven thousand employees work-ing in the Sears Tower were directed toward the Challenge Meetings. Samples needed to be secured from suppliers, audiovisual presentations designed, and the transportation of all the territorial heavyweights into Chicago at once had to be planned with military precision. Because Joe Moran told him that he wanted the visitors from the territories divided into five groups, Frank Tuma ordered that the four auditoriums on the technology-laden twenty-seventh floor be resubdivided into five rooms. There was so much money being thrown around the Tower as the Challenge Meeting approached that the $250,000 renovation was al-most executed on the basis of Tuma's zealous interpretation before Moran stopped the reconstruction of the Wacker Room at the last minute.

On July 3, an official announcement publicly heralded a major sales meeting to be held on August 6, 7, and 8, in Chicago, to focus on "1981: The Challenge Year." The memo noted that Ed Brennan would open the session with a speech that would be carried on closed-circuit televi-sion in forty-six locations throughout the Tower. The first historic meet-ing in Chicago was to be for the senior Field executives, the buying and merchandising organization, and the Headquarters staff. Then the whole multimillion-dollar event would be taken on the road to each of the five territories, so that every manager of every store would "receive" the Challenge.

Brennan helped design every aspect of the look of the event that could in any way be seen as symbolic, down to the half-circle flambeau with starburst golden rays thrusting from the edges that would be the central visual emblem of "Challenge 81." The insignia looked like the embossed halo placed behind a sanctified head in a Renaissance paint-ing, or the golden half-circle of a rising sun . . . or of a sun half-set.

Brennan came down to the twenty-seventh floor on the last day of July and walked methodically through the large beige meeting rooms. Moran's buyers had covered the walls of the rooms and all of the halls with Sears merchandise. It was hanging everywhere—Diane von Furstenberg bedsheets to DieHard motorcycle batteries. Everything bore the sorts of bright, aggressive colors that seemed to have faded during recent times.

Brennan was pleased, though he looked unusually pale and drawn. The "administrative exercise" of recent weeks proved the buyers could still move quickly despite what they'd been through. That would come in handy if he pulled off the rally.

As he got to the front of the Quincy Adams Room, where he would open the session the following Tuesday, Brennan decided he wanted one more touch. He ordered a huge banner to be printed and hung at the front of the room that said "SELL MORE UNITS" in huge letters. After all, every great rally in the public squares and great halls of history had a banner.

CHAPTER 10

The Challenge

I n the early morning of August 6, Field executives boarded buses at their hotel for the short ride over to the Wacker Drive side of the Tower. The visitors stared out at Sears employees wearing foam-plastic Challenge Year hats who were arranged on the red granite steps in such a carefully orchestrated array of nationalities, ages, and sexes that it looked like they were posing for a brotherhood poster. The brass in from five territorial and fifty-one group and zone headquarters went up to the twenty-seventh floor and mingled in the Jackson Room amid waterfall racks full of bright dresses, lamp displays, Winnie the Pooh garments, bicycles, and home fitness equipment that a nearby sign proclaimed was designed for "92 million exercising Americans."

More senior Searsmen filed into the Quincy Adams Room, where they were to attend the opening ceremonies, and throughout the Tower three thousand other employees took seats in front of various television sets to watch closed-circuit coverage of the event. Television sets glowed with the rising-sun symbol in conference rooms up and down the Tower. The entire buying-organization contingent from the Two North La Salle "ghetto" watched from their assigned seats on the mezzanine floor.

The lights were lowered in the Quincy Adams Room as three mammoth graphic renderings of the golden "Challenge 81" symbol rose slowly onto a projection screen that spanned the entire width of the auditorium. Then speakers all around the room began to blare a rousing song:

It's a Challenge Year.
That's why we're meeting here.
It's gonna be a great y-e-e-e-a-r.
Items we'll define,
All of the Challenge Lines.
We're gonna make a great year. . . .

At the end of the last verse, the lights came on to reveal the heavy-eyed old soldier Garland Ingraham standing at the podium at the front of the room.

"Good morning!" roared Charlie Wurmstedt's VP for advertising and sales.

"Good morning!" boomed back the deep response of tradition.

"*You* are a *great* bunch of people!" Gar said. Ingraham tended to speak in a voice so like W. C. Fields' that it often took first-time listeners several minutes to realize he wasn't kidding. This morning he had on a large bright-red tie with white polka dots.

"We usually sing at the end of a meeting, but I'd like to do it now," Ingraham said. "All the people in all the conference rooms throughout the building should open up the doors. Open that door back there for us. Now, Dick Priest, in the laboratory conference room two floors below street level, with his people; the people up in the heavy-nosebleed area of the sixty-eighth floor; Rita, my secretary; the girls at our department in room 4306 . . . I want the doors *open.* And with your help—all of you, *everybody* in this building—let's not just let a little sunshine in, but let some Sears enthusiasm out!"

As Brennan, Joe Moran, and a rather glum-looking Charlie Wurmstedt observed from the side of the stage, strains of "It's a Challenge Year" began to fall from the ceiling again, and many more mouths could be seen opening and shutting than there were voices raised in enthusiastic song.

When Ingraham finally began to speak again, he was interrupted by a funereal, quavering voice coming from the speakers overhead. "Mister Brennan," the voice said as angelic music rose in the background. "This is Richard W. Sears. From way up here, with a lot of your and my Sears associates. And we can hear all of you *very well.*"

From where he was sitting in front of a bedsheet-and-comforter display, Brennan managed to force his grimace into a smile, but his eyes fell slowly down into the plastic coffee cup he was holding.

Few people in the audience laughed.

Ingraham finally introduced Ed Brennan and disappeared behind a wall of stacked goods. Brennan strode slowly toward the podium to subdued applause that fell quickly into complete silence. He closed his dark-gray suit coat ceremoniously, never taking his light-blue eyes off the now sober faces toward the front of the audience. He held his head tilted slightly to one side, as if the weight of what he had in mind was real. Though he looked much older than many in the room had remembered young Eddie, Brennan still looked nothing like the men who'd looked the part in the past.

"It's the first time we've all been together for a long time," he said, his eyes slowly sweeping back from the front rows into the gray audience. "The world out there has changed in the time span that most of us have spent with Sears," Brennan said. As he mentioned the explosion of malls, the emergence of the discount houses, and the rise of specialty stores, his large hands encircled and gripped the podium. "I think because of the difficulties of the environment over the last few years, we have in some cases questioned ourselves and our abilities. But that really isn't the issue, and the issue isn't pointing fingers at each other and saying, 'Why aren't *you* doing a better job? Why aren't *you* providing *me* with better merchandise? Why aren't you doing a better job of selling the merchandise I'm giving you?' The issue is that we must meld together now and face this new environment with our great strengths. Many people have concerns about our future," he said, aware of the depth of concentration being trained on him now, "but the fact is that *we are a sound company.*"

Brennan's hands were moving in large arcs now above the silence. His hands described a new shape for each image. It was an oratorical manner the executives in from the South knew well. When he said "meld together," his long fingers came together and carefully knit his hands into a gesture of prayer, and when he lingered on the word "store," he cupped one hand and held it out with his palm facing upward. The store.

If Sears could put the right products in "vibrant, exciting stores" where the customer was well served, Brennan declared, the disaffected customers would return to the fold. If Sears executives would just stop believing it was incumbent upon them to *change* products and programs that came to them, and saw instead they should *add* to them, then some of the wounds could be healed. "All this company is, is one . . . big . . . store."

Joe Moran sat to Brennan's right looking dazed. As Brennan began to talk about one big store, Charlie Wurmstedt started to fidget at his side. Charlie crossed and uncrossed his legs, and then began to bounce up and down. The big sapphire ring he always wore began to wave through the air as he slapped at his knee. Sears stores the length and breadth of this country were most certainly *not* the same. Never were and never would be. The idea was *unethical.* Sears was the opposite of one big store. That was the whole idea.

Brennan described the new strategy of isolating several lines of goods as "Challenge Items" and "Challenge Lines." "The Field," he said, *"will give these lines complete and total support."*

"I would like to be able—if I were a territorial vice-president—to know I could get on a plane and go to Baton Rouge, Louisiana, and see the way the goods were presented; and the next day go to Norfolk, Virginia, and see them presented in a similar way. If Mr. Wurmstedt and I were to take a trip, I would like to be able to go to Los Angeles one week and to New York the next week, and we would see *great consistency.* I'm not talking about foolish consistency—like swim suits in Minneapolis in January—it's these *key issues.* And I'm not talking centralization; I'm talking about con-sis-tency."

But Brennan was indeed talking about a centralized corporate initiative dictated to the Field from Headquarters. It was to be supported by compulsory actions up and down the line, from television advertising to departments in the stores, and everyone in the room knew it.

Next Brennan described the new merchandise planning system that he had been working on since Eric Saunders had arrived in early June. He explained that a process would begin as a set of gross numbers in the Tower that would then flow down through the organization as a series of bargains. The numbers were to be called a "Challenge." "The Challenge flows down and the Plan flows back up."

"I'm looking for a 10-percent increase in sales for 1981," he said in a more resigned voice, "something that used to be easy for us, but something we haven't been able to do for the last few years." The beseeching gaze that fell over Brennan's strained face at that moment allowed everyone in the room to see that Brennan believed that if they couldn't end the "finger pointing" and turn the tide quickly, it was over.

"What we're looking to in the next few days is not just a merchandise presentation. We're looking to have some fun. This is a *fun business.* Because of the difficult sales experiences and profit problems that we've had in recent months, perhaps some of the fun has gone out of the business." He leaned hard on his palms and stared into the crowd. *"It's still there!* I know that most of the people in these rooms have never worked harder in their lives; they've never put in more time or agonized over more things or tried to motivate their people any more than they have over the last several months. And it can become discouraging when the results don't come in.

"But today we're talking about changing that pattern. I know we will remember: All we are . . . is a store. All we are is that collection of items, lines, and categories that make up the typical Sears store. . . .

"The General said in concluding his meeting in 1950, 'We are the leader, and the price of leadership is unceasing effort. We must keep learning, improving our methods and improving our organization. There exists ample opportunity for the future.' And I don't think I could end this speech with any finer words than that."

There was much low-pitched murmuring in the audience as Joe Moran waddled up to the podium after Brennan sat down. Joe's hair was combed back from his face, and he wore a wrinkled light-gray suit. After worrying aloud about the sartorial disaster area that was the largest individual buyer of goods in the world, Brennan had finally dragged Moran into a tailor's shop one afternoon while they were working in Philadelphia. He made Joe purchase several custom-made business suits, which in the brief interim had already become ill-fitting and rumpled. Joe looked tired—even by his own standards of debilitation—and as he stood with his face clenched tight as a fist in the spot Brennan had recently vacated at the podium, he also looked old.

The nonofficer Field men could be seen straining their necks to get a better look at the author of the infamous memos they'd been passing among themselves over the last two years.

"Mr. Brennan, the buying organization accepts your challenge gladly and with glee," Moran said softly. His voice was less gruff and wheezy than usual, but he spoke in tones so absent of affect and rage that it was hard for some of the Field visitors who didn't know him to believe that this was the mad king of the buyers.

"I pledge to you," he continued without glancing at Brennan, "to the entire Field organization, and to all the rest of the Sears family, the complete dedication and unremitting effort on our part that your challenge requires. This call to greatness that you have issued will be answered in part over the next two and a half days as one hundred and twenty-two of our buyers demonstrate for all of us how they have implemented the fundamental buying strategy of the company. . . . This company, as I am sure we all know, has many purposes. Some are social, some are economic, all are directed at serving the many publics that are dependent upon us. I think you can make a pretty strong case for the fact that almost one out of ten Americans depends upon us in whole or part for their economic well-being.

"The times are difficult, right?" Moran said, demonstrating his turning of a new leaf. "Competition is fierce. We're big and diffused and spread out. Say all of that; say it once, and then forget it. We've been around for almost a century and we're going to be here for another one. Mark this day and this time and this place; mark it well and firmly in your minds and in your hearts. What begins here now, I am convinced, is a new day in the proud history of our company."

Jumpin' Joe read pious words for forty more minutes, mentioning time and again in his emotionless singsong the sense of partnership he felt with the same Field operatives he had refused even to speak to a few weeks earlier. He spoke of his dedication to the same suppliers he had publicly threatened with extinction. He declared that for him, the many challenges Ed Brennan was setting before the retail company were a "call to arms": "Make no mistake about it," he said. "We are at war."

"Here begins for us the decade of our second century," Joe read, his tempo slowing near the end of the address. "Young again, and renewed again . . . You can count on us," he said looking over at Brennan, "to give purpose to planning and to make it an allied thing that unifies all of us in the pursuit of our goals. You can count on all of us, most of all, to win! Get out of the way, world! Beware, J. C. Penney! Look carefully, K mart! Behind you, Target . . . and all the rest of you! We mean to win and we mean to stay on top. And all of you, all of you throughout all of Sears, you can all of you count on us for firm resolve, for belief in ourselves, and for unshakable confidence in the capability that is contained in every nook and cranny of this great company and in its legacy, its goodness and its integrity. You can count on all of us, and we know that we can count on all of you!" Then Joe shuffled quickly to his chair and plopped back down.

Gar Ingraham came slowly back to the podium, looking rather nonplussed. There was the hum of whispers in the audience as Ingraham introduced Charlie Wurmstedt. Wurmstedt received only scattered applause from a room packed with his own executives, many of whom had come to Chicago expecting to witness the final victory of the Field over Headquarters. Brennan, after all, was one of their own; maybe not born of the stores, but at least bred in the Field reserve of the East—but this "sales meeting" was turning into something else.

Wurmstedt came up and flashed his huge smile. He offered a deep-throated, Ed Telling "Good morning!" and got a weak response from a few of the officers in the front. Then he looked back into the middle rows, where the familiar faces of many of the veteran group managers were located, the attendees with hair a bit grayer and ties somewhat wider than the others. "It's really . . . it's really such a privilege to have a chance to say a few things to a group like this, a group of fine merchants, a group of many good old friends, who I don't . . . get to see as often as I'd like to anymore."

The sadness in Wurmstedt's voice faded away and his tone hardened: "I don't know what I did to get this," he said, glancing off to the side of the stage. "I sometimes think that people of Irish heritage like Brennan and Moran must grow up in a family where they just talk all the time. It seems to just flow from them with no effort whatsoever. In families of my heritage, we didn't say too much. We listened a lot. And if you were going to say something, you said it rather quickly and got it over with, because you didn't get a long time to do it in. It makes me feel a little bit insecure to follow two such fine presentations. I will try my best not to disgrace the Field."

Brennan's eyes creased shut and his laughter at the suggestion of his garrulousness lingered after others had stopped, but the men in the front rows knew that Wurmy was blowing it. He'd started out with comments expressing his own isolation from the old Field hands, as if to apologize for what was happening to their historic sovereignty. His references to saying things quickly might have conjured the image of Ed Telling for some in the room, but Charlie had misread how carefully many of the Field leaders had listened to Brennan's speech. Then he'd used the word "insecure," at a time when only terms of strength and renewal were called for. He hoped he wouldn't "disgrace the Field," when every reference to a part of the company should have been evoked only as a part of the new whole, the larger order of the store.

Charlie told the crowd he accepted the challenge on behalf of the Field, and then quickly, as if he were reading a list, he promised that the Field would try to keep the shelves stocked in the stores and work with the new planning process. Wurmstedt said the Field accepted that Headquarters' promotional plans would arrive in the Field in writing, as a package, and that only one meeting per quarter would be allowed for Field input to those plans. He accepted on behalf of the Field that there would be more directed advertising. He said that he'd promised Ed Brennan and Ed Telling he'd be a credit to them both. Then he sat down.

Joe Moran turned to Wurmstedt with a grin. Then he gave him an exaggerated, playful elbow in full view of the audience. Wurmstedt looked back with shock and contempt at that obvious gesture of unity, until he got hold of himself and managed a smile.

Charlie had decided that, if he was going to have to acquiesce to the violation of sanctified principles he'd spent all of his life protecting, he wasn't going to use his allotted twenty-five minutes in which do it. He thought all the renaissance stuff was a lot of malarkey anyway, and he wasn't going to ramble on for the sake of some wet-behind-the-ears executive like Brennan who "took three hours to say sumpin' everyone else could spit out in three minutes." Charlie Wurmstedt had arranged the few words he'd had to say into short declarative sentences for all of a long career, and everyone from Ed Telling on down knew it.

Brennan then left the room in the company of his five territorial vice-presidents, in order, the crowd was informed, to deliver the Plan. Everyone else moved to an assigned room where the buyers were ready to begin their hymns.

No time had been allotted for participants to find a quiet corner and get together with their friends and allies to discuss what was happening. The executives were hustled quickly into a whirl of sound, light, and razzmatazz; of sexy models, talking alarm clocks, and computerized bench power tools that bleated and flashed warnings. For six hours—broken only by a fifteen-minute stretching break—seventy buyers hawked goods, one after another, at five-minute intervals. Box lunches were delivered to the twenty-seventh floor and were scheduled to be consumed in less than forty-five minutes.

As strange as the show was, there was something nostalgic and almost hopeful in it all. The most cynical anti-Parent visitor had to admit that, if nothing else, most of the five-minute performances describing new or improved merchandise were packed with an energy that had been missing at Sears for quite a while. Some of the buyers were able to conjure the old "tell-ya-what-ahm-gonna-do" screes by which the Parent merchants during the glory days had tried to sell the Field.

The old spirit of the sale was embodied in the performances of the apostle in charge of women's apparel, Wayne Holsinger. Wayne was a reformed "phys-ed major from the old neighborhood" who'd become a high-school coach just long enough to pick up the ability to march back and forth barking breathlessly at an audience. Holsinger still wore over-long sideburns like some of the store jockeys in from the territories, and he also shared with some of the country boys from the Field a penchant for plaid clothing and the venerable habit of calling the company "Sears *and* Roebuck."

Wayne marched up and down in front of a line of young female models dressed in yellow. "Whoa," he said, glancing back lasciviously at the models in a way that reminded old-timers of the antics of one Fred Hecht, who used to adjust and inspect the "crotch construction" of his ladies' lingerie on live models. "The guys in the old neigh-ba-hood would be proud o' me!" Holsinger crowed, shaking his head.

Suddenly, the famous fashion model Cheryl Tiegs appeared from the side of the stage, dressed in the same yellow jacket worn by the other women. The willowy Tiegs strolled across the stage and draped her arm gracefully around Holsinger, towering above the Sears merchant who'd recently guaranteed her a several-hundred-thousand-dollar windfall in exchange for the use of her name on garments. Holsinger looked up at Tiegs and then stared out at the group managers in the audience with an unmistakable "I-know-what-you're-thinking" double take.

The boys roared.

"Somehow, ya know, I never had yer attentions like this before," he said, as Cheryl Tiegs blushed noticeably. "You sure Burt Parks started this way? Seriously, folks, this line shows that we can have quality and provide it to the American woman; that she shouldn't be afraid of fashion."

"Aren't you gorgeous," he said to Tiegs, reaching up for her shoulder. "She's our kinda people. . . . I tell ya, boys, you'll go into the malls and you'll see these young girls now. . . ." Holsinger swept his hand over the scene behind him in a gesture that indicated how much the world has changed.

He escorted Tiegs down into the audience and propelled her over to several of the more powerful and hard-bitten group managers. "Meet Ralph Fiorelli. He's New Yawk, Cheryl!" Wayne boomed. "And over here, meet Pittsburgh. Here's Chic-aw-ga," he said, moving Tiegs along to the next man, who leapt uncomfortably to his feet, "and h-e-e-e-e-r-e's Philly, right here. . . ."

Wayne Holsinger had been surprised when the studies his buying group conducted indicated that Cheryl Tiegs was the most acceptable and powerful available image in the minds of Sears' female customers. Women such as Kate Jackson, an actress from the television show "Charlie's Angels," had been found to be much too sexually threatening to most women. Also rejected was Jackson's "Angels" colleague Cheryl Ladd, and the actress Bo Derek.

Cheryl Tiegs, a woman who looked her age at thirty-three, had a powerful mass appeal. Younger and older women seemed prepared to trust the blond native of a small town in Minnesota not unlike the birthplace of Richard Sears. Tiegs grew up subsequently in the Sears depot of Alhambra, California, site of the territorial headquarters. It even turned out that Tiegs had begun her modeling career on the cover of the 1966–67 Sears Catalog, a fact that aided Holsinger's efforts to sell her to the burghers of the sixty-eighth floor, despite her widely observed anatomical revelations in an issue of *Sports Illustrated* and her 1979 association in the gossip columns with her then husband's drug problems.

From the time Richard Sears placed the unmistakable visage of Teddy Roosevelt atop the torso of a catalog model displaying suits for portly men, a long history of national celebrities had been associated with merchandise from Sears. Film stars Gloria Swanson, Joan Crawford, Norma Shearer, Susan Hayward, and Ginger Rogers were all featured in the catalog, and the young Lauren Bacall got her start in the big book.

During the Jim Button era, celebrities were signed up to endorse and occasionally to help design and even buy products for the company, the most famous association having been struck with the actor Vincent

Price, who roamed the world buying fine art to be sold in Sears stores. Because of Price's efforts, works by artists such as Andrew Wyeth were offered in the stores for over $25,000, a phenomenon thought by many a store manager to exist in rather high contrast to the offerings in Joe Moran's drapery departments a few feet away. Ted Williams was hired to lend his name and prestige to sporting goods, and though his name had faded considerably as a consumer draw by 1980, the old lefty was still on the payroll.

Since the early 1970s, when a major investment in product lines endorsed by golfer Johnny Miller backfired, and a line of designer Anne Klein's jewelry failed to take off, celebrity programs had been discouraged, until Holsinger signed up Cheryl Tiegs to help promote apparel designed to draw more youthful customers. In a sense, the all-American "sex-is-healthy" imagery that surrounds Tiegs was well within the earliest company line on sexuality. The Sears Catalog had offered contraceptives and various aids and sexual nostrums at the beginning of the century. Sigmund Freud's books about the mind and sex and a book called *Sane Sex Life* were all available through Sears, until the company became decidedly dowdy and asexual—in both image and offerings— during the post–World War II expansion. Sears became more and more prissy in seeming counterpoint to the rise of sexuality in the marketing and nature of goods sold everywhere else. Cheryl Tiegs' presence at the Challenge Meetings correlated with the new wave of managerial virility represented by the arrival of Ed Brennan.

The buyers had also signed up the New York designer Diane von Furstenberg ("To be able to penetrate in every leetle A-mur-ican home is a very nice thing for a leetle Belgian girl," von Furstenberg enthused over her arrangement with the bedsheet buyers on one of the in-house videotapes). It was as if Tiegs and von Furstenberg—both of whom had been depicted semi-nude in publicly beheld photographs—had been hired to try to help the company get sexy again.

Tiegs' deal called for payments to her of between 3 percent and 6 percent of the cost to Sears of the goods bearing her name. Given the many millions of dollars being poured into the Tiegs "Challenge Line," scheduled to debut in New York early in the fall, the deal could easily end up rewarding the model with over a million dollars during her first season. In her little-girl hand, Tiegs wrote a personal note to her "friends at Sears" that was disseminated to Field participants, and many a hardened old group baron could be seen walking from one meeting room to another clutching the note and commenting about how "nice" the young lady seemed to be.

The colorful presentations continued at such a pitch that Ed Telling was able to take a back elevator down to the twenty-seventh floor and observe the Challenge Meeting unnoticed for a while before slipping back upstairs. Telling said he'd kill himself before impairing Brennan's ability to lead by causing a flurry of attention. "Even if it was just a refrigerator buyer speaking," he didn't want to draw notice or steal any thunder. During the opening ceremonies, many of the Field executives kept looking around the room in search of Telling, and his apparent absence was the subject of much disappointed conversation at the cocktail hour that preceded the voluminous dinner Brennan fed the visitors after the first day's events.

Ed Telling was never one to enjoy a sales meeting, but his presence at the revival meeting on the twenty-seventh floor would have at least assured some of the executives that their chairman hadn't abandoned them. Telling told *Fortune* magazine that he'd handed control of the merchandise business over to Brennan in order "to concentrate his attention on the changing nature of Sears." There had been considerable discussion among the veterans about what in the world this could mean. Shortly after placing Brennan's hands on reins connected to both sides of the retail business, Telling stunned the merchants again by declaring that for accounting purposes the "three major businesses" that make up Sears, Roebuck would now begin to report operational results separately. This meant that the mighty merchant would have to stand beside Allstate Insurance Company, and beside the nascent group of real-estate-oriented businesses being run by an outsider named Preston Martin, just when the core business of Sears was producing its sorriest results in modern memory. The move mystified even those executives who thought they knew Ed Telling, and further demoralized the embattled buyers and sellers.

Then, a few weeks before the Chicago rally, Telling had removed the territorial vice-presidents from the board of directors of the corporation, an act that completed the step-by-step removal of the old territorial kings from the plexus of authority begun with the McKinsey proposals and accelerated on the airstrip at Pueblo in the fall of 1977. Joe Moran would remain on the board for only a short time. Eventually only Brennan would represent the retailers on the board, and after Telling replaced the dismissed insider directors with two outsiders, the traditionally packed Sears board of directors contained a majority of outside directors for the first time.

The day before the Challenge Meeting began, Telling seemingly took yet another giant step back away from the embattled merchants when he announced the recruitment of yet another outsider to be a corporate officer and board member. The manager was to join Phil Purcell and other sixty-eighth-floor cronies immediately in what was becoming a separate "corporate" executive cordon arrayed around the person of the chairman. The new man on sixty-eight would be . . . a bean counter. Don Craib, the number-two man at Allstate Insurance Company, would come work in the Tower as a *vice-chairman of the board*—responsible for corporate administration. This was more than a step away from the hallowed traditions; this was a slap in the face. The move seemed particularly perverse to those Field soldiers who knew of Telling's oft-stated resentment of Allstate. "The spoiled child of Sears," he used to call the insurer. Everyone who'd spent any time with Ed Telling during his career had heard him talk about the "goddamned Allstate Insurance Company." Telling found Allstate's business impenetrable at worst and tedious at best, and, as did most of the old-line merchants, he believed the insurance company had been created only to provide paper reinforcement for the sorts of real things Sears provided for the nation.

Telling's elevation was particularly humiliating to the merchants since it highlighted the fact that Allstate was on its way to making twice as much money in profit for the corporation as the retailer, with one-third of the total revenue. A few merchants noted in the corridors of the twenty-seventh floor the day after the announcement that at least Don Craib had some good bloodlines to him. The insurance executive—an ex-Marine who resembled a younger J. Edgar Hoover—was the son of a much-loved merchant who'd served during the heyday of the Pacific Coast Territory. It was Don Craib, Sr., who'd effectively run the West during the years when Arthur Wood was sent out to be groomed for the chairmanship. The elder Craib was the mentor of John Lowe, and a noted rewriter of directives from Chicago.

But there was no getting around the fact that Telling had dealt the merchants another severe blow by placing an insurance man so close to the heart of Headquarters authority. Telling seemed to be creating a new structure designed to perpetuate the company in name, even after its core business fell away.

Maybe it was because Ed Telling had been defeated. Earlier during the summer, Telling paraphrased V. I. Lenin when he said that one of the good things about running Sears, Roebuck was that he didn't have to buy the rope to hang himself with. Not only had he removed himself from the other veterans, but he seemed to be systematically taking away their traditional rank in the corporate structure. He'd usurped their seats on the board, torn back the camouflage covering the collective balance sheet, and now he'd left them in the swirling hands of this eerily affecting young man named Brennan. The whole scenario smacked of betrayal.

After two solid days of presentations, pep talks, and big meals, Gar Ingraham took to the podium on Friday to begin the closing session of the Challenge Meeting. After the now familiar strains of "It's a Challenge Year" faded, Gar—who looked more and more like a crocodile as the years went by—made a brief joke at the expense of old Bob Howard, a long-time group manager who was best known for the amount of time he'd spent in the company of Ed Telling. Having thus invoked Telling and the nostalgic security of the old days in the Quincy Adams Room, Ingraham instructed all of the managers to remove their special "1981: The Challenge Year" name tags and to replace the rectangular badges with the circular yellow buttons they would each find in front of them, next to their official notepads. There was much nervous laughter rising from the crowd as hundreds of men with silvering hair placed large yellow "smile" buttons on the lapels of their gray business suits.

"Now," Ingraham said. Some Searsmen began to rummage meaninglessly through their briefcases, trying to avert their looks of horror. Others began to cough. "Now, when you're going home on the train tonight, if you're a Headquarters person; or if you're on the plane going home, wherever that is; somebody will say to you, 'What have you got to smile about?' And you'll smile like you-know-what 'cause you know something they don't know. *You know what's coming!*"

Several senior executives were then asked to go to the lectern to reiterate some of the myriad new planning, operational, advertising, buying, and selling principles taught during the three-day convention. Gar asked them to offer their "impressions" of the last few days.

Jack Kelly got up looking extremely distressed about his "smile" button and spoke of the catalog division's commitment to the new spirit. Kelly picked up Brennan's strain of near-confessional honesty about the true state of Sears' affairs by saying that while 350 million different sorts of Sears Catalogs had been sent out to twenty-five million American households during 1979, the company's dominance of the catalog business was slipping. The customer count had declined for the first time in twenty-five years during 1979; and just as smaller specialized operations were hurting the retail stores, younger, more aggressive catalog houses were moving in on the big book. "We've dominated this business for ninety-five years," Kelly said in his careful, articulate manner. "Now we have got to make it more convenient."

Jack Kelly felt truly awful about having to wear a "smile" button. It was a feeling he shared with many of the other senior executives in the room. It wasn't lost on Kelly and some of the others that they'd just been asked to leave the meeting in Chicago and go back home wearing generic smiles in the spot on their lapels where their own names had been.

Whether or not Gar had simply gone overboard and misinterpreted Brennan's intentions with the "rah-rah" stuff, the men had listened to their new leader say that he dreamed of traveling coast to coast and finding displays in Sears stores that looked exactly the same. The executives in the audience who felt most uncomfortable with their metal smiles tended to be those who'd entered the General's world after winning a war, at a time when the whole company wasn't as big as the current Eastern Territory. But the faces of those who were pained by the irony of wearing fixed smiles when there was so little to smile about were indistinguishable from the believers in the audience. There was no way of knowing if the executive next to you was thinking about going along, so every eye in the room was aimed up at Gar Ingraham as he returned to the podium and then walked away abruptly with a hand microphone.

"In Sir James Barrie's great play *Peter Pan,* there's a scene in there that never fails to move me," Ingraham said. "It's the scene when the little white spot on the stage that is Tinkerbell fades and dies." At this, the room went black, and a tiny circle of light appeared at Ingraham's feet. "Peter Pan, in those moments, appeals to the audience for a response," Gar continued. "He says, 'Tinkerbell is gone, but if we believe, she will come back.' Peter Pan exhorts the audience to tell him whether or not they believe in Tinkerbell.

"I don't think that this meeting or real-life Sears is analogous to Tinkerbell, but as relates to belief, I do think it's the same." Ingraham's voice then blasted through the darkness in a full shout: "Do you believe that Sears is unique?"

A single voice way in the back of the auditorium called back, "I believe."

"Do you think—do you believe that Sears is unique?" he asked again.

A small group answered, "I believe."

"How many of us *really believe* Sears is unique?"

More than half the crowd answered now: "I believe!"

Finally he asked, "Do you believe in Sears?"

As the crowd yelled back its answer, a giant "S-E-A-R-S" appeared stretched out across the huge screen in the front of the room.

Ingraham asked Brennan, Wurmstedt, and Moran to come to the front of the room before continuing. "I want you to do something that you don't do naturally," he said to the audience. "I want you to join hands."

The stunned crowd now came to life. Nervous, derisory laughter mixed with much low-pitched grumbling. Up until now, the vocabulary and imagery that characterized the session had been carefully derived from Field and Headquarters assumptions of old. Even the new Plan was composed of individual deals between free men. In the hallways, Field managers had actually marveled at the depth of empathy Brennan's Headquarters cadre exhibited for Field soldiers living in the red. Territorial visitors agreed that the buyers' wares looked better than they had in years. The buyers seemed to be addressing the reality of selling for the first time since the widening of the divide. There had even been conjecture here and there that perhaps senior management knew what it was doing after all. But here was Gar, asking them to wear "smile" buttons, to listen to him compare metaphorically the company and a dying fairy, and now instructing them all to hold hands.

On the stage, Ed Brennan looked pale and perturbed, but he seized Joe Moran's thick wrist and then took up a stricken-looking Charlie Wurmstedt's hand. Gar Ingraham would perform his "little personal things" one more time during subsequent Challenge Meetings before it would be suggested from above that he could well afford to lose the "smile" buttons and Tinkerbell story, but for now Brennan would play along with the games, so the three officers remained as still as statues as they stared out above the top of the crowd.

When Brennan was finally introduced, the applause was sustained, but it was more deliberate and appreciative than enthusiastic. Brennan stood above the silence that followed, leaning forward slightly, as if he were facing into a gale. He was wearing a very dark gray three-piece suit now, which was notably lacking in lapel-borne smiles.

"I really wasn't sure, when we decided to hold this meeting, whether or not the times were right, whether or not something we had done thirty years ago could be done again with a recaptured spirit," he said. "But it didn't take long. It was some time during the day on Wednesday that I think it became obvious to all of us that we were going through a tremendously worthwhile exercise. In fact, when I arrived home about nine o'clock on Wednesday evening, I said to my wife, 'I think this has been one of the great days in the history of Sears, Roebuck.'

"I am so proud of our buying organization I could almost burst!" he intoned with great feeling. "I think I only echo the feelings of our Field organization, and I would only ask if they agree that they respond right now."

The applause was long and sincere, the sort of clapping associated with affirmative nods of the head, acknowledgments of a job well done. The buyers really had tried this time.

Brennan maintained the crowd's rapt attention as he hammered out once again the commingled themes and strategies he was launching against a situation he said they all had to recognize was extremely desperate. There had to be peace among the warring divisions, and there had to be a reaffirmation of the old verities of good solid storekeeping and Searsmanship. The "questioning of everything" had to stop in the Field. He asked the local leaders to accept new formations and systems for the sake of the whole.

As if to separate himself once and for all from Gar Ingraham's impromptu hijinks and again draw a line between old and new, Brennan said, "Some of our meetings over the years were of great substance, but we didn't always put together enough enthusiasm. Then there were the larger number of meetings—where there was a tremendous amount of enthusiasm but there wasn't a heck of a lot of substance. Enthusiasm without substance," he said purposefully, "is meaningless."

There were nods and laughter in the crowd now. Applause began to punctuate each sentence, indicating the successful severing of Brennan's person from the failures of the past. "Embrace this planning process we have talked about. It will work," he promised them. "It will permit us to generate business and the much-needed profits that will make this company prosperous." Brennan leaned forward, paused, and lowered his voice. "We . . . are . . . a . . . great company," he said.

Managers who minutes earlier had been writhing with embarrassment were now mesmerized by Brennan's pleas. Brennan's honesty was touching; his plans were dreamy but tough-minded too. His hands drew pictures before them that lingered until a new image was described. All of it was illuminated by an affecting fervency and a strangely powerful sense of grace.

"Within this decade will be our centennial. We've talked about the '20s and the '30s and '40s and the '50s and the '60s. During this decade we will cross one hundred years, and it's our job to make sure that the company is stronger in its second hundred years than it was in its first hundred.

"We are a diversified company; we have great people and great strengths. Our *base* is merchandising. Last year we experienced over seven hundred and seventy-five million transactions in this company. We have over fifty million customers that carry Sears credit cards. That's a tremendous customer base. Our studies show that the base is intact. We are a *store,* and we must present ourselves to the customers as *a* store."

Brennan's hands fell to his sides. His head tilted to one side in a way that informed all the personnel in from the Southern Territory that a parable was coming.

"When I started in this business about twenty-four years ago with

Sears, I started as a salesman in Madison, Wisconsin. And, as it often happens with Sears people when they are not working, we would sit around over a cup of coffee or lunch and talk about our bosses. Typically, we would refer to the bosses as 'they.' I can remember sitting around as a salesman and talking about 'they' and saying to myself that we could do a better job than 'they' can. We referred to them always as 'they': *They* ought to do this; *they* ought to do that.

"Then, after a while, I moved to the next level of management—a division manager—and we would sit around and have lunch or a cup of coffee"—Brennan paused for a long breath now—"and I found that we were still talking about 'they,' only 'they' were a notch higher on the ladder. . . ."

The story followed the entirety of Brennan's route through the company. As a store manager he talked about "they," the group managers. As a group manager he talked about "they," the territorial vice-presidents. "I thought, perhaps when I became an officer of the company, and I got to come to Chicago, this would change. So I came to the Tower when I was a territorial vice-president, and I went to the board meeting and I listened to the discussion. They were talking about what was going on in the stores and the buying organization, about *our* management. Suddenly . . . it dawned on me." His voice rose now to a high pitch, and his clasped hands unlocked—unfurled, really, as if to illustrate the opening of himself and the light of his epiphany to the others: "It dawned on me, there . . . is . . . no . . . *they. They* is us! *We* is they! And that is what this company is about!"

Just a big store. *They is us.* It wasn't even in the sketchy outline of Brennan's notes. The story and the image just came to him as he stood there, and now almost everyone in the crowd jumped up and applauded wildly. You could have programmed rising strains from a violin section into the background, but in the end a great number of them bought it. The call for peace and unity and sacrifice was accepted as coming from one who in spite of his extreme youth shared the great heart that had been broken by the failure of time-honored ways. He was exhorting them to move beyond the pain and fear with him now.

As the managers rose to their feet, generating rolling waves of applause, it was clear that Brennan and his Challenge Meeting had successfully convinced great numbers of them that his enunciation of the unspeakable truth and extent of their failure was a confession they all had to hear. By renouncing some elements of the past they could revive and maintain others. In return for a repudiation of old certitudes, Brennan would personally encircle their fears and redeem their hopes.

Through a combination of skilled oratory, traditional demonstration, and overt ritual, the meeting had associated a great crisis with a great challenge, a great history of triumph with the possibility of renewed greatness in the future. The historical revivalism was laden with symbols and slogans that obscured the full import of new planning processes and centralized "top-down" selling programs, initiatives that would have been spat back out instantaneously only months earlier.

Ed Telling had asked Brennan the day he told him to come to Chicago to do nothing less than "destroy a thing called Headquarters and a thing called Field and create a thing called Sears," and now, in the gulf between buyers and sellers, between history and the future, old sanctities and new processes—between success and failure—Ed Brennan had inserted himself.

Plans were adjusted so that, rather than a scaled-down version of the Challenge Meeting's being presented in the capital cities of the five territories, the whole show, including most of the buyers, was taken on the road. The entire production was staged in each of the five territories. Six corporate planes were used to move people and displays between Chicago, Los Angeles, Philadelphia, Dallas, and Atlanta.

Brennan delivered his exposition—his "call to greatness," as Joe Moran called it—upon unity, planning, management, and history, five more times. Ten thousand Field managers, including all the store runners and the group-based merchandise managers (who had been stuck in the middle of the freeze between Field and Parent by virtue of their responsibility for moving goods into the stores) all heard his call for unity, as a cathartic atmosphere was re-created in a remarkably similar form in each city.

The arrival of so much firepower from the Parent would have been viewed as an utterly unacceptable invasion of territorial sanctity only a year or so earlier, but now it was welcomed with open arms. Even Brennan seemed overwhelmed on occasion by the collective desperation that was opening the minds of the company to a new reality and new ideas.

At one of the meetings, Brennan decided to take advantage of the emotional aperture to carry the level of historical repudiation he was seeking a bit further. He stared out at the store managers in that uncanny manner by which all of his listeners believed he was staring into their eyes, and said, "It will never be 1955 again." The simple phrase was repeated by the younger Sears managers for months afterward, because it was a slogan at once so obvious and so radical. A new leader had clearly emerged, one who had touched something deep inside the injured society by promising to make the company young again.

CHAPTER 11

The Purge

C harlie Wurmstedt soldiered on through Brennan's fall campaign. Brennan demanded that he delete his remarks about loquacious Irishmen and their respective childhoods from his opening remarks at the regional Challenge Meetings, and Charlie did as he was told. He watched as Brennan marched across the map of Sears, exhorting the troops to renaissance, and watched with bewilderment as large numbers of Field managers who received the itinerant Challenge responded with enthusiasm to the young president's efforts to reclaim the company's spirit.

"If you're a cynic," Wurmstedt heard Brennan caution, addressing directly the recalcitrants of the Midwestern Territory, the Southerners in Atlanta, the Southwesterners in Dallas, the inhabitants of the once-separate kingdom in Los Angeles, and the already converted soldiers of the East in Philadelphia, "then maybe this is the wrong business for you." Brennan stared deep into the collective corporate eye and proclaimed for everyone to hear, "It will never be 1955 again."

"And you gotta believe!" old Gar Ingraham's cry would continually rise as a chorus from some place in Charlie's head. *"Do you believe!"*

But Charlie—damn it—Charlie just couldn't believe, at least not with the requisite passion. And he knew that in Ed Brennan's Sears, just like Gar said, "you gotta." The smile on those buttons was Eddie Brennan's smile, and Charlie Wurmstedt had worn his own broad and toothy grin through a few too many selling seasons in a few too many towns, to suddenly adopt the kid's smile as his own.

Wurmstedt read his sanitized lines as the mammoth traveling troupe moved from city to city, but it hurt him badly to do it. He watched some of his store managers out in the territories of the Field rise to the Challenge, rise from their chairs and the depths of their despair to hail this new wind from Headquarters and this altogether different child of the stores with an energy he hadn't seen around Sears for a long time— but Charlie just couldn't seem to catch it. He would sit there after Brennan's charismatic call to arms and clap a few times, looking down between his knees past his sapphire ring for such a long time that people noticed. His sadness was particularly evident because Jumpin' Joe Moran was invariably sitting next to him clapping and cheering like a kid at his first World Series. Joe even turned to Charlie in the midst of a long standing ovation at the end of one Challenge Meeting and yelled in his old nemesis's ear, "Charlie, old friend, I fear you need a little public-relations work." Then Joe went back to cheering.

It had been only a year earlier that Wurmstedt had warned Joe Moran to "watch his back," so violent was the reaction to the way Moran was destabilizing the buying organization. Now the Headquarters newspaper was running the photograph of Brennan holding his and Moran's hands (to "assert belief in each other," the caption read), and crazy Joe was offering *him* free advice on how to get along. The whole thing was hard to believe.

For his part, Charles Christian Wurmstedt still considered 1955 a hell of good year. One of the best goddamned years he'd ever had. He'd ridden through the cornfields of the Midwestern zone for all of that year beside a big fellow named Ed Telling, a "man's man," who knew how to have a couple of drinks and a good game of cards. Ed the Elder had a damned good sense of humor too, in Charlie Wurmstedt's book. He could get to a point without making a public event out of it, and if the truth be known—despite what Ed Telling had just done to him by jumping Eddie Brennan over his head and making the kid his boss—he would still rather have spent a year in a county jail with Ed Telling than a single weekend in the company of this new Ed, with his eighteen-hour workdays, his astonishing piety, his humorlessness, and his strangely powerful sermons.

During the second week of September, just after the Midwestern Challenge Meeting, Charlie Wurmstedt got a formal letter from his old friend Ed Telling that offered him a way around ever having to believe. It arrived on Telling's own formal stationery rather then the usual interoffice stock, with the date centered below the bold *"Sears, Roebuck and Co., Sears Tower"* and the text arrayed underneath like words on a proclamation.

"The purpose of this letter," it said, "is to offer you the opportunity to take advantage of the 'Early Retirement Incentive Plan.'

"In recognition of your long service and valuable contribution to the Company, a special compensation plan has been designed, in addition to the Company's normal benefits for retirees. This is a one-time effort to encourage early retirement among Sears checklist [managerial] employees who currently qualify under the provisions of the Company personnel policy for retirement—i.e., that they are at least 55 years of age and have 20 or more years of service. You will have until November 28, 1980, to accept or decline the offer to retire early; and if you accept, your retirement will be effective December 31, 1980.

"Obviously this exception to normal policy would not be made to all eligible checklist persons without a compelling reason, nor would it be made unless the hope was that a large number of individuals would elect early retirement. Because the offer is unique and because we are urging serious consideration on your part to accept it, we believe a full explanation of the reasoning behind it is necessary.

"It has become increasingly clear that Sears, like other companies competing in a highly labor-intensive industry and confronted with predictable increasing wage and benefit costs, must conduct its business with fewer employees. Over the past several years, we have seen the reductions in the numbers of employees in our selling and distribution units. In spite of these reductions, our operating costs remain high. It is therefore clear that reductions must be made in the size of our checklist organization. Each of us should understand that while the current recession has accelerated our facing up to the need to take action, the action itself was inevitable and would have occurred even in a strong economy.

"The 'Early Retirement Incentive Plan' was adopted in the hope that it will provide an effective answer. The election by current checklist employees to retire early should provide us the opportunity to reduce the size of our checklist organization through the process of attrition rather than substantial numbers of layoffs.

"The program will be expensive to Sears. However we believe that it is so important that Sears demonstrate its interest in providing upward movement and future opportunities for its young people, a clear continuing commitment to affirmative action, and its desire to minimize to the greatest possible degree the necessity for layoffs that the expense is clearly justified. . . . There cannot be an extension of the time for decision nor is it planned that this offer will be made again."

The letter was signed in Telling's heavy scrawl.

. . .

Almost twenty-five hundred other Sears managers received the same letter, among them the most powerful executives in the corporation. "We've gotten old," Ed Telling said during a meeting called to plan the ERIP (pronounced "Eee-rip"), as it was soon known throughout Sears. "We need young blood. That's what Sears was like when it grew. It was young then, young and vigorous. But this old crew—myself included— we're suddenly sitting and rocking. We just sat and rocked for years. . . . You don't fight wars with old people."

But a fifty-five-year-old Sears executive with twenty years of hard work under his belt *was* a young man. The average age of the officer corps was around fifty-six, and even if *The Wall Street Journal* did contend in an article about Sears that this was evidence of an "elderly, entrenched bureaucracy" during that stormy autumn of 1980, this was hardly how it looked or felt from the inside. At fifty-five, the boys were just about ready to "have their innings," as Arthur Wood used to say. Most of them believed they could still buy the pants off an item or sell the hell out of the goods with as much skill and vigor as they'd ever possessed.

A few years earlier, when Congress superseded the official Sears retirement ages of sixty-five for general employees and sixty for officers by changing the legal, mandatory retirement age to seventy, Sears personnel executives went to the Department of Labor and contended it would cause a stasis in the ranks at Sears and clog advancement. Government officials countered with studies that indicated 75 percent of the employees would retire when they were sixty-three anyway. The personnel people said the government didn't understand anything about Sears, Roebuck. At the point when the government studies indicated veteran employees would leave in droves, only 20 percent of them had left.

For years the personnel department had known that many employees lied about their age in order to avoid retirement. Though retirees from Sears tended to enter an active afterlife, to a tremendous number of those still on the payroll, Sears, Roebuck was so much of a complete and clearly delineated life that retirement was feared as a state of living death.

The idea of inducing senior executives to leave the company by offering them money had been in the works since the emergency meetings during the spring of 1980 called originally to consider across-the-board layoffs. Though Brennan and Telling both opted for a program of reductions based on attrition at the time, it was clear to Charlie Bacon that something more drastic was needed.

After layoffs were rejected, Bacon commenced a study of an early-retirement program conducted to great effect by IBM. During the early summer, Bacon presented a proposal to Telling and Brennan that was modeled on the IBM plan. He even showed Telling a list of some of the more problematic officers who would be eligible to leave, the ones for whom the offer could be rendered "more voluntary than for others," but Telling rejected the proposal, saying that the ones he wanted out would probably stay. Telling thought they'd only lose the most talented veterans, who were confident of finding other work.

When Bacon came back to try again in July, the chairman was more interested. By then, Jack Kincannon and various of his taxation experts had become involved in figuring out a way to make the package of rewards attractive enough to convince older veterans to leave home. The ERIP they went on to develop would offer up to half-pay for three years to most of the early retirees under sixty-three. The rest would be able to take a large lump-sum payment without the attendant tax on such a windfall, as long as they placed the money in a tax-deferred Individual Retirement Account.

After Telling gave the new plan his blessing, corkboards full of familiar names were set up in the territorial offices and a master board was erected on the sixty-eighth floor of the Tower. Twenty-eight men, more than half of the forty-one company officers, were eligible to take the money and run, including Jack Kincannon, Gar Ingraham, Joe Moran, and Charlie Wurmstedt. At one point Charlie Bacon had all the members of his personnel department write down on a piece of paper the number they thought would take the ERIP and throw the paper and a dollar in a pot. Their IBM personnel-department contacts told them to expect no more than 25 percent of the executives to decide to stop working. After considering all of the old soldiers and warlords whose names were arrayed before them on the corkboard, most of them made guesses that day that fell well under five hundred acceptances, out of the 2,474 offers sent out above Ed Telling's signature.

Telling guessed that six hundred would take it, but he added, with only a glimmer of humor, that he really hoped they'd all leave. For all of his own career, Telling had been masterful in his ability to wait until the time was right to jettison colleagues. People who failed to heed his signs on the third pass were rarely just thrown out in direct contravention of the psychological contract. Somehow, people Ed Telling wanted away from him always seemed to be sick when they finally left, or so tired and sad that they themselves decided it was time to strike camp. But ever since Telling had busted down that venerated group manager

Richard Sears.

General Robert E. Wood (left), company president, and Julius Rosenwald, chairman of the board, ca. 1928. Wood had convinced company officers in 1924 that Sears should enter the retail field.

The West Side
Complex—the "Great
Works"—Sears'
headquarters until
1973.

The Tower.

General Wood with his secretary, Miss Richardson, 1954.

Gordon Metcalf, Sears Chairman Arthur Wood, and Chicago Mayor Richard Daley at press conference announcing construction of the Sears Tower.

SEARS CONGRESS OF MERCHANTS
"ON TO CHICAGO"
STEVENS HOTEL   MAY 4, 1950

A meeting of Sears merchants, May 1950.

OSCAR
CHICAGO
50-1087-8

THE HEADS OF THE FIVE
TERRITORIES, ca. 1973:

Edward R. Telling, East

John G. Lowe, West

Culver J. Kennedy, Midwest

A. D. (Dean) Swift, South

Alfred I. Davies, Southwest

The Alhambra Cube, John Lowe's Headquarters of the West.

Senior management of the
Merchandising group, 1980 (from
front, left to right): Ed Brennan (1st
row); Henry Sunderland, "Jumpin'
Joe" Moran (2nd row); Thomas Neal,
Bill Lochmoeller, Robert E. Wood II
(3rd row); Bill Bass Jr., M. E. "Burk"
Burkholder, Jack Wirth (4th row);
Raymond Kennedy, Charley Moran,
Thomas B. Sweeney, and Charlie
Bacon. Photo © Wm. Franklin
McMahon.

Ed Telling, November 1977.
Photo © Wm. Franklin
McMahon.

back in the Eastern Territory, and replaced him with Brennan, he'd maintained little patience for the cult of the old salt. As much as the many ersatz analyses of Sears' impending downfall had to hurt him, the Rip Van Winkle imagery publicly pinned on the company was particularly galling because Telling believed it was true. Telling said the "old crew" was lucky to be receiving Sears' "historic kindness," being paid to leave, because other companies would have done the deed in a less feeling way.

Veterans traveling with the Challenge Meeting troupe noted that during each rendition of the event the younger managers in the audience—the members of the generation of the Hay Committee young Turks—looked as enthralled by the spectacle of an end to the reign of the old ways as the older men looked unsettled by it. The reactions seemed to define a generational schism within Sears that appeared to cut across other factional lines and fall roughly between those who were working during the General's "On to Chicago" rally and those who didn't remember it at all. The anthropologist Margaret Mead once defined the "generation gap" that divided fathers and sons during the 1960s and 1970s as a split between those who were old enough to actually remember World War II and those who'd only heard about it. The generation gap within Sears was similarly marked on one side of the gulf by the shared experience of the last good war and the General at full bore, though the division had remained subconscious until the company reached a crisis.

The huge group that had known the General's leadership and now held Ed Telling's formal enticement to leave Sears was subdivided superficially between those who'd come to the company directly from military service in 1946, and those who went to college and joined the company two to four years later. But the two subgroups had moved through the years as one, fused by their sense that winning the war and doing battle for Sears, Roebuck were events situated along the same noble continuum. They'd grayed together in the ranks after a time, and in retrospect some of them saw that their beliefs about the company and the world around it—even their indomitable pride—had indeed become obsolete. Telling seemed to be offering them money now, not for having prevailed, but simply for having kept the faith so long.

The strange thing about it, though, was that, whereas the dominant executive style of their generation—the "Organization Man"—always called for managers to act much older than their years, most Searsmen believed they were young men all along. The General was the old one:

he was an old man at the "On to Chicago" rally in 1950 and old when
death finally pulled his hand from the reins almost two decades later.
They were the General's boys, and now Ed Telling, of all people, was
saying they were old. They all knew Sears would persist beyond their
tenure, just as it had been there before they came. But somehow most
of them never pictured the end this way—not for their bunch. It was like
they were being turned, like old velveteen jumpers after Christmas,
liquidated like so much shopworn goods. No matter what kind of six-
figure settlement was involved, or how unhappy the devastation of recent years had made the 2,474 senior executives considering the offer,
it still hurt like hell that the culmination of so much industry should be
a letter telling them they'd grown old.

As the late-November decision date approached, conjecture was rife
inside and outside of Sears over which executives would leave. The
business press asserted from the outside that both Charlie Wurmstedt
and Joe Moran would probably leave because they had been passed over
for promotion when Brennan came in.

The autumn decisions as to whether or not to leave the company
would be made against a backdrop of further fiscal disintegration. It was
clear now that 1980 would be a year of strong "negative growth" for the
merchants: one of "financial disappointments," as Ed Telling put it. Sales
for the third quarter of the year were down once again from a year
earlier. Net income from merchandising for the first nine months of
1980 was below $50 million—down from $236.3 million the year before.
This was before the $20-million pool assumed to be sufficient to pay off
the early retirees was set aside.

Inflation and recession combined to assault the numbers from the
expense side and in terms of real purchases to the extent that the once-
humbling experience of 1977 now looked like a triumph. Once again,
negative external economic events hit Sears much harder than they did
Sears' large competitors. Though the prime rate was approaching 20
percent, every other big retailer had a good October. Even *Montgomery
Ward* was up—a humiliating course of events—and K mart was up 12
percent.

By the end of the year, total corporate net income would be down 36.1
percent for the year, despite Allstate's almost $450-million contribution
to the bottom line. The bean counters made more than twice as much
money as the merchants. The stock price bottomed at $14.50 per share,
over $7 per share lower than a price high that had spurred the retirees
to revolt in 1979.

Moody's Investor Services followed S & P's earlier decision and lowered Sears' debt ratings because of the company's performance. *The New York Times* reported that rumors were sweeping the merchandise wing's four hundred thousand employees of "wholesale dismissals"—which the company denied—but more than a few ERIP candidates read the news, looked at the numbers, and listened to the gossip, and many of them wondered whether, if they didn't take the money, they might still get fired or laid off in the end. Most of the senior veterans had to admit that if the company was to crawl out of its dark hole a new pace was indeed in order, and many of them had to honestly wonder if they could keep up with the seemingly indefatigable Brennan, who was criss-crossing the country like a young candidate in the throes of a great campaign. And if the business failures and the specter of having to give up what remained of the sacred tenets that had guided their past wasn't enough to induce them to leave, then there was the cash. Telling's offer was indeed a generous one, and as the vets "put the pencil to it," only the managers just a bit over fifty-five years old felt that they would benefit financially from staying on. By and large, everyone over fifty-eight made out better by leaving, with only the relative psychological value of your future working life at Sears lending weight to the other side of the equation.

Charlie Meyer stopped in to see Ed Telling with his early-retirement offer in hand during early October. Telling's one-time boss in the East believed that Ed would have kept him around in some corporate sine-cure out of loyalty, but ever since Meyer had gone to Washington to be an assistant secretary of state—and thus "cut the umbilical cord," he said—Charlie had felt himself an observer rather than a master of events. Meyer had stepped aside graciously to allow young Phil Purcell to become Telling's planner, but the Sears patrician had little patience for his subsequent role as a vice-president for corporate public affairs. He couldn't abide the noisy protesters from the National Organization for Women or one of the other groups that had joined in the kicking of the company when it was down. Charlie claimed that somehow he'd lost his ability to "suffer fools gladly" while in Washington, but those who'd known Meyer for a long time wondered how you can lose something you never had.

"Ed," the last of the Tall Men said, "this plan is so good that I think I'm gonna take it."

"You son-of-a-bitch," Telling said. "You're gonna leave me here all alone."

But Meyer saw the twinkle in Telling's eye when he said it. The two men just grinned and shook hands.

Jack Kincannon was on record in the newspapers as not intending to leave Sears until the time of his scheduled retirement in 1983, but ever since Telling screamed at him in the officers' coffee room that day, Kincannon had been crossing swords with Telling at every turn. Jack argued vociferously against making the insurance man Don Craib a vice-chairman of the corporation, and Telling pointedly ignored him. After originally fighting the idea of a wholesale purge of his generation, Kincannon had worked hard to figure out a way to pay the older early retirees a lump sum. Lately Jack had become a vocal supporter of the ERIP, but Telling found occasion to criticize Kincannon's tax-related work on the plan in front of an audience.

It was clear now that Kincannon was sitting on a sidetrack. His once-fearsome power was waning by the day. So Jack Kincannon also appeared at Ed Telling's door one morning, though with less good cheer. "Ed," the chief financial officer drawled, "I know you don't much like me, and you know I don't much like you either. If you do one of these two-an'-a-half-year full-salary things you've worked up for some of the others," he said, referring to the remuneration John Lowe received when he left, "I'll just disappear from the company."

"Why, you don't have to leave, Jack," Telling said with a straight face. "Whyn't you stick around until you're sixty-five?"

But a deal was struck with considerable speed that exchanged a sum of money for Kincannon's departure. The announcement that Jack would leave Sears and be replaced by Dick Jones noted that, unlike other potential retirements from the senior ranks, the end of his career was effective immediately. Kincannon had most of the files he'd collected during all the years he was known as "the controller" shredded, but he decided to keep the one file marked "Ed Telling" and take it home with him to his ranch outside Dallas as a souvenir.

Jack Kincannon was not about to go quietly, and after forty-one years he knew exactly the manner in which Ed Telling would least like to receive his parting kick in the ribs. So yet another article about the turmoil at Sears, Roebuck appeared in *The Wall Street Journal* near the end of the late-November ERIP decision deadline: "Yesterday's heresies have become today's certainties at Sears, Roebuck, and Company," the article began. "Witness these words from Jack Kincannon, outgoing vice chairman and chief financial officer: 'It's absolutely essential that future chairmen come on stream with a broad basis of exposure and experience other than just knowing how to open and close a store. If you don't know anything except how to open and close a store, how does that qualify you to run a $25 billion complex?' "

The shot at Telling was shocking in that during all of its ninety-three years a CEO at Sears had never been criticized publicly by a family member. Kincannon's assertion was in many ways as profound as the one Ed Telling made to John Lowe that day on the airstrip in Pueblo, when he contended that Lowe had "lost credibility with your people." The blast had such a strong historical strain to it that insiders found it almost nostalgic. Headquarters aristocrats and powerful staff kings like Jack never did think anyone bred in the far-flung stores of the Field was smart enough to run Sears. Kincannon was expressing one last time the deep feelings of an entire school of thought, a now vulnerable camp within Sears that had been made to suffer the stupidity of store jockeys for a long time.

Ed Brennan wasn't at all surprised that the grapevine was carrying indications that a great many of his senior managers were leaning toward early retirement. The meaning of the Challenge included a demand for new standards—new staffing standards, new merchandising standards, new planning standards, and new standards to bear—and he knew many members of the World War II generation were simply too tired or mired in the past to adjust. But Brennan didn't want to lose certain eligible veterans, especially some of the wily old Headquarters politicians.

Brennan almost seemed offended when he heard that Jack Kelly wanted to retire. In the old days Kelly had worked beside Brennan's father in Department 45. The connection of a respected veteran like Kelly to his and the company's shared past was important to Brennan, and he didn't want Jack to go. He dispatched Joe Moran to talk Jack out of it, but all Joe did when he got there was talk about how much he was looking forward to retiring too.

Eventually Brennan called the old catalog man into his office to change his mind. Brennan talked about how well the Challenge Meetings were being received and of how essential Kelly and Joe Moran had been to their conception and execution. He mentioned that the idea for the meetings took form from Joe Moran's memory of the powerful "On to Chicago" meetings the General had staged back in 1950.

Brennan pulled out a large gray photograph he'd found that depicted hundreds of Sears executives arrayed around banquet tables, wearing wide lapels and low side-parted hair.

"Look, Jack," Brennan said, pointing at a face in the photograph. "Here's my dad."

"Ed," Jack Kelly said, "have you ever asked Joe where he was sitting at that banquet?"

"No," Brennan said. "Why?"

"Because he wasn't there," Kelly said with a slight sigh. "The 'On to Chicago' meetings were for retail people only. Joe and I were in catalog and we weren't invited."

No matter what Ed Brennan said to him, Kelly replied that he just wasn't going to stay. There were books he wanted to read, friends he wanted to see, and more than a few little catalog operations that could use his help. Jack Kelly hated the way the company had been torn apart, and he knew he could never feel quite the same about Sears again. Telling's proclamation about early retirement promised emancipation.

"I'm sorry, Ed," Kelly said to Brennan when Kelly was called up to the president's office one more time before signing his initials next to the "I ACCEPT" box on the last page of the ERIP papers. "I want to leave. I think I've run the catalog now longer than anyone save Richard Sears, and I'm just tired of this old place."

Brennan didn't want Jumpin' Joe Moran to bail out either. The Challenge Meeting preparations indicated that he could possibly make Joe Moran palatable to the very buyers he'd terrorized, that he could harness and redirect some of Moran's intellectual conceptions into programmatic language and systems that would help make the company work again. Others would perhaps look on and realize that if Joe could change, anybody could follow the new steps. Brennan always thought someone like Joe Moran could be tempered and balanced, given the appropriate managerial lead, and now that he was finally in a position to give it a try, the last thing he wanted was for Joe to retire.

Jumpin' Joe turned sixty a few weeks after he got his letter from Ed Telling. His family scheduled a big birthday dinner for thirty people to be held in the Metropolitan Club, the glass-enclosed restaurant off the Tower's sixty-sixth-floor skydeck where Sears executives' tables always bore matchbook covers with their names printed on them. Before the dinner, Joe told Jack Kelly that he'd been wrestling with the ERIP numbers and, as much as he wanted to bail out, the financial strains of supporting such a large family made it difficult for him. The stock price that many executives of his generation had always counted on to finance life after Sears was still well below his option price, and he'd just recently come to a salary level where a man with ten kids and a mother-in-law at home could save any money at all. But he'd still had enough heroics, he told Kelly. He'd given it his all. He was determined to announce his retirement plans to his family on the occasion of his birthday.

Old colleagues had been asking Moran what he'd do with himself if he retired since the day Brennan was catapulted over his head. Everyone knew the man had no hobbies after the doctors made him give up his roses, no recreation, and hardly any friends. He'd been talking about writing a big, serious book since he was a young man, but it never seemed to get off the ground. All Joe had other than his family and his dog was Sears.

The morning after the party, Joe shuffled into Jack Kelly's office to tell him he hadn't said a word about retirement at the surprise party. He'd decided to stay on board for the full ride—or at least for three more years, until he would become eligible for enhanced benefits under the standard officers' retirement plan. But Kelly and other buying-side vets knew Joe was staying for other reasons. Joe was in the midst of a monumental metamorphosis, a carefully mapped plan designed to reform himself as young Eddie Brennan's right-hand man.

Charlie Wurmstedt knew that Ed Brennan didn't like him any more than he liked young Ed. Some observers were surprised that Wurmstedt had lasted past Brennan's arrival at all. Charlie's comments about talkative Irish families and his general demeanor at the revivalist Challenge conventicles were all duly noted, so the general consensus was that if there was a secret politically oriented "hit list" on some corkboard somewhere, Charlie Wurmstedt was probably on top of it. But legal restrictions on voluntary retirement programs reduced the relative force with which retirement could be suggested.

Not long after Wurmstedt got his letter from Ed Telling, Ed Brennan sent Wurmy a message of his own by announcing that one of Wurmstedt's five territories would be eliminated. It was a decision made without the counsel of the senior executive vice-president, Field.

After the first Challenge Meeting held for the brass in Chicago, the Headquarters newspaper carried a photograph of big Bill Lochmoeller, the vice-president running the Southwestern Territory. The Southwest—site of the first outpost of Sears, the Dallas mail-order plant—was the smallest of the Sears territories, though it usually exhibited a relatively high level of profitability considering the logistical problems presented by its far-flung population centers. Under the heading "Field Reaction," a buoyant Lochmoeller expressed the territorial leadership's enthusiasm for the Challenge Meetings, which he said "will assure us of a very successful 1981 in the Southwest." But there wouldn't be a 1981 for the proud old territory, because it was to be split up and merged into the three contiguous territories. The palatial suite of paneled offices Al Davies had built in Dallas was to be evacuated, and the territorial staff would be rendered "surplus" or placed in jobs vacated in other territories by early retirees.

Whatever the merits of the decision on a cost-containment basis, Charlie Wurmstedt couldn't buy the way Brennan went about it any more than he'd stood by when Ed Telling began thinking about killing off a territory before the meeting at the Cricket Club in Florida. *He* was supposed to be running the Field, and he hadn't even been invited to the meetings pursuant to the single most radical alteration in the structure of the Field since the General erected the territories.

Wurmstedt decided to go ahead and take Brennan's hint. He'd take his trophies and the big brass plaque with an old Sears logo on it he'd salvaged from one of the original stores and he'd go home. But because of the way it was done, Charlie, like Jack Kincannon, wasn't going to go gently.

"Look, Charlie," Wurmy said when he phoned Charlie Bacon, "I know what you all want, but I also know that John Lowe got two years' full pay and so did Jim Button when you moved them out, and I want at least what they got. I've always done a better job than either of them, no matter what you guys may think."

Brennan called Wurmstedt into his office and said that he would agree to give him six months of full pay beyond the early-retirement program's stated December 31, 1980, retirement date, but only if Wurmstedt would agree to assist in the closing down of the Southwestern Territory during the time he received the compensation.

As of January 1, Brennan added, Wurmstedt would no longer be senior executive vice-president, Field. The demeaning title "assistant"—assistant to Ed Brennan—would replace his current one for the six months. It was widely known that Charlie Wurmstedt hadn't much liked being an assistant to Ed Telling back in the Eastern Territory, but they weren't about to let Charlie off easy. Just as Jumpin' Joe's efforts to become a good soldier of the new would be rewarded, Charlie's inability to ride the wave would not be overlooked. The company was in need of selfless gestures, not exhibitions of pride.

Brennan decided that as of January he would suspend altogether the job of senior executive vice-president, Field. The four remaining territorial vice-presidents henceforth would report only to him. Brennan reasoned that the job title Wurmstedt held had become such a symbol of what he now rather diplomatically called the recent "friction" between Headquarters and Field that a "suspension" of the McKinsey-born job title was in order. The Field's man in Chicago would be him. Brennan sold the idea of eliminating Ed Telling's old job to the chairman and then to the board of directors as a short-term fix, despite several directors' contention that it created too "flat" a managerial structure for a company that was being made dependent on one man's skill. But since Charlie Wurmstedt had "decided to retire," Brennan said, the move could be made with a minimum of trauma and maximum symbolic effect. The change would facilitate the "melding together" Brennan was calling for at the Challenge Meetings.

Charlie Wurmstedt had no intention of going to Dallas to close down a once-sovereign territory of Sears. He gave his secretary a phone number where he could be reached and went down to his house in Vero Beach, Florida, to be an assistant from there. Brennan called him one day and made him go to Dallas ("Like a little kid," Charlie thought), so he went for a day, and then returned to Vero Beach to wash off the blood.

As tough an old Sears soldier as Charlie Wurmstedt knew himself to be, the experience of being drummed from the corps of his calling injured him deeply. He'd only tried to help fix Sears in a manner he'd been taught to defend as right and honorable and good for all of a career. He believed in the defense of the Field, and he believed things would get better if they would just do what Sears used to do a little bit better, but all of it had been played out over the last few years under the pall of constant failure. The same strong ego that Charlie knew had propelled him from job to job at Sears—probably a few jobs higher than he should have traveled—was in shreds by the end of 1980. He felt utterly dispossessed from the only real home he had ever had. For all those years of wandering from town to town, Sears was home, and even though he knew where he'd be for a while, and finally had a chance to slow down and rest, for the longest time Charlie Wurmstedt couldn't sleep at all.

As the November 28 deadline approached, the veterans could be seen huddled together in little groups around the Tower. In the lunchrooms of the five territorial headquarters there was much warm talk of the golden years of unceasing growth, and bitter conversation about how needless all of the pain and contention of the last two years now seemed. An article in the Tower newspaper quoted a consultant who specialized in retirement issues on "the switch from the work ethic to the freedom ethic" the new retirees would have to face. "Suddenly," the consultant advised, "they can eat breakfast at ten A.M. if they feel like it, and they become insecure and lost. For the first time, they have to organize their own time."

There was an insidious self-sacrificial aspect to Ed Telling's inducement to his own generation that came up often during the discussion. The ERIP, Telling kept repeating, would "minimize to the greatest possible degree the necessity for layoffs." It was as if Ed was asking his own generation to purge itself from the ranks out of loyalty, for the good of the corporate commonwealth—like aged Eskimos set willingly adrift on an ice floe.

It became clear as the final day of decision approached that all the observers of the original corkboards who'd tossed a dollar in the pot two months earlier had missed the number of early retirees by miles. Instead of the upper estimate of five hundred executive retirees that IBM's experience suggested, some 1,484 senior executives—60 percent of those eligible—signed up to take advantage of the program. Far from the planned expense of the ERIP, the fourth quarter would show an extraordinary charge of another $45 million. Altogether, nearly $77 million would be requ.red to pay off the generation that would leave Sears together on a single day at the end of December.

Save a few holdouts like Ed Telling and Joe Moran, the leading representatives of an entire generation—the "lost generation," as it was known in the Tower by the time the acceptances were totaled up—chose to retire. Along with Charlie Meyer, Jack Kincannon, Jack Kelly, and Chuck Wurmstedt, the man now known throughout the company as "Tinkerbell," Gar Ingraham, decided to leave for the mountains of Colorado. The old baron of credit, Linden Wheeler, whose power had so amazed the Hay consultants when they first began to study the private society of Sears, was leaving. So was Vince Graham, Jim Button's once-indispensable numbers man. The chief corporate attorney, Lloyd McLellan, would retire to a home in California just a few fairways away from John Lowe. The corporate treasurer under Jack Kincannon was leaving, as was the vice-president of international operations, the vice-president of logistics, the vice-president of data processing, and the buying-organization apostle in charge of recreational merchandise. The personnel record cards that belonged to thirteen of the senior officers with terms of service between thirty and forty-four years—their service records reading as they did like cross-country railway schedules—would be stamped "Vol. Retirement (ERIP)." Eleven store managers in the Los Angeles group alone elected to leave, as did some twenty-one managers in the Headquarters product-testing laboratory. They were all going to leave together, just as they'd arrived.

"It's sunrise, not sunset," Ed Telling told someone from the press. "It's a rejuvenated company."

Ed Brennan would continue to contend, as he always had, that people never really leave Sears, Roebuck. Retirement was just the next stage of the company life. But the spectacle of so many farewell parties, so many boxes full of shiny loving cups, plaques, certificates, and all the other evidences of thousands of collective years of service to the institution lining the halls, looked to most observers like an exodus. For every one of them who felt dispossessed, there was one who felt relieved—

delivered from fear and sadness and the implication that you've grown too old. One retiree told *Sears Today*: "In my mind was the image of a big black door opening up . . . [revealing] blue sky and undulating green grass, and I thought, *'There,* the door to freedom.' "

Among the leavers were some of the company's very best, and probably some of the worst, but there was little doubt that the early retirees included residents of Sears who had taken the recent spiral of failure, the internecine warfare, and the reign of management by fear most personally. They were the ones who felt that they'd labored a lifetime creating something much better than all of that.

Not long before he left, Jack Kelly had received a phone call from Ed Telling. "Wanna go down and visit the Louisville group today, Jack," Telling said. "While we're down there, I want to look at their catalog operation. Come on down and meet me in the garage in ten minutes."

There wasn't much of a catalog operation at all in Louisville, Kentucky, but Kelly still went downstairs. He was surprised to find Joe Moran and Charlie Wurmstedt waiting in the garage too. When Telling arrived, the men drove out to Midway, got into a Sears jet, and were met in Louisville by the local group manager, as was the custom.

Telling instructed the group man to drive to the racetrack, where they all shared a long lunch and watched Joe Moran drop $150 on the horses before heading back to the plane. Jack Kelly never forgot how happy Moran seemed that day, or how relaxed Charlie Wurmstedt acted. Telling was as inscrutable as ever, but even Ed seemed at peace. There was something about the four of them—Telling, Jumpin' Joe, Wurmy, and himself—veterans several times over, goofing off together on a weekday afternoon, that he would always remember as an appropriate goodbye. Kelly sensed that Joe Moran and Ed Telling both knew that by staying on past December of 1980 they were in some essential way being left behind.

For his part, Jack Kelly was toasted at a brief going-away party before he joined his lost generation on December 31. On his Christmas cards that year, Kelly decided to include a phrase from an old spiritual. Under the printed lines of holiday greeting to his friends and former colleagues he wrote in his own hand, "Free at last."

Part II

The

CHANGES

. . . there is nothing more difficult to take in hand, more perilous to conduct, or more uncertain in its outcome, than to take the lead in introducing a new order of things. Because the innovator has for enemies all those who have done well under the old conditions, and lukewarm defenders in those who may do well under the new.

—*Machiavelli*

CHAPTER 12

The Great American Company

E d Brennan was president of Sears, Roebuck for only eight months. On January 1, the day after the departure of the early retirees, Ed Telling took Brennan's title as his own. Telling had decided to reconstitute the organization as something not unlike a holding company. A small "corporate" entity would preside over the three discrete businesses—the small Seraco Real Estate Group, the Allstate Insurance Group, and the Sears Merchandise Group—each of them run by a chairman and chief executive officer who would report to Telling. The old "twin offices" of the Sears chairman and president, along with the later office of the chairman configuration, would cease to exist.

The possibility of creating a structure in which the "Parent" was a corporate office, instead of one pole of a bifurcated merchandise company that happened to have a $6-billion insurance subsidiary on the side, was discussed during Arthur Wood's tenure, but Wood had decided the idea would never be tolerated by the merchants. Sears, Roebuck was the world's premier merchandising establishment, and the rest of the business entities bore at best a marsupial relationship to the true Sears.

But Telling's decree meant that the chairman of Sears would no longer run the merchandise company, and that the merchants would no longer run the corporation. Ed Brennan would continue to struggle with the retailer as a chairman moved down from the pinnacle. He would henceforth be chairman and chief executive officer of the merchandise group. The operative phrase used by Purcell and others on the sixty-eighth floor who'd helped design the reorganization was that the merchants had been "restructured down," leaving the chairman free, Purcell explained that winter, to "build the company."

From the perspective of the embattled merchants, the idea of Ed Telling building the corporation—whatever that was supposed to mean—was difficult to fathom, since, from most of their perspectives, the chairman, president, and chief executive officer of one of the largest corporations in the world had simply disappeared. One school within the internal populace held that Telling was rarely visible because he refused to leave the thinly populated beige cocoon of the sixty-eighth floor. Some said the chairman had receded into the company of Phil Purcell, there to plot new corporate adventures. There were rumors throughout 1980 and the early days of 1981 that he was down at his summer place in Florida. Some employees who'd heard the stories of Telling putting the entire Eastern Territory on auto-pilot and going home to do yard work contended that Telling never came to work at all anymore—like Howard Hughes.

There was a definitive sighting one morning when Telling showed up in the corporate archives on the fortieth floor and asked to see one of the official phone books from the early 1970s. He found the page that described the unquestioned authority of each territorial vice-president of his turf, and reports indicated Telling began to chuckle.

The planner, Phil Purcell, was still far more visible than the chairman, though young Phil's internal image as boy-architect of the new, and chief proponent of a thoroughly scientific manner of merchandising, had faded away even before the arrival of Brennan. He'd retained only his disconcerting status as an outsider within the inner sanctum, and he dwelled there as a constant reminder of Ed Telling's capacity for grand gestures. From the moment he'd come on board, Purcell had labored under a private mandate from Ed Telling to think about entirely new directions for the company, but since this separate charge was still a well-protected secret in early 1981, people wondered whatever happened to Phil, too.

As was observed of others who spent time with Telling, Purcell had begun to walk like the chairman, and the two held their mouths in a similar hard-set grimace when they lumbered, all loose-jointed and tall, down the sixty-eighth-floor hallways together. At thirty-seven Phil still had his sparkling schoolboy's smile, and at times he still exploded with a country-boy laugh so unconventionally loud and uninhibited by the standards of other corporate executives that it could make those of lesser rank or pedigree feel at ease.

For all his acknowledged brilliance, Purcell had gained a reputation within Sears for being somewhat distracted and disorganized. His desk was invariably a mess; his shirt tails often billowed up above his belt; he forgot his keys or grabbed the wrong set with regularity, and he would occasionally disconnect people on the telephone by mistake. During his early days, Phil impressed his absentmindedness upon several senior merchandise officers when, on a company jet that was halfway to California, he informed the others that he'd forgotten his suit coat. A radio call had to be made so that someone could meet the plane with a blue, pin-striped jacket that fit the corporate planner.

When Phil Purcell did concentrate his mind on something, however, he became, in the heroic vernacular of the business culture of the early 1980's, "scary" or "scary smart." Once his sights were trained on an issue, he appeared incapable of forgetting a single pertinent numeral, almost like a machine. It was at these times that he would cut off people talking to him as soon as he knew what they were trying to say. He would interrupt, saying "correct" or "wrong," and then move on to the next item of business. He had a habit of reading reports in front of the author with a red pencil in his hand, thoroughly marking up the memo during the first scan, and then handing it back across his desk without looking up.

There were notable exceptions, but veterans as prickly as Charlie Wurmstedt and Joe Moran figured Phil was all right. He might have acquired an elite education not available to most of the people he worked with, but he did adorn his office with cowboy art like a Field soldier, and after a few perfect Manhattans, the kid with the M.B.A. could hee-haw with the best of them.

But Phil never approved of the way so many Sears people made work and friendship the same thing, so, like Telling, he made it a point never to socialize with his colleagues. He and his wife, Anne, and the six boys stayed close to home in the pleasant North Shore suburb of Wilmette, where the family had settled when Phil was twenty-two. He was never the greatest Catholic, but when he was in town he would always join the family for mass at Saint Francis Parish in Winnetka, the suburb north of Wilmette. Purcell was raised Catholic among all his Mormon friends and relatives in Salt Lake City because his Mormon mother agreed to do so in order to marry Evan Purcell, Phil's Irish Catholic father. Purcell's mother was hospitalized when Phil was five years old, and she died when he was eight.

Evan Purcell showed up on the sixty-eighth floor to visit his son at work one afternoon, and word passed around the corridors that if you wanted to shake the hand of a man who might well be the only living *father* of a Sears, Roebuck and Company officer, the fellow could be found down the hall in Phil's office. Most everyone came by that day to meet the former insurance agent in from Salt Lake City. The senior

Purcell had carried much of the insurance purchased by Brigham Young University for twenty years. The Mormons were like that, Phil believed. For twenty years they gave a Catholic their business because he could do it better, but the moment age slowed him down, they took it away. It was tough, but Phil always thought it just.

The importance of taking responsibility for your actions and accepting the results of your shortcomings was a philosophical preoccupation of Phil's. He'd read widely in the work of the existentialist philosophers, where he found corroboration of his belief that people are a part of anything they do, that you are personally responsible for any and all "terrible mistakes" you make. Much of the effort within large organizations Phil had studied appeared to derive from a desire to avoid responsibility for errors, when the only justification for a large organization was the collective desire to make a material impact on the world. Making an impact, as the existentialists instructed, was imperative. Making an impact, in Phil's book, was the very purpose of work.

Purcell respected Ed Telling's contempt for the strain of well-bred Sears executive the General had bequeathed the company, because Telling understood that the elite managers "didn't really care about making a difference." It was like the guys back at McKinsey, who created nothing and contributed only *critiques* on real life. "If you're gonna run something, run something important," Purcell would say.

With his rigorous standards of action, Purcell never would have come to Sears if destroying the old system had been his sole mission. The destruction by itself would scarcely have advanced his dream of somehow harnessing the prosaic power he had first sensed within Sears during his time of wandering through the company for McKinsey. He wanted to direct that great force outward to create something new. Purcell had come to Sears because back in 1977 Ed Telling had told him that, during his tenure as chairman of the board, he was determined to go beyond cashiering company kings and breaking the spell of the past at Sears. Telling said he believed that even if the merchandise company was rejuvenated, the Sears empire could not retain its incomparable position above almost all other companies by relying solely on existing businesses. Telling believed Sears needed entirely new reasons for being. He said he wanted to retether the company to a more viable realm of the culture, and if that meant Sears should move, with all its financial power and resources, into an entirely new but growing sector of the economy—if that meant changing Sears so profoundly that it looked like something else when he was through—than that was what they would do. He told the thirty-four-year-old consultant that if he joined up with Sears, he would be central to his plans.

So all along, throughout all the days of bitter conflict during his first two years in office, Phil Purcell was quietly directing the work of a small group of "draft choices" he'd drawn from various research groups within the corporation. The group resided officially within his 702-P planning staff under the seemingly innocuous title "resource allocation." The small team dwelled among code names, unmarked folders, and shredding machines. Several researchers' wives were unaware of what their husbands were up to, despite the regular arrival of documents mailed, for security reasons, to their homes from corporations and other organizations located all over the world.

After first taking an objective look at the general merchandise and insurance businesses, and trying to project the state of both industries in 1990, Purcell's resource allocators were asked to consider the creation of a "third leg" of Sears. Ed Telling came to his chairmanship unsuspecting of the drift and dissension that would mark his early years of leadership, but from the beginning he sensed that the march of his generation's Searsmen across the map of the country had not so much slowed as simply come to the physical borders of the known world. The next battles would have to be fought on new planes, over new beachheads, and in a much different way. Phil Purcell and his secret team were therefore instructed to ponder both the possibility of sprouting a new business endeavor from existing resources, and the more radical and un-Sears-like idea of buying other corporations so large and different from Sears that the old retailer would be reconstituted as something completely new.

The original corporate strategic-planning committee Telling called together during the spring of 1978 was composed of Telling, Jack Kincannon, Charlie Meyer, Archie Boe (Allstate's veteran chairman), and Phil Purcell.

Telling told Phil Purcell his first hurdle would be to convince this tiny but powerful committee of corporate elders that the future was bleak enough to warrant substantial new ventures. By the mid-1970s, Sears researchers were collecting data showing that the company's domination of American merchandising had peaked backed in 1969, that there were simply too many stores in America to allow them to grow, and that these newfangled operations like K mart and the small specialty retailers in the malls represented serious competitive threats, but the warnings rarely made it to the sixty-eighth floor, and if they did the signs went universally unheeded. But as the internal armies of Sears grew bellicose and the business sagged, Purcell came to the little luncheons Telling convened that spring prepared to break through the wall of pride he'd observed as a McKinseyman.

By the late 1970s, his documentation showed the further loss of market penetration, the ravaging effect of Sears' erratic pricing and internal upheavals on the company's image, and the fact of the entire corporation's hypersensitivity to changes in interest rates because of the powerful business cycles that dominate the selling of goods. Retailing goods on a large scale had become one of the least profitable endeavors within the nonagricultural economy. The all-important margins in mass retailing were never meant to be enormous—volume compensated for that—but margins were shrinking all the time now, and the merchandise operation could expect no more than a 3-percent difference between the cost and profit of doing business. Back in January of 1932, Sears executives decided to spend millions of Depression-era dollars rehabilitating urban slums, a charitable gesture, officials of the time noted, because the project promised a return to the company of no more than the same 3 percent in profit margin.

The statistics revealed that whereas 80 or 90 percent of the profits had once come from the venerable art of selling goods, the actual profits that came to corporate Sears by the end of the 1970s were around 75 percent derived from various services, like installation, credit extension, or the provision of insurance. The rise of the two-income family had contributed heavily to the shift of disposable income from goods to services, and the trend was exacerbated by the fact that the America that Sears served was getting older.

In 1968, 9.6 percent of the population was over sixty-five. Only ten years later, that figure had increased to 11 percent of the populace. There was still plenty of wealth around—a vast net-worth buildup had occurred as each generation bequeathed the accumulated gifts of their life's work and savings to their children—but each time Purcell met with the tiny strategic-planning committee during the early days of Ed Telling's reign, he would hammer away again at the fact that the number of bread-and-butter customers available to Sears was being chiseled away.

"The sales are shifting to people forty-five years old," he'd argue. "The guy who walks in and says he's just had his first kid and just bought his first house, and he needs a washer, dryer, and a lawn mower, and tools— the Sears core customer—there are just going to be fewer of him in 1995. As night follows day, no matter how good we are, it's just going to be more difficult to make money."

Purcell reported to the committee that the state of Allstate and the property-casualty insurance industry wasn't very bright either. The insurer had indeed doubled its sales during several years of growth during the 1950s and 1960s, but the number of policies in force never kept pace with premium increases. The back-to-back industry-wide rate increases of some 20 percent during 1975 and 1976 had assisted significantly Allstate's stellar late-1970s performance, but premiums could only be raised so high before policyholders took flight. Though the gross premium returns for Allstate were still growing at rates just over 10 percent, arch-rival State Farm Mutual's growth rate was just under 20 percent per year. Allstate was a wealthy, strongly capitalized company, but it was still at risk. Phil Purcell would become quite animated as he attempted to apprise the strategic-planning committee members of this fact: "You wanna have a profitable insurance company?" he'd ask. "Well, it ain't gonna grow any faster—it just won't. There's nothing in the world you can do to grow into 10 percent of the market except cut prices. You've got total geographic coverage in this business. You've got total policy coverage. You aren't gonna grow; you're just riding the cycles."

Purcell and his research team spent a lot of time studying cycles during the early months of their assignment. Merchants live so completely within the span of various economic cycles that most regard them as fatalistically as they do the weather. Every Sears merchant knew that an economic slump would dampen the big-appliance business, but because people would try to put off buying new cars during periods of economic stress, the countercyclically situated automotive department would sell loads of DieHard batteries and other replacement parts. "If we can't sell refrigerators," the General declared once, "we can still sell baby chicks." Until the early 1970s, chirping little chicks continued to be sold in many Sears stores, and it was a rare store manager of the old order who could resist giving the messy job of throwing away the dead chicks and cleaning the coops on Monday mornings to his college-boy trainees.

There was already an internal cyclical symmetry between Allstate and Sears. If a hurricane came on shore in Texas, Allstate's claims awards were strongly affected—as were local Sears stores' chain-saw and tool sales, which inevitably soared. But the plethora of cycles, waves, and trends now buffeting corporate performance were not being adequately offset. The relatively small real-estate subsidiary capitalized to some extent on the raging inflation of recent times, but its harvest did little to offset inflation's injury to the retail wing. Sears was an utterly labor-intensive enterprise at a time when microchips were giving less populated businesses a distinct competitive edge. Demographic changes were moving people and their money in new directions, and, as Purcell demonstrated to the committee in report after report, Sears was not situated in the path of enough of them.

The committee's exercise in negativity, carried out as it was against the backdrop of decline and painful dysfunction in the Merchant, indicated quite clearly that some form of business diversification was needed. Even Jack Kincannon agreed that Sears should try to move to the other side of the curve, to sprout some line of business that was sure to be growing in the 1990s.

For Kincannon, and, to a slightly lesser extent, for Charlie Meyer, there was never any question about the source of such a new endeavor. One of the inviolable propositions spoke directly to the issue: Sears went outside its boundaries no more for new business ventures than it did for new talent. If people didn't want to saw wood with their arms anymore, the guys in the lab would put a motor on the blade for them. If their ice cubes looked too big, Sears invented a machine that would crack them into little pieces.

Allstate had grown up as a corporate offspring from a meager $300,000 investment in the idea that people accumulated enough valuable automobile stock to be interested in protecting it. The shopping-center development wing was home-grown, and the company had reaped huge dividends over the years from the buyers' efforts to combine small companies or acquire an equity interest in new businesses, or start factories from scratch with Sears seed money. When home building looked like a hot business early in the century, Sears began a "Modern Homes" division that sold beautiful assemble-yourself houses through the catalog until the operation was closed down during the 1930s. When it was decided that the retailing of books was a good business, Sears moved into it by agency of "The People's Book Club," an organization that employed a "People's Jury" to select books that were then listed in a magazine sent to subscribers called *The People's Choice.* The company founded the powerful Chicago radio station WLS (World's Largest Store), in order to communicate better with its rural clientele (the station was eventually sold off).

As for mergers and acquisitions, the General toyed with the idea of merging Sears with Montgomery Ward and subsequently with J. C. Penney during the combination-mad days of the late 1920s and early 1930s, but nothing ever came of it. Sears did own the *Encyclopædia Britannica* for a while, but the idea of buying up going concerns ran strongly against the grain.

"We should tend to the hearth, *lares et penates,*" Charlie Meyer declared to the committee with his careful New England diction. "Sears grows from within." The dictum was rooted deep in corporate pride. No other company could possibly match the separateness and moral force of Sears; none other, in short, could ever understand.

Raised as he was away from the Parent, Allstate's Archie Boe wasn't bothered by the idea of acquiring another corporation. Boe was a diminutive Iowa farm boy who spoke with a palpable twang. He was known to have a wife who thought Sears, Roebuck retail stores were without question the least exciting places she'd ever seen, and, for his part, Archie believed the merchants—with their tradition of growth only through the physical expansion of stores and improvement only through doing the same things a bit better—had been heading toward a fall for years. But Boe tended to keep his prognostications to himself. "I'll run my company, and you run yours," Sears Chairman Gordon Metcalf had once told Archie. "But don't you ever dare put your foot in our mouths. 'Cause if you do, we're gonna get ourselves a new boy."

Boe's bean counters worked out of a massive headquarters complex north of Chicago. Five thousand of Allstate's forty thousand employees worked there amid 122 manicured acres of grass, trees, long clean hallways, cutting-edge computer technology, and a progressive management atmosphere that was tuned regularly by ever-present management consultants.

Archie was a relative sophisticate in his knowledge of other businesses, in part because Allstate possessed a tremendous diversified investment portfolio as well as sophisticated computer-driven models that ordered the management of their $7 billion in invested capital. The models were cooked up out at Allstate's private think tank located near Stanford University in northern California. The insurer even had an aggressive venture-capital division that had provided seed money for hundreds of small companies, including notable success stories like Federal Express and the Control Data Corporation.

Boe arrived at one early strategic-planning meeting and suggested to Telling that, in the spirit of their ongoing discussions, Allstate should purchase the successful commercial insurance company of Crum & Forster.

"No," said Jack Kincannon. "That's no way to use Sears, Roebuck capital."

"It's Allstate's capital," Boe said as Telling looked on. "Besides, we'd be buying a company with capital, transferring our capital."

But Jack was death on the subject, so the Crum & Forster idea was passed by.

During 1978, a cigar-chomping veteran securities analyst named David Williams who was working with Sears Investment Management, the corporate unit that cared for the Sears Pension Fund money, had just completed a computerized analysis of a wide range of American industries. The analysis divided various industries in terms of the potential effect of external economic changes on sales, growth, and debt. Williams' report was essentially an exercise in what economists call "rational maximizing," the effort to derive higher gains from capital investment. The project was designed only to enhance the value of the profit-sharing-fund investment portfolio, so Williams was confused when the new planning officer called him to ask for a copy.

It was only after Purcell had drafted Dave Williams into his elite resource-allocation unit and asked him to write a paper called "Criteria for Diversification" that he understood that the new planning officer wanted to move Sears toward a level of investment the company had never experienced before. Apparently, Purcell and Telling had in mind nothing short of a full-scale corporate shopping spree. The "Criteria for Diversification" document Williams wrote called, not surprisingly, for endeavors that promised high levels of growth and profit into the 1990s, but it also stated that a new business venture for Sears should in some way relate to the corporation's strengths. Any suitable acquisition should be—if not already the biggest and the best in a given business sector— then at least a company that would quickly become the biggest, the best, and the most popularly revered, given the addition of Sears, Roebuck's reputation, money, and power.

The committee never formally abandoned the assumption that Sears could only grow from within—Jack Kincannon saw to that—but the concept of diversification through acquisition was actively entertained during meetings. Archie Boe put the thought of buying Allstate a life-insurance company on the table, but when Purcell's analysts did the numbers, it was discovered that the better life companies were selling at huge premiums over their book values in comparison with other businesses. Archie liked Lincoln National, but it might have cost over $500 million, and Boe had to agree that Allstate could develop its life-insurance wing internally much less expensively. Boe conducted research independently on what he still referred to as the "motor-car" business, but the rest of the committee was against the direction, despite Boe's assertion that the American Motors Corporation could be had for a mere $80 million and might well be rejuvenated simply by association with the Sears name.

Charlie Meyer weighed in with a proposal to acquire Wendy's, the fast-food chain. Meyer argued that Wendy's was cyclically counter to Sears' other businesses because people tend to buy more cheap food when money is tight. It was a cash business, as opposed to the credit-intensive Merchant. Phil Purcell was enthusiastic about the idea, but Ed Telling curtailed further investigation. After muttering something about having to feed and clean up after hundreds of baby chicks when he was an assistant manager in the stores, Telling was heard to say, "We're just not gonna have anything to do with food or manure."

There was a short pause before the committee moved on to its next item of business.

The more general idea of joining forces with another corporation, however, was beginning to captivate Telling to the point of preoccupation. As soon as the idea of combining Sears with another big, powerful, famous, and rigorously moral company came up during one of Telling's long discussions with Phil Purcell behind the big closed door on 68, the chairman didn't appear interested in hearing much more at all about the hallowed tradition of growing from within. After one discussion of the sort of ideals and ethical values the "third leg of the stool" would have to possess, Purcell said, "You know where we're headed with this? What we really want to create is nothing less than . . . the Great American Company. We probably should stop even considering any corporation for acquisition that doesn't fit that imagery."

"The Great American Company," Telling said with pleasure. "Yes."

So, as the merchants of Sears gazed back upon lost glory while they fell into warring factions and watched their customers leave them during 1978, the chairman of the board and his young aide spent time alone constructing the towering image of a new monument. Telling and Purcell drew up a list of corporations that in combination with Sears, Roebuck could render an organizational apotheosis of solid American values and strength. The list included IBM, AT&T, Walt Disney Productions, Standard Oil of California (which most everyone in the world but Ed Telling had agreed to call "Chevron" a few years earlier), and the Illinois-based farm-equipment manufacturer Deere & Company. The Great American Company template became a means of strategic analysis far more powerful than the technical data researchers fed to Phil Purcell. The true "fit" between Sears and some of the eligible great companies existed only in metaphors and images, most of them resident in the mind of Ed Telling.

Even Archie Boe was shocked when Phil Purcell came into a strategic-planning committee meeting convened in Florida during 1978 and said that he and Telling wanted to buy John Deere. Purcell and his team had been looking hard at the agribusiness sector, and a fellow expert in the ways of the tractor business had already addressed the small committee, but the idea of taking over Deere was unsettling. "If you are going to make a major investment in American greatness," Purcell argued, "you ought to go to an area in which America is assured of winning out on a global scale. America is going to win big in agriculture."

Research indicated that the two Great American Companies that would continue to dominate agriculture-related business sectors through the end of the century, and were also sufficiently large to be worthy of becoming the third leg of Sears, were the secretive, privately owned grain company called Cargill, and the traditionally well-managed farm-implement manufacturing company Deere & Company.

Closely held Cargill was run out of a high-security headquarters located in a forest in Minnesota, a state with a well-known special connection to the historical Sears. But Deere was run out of a rust-colored headquarters set amid the farmland near Moline, Illinois, the "farm implement capital of the world," and a place not unlike Telling's home town of Danville. Named for its founder, John Deere, the inventor of the steel plow, 141-year-old Deere was in the process of selling over $4 billion worth of farm and industrial machinery during 1978. It would draw from that revenue around $265 million in profit—a margin twice that realized by the Sears merchants. Deere operated factories throughout the Midwest, as well as in Canada, Europe, and South America, and some of them were by far the most futuristic industrial facilities in the industry. Deere had managed to become a low-cost producer while maintaining a huge network of dealerships throughout rural America, most of which were regarded by the citizens of farming regions with the sort of respect and loyalty those same people still accorded Sears. Deere had put as much distance between its own performance and that of tired old International Harvester as Sears had placed between itself and tired old Montgomery Ward. Reports indicated the internal culture of the company was hokey, fetishistic about honesty and fair play, and, though it wouldn't have seemed possible, almost as inbred as Sears.

The thought of putting together two of the most powerful and folksy institutions in the world was plainly moving to Ed Telling, and the idea of putting the consummately American companies together at a time when it would cause the public spotlight to move away from the merchandising debacle made the thought that much more attractive. Telling couldn't stop thinking about the Great American Company. His voice would take on dreamy, reverent tones when he said it—"The Great American Company"—just as Ed Brennan's voice changed when he uttered the word "store."

Telling decided to authorize Purcell to plan a friendly approach to Deere, and he told him to also direct the planning department to do a workup on the idea of buying Disney too. Sears, Disney, and Deere—the very concept was historic. Old Walt Disney would have seen the beauty of the combination. The Disney founder had collected one of the finest libraries of Sears, Roebuck Catalogs ever brought together before he died. The force of Disney's creativity and Sears' incomparable advertising and marketing power had already made the "Winnie the Pooh" apparel line a great success for both companies.

The beauty of both ideas was lost, however, on Jack Kincannon, who from the beginning said he didn't like the idea of taking Deere because they had too much outstanding debt.

"They have all that paper on purpose, Jack," Archie Boe said. "It's in a separate finance company; it's not that they need it."

Since Kincannon's position on any acquisition was becoming quite clear to the others, very little information about the move toward Deere, and even less information about Disney, was passed his way. But ascertaining information inside Sears was a particular specialty of Jack's, so, just before Kincannon left for a trip to the Far East during the summer of 1978, he discovered that Ed Telling had signed a letter written by Phil Purcell authorizing contact by Sears with the superstar New York merger and acquisition attorney, Joseph Flom. The purpose was an approach to Deere, and the revelation made Jack mad.

Kincannon hadn't been overly impressed by Phil Purcell from the moment he set eyes on the youngster. "Son," Kincannon said when he went to urge Purcell not to send the letter of inquiry on to New York, "just how many acquisitions have you been involved in?"

"Plenty," said Purcell. Phil, not surprisingly, thought Jack was a source and symbol of Sears' problems. He considered the financial officer to be one of the plain meanest men he'd ever met in his life, and he interpreted Kincannon's comments that day he came to his office as overtly threatening.

Phil Purcell recalls that Kincannon said, "From now on you are not to advocate or do anything unless someone first reports to me to find out if I agree with it. Then you will do what I tell you to do. If you don't, I'm going to audit your expenses."

Purcell remembers replying: "When you audit my expense account, you'll find that I basically report nothing other than a hotel room out of town—no lunches, no dinners. . . . Also, if I were your age and your size, I would open the door and get out before you get the living shit kicked out of you, because if you ever threaten me again, that's what's gonna happen."*

As the letter from Telling was being readied, the chairman of Deere & Company, William Hewitt, received a call from a Deere staff attorney informing him that an attorney from Sears had just telephoned to see if Joe Flom was on retainer to Deere. So infamous was Flom as a successful representative of acquiring companies that some large companies retained him so he would *not* be hired by other companies to orches-

---

*Kincannon denies that the confrontation was anything like this. He remembers asking the question about Purcell's previous acquisition experience, and noting to Purcell his "display of poor judgment" vis-à-vis the Deere approach, but he has no recollection of the argument as such.

trate a takeover move against them. The call, while well intentioned, proved ill-advised. Hewitt quickly located his old friend Arthur Wood, who was then in Dallas, and informed the former Sears chairman that the company he and only four others from his family had run for fourteen decades was decidedly uninterested in joining up with Sears.

Prominent among the guidelines under which Purcell and his planners were proceeding was the desire to avoid any hint of a hostile takeover. Only other sorts of corporations did things like that. If Sears was to move into a business realm like farm machinery where it had no operational expertise, alienating the existing management of a target organization could only hurt the cause. Much to Ed Telling's disappointment, the files on John Deere were closed.

Charlie Meyer complained that he was particularly disappointed in the way the approach was handled away from the strategic-planning committee. If Sears wanted to talk to Deere, he would have gladly set up a lunch with his old and similarly well-educated friend Billy Hewitt. Meyer believed the Deere idea was little more than a dream, but all they would have had to do was ask for his help.

Cargill was eventually deemed too impenetrable an organization, and several candidates in the high-profit-margin paper-products industry and others in the energy sector were studied and also set aside. The fields of entertainment and communications were next on the list, especially because of Disney.

The planners studied entertainment delivery systems, specifically the futuristic business of satellite-based television broadcasting. Purcell became interested in making a substantial investment in COMSAT General (a subsidiary of Communications Satellite Corporation), a company that was developing technology designed to make possible the first satellite-to-home integrated television system. Armed with the rudiments of the idea of creating a new high-technology network, possibly in concert with a Sears-owned Disney as a production center, Purcell traveled to Hollywood to find out about the availability of independent programming for such a venture. Phil felt rather overdressed as he listened to Grant Tinker, then the president of ABC, who held forth about his industry in a low-key, candid way while dressed in a sport shirt. Tinker sat beneath a gigantic photograph of Mary Tyler Moore. "What can be said about an industry in which the leading product last week was a piece of trash called 'The Dallas Cowboys Cheerleaders'?" Tinker said.

Purcell returned to the Tower feeling that perhaps the comparatively small but fast-moving entertainment business would never be compatible with the Sears wavelength.

. . .

Ed Telling had been chairman of the board of Sears for two years by the time discussions with COMSAT General progressed to a point where Purcell composed his first diversification proposal for the board of directors. By 1980, Telling's dream of carving his initials into company history by re-creating Sears had been subsumed in countless emergencies and daily humiliations. Terrible sales results, embarrassing annual meetings, bitter infighting, abortive peace conferences, vicious public assaults, the intransigence of Jack Kincannon, and the preoccupation of Phil Purcell and the planning staff with keeping the company from splitting apart for good, had conspired to obscure the secret mandate for change. The failure on both fronts—the sense of having made mistakes and false starts—was particularly painful for Phil Purcell, not only because of the standards he kept for himself, but because he had to watch Ed Telling withdraw further into his "loneliness" and silence with the advent of each new loss. Phil knew the chairman he'd come to help change Sears would never say, "You've failed me." And that made it all the worse.

Purcell believed that, despite Jack Kincannon, the Sears board would still go along with whatever Ed Telling wanted as long as the members were made to believe they'd arrived at the wisdom of the decision themselves. Throughout the months of bringing the board along toward an understanding of the need for diversification, Purcell's strategy had been to make several key board members believe that they alone had been briefed privately about the issue pursuant to one of the six or seven meetings convened each year. As the COMSAT deal neared execution, Purcell approached the long-time board member Edgar Stern to explain the entertainment and communications initiatives he had in mind.

Edgar Stern had considered actually working as an employee at Sears, Roebuck for all of a single afternoon. Julius Rosenwald's grandson was a young boy when his father took him to meet the General and see the Great Works on the West Side. Stern was taken on a lengthy tour of the bustling mail-order plant, but he knew enough about the way of things at Sears to see that he would have to start out a career at the bottom of the organization despite his lineage. As he watched workers rushing about, moving goods between chutes and conveyor belts, he became distinctly aware of the great expanse of his own time that lay between the dirty Victorian warehouse and the General's office in the administration building.

It was then that Edgar Stern decided to become an "investor" of his portion of the considerable fortune that was left over from his grandfather's efforts to give so much of his money away. It turned out that, in his own business dealings, Edgar Stern had dabbled in both entertainment and communications industries and had come away from the experience with the most negative of impressions. When Purcell approached

Stern with the COMSAT and Disney concepts, he was told that, despite its squeaky-clean image, Disney was still part of Hollywood, and Hollywood was simply too "sexy" a scene for Sears. Stern was unalterably and vociferously opposed to even a joint venture with COMSAT, because he felt that the technology of satellite communications was moving too quickly now. Even though Purcell and Telling were largely interested in a new technology delivery system, the company would still have to turn toward the untrustworthy producers of Hollywood to provide products to deliver.

Given the constant public criticism of Telling's leadership, Stern's opposition to the deal at a board meeting could lead to a humiliating scene, so the drawer full of entertainment files was thus closed before the proposals ever came to the board of directors.

The technical team working under Purcell was less than impressed with the Great American Company strategy long before the Disney and COMSAT ideas were put to rest. There was little that Sears could "bring to the game" for a Disney or a John Deere. "They're nice clean family folks like us," Phil Purcell finally agreed, "but what can we do to make them more successful? What would they do for Sears?"

Purcell instructed the resource-allocation group to turn their thinking back to an earlier criterion for diversification, the proposition that any new venture must "leverage off the existing strengths of the company." Purcell asked his scouts to reintegrate the prerequisite with Telling's more emotional call for an entirely new manner of corporate eminence.

The third leg should "drive more business past the existing Sears customer base," as Purcell put it. Three of four Americans still shopped Sears at least once a year. The Sears merchandise researchers in department 720 figured that almost nine of every ten Americans had some sort of business "involvement" with Sears now, if not as a member of one of the thirty-six million families of regular shoppers, or as one of Allstate's twenty million policyholders, then as a more casual user of Sears services.

Any new venture must "leverage off these strengths," instead of chasing some purely romantic conception of American virtue.

A few weeks after the 1980 annual shareholders' meeting, *Roper Reports,* a publication of the well-known polling organization, released a study that placed Sears atop the list of "most trusted American corporations." More than eight of ten Americans still had a favorable opinion of Sears as an institution despite all of the company's troubles. "Sears," Ed Telling had claimed before the audience at the relatively low-keyed annual meeting, "has the largest consumer franchise in the history of the world. All of Sears' operations owe their roots to the trust the American consumer has in our company."

All they had to do was figure out what goods or services Americans would need during the coming decade, preferably items or endeavors enhanced by a powerful sense of public confidence in the institution that provided them. Just as millions upon millions of people woke up each morning with complete confidence that their Sears Kenmore refrigerators had kept the orange juice cold, or that their clothes would become clean and dry because they'd purchased their household machinery from a local Sears, something needed to be found for which dependability and honesty and access would be of paramount concern to the customers.

Telling believed the right idea would come to him in a burst of magic, much as he had conceived the Great American Company, of creating an image possessed of such power that all offerings from the new combine would appear morally superior to the competition.

He finally felt the magic the day Phil Purcell reported to him that a consensus had developed among his planners that there could be no reach of the economy in which the "trust quotient" was more eminently exploitable—with the possible exception of the field of medicine—than in the organized act of storing and caring for people's money.

Maybe Sears could build the third leg by positioning itself in the flight path of the public's money. The "industry" of money had even acquired a new catchall name of late—the financial-services industry. The idea of entering an aspect of the financial world in a powerful way was complemented by the sort of cyclical symmetry that was discussed from the beginning: if people still trusted Sears but weren't buying enough of the Merchant's goods, then they must be socking their money away, or reacting to inflationary times by indulging in speculation.

The tradeoff between consumption and spending had been a subject of discussion inside Sears from the beginning. Richard Sears set up a banking department replete with savings and checking services in 1899. He offered his mail-order customers 5 percent interest on their money, in hopes that if the popular mood shifted toward a desire for more saving and less buying—as it occasionally did, especially during the intermittent financial panics that often beset turn-of-the-century business climates—he could still make some money and keep loyal customers involved with the company until they wanted to spend again. But people were more interested in buying from Dick Sears than saving with him, so he closed down the banking operation in 1903. A few years later the founder thought about trying to sell bonds through the catalog, but nothing ever came of it.

The General turned out to be somewhat of a purist when it came to handling money for the masses. He reluctantly expanded the availability of credit buying to a wider array of Sears goods, while being something of an early "supply-sider" when it came to the theoretical economic interplay between savings and consumption. Wood was singular among industrial captains of his time in that he supported aspects of the New Deal, but he never bought John Maynard Keynes' contention that the industrialized world would rise out of the Great Depression if cash could be cajoled out of personal savings accounts and into the act of consumption. The General explained all this in no uncertain terms to Keynes during a meeting in London during the early 1930s. Wood said government should keep its hands off people's savings and build new factories if it wanted the economies back in gear. The expansion of the industrial web that fed the Sears machine reflected the General's opinion, though the profitability of loaning to customers money that was borrowed at lower than prime rates was hard to ignore. The America Sears, Rosenwald, and General Wood lived in was ultimately about tools and durable clothes and glorious machines, and their company was nothing if not dedicated to what America was about.

For several decades Sears officials had even tried to obscure the fact that the company had become one of the most powerful and pervasive financial institutions in the world. That Sears had become one of the biggest lenders, borrowers, and users of money and other financial vehicles and commitments was thought inimicable both to the homey image of the company as the trusty store full of wrenches and miracle fibers located down the road, and to the spirit of institutional regulation present until quite recently in Washington, D.C.

By 1980, the chairman of the board of Citibank, the irrepressible Mr. Walter Wriston, had been calling Sears "the biggest bank in the country" in public for six or seven years and had for twenty years been warning fellow bankers that it was Sears that would eventually challenge the banks' domination of the financial establishment. In good times Sears made more money on its installment loans than any bank in the country. Allstate was already designed to offer the financial services—involving insurance coverage forms from which banks were proscribed by law—and Wriston contended that Sears was competing inappropriately with banks in light of the spirit of existing laws by offering loans, issuing its own financial instruments like bonds and commercial paper, and beginning to creep into the business of providing mortgages through the nascent Seraco Group. Wriston once confronted

Allstate's Don Craib at a conference in New York City, back when Craib was running Allstate's investment department. The insurance company had just purchased a savings-and-loan company out in California, much to the chagrin of the savings-and-loan and banking industries. "You guys are trying to take over the world," Wriston barked at Craib.

"We can't take over the world," one of Jack Kincannon's aides told the banking expert and author Martin Meyer in 1979. "It's not legally possible."

But by 1980, the legal restrictions on Sears' involvement in money-handling were falling away apace. Congress appeared determined to pass the "Depository Institution Deregulation and Monetary Control Act," the latest in a decade-old series of measures designed to repeal Depression-era restrictions and reintroduce unfettered competition to the once-restrictive business of finance.

From the earliest days of resource-allocation work, Purcell's team wanted to move Sears into a business realm undergoing change. Purcell and Dave Williams believed something unsettling should be happening in a new business environment that would allow Sears to exploit the state of flux. Some observers contended that the traditional business institutions that provide savings, investment, insurance, and other financial services to consumers were in the throes of changes as profound as any witnessed in fifty years.

More important, however, was the way the idea hit Telling. Now that money-handling felt right, Purcell knew it was up to him to validate the chairman's gut instincts with hard numbers. During early 1980, Purcell commissioned SRI International to conduct a customized study of the state of the emergent consumer-oriented financial-services industry. Much of the more aggressive thinking about how to open up the money business had occurred at SRI, the California research institution located not far from the Allstate research center in the suburbs south of San Francisco.

A growing array of hybrid, consumer-oriented financial products that relied on either technological systems or innovative methods of circumventing government regulations had already been devised by the time Sears began working with SRI. The world of high finance had been brought down a bit during the early 1970s, as pioneer product packages figured out how to pool previously elite financial instruments such as short-term commercial paper, and federal funds that sold only in such high minimum denominations (usually $100,000) that only companies or very wealthy individuals could afford them. These new pools of financial instruments, such as the one brought together under the auspices of the Reserve Fund in 1972, were repackaged and retailed to the public in the form of dollar-a-unit "shares" of a "money-market mutual fund" that reflected the underlying pool by paying substantially higher interest rates than government-controlled bank accounts—especially since inflation was driving borrowing rates higher. By 1979, there was some $45.2 billion invested in a wide variety of money funds—up from just under $4 billion only two years earlier.

Among the analysts working at the SRI campus in Menlo Park, California, was the noted financial inventor Andrew Kahr, who, by simply reading the labyrinthine statutes governing banks and other financial institutions in the United States since the era of post-Depression regulation, had already figured out paths around and through legal loopholes that led to new financial products. It was Kahr who'd assisted the brokerage firm Merrill Lynch in the development of a novel way to keep customers' cash in the house after they sold stocks. The Glass-Steagall Banking Reform Act of 1933 prohibited brokerage houses from "taking deposits," but Kahr and his colleagues designed a system by which funds from dividends, securities sales, or other money were "swept" automatically into a connected money-market fund held in the customer's name. The system was hooked together by computers, and it included checking, a margin account, and even a credit card. Merrill Lynch began marketing Kahr's invention in 1977 under the name "Cash Management Account."

Kahr did the work assigned by Purcell. He described the new frontier of financial services as a business sector potentially "cleaner" and more profitable and less labor-intensive than merchandising or insurance. The business appeared all but impervious to foreign participants, and in general an exciting sector from which Sears could "key off its strengths." But Andy Kahr sensed from the beginning that Purcell already knew all of this, and he was reporting to someone who'd already decided that money funds would be the trash compactors of the 1990s, that bond funds and limited partnerships would eventually be arrayed before the American consumer like so many food processors, and that Sears, Roebuck would in one way or another come to dominance in this new marketplace as it had once come to lord over the selling of goods.

Some economists were now auguring a coming growth rate of 15 percent per annum in the $100-billion "savings industry" and nothing beyond 9 percent for growth in consumer spending—this around the same time Ed Brennan took his officers out to the Skyline Country Club in Tucson to figure out how to move the customers' money *out* of savings and into his cash registers.

Just as the American banking industry's reluctance to lend American consumers money for goods led directly to the mammoth credit operations run by auto producers and big stores, the banks had allowed such a huge disparity to develop between what they offered their customers for deposits and the value of that money outside the banks' vaulted portals, that not only were innovative business thinkers creating new products designed to suck the banks' business away, but a spirit of deregulation had arisen that threatened to tear away all of the statutory bulwarks behind which American banks had done their business for many years.

Purcell's early discussions of the idea with the strategic-planning committee were surprisingly upbeat. Jack Kincannon and Charlie Meyer were comfortable with the idea of a financial-services venture. A home-grown enhancement of Sears' involvement in services it already offered made a lot of sense to the veterans. Retailers in general, and Sears in particular, had always moved opportunistically and authoritatively into areas poorly served by others. The boys had sold the hell out of automobile clocks and rear-view mirrors for years before Detroit manufacturers figured out that people wanted them. The idea of profiting from changing legislation was also present in the grand tradition. Sears' and Rosenwald's quick exploitation of congressional creation of the Rural Free Delivery system when they were building the original house was central to the mail-order empire's growth.

But Phil Purcell knew that deep within Sears were built numerous impediments to the sort of entry into financial services he now had in mind. Almost every element of the company's considerable participation in the financial world derived philosophically and technically from the sale of goods. Sears *was* American consumption; the people's cornucopia. Allstate existed to protect people's things; if something happened to your home, the insurers would help you get another and help you restock it at Sears. The corporation's involvement in real estate was predicated solely on building new places for people to shop.

Purcell believed that the real action in financial services was centered in businesses within or connected to the securities brokerage industry, a relatively small business sector—Sears spent more on *advertising* than all but a few brokerage houses in the country made in a year, and Sears corporate sales were larger than the sales of the entire brokerage industry combined. Stock and bond sellers also operated in a morally questionable world, by the General's still-prominent standards, and by any Searsman's standards it was a business realm that existed to cater not to the Sears portion of America—the "middle 80 percent"—but to the very rich. (SRI confirmed the long-held assumption at Sears that there are only around five million "affluent" families in America.) If the corporation could somehow enfranchise some of the "Sears forty million" to become their cash managers, the results would make the turmoil in the old Sears beside the point. But the century-old apotheosis of merchandise that dominated the internal consciousness of the corporation would have to give way if this was ever to occur.

With the help of SRI, Purcell began to draw up a list of consumer-driven, financially oriented businesses that touched people at various points along their "life cycle." It seemed that after buying a home (usually with the help of a bank), insurance, and durable goods (usually with a credit card), most middle-class Americans tended to move into other financial products only as they got older, and by then most of them were extremely unlikely to change bankers or move away from their first securities firm. The trick of Sears' entry into financial services would be to exploit the Sears image to draw elements of the customer base into a web of businesses early in the "cycle" of their lives.

Ed Telling dearly loved the idea of Sears' moving forcefully into the financial-services arena from the moment he heard about it, and he was perfectly happy to take full responsibility for any ruffling of feathers that might occur at the corporate base. The profit potential in moving money like a mass merchant impressed him, but he seemed almost mesmerized by the thought that a diversification effort by Sears aimed at the financial-services industry necessarily entailed an assault on turf controlled by the nation's banks. It just so happened that there was only one thing in the whole world that Ed Telling hated more than a bank—and that was a banker.

All of his life, Telling had agreed with Thomas Jefferson's contention that banking establishments are more dangerous than standing armies. Long after most country boys reared in the populist tradition had given up their mistrust of parasitic lawyers, big-city bureaucrats, and all varieties of local bankers, Telling had retained the prejudice in a pure and inviolate form, refining it slightly with experience over the years. With almost four thousand separate bank accounts in the company name around the country, Sears was possibly the largest single user of the American banking industry, but that didn't mean that Ed Telling had to like a bank.

Some executives who heard Telling rail on about the unmitigated idiocy of rural bankers figured they were hearing echoes of the traditional animosity between the kingpin small-town merchant and the local banker. His observations that bankers were universally "stupid and lazy; people you can never find when you need them and who are always there when you don't want them around," sounded much like the age-old accusations by merchants, who were conversely thought by bankers to be unsophisticated, sly, arbitrary in their practices, and irresponsible with the borrowed capital given them by local banks.

Telling knew the truth about bankers because he was "just a small-town banker's son" himself. He knew that getting a loan in America was "pure hell." He knew that banks don't trust consumers ("never have and never will"), and that savings-and-loan institutions only loaned everyday people money " 'cause they're statutorily required to do so."

Big banks were just little ones in pinstripes, in Telling's estimation, and because of the way inflation was devaluing money and due to the shaky state of many of the large-money-center banks' foreign-loan port-folios in 1980, the chairman noted that the general public and the press were beginning to join him in his lifelong convictions. A poll conducted by *Newsweek* magazine showed that public confidence in the banking establishment had plummeted from a 60-percent confidence rating to just 46 percent in a single year. Telling also liked the fact that over $100 billion that used to be in mattresses, socks, and passbook savings accounts had been transferred into money funds by the middle of 1980. Telling thought that all the banks ever had going for them was the shelter of protective legislation, a big customer base, and a considerable credibility with most consumers. They never did have a bit of marketing expertise.

Sears, on the other hand, could bring things to market like no other institution in the world when the machinery was in gear. As soon as Telling realized that legal changes and financial innovation had rendered it possible for a company that wasn't chartered as a bank to act like a bank anyway, he felt the magic he had been longing for in silence for quite a while. For the first time since he'd taken what he occasionally called "this goddamned job," Ed Telling saw light in the distance.

The merchandise business's sorry state only steeled Telling's resolve to move, even if it meant getting into businesses that would seem designed to siphon more money away from merchandising at precisely the moment the old Sears could least handle the loss. Sears was an institution of such size that it could have raised almost unlimited investment capital on its deathbed, if it came to that.

During the August 1980 Challenge Meeting, the Allstater Don Craib was recruited to be a vice-chairman in part so he could help engineer the move into money. Craib had been instrumental in the development of the venture-capital wing, and at one point had turned a chunk of Allstate capital into a 20-percent interest in a large West Coast real-estate brokerage house.

In October of 1980, Telling decided to tell *The Wall Street Journal* that he sensed "a very big financial future for Sears." The chairman revealed, in the same front-page *Journal* piece that opened with Jack Kincannon's parting blast at Ed Telling, that Sears strategic planners were even considering a move into businesses such as stock brokerage and personal finance. The *Journal* also quoted Purcell: "There is no reason why someone shouldn't go into a Sears store and buy a shirt and coat, and then maybe some stock. I don't consider that any more outrageous than the first idea, like that someone might buy a coat and tie and then buy auto insurance. . . . Any idea how preposterous Allstate sounded in 1934?"

Though Telling hinted otherwise in the article, Jack Kincannon and fellow strategic-planning committee member Charlie Meyer joined the ERIP exodus firmly convinced that they'd helped render the idea of Sears' buying another large corporation a "dead issue." To the veteran Searsmen, buying a company full of people who could never understand the meaning of Sears was like hiring mercenaries to fight your wars. Hired guns never fought in the right spirit. It was no accident that mercenaries were involved in the later battles of dying empires.

Both Charlie and Jack believed the Sears planning establishment was committed to "growing its own" financially oriented lines of business under the aegis of the consolidated operating group they'd given the name "Seraco" during 1980.

The Seraco misadventure was begun during the dark March of 1979, when Telling assigned a task force to look at the future of Sears in the real-estate business. The task force was chaired by the outsider Preston Martin, a Californian with a Ph.D. in economics and a love of all things Italian, who'd entered the corporate fold via Allstate's acquisition of his pioneering mortgage-insurance company in 1973. Allstate pumped $25 million into Martin's San Francisco–based company, PMI, which was one of several private mortgage-insurance companies created to provide high-risk real-estate customers with the chance to obtain a mortgage loan.

Before the acquisition, Press Martin was the California savings-and-loan commissioner under Governor Ronald Reagan and then chairman of the Federal Home Loan Bank Board under Richard Nixon. He'd been instrumental in the passage of legislation that formed the Federal Home Loan Mortgage Corporation (known as "Freddie MACS") and was widely considered the father of the trend toward low-down-payment real-estate purchases made possible by the backing of private mortgage insurance. The mortgage-insurance business was the sort of extra-bank innovation brought forth in the name of the consumer of modest means (and at the expense of the public image of banks) that intrigued Ed Telling. Martin had a variable reputation as an administrator, but PMI still turned in a 15-percent return on equity. And his background in deregulatory activities made him a logical choice to run the financial-services and real-estate operations under the consolidation and corporate restructuring that became effective the first day of 1981.

Seraco was to bring together the third-largest shopping-center developer in Homart; the California savings-and-loan Allstate purchased in 1976, now the seventh-largest in the state; the small mortgage-insurance operation previously owned by Martin; and Allstate's $50 million worth of varied real-estate investments. Martin began to hire talent away from various segments of the real-estate business, much of it coming not from the institutional development sector but from the world of retail selling. Taking a cue from Purcell's commitment to somehow driving more kinds of business past the customer base, Martin's team began to write a plan by which a big player like Sears could move into a business that had always been composed of small, local real-estate agencies or franchise agglomerations.

Telling took the strategic-planning committee away to a Napa Valley resort in northern California, away from the dark cloud that had descended upon the merchandise business in March of 1980. The order of business at the wine-country retreat included a discussion of "the year 2000" for Sears. There the tall, self-assured Martin delivered the long-awaited report his team of hired experts had prepared. It was an impressive presentation that included a proposal to develop an in-house "Century 21–type real-estate franchise system."

But the Napa Valley meeting turned out to be Press Martin's high point at Sears. The small mortgage-insurance business, which had enriched Martin by some $5 million when he sold it, was in the process of losing fully 3 percent of its market share in a little over a year. Losses were pouring in at a rate well over a million dollars per week. It was then recalled on the sixty-eighth floor that under Martin's direction PMI had "plunged" into risky second-mortgage insurance policies. It was remembered that Archie Boe and others at Allstate had "held Preston's hand" the entire time he ran PMI, such were the man's innumerable managerial deficiencies. The fellow was a plunger.

As with the early efforts to create the Great American Company through a large-scale combination, the creation of a plan for a significant real-estate and financial-services wing moved too slowly. The question of how Sears could build a grass-roots real-estate business without an army of brokers remained unanswered too long. As the upheavals of 1980 grew ever more ugly, the state of the Seraco adventure caused Ed Telling to note that Martin had been an "ivory-tower type" and a "suede-shoe operator" all along. And as soon as variations on this latter comment by the seldom seen chairman hit the planning grapevine, everyone knew that, for all practical purposes, Preston Martin had "had his innings."

After handing the Merchant over to Ed Brennan and withdrawing so completely from public view that there was debate among the rank and file over what had become of him, Telling had ostensibly turned away from his strategic-planning committee. On the rare occasions when the big door to Telling's office was opened, Phil Purcell was usually alone with him inside. Day after day—over 85 percent of his time, Telling figured—he and Phil sat around reading, cogitating together, and trying to figure out how to really make a difference. The General had once backed away from the others in the same way. In 1928, Wood left the running of Sears to his operators, disappeared with his maps and statistical studies, and emerged, the story goes, with his grandiose plans to create a web of stores.

Andy Kahr's SRI group completed their assignment to study the financial-services landscape early in 1981, and their final report included astounding statistical findings. Though it was known that a Sears credit card could be found in over forty million American households, conventional wisdom dictated that these were largely blue-collar people. A World War II–era study had indicated that half of Sears' customers didn't even have a bank account. But the SRI study indicated things had changed: Among households with incomes over $36,000 a year, 70 percent had a Sears card. Among households with a net worth of more than $500,000, 76 percent were card-carrying Sears customers. Even more shocking was SRI's contention that 73 percent of all stock-market investors who had made securities transactions involving at least $25,000 already had a card. Conversely, only 9 percent of the twenty-five million "active" Sears credit customers had stock-brokerage accounts.

The process of creating a new home-grown real-estate business and Sears-operated financial products like money-market funds continued under Preston Martin well into the spring of 1981, but early in the morning, before the other planning meetings of the day began, Purcell's resource-allocation staff would arrive at work with the latest privately commissioned research studies, with analysts' reports from brokerage-industry experts, articles, 10-Ks, and annual reports—all of which they'd received at their homes. After the computer turned off the Tower's day lights and turned on the low-energy, heat-generating night lighting system, the team stayed late to talk about the state of back-office politics at the brokerage house of PaineWebber, or the value of the real-estate holdings controlled by Merrill Lynch, because Telling had become committed to acquiring for Sears a major securities brokerage business.

In the past the old Glass-Steagall Act and subsequent laws separating active business and the storage of money would have threatened the corporation's ability to invest in common stock, if a brokerage house was a subsidiary. Sears' ownership of the California savings-and-loan would have been brought into question and generally would have been viewed with suspicion in Washington. But the spirit of deregulation had altered the climate in Washington. Laws were changing, and loopholes big enough to pass one of the largest companies in the world through were opened wide—so wide, the loophole honers like SRI's Andy Kahr instructed, that anyone brave enough ought to move in on Wall Street quickly before the holes were shut, or the banks caught on and took defensive action, or others moved in more quickly.

Phil Purcell usually wrote the full title of a meeting or an event he was to attend in his executive datebook, but the early pages of the red pocket-sized 1981 booklet he carried were covered with cryptic last names and code words. "Gorter" indicated a meeting to discuss mergers and acquisitions with Jim Gorter, the Chicago-based partner of the Wall Street investment bank Goldman, Sachs who was handling Goldman's Sears account. The account was first opened in the spring of 1906, when Richard Sears and Julius Rosenwald went to see Rosenwald's boyhood friend Henry Goldman about a $5-million loan to pay for expansion. Goldman convinced the men that elements of the general public might be receptive to owning stock in Sears, so the capital was raised by a public offering of shares. Goldman, Sachs had conducted Sears financial business in the evil city of New York ever since.

When the word "Williams" appeared in Purcell's book, it usually indicated another session with the resource allocators. The staff offices were moved, first from the thirty-seventh floor to the thirty-fifth, and then to a portion of the forty-fourth floor, but the constant activity and appearance of high-level personnel around the offices still drew attention. When Dave Williams emerged from the effluvium made by his ever-present cigars, office employees would ask him what he *did* at Sears.

"Shit, I dunno what they've got me doin'," Williams would shrug. "We allocate resources."

Ed Telling went directly to the board of directors during a meeting called in May 1981 and told them of his desire to move Sears into consumer financial services through acquisition.

The board reacted to the announcement with a long silence. Finally Donald Rumsfeld, the former Illinois congressman and Nixon aide, and current CEO of the drug-maker G. D. Searle, piped up, "Well, when's the press conference, Ed?"

But during the time of study and way-paving, the field of major securities houses suitable for acquisition began to narrow. In March, the
Prudential Insurance Company, the largest insurance company in the
country, purchased Bache, Halsey, Stuart, the sixth-largest securities
firm. During the early summer, American Express Company bought
Shearson, Loeb, Rhoades, the second-largest brokerage house, for $930
million. Around the same time, the engineers of Bechtel Industries
purchased the elite old-world investment company, Dillon, Read.

Dillon, Read was deemed far too rich for Sears' blood anyway by
Purcell's team, and Sears' secret research polls indicated that both
Bache and Shearson employed a few too many hot-shot, occasionally
irresponsible account executives, from the houses' customers' point of
view. As far as American Express was concerned, a meager thirteen
million American families—just 11 percent of the total—carried their
card, but the combination of Amex's credit-card base and a major brokerage house meant at the least that Sears would join some worthy and
powerful competitors in the financial-services field when, and if, the
corporation finally moved.

One afternoon Telling looked up from another lengthy report on the
financial, managerial, and market status of a targeted Wall Street brokerage house. The document included an estimate of how much Sears
would have to pay for the firm in light of its book value, price-to-earnings
ratio, the special multiples it carried by virtue of its status, its profitability vis-à-vis its industry, and a long list of other pertinent factors. Here
Sears could afford to buy up much of Wall Street. The biggest brokerage
house in the world didn't chalk up annual sales anywhere near those of
just one of the Merchant's territories. There were *groups* that brought
in more money. And here he was being stymied by facts about nickels
and dimes.

Despite the credit crush, the company could quickly get its hands on
around a billion liquid dollars. Sears also had a standing authorization to
issue almost $4 billion worth of new stock. There were unutilized lines
of credit as big as the Gross National Products of most countries. The
strength was there; it was just untransmitted into action by so many
years without direction or will.

For too many years the old hubris, the mesmerizing vision of the
corporation's unimaginable economic power, had been turned inward
upon the order. The era of incomparability with companies that pretended to do the same thing as Sears had passed so quickly into an era
of profound decline, public pillorying, and private criticism that the
relative standing of Sears with other companies had remained clouded

for years. Sears was a goliath, and it galled Telling deeply that it had ceased to act like one.

Telling reveled in those rare moments when life seemed to conform to the world such as it appeared in books, and there was something exquisite in the metaphorical possibilities all those documents full of names and numbers threw up in front of him now. He saw a big old country boy from Danville, Illinois, and his boy-wonder sidekick out of Utah turning the battered, outmoded Midwestern battleship and guiding it out of the narrowing stream of the past few years. They glided past the mouth of the harbor of the evil city of New York and moored the ship immovably just a few blocks from the meeting room at Fraunces Tavern, all in the name of the American people. The whole idea of the thing caused the two Searsmen to speak of it in an exaggerated "aw-shucks" vernacular inflection that was never far from either of their commands.

But it was Phil's job to chart the course, and Telling was getting itchier all the time. He was beginning to wonder if perhaps young Phil could use some assistance. "Ya know," Telling finally said to Purcell and his team of researchers as other, lesser companies bought into the money business from the outside, "you're all young people, and ah'm an ole man. You're gonna study this thing to death if you keep on like this. Let's just go in there and get started."

CHAPTER 13

Ed Brennan's
Thermidor

J oe Moran claimed all along that all he'd wanted to be part of was a revolution that "changed the face of Sears, not its soul."

But many of the merchants who remained after the flight of the ERIP generation were deeply injured by the corporate reorganization at the beginning of 1981, because it underlined Ed Telling's turning away from the wing of the organization that had embarrassed and frustrated him. He'd seemingly given up the task of retailing countless bits of the physical world and turned instead toward the metaphysics of insurance and finance.

There were rumors from above that the Sears Catalog might be discontinued in favor of an attempt to send out small "specialogs" to discrete groups of customers targeted by a computer. In May 1981 the 236-page summer catalog had been experimentally committed to a videodisk in preparation for the up to thirty million households that some studies indicated would be shopping by telecommunication instruments from their homes by 1995. With newspapers full of the possibility of new adventures directed from the sixty-eighth floor, there were still few indices of how much things had changed for the merchants more powerful than seeing the "handbook of the American people" composed in sound and light.

From the time of Don Craib's mysterious appointment as vice-chairman during the first Challenge Meeting, through the fall of the territorial vice-presidents from the board and the downward restructur-

ing of the merchandise business as a separate business, and then the
arrival in late 1980 and early 1981 of intimations and rumors of even
larger structural changes decreed from the sixty-eighth floor, the chairman and chief executive officer of the merchandise group counseled his
senior executive against overreaction. "The changes are evolutionary,"
Brennan would say. Joe Moran would join Brennan in asserting that the
new divisions alongside "the Merchant"—an old Allstate term that
would now refer to the "decentralized operating unit" that was the
retail group—were just examples of Sears' traditional business of merchandising adorned with different products.

Just after the January 1981 corporate reorganization was announced,
The New York Times reported in a long article about the changes that
the merchandise wing had contributed 66 percent of revenues but only
14 percent of profits in 1980. "Even though Mr. Brennan is considered
the company's rising star," the *Times* observed, "his group could find
itself last among corporate equals if profits do not recover."

"We're looking at our balance sheet from the standpoint of the advisa-
bility of redeploying our assets," the newspaper quoted Ed Telling as
saying. "The entities that promise the best return will have the first call
on capital."

Brennan chose to call the "restructuring down" an opportunity. Sears,
the Merchant, would gladly go head to head against K mart and Penney's, and if Allstate and the little internal real-estate and consumer-
finance venture wanted a piece of the action, they were welcome to it.

The mass departure of so many members of the old guard presented Ed
Brennan with the possibility of some eight hundred "key" management
changes. Brennan wanted people who were intellectually, physically,
and psychologically able to keep up. He talked of his desire to "implant"
people who "understood the language." But though there would be
young Turks elevated, the changes had to be carefully designed so as not
to openly repudiate Telling's three years of retail operation leadership.

Joe Moran's reformed presence was essential to this desired strain of
continuity, and Jumpin' Joe's ability to change tacks brazenly and in full
view of others was never so evident as it was under Brennan. Before
Brennan arrived, Phil Purcell and his aide, Joe Batogowski, had worked
hard to sell management on the importance of the sales technique called
"direct-response marketing." The new method seemed logical for Sears
since it involved advertising one or two well-priced items inside, or on
the "bangtail" flap of, the return envelopes enclosed in monthly bills.
Since Sears mailed out some twenty-five million monthly bills, and Allstate billed another twenty million customers, direct response seemed

an easy way to sell things for the cost of a stamp, and Batogowski argued the supposition at length in a memo.

But Moran disagreed. He wrote back to Batogowski at the time, calling him a "poor man" who was suffering from a "disease of the eyeball." Joe concluded the reply by writing the word "no" in each of seven languages and signing his name.

After Brennan arrived, Purcell and Batogowski took advantage of the attendant cease-fire and scheduled a meeting with Telling, Brennan, and Moran in order once again to attempt to explain the advantages of direct response.

As Batogowski finally began the formal presentation he'd been preparing and waiting to deliver for over a year, Joe Moran interrupted him. "Excuse me, Joe," he said, in the soft-spoken, almost gentle voice he'd adopted since Brennan took over, "but I think Mr. Telling ought to know some of the underlying advantages to Sears of a sophisticated marketing technique like this." Moran launched a forty-five-minute ode to the beauty and logic of direct response, covering every one of Batogowski's points without the aid of notes. He thought there might well be a billion dollars of new business in the venture for Sears. Purcell and Batogowski were still looking at each other and shaking their heads when Telling and Brennan told Moran to go ahead with his project.

With Joe's pen quelled and his role as chief subaltern highlighted daily by his subdued presence at Brennan's side, the Headquarters merchants felt assured that the period of what Brennan called "the excesses" was now over. Brennan had come to realize that only Joe was left among those with the historical love of the goods and the intellectual capacity necessary to help him recast the store, and by early 1981, the two former back-of-the-yard West Side Irish boys were rarely seen apart.

It was as if Joe had accepted that the kid was the true peacemaker. Brennan really did seem to understand by instinct things that Joe learned from books.

The return to Headquarters of Henry Sunderland was also deemed essential to Brennan's new administration. Henry would be brought back in from the Far Western Territory as the first "senior vice-president, administration and planning—merchandise." Ever the good trouper, Sunderland would serve Ed Brennan from this customized job title just as he'd served Ed Telling in the past.

Sunderland would be replaced in the cube-shaped headquarters John Lowe built by Bill Lochmoeller, the big man in the old "looks-the-part" tradition who was running the soon-to-be-closed Southwestern Territory. Lochmoeller began his career in a St. Louis store alongside Charlie

Wurmstedt, and the two men rose to be territorial administrative assistants around the same time in their careers. When Wurmy got the Midwest, Lochmoeller was given old Al Davies' suite in the Southwest. But from the moment Brennan arrived as president, Lochmoeller had distanced himself from Charlie. Lochmoeller wanted to believe. He was going to try hard to change with the times, and since Brennan didn't want to dissolve a historical territory and bust down its leader at the same time, the post-ERIP reshuffling would allow him the opportunity.

Twenty-one senior retailing executives were moved as the number of buying groups run by the officers reporting to Joe Moran fell from nine to seven. The total number of buying departments was "streamlined down" from forty-one to thirty-five as department managers retired and were not replaced. The Field's fifty-one retail groups in the four remaining territories were reduced to forty-six.

In February, Brennan created from his top officers a board of directors for the Merchandise Group. Soon afterward he announced that his own offices and the senior management of other merchandise-related operations would move to the forty-fourth floor of the Tower. Brennan told the interior designers he wanted his own executive floor to be "warmer" than the offices he was leaving on sixty-eight. Ever since he first came to meetings in the Sears Tower during the mid-1970s, Brennan had detested the sterility of the monolith. "It's like a hospital," he'd say, "so bland and low-budget, so colorless and without warmth."

The chairs on forty-four would be a bit more comfortable, the atmosphere a bit less formal, and though it wouldn't have seemed possible, even more all-American in its motifs than the sixty-eighth. There were American flags and weathered maps and old prints on the walls depicting coastal harbors and bucolic rural hamlets.

Brennan would admit in retrospect that he might have gone "a notch" too far in his opulent casting of the new base of operations for the Merchant, but at the time he believed he couldn't allow his managers or the important suppliers who came through the offices to think that the move to forty-four indicated that the merchandisers were something less to Sears than before. While Brennan accepted that the empire of selling goods was a "mature" enterprise, he still thought there was a lot more life in the old Sears than the strategic planners upstairs realized. If the merchants were to be the "last among equals," nobody would know it from the look and feel of the place.

The first quarterly review of the new planning system in 1981 indicated that for the first time the sales figures the Headquarters buyers expected to realize and the sales figures the Field expected to realize were the same. But Brennan knew that the Merchant could become thoroughly notched and calibrated, a machine so clean and obedient to data that nuance would become beside the point, and still fail unless he changed the nature of the business at the point it touched the customers. The call to "Sell More Units" contradicted the abortive strategy of selling fewer things at more profitable prices by gaining control over the suppliers and simply telling consumers what to do. If the sales side of the planning equation didn't grow, then the tendency of the operation side to retain margins by cutting would whittle the business down to nothing.

Brennan decided one way to find a new direction would be to take a look at the competition. On a cold winter day, Brennan and three other managers took a trip through the Midwest dressed in "sports clothes," which, according to Joe Moran, meant to most business executives "camel-hair overcoats, Gucci loafers, dress slacks, and a white dress shirt . . . with no tie."

Since senior retail executives dressed in sports clothes usually enter a store in groups—often at nine in the morning, when no other customers have yet arrived—store managers tend to spot this sort of reconnaissance mission in seconds. Etiquette in the industry usually calls for the manager to let the visiting executives meander through the store for a while before approaching the men to offer a tour. It's all part of the game, but it's one Sears had played only as hosts.

On the way home from the Midwest trip, Brennan said he was impressed with the Target store they'd seen. The creators of the off-price retailing chain, owned by Dayton Hudson, knew how to merchandise a store. It was clear to Brennan that Target's merchants were working from a common, predetermined, and scientifically delineated physical plan that was a far cry from the Sears way, where each store still reflected the tastes and experience of the manager.

Brennan believed the design of the almost nine hundred Sears stores no longer conformed to the aesthetic sensibilities or social and psychological motivations of the customers. Beyond the obvious grayness of the stores, he thought that the goods in most stores fought one another. Because matters of survival had so preoccupied Sears for several years now, the store managers had lost touch with the art of presenting goods in a pleasing way. They had concentrated on operating the hell out of a store for so long that they had stopped caring about which goods were adjacent to others, or how the assortment of items might affect the delicate desires of shoppers.

Here he'd been disseminating the unifying metaphor of "one big store," he'd even considered a new campaign of television advertising designed to "project the personality of Sears stores," and now, after looking hard at the competition, he'd realized his stores didn't have a personality to project.

"We have to make these stores live again," Brennan told his board. "We have to have vibrant and exciting stores again, and the only way I can think of creating them is to start spending a lot of money on experimentation. We haven't been able to rationalize spending a couple of million dollars on new store experiments around here for a long time, but when we build one dud of a retail store and blow $12 million in the process, nobody cares. We don't even spend money for new carpets, we've been so damned frugal. We think we're innovative because we were innovative once—a long, long time ago. We all had that mentality, but now we're gonna change it."

For decades, expansion had been the driving force of the company's grass-roots existence. Interior design was a frivolous, almost feminine consideration. Sears stores were supposed to look utilitarian and spare. They were stores the General ordained as emporia for men.

At various points before the post-war expansion, Sears store planning had been considered rather progressive. It was Sears that unveiled the first "completely sealed, windowless stores," to much architectural notice, during the 1930s. But large-scale experimentation had ceased during the 1940s, and since authority over the look of stores was then ceded to the territories, innovation—such as it was—tended to rest with the Field kings. The corporate billions controlled from Chicago were better spent on dropping new stores. Good goods sold goods, not the grandiosity of their display.

Brennan's decision to reopen the old West Side Headquarters as the site of his experimentation with new "platforms" for the goods was regarded as an act of liberation by the rank and file in the Tower. The majority of employees who'd grown up working on the West Side never got over the move downtown in 1973, and many of them dated the downfall of the company not from the point when sales withered and their pension fund dried up, but from the moment they were ordered to leave the gardens of their ancient outpost in the middle of a ghetto. By the time they moved, the neighborhood surrounding the plant had become so dangerous that Sears employed the third-largest police force in the state of Illinois. The three-block walk from the elevated-train station to the red brick complex had become a picket line of uniformed policemen. But it was hard to find anyone who didn't miss the old place.

For seventy-five years, nobody had "gone out for lunch," because employees had lunch together in the cafeteria or, if the weather was fine, in the gardens. The long main corridor of the administration building, with its endless linoleum, used to be like Main Street. You could see the General in the company of other brass hats on their way to lunch.

Quite suddenly, life got very vertical the day of the move downtown, as if the whole world had been turned on its side. Ed Telling realized, during his visits in from the East after the Tower was occupied, that he only saw people who traveled in his particular elevator shaft. Three- and four-decade-long friendships ended because of the configuration of the Tower. Nobody was particularly pleased about commuting all the way from the suburbs to the Loop and then having to commute once again to get to his or her desk. You had to leave an extra half-hour once you got to the Tower in order to move from skylobby to skylobby, past guards and too many heavy glass-and-steel revolving doors designed to keep at bay an internal, vertical wind that engineers contended would be so powerful without the doors that it could lift people up through the great Tower like shells through a cannon.

A study conducted after the move indicated that the tallest building in the world was universally resented by the workers it was designed to house. The giant moving sculpture with its five twirling forms that Alexander Calder created for the mezzanine was singularly unappreciated. The creation was known from corporate officer to departmental typist as "the screw." The cafeteria was a garishly colored amphitheatrical expanse that looked at all times like the floor of a national political convention. With its bright signs, each carrying the name of one of the United States, Field visitors thought the geographical motif some sort of Parent joke. Everyone knew the cafeteria had rats.

Sears workers used to brag about the fact that each light in the massive West Side complex was turned off at night in the spirit of corporate loyalty, but now a computer turned off the lights. Instead of the sound of children at play after school, a voice came over the intercom speakers at four o'clock every day to tell you if it was raining outside, because it was often impossible to tell from inside the upright city. When the robots first appeared, chugging down the halls and pausing at doorways to announce the arrival of the mail, employees wondered what had become of the sweet retarded people who used to deliver the mail out west, and the apocryphal rumor soon circulated that they had been fired to make way for progress. Those who'd been invited up onto the roof by one of the hundreds of technicians who kept the monolith running told of the terrifying wind up top and a light so blindingly bright that it felt like the Tower had been built too close to the sun.

Beyond the loss of family feeling experienced by the Chicago-based employees upon moving from the West Side, it often felt like they were working not in an office building, but in some gigantic scientific mechanism. There were things about the Tower that made people feel like decisions and plans were being made in places they couldn't see by things that didn't eat or go home at night.

Late in the spring of 1981, Brennan ordered the old brass plaques bearing phrases uttered by Richard Sears, Julius Rosenwald, and the General shined up, and small portions of experimental Sears retail-store departments began to appear in corners of the vast emptiness of the old Headquarters. The first new fixtures were designed to display color televisions and other home electronics, followed by experimental means of presenting athletic equipment. Brennan spent hours on end staring at new display concepts—most of them designed by a former art student from the Appalachian foothills named Claude Ireson, who worked for Brennan as vice-president in charge of national facilities planning.

The tall, aesthetic-looking Ireson—whose prominently boned, slender face was fitted with those round eyeglasses so popular in architectural and design circles—was still thought of by many veterans as "Ed Telling's window dresser," because the quiet Kentuckyan had indeed been the window trimmer in the Sears store in Rockford, Illinois, when the young Ed Telling was sent to manage it. Telling had included Ireson on the long ride through the ranks, and it was said that he liked browns and beiges because Claude preferred those hues.

The purpose of facilities planning for most of Claude's career was ostensibly to take as much money out of the cost of the construction of new stores as possible, so as to create an occupancy cost that would contribute to profits. But during the spring, Ed Brennan told Claude to start dreaming.

Ireson and his staff began to accumulate recent technical research on individual shopping patterns, and they worked to integrate subliminal habits of mind into their prototypes. Their data indicated, for instance, that, when confronted by a wall of merchandise, most people's eyes scan the accumulated objects as their eyes move across a printed page—from left to right and top to bottom. Claude's designers worked on displays by which the configuration of goods would cause a shopper to naturally "trade herself up" to the better products in the lower right-hand corner of a display.

Though Brennan regularly sent Ireson and his staff away to rethink proposals, he also became convinced that the "exercise" at the West Side was an important extension of both the spirit and the required sensitivity to old and new with which the Headquarters had mobilized to stage the Challenge Meetings.

The grapevine out to the territories carried word that at least Eddie Brennan was willing to move.

.   .   .

Morale was already shored up slightly by the announcement in March that Sears had chalked up its first double-digit monthly sales increase in three years. The merchants beat J. C. Penney's and K mart's monthly percentage sales rise in March for the first time since the first month of Telling's regime. Brennan knew that the rise was in large part due to particularly meager March figures during the 1980 credit crunch and the internal chaos that had led to his arrival, but it also appeared that the spring Challenge Items—which were now called the "Chairman's Challenge Items"—would be a huge success. Some of the departments housing the hundred carefully bought and advertised goods that had shown sales increases of only 3 and 4 percent during recent quarters were up 50 percent, 125 percent, and over 300 percent in some categories. The Cheryl Tiegs lines were walking off the racks; a gas grill offered as a Richard Searsesque "impossible value" sold like hell; forty thousand sofa sleepers priced at $199.88 apiece were unloaded during one week in February. The sleeper moved so well that Sears was bitterly attacked in the March newsletter of the Retail Furniture Association for taking a "step backward" from the industry's effort to convince consumers to buy more expensive furniture. The attack on Sears was carried under the subtitle "Up to Their Old Tricks Again," a choice of phrase that couldn't have pleased Brennan more. Brennan flashed a half-smile when he heard of the attack and admitted that he found the information "gratifying."

The positive sales figures were followed by the first positive securities-analyst's report about Sears in several years. Walter Loeb, a retail specialist with Morgan Stanley & Company in New York, issued a long justification of his decision to call Sears' deeply depressed shares good buys again. The document was entitled "The Battleship Has Turned." Loeb had mistakenly contended that Sears stock had bottomed out at $19 a share back in 1979, but the widely respected analyst's reports on Sears had been accurate enough over the years that news of his change of opinion sent the stock up a full dollar.

At the end of the first six months of the year, as the Merchandise Group reported profits of $103 million on sales of $9.4 billion—nine times the profits realized during the same period in 1980—the retail analyst from Mesirow and Company in Chicago joined Walter Loeb, saying that the merchant "had gotten its old aggressiveness back."

From the inside, though, the spirit of the Challenge Year was nothing at all like the old aggressiveness of the glory years. The old urgency was atomized, decentralized. It was inspired by a great leader or his residual myth, but carried out in thousands of individuated ways. The new spirit derived from Ed Brennan and because of his tireless, almost obsessive pace the implementation and practice of the new ways derived from him too. Brennan would appear at some outlying headquarters during a morning and appear again in a dark corner of a room at the old West Side Headquarters studying a new fixture in the afternoon. As Ed Telling was eventually nowhere to be seen, Ed Brennan was everywhere.

Almost every time Brennan wanted to make a quick trip to Mexico City or fly down to look at a few square feet of some store in Indianapolis, Joe Moran was on board. The remaining veterans from the time of Moran's management by intimidation noted that Joe's constant complaints about the pressure and his failing health had ceased when Brennan arrived. He never talked, as he used to, of the history of Sears executives who'd fallen from the strain; of Struthers, who died on the job; of Jim Button and his bad lung; or of the great Rosenwald, who was carried into work by his chauffeur in the end.

Joe once wrote in a memo that "to be under pressure is inescapable. Pressure takes place through all the world: war, siege, the worries of state. We all know men who grumble under these pressures and complain. But they are cowards. They lack splendor. But there is another sort of man who is under the same pressure, but does not complain. For it is the friction which polishes him. It is pressure which refines and makes him noble."

Joe certainly passed through the stress of war, siege, and the worries of state—such as exist in powerful metaphor within the polity of a large corporation—if not nobler and more refined, then at least intact. But Ed Brennan's efforts to turn the war-torn merchandise company had spawned a level of friction that appeared to be grinding the older man away.

Brennan could speak for hours in meeting rooms on the forty-fourth floor about a single process within the business, some seemingly innocuous connection within the vast organism that he could not set free from his mind until it was unfolded, examined, and replaced correctly. Then he'd get on a jet, fly to a meeting room in the Field somewhere, and begin to speak for hours again. *How* things were folded—how far apart were the hangers displaying dresses on the rack—was given the sort of thought and scrutiny that previous leaders had given to building the stores. His observations were enunciated as "principles," a word that rolled away from Brennan's fluid lips like the word "goods" and the word "store." The Challenge Year would even have its own calendar. After nearly a century of using a fiscal year that ended in late January at Sears, the company time-frame would now conform to the general calendar one.

Brennan was careful to remind his troops that, as demanding as the forces of order may have become, they were still far more benevolent than before. A "consistency of excellence" replaced in every case the dreaded term "centralization." Employees were now expected to be "accountable" rather than able to prove the quality of their "integrity" upon demand. Heresies and other evidence of disloyal behavior were called "intellectual dishonesty." Merchants were meant to take risks without fear of retribution, but Brennan also made no effort to obscure the fact that ultimate authority and sovereignty had not returned to their former residences.

When the 1980 corporate annual report was published in 1981, Ed Brennan's face dominated the forefront of the photograph of the Sears Merchandise Group officer corps. He was depicted turned brashly to one side with his eloquent hands forming relaxed fists. His twelve senior officers were arrayed in a chevron behind him, looking so small a fraction of Brennan's size that it seemed like a bit of trick photography. Several of the others—including Joe Moran—clasped their hands below their belt buckles. The four remaining territorial officers of the Field were situated in no apparent order in the background, interspersed among the others, as if to remind the most casual observer of how quickly things can change.

The spring leveling off of the Merchant's nose dive suspended the desperation long enough to highlight the size of the task still facing Brennan and his managers. Brennan would ride back to the Tower after viewing some of Claude Ireson's trendy new shelves and signs in frustration. If he was with one of the few officers he trusted with his thoughts, he'd lament that the best-looking fixtures in the world wouldn't help if they didn't display the right goods. Trying to discern which goods were the right ones for the Sears Americans of the moment was an exercise laden with historical precedent and emotion. Traditional dogma dictated that Sears "had everything." The boys bought and sold a large representation of the best examples of all serviceable, mass-produced artifacts; and the shoppers came into the stores in all their democratic glory and voted. If particular lines and items didn't make much money for the company, it was still considered the consumers' right to see them there on the shelves. Conventional wisdom argued that even unprofitable goods brought people into sections of the stores where they might notice and buy more profitable ones.

The buyers had made a circus of Phil Purcell's 1978 effort to cull their offerings via his Harvard Business School "matrix," and though Joe Moran had some success in forcing the buyers and sellers to configure their goods into disciplined "price points" (while cutting off some of the smaller suppliers that contributed to the overly large selection of goods), he'd so badly damaged the supply lines and demoralized the internal organization in the process that the system had seized up and simply failed to proceed. From the early days of Hay and McKinsey, the idea of breaking Sears down to observe, industry by industry, line by line, and even item by item, exactly where it touched popular desires in the most profitable way had been discussed, attempted, and subverted.

Brennan believed that the time of Sears, Roebuck's residing in public life as the official national cornucopia, the place where America shopped because it offered Americans all things save cars and houses, should become part of the company's past. But he also knew that the process of figuring out which of the 775 million transactions he mentioned at the Challenge Meetings were worthwhile could also undo all of the reconstructive surgery accomplished so far. "The fabric," he'd caution. "We just can't tear it anymore."

One of the largest impediments even to studying the problem of how to find out which of the 775 million transactions were worthwhile, and then how to target the goods more carefully, was the same one that had so frustrated Joe Moran that he instituted "the excesses." The available hard information about the consumer's-eye view of Sears—like the senior managerial perspective from the Tower—was only expressed in huge aggregate economic figures and conceptions grouped by region and national departments. The data were no more meaningful or useful or even changeable than the gross national product (of which Sears, in the wake of oil-price inflation, no longer constituted its former 1 percent) or any other Keynesian macroeconomic indicator.

Brennan realized that before the retailer would be fit to survive, a way would have to be found to tear back the historical and bureaucratic coating so he could study the organization's component parts. He needed to take the merchandise side of the thing apart piece by piece, and do with the goods what the Hay Committee had tried to do with job titles. He had to somehow draw knowledge from the guts of the company without spreading more fear. The spirit in which the Challenge Items had been purchased and sold had to somehow be transferred to a process that would necessarily end many of the participants' day-to-day purposes within the company.

Though he trumpeted the mid-year sales jump to anyone who'd listen, the blip on the line was little more than the result of the quick fixes Brennan had ordered when he unleashed the buyers in Tucson. The Challenge Items did not amount to a new store, and they would never be the source of the sort of profiting the company required. After carefully studying Sears' plight some time earlier, a writer for *Chain Store Age* had asked in an article if, in the end, Sears didn't "require total transformation." The article noted skeptically that the true transformation of a big retail business had only occurred three times in America since World War I, with the creation of K mart from the tired old Kresge chain in 1962; the redirection of J. C. Penney from a system of tiny shops into a modern mass retailer; and the transformation of the largest mail-order empire in the world into the world's largest chain of big stores by General Robert E. Wood.

But transforming Sears, the Merchant, the writer concluded, would have to be accomplished without the aid of external demographic and economic events, such as those that aided the other success stories. The general rise of discount shopping helped K mart; the phenomenon of the large shopping center assisted Penney's change; and the fact that the masses did indeed go out and spend significant portions of their net worth on the automobiles that filled up the ample free parking spaces surrounding the Sears stores certainly helped the General.

By the fall of the Challenge Year, as Ed Brennan looked toward the all-important Christmas season, it was clear his efforts would not be assisted by exogenous economic events; they would indeed have to be conducted in spite of one of the most destructive general economic environments to come along in many years. Though business leaders had been explaining that it was a recession that was causing sagging results for at least a year, it wasn't until the fall of 1981 that the industrialized world descended full-force into a synchronous recession of a magnitude not experienced since the Great Depression. Ed Brennan was going to have to try to turn the merchandise company at a time when a great number of the thirty-six million families he ultimately needed to return to the fold as believers would find themselves with less money, and often without jobs. He hadn't had the time yet to work his magic all the way down to the level of the stores, and the stores were where the recession would hit the hardest.

Then, as the clock next to Eddie Brennan began to tick louder that fall, the merchants were shaken again when, quite suddenly, Ed Telling re-emerged from the shadows.

CHAPTER 14

Fishing with Rod and Phil

Ed Telling never had much time for people called "power-brokers"; those sort of well-connected movers-and-shakers who'd apparently "gone to college with every damned body in America to hear them talk." But he was still smarting from the embarrassment and disappointment of the abortive approach to Deere & Company, he lacked confidence in his own investment bankers at Goldman, Sachs; and too much of the other work and research had come to nothing. As he had decided once to break with tradition by going outside to find someone capable of helping him when he became chairman, Telling decided during the summer of 1981 that Sears required a specialist to help navigate the course toward Wall Street.

Telling first observed the notably active mind of Roderick Maltman Hills during a late-1980 convocation in the Tower made up of an entire auditorium-full of lawyers—members of a professional class Telling tended to locate just a peg above bankers in his general estimation of things. Numerous Sears staff attorneys from the territories and Headquarters had come together with hired guns from a variety of law firms to discuss yet another series of suits and complaints against Sears—these brought by the Treasury Department, the U.S. Customs Bureau, the Securities and Exchange Commission, the Zenith Corporation, Corning Glass, and several labor unions. All of the actions contended variously that Sears had conspired with Japanese television manufacturers to dump cheap imported color sets on the American market. The TV buyers of Department 657 contended that they were faultless, that complainants had misinterpreted the Japanese trade regulations administered through the omnipotent Japanese economic development agency, MITI.

The meeting was held in the same drapery-deadened room on the twenty-seventh floor where Ed Brennan had issued his challenge a few months earlier. Ed Telling slipped into the back of the room, where he sat fidgeting and observing a consensus form among the attorneys at the meeting, which held that Sears should plead *nolo contendere*—no contest—to one of the lesser criminal charges so as to avoid the possibly far more adverse effects of a guilty verdict in the potent anti-trust portions of the cases.

Toward the end of the meeting, a stocky fellow out of Washington, D.C., got up and spoke in a deep, Northwestern variation on a country-boy twang. Rod Hills argued against the *nolo* pleading. He outlined the political ramifications of the proposed plea, the potential for negative publicity, and even touched on the moral issue inherent in a tacit admission that you had done something that you didn't actually believe you'd done. Hills contended that divergent legal strategies were guiding each of the four or five cases against Sears, and though the corporation might win some battles and lose others, they could easily end up losing the proverbial war because of the lack of a coordinated corporate strategy.

As he finished, Hills noticed that the big fellow in the back, who'd been pointed out to him as being the beleaguered chairman of Sears, was leaving the room. Hills thought Ed Telling might have looked disgusted when he left, so he was surprised when Telling had a Sears staff attorney call him at his law office in Washington and ask him to coordinate the corporate defense on the dumping suits. The assignment meant that Rod Hills began to spend a great deal of time in Chicago during early 1981, and as the year progressed, he found himself drawn—without realizing the novelty of it—into increasingly lengthy discussions with Ed Telling.

Hills was intrigued by Ed Telling's decided intolerance of bureaucratic functions—an unusual prejudice for the leader of a modern organization, and one Rod Hills respected and shared. Hills also sensed that, unlike most presidents, prime ministers, and corporate chairmen he'd known, Ed Telling actually believed that things could change. Most people who sat in control of large organizations in the modern world had never even entertained the fantasy of their abilities to steer the course of events fundamentally. But here was a fellow who never accepted that things don't really change anymore, though he'd soldiered for most of his life in one of the least changing or changeable organizations in the world. For all of his access to heads of state and peers of the remaining realms, Hills had never yet come across someone more intellectually attuned to the possibilities of power, or more willing to adventure with that power, than the little-known chairman of Sears. Telling, though he cringed at Hills' incessant name-dropping, was fascinated by the well-read lawyer's command of abstract analyses of institutions, people, and power. Both men realized that beneath the patina of meetings, financial statements, legal writs, and six- or (in the case of Telling) seven-figure paychecks that were the embellishments of their jobs, they were both more interested in the metaphysics of change. Telling and Hills began to meet for dinner and long conversations, though Hills remained unaware of how unusual these evenings were for Telling.

It turned out that Hills shared Ed Telling's skepticism about the regulations and laws enacted to protect "civilized forms of capitalism," such as those forms perpetuated by bankers. When Rod Hills had worked for his old friend Jerry Ford as a special adviser in the White House during the mid-1970s, he'd even chaired a committee on deregulation of the financial sector of the economy. Many in Washington considered Hills the spiritual and ideological godfather of the regulatory repeals Congress enacted during 1975 that reopened rate competition in the brokerage business on May Day of that year. President Ford moved Hills from the White House to direct the Securities and Exchange Commission, so he could monitor the changing brokerage industry in the wake of less civilized restraint.

Before going to Washington, Hills worked out of the Los Angeles corporate law firm Monger, Tolles, Hills, and Rickerhouse, and after leaving the SEC he was drafted to serve as chairman of the old mining giant Peabody Coal, until Peabody's directors undrafted him the following year. After his stint at Peabody, he operated out of the Washington, D.C., law firm of Latham, Wadkins, and Hills—this Hills being his wife, Carla, who worked above Rod in the Ford administration as secretary of housing and urban development, and who often overshadowed her husband in the various "public lives" he spoke about.

Rod Hills viewed the world as a mishmash of unconnected power trains, all there waiting to be hooked together by an inspired deal. He'd made a career of skillfully refining the face of the business economy by helping governments, big companies, and big shots do big deals. It was hard to open an annual report or a business periodical without revealing photos of Hills' dear personal friends. The man was like a perambulating Rolodex.

By the spring of 1981, the puff-chested figure of Rod Hills began to appear in the background as an away-from-the-table observer at some strategic-planning sessions, much to the consternation of the other participants. The budding personal relationship between the noted Washington rainmaker—with his cutting-edge vocabulary and his high-minded intellectual observations about the impending transformation of the world economy—and the introverted chairman of Sears was regarded with considerable skepticism on the sixty-eighth floor, and Hills sensed the scrutiny from the start. He sized up the dynamic of the sixty-eighth floor as a case of one peculiar and powerful personality encircled by a tight ring of sycophants dedicated above all other things to protecting him. Also in residence was one hot-to-trot young ideas man, who could pass through the wall at will, and who was masterfully controlling the flow of information to the chief. That was Phil Purcell. Hills was impressed with the technical planning papers Purcell's staff prepared about the future of financial services for Sears, but, as Rod was fond of saying when it was time to do a deal, "You can only prove so much with information; after a while you've got to fish or cut bait."

During the early summer, Telling invited Rod Hills farther inside when he asked him to scan the waters off Wall Street to see what was available. Without mentioning the name of his client, Hills inquired among bankers, securities lawyers, and analysts about the internal politics current within various still-independent broker-dealer securities firms. Trying to get a feel for which houses were ripe for the taking, he sought the guidance of his old friend the arbitrager Sandy Lewis, who helped make the connections that led to the American Express–Shearson deal.

After Hills returned from this first reconnaissance trip to New York in fee to Sears, Telling revealed to him that, though he was sure numerous worthy firms were there for the taking on the Street, what he really wanted, if he had his druthers, was the house of Merrill Lynch.

Merrill was clearly the Great American Company among the stock sellers. The firm was made in the image of a man who believed that the elite Wall Street products could be purveyed to plain people resident on the Main Streets of the heartland. Charlie Merrill's dream was to bring together several securities firms to create a business system capable of demystifying financial instruments like common stocks—"democratizing" them and making them truly common—just as Sears, Rosenwald, and the General had made available consumer goods that only the wealthy could previously afford. Merrill worked to create a network of local distributors to be there on the spot, right down the street from the local banker. He called his dream "people's capitalism."

In 1971, the CEO of Merrill Lynch, Donald Regan, pledged that the company would one day be a true "financial department store," marketing its expanded array of financial wares everywhere. Ten years later, after the success of such experimental products as the Cash Management Account that Andy Kahr helped create, the securities firm was moving into other financially oriented businesses, like real estate and insurance. Merrill Lynch had come to control 12 percent of the brokerage market, three times the portion owned by its nearest competitor. The company sold over $2 billion worth of paper and property during 1980 and reported $120 million in profit—a figure more than half as large as the profits reaped by the Merchant from close to $19 billion in sales.

As at Sears, the huge number of recruits hired on amid rapid growth had made Merrill Lynch a rather high-cost operation over the years. The company was divided into powerful operating divisions, each with its own support staffs, research centers, and traditions. The marriage of two plans and two strong traditions might easily lead to strife, for Merrill was already far along with its own plans to wrest business away from the banks.

But Telling wanted Merrill Lynch and that was all that mattered. He'd never given up the idea of a combination of companies that would create a new institution that was symbolically superior to anything before it. He figured that Merrill Lynch people were probably as close to real Americans as any other members of their fraternity. He loved the way they'd figured out how to hold people's cash like a bank. He liked the "bullish-on-America" stuff as well as the provincial backgrounds of some of their top executives. They even had an internal system of promotion from within that included a long period of training in the field. The acquisition of Merrill Lynch by Sears, Roebuck loomed as an all but pre-emptive gesture, a $2-billion-plus venture that in implication and potential transcended its material reality—like art.

The tiny cadre of Sears people close to corporate-diversification plans were never supposed to mention target companies by name. Each file in the resource-allocation office had a code name—most of them drawn from the names of counties in Illinois. The growing numbers of studies and financial analyses of Merrill Lynch were filed under the central code name, Vermillion. Vermillion was the county where Ed Telling had been born. It was the name of the street where Nancy's mom, Gertrude Hawkins, lived.

Though Phil Purcell's team was officially responsible for planning the foray, it was Rod Hills who made the first contact. During the early summer of 1981, Hills made a casual phone call to his "old friend" Roger Birk, the Merrill CEO, in which he paraphrased for Birk the evolving strategic direction of Sears and mentioned that, if Birk was interested, Ed Telling would like to compare a few notes with him. Hills said that nothing had been decided at Sears about what they wanted to do with their current or future financial-services businesses. The Sears leadership really didn't know if they wanted to buy a brokerage firm or not, but they would appreciate the chance to get together for a chat.

Roger Birk was nothing if not a cautious man. His fear of rumor moved him to restrict knowledge of the phone call to his top four officers. He added a fifth to the group when he nominated a senior strategic planner at Merrill Lynch, Wallace Sellers, to establish contact with Sears and lay the groundwork for a meeting. Phil Purcell flew to New York to meet privately with Wally Sellers, and over a long dinner at the Midtown restaurant Quo Vadis, the two planners decided the fit was right. They both agreed to take on the job of choreographers of the intricate dance by which their companies could come together. Soon afterward, Sellers and Purcell met again in New York to compare planning papers and personal observations of the two chairmen involved. They tried to come up with an agenda for the first meeting between Telling and Roger Birk. Both men felt they were laying the groundwork for a historic moment.

Before leaving on a trip abroad, Rod Hills helped arrange a secret lunch to be held in Merrill Lynch's Wall Street headquarters. Telling arrived in the company of Phil Purcell, and Jack Kincannon's successor, the ever-pallid chief financial officer, Dick Jones. Birk brought his number-two officer, Merrill President Bill Schreyer, as well as Vice-Chairman Dakin Ferris, and the chief financial officer, Greg Fitzgerald. The legal restrictions that dictated the course of action by a CEO once a formal offer has been made to buy a company rendered the conversation at lunch rather light and frivolous. Telling spoke about the weather, the Midwest, and a bit about Sears. He cracked a few jokes, to which the Merrill chairman responded quite slowly, Telling thought.

Telling figured that Birk was simply shell-shocked by the unspoken underlying purpose of the idle conversation, but Phil Purcell began to think the problem was that Roger Birk was a ponderous and unimaginative man—a "disciplined" one at best. Birk had come up through the operations side of the brokerage house and was known as a maker of decisions by consensus. A nice man, honest and well meaning—like Merrill's own Arthur Wood—but someone who sought out every member of his executive committee before acting.

Purcell saw that Birk was too timid to be of much use, and that, while Wally Sellers was committed to the deal, it appeared now that Sellers might have been too junior to bring Birk along into the game. As the lunch progressed, Purcell found himself wishing they'd worked through the obviously quicker and more aggressive Schreyer (who was to replace Birk two years later), but the fellow opposite Telling now was Birk, and the Merrill CEO let it be known that he was extremely reluctant to move with any haste.

As Birk argued to his officers later that there was no coherent plan by which to integrate the corporations, several of them sensed that he was worried about being remembered as the man who took Merrill over from the powerful Don Regan only to sell it to Sears. Sellers argued that the existence of two advanced expansion plans and two heavily textured cultures would serve to assure that Sears wouldn't swallow Merrill. Sellers reminded Birk that the availability of big capital was fast becoming the name of the game on Wall Street, and a combination with Sears would open limitless possibilities as well as strike a partnership that might truly be the Great American Company. But Sellers could see that the thought of such an act caused Roger Birk to panic. He eventually called Phil Purcell to confirm the Sears planner's hunch that the time was not right. Sellers said he was extremely upset about it, but any further negotiations would assuredly be very slow ones.

The Vermillion project was adjudged "dead in the water" at the end of the summer. Rod Hills believed Merrill could still be taken peacefully given the proper sort of dealing, but he sensed that the desultory character of the private contact between the two companies had disillusioned Telling. Rather than being the archetypal all-American broker-dealer, Merrill was in fact a sprawling enterprise replete with problems, tendencies, reticences, power pockets, formalities, and a leadership slow to rouse and in command of no taste to speak of when it came to a good joke.

From the beginning the criteria for diversification had included the necessity of friendly takeovers. The Deere initiative aborted the moment Deere's chairman warned Sears away. Sears was interested in buying a skilled and happy management along with the assets and good name of a target company, and the corporation could not afford to be tagged as a raider. Ed Telling added to this his own conviction that any substantive resistance to the idea of joining up with him and Sears by itself rendered a company unfit for consumption. Telling took the whole thing quite personally, especially after two and a half years of frustration in the trying. If the idea of wanting a company because of the way the combination resonated in his mind, or of not wanting it because of the lifelessness he said he'd glimpsed in its leader's eyes was conceit, then that's just what his casting off of the Merrill plan was.

With Vermillion closed, other files were reopened. Purcell had become enamored of the idea of buying PaineWebber, a prestigious wire house managed by Rod Hills' friend Don Marin. So Hills chatted with Marin as he had with Birk, but it was observed that PaineWebber had become embroiled in troublesome office politics, and the last thing Sears needed in 1981 was to buy up a house with troubles.

E. F. Hutton was considered next—quite briefly. Rod Hills supported an approach to Hutton, but Telling summarily vetoed the idea, solely because of Hutton's most recent corporate annual report. Telling perused the perfectly bound, shimmeringly opulent silver document and lifted it up in his giant hands wearing a look of horror. The report weighed a full pound and contained thirty-six pages of formal photographic portraits of Hutton functionaries, most of them posed in front of villas and ornate balconies. The cost of the report was over $340,000, and Telling was informed that the villas and lodges were all rented. "What in hell do we want with a company that has a *silver* annual report?" Telling said. "That's not our kind of company."

The chairman's intuitive approach to shopping for a major brokerage house frustrated the technicians working for Phil Purcell. With the assistance of SRI and several other private polling and consulting firms, the resource-allocation staffers believed they now knew more about the state of the brokerage industry than any observers on the ground in Wall Street. In the space of three weeks after the Merrill approach fell apart, Purcell's best numbers man, Jim Keller, designed a questionnaire, mailed it out to fifty thousand sample consumers, and processed the returned data in a way that rated all of the major brokerage houses on the basis of criteria that ranged from market share and demographic penetration to readings of public trust and depth of consumer commitment.

Keller's results ran counter to a number of the standard perceptions by industry insiders. For instance, the general public indeed thought quite highly of Merrill Lynch, but only from afar (the study called the popular perception a "halo effect"). The firm's own customers didn't agree at all. This was also true of American Express's recently purchased firm, Shearson, a company with a flashy image among the general populace but a customer base that, as Phil Purcell interpolated the report to Telling, "thinks they stink." This same negative rating by customers was true of the recently renamed Prudential-Bache. The top-ranked firm in the majority of the studied categories—in nine of the eleven measured categories—turned out to be Dean Witter Reynolds, the fifth-largest house in volume and, by most insider accounts, one of the least exciting firms on the Street.

The resource-allocation group's survey revealed that Dean Witter had unusually strong regional market penetration, by far the strongest presence west of the Mississippi, and a large number of account executives— second only to Merrill Lynch. They were the first securities firm to have established branch offices in all fifty states. The fiscal performances of Dean Witter—code-named "Will" in the Tower—were erratic at best. Profitability could range from $10 a share during a boom to red numbers in the face of a bear market, but the firm had the distinction of being the plain people's choice.

Dean Witter, circa 1981, was created from the merger in 1978 of conservative California-founded Dean Witter and the Reynolds Securities Firm, a smaller New York–based company. The "Will" file revealed that the firm's reputation for fair dealing was born of a legacy left by Mr. Dean Witter himself, the firm's own ghostly presence, who announced during the bleak year 1932 that he still believed "the most valued investment of an investment firm is its good name." Witter's heirs went on to develop the second strongest "Main Street" association in the industry. The number-two executive at the firm used to tell Merrill CEO Don Regan that Dean Witter was "the rowboat behind the *Queen Mary.*"

It was with a great deal of ambivalence that Ed Telling told Rod Hills to make the calls and connections pursuant to a meeting with the Dean Witter brass. On August 20, after flying in from Europe, Hills called the Dean Witter officer Robert "Stretch" Gardiner from the Concorde Lounge at Kennedy Airport. Gardiner was known as one of the most gregarious and, at six foot seven, certainly one of the tallest men on Wall Street. Stretch had run the Reynolds Securities before the merger, and Hills knew him from his SEC days. In his low-registered, matter-of-fact manner, Rod said he just wanted to set up a lunch. His "people" wanted to "share some thoughts" and talk about comparative philosophies and plans.

With all the takeover hysteria loose in brokerage circles at the time, the officers of Dean Witter had agreed previously that only the firm's chairman, Andy Melton, was allowed to speak to oncoming sharks. Gardiner called Melton out of Dean Witter's elegant private dining room, a place where haute cuisine was served daily on Limoges china and beside a glorious view of New York Harbor. Stretch told Melton that the noted wheeler-dealer Rod Hills was waiting for a telephone call at the airport. Dean Witter's lawyers had composed a little speech designed to address such a situation, and Melton had committed it to a slip of paper he kept in his desk. The statement was supposed to protect the officers from treading on any securities laws. The pace of corporate takeovers in 1981 and the exponential escalation of the size of acquisitions had so charged the process of management with intrigue that many executives, who'd risen to prominence by virtue of their ability to run companies rather than sell them, felt compelled to be cagey.

But Andy Melton was supposed to be a seasoned investment banker, so Rod Hills listened to him recite his speech impatiently.

"Come on now, Mr. Melton," Hills said. "Ed Telling of Sears, Roebuck just wants to come have lunch with you. Are you saying no to that?"

At lunch in New York the following week, Telling sat by quietly as Phil Purcell dazzled Melton and Gardiner with a presentation full of information and insights about their firm that they didn't know themselves. Purcell reeled off facts about Dean Witter and its customers that would have seemed impossible to collect without at least stirring up gossip on the Street. Stretch Gardiner was entranced by Purcell's performance. Ed Telling's bright-button boy—his "walking corporate staff," as Andy Melton would remember him—sat at lunch with reports and spreadsheets arrayed in front of him, but he never glanced down. He told the two men what Sears had learned about the depth of the unexploited "trust factor" at their disposal. He talked about the SRI study, and even tossed in the results of Jim Keller's most recent brainstorm—a quick survey of twenty-five thousand Sears customers that indicated several hundred thousand people might be willing to open a brokerage account for the first time if they could only associate stock trading with the trustworthy image of Sears.

Beyond the fact that Sears stock had lost its blue-chip glamour in recent years, Andy Melton didn't really know much at all about Sears other than that they sold pretty good appliances. Melton's personal dream for his own company after the merger with Reynolds was to recast the somewhat hokey Dean Witter as what he called the "Tiffany of investment houses," or the "Tiffany alternative to Merrill Lynch"— something in quite the opposite direction of the Sears, Roebuck approach to things. The idea of a system of entwined businesses, from retailing to finance to real estate to insurance, all of them perhaps connected by computers, all of them united in service to the rapidly changing desires of an American middle class long denied access to financial products they deserved, was in precise counterpoint to Andy Melton's dream.

Melton offered a few facts about his firm's success with its money-market account and other deposit-oriented products, but he said nothing that Purcell hadn't gleaned from the Dean Witter annual report. Dean Witter's chairman said he was only representing the stockholders of the company, and that he hoped Sears understood that the firm was not for sale.

Telling didn't much care for the cottony-haired and chubby-cheeked Melton's attitude, any more than he'd liked the reception Roger Birk gave him at Merrill Lynch. Wasn't it just like New York City, though? Just a bunch of people acting superior, people who thought they knew something about the world because they handled money.

Melton sensed Telling's irritation. He mused later that perhaps Telling's anger was the result of so many years of dealing with "ten thousand little suppliers, little corporations, to whom Sears appeared the most important thing in the world." Dean Witter's 1980 revenue of almost $750 million was actually dwarfed by the sales of several of Sears' top merchandise suppliers like Whirlpool, Sanyo, Singer, and Michelin, but Melton still figured Telling must have confused Dean Witter with some little factory if he expected to get something different from the lunch.

"You know, Andy," Stretch Gardiner said to Melton as they headed downtown, "we could have been a bit more outgoing in there. Our reserve could have been . . . misunderstood."

Melton was still thinking about the grand design Purcell had laid out for them. "You know what I can't get out of my head?" he said. "Could you imagine actually *trusting* your investment firm?"

On the way to back to the airport, Phil Purcell deemed the meeting a "fiasco." Then Phil sank down in his seat and joined Telling in his injured silence. It was beginning to seem a very long time since anything had gone their way. Tearing the old thing down had turned into a hell of a job, and building something new wasn't turning out to be any easier.

A few days later, the Securities and Exchange Commission approved Sears' application to create its own money-market mutual fund, and Telling quickly announced the formation of the carefully named "Sears U.S. Government Money Market Trust."

The pools of commercial paper, certificates of deposit, and government debt securities were paying investors 11 percent interest by early September 1981, as inflation and the clean track record of existing funds were drawing more money from 5.25-percent bank passbook accounts all the time. The home-grown Sears version of the product was designed to capitalize on the trust factor by investing much more heavily in government-backed paper than in other instruments. The association of Sears, the United States government, and the word "trust" was supposed to enfranchise the sorts of people who still worried about the product's safety. "Sears U.S. Government Money Market Trust": trust, trust, and trust.

A survey published in *Advertising Age,* a trade magazine owned by Crain Communications, the organization that published Joe Moran's leaked "yellow book" back in 1978, indicated that Sears could lure away *half* of all the customers already holding funds in another money-market account. The Sears name alone held the further potential of inducing one in four families that had no previous interest in a money-market account to open one. An incredible one in four consumers told *Advertis-*

ing Age they would transfer their savings and checking accounts to a Sears-run bank, especially if Sears stores had facilities for collecting and disseminating the money, and three in five consumers indicated that if Sears, Roebuck sold houses, they would shop there for a home.

"Our goal," Telling told reporters when he took the money fund public, "is to become the largest consumer-oriented financial services entity."

Those working closely with Ed Telling on the diversification effort knew that the chairman's early-September comment was in part directed at them. The "entity" still needed a chassis upon which the system could be constructed. Sears still didn't own a means of delivering consumer financial products. The idea of selling houses and other real estate was no closer to reality than it had been a year earlier, and Telling's frustration with Preston Martin and Seraco was now complete.

Rod Hills listened to the back-and-forth discussions about what was to be done in the aftermath of the unhappy Dean Witter lunch. Rod left town in late August for a family vacation aboard an oil tanker owned by his old friends at Chevron, thinking that it was the Middle American chips balanced on both Purcell's and Telling's shoulders that was keeping them from seeing that big business deals were pure things and quite separate from emotions like resentment. It all seemed to be more than a deal was meant to be to both of them. In Phil's case, it was clear that, despite all of his elite training, he was obsessed with something he called the "real America." Purcell borrowed a term from the Sears merchandise-assortment categories and spoke warmly of the "basic-basic" sorts of people he respected.

Hills returned to Chicago on September 11 to find Purcell and Telling still unresolved about whether to approach Merrill Lynch again, to talk again to Dean Witter or another firm, or just to forget about the idea and try to grow their own organization. Hills said he still smelled a living deal in the Dean Witter approach. He wanted to re-establish contact with Gardiner and Melton before somebody else bought up their best second choice.

Hills stayed late at the Tower and had dinner that evening with Telling and Purcell. After a few drinks, Rod began to push more aggressively for another approach to Dean Witter. He turned away from Purcell and talked to Telling. Hills noted the Sears chairman was much less expressive now than when they had first talked of great combinations and new eras. Telling appeared to care little for his empire of stores, and it was hard for Hills to see how he had managed such a long career in retailing. Telling was as intellectually and emotionally ready for action as anyone Rod Hills had come across in a long time. He was a gifted student of what Rod called "the art of the possible." A grand romantic,

Hills thought. But he'd been tripped up by circumstances of late and was losing heart.

"You could get Dean Witter for a good price, Ed, and I bet the difference between Dean Witter and Merrill Lynch in the end is about two years of your kind of advertising." Hills looked over at Phil Purcell. He thought Phil was one of the brightest people he'd come across in ages, but he was untrained in casting bait or navigating the intricate flow of deals. "It's time for you guys to fish or cut bait," Hills said.

Five days later, Ed Telling received a call from Dick Sharp, the president of Simpson-Sears Limited, a Canadian retailer in which Sears held such a large equity interest that a Searsman sent from Chicago usually sat as president. Sharp told Telling that he wasn't sure what was going on, but he'd just gotten a call from a Simpson-Sears outside director who was also president of the largest Canadian real-estate brokerage company. Sharp said that William Dimma, of Toronto-based A. E. Le Page, wanted to talk to Telling about Coldwell Banker, the largest real-estate brokerage in the world. Allstate and A. E. Le Page had each owned around 21 percent of Los Angeles–based Coldwell Banker since February of 1970, when both parties agreed to stop buying shares of the expanding residential and commercial real-estate concern.

The inquiry could have meant that Le Page wanted to sell their interest in Coldwell Banker or possibly buy out Allstate—and Telling guessed it was the latter.

Telling told Sharp he'd call him back.

Telling had been thinking about buying Coldwell Banker ever since he'd soured on Preston Martin's plan to created a major real-estate company through internal development. Six months before the call from Canada, he'd sent his vice-chairman Don Craib to Los Angeles to feel out Coldwell Banker's feisty broker/managers on the subject of joining up with Sears, but the approach was viewed as something far short of a genuine effort in Los Angeles, and Craib carried back news that sounded like another rejection.

Rod Hills was in the Tower when the call came in from Canada. He agreed with Telling that there would be little reason for Le Page to want to talk unless they were going after the American realtor. He was also agreed that Sears should try to pre-empt Le Page quickly and avoid an expensive open-ended bidding war. Phil Purcell joined Hills in Telling's office, where it was decided that Sears could attempt to play the "white knight" to Coldwell Banker's damsel by offering to intercede as a preferable alternative to foreign ownership.

Telling was decidedly unimpressed with the idea of contacting merger-and-acquisition specialists such as the people at Goldman, Sachs. He'd been burned by a takeover maven back when Deere came up, and he'd had just about enough of New York financiers.

"Well," Hills said in his deep pioneer's drawl, "I'll give it a shot myself, then." He walked over to Telling's desk and put in a call to Wes Poulson, the chairman of Coldwell Banker. Poulson and Hills had tossed footballs back and forth when they were at Stanford together (" 'Course they did," Telling said, shaking his head). Poulson's secretary said he was out of the country.

Wesley Poulson took Hills' call on Friday, September 25, at the Château du Domaine Saint-Martin, a small hotel perched high above the Côte d'Azur in the village of Vence. Outside, the worst electrical thunderstorm Wes Poulson had ever seen lit the sky over the Mediterranean. Poulson had been a few classes ahead of Hills at Stanford, and his relationship over the years with Hills and his wife, Carla, had been casual at best. But he considered Rod Hills to be "the best name-dropper in the whole world," and he knew enough of the nature of Hills' business interests to understand that Rod was not calling him in France on his own behalf.

"Wes," Hills said over the crackling connection, "now, I don't know how serious this is, but I'm just calling to warn you that A. E. Le Page seems to be interested in buying you. Now, Mr. Ed Telling and Sears aren't at all interested in something like that—Sears is a benign, friendly holder in this—but I'd like to have the opportunity to convince you that you ought to consider coming into Sears. There's a lot of good work being done here that you would find interesting."

Poulson had been expecting a call like this for years. He couldn't tell from Hills' approach whether Sears would go so far as to play their best card if he balked—a threat to sell their 21 percent to Le Page, a far smaller and lesser outfit than Coldwell Banker. He needed to gauge their seriousness: "Well, I've gotta listen to you, Rod. I'm here on vacation with another couple, but I'm due to come home in two days. I can meet you at my office in Los Angeles."

"Why take a chance, Wes?" Hills said quickly. "I'm free at the moment, and there's a chance these guys up north might be serious. I can't tell you *how* serious, but if you and Anne wouldn't mind, I'll come meet you in Paris on Sunday around lunchtime. Let's spend the afternoon talking and have dinner. Then I'll fly you and your friends home in a Sears plane."

Hills covered the telephone and looked over at Telling. "Can I use a plane?" he whispered.

Telling nodded.

While a jet was being readied, Phil Purcell pulled the research file on

Coldwell Banker and huddled briefly with Hills to present a skeletal pitch about why a marriage between the two companies made sense. Phil described the fit between Sears' existing shopping-center developer and mortgage businesses and Coldwell Banker's network of residential-housing and commercial real-estate brokers.

Hills said he wanted to take the file with him to read on the way to Paris, so he threw it in his briefcase and rushed to the airport late on Friday evening. The jet stopped in Washington, because Rod and Carla were hosting a tennis party the next day for the Swedish ambassador and several other dignitaries. Rod figured he could have a glass of wine, work one circuit of the crowd, and still make it to Paris by Sunday morning.

Late that same Friday evening, William Dimma of A. E. Le Page was sitting in his library at home when he finally got a return phone call from Dick Sharp of Simpson-Sears. Sharp began to stammer incomprehensibly. He began one sentence after another that had no ending. Dimma couldn't understand much of what Sharp was saying, but he heard something about not being "fully authorized" to return his call of that morning. Dimma quickly begged off from the torturous conversation and called the Le Page board chairman (and a Coldwell Banker board member by virtue of their considerable holdings), Gordon Gray. "I just had the goddamnedest telephone conversation," Dimma said. "I don't know if you're interested in playing David to a Goliath, but I think Sears is about to make a run at Coldwell Banker."

When Wesley Poulson emerged from Harvard Business School in 1953, the world of Wall Street was finally shedding the last vestiges of the Depression-era stigma that located it as the national cynosure of ruinous greed. Serious young elites from his Harvard class were once again joining securities brokerage firms and investment banks, but Poulson, a Chicago boy by birth, decided, some fifteen years before it became the place for bright young men to be, to cast his lot with the still utterly unacceptable hawkers of American real estate. Poulson was thirty-eight years old and already an extremely wealthy man when he became what's known in his business as a "reformed real-estate man." He stopped selling and became the senior manager of the country's largest full-service real-estate company, which under his leadership had expanded and acquired until it operated 382 real-estate offices around the country and employed a sales force of seventy-four hundred people. The blue-and-white Coldwell Banker aegis had become unavoidable during Poulson's thirteen years of leadership, rising as it did from so many rural tracts and jutting from the side of office buildings and stores.

Lunchtime salads at the California Club and a compulsive regimen of jogging had kept the fifty-one-year-old Poulson as trim and lean as a middleweight. He tended to bob his head and bury his jaw behind a twitching deltoid like a fighter when he became agitated, and he was known on occasion to express displeasure by offering to "pop a guy." Poulson was given to straight talk, huge tie clips, Cyrus Vance half-glasses, quick and sardonic comments, and the occasional longer tirade concerning his pet peeves—grossly overweight people in general and fat business executives in particular.

Wes Poulson never for a second thought you "had to be a brain surgeon" to understand the rudiments of the real-estate business, but during his time as manager of the seventy-five-year-old real-estate institution, he'd applied himself to becoming an unusually serious student of the economic underpinnings of the trade's hypercyclical business environment. Poulson could talk for hours about the advanced research being done on economic cycles and business developments in academies around the world.

Since 1974, Poulson had been telling his stockholders that the vertical integration of the real-estate business was going to become so pronounced that the profitability of the pure brokerage businesses would eventually be crippled by bigger players. In 1978 he prophesied that within ten years the trend toward "ancillary services" would bring competitors like big banks or insurance companies into Coldwell Banker's game. He'd kept a huge chart in his downtown Los Angeles office that listed 120 large corporations up and down the left edge and a long list of specific financial services across the top. The numbers of blue squares filled in as companies added to their repertoire of offered services were multiplying more quickly all the time lately. Sears was listed high in the upper left-hand corner of the chart.

Poulson had become convinced that the trends at a company like Merrill Lynch, where financing, brokerage, insurance, and several other services were offered, could eventually close a company like Coldwell Banker out of the business of selling homes and other real estate for good. Getting people mortgages was becoming a booming business function, and brokering was just a single piece of an emergent whole. As, with inexorable cycles, the best you can do is try to stay ahead of the curve, so for some time Wes Poulson had believed there were only two questions about the future of Coldwell Banker—when and who.

It was hard to find an open restaurant in Paris that Sunday night, but Rod Hills and the Poulsons eventually settled on Chez Michelle, not far from the Gare du Nord. During the afternoon, Hills had delivered an impressive rendering of what Ed Telling—"an old-shoe type," as Hills de-

scribed the chairman to Poulson—had in mind. Hills believed in a negotiating tack that dictated price talk only during the closing rounds, but
after several hours of pleasant conversation in the afternoon, Hills began
to leaf casually through Purcell's file on Coldwell Banker as Poulson
looked on. He passed by documents written by Preston Martin that
urged a grow-your-own approach to creating a Coldwell Banker–style
real-estate operation, pausing at one sheet of paper long enough for
Poulson to get a look. The page included a test of "price sensitivity" on
Coldwell Banker, an analysis of the range of the price per share Sears
might have to pay. Poulson noted that the range was between $37 and
$47 a share. Nothing was said at the time, but it would later be remem-
bered that Rod Hills had encountered document troubles before in his
life: a member of the House Intelligence Committee once tried to get
Hills fired from his White House staff job for losing a folder containing
national security data.

At dinner Hills said he wanted to negotiate a definitive agreement
within five days. Poulson laughed the comment off, but after dinner he
phoned Los Angeles and scheduled an executive-committee meeting for
Tuesday.

The couple from Los Angeles traveling with the Poulsons still didn't
know who Rod Hills was or why he'd come to Paris when they boarded
the plush, unmarked Gulfstream jet the next morning. After unsuccess-
fully scouring the plane for an insignia or a marked matchbook cover,
the two travelers gave up and settled into the plush seats in the back of
the plane for the rest of the free ride home. Rod Hills got off in Connecticut to attend to some other business. He told Poulson he'd meet him in
Chicago the following evening.

Though Poulson had been warning his colleagues to expect a takeover
move for a long time, he knew that approaching the other big wheels
at Coldwell Banker would be unlike the approach of most CEOs to a top
management group with news of a suitor. Just as Julius Rosenwald had
proclaimed the independent status of the buyers at Sears, and the General had designed his democracy of store management, Coldwell Banker
was actually a loose confederation of extremely entrepreneurial real-
estate salesmen, many of whom had ridden the California property rush
long enough and with enough skill to amass sizable personal fortunes.
Poulson could run his finger down the list of his top people for five
minutes before he got to somebody who wasn't worth well over a million
dollars. The key people all had over $4 million, and a few of them had
accumulated $50 million. Wes Poulson was the president and chairman
of the firm, but he was surrounded by Coldwell Banker principals who'd
never stopped selling long enough to ponder cycles or try managing
others. While Poulson knew none of them would be averse to becoming

suddenly much wealthier by virtue of the effect of an acquisition on the value of their shares, he also knew that his partners would resist the idea of being engulfed unless the conditions and the price were right.

When he arrived in Chicago, Poulson brought along the firm's largest insider stockholder, a deceptively laid-back Californian named Forrest E. Olson, as well as two other top executives. Poulson's acquisition of Forey Olson's large southern-California residential-real-estate company was an early step in the creation of a system of local house-sellers that was to complement Coldwell Banker's flashier commercial-real-estate business. Olson had been given a great deal of latitude in his subsequent building of the operation, and he knew that it was his mass distribution system Sears was after. Olson had been a Sears-watcher for years. His mother worked in one of the Far Western Territory stores as a cost accountant, and Olson himself had worked in a Sears automotive department during the Christmas season of 1944.

Poulson had promised his executive committee that he, Olson, and the others would go to Chicago and "size up Ed Telling." "There's no such thing as a white knight," Poulson said, "only various shades of gray. But we've gotta go listen."

On the way to Chicago, Poulson mentioned the price range he'd spied in Rod Hills' file. "If they stick with $37 a share," Forey Olson said, "I'll personally lead the rebellion in the board of directors."

Poulson's team joined Telling in his office late on Tuesday, September 29, for a relaxed conversation about the state of their respective businesses. Wes Poulson talked a bit about cycles, and Telling spoke of his hopes that his young managers working downstairs would turn the Merchant around. He added that he was sure the Sears stock price—which languished at around $16 a share—was due for a rise.

Poulson realized from the start that Ed Telling was far from the "old shoe" Hills had told him to expect. He looked to be more than a bit overweight, but Poulson sensed an unusually wily mind working behind the gentlemanly country-boy veneer. His suspicion was confirmed when Telling suddenly excused himself from discussions just as the subject of price was raised. The strategy allowed one of the three Sears negotiators—Rod Hills, Phil Purcell, and an aggressive, dark-haired thirty-four-year-old investment banker from Goldman, Sachs' merger-and-acquisitions department in New York named Geoff Boisi—to leave the room periodically with a new proposal and come back with a decision from Telling. The chairman would thus remain unsullied by haggling, above the butting of heads. Poulson thought the tactic far from old-shoe in conception and effect.

Neither Purcell nor Hills was particularly pleased by the presence in Telling's corner office of Boisi, the Goldman, Sachs pugnacious boy-wonder of takeovers. Purcell thought that Sears' long-time investment bank had been collecting consultation fees in exchange for little help during his nearly three years of strategic work—the bankers had been less than helpful in Sears' effort to get Seraco going, and useless in the conduct of other business concerning the Merchandise Group's failing international operations.

Rod Hills was still smarting from Goldman, Sachs' effort to take him and his law firm out of the transaction altogether. Representatives from Goldman had suggested to Telling that they preferred to do a deal with the aid of one of the Wall Street legal firms they already knew, and Hills had been woefully insulted by the attempt to freeze him out.

Within a half-hour of Ed Telling's exit from the negotiations, Geoff Boisi had positioned himself rather immovably as the guardian of Sears' "final offer" of $37 for each of Coldwell Banker's five million outstanding shares, and Wes Poulson was bobbing and weaving in full readiness to pop the young banker square in the nose. Thirty-seven was the price the team from California knew to be the "low-ball" offer. At several points during the acrimonious discussions, Purcell believed the Coldwell Banker delegation was going to walk out over Boisi's consistent and, Purcell thought, arrogant contention that Wes Poulson was "crazy" to think that the underlying value of his business was worth more than $37 a share. Because of the rapid expansion of the company, both Poulson and Olson had been part of numerous acquisition proceedings, and they weren't enjoying Boisi's remedial tirades about what they didn't know. If they walked, Phil Purcell had decided to punch the whining Boisi in the nose himself.

The negotiations broke and recommenced, continuing late into the night. Every so often Purcell would return from a visit to Telling with a comment like "Chairman Telling says that, the way he understands business, a $7.99 wrench is for sale at $7.99. He says the price is the price."

During the breaks, Poulson talked to his colleagues about fighting off both Sears and Le Page and trying to go it alone. He'd raised the idea before of Coldwell Banker's buying its own securities firm so as to assure its clients access to mortgage loans.

By the next morning, it had become clear that the best solution that could possibly come out of the negotiations was a proposed price from Sears that Poulson would then take to his board of directors without the pledge of his personal support.

By mid-morning that last day of September, the Sears side had made its final offer. Poulson agreed to take a written offer of $41 per share to his board during a meeting called for the following Sunday. Poulson and Forrest Olson both said they wouldn't commit themselves to voting for the proposal. Olson added that he was impressed with Purcell and Telling's business plans, but he believed that $41 was too low a figure even to submit to the others. For one thing, part of the offer was in Sears stock, which Olson felt would never return to approach its former strength.

Wes Poulson felt himself slip into what must have been a mild state of shock on the way back to Los Angeles. Through the haze of his severe physical exhaustion, he did know that he'd taken a shine to Ed Telling. They wouldn't know what the hell to make of him at the California Club, and Poulson liked that. The Sears chairman had mentioned that he would want Poulson to run much more than Coldwell Banker for him after the marriage was consummated, but Poulson couldn't get it out of his head that his band of hot-shot sellers of California dreams wouldn't do too well on a tight lead. On the plane back home, he began to think that the whole idea, though possibly inevitable, was a big mistake.

Rod Hills didn't tend to get tired when he was doing deals. His bright-eyed, morning-rooster quality never seemed to flag. He could eat heavy meals according to the schedule of whatever time belt he ended up in from day to day. After Paris he'd seen to his business in Connecticut, and he'd made it down to Washington again in time for his son's birthday party. He was in Chicago to greet the entourage from Coldwell Banker, but he excused himself to fly briefly over to Detroit for a board-of-directors meeting before returning again to the Tower.

Phil Purcell had developed a grudging respect for Hills' energy, as well as for his creativity in negotiation. He was masterful at yanking discussions back just as they touched the edge of failure. It was Hills who decided—without knowing how appropriate it was to Ed Telling's style—to set the chairman up as an exalted off-stage presence during the Coldwell Banker discussions, and Hills who'd come up with the compromise of a written offer in lieu of a final handshake that was clearly not forthcoming. Hills' performance was all the more impressive to Purcell because he knew that each time Rod Hills excused himself momentarily from the Wednesday negotiations in Telling's office, he was going into another room with Ed Telling to try and light a fire under the Dean Witter deal again.

Hills had been trying to convince Telling to let him re-establish proceedings with Gardiner and Melton ever since their lunch in New York. While Rod was traveling in Kuwait just before the Coldwell Banker opening appeared, Gardiner and Melton had dropped in on Telling for an informal dinner at the Tower, but when Hills returned, Telling told him he was reconsidering an approach to PaineWebber instead. Hills insisted that Sears could buy Dean Witter if they only pushed a bit harder.

Every time Stretch Gardiner began to think the approach was over, Rod would phone or show up again in his office. The day Hills returned from Paris, he'd called Gardiner from the airport. "What the hell's going on with this?" Hills said. "Are you interested in this or not?"

Telling agreed with Hills that the addition of Coldwell Banker might move Gardiner and Melton to action. A takeover of the huge realtor would be seen as strong evidence of Sears' commitment to becoming the sort of financial-services Goliath Purcell had described during their first meeting.

During one of his exits from negotiations with Wes Poulson, Hills located Gardiner and Melton in Washington. They were hosting a Dean Witter reception at the Corcoran Gallery that night for participants in a World Bank meeting. They were due to spend the night at the Jefferson Hotel after the party.

A Sears jet was rolled out late Wednesday night, and Rod Hills headed for Washington. He joined Andy Melton, Stretch Gardiner, and Gardiner's wife, Elizabeth, for breakfast in the small traditional dining room off the lobby at the Jefferson. "Look, this has gone on long enough, and the time has come to move," Hills said. "I'm going to give you some market information that we think will interest you. We're about to make a deal for Coldwell Banker." He paused, concentrating a stare on Gardiner. "I've got a plane waiting at the airport to take us to New York. Let's get up there and get some papers drawn up."

The information about Coldwell Banker was indeed a powerful factor to Stretch Gardiner. During the winter of 1976, back when he ran Reynolds Securities, Gardiner was sitting in the Abu Dhabi airport with the managing director of a Paris-based bank that owned 16 percent of Reynolds. "If you had all the money in the world to buy a company," the banker said, "what would you take?" Gardiner said he'd buy a California real-estate company called Coldwell Banker. An emissary was subsequently dispatched from Reynolds to approach Coldwell Banker, but he was sent home with a firm rejection. Wes Poulson was apparently not about to let Coldwell Banker get swallowed up by a small fish.

It was Gardiner who'd put in an early-morning call to Andy Melton to propose a merger of Reynolds and Dean Witter the very morning Melton took over leadership of the firm from the last of the Witter family members. Stretch didn't even take off his hat in his rush to make the call, such was his conviction that the smaller securities firms were a thing of the past. He'd written one of the occasional in-house "thought pieces" he penned every so often since the merger about the idea of an enlarged

Dean Witter Reynolds' joining forces with an even bigger company like Sears, Roebuck. It always stuck in Gardiner's head that Sears spent as much on advertising in a year as Dean Witter collected in gross sales revenue. Gardiner shared Wes Poulson's belief that the domination of the world of finance by a few "superpowers" was inevitable. Instead of a chart marking the inexorable progress of the phenomenon, he kept the early speeches and business plans of Merrill Lynch's founder, Charlie Merrill, in his desk. Merrill saw the future in 1940, Gardiner thought, and it was a fantasy to think you could buck the trend toward the integration of power and resources.

Stretch was by far the more easygoing of the two Dean Witter leaders. He had a deep orator's voice, an easy laugh, and the languorous presence of many very tall men. His visibility in a crowd was augmented by his inevitably tanned, somewhat florid face and straw-thick white hair, which traveled so high above most people around him that it looked from a distance like a snowcap. Gardiner grew up within a powerful strain of tradition on Wall Street. It included the Pawling School, then Princeton. As an Army captain in Germany he won a silver-and-bronze star before hitting the Street. He was a member of two urban clubs, three country clubs, and one hunting club in Essex Fells, New Jersey.

Rod Hills liked Stretch Gardiner. Everyone did. But Gardiner's personality was less involved in Hills' direction of phone calls and visits toward the number-two officer of Dean Witter than was the fact that after Dean Witter's takeover of Reynolds, Stretch owned about 130,000 shares of Dean Witter stock—about 110,000 more shares than Andy Melton controlled.

It was always surprising to observers of Dean Witter that it was Melton—a native of the lower-middle-class Long Island suburbs and a graduate of Villanova University rather than Princeton—who contended that the future of Dean Witter was reflected in the carriage-trade browsers uptown at Tiffany's. Melton came to Wall Street during the war and got a job with Smith Barney, a brokerage house known for its policy of hiring only graduates of Yale University or former U.S. Marines. Andy had been a Marine.

Melton rose from the sales side to run the sales operations as well as the syndicate department for Smith Barney. The syndicate is a deceptively named department in Wall Street houses that deals in underwriting new securities issues. Since most stock and bond issues are underwritten by a number of financial firms that share in an offering, the syndicate man tends to be a high-profile figure on the Street. Syndicate men could be seen around town consuming lunches worthy of merchandise men, and Andy Melton was well known and personable enough to be well liked.

After twenty years of success in the senior ranks of Smith Barney, alongside many better-born and -educated colleagues, Andy Melton's career was suddenly blocked. Personal problems affected his work, and Melton was moved aside before he eventually left the firm. His personal tragedy became a much-repeated decline-and-fall story in financial circles, but after a while Melton pulled himself together and began to work his way back up through the ranks of Dean Witter, all the way to the top. "The book" on Andy Melton was thus rewritten in some quarters so as to include the part about his amazing comeback, but those who worked closely with Melton knew that he'd come back as a far more cautious, less trusting man.

When Reynolds and Dean Witter got together, Stretch Gardiner accepted a clear number-two role in deference to Witter's size. At one point during 1980, Melton held the titles of "chairman of the board," "chief executive officer," and "president," while Gardiner was just a vice-chairman of the board. Stretch became associated with the operations side of the business, and when Dean Witter's less-than-efficient "back-office" operations group was blamed for unforeseen losses in 1979, Gardiner ended up with the blame.

Melton continued to concentrate on making Dean Witter the investment banker to the biggest companies and government agencies, rather than a brokerage house for Main Street, while Gardiner had become fascinated by technical systems of distribution by which the retail side of the business could expand. The man from Dean Witter sought the "Tiffany alternative to Merrill Lynch" while the Reynolds man wanted the company to be Merrill Lynch unadorned. By 1981, students of the brokerage world saw this ironic conceptual division as just one of many residual divisions between the Reynolds and Dean Witter elements in the merged company: the small but elite Wall Street house and the Main Street wire house from San Francisco that had never really formed together as a whole.

After breakfast in Washington on Thursday, Hills, Gardiner, and Melton flew to New York and rode in a limousine to Dean Witter's company apartment in the Carleton House on Madison Avenue. The slightly ragged apartment on the fourth floor of the Carleton had been the scene of the original, unsuccessful meeting between the Dean Witter leaders with Telling, Purcell, and Hills. The apartment was lined by strangely institutional green carpets, and the furniture was covered in Sun Belt hues that matched the ghastly motel-room art on the walls.

After a few hours it was decided that they would work throughout the following day trying to strike a bargain. The men took turns calling lawyers on the phone sitting on a small desk near a window. Eventually Hills called Telling. "I think we're ready to go here," he said. "You and Phil better come on in."

After Hills collected Telling and Purcell at the airport early on Friday morning, Andy Melton received the three men at the Dean Witter apartment. Melton immediately announced that he'd set up a meeting downtown so that Phil Purcell could present his brilliant financial-services rap to some of Dean Witter's senior executives. Purcell glanced over at Telling. This wasn't part of the deal, and as Melton stood there waiting for Purcell to leave, Purcell realized that he was being purposely moved away from the action. But Telling nodded at him, and Phil took a taxi down to the Vista Hotel, located at the southern tip of Manhattan, just a few blocks from Dean Witter's headquarters.

As soon as Melton sat down with Telling and Hills, he mentioned the price he expected to be offered for the firm. "Come on, Andy, we agreed to talk price at the end," Rod Hills interrupted. "Only at the end."

"I just want you to know the range." Then Melton suddenly stood up and announced that he had an important luncheon engagement to attend to. He excused himself and walked out of the apartment.

The price Melton had mentioned was almost $20 per share above anything Sears had in mind, and as Hills looked over at Ed Telling, who was staring hard at a wall and quietly mouthing the price Melton had mentioned—as well as something else that looked like "*luncheon* engagement?"—he realized that the day might be longer than he'd thought.

"I guess if we're into price already, we better get Geoff Boisi," Hills said. Boisi was on his way to his first meeting as a trustee of Boston College, where he had been an undergraduate before Wharton and the fast track. He was traveling in a Sears car when a call from Rod Hills came through on the two-way radio. After subsequent phone calls to Dean Witter, a meeting was scheduled to commence at the uptown offices of Dean Witter's law firm, Sullivan and Cromwell. As Hills left the apartment for the talks, he told Telling he'd call him as soon as something broke.

Ed Telling didn't mind cooling his heels all alone in the ugly room—for at least a minute or two.

Telling had long been aware of the anomaly inherent in being at once a confirmed loner as well as someone who got a bad case of cabin fever after only a few minutes in his own company. He didn't like being inside a hotel room now any more than he had during the nights at the end of his long days riding the zones and groups of the Field. All those years of Holiday Inns and sitting silently in cars surrounded by corn, he'd always been a little happier if there was at least somebody else sitting there. There was a time when Sears made him ride with a tragic ruin of a man, a fellow named Carpenter, whom Telling had to practically carry between numerous motel rooms and the back rooms of many stores. Telling covered for Carpenter at every turn while he was drying out, while all the time Nancy was home trying to take care of the family. But even Carpenter was better than being alone.

He was alone now, and alone in New York City, and thinking about things that he'd been forced to endure. He'd been judged one of the nation's worst executives; he'd been inveighed against in the press, attacked by his own retirees, betrayed here and there by colleagues, sued by somebody every time he turned his back; and now was frustrated to hell in his effort to spend a couple hundred million dollars. It was enough to impair a man's sense of humor, no matter how much he talked himself up in the mirror in the morning.

He gazed around the empty Dean Witter apartment, a seedy place with deep, empty closets and only crackers and full cases of Scotch in the kitchen. Telling didn't "understand" Andy Melton's behavior. When he told people he didn't understand something—Telling would usually say something like "Well, I guess I'm just so goddamned naïve and dumb that I can't un'erstan' that"—it really meant that he rejected the thing to the point of barely contained rage. If Ed Telling didn't understand you, it usually meant you were headed for trouble. He had a faint sense now that a couple of big-city operators were playing games with a couple of small-town boys from the Second City—a couple of pretty tired-out people at that—and as he paced the awful carpets of the apartment and watched shoppers who would never in their lives register on the sales charts the researchers kept in department 720, as they moved back and forth in front of the shops on the east side of Madison Avenue, Telling just found the whole situation hard to understand.

After Phil Purcell had delivered to three Dean Witter officers at the Vista his canned rendition of what a new Sears, geared for the future, would look like, Andy Melton called and asked him to come back uptown to the Sullivan and Cromwell offices. There he would find Dean Witter's attorneys, two more Dean Witter functionaries—investment bankers this time—as well as Rod Hills. Purcell hoped that Melton's charade indicated his efforts to build internal support for the deal, but it crossed his mind that the important lunches and office jockeying might mean the presence of another suitor. When he realized that Rod had left Telling alone in the green suite, he knew Rod had made an error.

Hills, Geoff Boisi, and Purcell sensed from the start of the meeting at the Park Avenue law offices that the two Dean Witter bankers—Frank Richardson and Tom Murtaugh—were not particularly interested in working for Sears, Roebuck. The two men gave short presentations of their position as to price, which they presented as immovable at $78 a share, a figure that would have multiplied out to more money than American Express had paid for Shearson, a firm twice the size of Dean Witter.

Geoff Boisi was crankier than usual; he began to lose his temper early in the meeting. But Phil Purcell, after watching Boisi's effect on the Californians two days earlier, was determined to carry the conversation. He and Telling had come to town prepared to pay between $46 and $50 per share for Dean Witter, so he ran through some of the multiples of price-to-earnings and price-per-account-executive that had been paid in other deals as evidence of a fair price in the 1940s, but Murtaugh and Richardson argued at length that it was the ratio of Dean Witter's stock price to its book value that was salient.

Frank Richardson was in fact quite ambivalent about the proposed acquisition. He owned a lot of stock, but he found it hard to believe that ownership by Sears would in any way aid his investment-banking and deal-making side of the firm. His more immediate problem, however, was that Andy Melton had called him and Tom Murtaugh into his office only the previous evening to reveal that a deal was pending, and Richardson was still utterly unprepared.

From the moment he sat down with Richardson, Rod Hills thought he recognized the man, and just before Geoff Boisi began to scream, Rod remembered he'd been Richardson's lawyer once in California. Rod lived in a small world.

"How in the world can you ever say such an *absurd* thing!" Geoff Boisi began to yell when the Dean Witter side entrenched. "You just can't say that! There's not a single transaction on record that could ever lead you to that price."

Continuing would be fruitless, so Phil Purcell rose to excuse himself. He'd been wondering for several hours how Telling was holding up all alone.

"Well, I'm just fine," Telling said with a decided edge in his voice when Purcell phoned. "Jus' fine. Spent four more hours with myself than I have since I was in the Navy. Been sittin' here all by myself. . . . Worse than that, I found a bottle of Scotch, but I don't know whether to drink it in case these boys are coming back here. I've eaten every goddamned cracker in the place already."

"You wouldn't believe what's going on here," Purcell said. "You just wouldn't believe it."

A short time later, while Murtaugh and Richardson were out making a call to Andy Melton, Hills, Boisi, and Purcell walked out of the Sullivan and Cromwell offices and headed back to the Carleton. They found Telling standing in the middle of the room looking at a wall.

Rod Hills said that he was sure Melton would call. They agreed that if he did Purcell should answer the phone and say that Telling would call Melton back, to give them more time to decide what to do. The telephone on the small desk rang a few moments later:

"This is Andy Melton. May I speak to Ed Telling, please?"

"This is Phil Purcell; Mr. Telling's in the bathroom."

"Well," Melton said. "My boys tell me there's no point in having any further discussions."

"That's a bit disappointing, Mr. Melton. Are you at a number where Mr. Telling can call you?"

When Purcell relayed the message, Telling began to pace back and forth. "I don't understand this at all. What is this?" Telling phoned back five minutes later. "I've found myself all alone in New York City today, Mr. Melton. Haven't seen ya' all day. I've eaten everything in the place—which I might add was just cookies and crackers—and I'm just about to start in on your Scotch . . . if you don't mind."

"Drink the whole bottle," Melton said.

"I'm having a little trouble understanding all this. No need for us to talk anymore," Telling said. Then he hung up.

Telling led the group quickly down Madison Avenue to the high-ceilinged rococo dining room at the Helmsley Palace Hotel. It was already late in the evening. Geoff Boisi said the problem was that Rod Hills had set up a one-day negotiation session for a deal that could only have been settled in four days. Hills was indeed anxious that the Dean Witter deal be concluded that Friday, because he thought it essential that Wes Poulson be able to tell his board about Dean Witter at the meeting in Los Angeles on Sunday. Wes needed the added firepower.

Several drinks were consumed, and then a few glasses of wine. Geoff Boisi began much more aggressively to press his assertion that they'd made a mistake in trying to work the deal in one day. "I think you ought to call Andy Melton and start it back up," Boisi demanded, leaning toward Hills.

Phil Purcell was still fuming. "They've treated us like some lower form of life," he said. Purcell eventually agreed with Boisi that Hills should at least call, if for no other reason than to demand an apology.

Hills refused. He said the deal was stalled. There were no SEC problems, and after the weekend they'd probably have Coldwell Banker to wave at Melton.

All through the subsequent bottles of wine, Purcell and Boisi badgered Hills as Telling sat quietly, apparently lost in thought. "Goddamn it, Rod," Phil Purcell said, "get up from the table and make the call."

"No," Hills said.

Finally Telling said, "Why don't you go call, Rod."

Hills agreed to call, but he said he would call Stretch Gardiner to say that his people thought Andy Melton had been less than gracious and therefore had an obligation to repair relations with Sears. Gardiner picked up the phone just after eleven o'clock. He told Hills he understood his feelings, but added that having investment bankers present had been a mistake. If the merger occurred, then Sears would come into ownership of an active and growing investment-banking department in Dean Witter. Geoff Boisi's behavior caused the Dean Witter side to wonder if it wasn't in Goldman, Sachs' interest to make the deal unreasonable, so as to keep their Sears business in the future.

Gardiner was getting up very early the next morning to go address an American Bar Association meeting in San Francisco. He said he and Melton were so afraid of rumors that they'd decided to keep all their previously scheduled business appointments. The reason Melton left Telling alone at the Carleton was not to open negotiations with another company but to have lunch with an insurance-company executive who was trying to gain acceptance into one of Melton's New York clubs.

After the phone call, Telling finished his wine. "When somebody tells me to go home," he said, "I go on home."

They came home early the next morning—Saturday—only to hear of new problems in Los Angeles. The Sears attorney who was supposed to deliver the written offer was being avoided by the attorneys assigned to receive it for Coldwell Banker. Rod Hills found out that Forrest Olson and another major Coldwell Banker executive, Rod Briggs, had soured on the deal completely.

When Wes Poulson left Chicago after negotiations in the Tower, Phil Purcell said to Telling that the Coldwell Banker CEO was headed for a difficult and emotional few days. "Wes Poulson's life is going to become very interesting now," he guessed. Phil saw Poulson as a latter-day corporate king who was faced on one side with the specter of being swallowed up by a much larger company and on the other side by a group of powerful "medieval barons," as Phil put it, men who really controlled the kingdom Poulson ran at their behest. The issue was complicated by the fact that the barons also happened to be Wes Poulson's close friends, with whom he'd built the business over the years.

Though there was indeed trouble in Los Angeles, it appeared that Poulson remained committed to pushing the deal, but the avoidance of the formal documents indicated his difficulties with the others. It was decided that Purcell and Hills should fly out to Los Angeles right away to see if they could improve the odds. Before they left, Telling and his team of outsiders—Hills, Boisi, and Phil Purcell—reviewed the sorry events of the previous day in New York City. "The girl took a walk and we oughta say goodbye," Purcell said. "There are still other alternatives." It was agreed that Sears wouldn't even respond to a subsequent overture from Melton or Gardiner. As Hills and Purcell were about to head west, a call came in from Washington indicating that Andy Melton was calling all over the District of Columbia in search of Rod Hills.

Melton had retreated to his summer home in Vermont right after talks fell apart on Friday. He wasn't about to lose sleep or a weekend over Ed Telling's injured feelings. If the chairman hadn't enjoyed his day of solitude in New York, then Melton figured he should address the members of his own staff who had left him alone. He was much more worried about the loss of a good deal. He talked to Gardiner from Vermont and then phoned some of Dean Witter's outside directors, including one of his own mentors, the retired investment banker and former chairman of Smith Barney, Hugh Knowlton. Knowlton convinced Melton to try again. That's when Melton began to look for Rod Hills.

Hills called Melton back from Telling's office without indicating where he was. "Well, Andy," Rod said, "I have no idea what the Sears thinking is now, but from the tone of the meetings I assume they've forgotten all about you. As you know, they are trying to close the Coldwell Banker deal, so I don't think it's a good time to talk to Ed Telling again. Maybe some other time."

"Ed," Hills said after hanging up, "I think you oughta sweeten the deal by a dollar a share on Coldwell Banker—move the price up to $42 to help Wes sell it."

"You're crazy!" Telling roared. "A deal's a deal!" Purcell was bone-tired from all the long hours, tension, and travel, and he was more then twenty years younger than Ed Telling. For over three years he and the chairman had been trying to enact a reconstruction of the aging empire, and now all of their work, all of those thousands of hours of study and talk about creating a new corporate future, had come down to two shaky deals being played out over just a few debilitating days. It wasn't the prospect of a $1.00 sweetener that would cost Sears around $4 million that had provoked Telling.

"Wes is a good man," Hills said softly after Telling clammed up again and turned away. Rod began to gather his papers together for the trip to Los Angeles. "He won't back away from the deal, but it's clear he's having problems with his people." Hills had seen many a good deal fall apart because a businessman couldn't stop himself from relating to an acquisition as if he were purchasing some real estate or a refrigerator. It just wasn't the same. Acquisitions were lofty rearrangements, not simple exchanges of value. The buyer had to be sufficiently in control of his ego to let the seller feel like he screwed you over a bit if a deal was to succeed.

Hills saw Phil Purcell smiling at him after they boarded the jet that Saturday afternoon. "Telling says we should throw in the extra buck," he said. "But we aren't to offer it unless he asks."

"Wes Poulson won't ask," Hills said.

The Sears lawyers had still been unable to formally deliver the written offer to Coldwell Banker when Hills and Purcell met Wes Poulson in downtown Los Angeles for breakfast at eight o'clock on Sunday morning. Poulson's board was due to convene at noon. "Your attorney's a little hard to find," Purcell said. "He seems to be avoiding delivery of a document. If it ever gets to you, you ought to read it, Wes, because the price Sears is willing to pay is now $42 a share."

Forrest Olson and Rod Briggs both changed their minds and decided to vote for the takeover when they heard about the extra dollar. They didn't say so at the time, but the dollar seemed to alleviate some of the weight of culpability involved in voting for a change at Coldwell Banker that could potentially serve to end the company's freewheeling style.

The board voted unanimously to be acquired by Sears. Even Gordon Gray, the chairman of A. E. Le Page, said he felt that Poulson had made a good deal for his company and shareholders. After the vote, the public-affairs people on the sixty-eighth floor in Chicago prepared a press release announcing an agreement "in principle." The statement mentioned that upon completion of the merger, Mr. C. Wesley Poulson would become the new chairman and chief executive officer of the Seraco group.

Poulson, Rod Briggs, and a few other senior Coldwell Banker people decided to go out for dinner with Hills and Purcell Sunday night. Wes Poulson and Rod Hills smiled at each other when the entourage encountered difficulty in finding a decent restaurant that was open on a Sunday night. Their dinner near the Gare du Nord had occurred just a week earlier.

Over his first perfect Manhattan at the Bona Ventura Hotel—straight up and with a twist—Phil Purcell began to worry. He began to wonder, almost in a panic now, whether the thing would work, whether he'd helped engineer a brilliant commercial maneuver or a tremendous mistake. All his life he'd made plans for others—but this one had suddenly become real. He told himself it was only natural—psychologically natural—to pass through these dark thoughts. After a while he shook it off, but he couldn't stop thinking about how strange the dinner felt. He could sense that Wes Poulson and the other Coldwell Banker boys were also circling a wheel of emotions. How interesting it was to have all those countervailing tensions, the intersecting dramas of so many people's lives held together in stasis for the space of an apparently run-of-the-mill meal shared by a bunch of very well-paid guys in business suits.

The next morning the market price of a share of Dean Witter Reynolds stock began to exhibit all the telltale signs of "informed accumulation." The price had been jumpy during the final moments of trading on Friday, as Telling paced the living room on Madison Avenue. Telling was well aware of the incomparable potential of the Sears, Roebuck grapevine, but he was sure that the leaks came from the Dean Witter side. On unusually large volume, the price had jumped nearly $4.00 a share by Monday's close.*

Phil Purcell flew back to Chicago alone on Monday morning, because Rod Hills had to tend to another deal in Los Angeles. Hills dragged himself out of bed and drove out to a board meeting at Santa Fe International, a complex located next door to the Far Western Territory's cube in Alhambra. Hills had been helping set up a deal by which the government of Kuwait would purchase the American engineering firm, and the board meeting he attended happened to be the one where the directors were asked to approve the takeover. The meeting lasted until two in the afternoon, when Hills hitched a ride to Washington on Santa Fe's Jetstar. Hills was supposed to meet with the head of the Justice Department's anti-trust division to explain the sensitive Kuwait–Santa Fe deal when he arrived, but the Santa Fe jet developed a leak along the way and had to stop in Houston for repairs. Hills got to bed at five o'clock in the morning, only to be awakened an hour later with the news that Andy Melton was trying once again to re-establish contact with Ed Telling.

Though the movement was obscured by the assassination that day of Egyptian President Anwar Sadat, the Dean Witter stock price rose again on Tuesday morning's opening, partly in response to a *Wall Street Journal* report of street rumors about Sears, Roebuck's determination to acquire one of the major stock-brokerage firms.

Telling grumbled to various sixty-eighth-floor cronies about Andy Melton for quite a while before he finally took his call. Telling's assistant, Pat Jamieson, had been telling Melton that the chairman was too busy with the Sears board of directors, who were in town to hear about the

---

*A week later, a $37.50 investment in a Dean Witter call option—the contractual right to purchase shares at a specific future price—that was bought before the approach would be worth $1,300.

Coldwell Banker deal, to talk with him. When Telling finally called Melton back, he heard enough conciliatory talk to offer to send a Sears plane to get Melton in New York. Telling decided that this time he'd deal on his own turf; at least he could get home for dinner if things went sour again. By the time he got off the phone, Phil Purcell was already scraping himself out of a chair opposite Telling's desk to go back out to the hangar and fly east to get Andy and Rod.

Rod Hills was explaining the logic of the Santa Fe deal to his old friend Bill Baxter, the director of the Justice Department's anti-trust division, when he was called out of the meeting to take an urgent phone call from Chicago. Hills came back into Baxter's office and said he had to leave for the airport. "Bet I'm back here in a week with another deal to tell you 'bout," Hills said as he rushed out.

Phil Purcell picked up Hills in Washington; then Headquarters' big G-II continued on to Newark Airport, where Andy Melton was waiting. Melton and Telling had agreed to try to talk alone, chairman to chairman, so only one lawyer boarded the plane with Melton. Hills had remained quietly in touch with Stretch Gardiner, and from their conversations he'd surmised that Andy Melton's reticence could be overcome if Ed Telling would only switch on the "grandfatherly" charm he would on occasion flash, with great effort, at someone he didn't know or understand.

Before the jet took off, foul weather and traffic-control tie-ups delayed the flight on the ground for several hours. Dinner didn't commence in Chicago until after ten o'clock, but Rod Hills noticed immediately how gracious and friendly Ed Telling was being toward Melton.

Telling took Andy Melton aside at the end of the dinner. In deference to what Hills considered to be Melton's mercurial personality, it was decided that this time Telling should play Mr. Inside and let his aides wait in another room. "Mr. Melton," Telling said, "let's just you and me sit down and get all these lawyers out of the thing."

He led Melton to the comfortable square club chairs located in the far corner of his office, opposite his shelf full of old books and Eskimo sculpture. There the two chairmen began to bargain.

An hour later Telling walked down to CFO Dick Jones' office. Jones, Hills, Purcell, Geoff Boisi, and several other Sears and Goldman, Sachs officers were waiting inside. "He's down to fifty-two bucks a share," Telling said.

Sears had opened the serious bidding at $47, with an underlying assumption that it was still a good deal at $49. The consensus in Jones' office was that the deal could be had for $49 and that Telling should not go a nickel higher. "Forty-eight is plenty," Purcell said. "I'm sure you'll take him at 48."

"Give him 50," Rod Hills said. "Whatever we do, we'll end up paying 50."

"You can get him lower," Purcell insisted.

As Telling went back into his office to resume haggling, Phil Purcell was once again struck by the intensity of his feelings. Maybe it was the fatigue, but over his entire career in business he hadn't ever felt as attuned to a moment.

At four o'clock in the morning New York time, Stretch Gardiner was awakened by a call from Melton. Melton said that Telling had agreed to a price of $50 a share, much of it to be paid in Sears "paper." Gardiner agreed with Melton that $50 was a price that the Dean Witter board would accept, and the tax-free status of the paper exchange would obviate questions about the value of Sears' less-than-popular common stock. Melton suggested that Gardiner should get over to the Stock Exchange and stop trading in their stock first thing in the morning (the stock had closed another $5.00 higher on Tuesday). Sears and Dean Witter functionaries would hammer out the details in New York the next day, Melton said, so that an announcement could be made after simultaneous Dean Witter and Sears board meetings they agreed to schedule for Thursday.

The signing of a definitive agreement between Sears and Coldwell Banker occurred the next day, a few hours after a Sears team was dispatched to New York to hammer out a similar document pursuant to the acquisition of Dean Witter. When Purcell and Hills arrived at the Park Avenue offices of Wachtell, Lipton, Rosen, & Katz—Goldman, Sachs' attorneys—they agreed that a young lawyer from each side should do the "tablework" and "put the nits and lice" on the final contract.

The haggling over subclauses and options dragged on past dinner, when Hills and Purcell decided to remove themselves from the tedious discussions: "I can't listen to this shit anymore," Purcell said before he left. "Bob," he said, turning to Bob Burgess, the lawyer working for Sears, "if something needs to be decided, come find me." Purcell's spirits seldom soared in the presence of lawyers, but he was particularly irked by the lengthy discussions he'd just heard about personal compensation packages for Melton and Gardiner. When Telling and Melton shook hands on $50 a share, Telling believed they'd agreed there would be no more demands from Dean Witter. The talk of pensions, insurance, and other personal benefits was not part of the deal.

At 4:00 A.M. on the day the Sears and Dean Witter boards were both scheduled to meet to approve the deal, a document was sent to the word processors, as word continued to come from Sullivan and Cromwell that serious problems still existed. At 2:00 P.M. Purcell heard that Bob Hiden, a Sullivan and Cromwell partner, had declared that Dean Witter would not sign the document unless certain further changes in a comparatively minor clause were made.

Phil was bouncing hard now on the end of his lead. "Bullshit!" he remembers screaming at Hiden on the phone. "We're not going to do it! The Dean Witter board just approved the deal and now you're telling me you want to renegotiate. The answer's no! We won't renegotiate one damned word."

"Phil, you've got to get your emotions out of this now," Rod Hills said after coaxing Purcell into a hallway. "The boss wants a deal. We won't give anything away. Let me play out the last act. All we're here for is to make a deal."

Rod Hills had long believed that anger was an appropriate emotion to drag into a deal only if it was of the utterly disingenuous sort, trundled into a tense situation solely for effect. But Phil's anger was real—much of it, he realized, directed at Rod.

His suspicions about the object of Purcell's ire were confirmed when Hills agreed to renegotiate a small number of points—three at the most—so as to avoid a delay. He suggested that Telling call Andy Melton and work out the three points privately. Purcell was already incensed by Hills' propensity to speak in the name of Ed Telling. Phil saw that as his role, if anyone could presume to do such a thing. Hills had been inserting himself inappropriately ever since the Coldwell Banker deal broke.

"This is bullshit!" Purcell kept saying to Hills. "Pure bullshit." Purcell got Telling on the phone. "We don't have to respond to any of this," he said. "I don't even think Melton and Gardiner know what this lawyer's saying."

Telling said he was inclined to negotiate the snag, and Purcell stormed out of the room, announcing that he would have nothing more to do with new concessions.

"Our boys are scraping again," Telling said to Melton on the phone.

"Yeah, the lawyers are getting in the way," Melton said.

By late afternoon on Thursday, minor changes had been typed into the word processor. After further mechanical problems threatened briefly to delay the public announcement, the acquisition of the Dean Witter Reynolds organization by Sears, Roebuck was made public in Chicago and New York late on Thursday, October 8.

Rod Hills convinced Phil Purcell to come get drunk with him at the City Lights bar on top of the World Trade Center. Over the top of one of Purcell's several perfect Manhattans and Rod Hills' Bombay gins ("You only drink straight stuff when you got it done," Rod always said)

—as the island lights of New York Harbor glimmered far below them—
the two Westerners finally smiled at each other, and then they both
leaned back in their chairs and began to laugh.

The final votes of the Dean Witter and Coldwell Banker shareholders
wouldn't be tallied until just after Christmas, but by the night of October
8 it was already clear that Andrew J. Melton would become chairman
and chief executive officer of a new Sears entity called the Financial
Services Group, Stretch Gardiner would stay on as president of Dean
Witter, and both men would enjoy a substantial salary increase over
their 1980 pay. Melton would earn $500,000 in base salary—over $100,-
000 per year more than any of the Sears lifers running the much larger
retail territories. And he would hold an organizational portfolio co-equal
with Ed Brennan's. It was all in writing, there for anyone to see.

What was never committed to public documentation was the comment Ed Telling was heard to make after Hills and Purcell reported to
him Melton's last-minute demands for a better employment deal for
himself. Telling had experienced difficulty in understanding Melton
from the moment the two men first sat down together, and though he'd
smiled at Melton and tried to charm him for weeks since then, Andy
Melton's last-minute gilding of his own parachute had been a mistake.
"Son-of-a-bitch," Ed Telling said when he heard about it. "Fella's gonna
pay for that."

The fat personal contracts Melton negotiated served the ancillary
purpose of dispelling some of the rumors that raged through the Dean
Witter organization when the takeover was announced. It was feared
that a hokey bunch of store runners could never stomach a securities-
firm milieu in which twenty-five-year-old account executives made several hundred thousand dollars a year more than the top managers. Some
of the Dean Witter stock and bond sellers were so successful that they
employed up to four private assistants, whose salaries were paid from
the broker's own earnings. Others, who were just beginning to learn the
stockbroker's trade, still earned more than successful Sears merchandise
executives with thirty-five years of service in the Field.

During November, Telling decided to make a somewhat limited public appearance on Wall Street, almost three years to the day since his
appearance before the analysts at Fraunces Tavern. He went to New
York to appear with Melton and Gardiner in a videotaped question-and-
answer session in front of Dean Witter employees brought in from
Tennessee, Washington, Minnesota, Chicago, Arizona, and several other
states. The resulting tape was called "The Organization," and it was
circulated throughout Dean Witter to great effect.

Telling sat in a chair between Gardiner and Andy Melton, wearing his grandfatherly smile. Melton spoke first, saying that the audience was assembled to discuss the "proposed merger." He continued with obvious hesitation to talk about the changing structure of the securities industry and Dean Witter's need for more capital. Melton described his negotiations with Sears as having been "the kind I would have hoped for."

"If Sears' motto is 'Trust Sears,' " he said (which it never was), "I do."

Telling looked out at the younger Dean Witter employees from the chair between their white-haired leaders and started to grin. "It's good to learn that all financial people aren't elderly white-haired men," he said.

The camera panned across the faces of some of Dean Witter's most demanding and well-known middle-level employees, who were specially selected to avoid the accusations that the audience had been packed.

Telling was asked about the level of corporate independence Dean Witter would be allowed to retain.

"We discovered long ago that decentralization . . . well, whatever you wanna call it . . . is by far the superior management technique," the chairman said. "In the merchandise group we've always been very decentralized—almost to a fault in some cases. It was even down to an individual store manager having such great authority that he priced his own goods. Now, that might not mean much to you, but to a merchant . . . that's called independence. We've all grown up in that atmosphere in our company and we fight to protect it."

Stretch Gardiner chimed in with the observation that there were already "totally independent entities" within the Sears family.

" 'Totally independent' might be . . . a little strong," Telling corrected, never allowing his grandfatherly half-smile to lapse for an instant.

Nobody on the sixty-eighth floor even bothered to inform Preston Martin about the acquisition of Coldwell Banker until it was done. Once Telling had expressed his displeasure with Martin and his handling of the Seraco Group, all information made a detour around him. Preston Martin had no history at Sears, so, unlike Jack Kincannon's, his corporate demise was instantaneous and noiseless. By the time of the acquisitions, the wisdom of moving Martin aside had been underscored by the sorry results of Seraco's Allstate Savings and Loan division, which was losing a million dollars every two or three weeks after a long run of black numbers under Allstate management. In October it was announced that Preston Martin would become a "special assistant" to Ed Telling, since

Wes Poulson would be taking over the remains of Seraco from Martin on January 1, 1982.

On November 17, Preston Martin resigned. An agreement was struck by which he would receive $492,000 in aggregate payments in lieu of his planned compensation through the end of 1983.

The day before Christmas, Ronald Reagan appointed Preston Martin, a man described as a pragmatist, to be vice-chairman of the board of governors of the Federal Reserve, an organization housed in offices lined appropriately with Italian marble, and dedicated by charter to the protection of the sanctity of America's banking institutions.

The pieces of a new dream had finally been drawn in—big, diverse businesses that could combine as a sum greater than the proverbial parts. Now Sears could continue to "democratize" products that were previously too expensive or sophisticated for everyday people.

The automatic washing machine was an artifact owned only by the rich until Sears democratized the machine in 1942: $37.95—three bucks down and four more a month on time. The process was at the core of the entire industrial revolution—the humbling of products: buckles, buttons, and beer—and the efficient distribution of previously unattainable things to the huge pools of human desire called markets. Now the possibility stood before them of starting the cycle all over again.

Sears could spin a grand, gilded net for the people that included housing, mortgages, all manner of insurance, variations on banking sources, investment services, and, of course, consumer goods. People could get a house from Sears again. When the system was up and running, they could even get the money to buy the house; get the stuff that goes in the house; and the services that ensure the sustenance of the house if something unforeseen happens. People would be able to save their money at Sears and spend it there too, and perhaps some day the whole thing could be intricately connected by machines. People's televisions and telephone would connect them to the system. Sears, Roebuck could become the chassis for the whole of a citizen's material life.

A few days after the acquisitions were described on the front pages of newspapers across the country, Citicorp's Walter Wriston declared, "I said ten years ago that Sears would be our principal competition in the 1980s—and no one would listen to me then. Now they're listening." A few of the articles mentioned the results of the SRI and internal Sears research studies, such as the discovery that 7 percent of all Americans involved in stock transactions of $25,000 or more each year carry Sears cards. "These new competitors," Wriston said, "unhindered by archaic laws, are rapidly taking over the financial services business." By the end of the fall, magazine articles were already referring to Sears, American Express, Prudential-Bache, and Merrill Lynch as "the new super companies."

Whenever Telling was asked what an old general merchant could possibly know about money, he would just roll out the figures, as if to say that what he knew meant nothing next to what he had. He'd talk of the 852 stores; the 2,388 Sears Catalog outlets in small towns; the 324 Dean Witter brokerage offices; the three thousand Allstate offices, free-standing outlets, and booths in most of the retail stores; and the four hundred Coldwell Banker offices. There were around eight thousand Dean Witter employees dealing with the public and ten thousand more who worked for Allstate.

The company's distributors already covered the map, like so many railway-station agents waiting for Richard Sears to send gold watches down the line. The pinpoints of the network just needed to be wired together and switched on. If Telling hadn't constructed the Great American Company by dint of deals, he'd made deals that held at least the possibility of such greatness.

If there was any irony in the way Ed Telling stepped forth after three years, it was in the fact that from a decision to find new roads leading away from the chaos and contraction of the company's traditional merchantry had come a master plan predicated in large part on the resurgence of the Merchant.

A chart somebody drew up at the rating agency Moody's Investor Services showed that the combined profits of the Sears financial-service entities in 1980 would have totaled $500 million, compared with just $200 or so million for the once-mighty merchandise business. But the power source that would light the new network had to be the Merchant, and the transformer that would make it a success was the loyalty and trust the Merchant still drew from the American heart.

The startling October announcement now trained a national spotlight down hard on the merchandise wing of the company, just as Ed Brennan's numbers began to reflect the full brunt of a worldwide recession. Within weeks of the acquisitions, the mid-year surge that had caught the eye of several analysts, when the Challenge Lines and other quick fixes Brennan had designed kicked in, sputtered so badly that sales for November fell below those of 1980, and below the performances of K mart, Penney, and Montgomery Ward. Almost every single department was falling short of the profit target inscribed in the Plan, and though the stores were reporting better sales by the first few weeks of December, the merchants had other reasons to be glum. The Sears credit-card operation, which was such an inspiration to the ideology behind the new corporate ventures, was lightening the corporate coffers at a rate of a million dollars a day. Whereas the total credit loss of $25 million in 1980 was considered a disaster, in 1981 losses just to personal bankruptcies among the customers would top the $50-million mark. Over a quarter of a million credit accounts were delinquent.

Just as Brennan had feared, the recession was erasing all ameliorative programs he'd set in motion. All the temporal gains of the Challenge Lines were subsumed in red numbers. The buying organization persisted in operating in a way that didn't reflect the stores, and the stores—where the recession battered the company the hardest—were still mired in chaos. Though Ed Telling had stunned the business world by spending a billion dollars in a week to complement his famous stores with bright possibilities, Christmastime in the stores was absent of good cheer.

CHAPTER 15

A Christmas at Hicksville

The big store in Hicksville, New York, sits on a concrete plain not far from the birthplace of Walt Whitman, who grew up twenty-five miles east of Manhattan in a quiet Long Island village surrounded by farms and Indian burial mounds. The poet was mesmerized by the "chainless enterprise" that characterized his times, and much of his long life was spent observing and recording the rhythms, sounds, and smells of a young democracy creating "great commercial emporiums" for the new world. But when Walt Whitman died, six years after Richard Sears began to sell watches through the mail, the countryside near his birthplace still moved to the prosaic cadences of the growing seasons.

Harvest time on Long Island—at the Sears "A" store, number 1264—still smelled of grain in 1981 . . . hot, popped, and buttered. The recession-Christmas brought so much heat and movement into the aisles of the store that the cloying odor of popcorn oozed forth from its usual haunt in the candy department and traveled through the overheated sea of shoppers like a squall. It wafted past children in night braces, children displaced from strollers by their full weight in goods; past children crying, and others full of pre-Christmas joy. No "member of the Sears family," as Ed Brennan suggested the employees of Sears should be calling themselves with pride once again, was able to smell the popcorn, because after a while the scent is as gunpowder to soldiers at war, apparent only in its absence. But the smell was there; like the burial mounds under the expanse of parking lots that covered the region.

As the final week of shopping days before Christmas commenced, telephones rang unanswered in every department of the store. So many transactions were ratified by Hicksville's portion of the forty thousand electronic cash registers in the system that their electronic bleatings ran together into a single penetrating tone. Six registers were stationed at each "central cashiering island" located, as part of the recent experimentation, in the middle of the aisles. Employees stood at the islands surrounded by wide-eyed customers who were consistently reminded to arrange themselves behind lines painted on the floor. Above the central cashiering islands, hidden in the ceiling of the store, were secret observation posts where moonlighting policemen stared down through a metallic mesh at the fast hands of family members, making sure no one stole from Ed Brennan's till.

Beside the registers sat thick dog-eared computer printouts announcing hundreds of last-minute markdowns. During the weeks after New Year's thousands of price increases would outnumber the decreases by a hundred to one as inflation continued to flame unabated, but until Christmas the big store was on sale. It said so in the computer paper—somewhere.

Customers often crossed the lines on the linoleum in frustration, and began to help beleaguered cashiers search the grubby pages of continuous-feed paper for a price. After the figure was located, an unwieldy seven-page form, number 16117-025, was threaded carefully into the side of the machine so it didn't tear. Then an endless series of numbers were punched into the whirring data terminal as lights flashed and buzzers and synthesized bells sounded. All buttons were to be pushed in the proper sequence, ending with two jabs to the "Sub-Total." If the cashier forgot to subtotal twice, the computer would still figure sales tax into the equation, but since the employee would have tripped one of the thirty-three error messages programmed into the "fallout" region of the ten-year-old electronic checkout system, he or she would arrive at work the next day to find what the younger employees called a "note from the computer" reminding the worker about subtotaling twice and asking that the error not be repeated again.

Over fifty million people reside in what the Sears research department on the forty-first floor of the Tower deems the "market region" of the "A" store at Hicksville, and by virtue of their shopping habits they have made Hicksville one of the two or three most successful stores in the company. In light of the store's proximity to Manhattan, where the General vowed as a matter of principle Sears would never do a lick of business, the awesome selling power of the store was a pleasant irony that local Field managers enjoyed pondering. Wood's interdiction of stores in the Evil City had remained unviolated, but because of the General's own system of building Sears retail markets on prime suburban sites spaced an average of twelve miles apart, Sears, Roebuck had still become the largest retailer in metropolitan New York. Manhattan Island constitutes the most concentrated and powerful place of buying and selling in the world, and it houses some of the most well-known and sophisticated retail institutions ever conceived, but by encircling New York during the belated period of growth finally granted the Eastern Territory during the 1960s, Ed Telling's old New York group of stores had become the low-profile retail giant of New York—as well as one of the largest customers of New York City's manufacturers and, lately, the owners of one of its big Wall Street money firms. By Christmas of 1981, the New York group—just one of forty-six Sears retail groups in the Field—was completing a year in which it would sell more than $800 million worth of merchandise, and this would be a disappointing year at that.

In 1964 the huge flagship store in suburban Hicksville was launched into what the Reverend Martin Luther King, Jr., that same year called a "vast ocean of material prosperity." The expansionist Sears chairman of the time was Austin Cushman, who declared as part of his "Today!" program that a Sears store should open somewhere in the United States every few days. Though he would be remembered as one of the visionless caretakers on the General's list of anointed epigones, Cushman in his time displayed the hyperactive personality of the ex-appliance salesman he was. He had a thing about people who exhibited what he called "tired blood," and he was heard to rail often that there was no place at Sears, Roebuck for a man whose blood got tired.

Cushman also had a thing for huge, California-style, free-standing retail stores surrounded by acres and acres of free parking. Back when he ran the Far Western Territory, before ascending to the chairmanship and letting Arthur Wood sit in the territorial chair for a time to gain experience, Cushman made his name in the company by constructing mammoth, single-story, high-ceilinged cathedrals of consumption like the incomparable "A" store he built in Torrance, California. Cushman's West Coast Sears stores were sprawling monuments to the times, huge, well-insulated coverings where the ethos of American industrialism could couple with the ethos of American consumption with plenty of room to spare. A Sears chairman's pet project was still tolerated by the territories in 1964; thus a store built during Cushman's tenure, like the Hicksville Sears, looks exactly like the store at Torrance. So do one of the big stores in Washington, D.C., and the store outside of Cleveland in Middleburg Heights, and the one since closed down at St. David's, Pennsylvania. The Californiate land-hogging stores were *planted* in a wide variety of climates, in spite of a huge differential in construction cost due to comparatively higher land prices in the East during the early 1960s. The implantations underscored the dangers of centralization. The stores were emblems of the balance of power within Sears at the time, and no less symbolic of the Far Western Territory's imperial moment than the Victorian post office in Dublin, or the President's House in Delhi.

The Hicksville Sears store is located on a street called Broadway, though its former dominance of the roadway is obscured now by Dunkin' Donuts, the Pearle Vision Center, Roy Rogers, a Gulf station, the Garden Center, McDonald's, a Dollar Savings Bank, several hundred other free-standing specialty stores, a few chained shopping centers, and two or three other big stores. Broadway is really a parking lot striated by yellow lines and made uncrossable by the speeding automobile traffic that runs between stores. It is a classic "open-strip center," a relic that represents a stage of commercial architectural development that was superseded a few years later by the thought of putting a roof over a clutter of shops and calling the whole thing a mall.

Inside the main door of the store, Sears Christmas shoppers were greeted by Cheryl Tiegs. She smiled at them from posters and clothing racks, from back-wall photos and even from price tags. There was a life-size, full-length photographic portrait of Cheryl Tiegs looking contemplative before bedtime in her Sears lingerie, flanked on either side by two apple-cheeked mannequins wearing Cheryl Tiegs underwear, both of them turned inward slightly toward the portrait of Tiegs, like twin fashion-conscious bodhisattvas.

The Cheryl Tiegs product line on which Brennan and his team had banked so much of the their 1980 effort premiered in New York just after the 1980 Challenge Meeting. A double-paged, artistic, and rather un-Sears-like spread appeared in the decidedly un-Sears-like pages of *The New York Times'* Sunday magazine section on December 7, announcing simply and with unintentional irony that "It's got to be Cheryl Tiegs."

During the 1981 spring annual meeting in Minneapolis, an otherwise sober and guarded Ed Brennan brightened noticeably at one point in the proceedings and said, "We have a surprise for everyone." Then Cheryl Tiegs bounded into the grayness of the meeting from behind a drape, to the hysterical cheers of her home-town supporters. Tiegs had by all measures "peaked" during 1978, when she made the cover of

Time magazine, but by late 1981 she'd had a personal turnaround and been reborn as a symbol of the New Sears: a mature model representing a mature retailer. That her breasts had been bared in a national magazine, that she'd been publicly associated with her former husband's arrest on drug charges, and that during her Sears period she'd married an erstwhile playboy and wildlife photographer didn't seem to matter as much as the fact that America, in 1981, wanted to look like Cheryl.

The waning of Tiegs' high-fashion period and the coming of her massification through the marketing might of Sears corresponded to Joe Moran's "style clock," which dictated in a famous 1979 white paper that Sears' proper involvement with a "look" comes a bit past the hour of high style.

Though the apparel department continually dispensed the fiction that Cheryl Tiegs actually designed the clothes bearing her name, it was clear that it was her face—the face that once peered from covered wagons, the same face that Richard Sears placed atop the long, perfect bodies of the woodcut Americans who populated his catalogs—that had helped Ed Brennan plug the dike during the middle months of 1981, before interest rates and recession laid into the numbers and exposed the Challenge Items holding action.

Tiegs was "exposed" to the managers of the Field throughout the winter, and territorial observers felt that the morale value of her presence did much to boost the selling spirit in the stores. The Tiegs spring-1981 collection of jeans, bathing suits, blazers, skirts, blouses, and lingerie accounted for over $40 million in sales. The Tiegs label was now displayed on some 20 percent of the women's apparel sold by Sears. Ed Brennan told securities analysts at a September 1981 conclave that the assortment was "the biggest single success story we have had on a new line at Sears in memory. . . . Maybe not in history," he added, ever cognizant of the past, "but certainly in memory." Now, as crowds invaded the pastel corner of the store at Hicksville dominated by the model's image, managers in Chicago said that 1981 would end with the line's accounting for over $100 million in sales—some $5 million of which would be remitted, by prior agreement, to the personal account of one Cheryl Tiegs.

There were screams coming from the jewelry counter at Hicksville.

Though the image of Sears as the place for big appliances and other hard goods dominates public perception, the company sells a great deal of jewelry. Lady Bird Johnson bought jewelry and even her wedding band at a Sears jewelry counter. Sears was until recently also the largest merchant of mink in the country. Diamonds were among the first items Richard Sears added to his watch inventory, and modern customers of the diamond facet of the Sears jewelry stations still receive a parchment-like document similar to the one pledging a stone "free from flaw or imperfection" that Richard Sears used to send through the mail.

But the soaring levels of trust and commitment to Sears indicated by the large number of customers who think of Sears for diamonds was gone at the jewelry counter at Hicksville this day. The oval counter, located for some reason between luggage, typewriters, and children's wear, was surrounded by enraged customers standing five deep. They formed a fiery ring of anger and noise around the young women inside the circle. Several of the customers were complaining that they'd been waiting twenty minutes to "see" a camera, pen, or watch that was locked in a case outside the jewelry pit. The key to the case had been misplaced, even though it was attached to one end of a piece of wood the size of a baseball bat. By *seeing* the goods, the customers really meant they wanted to touch them, and in their separation from the physical fact of the objects their collective anxiety rose higher. One dark young man in a Sears A-line T-shirt even began to scream: "I'm not a piece of shit!" he roared, leaning over the jewelry counter. "I want respect!"

The reaction of a young store clerk named Brenda was to appear unable to see the man. She looked past and through him, offering to serve other customers. Eventually she paused briefly to mention to the man that the customer-service department was located in the basement in the event of his desire to pursue his complaint, a comment that caused him to clutch a large medallion hanging from his neck and throw it behind him so that it hung from his back, a gesture obviously akin to the dropping of gloves during an ice-hockey match.

Another part-time Sears employee, who had recently retired from his job as principal of a local elementary school, intervened, trying to calm the man, but the customer began to poke the part-timer with his finger, prodding him in the heart, just above his beige-and-brown "Welcome to the Friendly World of Sears . . . Courtesy Is Caring" nameplate.

Brenda stood by with one hand on her hip, staring blankly into the customer's eyes.

A few days before the angry man almost climbed over the case to get Brenda, another customer had stapled his finger to get her attention. An elderly woman came into the department several times each and every day as Christmas approached, to inquire after a "fine writing instrument, like the pen at my bank," only to wander away disappointed each time. During a lull one afternoon, a lady with bleached white hair falling over her weathered skin paused in the aisle in front of the diamonds, extended one leg in front of her, and as she yelled "Yippee!" kicked a black spiked high-heeled shoe high into the air toward the rent-a-cops in the ceiling. It landed near the typewriters.

The veteran Sears department manager in charge of both jewelry and stationery supplies contended to her workers that emotionally disturbed customers were attracted by the brightly colored Christmas cards near the jewelry case, but all over the store, otherwise stable personalities appeared jangled by the miasma of odors, noise, and heat. Male shoppers seemed particularly ill at ease on the "soft" side of the store, where the jewelry counter, the Tiegs displays, and the rest of the apparel were located. They preferred the "hard" side, where the tools were displayed, the side where men were in control and among men.

Though his ghost had been systematically banished from higher corridors of the company in recent years, Robert E. Wood still walked unfaded through the aisles of the "hard" side of the big stores. "Forget the first and second floors," the General used to say, back when the multistoried stores carried clothes and other nonmetallic goods there. "The money's in the basement." The store was hard, utilitarian, rather colorless, and dead honest. Clothes were there to occupy the little lady while the men conducted the serious business of buying durable tonnage downstairs.

The schism between the hard and soft sides of Sears had been obscured by other factionalisms in recent years, but it still ran up and down the merchandising organization. The apparel buyers had always felt like second-class citizens, and some of the fiercest battles during the Hay Committee analysis of the purpose and value of jobs at Sears were not between Field and Parent, but between soft- and hard-line buyers. Much of the underlying bitterness surrounding the closing of the New York buying office and the ghettoization of the transplanted buyers at Two North La Salle harked back to the old hard/soft dichotomy. For years soft-side merchants from Headquarters had been calling the Sears stores drab, dull, and inimicable to the act of shopping for high-profit pretty things. But the look of the stores was still dominated in 1981 by managers who believed Sears was built to serve the General's half-century-old image of men.

The hard sides of the stores were the last repair of the professional conservators of the ways of Sears circa 1955. By Christmastime 1981, they also constituted the single most demoralized group of employees in the organization. For every deracinated middle manager yanked from a plush office in the Dallas headquarters of the now dissolved Southwestern Territory and cast into some operating job in some God-forsaken group office in Oklahoma City, there were three Sears dogfaces known as "big-ticket guys" just a bit more disgruntled with the turn of corporate events in recent years. The days of Sears hard-line salesmen selling the hell out of the best Kenmore washing machine or the finest chain saw in the entire civilized world, of single-handedly loading entire suburbs with Sears "white goods," seemed long gone to most of the guys in the plaid sport coats and frayed "lucky" ties who still stalked the hard side of the stores.

There were subcultures inside the subculture of big-ticket hard-side sellers at Hicksville. The tool men in carpenter's vests and feed caps tended toward a more macho style than the guys sitting idle and depressed in the comfortable chairs in the furniture department. The white-goods boys who retailed the washers, dryers, and refrigerators were by and large the most skilled orators, but all the big-ticket guys shared in the tradition of American salesmanship that so inspired and charmed the young Eddie Brennan, back when he learned how to sell suits from the fast-talking commission salesman at Benson and Rixon.

The most hard-bitten hunter/buyers and toughest zone-riders in the Field shook their heads in wonder when the big-ticket boys came up. A booklet given to managers in the Field warns that psychological tests indicated that the big-ticket seller is "a different breed of cat." The big-ticket guys at Sears were the last of the pitchmen—anachronisms, who'd contrived to prosper because most people see and hear pitches only on television—and any floor man worth a damn can do better then that.

Joe Moran's departed sidekick, Ira Quint, had come to work at Sears because of a big-ticket man's rap. Quint was a student at Harvard when he wandered into the department of the white goods and was enchanted by the ode to the Sears Kenmore refrigerator he heard after announcing he was only browsing. After the pitch, Quint asked the salesman why he had taken so much time on a browser. "You're a browser today," said the man. "But in a couple of years, when you're married, settin' up house, you're gonna come back in here and buy one of these things from me."

The hawkers on the hard side of the stores—especially in urban areas—are masters of applied sociology. Any number of them can see a sale on a customer's face at twenty paces. A Los Angeles–based master of the rat-a-tat-tat vulgate of his trade, a hulking, bearded man named Jack Morgan, given to racetrack neckties the size of kites, once explained that "after twenty-seven years of bargaining, you just sort of learn what it takes to keep a sale alive. Once you start a pitch you never let 'em leave. It's like a long tango, and you keep on dancin' till the music stops."

Morgan worked washers, dryers, and refrigerators on the hard side of his store with a Hispanic big-ticket man named Pablo. "Man 'ud *live* in the store if they let 'im," Morgan said. "He was out sick one day two years ago and his wife sent him back to the store by the middle of the afternoon because he was makin' her crazy practicing his pitch in front of the mirror."

Jack Morgan claimed that Oriental customers were the toughest sells. "They'll pull the exhaust flap off a white goods and then say they'll take two if you take a hundred bucks off the price," he explained. "But an Oriental's still an easy sell compared to an Armenian. An Armenian makes an Oriental seem like a cakewalk.

"I've had my troubles with the Spanish, because I don't speak. You try to talk real slow to 'em and they walk out on you. You can't trust the little kids to translate right, even though the kids speak English. Besides, nobody in the world can deliver another man's pitch."

With new housing starts diminished by half since the beginning of 1981, sales of the goods that fill new homes had suffered terribly from the recession. But most big-ticket salesmen still blamed the company for their problems. "They want me gone," said a middle-aged hardware jock at Hicksville. "The salesmen in this store make more than the managers. They hate our benefits, and I know that if I left they'd have a party. There's no place to go at Sears now. It's a company of part-timers, and I, for one, don't blame part-timers for not caring and treating the customer like shit. Full-timers are the only ones that care—I used to care, before they turned on me."

The Sears big-ticket salesmen had lately fallen victim to one of those seemingly inconsequential managerial snafus that occur frequently when large companies lose control. As the roaring sales success of post-war Sears began to flatten out during the early 1970s, the lot of the professional salesmen of the Field, whose incomes derived from a percentage commission on items they sold, took a sudden turn for the worse. Their pay ceased to keep pace with the general cost of living, and it no longer matched the "earnings curve" of the rest of the company, especially after a long-planned across-the-board increase was granted to all noncommission store personnel in 1974.

It was thought in the Tower that one of the reasons Headquarters couldn't seem to stop the Field salesmen from practicing bait-and-switch selling and other illegal sleights of hand during the mid-1970s was that they were angry with management over compensation. During the slow times, salesmen lived on a "draw" against future commissions, and if they never met up with the draw they took home, they were occasionally fired. A sweeping initiative was obviously needed to rectify the situation, possibly a new pay formula that would take away the commission sales force's dependence on a department's performance and on the vagaries of the economy in general.

An up-and-coming young Headquarters executive named Bruce Davis, who had been an assistant in the personnel department specializing in time-card compensation, was given the task of coming up with a new pay plan for the thousands of Sears big-ticket employees. He proposed a new system that would replace the pure sales commission with an hourly wage supported by an "earnings floor" and augmented by a factor drawn from the employee's sales performance during previous years. Each time a salesperson passed a new dollar sales barrier or "bracket," spaced at intervals of around $15,000 in sales, another twenty-five cents would be added to his or her hourly wage for the coming year and beyond. The plan appeared to maintain the motivational advantages of commission selling without some of the downside risk of a pure commission or the alternative "draw" against future commissions.

Bruce Davis, Charlie Bacon, and a large entourage from the Headquarters personnel department hit the road to sell the new program to the territories during 1975. The idea was received with general approval everywhere but in the West, where John Lowe declared the initiative a mistake. But John Lowe didn't care for much at all that came out of Chicago, so his skepticism was ignored.

A large number of store managers throughout the company were also against the program; many of them said that no impetus to sell hard could ever replace a commission. But the store jockeys of the Field were a reactionary lot anyway, and their senior managers bought the new plan. Eddie Brennan was up in Boston at the time, running the group. The idea seemed to him a fair way to lift people's incomes, which it might well have been if things had worked out differently.

The first year under the new system, the personnel department figured it saved the company some $23 million, but the second year was 1977—the year of the great selloff, when Sears racked up a 17-percent sales increase by "giving the store away." The big-ticket boys went wild in 1977. They crashed through barrier after personal sales barrier, bracket after bracket. Line managers in the stores and executives in the groups watched the salespeople's guaranteed incomes for 1978 fly past their own. Within a few months, the highly paid big-ticket guys were sitting in the comfortable chairs in the furniture department, because the strangulation of the business in 1978 had begun. Salespeople were pulling down around $35,000 a year for writing up two or three sales checks a day. Their incentive to sell was gone, the tap on the business had been turned off in the Tower, the company structure above them was embroiled in political turmoil, and Sears was left with a vastly bloated payroll at precisely the time when the company could least afford it.

The muddle was a small sideshow to the war between Parent and Field, and the official line from the Tower was that the big-ticket pay plan had been too hastily implemented without proper testing. Accordingly, Bruce Davis was exiled to the corporate Siberia of a personnel job in the Dallas–Fort Worth retail group. Davis stayed on at Sears for a time, warmed by the dying glow of his once-rising star, then left the company some months later, saying he was bound to do the Lord's work as a seller of Bibles.

It was said in retrospect that Bruce Davis was the victim of his boss's— Charlie Bacon's—preoccupation with the larger political crises facing Ed Telling at the time when Bacon had told Davis to draw up his ill-fated program. The "Davis big-ticket pay-plan affair" was one of the many smaller management dramas obscured by the magnitude of the struggles for control before the arrival of Brennan, but by the time he was exiled to Dallas, every buyer in the Tower and every merchandise manager in the Field whose department in the stores had been pulled off of commission thought that perhaps their goods weren't moving because of a fellow they'd never met named Bruce Davis. Bad luck allowed Davis to enter the pantheon of important corporate figures associated with the old order of things, and for a short time thousands of people felt strong emotions at the mere mention of his name.

It was common knowledge on both sides of the Hicksville store that each new shopping day before Christmas ushered a new level of desperation onto the floor. For a decade, retailers had noted that shopping was more concentrated each year on the last few days before the holidays. Saturday was a big day anyway, but the Saturday before Christmas was "Super Saturday" at Sears stores all across the Republic. There was adrenaline clouding the air, and reasoned expediencies collided hard in the aisles with unsheathed acquisitive impulses and random rage. When people got so angry that they began to yell at the employees, they tended to mention the number of years they'd been believers in the company: "I'm shopping here a lifetime!" was heard often.

"Forty-one years!" screamed a middle-aged woman on Super Saturday. "Now it's K mart!" A thin white line grew around her lips. In leaving her selections on the counter of a central cashiering island, turning on her heels, and taking her custom elsewhere, the lady became a "lost-sheep" shopper, in the lingo of the trade, and yet another example of the "draining power" measured by the market researchers on the forty-first floor.

Hicksville customers would draw aged and cracked Sears credit cards from their wallets—wallets that often contained only a Sears card and some cash—and wave them before employees like sabers as they offered disquisitions upon their lifelong relationship with Sears. If the card had a blue edge, every employee knew to be especially pleasant, because this was the card carried by someone on the "checklists" of executive employees of Sears and their families.

Sometimes after toting up a sale for a card carrier the computer would send back a message to the cashier that the card was invalid; that a credit limit had been exceeded, or, worse, that it was a "husband-only" card. The personal problem a shopper might have with his or her account was suddenly made public, and the transaction became a charged personal issue that drew the attending clerk into an emotional drama. If the computer said no, the employee became a representative of a vindictive bureaucracy, every collector of past dues, and every repossessor of private property. The anger drawn out by a credit rejection was considerable. Back at his first store in Danville, Illinois, the young Ed Telling had once had to pull a customer off his credit manager, and many of the old Danville Searsmen remembered Telling best because of the way he held the man in the air by his collar with one hand as he carried him out of the store. During 1980, a customer at the service desk in Pasadena, California, tore her heavy-gauged Sears card in half and ate it in an act of defiance.

The act of shopping appeared to bring the customers together just as the building tension of the Christmas rush galvanized the employees. Young and old, hard and soft, the employees merged as one to fend off customers. A survey indicated that only 13 percent of the customers at Hicksville thought the employees were polite, this at a time when Ed Brennan contended to his officers that 69 percent of the people who left Sears to shop in a different store did so because a store employee had been rude.

Families of customers and groups of friends roamed the Hicksville store in packs. Shopping together was less an act of pleasurable social interaction, a shared experience of the nation's prime cultural activity, than it was a system of mutual protection. It seemed to the customers in the store that their inalienable rights were constantly in danger of being violated. People wary of the long-range psychological consequences of screaming at their children bellowed in full voice at adolescent shop-clerks about their "rights." The former highly mannered mores of shopping had been replaced by the edicts of a consumer movement. The absence of a sense of public awe in the emporia was one of the things Ed Telling could never understand. The way people acted in stores made it a lot easier for Field people to face being promoted up and away from stores and to turn one's attention to other arenas.

Several consumers at Hicksville admitted they were just angry. Some had lost jobs during the recession. Others said that, with inflation rising lately past 20 percent, on an annualized basis, they felt they had to buy things they could barely afford now, before the prices soared beyond possibility. They'd worry about paying the bill later. After all, the inflation rate was higher than Sears' credit charges, so in a sense buying like crazy on the card was a way to stay ahead. But it still made people mad.

Special super-short-term super sales were announced periodically over the loudspeaker system on Super Saturday, a selling technique most of the old guard—and Ed Brennan—disapproved of as emblematic of the desperation that set in at Sears during the mid-1970s when the bargain-basement five-minute-sale techniques first appeared in the stores. Sears, Roebuck began holding major sales, like anniversary sales or Sears "Value Days" sales, during the shoppers' nightmare year of 1933, but the sort of flashing-light, high-intensity sales derived from the "shipwreck sales" and "distress sales" of old were associated, during the post–World War II years, with lesser retailers in need of such ploys—like K mart. But in late 1981 the group and store administrations still controlled the style in which price concessions were heralded to the shoppers, so short-term mass sprints from one end of the store to another still occurred.

The brief sales only exacerbated the existing state of confusion in the store. Customers and employees alike seemed confused by the helter-skelter arrangement of the goods. The number of price changes listed within the fat piles of computer printouts next to the registers were so confusing that items were often checked out at old prices. There were electronic guns attached to the data-terminal registers that were supposed to speed up the checkout process by reading prices off an electronic tag on the merchandise. But the guns rarely worked, and cashiers would pass the device over and over the label in frustration until the package broke. The lines behind each register were up to forty yards long by the middle of Super Saturday, and every two or three minutes a customer could be seen leaving the line, putting his or her would-be purchases on the nearest flat surface, and stomping out of the store.

Back in 1950, the General contended that Sears was different from other retailers because their customer policy was still predicated on Richard Sears' novel belief that the American people were overwhelmingly honest, but the most casual observation of the Christmas fury at Hicksville revealed petty larcenies at every glance. People stole the envelopes from behind Christmas cards with impunity. Others grabbed handfuls of Smurfs from a large box and put them in their pockets. A table near the entrance to the cavernous basement storage area was filled with empty boxes from every department that used to house goods, and behind the entrance to the stockrooms were cages full of calculators, cameras, and phone-answering machines that were locked up to protect them from pilferage by members of the Sears family.

A man muscled through the crowd around the jewelry counter late on Super Saturday and said that he was with store security. He helped out by answering the phone near a case housing three versions of the Sears Phone Minder telephone-answering machine. Then he took one of the machines out of the case—the Sears' Best model—and walked toward the exit. A woman met him just beyond the Pittsburgh Steelers sweatshirt rack with a large bag, into which he slipped the Phone Minder. All of this was observed by the security men behind the fake ventilation ducts in the ceiling, so when the couple walked into the icy parking lot, a guard was waiting. A game of keep-away ensued, in which the man and woman tossed the machine back and forth over the head of the lone security man until others arrived to subdue the couple and wait for the police.

The machine never made it back into the display case before Christmas, and when customers asked where the Sears' Best Phone Minder was, the clerks replied that they'd been told by management to say nothing at all about the missing item.

Even the more seasoned big-ticket vets thought the Christmas rush of 1981 was the craziest in years. The soft side of the store was in a constant state of siege, and each of the central cashiering islands seemed like a bunker under a firestorm.

Sears always dwelled in the gap that separates what people wanted and dreamed about from what they already had. In the same wide expanse of American possibility that held Walt Whitman's poetry, many of the world's religions, and more than a few revolutions, Sears had become one of largest, richest, and best-known organizations in the world by directing into the divide an unceasing flow of things. The gap was kept wide by pictures and words in the catalog and later by nearly a billion dollars' worth of advertising in newspapers and on TV, and it was made traversable by Sears' low prices, by the convenience of its catalog and stores, and by the medium of available credit.

The company was a meeting place of desire and reality; its stores were American agoras. Sears had dispensed the gifts of the modern era to several generations. Having acceded to a level of economic success that warranted a shopping trip to Sears was a rite of passage for a population as large as that of France. Things from the company helped Americans manicure contrived Edens in private quarter-sections called backyards. The trees in the boggy new suburbs the customers built grew strong enough to support Sears birdfeeders, and then Sears aluminum swings. The company was a part of a huge segment of the population's experience of growing more secure, more comfortable, and freer, and to many of these credit-card-carrying citizens the institution mustered, if not an overt loyalty, then at least stirrings of nostalgia for a purer and less beleaguered time in their lives. Sears had come to be a private institution that served so public a purpose in the minds of so many people that the values—honesty, fairness, politeness, orderliness—and even the public image of a company that symbolized *success*, had become things consumers had come to demand and expect of the company, like citizens demanding their rights.

But lately dysfunction had suffused the store with anger and fear. Connections were not being made, and as the sides of the company had lost touch with each other, so the customers appeared infuriated by the inability of Sears to service their material and emotional needs.

Only when the young employees at the registers believed violence was imminent were they allowed to pick up a telephone and demand that the person on the other end "Send the Flyers!"

Usually the Flyers traveled in twos or threes, walking to the rescue shoulder to shoulder and with great speed, their high-heeled boots clicking over the linoleum. Many of the Flyers had haircuts that made them look like miniature Cheryls climbed down from the end-stands of the Tiegs displays. None of the better Flyers had graduated from high school yet, but when the most seasoned cashiers saw them approaching a besieged island, they felt like the cavalry had arrived. The Flyers would bull through the crowd, duck under the counters, and punch an idle data terminal to life in an instant. Then their painted fingertips would begin to fly, the lines would move, and disaster was averted.

All of the employees at Hicksville this Christmas had taken a company entrance examination before they were hired. The test was developed by a University of Chicago psychology professor named Dr. L. L. Thurstone, who in 1942 received a $50,000 grant from the company to develop a test that would cull those candidates for employment unfit, by virtue of insufficient intelligence or "schedule of personality traits," to join the Sears family. All the kids in the Hicksville store had taken the same Thurstone Temperament Schedule exam first used in 1948. The test asked them, "Do you like to hunt? Do you like to wrestle? Do you swear? Are you fidgety? Do you yell at games along with the crowd? Do you have trouble giving orders to servants?"

If they passed the test, the new hirees were shown a short film about Sears and asked to read a *Getting Acquainted* booklet that still contended, in 1981, that Sears was in fact five sovereign territories.

Most of the part-time and full-time employees in the Hicksville store designed to serve men were women. Of the almost two hundred thousand sales and clerical personnel working for the company, women were nearing 70 percent by late 1981—compared with 41 percent of the total employed work force elsewhere. It was in the nation's stores that women finally made their late entry into public life, first as shoppers, and later as shop clerks. By the 1980s Sears and most other retail institutions depended on a solidly female, largely part-time work force.

Hicksville had 241 full-time employees on its payroll during the Christmas rush and 552 part-timers, almost all of them being paid the hourly minimum wage. Since 1978, executives of the territorial and Headquarters personnel departments had convened meetings to discuss "the teeny-bopper concern." It suddenly dawned on management that the stores would soon be dependent not on women but on children. The issue of part-time employment—especially that of very young women— had been debated at Sears since 1913, when Julius Rosenwald testified before government tribunals about the working conditions of the young girls at the West Side catalog plant (at the time Rosenwald defended a pay scale of under $5.00 a week for girls under sixteen).

As was the case with the young Flyers, who came to the rescue so full of youthful energy and poise, it often appeared that Christmas in Hicksville that the Sears teeny-boppers were the employees best equipped to stand the strain and fight the battles that now raged in the stores. Many of the young part-timers came to work in the afternoon after spending a few hours being "mall rats" in the enclosed shopping center across the uncrossable expanse of Broadway. The young workers seemed less disgruntled about investing so much of their seventeenth or eighteenth Christmas season in fee to Sears, Roebuck than did the big-ticket boys making four times their wages. They were more attuned to the aggressions of shoppers in 1981 simply because they had grown up as consumers in the 1970s.

Except for their meager paychecks, the young workers expected very little in return from Sears, but they felt no great loyalty either. Most of them were middle-class kids who lived nearby, and most had worked at Arby's, or Shoetown, or at one of the other shops on the Broadway strip at one time or another. It didn't really matter. While the size of their ranks had been growing at twice the rate of full-timers for a decade, the part-timer turnover rate at Sears ran at 125 percent.

A few of the Hicksville Sears part-timers were taking a year off from school to save up money to pay for college. Others were already students in a local college or high school. When a part-timer called in sick it was often because he or she was home studying for an exam, so other part-timers would try to cover. There was a great deal of after-hours dating among the young part-timers, and no matter how much noise and anger surrounded a selling counter or a cashiering island, the kids still seemed to be able to gossip constantly with impunity.

The full- and part-timers hailed from different generations, from different worlds and ideas of company and work. Only under fire did the work force of Hicksville begin to draw together. The big-ticket boys resented the young employees' energy and resiliency, and full-time managers admitted that it was not so much the lack of company loyalty that irritated them about the teeny-boppers as it was that their ignorance of the fact that they were laboring amid the rubble of a business empire in decline, of a family fallen into disunity, allowed them to avoid knowing how awful it felt.

The Hicksville store employed a store manager, an operating manager, two merchandise managers, a controller, a credit manager, a customer convenience center manager, a personnel manager, several receiving managers, a security supervisor, and a visual merchandise manager. The younger employees all figured that the Sears managers in the store were distinguished by their access to coffee breaks, because, other than the store manager, it seemed that the big shots at the store and some of the veteran salespeople could usually be found sitting around in the lunchroom eating "Searsburgers" and talking about the old days.

The walls of the basement lunchroom were covered with pages from old Sears Catalogs, plaques bearing bronzed DieHard batteries, bronzed hand tools, and other bronzed artifacts representing past sales triumphs. The lunchroom was next to the executive office suite and a training room that housed a dummy data terminal, chairs with attached desks for taking quizzes and notes, and a television monitor on a stand where videotapes entitled "Challenge 81," "Promotion Selling," "Bait and Switch," "Challenge 82," and "The World of Sears" (the one the new part-timers were shown) were all piled in disarray.

Away from the battlefront, the veterans sought out only their peers. Over many cups of coffee they commiserated about how nothing had really been right at the store since night hours crept into retailing and then expanded until the store was open six nights. Then Sunday fell, and pretty soon the family feeling started to leave. Hours were staggered. And then, as the red ink began to flow through no fault of their own, little kids began to appear with Sears badges on their chests, little children with "smile"-button faces that were still bright and young at nine o'clock at night.

All the employees funnel down into the basement at closing time. Some wait to slip bags of money to a woman in a cage, and others wait in line to slip their time cards into the clock at the door. Other employees shuffle out of the data-processing room, a place that continued to glow green and bright as most people left the store. The data workers usually looked even more bloodless and exhausted than the shop-floor veterans. They emerged from their backroom blinking like miners coming up into the light.

There was little discussion in the punch-out line. Employees tended to look up at the bulletin board full of corporate announcements by store, group, territorial, and even a few from Tower-based administrators. There were announcements of numerous retirements from the store and news of two Christmas parties: one sit-down dinner at a restaurant for full-timers only, and one "annual luncheon" for all employees, which was a several-hour-long function to be held in the lunchroom on December 23, complete with a raffle. All employees were invited to attend, in staggered shifts of twenty minutes each.

In the parking lot, the veterans walked directly to their cars, parked, at management's insistence, in the corners of the huge lot. The part-time kids stood around in the cold for a while, clearing their noses of popcorn as they flirted and made plans for the evening. It was still Super Saturday night, and with the crack of the time clock Sears had ceased to exist for the kids. Few of them had heard of Ed Brennan, and some weren't even aware that Sears was run from a tall building in Chicago, Illinois. Most of them knew that eleven weeks earlier Sears, Roebuck had been mentioned on the news and in the papers, and several of them had heard rumors from the big-ticket sellers that the recent corporate shopping spree meant that Sears was going to bail out of the merchandise business very soon.

Several young employees waded through the sleet to their jacked-up cars, parked alongside the free-standing Sears auto center, which, true to Hicksville's California roots, had sixty service bays. The car radios reported the Christmas news of bread riots in Poland. The American auto industry had become an economic disaster area. Retailers *had* to have a big Christmas this year. After adding recent losses of 1.5 million jobs, fully nine million Americans were now unemployed.

Across the parking lot, on the other side of Broadway, loomed what had until recently been a big store in the Korvettes retail chain. Korvettes had closed its fifteen remaining stores and died quite suddenly a year earlier, on Christmas Eve. A sign in front said "Always Open," when in fact the Korvettes was now always closed.

The dead store seemed black and haunted. Inside, mannequins lay on their sides, stripped and smudged with black like victims of the plague. As professional retailers, habitués of last-day close-out sales, and every-day consumers in places like Poland already know, there are few things as sad and hollow as a dead or dying store. The signs of a gravely ill store appear first as holes, empty spaces between the goods. Then the lights grow dim as the holes spread. The illness metastasizes toward a state the industry calls "overspaced." The parking lot then begins to look like a drained pond, full of debris. Eventually the lights go off, and the store just rolls over and dies.

Ed Brennan believed stores are like children at first. They begin all bright and full of promise. The first months of their lives they have to be nurtured, loved, and eventually disciplined. Changing the fundamental character of a store after the imprint of its early days is next to impossible. Stores grow old after a while, and, like people, they lose their faculties. Then, sometimes after only a few misbegotten months and sometimes after a century, stores really do roll over and die.

All the Sears managers—from the forty-fourth floor of the Tower to the store lunchrooms—talked about dead and dying stores and chains of stores like old people rehashing the obituary pages. "Ya hear about Goldblatt's?" someone would say. Then a brief, respectful silence would accompany fatalistic nods all around. A retail failure like the fall of W. T. Grant—the billion-dollar, thousand-plus-store, seventy-year-old outfit that a legendary ex-Searsman, Bob Anderson, had attempted to save before it closed down in 1976—was discussed often.

Korvettes had been a noble combatant since its founding in 1948— some called it the first of the true discounters. The famous 1964 quote from *Fortune* magazine that the outside consultants who came to Sears in the mid-1970s heard so often—that the paragon of retailers was number one in the United States and number two, three, and so on—was in fact borrowed from a comment by Jack Schwadron, the merchandise chief of Korvettes at the time.

By the dark Christmas of 1981, talk of sick retailers had taken on a particular poignancy within Sears, for most professional students of retailing contended that Sears and several other big chains were bound to decline to the edge of extinction because of something called the "polarization" of the American retail market.

The theory held that the small mall-based specialty stores and the discounters on one pole, and the upscale department stores on the other pole, were pulling the traditional middle-class customers away from

Sears in one direction or the other. The image placed Sears in a market version of purgatory. The little shops feasted off Sears' reputation, draining the power from its incomparable advertising budgets, corralling its lost sheep. Meanwhile, big stores without so much weight of history were underselling the Merchant and garnering more profit from cheap goods and low-expense overhead.

The polarization theory made some sense of the abject failure of recent years. Sears was sinking as a retail institution because the midsection of the nation had left it. The company careened up and down trying to find the customer—moving prices up in 1975 and 1976, down radically in 1977, and then back up in 1978, when Jumpin' Joe tried to get back the 2 percent. But polarization meant that they were searching for a market that was no longer there. The internal wars were just symptoms of the true disease. A store like Hicksville was by 1981 nothing but a mine holing out its last vein, a Korvettes in the early stages of disintegration. No wonder there were rumors flying through the industry about Sears' getting out of retail. Telling must have seen it himself.

Maybe Sears could be one big store, as Brennan promised, but if the big store was cast in the image of Hicksville—one of Sears' best—then it would look like a dingy battlefield of space filled with screams, beeps, fear, madness, desolation, children, and things to buy. Democratic vistas gone haywire on a strip called Broadway; the whole thing moving, as old Walt Whitman had it, toward "the sure-enwinding arms of cool-enfolding death."

CHAPTER 16

Dark Times

The merchants of Sears missed their December profit goal by $10 million. All over the country, exhausted retailers stepped back from their quieted stores and considered the hard work they'd put in during Ed Brennan's Challenge Year. It was hard not to think that a lot of it had occurred "under a bushel basket," as Ed Telling was fond of saying.

Early in 1982 their phantom chairman of the board came forward and gave one of his rare speeches. "We are facing up to the new realities of the American marketplace," Telling said. "The American economic, political, and social condition has undergone a radical change, a change that calls out for new products, new services, new ways of doing business. Old institutions which adapt to these changes will survive and prosper. Those that do not will falter and fail. After all, the underlying principle of the free-market system is that the chance of failure is as important as the right to succeed."

Anyone who'd ever been within a hundred yards of Ed Telling when the subject of banks came up would have looked at the speech and understood the point of his reference to old institutions, but the merchants were feeling sensitive these days. In considering the way Telling had "stunned the financial community" by snapping up Dean Witter and Coldwell Banker, *The New York Times* wondered if the move meant that Sears had "run up against a growth ceiling in its retailing business." The *Business Week* cover story about the corporate changes included the prominent assertion "Unable to grow in retailing, it [Sears] turns to financial services."

Meanwhile, the recession had coaxed out of university economics departments a "polarization-of-incomes" theory that explained the Merchant's decline. The "new realities of the American marketplace" now included the general assumption that the economy was reorganizing in such a way that income redistribution was drawing the middle class apart, thinning its mass like an overstretched rubber band. The number of families falling into an income-based definition of the American middle class Sears served was indeed dropping, from around half the families in the country to 45 percent, and as the ranks of the rich and poor swelled, the resulting "polarization" of the retail marketplace would strand a company like Sears. After serving to define what middle class meant for several generations, the old Sears, having outlived its usefulness to its clientele, would eventually decline and die. It was all there in the shape of the lines on the charts.

There was something strangely comforting about the polarization theory to many embattled Sears merchants. It explained away some of the neurotic behavior of recent years and indicated that perhaps the pain and confusion were not the result of some failure in themselves. There was an epidemic, a destructive "trend" that was even bigger than Sears. In 1976, the secretive, internal Sears "National Image Survey" showed that 20 percent of the shoppers in the country said they shopped Sears "most often." By 1981, this figure had fallen to 14.2 percent, a humiliatingly precipitous descent—unless it was envisaged as part of a changing economic reality as inevitable as the changing seasons.

And the polarization theory *felt* true. It explained how it was possible that legions of Sears buyers and sellers who'd bought and sold everything a middle-class, "basic-basic," power-mowing, casserole-consuming, hedge-trimming, winterizing, God-fearing American could ever have wanted were having so much trouble recognizing the customers now. Sears merchants of yore never had much trouble locating the customers, because, from the day the General "turned the stores loose," the customers were just like them. But the customers had changed. They seemed . . . well, almost kinky, and sort of nasty. They thought differently and shopped differently and acted like they no longer appreciated the great good gifts of American know-how and the freedom to shop. *Children* had learned to be fickle consumers now. They were more sophisticated and demanding in a store than the average mother of only fifteen years earlier.

Since 1975, the research department had reported that something strange was happening to the customers. Jim Button noted a "disturbing militancy" among the customers at the time, "the tone of an adversary

venting rage at 'the system' rather than expressing a genuine and under-
standable desire." Joe Moran echoed Button during the late 1970s when
he noted to his apostles that "the American retailer is dealing with a
disenchanted, angry consumer."

After a year of busting themselves up trying to do better, many a
Headquarters and Field merchant had to admit that he knew what Ed
Telling meant by new realities. The Sears American—*Homo economicus
Searsus*—was headed for extinction. Maybe what the experts had to say
about them was true. Maybe the day of the big general store was over.

The problem with slipping down into this warm stream of inevitability
was that the boss merchant wouldn't buy it. The middle class not only
still existed, Brennan argued to his managers, but it was plenty big
enough to keep Sears the most powerful store in the world forever. The
trick was to make the company respond to what the middle wanted now.

"This polarization crap!" he railed before his inner circle. It was some
high-brow rationalization. It was just another way of describing competition—strong, vicious competition. It was competition that post-war leaders of Sears had allowed to flourish in their arrogance, while they preoccupied themselves with the appurtenances and politics of empire. It was
competition that could indeed bleed Sears white, but plain old competition was all it was. It was not a bit like the seasons' changing. It was like
war.

Brennan quoted lists of statistics the research department had sent
upstairs to prove that "the franchise" was still there. There were over
twenty-four million credit customers who regularly shopped the stores,
he said. Another twenty-four million families used the catalog regularly.
Since it was discovered that twelve million of the catalog customers did
not have a credit card, thirty-six million American families were still
shopping Sears regularly. Three of four adult Americans still walked
through a Sears store at some point during a year, even if it was out of
some atavistic habit.

"We don't *need* new customers," he told the troops as he moved
across the corporate landscape during the early days of 1982. "All we
have to do is leverage off the legacy, off the huge customer base we
enjoy, and sell them more goods."

Everyone in the company knew that K mart had expanded into new
locations at rates up to 15 percent a year for well over a decade. The
discount houses had grown from dominance of just 2 percent of the
retail market in 1960 to ownership of 15 percent of it by the Christmas
of 1981. But Brennan pointed out that Sears', Penney's, and Ward's
share of the market had remained relatively constant all along: the

discounters were drawing their customers from other stores. A McKinsey study of segmented shares of the general merchandise market showed that, as the discounters' share of retailing in America rose from 7 percent to 32 percent, the *department stores'*—not the big chains'—share fell from 71 percent to 42 percent.

Better yet, the defecting hordes of Sears customers enumerated in the National Image Survey was a mirage: "They aren't leaving the fold altogether," Brennan declared. "They are just shopping the competition more often and shopping Sears less." Closer study of the surveys revealed that the basic franchise was still intact. The Sears part of the nation had remained almost canine in its loyalty. "They didn't leave us," Brennan said. "They just bought less stuff."

A booklet was printed on the occasion of the second series of managerial Challenge rallies held to inaugurate the "Action Year," the name Brennan had given 1982. The pamphlet included a grainy, almost impressionistic photograph of the chairman and chief executive officer of the Merchandise Group above a quote from Brennan's closing speech. Brennan's hands were clasped just in front of his lips in the picture. If the look on his face hadn't been so full of perplexity, it would have looked like he was praying. The adjacent quote was a restatement of the metaphor of the big store augmented for the Action Year: "What are we? We're a store: a store with all the items, lines, departments, advertising, signing, fixturing and credit. But, we're more than a store. We're different because we have a heart and soul. We have a spirit based on several generations that came before us. We have been left a legacy to nurture and to build on. We have a responsibility to pass on to the people who succeed us, a company stronger than the one left to us."

Brennan believed that, with the deepest divisions between management factions now fading, the source of the continued failure of the company could be found in "the last three feet," an old retailer's reference to that final, all-important space between both customer and employee, the consumer and the thing consumed. If any strategy for bringing the sheep back home was to work, the people in the stores just had to be nicer. Brennan would simply not accept the disappearance of public civility from the arena of the American store.

In an issue of the company newspaper he went so far as to declare, "The problem with the world today is that people are not very nice to other people who buy goods and services from them." It was a problem not for the company or the industry, it was *the* problem with the world.

Brennan starred in a videotape designed to kick off the 1982 "Courtesy Campaign." The tape was compulsory viewing in office lounges and store training rooms across the country. "I'm Ed Brennan," he said, looking intense and passionate on the screen, "and I'm here to ask for your help." He admitted that the state of the "Sears family" was not what it used to be before retailing changed. As during the first Challenge Meetings, Brennan stepped away from the past by leveling with everyone. He said they could maintain the sense of family and mutual respect, but they had to be more friendly. "We used to have many markets to ourselves—today we don't." The homiletic was designed to be heard and seen by part-time employees Brennan knew would never feel the sort of sincere devotion the full-timers used to exhibit. But he believed fervently that everyone wants to be a part of something.

Surveys indicated that the company newspaper was believed by only half of the employees, and most of them thought that executives suppressed stories as a matter of course—which they did. In the South, Brennan had observed the ineffectiveness of written pronouncements, so he began to experiment with the technological transmission of his vision. Closed-circuit television broadcasts of profit-sharing information had been used in the Tower since 1975, but, unlike Allstate, the Merchant had made limited use of videotape as a management tool, largely because no major leader of the corporation felt comfortable with the medium.

By early 1982, Brennan had a library of videotapes in a cabinet in his office including countless speeches and early experiments in regular internal programming for employees. The first "Fifteen Minutes" program was to be unveiled in March. The premier would feature an interview with Brennan, who would field questions about the battles ahead. "Fifteen Minutes" would be broadcast throughout the Tower and distributed on tape to the stores.

The videos and personal appearances were supplemented in *Sears Today* and the territory papers with man-on-the-street reactions to Brennan and reports on his constant movement, rather than the old press-release-style information published under an executive's name. "His warmth really impressed me. The time went by so fast," commented one time-card employee after hearing Brennan speak for the first time. "I was honored to be in the presence of Mr. Brennan," said a black man, who was depicted in a photograph next to his quote. "He came in here and he *knew* me," testified a store manager. "I was ten feet off the floor."

The media campaigns of early 1982 were only holding actions. Though Brennan honestly believed that polarization was a lot of rarefied crap, he also accepted that retailing on a mass scale had changed. Retailing was a killer-game for pros only now. Customers had to be located with crosshairs and hit before they left the aisles.

Sears was drawing life daily from a store of public trust that was inventoried in the past. The company simply had not kept pace with the way people had changed. The entire system by which Sears bought, ordered, and displayed its goods had become inimicable to giving the customers what they wanted and how they wanted it. The stores were in chaos because, just as customers had celebrated the joys of a century of rising prosperity in the aisles of markets built by Sears, the public was now trundling more current emotions and desires into the stores and finding the place so wanting that it felt like they'd been betrayed. The stores and the systems that served them still dwelled in 1955, and, as everyone in the Merchant knew by now, it would never be 1955 again.

Brennan said he wanted to bring the store back to its roots as a place representing convenience. The great ideas—the catalog, ample free parking, the credit card, and maybe this financial-services venture— were essentially about convenience. The technological systems had to be capable of moving the unruly checkout lines and handling price changes. The goods had to be more readily accessible.

Brennan was beginning to believe that the age-old design of a big retail store as a variation on the great bazaars of the past must end. The big stores of Sears were still designed for men, and to a lesser extent for women with time on their hands. If things were comparatively hard to find and illogically arranged in Sears stores, then the consumer could encounter other things to buy while conducting a leisurely search. Brennan wanted the stores to look jazzy. He wanted stores that reflected a current acquisitive style. And he wanted one big store that reflected all this as truth.

The way the stores of Sears, Roebuck looked and were organized, however, was the logical conclusion of an intricate economic system. The departments in the stores were still reflections of Headquarters' power and politics, refracted through the prism of the remaining territorial prerogatives. Even after the ERIP, most stores were still run by veteran managers who believed their purpose was to imprint their stores with aspects of their own personalities.

The seemingly innocuous task of changing the collection of goods within the boundaries of a given department augured deep trauma for the Headquarters status quo. Of course the telephone-answering machines should never have ended up next to the Christmas cards and the diamonds at the Hicksville store. People don't think about things that way. The arrangement was neither logical nor convenient. Video toys and games should certainly not be housed in the sporting-goods department, next to the basketballs, but the games resided in sporting goods

because the Headquarters buyer for that department was more powerful than the buyer over in electronics, so the day a young Californian
named Nolan Bushnell wandered into the Tower to tell the buyers about
his start-up company, called Atari, he was routed to the kingpin of
sporting goods. The reason the phones and answering machines were
next to Christmas cards was that a series of buying-organization managers of Department 3—titularly the stationery department—had somehow exercised such entrepreneurial authority that they'd managed to
corral cameras, phones, binoculars, clocks, and greeting cards into their
purview.

More sacrosanct than the various historical boundaries was the persistent animating creed: "Sears Has Everything." Phil Purcell discovered
how the organization had developed antibodies to protect itself from
any assault upon this central tenet when he attempted to make the
buyers "harvest" their less powerful items and lines through the use of
the "matrix" model. Joe Moran had been somewhat more successful in
cutting down the gross number of things Sears bought and sold through
his strong-arm tactics, but there was still no coherent philosophy of what
sorts of things Sears should and shouldn't sell, other than the belief that
any honest product worthy of an extended production run should be
retailed at Sears.

In reality, Sears no longer had everything in the way of the specialty
stores that lined shopping strips and malls. If Sears carried eight examples of running shoes, then a running shoe store carried twenty different
models. The experience of the Challenge Lines and Challenge Items
had confirmed to Brennan the efficacy of concentrating corporate resources like buying skill, money, scientific design, and floor space on a
carefully winnowed-down assortment of goods.

Lines had been dropped over the years. Homes, motorcycles, uni-
forms, silos, surgical instruments, and live animals had all been phased
out in the past, but efforts to prune lines and items threatened too many
careers and were now associated with the Draconian measures visited
on the buyers before Brennan arrived. The term Brennan chose to mute
the cultural destructiveness of filling the stores with a carefully aimed
assortment of goods was "dominance." "We have to mean something
again," he said. "We have to stand for something in every line we carry.
Where we can't purvey an image of 'dominance,' then let's get out of
that business."

Brennan asked Joe Moran to join him in a conference room on the
forty-third floor. The purpose of the exercise was to "take the store apart
on paper," by trying to analyze the course and power of each item Sears
carried from factory to store. Every one of the 850 product lines bought
by Sears was to be considered. Brennan told Moran the exercise would

take all of a few days, but it continued on through weeks of dawn-to-dark work.

Work sheets indicated Sears still dominated 75 percent of the American bench power-tool market, 40 percent of the automobile-battery business; 37 percent of the laundry-machine business, and 25 percent of the lawnmower business. But there were other lines taking up space in the stores that hardly meant anything at all to Sears or the public.

Buyers were to come sit across from Brennan and the subdued figure of Joe Moran, and they were supposed to tell the truth. The exercise was intimidating to many of them at first, but after a while the sight of Brennan and Moran dwelling day after day on one of the working floors in the Tower, immersing themselves in the reality of goods like that, had a powerful effect on many of the buyers. Several of them actually looked up at Brennan during a review session and said, "You know, my line shouldn't exist." A few even said, "My whole department shouldn't exist."

Brennan found the selfless admissions to be moving in the way of sacrifices people make during wars. He'd heard the Sears buyers' oaths and creeds and observed their resistance to observation from above since he was a boy, and he knew that, in disgorging so much information, the buyers were offering up to him prerogatives they had been taught to protect at all costs since their corporate infancy. The size of the gesture indicated how many of the company's historical precepts had been given up, and it also revealed how much latitude "the people," as he often called the employees, were now willing to cede up to him.

"These have been the most exciting days of my career," Brennan said to an assembly of buyers after the first wave of hands-on product review was completed, "because now we can do anything we want."

Joe Moran had dreamed of tearing back the armor and studying the buyers' wares for a long time, so he reveled in the discussions of the true meaning of goods and their relationship to popular material desires. Joe had become entranced by the audacity of Brennan's vision. He knew that there was a connection between the endless sifting on forty-three and Brennan's recent charge to Claude Ireson and his designers to pull together their West Side experimentation and draw a picture of a new store by July. Joe understood that he had in mind the creation of a new business system and a new business philosophy in the physical fact of a retail store, and Ed Brennan knew that Joe was one of the only people in all of Sears capable of fully grasping what he was up to.

From all outward appearances, the two men had developed a powerful working relationship. But if Ed Brennan looked haggard from the strain of what *Business Week* had recently called his "Herculean task," then Joe Moran looked worse. His weight seemed to fluctuate daily. He would puff up and overfill the tailored suits Brennan made him buy, only to shrink down again as if someone were letting the air out of him, the fine contours of his fancy suits getting lost in empty wrinkles and folds. Joe's boxy face became so slender that his big squarish glasses looked comical on the end of his nose. You could hear him drawing breath from across the meeting table on forty-three, and sometimes you'd see light disappear from his eyes. But he still showed up at each and every one of the endless meetings, at each marathon session during which he and Brennan planned their descent into the next level of the company— there to investigate, reorganize, and reconstitute, in their quest to work all the way down to the aisles of each store.

Brennan sat at Joe's side during a brief celebration of the thirty-fifth anniversary of Moran's arrival at Sears as a copywriter-trainee. After a round of roasting by the remaining apostles, Jumpin' Joe said he had a tear in his eye, and that he now knew how it felt when you get ready to die. Then he turned to Brennan. "I knew his dad and his Uncle Jerry," Joe said. "There's a great personal tie here that I've never been very good at showing. I've had a love affair with Sears for thirty-five years," he continued, turning now to the others, "and if I didn't I wouldn't have stayed on.

"I don't think there is anything that would have been more unusual thirty-five years ago today—for me, or for anyone who knew me then—than for me to have become a settled American businessman, still working in the same company after all this time. Anyone who would have said it would have been laughed out of the old neighborhood. I was about as far to the left as you could get in politics, social behavior, and my general attitude toward everything. If a lot of people were for it, I was against it.

"But I've learned through this period of time, a time that spans several wars and hopefully won't span any more, one principal lesson. You can't see it alone—you can't see it unless you have people who have touched you help you see it—what you can see is the utter inconsequentialness of so much we think is important. You can see the irony of so much; the smallness of life and its foolishness. And behind each one of those things are the wildnesses that most of us have experienced in our lives and our careers. But the most satisfying thing is that, having arrived at a point where I can say these things, I can still say that if I had it to do all over again, I would do it the same."

Joe really wasn't feeling right at all, and he knew he should have seen to his health already. He'd heard that Brennan was worried about him, so he was aware that, unlike in the past, his ghost-like visage gave his aches and pains away. In the wake of the departure of most of his generation, there was nobody left to remember his heart attack in 1959, and hardly anyone ever did find out that part of his lung had been removed during two operations performed several years later. Keeping that stuff off the grapevine was one of the benefits of being known to disappear every so often—that and the help of company friends.

Joe didn't see many of the guys who'd bailed out anymore. He talked to Ira Quint on the phone once in a while, and to a few others who'd retired, but the wounds opened by his final break with Jack Kelly would probably never heal.

It was only on rare occasions now that Joe was able to repair to his office, close the door, collapse into his desk chair, and do some thinking amid the dark, moody oil paintings that depicted hard-rushing streams, foreboding black storms, and ominous landscapes.

The professional art consultant assigned to decorate Joe's first executive office, on the sixty-eighth floor, made the mistake of asking him for an appointment so that she could get a sense of the sort of art that would reflect "aspects of himself." The consultant, a Toronto-based dealer named Helene Maslow, sat in front of the disheveled lump of a corporate executive for only a few minutes the first time they met.

"My *self*," Jumpin' Joe scoffed. "I would never reveal my *self* on the wall of an office."

The personal selection of office art was one of the few material perks that came with being a Sears executive. General Wood preferred his series of fine Pennell lithographs celebrating the Panama Canal he'd helped to build. Arthur Wood, of course, had his own Monet, and other impressionists and masterpieces. Jim Button had his Buttons, and Maslow had assisted Telling in securing his Eskimo sculpture, his Picasso lithograph, and the one print of an English golf course near the fens where Telling believed his ancestors might have lived.

But Moran made Maslow wait three months before granting her another chance to buy him some art. All the while others on sixty-eight—including Telling—tried to convince Joe to see the consultant again.

When Maslow sat down the second time, Joe immediately began to talk about Plato's perception of the purpose of art. He lectured on at great length, moving through the Renaissance and into the Enlightenment. He lingered with pleasure over the work of the Romantics of the nineteenth century. "Before this," he told Maslow, "artists were craftsmen, but a revolution in thought diminished the role of religion, and it fell to the artist of the mid-nineteenth century to evoke a new religion. They stopped being craftsmen and became emotive geniuses. I like Turner. He used prisms—technology—to say a great deal about light. I love the masters of the Hudson River School, the Regionalists. I love the

American Luminists—their work is thoughtful. What I don't like, inci-
dentally, is second-class, office-wall art."

After a great deal of searching, Maslow finally found some oil paintings
that were in fact of the Düsseldorf School, but which resembled in style
and feeling the much more valuable Hudson River School canvases
Moran had mentioned. Joe was overjoyed by her finds.

When the move was made to forty-four, Joe had one of his favorites,
the largest canvas, placed directly behind his chair. It depicted an otherwise sunless forest illumined by an eerie ray of light. Ethereal sheep
grazed in a clearing in the distance, and heavy clouds filled a dark sky.
Segments of foliage looked so thick and overgrown that the forest in the
painting looked like the forests in fantasies. If a visitor walked behind
Joe's chair and gazed closely at the painting, there, lost in the many
cracks on the surface of the old work, and obscured under the evanes-
cence of a huge spreading tree, he could make out the image of a tired
soldier in what could be a kilt and a dog resting at his side. The figure
looked like a tin soldier of some ancient guard collapsed against the tree
in apparent exhaustion, his rifle resting inviolately beside him and his
hands hanging limp at his sides.

One visitor was brave enough once to ask Joe Moran why he adorned
his office with such dark paintings.

"Because they're pictures of my soul," Joe said.

But during those endless winter and spring days of hard work during
1982, Joe told his family that his spirit soared. He loved thinking hard
about the goods. The spirit of collegiality he'd always desired was beginning to suffuse the tiny group of intimates around Brennan. He said that
when he did finally retire, he wanted to write a book about small-town
America. But for now Sears was the fertile source of his material. The
company contained the stuff of moral conflict and human drama, as Joe
reiterated to his kids over dinner at night—all of it available to the
observer on an epic scale. For thirty-five years he'd been a student and
chronicler of Sears life, and, but for a brief time when the dramas
engulfed him and made things too real, it was a fine way to live.

After a spring meeting about the ongoing line reviews Joe Moran called
Frank Tuma into his office to discuss a meeting of major suppliers scheduled for April. "Write me some notes for a speech as if I won't be there
to deliver it, Frank," Moran said. "I'm bleeding inside, and I have to go
to the hospital."

Larry Moran, Joe's fifth son among the seven boys in the clan, received
a phone call from his mother at his home in Minneapolis, Minnesota.
Margie Lou told him that she and his father were flying up his way to

visit the Mayo Medical Clinic. Larry and his wife went to the airport on Mother's Day to meet a Sears jet bearing his father, mother, and another, strikingly sober man who, while appearing quite young for a Sears executive, for some reason wore his hair in a style appropriate to a gentleman in his sixties. He was introduced to the young couple as Ed Brennan.

Though the work of experimentation and close examination of the guts of the business had become the central focus in Headquarters by the time Joe entered the hospital, the day-to-day performance of the company compelled Brennan to issue assurances of survival in his videotape and other communiqués. "We are an institution," he reiterated in the company newspaper. "We are the company that year after year shows up as one more consumers trust than any other organization. We are here for the long haul."

The year began with a streak of such bitter cold that sales were depressed in all the stores, but January was still the Merchant's best month in relation to the rest of the retail industry in years. Brennan took great pleasure in telling a group of assembled buyers that Sears' sales were up 6.1 percent in January 1982, while Penney's sales were down .6 percent and sorry old Montgomery Ward was off 10.1 percent.

Even the veterans who still worked from habit admitted that fiscal comparisons with Montgomery Ward were too depressing to consider seriously. Competition with the "other" Chicago mass retailer had been absurd since 1954, when Sears outdistanced Ward by $2 billion in sales. But on the receptionists' desks in the foyers of almost every Sears floor in the Tower felt boards were still displayed reporting daily stock-price quotes for Ward, Penney, and Sears. K mart remained unworthy of mention.

Despite the good January showing Brennan trumpeted vis-à-vis the traditional competition, the sales goal for the month was missed by $40 million, 4 percent short of the goal set out in the Plan. The recession doused every spark the Merchant offered up. The stock price was up, but that was because of Telling's financial-services initiative.

During the second quarter, the Sears retailers racked up almost $5 billion in sales and contributed around $75 million to profits, but Allstate sent $113.7 million to the bottom line on less than $2 billion in revenue.

Operational cost-cutting was elevating the Merchant's general performance, but several remaining operating impediments still stood in the way of further change. The selling system was particularly inefficient at the level of the cash registers in the stores, where one of the most expensive computerized checkout systems ever built to keep detailed customer accounts as well as to track inventory status was woefully overloaded. The number of price changes alone was inciting customers and employees alike to riot.* The piles of ragged computer sheets, the long lines, and the useless optical scanner guns had become universal objects of scorn. For all the millions of dollars in computer equipment, the over six hundred minicomputers and just under forty powerful IBM 370's serving the stores simply did not connect decisions to sales.

After the interlocking business-planning system made its first successful movement down into the organization and back up again, Brennan had rewarded his protégé, young Eric Saunders, with the opportunity to manage the powerful Atlanta group of stores. But in May of '82, he recalled Eric to the Tower to become the Merchant's vice-president for operating. Brennan told Saunders that, while the buyers were working through their programmatic soul-searching, and Claude Ireson's team was working to design the sellers a new store, the operators should work to figure out a new way to organize the dynamics of a sale in the store.

Saunders assembled a team and began to study state-of-the-art automated pricing systems. Within weeks, experiments were being conducted with new prototype technology in a test store near Milwaukee. Saunders had come to believe that the mammoth network of store computers and terminals could all be drawn into an integrated system—but he figured it would cost a sum of money in the middle "eight-figure" range, and would take a great deal of time.

By the middle of the summer, Ed Brennan began to exhibit the telltale signs of a man running himself too hard. If Brennan wasn't on the West Side or at a store test site or meeting a consultant from IBM or a store graphics designer, he was attending another meeting with the buyers. After Joe Moran entered the hospital, the seven buying-side vice-presidents reported directly to Brennan, and he had become much of what the territory kings used to be to their people. He was working as Charlie Wurmstedt and Joe Moran combined. With the sole assistance of Henry Sunderland, Brennan was now operating the old Parent and the Field manually. He'd turned the weight of the thing onto himself, and the consensus was that the strain showed. There was open discussion

---

*The original purpose of fixed prices in public marketplaces was rooted in the desire of managers and entrepreneurs to control the activities of clerks and salespeople. As organizations grew, storekeepers could no longer trust employees to haggle efficiently, so they set the prices themselves.

in the senior ranks about how very much older Eddie Brennan looked, and his old colleagues in the South were shocked at how the youthful star they'd sent north had become bloated-looking and quite gray.

Tests indicated that cancer was absent from Joe Moran's lymph nodes, and the doctors felt that they'd removed all of the tumor they found in his bladder. There were various complications due to the general state and history of Moran's health, but his prognosis was considered quite good.

Brennan ferried Joe between various specialists in a Sears plane and then back home for recuperation. They continued to "talk the business" and "take apart the store" as they traveled. Brennan told Moran he was thinking of bringing all the territorial, group, and even the store managers to the Tower at the same time for the third round of annual Challenge Meetings. He said that 90 percent of the managers of the Field had never even seen the Tower. He felt it was important that they take a look at the monolith.

In May another series of large meetings were held in Chicago. Representatives from Sears' best suppliers were brought to town for an event called "Partners in Progress," a term used first by the General. Brennan and Moran had decided that the old Sears "Symbol of Excellence" awards, which had been handed out rather arbitrarily in recent years to source factories, should conform with the new disciplines and new ideas. Moran wrote a memo expressing his reasoning: "There are sources listed in the book [the Symbol of Excellence book] that couldn't *spell* quality . . . some of them haven't had a new idea since 1740 B.C." Joe contended that there were 384 different standards for judging a source, just as he'd once enumerated thirty-four central criteria for judging the worthiness of a person seeking a job.

At one of the dinners that May, Frank Tuma used all of his bureaucratic skills to stage a surprise event for Joe Moran. Several musicians hoisting tubas suddenly appeared at the banquet, and they proceeded to play one of the only pieces of music that featured the instrument Joe Moran talked about so often. As the sonorous oompah tones filled the room, executives turned and looked at Frank Tuma, who was teary-eyed and lost in thought. Frank couldn't believe Joe Moran hadn't made it to the event, but the doctors had said no. One afternoon soon afterward, Tuma went out to see Moran at the suburban community hospital he was in, and all Frank could do was sit beside Moran's bed with a lump in his throat. He'd always figured Joe Moran was invincible, and now the old paratrooper looked pretty sick.

.   .   .

In June, Telling's long-time sidekick, Henry Sunderland, suffered a heart attack. It was hard to tell when Henry was sick or run-down because he always had a rather haggard, almost cadaverous look about him, but before the attack, Henry had begun to look particularly tired.

With Henry gone, Brennan was now alone. Just as he felt that he was beginning to see the possibility of extending his grasp out to the far edges of the organization, just as he was almost in a position to "lift the base," the only two people whom he'd allowed to share true responsibility were out of commission. Brennan tried hard to cover all the jobs—jobs that would have been more appropriately carried out by ten or twelve skilled managers—but he knew the situation was serious. "It's not healthy," he admitted. "The entire corporation is vulnerable." But he just wanted to hold out until Joe came back.

The scoreboard was reflecting the fact that the recession had utterly killed off the household-durables market, from which Sears drew half its business. Sales for 1982—after all that work—weren't even up 2 percent over 1981.

After a hopeful array of hospital reports during August, Brennan was informed on Labor Day that Joe Moran's cancer had in fact metastasized across the entire surface of his lungs. There was no further opportunity for heroic medical intervention.

A few days later, Brennan found out that his young brother, Bernie, was coming home to Chicago to be the number-two executive at Montgomery Ward. Every one of the long articles about Bernie's appointment mentioned the interesting symmetry of two brothers from the same "retailing family" rising so prominently to leadership of Chicago's two biggest retail organizations. One analyst noted that Bernie Brennan, in conjunction with Ward's chairman, Stephen Pistner, would constitute a "one-two punch"—like Brennan and Telling at Sears. Neither Ed nor Bernie would comment to the press upon the younger Brennan's installation at the other Chicago retailer, but a friend of the family noted in one article that the Brennans were "the Irish the Kennedys should be."

After he got out of the Navy, Bernie Brennan had come to Sears as a trainee, eventually ending up among the furniture buyers as an assistant. By then Ed had decided to break with family tradition at Parent and go out to distinguish himself in the stores of the Field. During the mid-1970s, people used to confuse the two brothers when Ed would come in from the field for Hay Committee meetings. Both Brennan kids—one in Parent and one in the Field—were considered pretty hot young merchants by the old-timers; though the question of who was better was rarely raised, it was generally acknowledged that Bernie was possessed of a mean streak that seemed absent in Ed. Bernie worked for Joe Moran's old sidekick, Ira Quint, for a while, and Quint couldn't help noticing how Bernie always begged off from trips that would include a stop in his brother's territorial bailiwick of the time.

In 1976, as Ed's corporate star ascended in the trail of Telling, Bernie quit Sears to join a Jacksonville, Florida-based discount operation called Save-A-Stop. Just before he left, a personnel officer asked Bernie why he was abandoning a promising career in Chicago. "Because," Bernie said, "there's only room for one Brennan at Sears."

After he left Sears, Bernie developed a reputation as a hard-charging retail executive who called long weekend meetings and demanded a rigorous regimen from his employees. They called Bernie "the purple people eater" at Save-A-Stop because of his demanding ways. Bernie had Ed's near-photographic memory and assimilating skills when it came to numbers, and he projected energy in similarly dazzling displays. Bernie had been given equity in Save-A-Stop when he came on board, at a time when the company's shares were trading for a dollar. The stock price had risen to $16 a share by the time Bernie decided to come home. While Bernie was in Florida and Ed was running the Southern Territory, Ed would occasionally entertain other Searsmen at his vacation home in Sawgrass, along the northern Florida coast. On several occasions, Bernie Brennan was in attendance. It was said the two brothers played tennis together, something many a Searsman and Save-A-Stop employee would have paid to see.

Nobody at Sears was very happy about Bernie's decision to come to Ward's, including Ed. Ed called his younger brother on the phone and asked him how he could have done such a thing, and several Sears executives on the forty-fourth and sixty-eighth floors wondered aloud why, if Bernie Brennan had something to prove, he couldn't have done it in another way.

Several visitors to Ed Brennan's office on the now silent forty-fourth floor that September were made uncomfortable by the darkness that surrounded the Merchant's chairman. On one occasion he ordered coffee and cake to be brought to his office while he told a retired catalog executive and another visitor, an old pal of Arthur Wood's who made store fixtures for Sears, about how the Merchant had become a family again. He talked about how constantly he attended to the ailing Joe Moran. Brennan talked on and on, though the two men mentioned several times a pressing appointment they had.

"Guess he's just excited about all the things he's doing," the old catalog man said as the two finally left the office.

"No," said the other man. "Something's very wrong there."

. . .

On September 28, in the middle of his thirty-sixth year with the company, at the beginning of the sixty-third year of his life, Jumpin' Joe Moran died at Holy Family Hospital in Des Plaines, Illinois. As was standard procedure, his Sears service card was pulled and, at the end of a list of eleven job titles, the card was stamped "Deceased."

Joe's friends from within the company filled Saint Anne's Church in Barrington on Friday morning, October 1. There never really had been many friends outside of Sears. His life was essentially a matter between Joe, his family, and Sears, Roebuck.

After communion, Joe's oldest son got up and read one of the countless poems that his father had ascribed to memory some time during his youth. It was a favorite of his father's by Stephen Spender:

I think continually of those who were truly great.
Who, from the womb, remembered the soul's history . . .
What is precious is never to forget
The essential delight of the blood drawn from ageless springs . . .
The names of those who in their lives fought for life,
Who wore at their hearts the fire's centre.
Born of the sun they travelled a short while towards the sun,
And left the vivid air signed with their honour.

The ERIP veterans who'd grown up at Sears with Joe sat together in rows and mingled together in large circles outside the church when the funeral ended. More than a few said that Joe must have worked himself to death. Over time, the period of Moran's mortal illness would seem to extend back into their own company histories, so that the response of many of them to the memory of how Joe Moran turned on his corporate brethren would be, "Yes, but Joe wasn't feeling well at the time."

To Moran's ten children, the wake and funeral provided opportunities to finally meet and look at characters who'd been made mythical to them over a lifetime of their father's dinner-table stories. On only one other occasion had they been able to put faces on the colorful host of names Joe always told them about. That was over ten years earlier, at the wedding of Peggy Lou, one of the daughters. It was then that they met the legendary Clem Stein. Aside from being one of the most flamboyant buyers of the old school, Stein was a world-class card player who used to drive to work in a Rolls-Royce, and he was prime among the epic characters the kids had come to know at dinnertime. At the wedding, the Moran horde had surrounded an astounded Stein and waited in line to shake his hand. A few years later, the kids learned at the dinner table that, when the time came that the company had to change, Clem and their father had fallen out over what was to be done. It was all part of the ongoing parable—the story of life through the veil of Sears—ended now in the fall.

From the beginning of the ordeal of their father's illness, the Moran kids had been amazed at the devotion exhibited by Ed Brennan. Brennan stood at the door of the church and greeted people as they arrived. At the wake he ushered executives over to meet Margie Lou Moran, who at one time had driven from the Irish West Side to her job as a Sears copywriter with Ed Brennan's Uncle Jerry. Brennan didn't leave Margie Lou Moran's side for several days after Joe died.

One afternoon Brennan arrived at her home with an illuminated copy of a testimonial to Joe, in the company of a stiff and grim-faced Ed Telling. Before they left, Margie Lou felt her broken heart go out to the chairman of Sears. The big man's obvious discomfort turned into even more obvious pain when he tried to express his feelings.

The children each wrote Ed Brennan notes of thanks and Brennan responded personally to every one. That none of them or their mother had ever met Ed Brennan before their father took sick was obscured by the constancy of his presence at the end.

It took a long time for Brennan to rally from the loss of Moran. Jumpin' Joe, who never once stopped calling him Eddie. All that knowledge and history and color, gone when he bailed out and left Ed Brennan alone.

CHAPTER 17

Maps

├─────────────┤

In the spring of 1983, a company plane from Chicago once again carried change to the old separate kingdom of Sears. Brennan and his team from Headquarters were scheduled to arrive in Los Angeles on April 5, five and a half years after Ed Telling's jet landed on an airstrip in Colorado before his showdown with John Lowe, the maverick king of the territory, and four years, almost to the day, from the time Telling came west to preside over the disastrous annual meeting held in the glass-covered, cube-shaped headquarters John Lowe built in a dry valley at the height of his reign.

Ninety minutes before the Headquarters plane was due to arrive, members of the senior executive corps of the Western Territory (the term "Far West" or the locally preferable "Pacific Coast" having gone the way of the term "Parent") paced the cool, slate-lined lobby of the territorial office building, each of them clutching an official itinerary that broke April 5 into increments as small as fifteen minutes. Sears employees came in out of one of those rare Southland days so unusually clear and bright that the craggy San Gabriel range rose in the distance like a photograph. Several of the officeworkers paused to stare quizzically at their leaders as they circled each other in the lobby, then they entered the elevators and began to spread the word that something was happening downstairs.

Some of the managers in the lobby were worried about their tans. "It's from golf at Palm Springs," apologized the territorial manager for public affairs. "But I was out there with Woody." Woody was Forrest R. "Woody" Haselton, the forty-four-year-old executive vice-president Brennan had installed in the Western Territory seven months earlier. It was probably better that the PR man's color was acquired under a sun shared by a corporate officer, but if the numbers had been better, the tans wouldn't have mattered.

"Hollywood Joe" Duggan, the territorial director of facilities planning in the West, owned the best suntan in the Cube, but Duggan seemed the least concerned about it. His color was offset strikingly by a head full of snow-white curls, by a prominent diamond ring, a slender and auda-ciously colorful non-Sears necktie, and, of course, the nickname "Holly-wood Joe." Duggan pulled all of this off, in part, because the facilities-planning boys throughout the company occasionally tended to be a little "artsy" by Sears standards. Since they also were responsible for each territory or retail group's huge real-estate holdings, facilities guys were also given to a bit of the flash that characterizes the commercial-real-estate sellers and shopping-center developers with whom they'd part-nered to transform the landscape of a place like Los Angeles, over the years.

Woody Haselton strolled into the lobby and announced it was time to form a caravan and go pick up the brass. Haselton was a short, somewhat portly man with graying, television-anchorman sideburns and glasses. Woody was an open man, and an easygoing manager, who usually pre-ferred a somewhat pedagogical form of corporate communication, but one thing Woody Haselton had learned to do as well as anyone in the territories by 1983 was talk like Ed Brennan. Haselton studied under Brennan as a group staff manager during Brennan's days in Buffalo, New York, so when Brennan charged him to "bring some Eastern Territory disciplines" to the West, he knew what that meant. Woody knew the secrets of the East. He'd experienced the South after Brennan. Woody spoke "the language."

The West had been entrusted to the long-time veteran Bill Loch-moeller when Henry Sunderland was recalled from his pacification du-ties in Los Angeles, but by the middle of 1982, Brennan decided it was time for the sixty-one-year-old Lochmoeller to retire in favor of a younger man. When he first arrived in California, news had trundled along the grapevine about Lochmoeller's purchase of a beautiful home in the genteel L.A. suburb of San Marino. The home had once been occupied by a businessman named Harry Carl and his actress/wife at the time, Debbie Reynolds. It was soon said on the sixty-eighth floor that Lochmoeller thought he was a goddamned movie star. Never mind that Lochmoeller bought the big San Marino house from Henry Sunderland, or that Henry was known to tool about the Los Angeles freeways in a bright-red Porsche. Henry Sunderland was an Eastern Territory guy at heart, and in the end, big Bill Lochmoeller just didn't have the bloodlines or the sales and profit numbers to handle the movie-star image. If he'd turned the numbers he could have stayed on until he was sixty-five—but he didn't. Now he was gone to the timeless golf course, and it was Woody Haselton who'd been told that the West *had* to do better this year.

Brennan sent the Maine-born manager to the West after Woody had run the Greensboro, North Carolina, group of stores for only eighteen months. Brennan told Haselton to "have fun" with his big new job. "Build a deep understanding of the territory, Woody," the boss said. But there was a new urgency coming from the forty-fourth floor in 1983, and lately Woody Haselton had felt the screws turning. The spring sales were coming in, and it looked like the Eastern Territory was going to clobber the West. The spring was traditionally the Sun Belt's time to shine.

Brennan believed the West needed changes now of a magnitude that required his presence in Los Angeles. "Streamlining" was the term, the act promulgated under a formal presentation process called a "territorial overview." The whole thing was top-secret, and none of the local executives on their way to the Burbank airport had ever seen a single day of meetings during which so much that stood could fall away.

Each territorial executive was assigned to drive his Headquarters counterpart back to the Cube. Woody was supposed to fetch Brennan; Joe Duggan was assigned to pick up Claude Ireson; and so on. The matched job-title transport system had served Brennan well during his constant barnstorming in the Field, because it allowed him and his inner circle to speak to local managers off-the-record before the intricate public ritual of the Headquarters visit commenced. The system also served to break up the inward focus that naturally coalesces a group of outlander managers anticipating the arrival of representatives of central authority, especially, in the old Western Territory. In the past, a visit from Chicago was cause for any retail territory, group, store, or mail-order facility to swab the decks temporarily, spruce up the ledger books, and generally rally round itself long enough to smooth-talk the Parent visitors for a while before sending them back to Chicago, where they belonged. The visit was one of the periodic exercises that served to unite the autonomous localities, and the Chicagoans tended to suffer the show with the knowledge that it was all good for the sake of the whole. But Brennan's carefully designed car rides helped remind a local operating manager, for instance, that, when push came to shove over issues of fundamental policy or ultimate loyalties, his long ride with Sears, Roebuck now depended on a fellow who worked in Chicago.

The caravan rolling off the freeway and down Main Street in Alhambra included a Ford LTD, a Continental Mark III or two, some Japanese imports, and Hollywood Joe Duggan's Jaguar—limos were still abjured on such occasions as inappropriately un-Sears. The entourage pulled up in front of the Cube, and all the Chicago visitors except Ed Brennan went directly to an executive conference room dominated by a table big as a whale. The fifty-foot-long grainy wooden conference table was shaped like one of the contoured Victorian coffins that Sears had sold for decades through the ever-popular tombstone catalog. In front of each of the chairs surrounding the table was a dish full of Life Savers and chewing gum, and a huge three-ring notebook in a high-tech hue of gray. "WESTERN TERRITORY RETAIL ADMINISTRATIVE GROUP REVIEW" was printed above an embossed rendering of the name of the participant assigned to that seat.

The gray books remained closed as the sixteen executives spoke of basketball and the weather and waited for Brennan. Each Chicago visitor sported a gray business suit that matched the puffy gray pallor that so much work and early-morning travel had made a regular part of their physiognomies. As some of the locals had feared, the Californians looked rested and tanned in contrast.

After Henry Sunderland had his heart attack and Joe Moran passed away, Ed Brennan decided to rebuild a small group of acolytes that included a few durable men even younger then himself, but even the youngest of the Headquarters visitors appeared run-down from the effort of keeping up with Brennan in 1983.

Eric Saunders was collapsed in his chair on the visitors' side of the huge table, alternatively blowing his nose into a handkerchief he held in one hand and applying Chapstick to his lips with the other. Claude Ireson, who was standing off quietly in the corner, staring into the air autistically, rarely got colds. Unlike Eric, who chainsmoked and ate too much, Claude trained for the pace like an athlete. Claude got up early every morning and ran the roads of whatever town he was in that day, for miles and at a healthy clip.

Ireson was such a shy and sensitive man that his position as planner, stylist, and tastemaker to the revivified management team was hard for some to understand. The fact was, if Claude hadn't been born a dirt-poor country boy who saw Sears, Roebuck as the only difference between a decent job and a life in the mines of Appalachia like his daddy, he probably would have spent his career in deep frustration over the paucity of beauty and light that characterized the aesthetics of Sears. By virtue of attrition, Claude was now a veteran on Ed Brennan's roster, and though few people realized it yet, he was probably the most essential executive to the work of 1983.

The wiry fellow now circling the conference room pounding people's backs, remembering "way back when," and calling several of the Los Angeles executives "mah boys," was the fifty-seven-year-old veteran of thirty-three company years, the light-opera sergeant-major of a Field manager, William Bass. Bass had been running the Eastern Territory when Brennan decided to restore Charlie Wurmstedt's old title, senior executive vice-president, Field. The job would clearly never again carry the authority or historical poignancy it had had under Telling or Wurmstedt, but Brennan restored the post less for symbolic value than because he finally realized he couldn't do it all himself. Bass didn't want the job at all, but as a good soldier of the old school, he'd answered the call.

The other man Brennan drafted into service on the forty-fourth floor was absent from the Los Angeles meeting. Joe Batogowski hadn't had a vacation in years, and he needed a rest.

Just before Joe Moran died, Brennan sat on the edge of Moran's bed and they discussed Joe's successor. Most observers felt that the General's grandson, Bob Wood, had the inside track on the top buying job if Jumpin' Joe didn't make it, but most of Brennan and Moran's discussion centered on Batogowski. Moran's opinion of "Bato" had mellowed since the days when he found the boyish-looking merchant's can-do style irksome. Moran would never forgive Batogowski's contention that his golden prose was analogous to the work of Erma Bombeck, but it had to be acknowledged that Bato got to work in time to watch the sun rise up from the lake, and was one of the only executives in all of the buying organization with the stamina needed to keep up with Brennan. He had a couple of decorations from work in the line of duty: there was the novel Betty Crocker apple-pie-scented scratch-and-sniff cookbook that sold like hell, and he'd come up with the snappy slogan "We install confidence" when he was running the auto-and-recreation buying group under Moran. He had the touch when it came to goods; he had lots of kids; he had a decent reputation in the Field; and because he was tight with Phil Purcell from their 702-P days, Telling even knew who he was.

So from his deathbed Joe Moran relinquished his doubts and swallowed his abiding distrust of a man with such limited literary acumen. The younger Joe was told about his appointment as the new merchant prince ten days after Moran's funeral.

"I ask you all," Batogowski said to the buyers at a meeting soon afterward, "please, do not compare me with Joe Moran. We share a first name and we were both paratroopers. But that's where it stops. I was and I remain today only a devoted student of Joe's.

"The thing that Joe was—all that time—was *consistent*. Everything he wrote in 1950, that he wrote in 1960, and that he wrote in 1970—he was consistent in what he advocated for merchandising."

Some of the former apostles in the audience couldn't believe the consistency stuff. Bato was ascribing characteristics that everyone knew were Brennan's and only Brennan's to his departed predecessor, the master of the flip-flop. If anyone was intimate with the audacious attitudinal changes of Big Joe's mind, it should have been the kid some called Little Joe, who saw Moran daily at the height of his erratic, self-justifying, and terrible zeal.

Brennan had rallied from his darkness of the previous fall. He'd apparently decided that, for all of the fast airplanes, computers, and videotape facilities at his disposal, the only way he could transmit the new "personality" Sears required was through others who understood. He'd taken on a veteran gutter-brawler retailer and good old boy in Bill Bass; the youthful former bag-carrier Joe Batogowski; the Telling hatchet man Henry Sunderland (Henry had returned to work the month before the L.A. trip but didn't travel); the smart and stuck-up kid Eric Saunders; and the quiet and artistic Claude Ireson—and he'd formed them behind him as a management team.

And now, as was his habit, he kept them waiting quite a while—long enough for everyone to sit down and settle down around the huge table. Long enough, perhaps, for all of them to look toward the door.

Late in November of 1982, Ronald Reagan finally admitted that the recession had twisted the American economy into a "hell of a mess." A few days later, a reporter from *The Wall Street Journal* noticed Sears big-ticket home-fashions salesmen sitting in the unsold furniture at the big store in Paramus, New Jersey, and duly reported the fact as a symbolic economic indicator on the front page. Christmas in the Action Year was far from a sellout, but when the year was toted up, Sears had at least returned to its position as the largest gross-profit producer in the retail industry, a position the company should never have relinquished in light of its incomparable size.

Much of the improvement, however, was because of a turnaround in credit-department numbers. During the summer, government credit controls had been revoked and interest rates began to ease slightly. The Merchant ended the year with an $18-million profit in the credit-card operation, in contrast to an $83-million loss in 1981. But the reported "record profits" failed to match the profits chalked up to cries of panic back in 1978,* and they were profits drawn from sales figures that were below those of 1978—the year Joe Moran shut down the business at the tap.

Chain Store Age published one of its long considerations of the Merchant, which this time posited that in 1983 Sears must show once and for all if it had the potential to revive. The article cast doubt on the possibility that the numbers for 1983 would exceed those of the mirror-and-pulley job of 1982. What was at risk for the Merchant in 1983 was nothing less than its "niche as America's store." The graphics attending the article were devoid of the inevitable images of the Tower leaning to one side or being cracked in two. The Tower was shown instead as a chess piece on a chess board, though it was unclear if the piece was meant to be the roving and dangerous queen or the defenseless king.

The first quarter of 1983 proved out Brennan's hunch that Sears was at least better positioned to rise up with an economy that seemed determined to climb up out of its hole from the moment the President pronounced it a mess. Retail profits were up to $16.2 million compared with a $23.2 million loss during the first quarter of 1982. In March alone, $382 million worth of appliances were sold at Sears to newly confident consumers—an all-time record. Even the suppliers were finally reporting a revival. Whirlpool was up almost 50 percent during the first quarter, and sales at most of the other big factories were improved by at least 25 percent over 1982.

A few days before the Headquarters visit to Los Angeles, an issue of *Fortune* magazine electrified the management of the corporation when it carried an article called "Sears' Overdue Retailing Revival."

The Tower had refused to cooperate with the *Fortune* reporter on the piece out of residual hurt over the devastating 1979 piece, "The Leaning Tower of Sears," which had questioned Telling's native aptitude for management and cataloged some of Joe Moran's excesses. The public-affairs officers figured that *Fortune* would just quote some professor on the inevitable polarization of retailing anyway, tolling again the big bells and breaking out the black crepe for the Merchant. But the article turned out to be hopeful and positive. At one point the writer even suggested that some of Sears' management techniques were "worth considering by anyone charged with getting a drowsy corporate elephant on its feet and trotting."

Ed Brennan actually had in mind a corporate organization metaphorically sleeker and more agile than an elephant, and the state visit to the

---

*Accounting changes during 1981 call for an adjusted figure to be considered in order to compare 1978 and 1982 profits for Sears.

Cube on April 5 was part of his determination to make 1983 the year when he utterly changed the nature of the corporate beast forever. Brennan preferred to index his performance via the popular and less malleable gauge called "return on average shareholders equity." The "ROE" cranked out by the unstoppable Sears of 1955 had run up to 16.1 percent. Brennan was shooting for a 15-percent return for 1983, twelve percentage points above the dire performance of 1980.

He knew that his cost-cutting and physical-contraction program was verging into critical areas now. Under cover of the state of shock in which he found the company when he arrived, Brennan had administered anesthetics with challenges and hope. The spirit of healing made the subsequent amputations, the closings down, the terminations, and the deracination of people as in great floods and plagues appear almost humane. His personal attendance to the streamlining of the company was as necessary to success as the presence of a master surgeon. He knew now that the sutures were straining, the fabric ready to tear, but he had to keep the operation going.

By winter's end, fully a hundred thousand employees of the Merchant had been taken out of the organization. The interlocking planning system of targets and challenges had so successfully overshadowed staffing regulations and moral guidelines from the past that over sixty thousand of the hundred thousand departed employees turned out to have been of the expensive, full-time variety. Whereas there were once twenty thousand employees in the executive or "checklist" category of the merchandise company at the peak, there were now fourteen thousand. Five sovereign territories had become four; fifty-one once-independent Field retail groups had become forty-six; and 110 different distribution facilities and warehouses had been cut to nearly half that number. Some 4,228 certified freight carriers trucked Sears goods around America when Brennan arrived, and now—with some help from transportation deregulation in Washington—there were 210 carriers, and plans that called for cutting the number to 170 by the end of '83. Brennan figured that, given the way the cost of running Sears was ballooning when he arrived in 1980, he was now running the company at one-third of what the costs were projected to be by now. He consoled himself on occasion with the thought that his cost-containment drive was piling so many millions of dollars into net profit that the addition would eventually be enough to have paid for Dean Witter.

But the best thing about the slimming down of the Merchant, he said, was that it was bringing the organization into contact with the state of the real working economy for the first time in years. Brennan could feel the ground now, and he believed that, after a few more months of surgery, the Merchant could be past its time of being so big that it was seriously injured by an economic downturn and unable to capitalize on an upward surge. All of this, he knew, did not mean that the old company would prevail. It would only serve to put Sears back in the match.

Brennan grasped a few of the more available hands as he entered the meeting room. He squeezed hands briefly, wrapping his face into a squinty-eyed grin for the duration of the greeting, then moved on to address the next man, warmly, very quickly, and always by his first name.

"How are you, Mr. Brennan?" one executive said.

"Welcome, Mr. Brennan," said another.

As with so many people of his heritage, Ed Brennan was becoming more handsome with age. Time appeared with a certain distinction on his once-too-smooth brow, and the tiny white forelock atop his high-swept pompadour had silvered elegantly. His face had filled out into better proportion with cheeks he always felt made him look chubby.

Far from the pastel double-knits he wore in his Sears youth, Brennan now sported beautifully cut three-piece suits. Before taking his seat at the long table, he swept off his suit coat and whirled it like a cape onto the back of his chair. The jacket bore a brilliant red lining decorated with circular, silver ornamental details. The vest underneath, conforming closely to what the press had taken to calling his "wrestler's physique," revealed the same bright material on the back panel. It was a pattern suitable to a riverboat gambler.

Brennan leaned back and unpocketed one of his A and C corner-drugstore stogies and allowed a rather long, silent pause as he attended to the ceremonies of the cigar. He began to speak without looking up, knowing without having to look that everyone at the table was watching. "You know, I came out here in 1958 when I was just a few weeks out of a store in Oshkosh, Wisconsin," he said, still looking at no one in particular. "It was pre-jet times, and it took forever to get here. I got a lot less attention that trip." Now he stared across at the executives arrayed along the Westerners' side of the table, his eyes brightening. "Don't know exactly why."

Woody Haselton strode to a podium as the lights dimmed. The entire wall behind Haselton was suddenly alight with graphics identical to the pages in the gray books, each of them attesting to the wisdom of the proposal at hand: to dissolve two more of the territory's nine remaining administrative units. Haselton's report included an estimate of the potential reduction in territorial expense the closing of two more former baronies would yield to a percentage figure replete with three digits to the right of the decimal point. Woody analyzed the proposed restructuring in terms of overall demographics, distribution issues, personnel store mix, and numerous other factors—including the political, moral, and morale implications of once again drawing a scalpel across the territorial organization.

The hail of slides lighting the wall showed how profoundly the campaign of structural consolidation had already altered the map of Sears. The geographical logic of the territorial structure was gone. The Eastern Territory stretched from the Canadian border into South Carolina, and the South now included Miami, Florida, and El Paso, Texas—combinations of American puzzle-parts that would have been inconceivable only a few years earlier.

Joe Duggan presented a more detailed consideration of the streamlining proposal with the aid of maps rendered with microscopic precision. The maps reflected in Ed Brennan's clear blue eyes, and registered, as with others who had the business in their blood, in a way people outside the fold would never understand. In a map, Brennan saw towns that weren't marked and invisible rings around those towns that described markets. Inside every black dot that was to him a Sears store, he saw people—some of them long dead. He saw rivers and highways that only locals in the region could name. He wore a choropleth map of the Republic in his head as naturally as other people knew their way home from work.

It was part of the Sears way that those most observant and skilled at being cross-country travelers in fee to the company eventually rose up to be office-bound company cartographers instead. But the difference between Brennan and the others who read the maps was that he carried in his head another, much simpler and cleaner map with an entirely different set of dots and crossroads on it. Bringing the image of Sears inside Ed Brennan into conformity with the one on the wall was the unstated purpose of everyone in the room.

When the slide that said "Mid-Cal Group, Strategic Relocation of Stores" flashed onto the screen, Brennan said, "Stop."

"Where are you gonna put Stockton?" he asked.

"The Pacific Coast group," Duggan replied quickly.

Brennan nodded.

A few slides later he interrupted again, when a map of the Central Pacific group appeared. The group organization was one of two headquartered along with the territory staff in the Cube. The plan being considered called for the group to absorb some of San Diego's stores as well as surplus personnel if the San Diego group structure was killed off, per the suggestions in Phase I of the restructuring plan.

"Why does Central Pacific have such profit problems?" Brennan queried, looking over at Woody Haselton. "Why do they march to such a different drummer?"

"It's their history," Haselton said evenly, looking over to Bill Bass, the titular Headquarters protector of the Field; Bass was silent.

It was then the turn of the territorial personnel manager, a sober-looking man named Steve Thorpe, to outline the "people problems" inherent in closing down two long-standing group offices. Fifty-five middle and senior managers, including the two veteran group managers, would become "surplus" as a result of Phase I. Thorpe recommended offering to relocate only those employees with "long-range potential." He said that the blow to those not making the cut could be softened with retirement seminars and the offering of a modified golden-parachute termination package that had been developed recently for such purposes in Headquarters.

Thorpe paused to note that being middle-aged and laid off in San Diego, California, or Seattle, Washington—the other site of proposed closing—given the unusually desperate economic situations in those towns in 1983, would be seen as nothing other than an imposed hardship on the executives. It was hoped that most of the managers in the Seattle group would accept demotion to stores in the Seattle metropolitan area. There wasn't much of a market for a fifty-year-old, $50,000-a-year retail executive anywhere else in Seattle, Washington, so it was assumed that the demotions would be accepted with reluctance, but Thorpe reminded his audience that Washington State and California were the two most litigious states in the union when it came to employment issues. Sears had been ordered to give a million dollars to a California employee in a wrongful-termination suit a few years earlier. Another judgment against the company for $5 million was still in the process of appeal, and fifty-one other, similar lawsuits were pending. Such were the risks of streamlining.

"The grapevine is already hot," Thorpe said. "The fear caused by rumors of layoffs is already affecting the quality of people's work. Sears is their womb, and a lot of them know they won't survive outside of the womb."

"So they can feel it coming," Brennan said in an almost wistful tone. He was often amazed at how tightly strung the company had become of late. Every gesture resonated.

"Ever notice how, when it's the right thing to do, the people always know it's comin'?" Bill Bass said in his raw twang.

"O.K.," Ed Brennan said softly as the lights were turned back up. "Go ahead and do it. There are large people concerns, but they have to go.

Do it with compassion. We'll try to make it as easy as we can from Chicago."

The whole thing took only ninety minutes. The net savings from the closings, when all of the payroll, Social Security, tax, data-processing, communications, maintenance, supplies, equipment, interest, insurance, rent, fuel, and accounting costs were tallied up, would be $5.5 million—almost exactly the amount of money lost a year or so earlier when some buyers picked up a few more electronic games than America wanted to own that year.

Brennan stood in the hallway outside the conference room as employees made detours from other parts of the floor to look at him, keeping a fair distance but staring at his face. "It's not just the money," he said. "As soon as you start to think about consolidation as a pure money move you're in trouble. That's how companies spiral out. Saving money is a by-product of making this thing easier to manage. It's also a process designed to put the best people around the table. One thing that happened here at Sears was that there were people who thought they were better than they really were. This way, only the cream will rise to the top."

Phase I of the plan just presented, for instance, would make two well-known group managers, two of the top hundred people in the company, surplus employees. There was known to be a group manager's job open in Denver, but Brennan wasn't going to give the post to either veteran. The two men could either retire or be demoted.

Brennan spoke often of the curse of people who thought they were better than they really were. It was as if he could suffer people who were only nominally competent more easily than those who were competent but believed themselves superior.

As Brennan took long, high-stepping strides down the hallway, many of the gawking Cube employees backed away toward the walls to let him pass. At one lobby a man as browned and well weathered as an old boot stopped Brennan and the entire entourage of executives behind him. The older man pulled off a powder-blue golf hat. "I took the ERIP. I took the golden handshake," he croaked.

"I remember you, Mike," Brennan said.

The retiree beamed. "You do? Well, I just want to tell you you're doing a great job. We're very happy again."

Brennan was genuinely pleased. A few weeks earlier, another retiree had approached him and proclaimed that he wished he were young enough to be part of Brennan's campaign. The early-1983 rise in the Sears stock price to over $30 per share—fueled almost entirely by the élan generated by Telling's financial-services adventure—had done much to lighten the spirits of the retirees, but Brennan still regarded retiree morale as one of the control standards by which he could take a reading. He said recent retirees reflected the sentiments of many of the veteran employees still working in the middle ranks of the company.

"We were such a successful company," Brennan said, continuing along the corridor. "It was wild. We just kept making more money and more money, but we never dealt with things like the disposition of assets. Now we've closed down groups; we've closed down hundreds of warehouses—and we've even closed dozens of stores. Ten years ago, we closed one store in five years. It took us a long time to accept that stores die. But they do die. They lose their energy and they die. Like people."

A few years earlier, Charlie Wurmstedt and Phil Purcell had signed their names to a $2-billion long-range plan that called for the construction of 239 new stores in 1983. Brennan would build fourteen new stores during the year, and he planned to close many more than that.

After lunch the Chicago visitors returned to the big conference table. The other side was occupied this time by the Field executives in charge of the Los Angeles group. Their leader was an amiable terrier-like man with a graying flat-top haircut and a wrinkled, asymmetrical face. Howard Lasky had been awarded the group that still accounted for 90 percent of the territory's profits when "Burk" Burkholder went to replace John Lowe in the Midwest. Lasky, who was just shy of sixty, made his reputation during years of wandering in the deserts of the territory, running stores. John Lowe once sent him to straighten out an infamously unruly store in Gary, Arizona, where no fewer than fourteen separate trade unions had managed to gain a foothold. Lasky tended to keep the fact of his rare 1950s M.B.A. from Stanford to himself.

For a Field warhorse, Howard Lasky had weathered the recent winds of change far more successfully than most of the now departed Searsmen with whom he'd grown up during the glory days of the separate kingdom, but Howard would never lose his reputation in the Tower as a hard-assed Field drone and small-time vassal of the old order. Somebody was invariably present who remembered that, back when he was running a group in Arizona, old Howard was the sort of Westerner who used to let visiting buyers take him and a bunch of his boys out to a fancy restaurant, where the Field men would run up a huge tab just to get a little bit back from the Parent.

The beginning of Lasky's review of the state of the Los Angeles group of Sears stores was like an economic history of the entire region. Maps showed the first stores the General had dropped in the central neighborhoods of the city during the late 1920s, and maps showed the addition of later stores that served Americans fleeing dust and poverty, who came to the sunny western edge of the country in search of the freedom to assemble a life in reflection of the one portrayed in the Sears Catalog. Other maps showed the arrival of the arterial freeways that connected the paved-over orange groves and paved-over foothills and the endless patio plains of southern California, marked everywhere with the stars of Sears stores. The towns Sears customers settled in, like Glendale, California, grew by some 2,000 percent during the decades before the war. Every time a new store opened in the Los Angeles group, there were parades, speeches, and new sales records. By 1964, the forty-four-year-old group manager, John Lowe, ran sixteen powerful "A" stores. Between 1960 and 1970, general merchandise sales in the Far West grew 70.3 percent, while in the rest of the nation they increased by 43.8 percent—and the general merchandise market in California was utterly dominated by Sears.

As the review continued to flash behind Howard Lasky, the dots of stores from other companies appeared. Then they slowly surrounded the once-inviolable Sears outposts. Some 275 dots representing other "majors" surrounded twenty-six Sears stars on Lasky's more current maps. Huge retail garrisons appeared on the screen called shopping malls. For all of its identification with the creation of the American shopping center, twenty major shopping malls were opened during the 1960s and 1970s in Los Angeles without Sears, Roebuck's participation. Millions upon millions of feet of new store space had come into Sears' sights and passed unchallenged. Many of the Sears stores of the era were misplaced; many of the stores located in the malls were unaltered from the free-standing store designs.

Lasky ran through an in-depth analysis that compared his stores in terms of their age, volume, net profit, selling space, and level of catalog orders. He broke down the nature of the markets surrounding the stores using sophisticated delivery studies, Zip Code studies, telephone studies, studies of appliance delivery schedules, "consumer-inclination" research, analyses of driving distances to the stores, local image studies, and credit-card "penetration" treatments. Maps chained with aggressive coded colors ripped across the wall behind Lasky. Maps subdivided the seventy-six-mile-long group into subregions like "the San Fernando Valley stores," the "Greater Los Angeles stores," and the "minority/low-income stores," which were highlighted in a bright shade of gold. Lasky's group contained stores that had sold over $30 million worth of goods in the late 1960s but were now producing less than $10 million in sales. The pioneering store in Glendale that once racked up forty million 1965 dollars in sales was now forty-one years old and sadly infirm. There were other once-proud old stores in Los Angeles that were even sicker than Glendale, especially those in the inner-city markets around the oldest neighborhoods.

Brennan was again stripped down to the scarlet waistcoat adorned with ornate silver baubles. "We really smothered ourselves in this town, didn't we? These were some good stores. Long Beach," Brennan said in agitation as he paused at a page in the book in front of him. "Number one in the company at one time." A mall had moved in across the street from the Long Beach store and conspired with the diminishing buying power of local inhabitants to strangle it. Long Beach had just been closed down.

"What about El Monte?" Brennan asked of another struggling store in an old center-city neighborhood.

"It's a densely Hispanic trade area now," Lasky replied. "If we shut it down, we'll recover 61 percent of the business. The group will lose $273,000 in profit, though, so we want to try downsizing the store."

Downsizing was a method of removing the dead zones and centralizing the selling space of an overly large store to make it look less sick and make it less costly to run. Brennan had tried downsizing in his time, and he believed it to be an expensive and fruitless exercise in postponing the inevitable. "I think we have to ask ourselves if we really want another dollhouse-sized store. You know we closed down the Chicago State Street store—the great *State Street* store. It cost us $3 million to do it, but we just weren't going to postpone the inevitable any longer."

Few stores in the system were as emblematic of tradition as the huge Depression-era store in the middle of the company's home town. Everyone knew State Street had been losing millions of dollars a year for a long time—dollars that were considered well worth losing in light of the symbolic consequences of closing it down. But Brennan took it down, altering the symbolism profoundly. The message on downsizing El Monte was quite clear.

The review went on to consider the fate of six or seven other stores, most of them in the poorest areas of town. The possible closing of the urban store on Pico Boulevard was discussed from the perspective of "political repercussions." When Pico opened in 1939, a noted rival merchant contended publicly, "In my long experience in the retail field, I have yet to witness a retail unit which equals Sears' Pico store in practical efficiency, merchandise engineering, operation, layout, and presentation of merchandise." People came from miles around to see Pico's rooftop parking lot.

Howard Lasky said that Los Angeles Mayor Tom Bradley, whom Lasky considered a "good friend to Sears," did a lot of his own shopping in Pico, and that every time Lasky saw Bradley these days the popular politician said, "You guys aren't gonna close down Pico, now, are you?"

"What did you say?" Brennan asked.

"I coughed," Lasky said to the accompaniment of much laughter from the Los Angeles side.

"Sir," said a very young, dark-haired fellow, clearly directing his voice across to Brennan. "There are some other alternatives to downsizing and closure." The speaker was Fred Bruning, a thirty-two-year-old territorial real-estate manager, who worked under Hollywood Joe Duggan. Bruning was not even seated against the Los Angeles edge of the big table. He spoke in a clear, earnest voice from a chair against the wall. Several of the older managers grimaced when Bruning began to speak: he was in attendance only for his encyclopedic command of territorial numbers, not his goddamned opinions. But Bruning proceeded to put forth his belief that Sears could save a great deal of money, as well as mitigate the social effect of closing several older stores, if the company would help build a new shopping complex in the middle of a predominately black trade district called Crenshaw.

Fred Bruning had been warned several times that his pet project was an inappropriate subject for a meeting of the magnitude of the April 5 Headquarters review, but he had become quite passionate in his belief that the Crenshaw mall was a good thing for the company. He'd been spending many of his free weekends observing all the bitterness and anger that manifested itself in some of Sears' inner-city stores near Crenshaw. He'd attended meetings about the new shopping center with members of the City Council, and applied his prodigious analytical skills to the business prospects of the project.

In the darkened conference room, Bruning said that his research indicated that the new mall would serve a market of eight hundred thousand people with an average income that was only a thousand dollars per family below the Los Angeles–Orange County median. "With a lot of support from the city, and a lot of support from the state and maybe two other 'majors' [other big retailers] like May and Broadway," Bruning said, "we could put up a two-level, up-to-date regional shopping center that would revitalize the entire Crenshaw-Wilford district around Martin Luther King Boulevard."

Bill Bass broke the long silence that followed. "Crenshaw's not a very good-looking area," he said weakly.

Brennan leaned forward, put his chin in his hand, and looked over at Bruning with an intrigued, somewhat quizzical gaze. The startlingly youthful-looking real-estate manager stared back without expression.

After graduating from law school in 1977, Fred Bruning had decided to come to work as a lawyer for Sears, Roebuck because of the incredible

scale of things at the corporation. Where a young associate in a downtown Los Angeles firm would have been lucky to deal with a personal
or corporate matter involving tens of thousands of dollars, Bruning was
handling $12-million lawsuits for the Far Western Territory during his
first year. He got interested in the high-gear world of California real
estate at about the same time Sears was opening its veins and entering
the throes of upheaval and exodus, and soon Bruning found himself—at
the age of twenty-eight—in charge of around one thousand pieces of
Sears real estate worth many millions of dollars. A history of long lunches
and free football tickets shared by real-estate developers and their Sears
West Coast territorial contacts over the years ended with Fred Bruning's appointment. As a member of the Bahai faith, Bruning figured he
was one of the only real-estate men in the business who didn't drink.
Bruning's secretary called him Fred.

As committed as Bruning was to a Crenshaw center, when the discussion returned to the military nomenclature and thrusting imagery of
stores and markets locked in conflict, he dutifully supplied Brennan with
acronym-laden real-estate data like a teletype machine. A developer was
planning to build a shopping center in a region ten miles west of Alhambra called Glendora, and there were fears that the new center would
detract from an extant Sears store. Bruning outlined a battle plan by
which Sears could make it look like the company was considering construction of another shopping center that would steal business from the
proposed Glendora project. The idea was essentially to scare the Glendora developer into abandoning the project as too risky, and therefore
save Sears the cost of relocating in the new center. Bruning would never
be part of a direct lie to a developer, but these sorts of sleights and feints
were all part of the game.

A detail of the San Fernando Valley came up, and Bruning contended
that the store in Canoga Park was being squeezed to death between two
plainly superior malls.

"Canoga Park," Ed Brennan said, his voice losing its utilitarian edge
for a moment and turning wistful. "The old San Fernando Valley store.
Johnny Hawkins ran that one. Old Johnny." Brennan was staring up into
the smoke from his cigar. Johnny Hawkins was one of the great characters of the glory days, a buddy of the peg-legged wild man, Stan
Donough, at the time Donough roamed the Pacific Coast Territory in
a helicopter he kept on top of the Seattle store. Hawkins knew Ed
Brennan's step-grandmother, and he was there when Katy Brennan—
Luke's second wife, a life-long Sears employee—laid the cornerstone for
the Sears store in the suburb of Pomona.

"We've got to get ours back in Los Angeles," Brennan said, locking
back into his more careful, oratorical voice. "We're out of the action in

this group. We used to *own* this city. We owned its markets and we taught the industry here a whole way of retailing. Ward moved in and cut us; then the discounters; and we should have seen it coming. But now the others are stumbling too. We're going to see Fed Marts—and Woolcos and even K marts—closing down here too very soon. We can win our place back if we just leverage off the existing base and sell them more goods. I know we can get it back." He turned to Lasky. "I want the key to our strategy to be the Valley; our franchise is in the Valley."

The following morning Brennan's entourage headed toward Disneyland to look at one of the Orange County stores. Just seven suburban stores in Orange County accounted for half of the Los Angeles group's profits. It stood to reason that Brennan would want to go to the suburbs. The Sears "franchise" in Los Angeles dwelled in Orange County and the San Fernando Valley. The seven aging stores in the gold-colored "minority/ low-income" subsector of the L.A. retail group all together barely surpassed one-half of 1 percent of the group's profit. But it was still not without irony that the old Sears stores of the neighborhoods had no place on the map in Ed Brennan's head, nor was it less than ironic that his entourage navigated the interchange near the great store called Boyle as the executives headed south. In many ways the spirit of Sears, Roebuck that made Ed Brennan love the company, that sense of respect for goods and the institution of Sears, persisted in its purest state now in the barrio, in stores like Pico, El Monte, and Boyle.

So many freeways come together in the East Los Angeles district called Boyle Heights that fully 12 percent of the district's land was covered in roadway by the end of the 1940s. The fifty-six-year-old tower atop the Boyle Street store rises above the knot of freeways from a bed of taco stands, Mexican *mercados,* and corner hot-dog stands. The brickwork and the old-fashioned Sears logo make the sprawling store-and-warehouse complex look like an Art Deco pavilion from one of the many industrial expositions held in the era when the General had opened Boyle. The store was once number twelve in the country, but now the acres of ample free parking are never filled to capacity, and crowds of people sit on the steps or lean against the walls in the shade, as people do in front of stores in Third World countries.

The people of East Los Angeles now represent 30 percent of Los Angeles' total population. Ninety-four percent of the immigrants to the city live east of the river. The first influx of Mexican Americans into the Boyle area occurred during World War II, when the Japanese residents were shipped to holding camps pursuant to an executive order.

Most of the shoppers from Mexico inside the Boyle store came to

Sears, in part, because the Sears stores built in the cities of Mexico had served, if not as supply houses, then at least as the prop closet to the dream of middle-class life. After middle-class life eluded all but a handful of Mexican citizens, millions of them moved north of the border to buy into a world they knew existed in part via Sears. Newcomers could even get a credit card from Sears and thus become card-carrying American consumers. The looks on the faces of the families of Hispanic customers wandering in the Boyle store revealed the reverence for the glory of the goods that Ed Brennan and Ed Telling often lamented was lost to most people.

Beyond the stores of the barrio, Sears had rather quietly become the second-largest employer in East Los Angeles. To many members of Mexican American households in East L.A., a job working for Sears was as valuable as the green document that made it legal to work at all. If a high-school graduate was bright and industrious but unable to go to college, than he or she could still do the family proud by going to Sears.

Most of them would go to work in the ancient catalog warehouse next to the Boyle Street store, where territorial catalog orders are still filled by a system and even some machinery that were designed for Sears by a German industrial engineer in 1906.* The ancient plant had been one of the eleven capitals of Sears during the golden days of the catalog. The "control store" at Boyle had published a regional catalog for many years before the era of the stores. The Far Western territorial headquarters was housed in the brick tower until John Lowe ordained the building of the Cube.

Workers still careen about the four and one-half million square feet of the catalog plant behind ramshackle wooden pushcarts. Many of the carts are ornately decorated with bright fiesta colors, religious iconography, and invariably the name of the "picker" powering them along past acres of goods in the deep gorges of the aisles. The pickers are largely women, and they move over the ancient wood-block floors past pictures of saints, signs that say "Beat Seattle," and photographic portraits of Ed Brennan, at a pace that reflects the dispensation from Boyle of some three hundred thousand pieces of merchandise every month. The place is full of exotic sounds that most of the customers receiving the goods would find hard to understand. In a much newer section of the facility,

---

*It was Sears executive Otto Doering's "schedule system" of "picking and packing" orders that, according to company lore, Henry Ford was said to have studied in the Chicago plant before designing his own production system for putting together automobiles. It was not, as lore has it, Julius Rosenwald's production line.

a largely male work force loads semis arrayed under signs indicating many of them are heading out to small towns like Sanisville and Crescent City.

As part of his charge to pacify the maverick Far Western Territory, Henry Sunderland decided that changes were needed at the old catalog plant where he began his own career in 1952. In the Draconian spirit of the early days of Telling's regime, Sunderland told the plant manager at Boyle to trim the work force and generally alter the atmosphere of complacency with stronger management. In less than eighteen months, more than 30 percent of the full-time employees at the plant were laid off, many of them immediately replaced by part-timers.

As the size of the force reductions became known, female pickers left their wooden carts in the aisles and screamed at their supervisors in tears. Several of them threatened to kill themselves if they were laid off, and a few plant managers were warned by male employees that their throats would be slit if the layoffs continued. The layoffs were conducted without the slightest sensitivity to the cultural characteristics of a work force that was 70 percent Mexican American. Proud fathers of large families were fired and their wives and children were hired back as part-timers. The heads of female-run households were laid off while other intact families were spared. Hispanic department managers were forced to terminate people from their home towns in Mexico, and others fired their own cousins by company decree.

The turning of the screws at the Los Angeles plant engendered a sort of rage that was more personal than economic. None of the managers at the plant were surprised when this un-Sears-like managerial behavior caused leaders to surface from the work force who called for resistance. Union organizers appeared outside the plant, so Headquarters sent in its crack employee-relations specialists to orchestrate the Sears side of the union election. Around the time Ed Brennan was drafted to Chicago from Atlanta to try to stop some of the "excesses" of the moment, the workers at the L.A. warehouse voted to become members of a local affiliate of the International Brotherhood of Teamsters, the labor union that had once promised to organize all of Sears during the 1960s. "No union could ever have as great and as personal concern for the well-being of employees as the company itself," personnel chief Wally Tudor said at the time. And at the time, Wally was probably right.

The second-generation Sears Catalog man managing the Boyle warehouse in the spring of 1983 figured that the feelings of betrayal brought about by the mismanagement of the plant would be felt for another

decade. Woody Haselton reflected that the upheaval in the old warehouse was the result of "the distant moral judgments of the time." But
the tragedy at the L.A. plant was as much a matter of pervasive sociological ignorance as it was the result of Henry Sunderland's overzealous
imposition of Ed Telling's will to crack the old power centers.

High-level interest in Sears' relationship with poor people and minorities—and to some extent with women—had diminished considerably
during the period of struggle for direction and survival. In retrospect,
attendance to minority issues reached its zenith during the administration of Arthur Wood. At the insistence of the Headquarters personnel
department, Telling had allowed consultants into the Tower to conduct
forums through which women and black employees could express themselves—Telling even attended a session or two in which the managers
presented long lists of grievances—but, as with so much of the nation
and its working institutions during the era of Ronald Reagan, the leaders
of the company were no longer interested in the particular problems of
minorities or women much beyond the limits of the law.

The still-unresolved legal action against Sears by the Equal Employment Opportunity Commission had taken on a life of its own. The
original forty-two claims of sex discrimination by Sears in its hiring and
promotion procedures had been whittled down to a handful of remaining complaints. A vast array of professionals had been hired—from attorneys to statisticians to feminist historians expert in the traditions of work
aspirations among women—and employment patterns and practices
within the company had been observed and quantified repeatedly in an
effort to shore up Sears' contention that the Merchant did not discrimi-
nate by policy.

Meanwhile, the combined effect of the ERIP, Brennan's program of
attrition, and the personnel department's diligent monitoring of affirmative-action rules had profoundly changed the makeup of the internal
population. Since the late 1960s, the number of black employees had
more than doubled; the number of women in the "officials and managers" category almost doubled; and the number of Hispanic employees
had tripled. White middle managers sat in the lunchrooms now and
talked about how none of their male children would ever stand a chance
at Sears these days.

The statistical alterations were viewed from most offices on the sixty-
eighth and forty-fourth floors as procedural necessities, but the corporate mind was in many ways more closed to the issues behind the procedures then ever before. Though Telling continued to shock the people

around him by bringing more women and blacks onto the corporate board of directors,* the officers corps of the company was still one of the most ethnically and religiously homogeneous in all of corporate America. There were still no women officers ("One thing about the ERIP program," a female middle manager commented in early 1983; "all of a sudden old Sears was no longer run by old white men; they were middle-aged white men after that"). The corporate heirs of Julius Rosenwald included not one Jewish officer, and though there was a single black officer in the merchandise company—the buying organization vice-president, Bob Johnson—he referred to himself with a wry and knowing smile as a "senior presence." Johnson felt the company had sold many of the other black management trainees hired during the 1960s a bill of goods.

If the official attitude toward hiring had retrogressed under the cover of statistics, attitudes toward minorities and poor people as customers bore all the absence of logic and evidence of psychological avoidance entailed in classical scapegoating. There were many stores in the system that catered to less wealthy urban customers—like the one at Boyle Street, the big store in Oakland, California, the Philadelphia Northeast store, and the one in Brooklyn, New York—that did quite well. The Oakland store, with its solid customer base drawn from four hundred thousand black shoppers, made the white elephant of a store built not far away in wealthy San Rafael look ridiculous. The official line on minority marketing derived from a Telling epigram: "We never leave a market; a market leaves us." But younger employees, like the demographics wizard Fred Bruning, believed Sears had repudiated its tradition of drawing power from the act of serving shoppers of humble means, in large part, because the lives of humble shoppers in America no longer resembled the childhoods of the men of once-humble means who ran the corporation. Most people of modest means just weren't white anymore.

The untapped potential power of the Hispanic market in Los Angeles was a case in point. There had been some effort in California and Florida to provide a Spanish index for the catalog, and a special wing of an advertising firm had been hired to advertise in Hispanic communities, but the markets were largely ignored.

Nobody in the Cube ever told Bruning to forget his dream of an urban

*Telling assured the stockholders at an annual meeting that the "fine ladies" on the board were there because of their accomplishments and expertise, not because they were women. "The fact that they might be more attractive just makes our board meeting more interesting," he said.

mall for the Los Angeles ghetto, but he was consistently aware that he was shouting over walls when he spoke up as he did at the group review. He'd seen it in the way managers flinched at the very mention of Dr. Martin Luther King Jr. Blvd.

Ed Brennan once ran a minority-neighborhood store for Sears, and he talked often of the rioting that overran his Baltimore store in the wake of the assassination of Dr. Martin Luther King in 1968. One evening there were fires and rioting and armed troops in the streets in front of the store, but on Monday morning all of the black maintenance workers at the store showed up to clean up the mess. They helped him load up a truck with merchandise and take it down to a local church, where it was sold to people who had been burned out.

Brennan spoke often of two lessons he'd drawn from the riots as he sped from town to town in early 1983. He'd learned that what might appear as the worst sort of turmoil from the outside, despite visible flames and murderous rage, in fact looks much less terrible and more manageable when viewed from the eye of the storm. He also said he'd learned something from the actions of his store employees he'd always wanted to believe anyway: that people—specifically Sears people—were basically the same everywhere. Black or white, Field or Parent, time card or checklist, us or them. People are the same. "All of us can live anywhere," he'd say. "We have a common world here at Sears. We can transfer anybody anywhere. Sears people even *look* the same, from Hawaii to Hicksville. We're all interchangeable pieces on a map."

Fred Bruning realized that Sears had strayed so far from reality in recent years that it was a gargantuan task just to get senior managers to understand what had happened to the suburbanites of the middle classes. The boys had looked inward for all those years. So, for now, Fred Bruning understood why Brennan wasn't going to visit Boyle or Pico or El Monte or any of the stores like them throughout the empire—at least not this year.

Brennan's troupe was spending the night in downtown Los Angeles at the Japanese-owned New Otani Hotel. Touring officers from Chicago had for decades stayed at the aging Hilton Hotel out in Pasadena, but Brennan preferred the efficiency and convenience of the New Otani, and it was to a small room off the hotel's Commodore Perry Restaurant that he summoned the top Western territorial officers, along with How-ard Lasky and the manager of the Central Pacific retail group (they of the separate drum-beat), for cocktails and dinner.

As so often happened after one of those elongated days of work that start in the dawn of one time zone and end in the dusk of another, the

6:00 P.M. drinking time led to loud and cheerful talk of the past. By 6:15 the dark room was already filled with cigar smoke and loud laughter. Brennan hadn't arrived yet, but Bill Bass, with Woody Haselton as straight man, was already in full cry.

The best of the talk among Searsmen at cocktail time was drawn from the raucous vernacular tradition of early American fast-talkers. The talk had descended from the old gamecocks: from the boasting orators of the wilderness and ringtailed roarers of the forest. With the departure of so many other old crowers in the ERIP, Bill Bass was left as one of the last, best roarers in the company, a reigning master of hee-haw. Bass' verbal legend was predicated in large part upon a famous roasting he once administered to one Ed Telling, whom he served as an assistant when Telling first came east to the New York group. There was a recording made of Bass' audacious comments about Telling's delegation of authority and managerial lassitude: "Let me tell you briefly what he did for me," Bass told the crowd. "The man did many things, and I could cite just a few of them. I won't elaborate too long here because it would take me hours to tell you what he did to me, but I noticed one thing immediately: he streamlined his office. All mail, all complaints, all *work* went immediately to me. He was able to operate much more effectively then, with an even lower profile than before. He eliminated all hardships caused by this work, because he gave me a key to the building. I could come early and I could stay late." The recording was still passed among senior executives like precious contraband; not only for Bass' inspired oration, but because the usually subdued Telling could be heard belly-laughing hysterically in the background.

"What about White Plains, New York?" Bass crowed to the small crowd that was gathering around at the New Otani. "Wanna talk about some gutter-fightin', street-brawlin', hard-sellin' times? Let's talk about the great greasy hole that was White Plains, New York—whoa!" After each outburst, Bass' face would reassemble into a tough-guy look, his jaw set so tight it looked like there were springs under his skin. Then his eyes grew bright again, and his chin protruded like a dare: "The *East*, baby. The great territory of the East. The East was hardball territory in my day. Every sale was a war! Show me somebody who knows how to live from the fat o' the land; who knows how to protect his profits in a store in the pits, and I'll show you a manager. That's the story of the East in a few words. *You* know what we did to the New York group, Woody. We cleaned up the New York group in eighteen months. A-a-teen months!"

"Do I get eighteen months out here?" Haselton queried on cue. Woody had worked closely with Bass in the past, including a stint as Bass' executive assistant at Eastern Territory headquarters.

"Naw, not you, Woody," Bass barked. He slipped his free arm around Haselton and raised his glass high. "*I* say Woody Haselton doesn't need eighteen months out here. Not the man who turned the great black rathole of Greensboro, North Carolina!"

"But I had eighteen months in Greensboro," Woody said, punching back his glasses from the edge of his nose.

"Up in Seattle, they might say Boeing's got 'em down," Bass continued as if hadn't heard. "The economy's down on top of 'em. But I ask you, did they ever hear of Greensboro, North Carolina? Furniture capital of the whole world? The place where an industry just rolled up and dah-ed? The very place I sent mah boy Woody Haselton? And what did he *do* with Greensboro, North Carolina?"

Bass rose to his toes now. "Tell us *what you did!*"

"Fourth-largest group-sales increase in the company," Haselton said softly, "but I had eight—"

"—and I say to you," Bass cut in, "that any man that can live off the fat o' the land in Greensboro, North Carolina, doesn't need eighteen months to turn the Western Territory!" Bass slapped Haselton hard on the back and quite literally strutted away from the circle of laughter to get another drink.

The company psychologist once did a clinical study of the psychic toll exacted in Bill Bass' career at Sears. The results were judged a paradigm for how not to treat a man. Bass came to Sears via Baltimore, Maryland, the paratroops, and Johns Hopkins University, and though some of the eighteen jobs the company had given him since then were so wonderful that the thought of them still fills his eyes with tears, other jobs Sears gave Bill Bass were like the trials of Job.

Bass figures that Sears has almost destroyed him and his family three or four times in his thirty-three years with the company. They made him partake in the company's union-busting up in Boston during the mid-1950s, something he still can't believe the company could have done.* They gave Bill Bass more than one crooked manager as a boss, and worst of all, every time he felt as though he'd finally found a place to call home, they made him leave again.

One time they sent him to manage a tiny store in Rockland, Maine,

---

*An outside expert in "union troubles" named Nathan Shefferman was hired to assist Sears' anti-unionization efforts in the mid-1930s. Over twenty years later, Shefferman's use of techniques like infiltration, intimidation, and vandalism were made quite public during the Senate McClellan Committee hearings under questioning by the young attorney for the committee, Robert Kennedy.

where he wrote the townspeople's wills for them. He was guest of honor at their christenings, marriages, and funerals. Bill Bass could have stayed there in Rockland forever. It was a good, clean place, and he felt close to his family, important, and safe. Feeling safe was an important draw of the Sears life. The reason that an M.B.A. like Howard Lasky had come to work among men without high-school diplomas was that there wasn't much turnover. You were safe with Sears.

But every time Bill Bass thought he'd found a little peace, Sears made him move. He moved several times at the behest of the man he called "Big Daddy." Bass used to drive all the way from his home in New Jersey to Ed Telling's home in Connecticut to pick him up in the morning. He loved turning the New York group on its head with Ed Telling, and he even enjoyed trying to run the black hole of a store at White Plains, New York. But when Bill Bass' wife died, and he realized that he and his beloved wife had spent so many of the years they'd had together doing things they didn't want to do in places they didn't want to be, it made him almost too bitter to work.

He was sent to run a store in Allentown, Pennsylvania, and after a few years there he thought he would be O.K. if he stayed. But Telling called and asked him to go run the Washington, D.C., group of stores. Bass knew that the prestigious manager's job in Washington entailed diplomatic parties and public appearances. He wasn't confident enough of his social background and he didn't want to leave Allentown, but Ed Telling had asked him to move, so he moved. At least the job of running the Eastern Territory after Dick Jones came to the Tower put him closer to his children, even if it did mean having to attend those awful peace-and-planning meetings with Charlie and Joe before young Brennan came in.

The day Ed Brennan called him in Philadelphia and asked him to move to Chicago to become senior executive vice-president, Field, Bass thought first of how much he'd enjoyed being near his kids in Philadelphia. He also thought about the fact that he'd worked like a dog since he was ten years old, about all the trials and testing the company had already put him through, and about how he really wanted nothing more than to retire from Sears, Roebuck and have some time for himself and his children. Bass was impressed with Ed Brennan, and he respected the young man's unmatched knowledge of the business. He realized too that his reputation as one of the last of the old-time Field warriors and his widely known personal relationship with the recondite Telling could be helpful to Brennan's campaign, but Bass still said no. He'd given the company enough, he told Brennan, and he simply refused to go.

Late at night a few weeks later, Brennan sat Bass down in an airport lounge and begged him to come help him in Chicago. The company needed him, Brennan said.

"I've given everything to the company," Bass said. "I've lived my whole life in the territories, and I just won't move. I want to stay near my kids, Mr. Brennan."

Beneath the wow and bang of the seller's song and his tough farmer's face, Bass protected a well of powerful emotions. Occasionally a feeling could be seen to flicker across his face, only to be drawn back in like a mitt closing around a fastball. But in the airport with Brennan that night, the feelings that came over Bill Bass caused his face to soften beyond his control, and he began to cry. "I don't want to come," he said.

Later the telephone call came from Telling. Bass had been called, and so he went. He bought a two-bedroom condominium across from a mall in the Chicago suburbs. The widow who sold him the place was overcome by emotions the day she had to leave her home, so Bass sat at the kitchen table with her as she cried, and told her he understood.

His presence beside Brennan since coming to Chicago had been comforting to Field employees of Howard Lasky's vintage—those too young to retire in the ERIP but too old to lose their residual belief in the sanctity and sovereignty of the Field. Bass' powerful love-hate feelings for a life in retailing came in handy when he commiserated with managers about the thankless nights and weekends of labor.

Nobody could play the ringtailed roarer of Sears at drinking time better than William Irwin Bass, because no member of Brennan's inner circle was as truly nostalgic for the lost communitarianism of the world of the stores, or more cognizant of the little pieces of their lives the people of Sears used to leave behind every time they moved along.

Bill Bass stood more quietly now as others at the reception talked of towns they'd known. Though the day's work had been dedicated to rearranging the map of Sears, the heavy liquor and the end of the day brought back older maps that were as deeply emblazoned on the minds of the veterans as their memories of childhood. Particular care was paid to the romance of small places, of stations on rail lines that ran from "nowhere-in-particular to nowhere-at-all."

"That was back in Paducah, Kentucky," somebody would say. But it hadn't really been Paducah. The shared references to Paducah; Splitlip, Alabama; Sheheyus, Washington; Keokuck, Iowa; and, on occasion, to East Bumfuck, Iowa, referred to the generic essence of the sort of places most senior American managers making big six-figure salaries had never even seen, let alone served. The stories were all told in the transrural twang that was found from coast to coast in the Field. Great care was taken to pronounce the names of towns and cities like locals. They said "Loo-*ah*-ville" instead of "Loo-*ee*-ville" and "Sin-sin-nat-*ah*" instead of "Sin-sin-nat-*ee.*"

There were numerous stories during this and most Sears cocktail hours attesting to the kindness and warmth a big-city Searsman could find at one of the thousands of tiny catalog store outlets through which the company still served its rural franchise. Most of the "CSOs" were little more than a single room with a Kenmore freezer or two, maybe a display television set, a couple of frayed Sears Catalogs on a table, and a local functionary who knew the business of everyone in town. "Ran outa gas near a catalog store outside o' Cottonwood Falls, Kansas, one time," a Western Territory man said. "Nicest folks I ever met in my life."

Ed Telling would occasionally explain why he hated to visit the catalog stores, or CSOs—in fact had refused to do so ever since he'd become powerful enough to travel on his own schedule. Apparently Telling's predecessor as head of the Midwestern Territory, an unusually gentle fellow for a territorial lord of the era named Cul Kennedy, was traveling some backroad en route to a catalog store in rural Indiana when he suddenly died. "So that's why I won't go to some goddamned catalog store at the end of the earth," Telling would say. " 'Cause I don't wanna end up like ole Cul." Telling was a small-town boy who loved to love the idea of small towns and hated to set foot in them.

When Brennan finally entered the room, the pitch of conversation diminished immediately, and the focus shifted to him. His entrances always subdued the largest room. In a crowd Brennan really did appear to most seasoned assessors of others to reside just above the din of the talk around him. There was a palpable aura edging his presence. Even Bill Bass, who had lived within the tiny personal orbit of Ed Telling, felt it. "He's just . . . different. I don't know exactly what it is. He's just different," Bass would say.

As soon as Brennan stepped toward a conversation or trained his gaze on a speaker, the focus would always transfer. Brennan knew as much about company lore as anyone in the company. He'd moved from town to town as often as Searsmen fifteen years older than him, and he'd known about traveling the roads between Sears depots since he was small. For several years after his mother left, he used to pick up Bernie and take him down to the Chicago Greyhound Station at 16th and State. The two little boys would board a bus and ride for five days and five nights to see their mother in Mexico City. Brennan's father never approved of the adventure, but the boys must have made the trip a half-dozen times, all with money Ed saved up for the journey delivering papers and doing odd jobs. Brennan knew a lot about the tolls on the road, he could hear the company twang in roarings and sentimental musings of the cocktail hour, and he enjoy a few glasses of liquor as much as the next man, but the territorial executive in the private room off the Commodore Perry who'd been describing a stretch of his career when the company asked him to move every four or five months still waited until Brennan passed before resuming his tale.

"So one of my daughters—she ends up with six schools in six states under her belt and she's still a little girl," he continued. "The last time I just came home with the look on my face"—everyone in the crowd nodded at the mention of "the look"—"and she starts blubberin'. 'No, Daddy,' she says. 'No. Do we have to do it again?' " The people standing around the speaker—including Woody Haselton, who had left a child in school back in the East when he was called to live in Los Angeles—chuckled at the remark, but the laughter held a shared sadness, and a sort of resignation that everyone in the circle immediately understood, because talk of children was one of the few acceptable ways that the people of Sears talked about sacrifice and pity and love.

You could talk about your success as a father by talking about the successes of your kids—especially if they were athletes—and stories of children flying home from college in order to celebrate a promotion was an acceptable way to indicate how important that promotion really was. But just as often, the talk of kids was really about a strong sense of guilt over having subsumed people you love within the larger purposes of a corporate family.

Some years earlier, a few personnel executives had begun to worry about the interior lives of the Field soldiers. They all seemed to be so tough. A professor from Michigan State University was brought in, and groups of store runners were told to listen to the professor warn that they could ruin their families if they didn't open up. Most of the boys laughed off the lecture, but later a personnel executive passed by one of the hardest old curs in the Midwestern Territory, who was talking on a pay phone and smiling—a facial arrangement he was known to abjure as a matter of principle.

When the store manager hung up, he saw the personnel man staring. "Jus' now did something I haven't done in twenty-five years," he said. "I told my wife I loved her."

Careers were marked as discernibly by the notches the men perceived on their families' psyches as they were by bonuses and trophies. But since by the time most of them saw the damage it was too late to change things, all they could do was make the phone call a quarter-century too late, or mention a child's success despite the life, or slip a reference to a child's begging not to move to her sixth school in six years into talk over drinks, and feel in the boozy bittersweet nods of company kinsmen the passing warmth of others who could understand.

Part III

The

RACE

In the modern world, and still more, so far as can be guessed, in the world of the near future, important achievement is and will be almost impossible to an individual if he cannot dominate some vast organization.

—*Bertrand Russell*

CHAPTER 18

The Run
for the Roses

A few weeks later, on one of those perfect Chicago spring days when
sunlight bounces up off the top of the lake, Sears hosted a luncheon
at the Drake Hotel for the largest agglomeration of financial analysts
ever assembled by a company. Over two hundred distinguished visitors
from thirty different cities were served pre-noontime cocktails at the
grand old lakeside hotel. They gathered in an antechamber that had
been transformed for the occasion by luminous photographic murals of
futuristic Sears stores and life-size experimental booths designed to ped-
dle Allstate's insurance, Dean Witter's stocks and bonds, and Coldwell
Banker's houses in Sears, Roebuck's retail stores.

The analysts clustered around Sears people wearing blue "Hello My
Name Is" patches on their lapels. Many of them could be seen glancing
up from their Bloody Marys to sneak a look at Ed Telling, the daring
hero of modern management about whom none of the guests knew
more than what they could glean from their inside sources at Sears—and
that information seemed coated by myth.

The chairman of Sears stood away from his guests behind a protective
cordon of blue lapel patches. His mouth hung agape, and he gazed up
over the top of the encircling crowd, his face so completely still that the
network of lines that crosshatched his heavy cheeks and jowls looked
like cracks. His thick legs were splayed out to the sides; his belly protruded from his open suitcoat. As he rocked back and forth slightly on
his heels, one of the hands clasped behind Ed Telling's back squeezed

rhythmically two meaty fingers of the other hand, like a beating heart.

For five and a half years now, Ed Telling had managed to put on a public face that kept strangers at bay, and just because the wizards of the metropolis, these so-called professional observers of the state of the company now drinking his booze, had changed their tune of late—and helped to add twenty bucks to the stock price in a year—he wasn't about to turn into some glad-handing, high-profile phony like Lee Iacocca. So the chairman of the board stood there at cocktail hour looking for all the world like an actor playing the jerkin-clad, drooling dullard son in some Elizabethan farce. Ever since the media had focused all the light upon him, an almost universal *"That's* the chairman of Sears, Roebuck?"* attended Telling's rare public movements. But the foreboding veneer had served the purpose of keeping reporters, securities analysts, government types, and fellow corporate big shots from getting too near him. Occasionally people had attempted to flatter him—and flattery was the worst of all. "If ya come up to me and say, 'You big dumbbell, you'—now, I can un'erstan' that," Telling said, "I can handle that. But I just don't take to flattery. It just sets me on guard like nothing else."

It was just the way he was, management hero of the 1980s or not.

Telling figured the excessively remunerated professional observers of Sears who had once baited him at Fraunces Tavern understood as little about the healing of the empire as they had about the internal combat and fiscal panics that had almost brought the whole thing down. But even the most casual Sears-watcher in April of 1983 could tell that the corporation was on a roll.

The first-quarter performances of all of the business groups conspired to push profits up 130 percent over the year earlier. It was openly acknowledged that the first quarter of '82 had been a recession-plagued disaster, but, still, the numbers were impressive. A new Roper study indicated that 84 percent of the populace now had a favorable attitude toward Sears, the highest rating of any corporation in the country. A Chicago appeals court even threw out the $8.1-million judgment against Sears for stealing young Peter Roberts' ratchet-wrench design.

A new tone was apparent within days of the acquisition of Coldwell Banker and Dean Witter. Telling's electrifying initiative; his late-round rise from economic canvas to unload a secret punch; the strange captain's creation of a new-model company, suddenly boundless—the acquisitions were pegged instantly as an act of genius. "With merchandising on the mend," *Business Week* contended, echoing much of the business press, "Sears is poised to make a big splash in financial services."

The same *Gallagher President's Report* that had named Telling one of the nation's twelve worst executives of 1978 named him one of the nation's twelve best managers of 1981. *Advertising Age* followed suit by including Telling in its list of the ten people who most auspiciously made the news of 1981. So many glowing articles about Telling and Sears appeared in the immediate wake of the takeovers that the public-affairs department on the fortieth floor collected them in handsome offset booklets as thick as some urban phone directories.

From the pages of *Newsweek* to the London *Financial Times,* photographs of Ed Telling were printed next to descriptions of a "new Sears" that was "aggressive" and "hungry" and as widely feared as it was respected. Mighty Sears, Roebuck was going to eat up less powerful competitors just as it had consumed competition during the epoch of corporate invincibility in the 1950s and 1960s. But now it was the money-handlers who were afraid of Sears, not the retailers of ovens and hosiery. A phrase could be heard on Wall Street during the middle of 1982 that characterized the trepidation with which the financial community regarded the new hybrid leviathan Telling had made. "The only thing we have to fear," the adage warned, "is Sears itself."

Ed Telling—of all people—had become the corporation's first major public figure since the General. Internally, the Telling legend had been revived and transmitted deep into the organization. The old stories of Telling in the East were dusted off: about his going home at noon to rake leaves, and the time he moved the New York group offices out to New Jersey before Headquarters gave the O.K. The status of anyone who'd ever worked for Telling soared, and those who had actually met their barely visible leader told others of the experience in tones quite similar to the old "One-time-I-met-the-General" stories.

All the trappings and forums of public authority were readily available to the unapproachable man now standing at the analysts' gathering, but Telling was rarely interested unless he could be convinced by members of his inner circle that it would significantly benefit the company. Telling still wanted his trips away from Chicago to be brief enough to get him back home for dinner with Nancy. He wouldn't even stay for dinner at the elite Business Roundtable Annual Meeting in Washington on a night when Don Regan, then secretary of the treasury, and Senator Ted Kennedy were scheduled to join the business leaders. Telling said he'd never thought much of Kennedy anyway.

Telling did see fit to go public in an aggressive and surprisingly political way during a speech he gave to the prestigious Economics Club of Chicago. The speech was laden with hints of the financial populism and anti-bank prejudices that had motivated his thinking before the 1981 acquisitions. Telling offered the members of the Economics Club a review of two decades of deregulation of the American financial system, from the early reports of the Commission on Money and Credit to government studies during 1975 that led to the landmark Depository Institutions Deregulation Act of 1980. He went on to list some of the many new conveniences that a freer financial marketplace had created for consumers, singling out money-market funds, cash-management accounts, discount brokerage houses, electronic funds-transfer systems, the prospect of conducting financial business at home, and the future advent of "one-stop shopping" for all home purchases as examples. "Despite our need for efficient mechanisms for capital formation, we maintain one of the most inefficient and most undemocratic financial systems in the world." But now, he declared, "because American Express, Merrill Lynch, Sears, and others have responded to the forces of the marketplace, we will have a new financial-service system. It is too late to turn back."

Telling denied that his arsenal of huge financially oriented companies covering such a broad range of businesses would bring an undue concentration of financial power under the company's control. If the banking establishment felt surrounded by potentially more efficient, popular, and cheaper financial-services systems—rather like Sears once looked from the viewpoint of the local general stores of American Main Streets and like the discount retailers once looked to the managers of Sears—then Telling had a philosophical thought for them: "We will not always have the fifteen thousand banks that we have today—after all, England has only ten banks. . . . Our free-market system, like Darwin's understanding of natural selection, means only the fittest will succeed. Institutions that have evolved into dinosaurs must face the inevitable process of natural selection."

The Economics Club speech was widely reprinted, and its saber-rattling content was taken as a further indication that Sears was alive and dangerous again.

Phil Purcell towered above fifteen Wall Street analysts as he headed out of the anteroom and slowly moved the circle around him into the banquet hall. Purcell had positioned himself near the distracted chairman of the board, and he would occasionally glance protectively at Telling, in case the wall of Searsmen chatting amiably about angiograms failed to keep the more aggressive analysts away. Next to Ed Brennan, who held court in a far corner of the decorated anteroom, Phil had drawn the largest crowd. He was still attempting to field questions with the utmost boyish charm and wit as he approached his table. "Oh, please!" he said, throwing his hands up in mock horror. "Please don't say the word 'bank'; we can't even *appear* to be a bank."

"Why not, Mr. Purcell?" asked a white-haired gentleman in for the day from New York.

Purcell paused for a second to physically suppress a wince rising from the unmitigated ignorance of the query. "Because there's a *law* in this country against it," he said. He took a deep breath and then patiently reviewed the central tenets of the Glass-Steagall Act of 1933—the congressional legislation that mapped out the institutional boundaries of American banks, the Federal Reserve system, and even the nation's financial-securities firms, one of which paid the man who asked the question several hundred thousand dollars a year for his analytical expertise.

Phil Purcell used to think that talking to reporters and analysts was fun because their "limited knowledge base" made it possible to make them write what you wanted them to write, but ever since Sears had changed the game on its chief spectators, the process had become frustrating. Nobody outside the company seemed to have a knowledge base that covered what Sears did now. The corporation was now the largest retailer in the world, as well as this country's second-largest property/liability insurance company, thirteenth-largest life-insurance company, largest residential- and commercial-real-estate brokerage, largest institutional-shopping-center developer, and seventh-largest securities brokerage firm.

For years a fraternity of retail analysts had followed Sears for the large banks, brokerage houses, insurance companies, and other institutional investment concerns, but since none of these companies employed experts whose knowledge extended to all realms of the new Sears, the French Room at the Drake was full of insurance, real-estate, and banking experts who knew as little about stoves as the veteran retail mavens knew about securities.

Telling seemed almost jaunty as he approached the lectern to address the analysts. He rocked back and forth as he welcomed the crowd and then continued in the affectless speaking voice he used when reading corporatese in public. Ever since one long-time member of the Sears board of directors had noted to the chairman that his habit of clawing at himself like a third baseman before a large audience was distracting at best, Telling had curtailed the public scratching. His thick hands were curled tightly around the rostrum as he reported the recent fiscal success of the business groups. Laughter punctuated his description of the company's "new, well-rounded merchandising philosophy," because as Telling read the words "well-rounded," a photograph of Cheryl Tiegs appeared on a screen behind the chairman. But the giggling ceased abruptly when Telling veered from his script and gazed into the audience. He would never enjoy this public side of the post, $1.4 million a year notwithstanding.

The chairmen of each of the Sears business groups, along with the company president and the chief financial officer, sat stonily on the high podium to either side of Telling. None of the barons of the new Sears even smiled when the crowd laughed.

Since Telling had broken the power of the old territories, the company had remained empty of internal kings, but the heads of the business groups had certainly risen to the status of powerful peers. The CEOs of the operating groups sat now on the corporate board of directors, in the same insider seats formerly occupied by the territorial leaders, and, as with the once-sovereign territories, the business groups were encouraged to engage in intramural competition.

Through his unusual combination of action and inaction, Telling had caused the seven senior managers on the dais—and one sitting below in the audience—to envisage themselves aligned shoulder to shoulder in an overt race for good numbers, for their share of corporate capital, for personal remuneration born of superior performance, for the ear of the chairman of chairmen, and lately for the golden prize of succeeding Edward Riggs Telling as the next chairman of the board.

The revisionist tales making the rounds in 1983 included the assertion that there were only three things Ed Telling had hoped to accomplish during his tenure as chairman of Sears. The description ignored his commitment to smashing the localist power enters, reining in the kingpins of the buying and Headquarters staff organization, purging the recalcitrants of his own corporate generation, and the like. All Ed Telling really ever wanted for Sears was to establish a planning mechanism for the corporation, to diversify its businesses, and to work out a better means of succession. The lack of viable candidates for the job at the time he had been chosen to be leader was almost sinful, and he vowed it wouldn't happen again.

It was incredible to think that the time had come to think beyond the Telling era. Telling told his intimates that he was looking forward to retiring when, in less than a year, on April Fool's Day 1984, he reached the age of sixty-five. He said he couldn't wait to "gaze out over his feet at some water somewhere."

As the company bylaws dictated, he had met once each year since 1981 with the outside directors of the board to discuss potential successors, the last time being a breakfast meeting two months before the analysts came to lunch. If Telling kept with company tradition, he would pull his personal choice from the "pool" and present the name to the board at their last meeting of 1983, scheduled for November. A formal announcement could therefore be made to the public at the annual meeting the following spring.

So, by the time of the gathering of the analysts in the spring of 1983, there was a horse race shaping up at Sears. The grapevine carried the word that Telling had already made one of his Delphic comments to each of his would-be successors. The next chairman of Sears, he'd said to each of them, would have to be "quick and tough." He hadn't said much more about the matter to anyone, but he had made it quite clear to all concerned that for the first time in the company's history the field was wide open to outsiders. Respect for the tradition of drawing the chairman from the merchandise company would no longer be a foregone conclusion.

There were entries in the derby this time that wouldn't have been admitted to the barn in the past. The disparate characters and backgrounds of the eight men thought to be Telling's own favorites for the office demonstrated as profoundly as any other measure the astonishing difference between the corporate society that was Sears, Roebuck during the beginning of the reign of Telling and the one that existed near the end. Only two of the eight barons were even of the true company blood, and one of the two was by traditional standards too young by a decade to carry a Sears chairman's bag. The run for the roses would include six late entrants who fell so far outside the bounds of what company tradition would deem acceptable that most of the company lords of even five years earlier wouldn't have taken their phone calls. If the changing of Sears was confusing to many of the analysts, it was also incredibly exciting to outsiders. More than a few of the analysts at the Drake had come great distances just to view the field of possible heirs, all displayed like this in a row.

Farthest to Ed Telling's right on the dais sat the senior Searsman from Wall Street, the chairman and chief executive officer of the Dean Witter Financial Services Group, Robert M. Gardiner.

It was only a matter of months after the acquisition of Dean Witter that Andy Melton was replaced by the astonishingly tall hail-fellow-well-met known in all corners of the Manhattan financial district as Stretch. Few people knew of Telling's October 1981 pledge to make Andy Melton pay for the last-minute hitches and personal demands he threw into the deal, but none of the senior Tower-based managers at Sears were surprised when Melton resigned his chairmanship in July of 1982 to devote more time to "Sears duties."

Melton's reputation had been tainted from the start by gossip about his management habits. He apparently demanded that his own staff review in advance all agendas and even the slides to be used in meetings he was supposed to attend in Chicago, and he was considered a nitpicker and blitherer after the meetings began. During one session on the sixty-eighth floor, Ed Telling turned to the Sears officer next to him during Melton's presentation and said, "Can you tell me why we're sitting here?"

In July 1982 Sears floated a $200-million bond issue through Goldman, Sachs instead of using Dean Witter's bankers, and Melton had dissented from the action in a style that those knowledgeable about Ed Telling realized would not serve him well in the long run. They could see the future of the relationship of Ed Telling and Andy Melton in some of the photographs printed in New York newspapers after the takeover. The picture of Telling was often one of the older ones, back when he sported goofy black-rimmed glasses and a Sears, Roebuck Field soldier's flat-top haircut, and invariably had one side of his shirt collars hiked up showing several inches of the noose of his necktie. The attendant picture of Andrew Melton, Jr., could have been lifted from the wall of an exclusive Manhattan men's club.

Ironically, the defensive, holier-than-thou image wasn't really Andy Melton at all. He was by Wall Street standards an old foot soldier himself. But he was never destined to be part of the Sears family. He was pegged. And when he was granted more time to spend with his family at the farm in Vermont or his home in Florida, few people at Sears were sorry to see him go. Melton would continue to run one minor wing of Dean Witter (because it was written into his contract), and he would remain as chairman of something called the Financial Services Planning Committee, a high-level interbusiness group entity that was supposed to figure out how to tie the new Sears into a whole. The committee had been dominated from the start, however, by an underlying Financial Services Advisory Committee, a purported staff-support group chaired by Phil Purcell.

The ascension of Stretch Gardiner to the top job at Dean Witter inadvertently quieted the four-year-old cultural conflict at the wire house between the Dean Witter people and the old Reynolds Securities employees like Gardiner. The Sears overlords were cognizant of having acquired Dean Witter's cleavages along with the brokerage house, but they sensed that the top management shuffle wouldn't destabilize Dean Witter, simply because everybody liked old Stretch. Gardiner had worked hard at appearing more capable of converting to the Sears religion all along. The loyalism was tempered rather attractively, Telling thought, by indications from Stretch that he didn't give a damn one way or another about corporate politics. Telling teased him on occasion about how rich he was (the enhanced value of the almost 405,000 shares of Sears stock he got in the merger made Gardiner a larger shareholder than either of the Rosenwald grandchildren on the Sears board, as well as a man worth in excess of $15 million), but it turned out that for all his money and his suede-shoe club memberships, Stretch was at heart a kid from rural Maryland who went to Princeton because the basketball coach liked the fact that he was six feet eight inches tall. Ed Telling liked tall men from farms who could let the world slide every now and again.

The business under Gardiner had performed well, largely because a powerful financial surge had brought life back to the retail broker-dealer business. Most of the new financial products Dean Witter brought to market in the spirit of Telling and Purcell's financial-services dreams— such as the Sears U.S. Government Money Market Trust—had been quite successful, though an experiment in the sort of direct-response advertising Joe Moran had suddenly promoted during 1982 had been a notable failure when monthly Sears bills that contained offers and infor- mation about Dean Witter IRAs failed to generate a response.

Stretch Gardiner was skeptical when he first heard of Telling's com- mitment to selling stocks and bonds in Sears stores: he believed securi- ties customers were wealthier than the store clientele. But by the time a couple wandered up to an experimental test of the Financial Services Network booths in Cupertino, California, and opened a $2.9-million brokerage account, Gardiner had become a supporter of the grass-roots money network that had animated Ed Telling's dreams from the start.

By Tower standards, Wes Poulson had been judged a health nut. He made a fetish of his tennis game and the lengthy morning run he'd made seven days a week for eleven years now. The man even ordered salads as a main course.

Poulson, conversely, was struck on each of his many journeys to the Tower since the buyout by the bulk of his new colleagues at Sears: "There's not a Sears guy up there who couldn't stand to lose fifteen pounds," Poulson would comment. "I mean, you ever see the bellies on those guys? They sit around and eat those huge steak dinners, and the only ones who aren't fat have just come off a bypass."

Wes Poulson tended to be unusually open about his viewpoints for a corporate manager who worked for someone else. His jutting-jawed frankness was prominent during several of the "setting-the-record- straight" sessions that were convened at his request during the year after Coldwell Banker joined the family. Wes worked for six months without a day off after the merger, seeing to the task of convincing his company of wealthy entrepreneurs that life as employees of a Midwestern Goliath could be made bearable.

Poulson remained skeptical of the staff executives who worked for Ed Telling, especially the financial men. When the Homart shopping-center development wing of Sears was transferred to Poulson's control, the Tower managed to transport a seasoned Sears financial controller of the venerable Jack Kincannon, professional-son-of-a-bitch school from the Western Territory's Cube to the chrome-and-recessed-light-laden downtown Los Angeles headquarters of Coldwell Banker. Poulson and the other Coldwell Banker executives were unimpressed with the "old Sears firehorse" in their midst. From the moment he came to work among the real-estate sellers, Dick Callaghan was regarded as a Sears spy, an image Callaghan tended to support by his habit of introducing assertions with the phrase "Management wants you to." Within weeks the controller found himself uninvited to meetings, denied the Coldwell Banker executive perk of a company car, and generally subjected to a campaign of overt shunning worthy of a primitive African tribe or a middle-class American high school.

Chief house-seller Forey Olson was so convinced that Callaghan was passing information to the Tower that he began to feed him disinformation. When the bad information came back to Coldwell Banker from Chicago, Olson challenged Callaghan in an executive-committee meeting, clearly referring to the Sears representative as a spy. Callaghan applied for a transfer and was eventually moved back home to the Cube, where people were nicer to him.

The salad-chomping Poulson was already regarded with skepticism in the Tower before the Callaghan incident because of his penchant for rather trendy, cutting-edge management theories of the sort that were rarely heard on the sixty-eighth floor, largely because Telling thought most of the stuff was stupid. But Poulson was enamored of technocratic think-tank-style polling of elite expert opinion such as Delphi Studies, and he was almost religious about his belief in the power of economic cycles such as the one that had taken some of the thrill out of the real-estate business in 1982. Coldwell Banker had been involved in the sale or purchase of more than forty-two thousand American homes in 1982, but the business seemed to have peaked in May.

Despite the sluggish performance, Chicago had been supportive of Coldwell Banker's aggressive strategic goal of eventually controlling fully 20 percent of the American residential-real-estate market. Around the time of their acquisition of a Baltimore-based firm in January of 1983, Poulson figured his sellers controlled 8 percent of the market.

Observers of the company horses couldn't help noting that the fifty-three-year-old Poulson was one of the brightest guys in the organization in 1983, or that Ed Telling appeared to like him despite his cage rattling, spy expunging, and highfalutin theorizing. The two men were known to share a tongue-in-cheek appreciation of the mounds of awful kitsch modern corporations generated as cheap, giveaway gifts. They both liked tacky lapel pins, ball-point pens with the corporate logo on the side, doormats, and feed caps with adjustable plasticine headbands. Poulson would leave a Coldwell Banker wristwatch on Telling's desk during a visit to the Tower, and Telling would present Wes with a power-table-saw tie clasp he'd lifted from a hardware buyer. You couldn't read too much into the relationship, but it was worth remembering that beneath the Californiate, maverick exterior, Wes Poulson was a Midwesterner born.

Long odds, to be sure, on the Californian, but with Telling you just never could tell.

Archie Boe sat to Telling's left as the chairman read his speech to the analysts. With just his small scholar's face, dwarfed by huge glasses, peeking over the top of the long table, the corporate president looked every bit like the caricature of the Allstate Insurance executive described in so many derisive jokes told among the merchants over the years. The corporate presidency had faded away after Brennan shed the title for his chairmanship of the Merchandise Group, but in March 1982 Telling asked Archie to come downtown to help out with the "integration" of the new businesses, to keep the Tower staff from treading on the newcomers' toes, and, at the same time, to temper them if he could.

Shortly after his arrival, Boe was the center of what the public-affairs department called a "PR nightmare," when Brennan's merchants in the Midwestern Territory streamlined away the tiny Sears store in Estherville, Iowa, birthplace of one Archie Boe. The national press picked up on local interviews with Boe's widowed stepmother, who remembered young Archie as "the most different child our family ever knew." The woman allowed that she was saddened by the abandonment of Estherville by the big-city corporation that the townspeople clearly believed their own Archie Boe controlled as its president. An Estherville Chamber of Commerce official was quoted with some authority as saying that the store was being closed so that Sears could put the money into its new financial-services businesses. Formal appeals to Boe were made, but the store remained closed.

Boe was committed to keeping the merchants and former merchants from moving in on the new divisions. He knew that the freedom to contend to subordinates that they still worked for an independent company was an essential tool each group leader needed if integration was

to proceed. Boe had spent much of his career protecting the individualism of Allstate from encroachment from Sears. But now Archie *was*
Sears. He chose to ignore the irony, because he'd believed for a long
time that the old corporate ways needed changing.

From the Merchant's point of view, having an insurance man as president of Sears would have seemed laughable before Telling took over,
but by 1983 it really wasn't such a big deal. However, the idea of an
ex–insurance man actually running the show was utterly terrifying to
the merchants who still dominated the corporate population below the
new barons. Telling was known to enjoy wandering into Boe's office
during the chairman's solo saunterings around the sixty-eighth floor. If
Telling had one of his greasy paper bags full of popcorn with him, Boe
was always offered some. If the chairman wanted to send out to the
South Side for some lunchtime gizzards, Archie was always asked if he
wanted to go in with him. "What 'bout Archie?" Telling would say, and
someone would wander off to find the president. Archie didn't trust
bankers farther than he could throw one, and he knew the value of
well-grilled gizzard.

Because Boe was only a year younger than Telling, he was considered
the most distant outsider in the running. It was generally assumed that
Archie had been kicked upstairs to let Telling observe how Don Craib,
the younger and stronger contender from Allstate could run, but there
was still one unsettling scenario involving Boe: if a decision between a
merchant and a nonmerchant was considered too difficult and destabilizing for late 1983, a one-year holding action might be called for in the
form of the short-term chairmanship of Archie.

Sitting next to Boe and looking nothing at all like the stereotypical bean
counter of years past was the big-shouldered and forever confident CEO
at Allstate, Donald Craib. All of the executive money out in Northbrook,
Illinois, sat square on the nose of the fifty-seven-year-old Craib, and to
the Allstate world-view his ascension to the chairmanship had been all
but preordained by events. Why else would Telling have drafted Craib
to the Tower as vice-chairman of the corporation during the secretive
months of planning and abortive acquisitive actions between 1980 and
the purchases? Telling knew then that the corporate future was in financial products. The chairman had clearly kicked Archie Boe upstairs to
let Craib have his requisite time as divisional CEO, and therefore be
co-equal in experience with the other business-group CEOs he was
clearly destined to manage.

On top of everything else, the high-stepping ex-Marine and J. Edgar

Hoover lookalike was a dyed-in-the-wool son of Sears. Craib grew up in the aisles of the Pasadena, California, store, then the one up in Bakersfield, and then in the big store next to the catalog plant at Boyle Street where his father was the manager. Craib's dad was a conservative Scotsman who wouldn't spend a dime of the company's money unless he got $3.00 back. Craib, Sr., taught the gospel of Sears merchantry and the rights of territorial rule to the young John Lowe, and he was the administrative hand behind Arthur Wood, during the former chairman's grooming in the field as head of the Far Western Territory.

Craib, Jr., worked part-time in the many stores his father ran. He met his wife at a Sears store, where she was working in the personnel department. His studies at UCLA were directed toward a life as a Sears merchant, but because of his father's senior position in the territory, he was told he would have to start out in another territory. At the time the separate kingdom of the West was in full flourish, and the option was rather like being told to join the Coast Guard instead of the Marines. Since Craib didn't want to leave California, he went to work as a $225-a-month claims adjuster for Allstate and eventually did quite well for himself.

Craib's twenty-eight-year-old son worked as an attorney in the governmental-affairs department Sears maintained in Washington, D.C., thus rendering the Craib legacy less pure but just as multigenerational as the Brennans.

The Allstate grapevine was working overtime by early 1983 in an effort to build the image of Craib as a singularly gifted general manager and a quick, no-nonsense decision-maker. His years of experience in managing Allstate's investments would certainly come in handy in the new Sears, and the fact that Allstate had become involved in advanced computer and telecommunications technology so much earlier than the Merchant was worth noting.

But for all of the hipper, higher-tech management jargon heard in the hallways in Northbrook, the insurance company had historical characteristics not dissimilar from Sears'. Allstate's agency system and its personal-insurance lines were once the envy of the insurance industry, but this was no longer the case. Some contended the decline was a result of the company's holding on to its independent, jack-of-all-trades-style agents, spread over more than three thousand outlets in six territories.* Recent attempts to streamline the organization had caused consterna-

*Much of the Allstate information comes from the noted academic observer of Sears, its subsidiaries and history, Professor John Jueck of the University of Chicago. Jueck was the co-author of the classic academic corporate history of Sears through the end of World War II, *Catalogues and Counters,* and though it could have been a coincidence, a similarly

tion at the grass roots over a reported "loss of freedom," and while profits at Allstate were still quite high—especially in relation to the Merchant's wafer-thin margins—the company did seem to be up against a growth ceiling. Whereas all of the other heads of business groups could show their stuff in 1983 in juxtaposition to weak performance in 1982, there wasn't a lot Craib could do to hype his numbers without conducting a campaign of cost cutting and premium raising that could tarnish his image.

There was also the potential problem of Craib's personal style. He wore shoes that buckled at the side, and he worked in a huge suite of white-carpeted offices in Northbrook that housed a portion of his distinguished collection of Oriental China and some stunning and suspiciously delicate Japanese prints. He made trips back to California a bit too often for the tastes of the Tower cognoscenti—even if he did get free tickets by virtue of his seat on the board of Jet America Airlines.

But Craib was still Allstate's man, and the myth-making machinery was working overtime for their candidate that spring. "A bull of a man," one vice-president was heard to say at an intercompany affair; "Knew how to merchandise a store at the age of four," said another. Craib was without a doubt the best hope the insurers had ever unveiled—a bean counter with balls—and given the new corporate direction, indicative to Allstaters of Telling's lack of faith in the future of the Merchant, Don Craib seemed to be running with even odds.

If the next chairman had to be a man with the word "financial" on his résumé, most of Ed Brennan's merchants would have preferred him to be the vice-chairman and chief financial officer of the company, Dick Jones.

The alarmingly pale and softspoken choice of conservative betters in early 1983 went up to the podium at the Drake to describe the company's financial status after Telling finished. In some ways Dick Jones' style appeared even more Searsy than the chairman's. His country-boy twang was far more pronounced then Telling's, and he'd even retained an unreconstructed pronunciation of the word "insurance." He said "*in*-surance," like some rural auto-policy huckster. Jones had worked very hard to get to know the financial-securities specialists sitting in the French Room, and many of them knew that the Sears CFO had known

---

encyclopedic history of Allstate's first fifty years assigned to Jueck, which included in draft form a close examination of good and bad company policies over the years, was aborted by Craib when the corporate-succession competition began.

almost nothing about corporate finance when Ed Telling brought him in from the Eastern Territory to supplant the imperious Kincannon. The resultant "book" on Dick Jones was that he was a man of giant intellect, a manager's manager, who had figured out how to run one of the largest private financial-supply systems in the world by reading books.

Jones was born in Eldon, Missouri, and had joined up with Sears in 1950 after graduating from Olivet Nazarene College. He'd experienced all the rigors of life in the post-war Sears Field, including no fewer than three separate store assignments as only an assistant manager. In 1963 he was finally given his first store to run, in Freeport, Illinois, by a local zone manager named Ed Telling. Jones ran the powerful Washington, D.C., group of stores for a while, had served as Telling's administrative assistant in Philadelphia, and had run the Eastern Territory after Telling and before Bill Bass. Jones was crushed when Telling gave the job of senior executive vice-president, Field, to Charlie Wurmstedt. He thought sure the job would be his if loyalty to Ed Telling was any measure of worthiness.

At fifty-six, Jones was about the right age to be a corporate chairman in America. His status as a Telling insider, coupled with the fact that his financial track record might mitigate the impression in the financial-services wings of the company and outside business community that the Merchant still ruled, made Jones seem a logical choice.

The bad thing about Dick Jones was that he seemed too damned *good.* He was a devout Nazarene Christian, and a sense of ethical responsibility oozed constantly from his gentle demeanor. His smile was so full of compassion and quiet endurance that you were forever expecting him to yank a Bible from his pocket and call you "friend." Jones tended to wear very dark, often black suits, which showed off the bloodlessness of his face. Amid all the talk of diversification, wags up and down the Tower a few months earlier had passed along the rumor that Sears was considering entrance into the lucrative undertaking business and Dick Jones was slated to run it.

If it had been 1973 instead of 1983, Jones would have been the logical choice for chairman. He would have kept Sears out of the papers, away from governmental interference, and generally out of trouble during those difficult days of corporate scrutiny. But that former demand for more ethical corporate leadership had dissipated. Nineteen eighty-three was a year of tough and agile executives, of leaders who grinned on TV and promised to meet the Japanese challenge head on.

Still, a number of people close to Ed Telling and a significant segment of the ERIP group believed Jones would receive the mantle when it was passed. The smart money argued this would occur in part because Jones' tenure would virtually assure the subsequent succession of Dick Jones' friend, Ed Brennan. Most members of the company establishment had to agree that Brennan was simply too young to be the chairman of the board of Sears, Roebuck, but if Dick Jones was given the job for six or seven years, then control of the company wouldn't have to pass out of the hands of the merchants, possibly until the next century.

"I'd be happy to answer that question," Ed Telling boomed back after receiving a query about merchandising from the audience in the French Room, "but I betcha Ed Brennan here is anxious to speak."

Brennan leaned out over the speakers' table looking dark and youthful between the white crops atop Gardiner and Jones. He carefully folded his hands in front of him and licked his lips, as he tended to do, as if readying precision instruments for action. His eyes rose from a downward gaze, then his face, and suddenly the low-level chatter ceased all at once.

The analysts and the media had all adopted Brennan's own vocabulary in recent months to describe the Merchant. Their descriptions of the once-medieval retail merchandise company in articles and research reports now included his words and phrases: "vibrant," "exciting," "dominant," and "It's still Sears, but it's different." Brennan had promised to pull off the consummate retail trick—wringing more business out of stores you already have instead of building new ones. He said he would soon unveil a new selling machine that would shock the industry.

What he had to say when Telling called on him was comparatively mundane—Brennan mentioned offhandedly that the Merchant's sale of $300 million worth of surplus goods at discount already made Sears the fourth-largest American discounter.

There was little Ed Brennan could say to deny the fact that his Merchant was shrinking just as the businesses run by the other men at the same table were poised to grow. Wes Poulson and Forey Olson had their go-ahead to buy up local real-estate agencies everywhere, and Stretch Gardiner had been told to hire brokers and expand outlets aggressively. The contribution of the Merchant to the corporation's 130-percent income rise during the first quarter was impressive, but the whiffs of corporate renaissance still rose most prominently from the awesome power of financial services.

Ed Telling spoke of the awesome power of financial services. The press spoke of financial services, but the way everyone "spun a web around finance" really irked Brennan. Financial services weren't so complex or fancy to him. It was like the old store-manager's trick of obfuscating the essential simplicity of their tasks with nomenclature and hype. But for all of his faith in his campaign to harness the awesome power dormant within the merchandise empire, Ed Brennan still sold sweat socks, bedsheets, and claw hammers.

There were two scenarios that observers like the Don Craib supporters in Northbrook actively feared. One was that the charismatic young man of the Merchandise Group would actually lift the Merchant up so high over his head during 1983 that the retailer would glisten with its old light, and that, in the spirit of the managerial idiosyncrasy that had characterized many of Ed Telling's big decisions over the years, Brennan would get the job despite his age. The other scenario was that Telling would take his demonstrated faith in men from outside the fold to its outer limit and pass up all obvious contenders on the payroll in favor of the ultimate outsider. Evidence of the real possibility of such an act was presented by Telling's growing dependence upon the compact fellow sitting thin-lipped and stern at the end of the dais, Mr. Roderick M. Hills.

Rod Hills' presence inside the company in 1983 was more unsettling to the status quo than Phil Purcell's entry into the upper ranks had been five years earlier. As a hot-shot Washington, D.C., mover-and-shaker with almost no experience as a manager, Rod Hills was far more distant from Sears traditions than Stretch Gardiner, or Hills' old college buddy Wes Poulson. But Ed Telling liked Rod Hills. He liked the way Hills bullied his way through the labyrinthine process of buying Sears some new businesses—liked it so much that Telling flew out to Washington two weeks after the acquisitions were closed to present Hills with a pale-green Sears, Roebuck bank check with the words "One Million Dollars" situated just below Hills' name. The Hills firm made around $4 million from the legal work generated by the two deals, but Telling wanted Rod to have something for himself. Telling came to town with the check the day an Air Florida jet crashed into the Potomac during a storm, and the resulting confusion and bad weather kept the Sears chairman grounded in town for a rare long dinner away from home with Rod and Carla Hills. Hills ended up giving the money to the firm—he made plenty of money—but he would never forget the gesture or the warm feelings at dinner that night.

Telling also liked the hell out of that hard-charging speech Hills had written up for the chairman's evening with the Chicago Economics Club. His call for the further democratization of the American financial system was well received in numerous quarters. Members of both the

Senate and the House wrote Telling with their compliments, and the chairman wrote back to say that the speech the legislators admired had in fact been the work of Rod Hills.

So much Sears legal work began to come to Hills' firm that Hills eventually engineered the acquisition of a twenty-lawyer Chicago firm and opened up a branch of Latham, Wadkins, and Hills on the sixty-ninth floor of the Tower.

His long days in the company of Ed Telling after the acquisition of Dean Witter and Coldwell Banker constituted the most satisfying time in Rod Hills' professional life. He and the chairman read books and reports together, and they talked about what could be made of the future of an institution with almost limitless resources and the will to change. Their discussions were cast in conceptual, almost artistic terms that seemed very far away from running a store. Hills wondered how Telling had survived his years of climbing the ladder among such basic people, and he wondered how a man could run a company and have kept his intellect and sensitivity a secret.

Hills was interested in the intricate webbing of the international economy, particularly in the fast businesses serving international trade. Telling invited Hills to sit in on some strategic-planning committee meetings in which a Sears world-trading venture was discussed, but though little came of the idea at the time, Telling seemed so personally interested in the concept that Hills went ahead and inserted a paragraph in the Economics Club speech that announced the coming of a Sears trading venture. Telling left the paragraph in the speech, and Hills was present to observe the shock on the Sears officers' faces as they listened to the late-February 1982 public proclamation of a corporate initiative to which the sixty-eighth-floor staff hadn't give a second thought.

Not surprisingly, the Sears World Trade Company came into being in March 1982. A veteran merchant from the buying organization named John Waddle was appointed president. The early aspirations of the unit were not unlike those of a Sears foreign-trade unit once established in 1934; the idea was to use the far-flung Sears foreign buying offices to move American consumer goods around. But Hills kept insisting to Telling during their private discussions that Waddle was not setting up a "true" trading company. Hills envisaged a global business venture modeled on the legendary Japanese trading companies—the Sogo Shosha—nine of which accounted for over $300 billion in annual sales.

The trading Goliaths of Japan like Mitsubishi and Mitsui grew large and ubiquitous in service to an economy in need of resources from abroad and access to internationl markets for its finished products. The Sogo Shosha became the consummate "middlemen" of international commerce, accounting for fully half of Japan's foreign trade. The firms were heavily leveraged, highly entrepreneurial, and, in the case of a few of them, vertically integrated with numerous manufacturing, mining, and financial companies. The Japanese, Hills argued, understood that a true trading company was much more than a goods peddler. He said that Sears could develop its own corporation of highly mobile commodities traders, merchant-banking specialists, consulting groups, and other services, preferably in concert with another powerful partner interested in a joint venture.

Eventually Hills even offered to do the job of taking Sears worldwide himself. For half of what he'd made the previous year as a lawyer, or half of $550,000, he agreed to sign on full-time in order to make a new company from parts he vowed to assemble himself. On September 9, 1982, he signed a contract, and a few weeks later he flew to the Far East as the new chairman of Sears World Trade, to announce his intentions to take on the world on the home turf of the great Oriental traders.

Just a few weeks before the gathering of analysts in Chicago, Sears had purchased an expensive new headquarters for the trading company located over an entire historic block of Washington, D.C., just down the street from the White House.

All of the other business-group chairmen were supposed to take their day-to-day administrative issues with corporate Sears to Archie Boe, but Rod Hills reported directly to Telling—and the little cockalorum still knew so little about Sears, Roebuck that he called the territories "regions." In 1983 Hills still thought that Ed Telling used to run the "Northeast Region."

It was remembered now that, for all of his brilliant foisting of responsibility on the most unlikely around him, Ed Telling had probably made a few bad choices along the way. There was Charlie Wurmstedt. Some put Joe Moran in the category, too. The idea of a chairman of Sears, Roebuck's coming from anywhere other than the Merchant was destabilizing enough, but the thought of a man like Hills having the ear of the chairman was just terrible.

Occasionally people with nothing to lose ventured to confront Telling about Rod Hills. Telling had utterly confounded members of his inner circle by establishing a golfing relationship with the man he'd crushed and disposed of five years earlier, the former merchant prince Jim Button. It was Button who finally turned to Telling on a golf course one afternoon and said, "Rod Hills is a big mistake for you. He's going to hurt you, Ed."

"Rod Hills is gonna get you in trouble," Archie Boe said to the chairman a few months later. "Hills is a wild man by my lights."

Telling looked back at Boe and responded calmly. "What Rod Hills does is gets things done," he said.

The deepening relationship between Telling and Rod Hills made Phil Purcell crazy. *He* was supposed to be the inside outsider. Phil watched the proceedings at the Drake from the audience—a baronet now, who was stationed far from Ed Telling's right hand, out at the eastern edge of things.

Stretch Gardiner was sitting next to Ed Telling when the chairman traveled to New York in 1981 to promise Dean Witter personnel, "Whatever you have now, you'll continue to have." But during the summer of 1982, Telling sat down again with Gardiner to discuss the idea of giving Dean Witter something more. He wanted to send Phil Purcell out to be the number-two man at Dean Witter. With Gardiner's approval in hand, Telling then broached the idea with Purcell: "I hate to ask you this, because I know you and Anne and the kids are happy in Chicago," he said, "but you and I have talked about how you oughta do something different from what you're doing some day. Stretch wants you to go work for him. Stretch says you can be the CEO and he'll be the COO, but we both know that's a bad decision, so you think about being president and chief operating officer out at Dean Witter and let me know."

Phil Purcell knew well the sound of something that was already done in the mind of Ed Telling. He also knew that someone hailing from outside the old order had even less opportunity to say no. So, during the late-summer rumblings of the most powerful bull market to come to Wall Street since the Depression, Phil Purcell moved to New York City to learn how to work on the line.

Phil managed to retain his Chicago post on the corporate strategic-planning committee, and though he was officially based in New York now, he had decided to leave Anne and the six boys in Wilmette. After he got the job in New York and was packing up to go work "on the cutting edge of the company," as he put it, a middle-level staffer dropped by to wish Purcell well. "I'll need it," he said. "I've only got two years."

Purcell was thirty-nine years old in 1983, and the idea of his being handed the reins—with the attendant probability of a tenure of nearly three decades in control—seemed more than unlikely. He still wielded considerable clout in the Tower, which he demonstrated in managing to wrest Allstate's huge California Savings and Loan from the insurers and having it transferred under the Dean Witter column of the ledger sheet in January 1983. But it was a tough time to be "out of the corporation."

He was working as the Searsman at Dean Witter, an outsider twice over. His mentor was soon due to pick a successor and leave, just as

Purcell appeared to have been supplanted as the master planner and senior tactician. Compared to the others—Gardiner, Poulson, Craib, Jones, Brennan, and even Rod Hills—Phil was barely senior enough chronologically or organizationally to be considered a runner in the race.

Some readjustments were in order before the guard changed. The systematic destruction of the historical power centers of a corporate empire was hardly the sort of thing you could put on your résumé. Phil Purcell knew that his corporate future was predicated on his ability to help make the financial-services dreams he and Telling had entertained during their time together come true. Phil knew that in Telling's vision the new Sears was all supposed to hook together like a backyard jungle gym from the catalog. The new baronies had to be bundled together like the five separate but indivisible structures that stood together as the Sears Tower. The sum was supposed to become more than its parts, and Purcell knew that whatever he could do to move Sears closer to that equation would help his own cause.

"This isn't about steel companies' buying oil companies," Telling liked to say, referring with disdain to other mergers and acquisitions that had taken place in the general takeover frenzy that followed the Sears adventures. "What does that benefit America? All that does is add two and two and make four. Are more people working? Are more things being created for people? We're involved in making a new industry, putting two and two together and making seven."

Even Telling had adopted the current buzz word, "synergism" to describe the end result of knitting all the new businesses together. Before the deals of 1981 were even closed, Wes Poulson and his top officers, and Gardiner, Melton, and theirs, were brought to the Tower. Ed Brennan gave the visitors a tour of the Merchant's floors and told them of his plans to turn the ship. Three or four officers from Allstate came downtown to participate. Ed Telling appointed them all to committees that were mandated to go ahead and dream.

The original Financial Services Advisory Committee Phil Purcell ran included no fewer than seventeen subcommittees made up of numerous stars from each of the business groups and charged with studying ways of intermingling the businesses. Some studied ways to use Sears' massive census-sized mailing list to sell new products; others explored ways to share consumer data between companies. They talked about ways to offer discounts in one business so as to build business in another; ways to sell the new financial-service products in the stores; ways to wire the entire system together technologically with computers and operationally through the use of a single universal credit card.

The committee members entertained dreams of a huge computerized state-of-the-art delivery system called Sears. The system would store a family's capital in a fluid account from which the funds could move laterally. A family would buy consumer goods at the stores or through computer connections. The family house would be purchased from Coldwell Banker, financed through mortgages backed by innovative Dean Witter securities. The family's insurance would come from Allstate; their stocks, bonds, savings instruments, and every conceivable sort of service, from Sears house-painting to Sears medical clinics, would all be charged to their central Sears account. The system would automatically pay down mortgages, pay off personal loans, and pay all the monthly bills. The system could even help decide how to manage money for the consumer, based on sophisticated analyses of individual tax statuses, interest rates, and investment opportunities. Cash would be available in machines in every store, and eventually on every streetcorner.

A new level of "pecuniary decency" of the sort economist Thorstein Veblen considered a utopian potentiality would be granted to average citizens by the same company that had helped make consumers of their parents and grandparents in the first place. The embellishments of modern life would all be had conveniently via the system, all of it dispersed from the central warehouse of the future.

The analysts at the Drake heard about the successful experimental booths already in some Sears retail stores that sold securities, various investment funds, and loans. They were told of programs such as one that rewarded a buyer of a new home from Coldwell Banker with a book full of coupons promising large discounts on big-ticket items at Sears stores. The analysts had already been exposed to countless articles that referred to Sears as a "supercompany" along with American Express, Merrill Lynch, Citicorp, and one or two others. Articles about the emerging financial-services industry usually appeared with charts and checklists that compared capital availability, number of consumer outlets, and the number and range of services each supercompany offered. Each chart showed Sears to be the biggest as well as the one offering the largest array of services.

Meanwhile, the field was being flooded with new competitors. An SRI survey a few weeks before the meeting indicated there were now some forty thousand depository institutions capable of offering a large range of consumer financial services to Americans, whereas in 1980 thirteen thousand companies were in the game. Telling had figured all along that others would make forays into the new industry. "Hopefully," he said at the time of the purchases, "we'll be a few miles down the road when that happens."

It appeared now that Sears did have the drop on the rest of the pack, but there was still a great deal to be done to make it all work. There were regulations to slalom around and loopholes to shimmy through. There were missing links that were still needed before Sears could claim dominance of the key activities in consumers' financial lives. Finding the missing links, monitoring the rise and fall of impediments to forming the business chain, keeping an eye on the internal competition, and learning to run a brokerage house were all part of Phil Purcell's overfull agenda.

"Mr. Telling," said the noted retail analyst from PaineWebber, Stu Robbins, "would you tell me how capital is allocated now in the corporation?"

"No," said Telling. The chairman then scanned the room for the next question.

Shorter-term tactical plans and the baronial requests for developmental funds Robbins asked about, were in fact reviewed together on a quarterly basis by the corporate staff. Telling put such great stock in the power of this sort of head-to-head competition that he'd even rearranged the yearly compensation of his would-be heirs so as to make the carrot bigger. Brennan's salary, for instance, was arranged so that the long-term confluence of various incentive bonuses could reward him with one and a half times his more than his $700,000 yearly base pay.

"Mr. Telling," said someone from the back of the room, "I was out in Alhambra at the annual meeting of 1979, and I'd just like to wish you luck at the annual meeting this year."

Telling sort of liked this. "You're very kind," he said with a nod.

Telling thanked his guests for coming, and over half of them moved quickly to the door en route to catch planes. The rest stayed to mingle in the French Room.

Ed Brennan took up a position in a corner of the room. At the end of each question asked by a member of the large crowd surrounding him, Brennan's head would fall to the side, and his smile would be transformed into a look of deep contemplation. He imparted a sense that the query had been full of unusual intellectual and moral seriousness. He would respond to protestations of abject flattery with a similar look. "It's fascinating that you should perceive that," he'd say, and then he would ask a question of the flatterer. Brennan had learned how to make people feel rather good about themselves.

But the whole idea of these "analysts" presuming in any way to understand what he was about actually irked the hell out of Ed Brennan.

Always had. He believed only six or seven of the retail experts really knew their stuff, and he would never get over the six-figure salaries the analysts made.

The dean of retail analysts, Walter Loeb of Morgan Stanley, who had been the first to prophesy the comeback of Sears in his April 1981 report, "The Battleship Has Turned," ventured forth bravely to the podium to engage Ed Telling in conversation. Telling smiled and nodded at what Loeb was saying, but the chairman's eyes darted around the room the whole time, as if he was looking for help.

Ed Brennan looked over the circle around him to observe Loeb's gesticulations. "We made him a hero," he said. "He went thumbs up and we made a hero out of him."

The retail analyst from First Boston Securities, Maggie Gilliam, came up to Brennan and began to ask about the prototypes for this "new store" the industry had been told to expect from Sears. Midway through her words of praise for his leadership, Brennan's eyes narrowed. He'd spotted a fellow from Standard & Poor's, the Wall Street securities-rating agency. Brennan interrupted Gilliam momentarily and coaxed the S & P man over to the circle with a hearty grin and handshake. As Gilliam went on about her sincere good feelings about the Merchant, Brennan stared into the Standard & Poor's fellow's eyes wearing a big grin until the fellow looked up with a grimace of acknowledgment. Brennan had once endured a session with the man and his supervisor at Standard & Poor's headquarters in New York. He and Dick Jones had been summoned there, Brennan felt, to explain themselves. Questions were asked as if he didn't know what he was doing, didn't know his business. Now Brennan held the man in place with his eyes as the First Boston analyst sang his praises. Brennan never forgot somebody who presumed to tell him about his business.

Ed Telling seemed to have sensed this about the kid from the start. During the spring of 1969, when Brennan was thirty-five years old and running the Baltimore North store, he was warned via the grapevine that the recently appointed vice-president in the Eastern Territory, the fearsome Ed Telling, was coming to visit. He was told to be prepared to cough up every record he had for the legendary tough manager's perusal. He was to have his profit-and-loss statement, his condition report, his payroll ratio studies, and even his employee record cards available. He was also told to be ready for lashing criticism.

Telling arrived and began to saunter around the store. After a few minutes he turned to the stiff young manager. "Got any coffee in this place?"

"Yes, sir," Brennan said.

They had a cup of coffee in Brennan's office, and then they went up to the roof so Telling could see the fine view of Baltimore the old three-story store offered. Next Telling said he wanted to go home.

"How much money you gonna make this year?" Telling asked as he walked out to the parking lot.

"Two million, sir," Brennan said.

"Guess I won't have to worry about North Avenue anymore," Telling said. He drove away and he never came back to the store again.

It had been like that between them ever since. Through each of the countless moves Brennan made as Telling catapulted him up through the ranks, there had been little said. Observers noted that the relationship between the two men was much more formal and emotionally distant than the usual gin-rummy level of affinity Telling shared with Charlie Wurmstedt, Henry Sunderland, Bill Bass, and several others. Brennan was never very good at small talk and ironic humor, whereas Ed Telling thrived on small talk and jokes about farm animals.

While Telling had carved a canal through the company that was customized for Eddie Brennan's passage, the kid had never been invited to become one of the boys. Brennan was not one of the Eastern Territory faithful like Bass or Charlie Bacon, men who could sit around with Telling, chew gizzards, and hee-haw. The stiffness between them, and Brennan's rather unnatural laugh in Telling's presence, actually made others uncomfortable. Telling could never have been called a mentor to Brennan as he was to Phil Purcell and several others. He was more like a presence.

After leaving the hotel, Telling trudged off by himself into the sunshine of the sort of perfect spring day that almost makes a Chicago winter worth the effort.

None of the men who might inherit his leadership would ever presume to escort Telling somewhere. Even Rod Hills knew better than to try to pour the chairman's coffee. Telling knew that the potential grooming of some eight powerful managers would eventually mean that seven of them were groomed falsely, and that, given the veritable cult of the chief executive officer that was animating men of great ego and ability throughout the nation in 1983, this perceived false grooming might end up having adverse ramifications. But he figured that he had to do it this way. He'd worked hard to change an unchanging company so that the field of men who might get control of it from him could include West Coast real-estate men, Wall Street back-slappers, a couple of bean counters, some youngsters, and even a cowboy mover-and-shaker out of Washington who claimed to know everybody worth knowing from Abu Dhabi to the Manila Bay.

He had to make them all run out in the open, even if it did make him feel even more alone.

"There was a time when I felt like I knew everybody around this place," Telling said as he lumbered through the busy lobby of the Tower, recognizing no one. "Guess this is how you realize your time has come. If you haven't made your peace with retirement after forty years or so, then there's something wrong. You wait for it such a long time. I won't miss catching the early train."

CHAPTER 19

The Store of the Future

There's more for your life at Sears.

The new motto was plastered across everything. Soon the phrase would be unleashed upon every functioning eye and ear in North America. In the meantime it appeared on stationery, notepads, banners, name tags, and at the top of the lengthy agenda describing the gala mid-spring christening of the long-awaited new store. The opening rally began in the gray television-monitor-lined Wacker Room on twenty-seven.

"Good afternoon!" Bill Bass roared at Headquarters managers and senior Field attendees who'd flown in from as far away as Peru to join in the two-day event.

"Good afternoon!" thundered back at a pitch so unusually loud and prolonged that a smile appeared on Bass' face. The Field was ready to see the future.

"I just gotta say it," Bass said. "After bein' in here these months, it sure looks good to see the Field in here after working with these . . ." Bass' voice trailed off as a pleasant titter ran through the rows of Field executives. Good old Bass. The boys loved it.

"I said to Mr. Brennan," he continued, " 'Last night I had a hard time sleeping because of thinking about this meeting.' "

As the pace of renewal quickened and the pressure to regain the Merchant's rightful place at the center of the corporation intensified during 1983, similar proclamations of insomnia had become an inevitable embellishment to speeches by members of the inner circle. "I couldn't sleep," Bass continued, "because I kept thinking of being seated here in the room with the key management of the Sears Merchandise Group. Headquarters and Field—here together. This is the most exciting time of each of our careers."

The beginning of the meeting was devoted to the Merchant's five-year strategic plan. The business plan for 1982–1986 had already been presented to Telling several months earlier, but Brennan had asked Bass, young Eric Saunders, and a wan and decidedly post-surgical-looking Henry Sunderland to present the usually top-secret long-range goals to the line managers in the spirit of transdivisional unity.

The five-year plan called for the company to add $10 billion in sales to the balance sheet and close to a billion dollars in enhanced profit. "But the days are gone forever when we can increase sales just by building new stores," Henry Sunderland told the crowd. No territorial employee could have ignored all the stores going dark of late. The message was that the Merchant would grow and stay big by virtue of something other than the old expansionism.

After the plan was described, the lights dimmed and the screen across the front of the Wacker Room lit up like a firefight. Hissing television sets along both sides of the room glowed bright as images of gleaming steam irons and other dazzling-looking goods appeared in exploding colors to the accompaniment of heroic synthesizer music. An "overview" of the planning behind the soon-to-be-unveiled new store was presented by the forty-two-year-old planning VP for the Merchant, Mike Bozic.

Bozic was a Bill Bass discovery from the Eastern Territory, but, more important, the serious-looking, bespectacled young officer was—along with Woody Haselton, Eric Saunders, and several others—one of Ed Brennan's "young tigers." Bozic and the others now constituted a clearly discernible group among senior managers. They could be seen at meetings glued to their seats, nodding thoughtfully as Ed Brennan intoned phrases and reiterated little apologues they'd all heard hundreds of times. They loved to use the new audiovisual technology now available to corporations. They'd picked up on Brennan's fascination with communications, and lately their computerized, laser-enhanced performances had become reminiscent of rock concerts. Unlike Henry Sunderland and Bill Bass, Bozic, Saunders, Joe Batogowski, Woody Haselton, and the other young tigers abjured the vague transprairie twang when they faced an audience. Success in the new Sears meant knowing how to wow a crowd. The veterans would still muster the traditional drill-sergeant's Sears hello, and a few of the buying organization's departmental national managers could still throw a fair nod-and-a-wink, hand-up-the-lingerie routine when called upon, but the young guys went in for a bit of flash.

The extravagant colors and blaring music continued as the leadership was exposed to the new national advertising program that would soon permeate the environments of 88 percent of all Americans between eighteen and sixty-four. The old battles over the control of advertising were just memories now. Instead of fiddling with local advertising all day, Brennan had told the Field leadership they were to become good marketers. They were to concern themselves with how the goods looked in the stores. There was still powerful advertising of items on the group level—a single newspaper ad in Houston a year earlier had caused such a run on Pac-Man units that four thousand of them checked out of local Sears stores before lunch—but the onus was essentially on Headquarters to "get the mystery out of the can," as Jim Button used to say after he came up with the idea of having television ads showing Sears paint being slathered on the sides of the White House, the Old North Church in Boston, and even John Paul Jones' home.

It was never discussed, but Sears national advertising campaigns of recent years tended, however subconsciously, to reflect prominent strains of thought present inside the company at the time. The declaration "Sears has everything" mirrored the true power and merchandise philosophy of its time. The 1981 "You can count on Sears" campaign corresponded with the budding realization that all was not lost, and that a franchise galvanized by trust was still there for reclaiming. During the early days of experimentation with a new look for the stores, Brennan liked the apparel department's "You're in for a change with Sears." Then, in the fall of 1982, he decided that something containing a larger and more definitive promise was in order.

The advertising agency Needham, Harper, and Steers—the same group that came up with McDonald's' "You deserve a break today"— was set to the creative task at a meeting Brennan held a few weeks after Joe Moran's funeral. Whereas McDonald's had managed to create an image in which "perception exceeds reality"—the hamburgers were not always good, and servers rarely sang in unison—Sears suffered from popular expectations that were difficult to satisfy. The new campaign was supposed to alter the perception while Brennan hammered out a new underlying reality. The result was "There's more for your life at Sears."

Everyone in senior management knew of the abiding respect Brennan had for the McDonald's organization. Early in his career, at a time when Ed Brennan thought that perhaps his personality and skills were better suited to running his own show, he almost left Sears to open his own McDonald's franchise. He eventually decided to see how far he could get with Sears instead, but he never stopped talking about the superior management of McDonald's. During the work of the creation of the new store, Brennan was often heard to wax eloquent about the pleasing uniformity of those hamburgers—edible "smile"-buttons—so many billions of which had been professionally served.

The television sets in the Wacker Room showed various examples of the new campaign as the catchy theme song blared at high volume. Images of futuristic Sears stores mingled with shots of Arnold Palmer and Cheryl Tiegs. After several renditions of the thirty- and sixty-second "More for your life" fugues, observers in the audience began to clap along with the refrain. In the reflected glow off the screen above the stage, Ed Brennan could be seen up front, swaying slightly and swinging his arms.

The applause was loud and sustained when Brennan was introduced. The clapping continued until he bowed his head in a way that always hushed a crowd. Brennan would still have a chance to address his managers at the major banquet planned for that evening, but he wanted to begin to prepare them.

"If you are tonight the way I was last night," he said, "then you will be very anxious for tomorrow to come. Then you'll have a chance to go yourself to our Store of the Future.

"We've accomplished a miracle. It's all come together in just ten weeks. It's not just a way of presenting goods. It's . . . it's an in-depth *analysis* of our business.

"Three years ago this day we were concerned that the fall of 1980 could be a disaster." Brennan reviewed the subsequent Power Plus 80 programs hammered out in Tucson, the decision to spend money into the void by increasing advertising, the creation of the Challenge Lines and Items, and the more traumatic and painful process of admitting after so many years at the top "that the world of retailing had done an end run on us."

"Over the years we became extremely reluctant to change. We didn't change our stores or the way our lines have been grouped. And as I said in 1980, and as you will see tomorrow, it can *never* be 1955 again."

The formal banquet thrown for the Store of the Future that evening was held at the grand old Chicago Club, the elite clubhouse for well-positioned Chicagoans of money and distinguished bloodline for over a century. As un-Sears-like as were the traditions of the Michigan Avenue institution, the club was still prominent in company chronicles. Some of the mid-1970s meetings Brennan attended as one of the aggressive young Turks of the Hay Committee occurred at the club. The reading room was where six years earlier Arthur Wood had informed Ed Telling that the mantle would be his, and where in April of 1980 Telling had hosted a reception to introduce Ed Brennan to the Chicago press. It was toward the bar at the Chicago Club that the despondent Dean Swift had kicked his Coke can after learning what had happened in the reading room between Wood and Telling. The third-floor dining room was where Gentleman Jim Button, having submitted to Ed Telling's and Joe Moran's subversion of his authority, raised his glass and uttered, "Here's to you, fellows," before he quit.

The hideous gilt-and-green banquet room with its ponderous chandeliers and oil paintings blackened by generations of cigar smoke was the scene of one of the General's more prophetic addresses, in March 1947. Amid his dissection of the burgeoning empire into self-contained territories, General Wood asked the assembled board members, officers, and senior executives, "Can a company grow too big? Will it become too unwieldy? Will it become a great bureaucracy? Will it get beyond control of its officers? The adage of the prize ring is still true," Wood answered himself. "The bigger they are, the harder they fall. The company is too vast and complicated today to be administered by any one man."

Brennan was the only one who appeared completely at ease amid the mountains of fresh seafood and the moribund elegance of cocktail hour that evening. Though many of the officers attempted to mingle, most of the Headquarters buyers and the sellers in from the Field tended to draw into separate drinking circles until the table assignments in the main dining room rearranged Field and Headquarters personnel into a more appropriate configuration.

Dinner would be steak. In fact, dinner at every single official Sears function since Brennan had returned the working feast to prominence invariably consisted of a variously embellished piece of steak. During the heaviest seasons of big meetings in the spring and late summer, the average top manager at Sears could eat steak four or five nights a week. Without a hint of irony or the most tenuous of connections' being made to the ever-present piece of red meat sitting in all its high-fat glory beneath all corporate dinner conversation, open-heart bypass surgery had lately become a popular subject of conversation. Henry Sutherland's bypass was only one in a large number of similar procedures performed on other executives. Former officers Jack Kelly and Gar Ingraham had had cardiac bypass operations performed while they were still actively employed, and the popular VP for public affairs, Gene Harmon, was just about to have his. There were even debates at the tables these days over whether the surgical teams at Chicago's Northwestern University Hospital, Rush-Presbyterian St. Luke's Medical Center, or the hospital up in Milwaukee that Jack Kelly had used were superior craftsmen. For decades, discussions of medical problems was proscribed by a tradition that held illness as a possible impediment to promotion, but bypass surgery was essentially a management tool for the modern era. Like steak.

"Why, look-ee there," said one Midwestern group manager in a boisterous, contrived country voice as he approached a table dominated by Chicago-based executives. The Field man leaned down as the steaks were being marched out of the kitchen to carefully examine a hard-boiled egg that was brimming with imported capers. He looked around the table with sardonic confusion: "Say! Any o' yoo boys know how come they got that egg all loaded down with peas?" The old soldier picked up his four-page menu with "There's More for Your Life at Sears" printed on the cover, and took his seat with great pleasure.

The next morning, buses converged outside the Vernon Hills Sears store several hours before the rest of the shopping center would come to life. The long, colorful hallways of the mall were empty, the rows of shops darkened like a carnival after closing time. The visitors were directed through the cool dawn toward a door at the side of the Store of the Future and they emerged blinking and disoriented in the new big-ticket appliance department.

As Headquarters executives began to subdivide the Field managers into seven tour groups, none of the out-of-towners seemed able to turn their heads from the gleaming washers and dryers positioned under carefully trained high-intensity spotlights. The appliances were silvery black, like some foreign racing car. "Somebody's made the goddamned white goods black," a visitor was heard to say.

The tour groups were supposed to travel to a rigid timetable between seven "stations" spaced throughout the new store. At each station, a buying-organization executive was to deliver a brief address about the new way of merchandising such as it would be in his portion of the Store of the Future.

But as the groups spread out, the silent, squinting tourists were drawn into corners by one glittering thing after another. Where there wasn't a shock of color or a stream of light, there was an unremitting configuration of goods stacked up and thrust forward like a feast. Row upon piled row of television sets—the "wall of eyes," as it was called—were arranged in the steel-gray-and-chrome electronics department. The sets were arrayed so that, as the average consuming eye began its natural and average movement from the upper left-hand corner to the right and then from top to bottom, it ended at the most expensive television set, which was replete with a remote-control device that did everything but open your beer. The older Field men smiled with pleasure at the wall of eyes, and at the video cassette recorders, microwave ovens, and even the trash cans that were arranged in a similar pattern. Many store-jockies of the old school believed that a customer would "trade herself up" to a better product if things were arranged as people read books, left to right and top to bottom, but now it was part of the store. After much consultation with data and experts, the planners of the new store found that the old wisdom happened to be one with science.

A delicately appointed jewelry-and-cosmetics department had been constructed at the entrance to the store from the mall. Above the refit-ted display was a riveting frieze made of backlit photographs of women called "American faces like yours." The welcoming faces were beautiful but unintimidating. The ladies appeared respectively nice, cool, con-fused, silly, quiet, experienced, outgoing, knowing, meek, vivacious, a bit mean, and the one on the end to the right looked as rich and eques-trian as any face out of *Town and Country* magazine, but even she seemed sort of pleasant at heart.

The store was as alight with gleaming colors as the stores the visitors ran were mired in beige and muted shades of gray. Segments of colorful carpet were aligned in a juxtaposition carefully designed for maximum stimulative effect. Things had been repackaged in colorful boxes that were keyed to nearby walls. Bright soft sculptures, including what ap-peared to be the lower half of a telephone lineman—outfitted from utility belt to toe by Sears—were on the wall above the shoe depart-ment. The quality of color and light changed from a bright-maroon rug in apparel to warm Santa Fe burnt-red tiles in kitchenware, so as to announce subliminally a shopper's passage from one new subregion of the store to another.

Brennan's determination to replace the blunderbuss approach to sell-ing with carefully sighted sniper rifles was evident everywhere. Thirty lines were missing from the new store. Where there were twelve models of hand-held "ghetto-blaster" cassette players in the old store, there were now seven players arranged in a way that still indicated Sears' national dominance of that product market. Every line was to be a Challenge Line, Brennan had said. Every display had to relay a sense that Sears, Roebuck is the biggest and best player in that particular business. The mountainous stacks of individual cans of motor oil in the automotive department were designed as a testament to a company that sold America forty million quarts of the stuff each year. The wall of car batteries included a huge Mercedes-Benz DieHard battery, not because the members of the Sears franchise owned many Mercedes-Benz cars, but because everyone in America had to know that when your car dies out on the highway, the Sears store less than fifteen minutes from just about any road in the country is *the* place to find your new battery. The

same strategy was evident in the blue-jean department, where the traditional Sears private-label jeans were joined by Levi's and Wranglers.
Sears would no longer be the place for everything, but it was most
certainly the place for jeans. The Merchandise Group had instantaneously become Levi Strauss' largest customer when the decision to carry
the product was made.

The famous Sears private brands, like Toughskins, DieHard, Roadhandler, and Craftsman, all thrived during the era of the Miller-Tydings Act,
the Depression-era legislation that allowed manufacturers to set a minimum selling price for the branded goods. All retailers had to honor the
price by law, so Sears circumvented the rule with considerable
creativity by growing its own brands. The Act was repealed in 1975, but
the spirit of the brands remained within the organization. Carrying
national brands ran counter to the populist commitment to small suppliers retained by many at Headquarters, but Brennan wanted "dominance" in the new store, and dominance in jeans meant Levi's.

Two hundred lines had been torn from the departments to which
powerful political and personal forces of the past had relegated them,
and many of the haphazard configurations of products that confused and
infuriated customers in a store like Hicksville had been adjusted.

The whole store had been reassembled so that everything was thought
out, cut to fit, and built in like the interior of an expensive sailboat.
Photography products were moved to an area where more sales assistance would be available. Office furniture was stationed near the furniture department. Telephones were together in a separate display, and
computers and electronic office products were now contiguous to other
electronic items.

The tour groups in the store were drawn from display to display along
the "racetrack" configuration Claude Ireson and his team had built by
the "strike zones" Claude had designed. The zones were scientifically
tuned areas where the bright-maroon carpets gave way to another, even
brighter color. The eye would be drawn to the strike zone unconsciously, to a Cheryl mannequin or an appliance illuminated by pin spots
designed by the best lighting man in the country. The zones were like
crosshairs aimed at shoppers as they traversed the store.

Claude Ireson knew which kinds of customers turned left when they
came off the mall and which ones turned right. He knew about sub-
conscious "levels of communication" by which the acquiring eye runs
first to the ceiling—Level One—and then to the very tops of the displays, Level Two. Claude had built hidden signals into the store that
would herd the shoppers along by force of their own instincts. It was not
unlike movement in the ant colonies and beehives Claude had often
pondered while studying the customers. The customers wouldn't know

why they stopped and made a decision at the exact spots where Claude laid his focal traps and pin-spot targets any more than an ant or a bee understood such things, but Claude knew.

Ireson had learned that the average Sears shopper was a 64.8-inch-high variety of female, so the display fixtures in the new store were scaled up in some cases and down in others. The ceilings had been dropped three feet below the rest of the store in the furniture department, because research indicated that the resulting sense of intimacy was conducive to good shopping. Ireson searched far and wide for new mannequins to wear the headbands and aerobics outfits he wanted under the spotlights in his strike zones, but nothing seemed right. He finally found a small company that had developed a production process that involved dipping people—including small children—into a pliable material and creating dummies so life-like that some of the people on the tour that early morning thought they looked like human beings frozen into a state of suspended animation.

"Jesus, Claude," somebody said to Ireson as they stood before a rigid child.

"We might have taken this one too far," said Bob Brothers, Ireson's right-hand man in the facilities-planning department.

Claude "understood" the Brennan reformation as fully as any man in the coterie. He'd begun his redressing of the store in 1982, when he took a group of his most creative design staffers to a resort near Chicago and told them to start dreaming. Schools of thought emerged, promoting various styles for a new design—post-modernists argued for a high-tech look for the total store and all displays, while traditionalists wanted something warmer in reaction to the years of masculine austerity.

Brennan told them to shop the competition. If a competitor had a better way of presenting the merchandise, they were to steal it. When a newly designed K mart opened in Indianapolis, a facilities-planning team was dispatched immediately to check it out. They attended numerous conferences on store planning, hired outside consultants specializing in everything from the relative anthropomorphism of mannequins to the mass psychology of color.

In a relatively short time, Ireson managed to design a prototype store that was modern and sleek without being offensive to the tastes of the great middle of the franchise. The best science of store design money could buy existed under the surface of the Store of the Future, but at a deeper and more profound level, Claude had managed to model the whole thing upon Ed Brennan's vision of how the one big store of Sears should be organized, peopled, and controlled.

Within a year, the Stores of the Future that Brennan planned to spread across the Republic as new stores or "retrofits" would all be "plan-o-grammed." Each high-tech cube-shaped bin, each back-wall display, each strike zone would be so carefully mapped that a buyer would know the exact dimension of the hole he or she was to fill in the store. If a buyer bought too wide a range of goods to portray the required aura of dominance, or bought too much to fit in the assigned rack or bin, then that buyer would fail. The new store would end forever the days of buyers' purchasing a wide array of manufactured goods and then haggling with up to a thousand storekeepers and managers in their efforts to sell their wares. The days of a departmental aesthetic's arising from a constant series of acceptances and rejections by store managers would end.

"The environment in which merchandise is housed and the merchandising of the environment have to be one," Brennan had stated. "This is the Store of the Future."

Eric Saunders had the presentation at his station behind the prototype checkout counter down to several seconds less than his allotted time. After a great deal of study and debate over the proper shape and position of the checkout islands, it was decided that a battleship configuration would provide the greatest assistance to shoppers with packages, as well as cool some of the emotional contagion that had turned the cash-register lines into combat zones in recent times.

In October of 1982, Brennan had increased the pressure on Eric and his operating specialists to come up with new technological ideas, and after a long series of meetings with both IBM and the "data terminal" makers at NCR, Saunders threw the issue back to Brennan by announcing that the entire computerized checkout system in the stores should be scrapped. He proposed a new system that would not only speed up the "point of sale" process, but would also allow sudden price changes to be programmed into the chain at a more central level. Both IBM and NCR had agreed to cooperate with stepped-up production of new hardware so that the system could be installed in some stores during 1983. The only hitch was that the project would cost $25 million.

"I guess we'll have to move the budget around a little," Brennan commented before giving the go-ahead.

Eric demonstrated an example of his new "intelligent" cash registers for the Field visitors at Vernon Hills. He explained that besides cutting down the transaction time, they did an instant credit check and automatically alerted a stock clerk to pull larger items from inventory and have them waiting in a special parking spot at the side of the store before the customers arrived. The optical price-scanners actually worked, and, best of all, price changes were programmed into the system from above, so the inevitable dog-eared computer printouts were relegated to the ash heap—along with any residual control of prices at the grass roots.

Eric said he expected to have the new system installed in 478 stores, accounting for 87 percent of the company's volume, by the 1983 Christmas rush. Saunders laconically handed everyone a sample sales stub as a souvenir of the day, then leaned his hip against the battleship island, crossed his arms, and waited for the next group to arrive.

Toward the end of the formal tours, Ed Brennan appeared at the top of the escalator leading to the second floor, wearing a beautiful three-piece suit and a tranquil half-smile. No one but the officers flanked at his side and a few of the buyers who'd borne the brunt of his wrath could have known how close to the wire the final ordering of the store had come, or that late at night just a day earlier Brennan had become so enraged with the state of the kids'-clothing department that he'd ordered the whole thing torn to shreds. Brennan looked unusually healthy and glowingly tanned, like some youthful candidates for higher political office ready to hit the campaign trail.

From the moment a visitor stepped onto the escalator, he had only a few seconds to decide on an appropriate facial expression.

Brennan stood at the top staring at each Field man in turn. He allowed his officers to accept the appropriate comments offered by the managers as they were delivered before him by the escalator, while he concentrated on the faces of those at the bottom.

"It's ten years too late," more than a few of the visitors said.

"Twenty years too late," one of the officers would reply.

Field attendees dispersed and mingled among the early-morning shoppers before the buses were scheduled to leave. After a short time, they began to coalesce again into small groups to talk quietly with those who could be trusted.

It really was a hell of a good-looking store, a store nearly fit to compete with the rampaging corporate modernism that had turned the sixty-eighth floor into a place haunted by strangers in from the coasts. It was a store that might cool the fury of shoppers, which had so troubled them all in recent years, and it looked like a store that could make a group or store manager look pretty good on the bottom line too. The way they'd figured out how to mark everything and rewrite the display signs so that any moron could understand what was being sold would certainly take some of the pressure off the sales personnel, and it wasn't lost on the Field managers that the new store could be run by only a handful of full-time employees.

Though the store was the sort of thing the Field could be proud of, it was still a Headquarters store. Everyone in the company with more than eight years under his belt had grown up knowing nothing if not that Chicago didn't know jack shit about a store. Now they'd gone and built themselves a store—and a pretty fair one at that. Brennan had sent the buyers out to wallow in the lowly day-to-day reality of the store, just as the Field always said they would never do—but they'd returned to help create a store full of tricks and mirrors, and the whole kit and caboodle was wired up to the Tower. This bright place full of warm lights, black washing machines, and mannequins that looked like live children dipped in liquid cellophane was a great deal more than a suggested grouping of goods and some flashy new fixtures from which Field managers could pick and choose and decorate their stores accordingly. It was the Store of the Future, the "one big store" of Brennan's heart and mind made real.

It was the consummate exercise in what the old pugilist-king of the Southwest, Al Davies, used to call "superimposure" from Parent. There was something in this new store that was meant to seize them up, to sort of laminate them as Searsmen and then arrange them under a spotlight in a preordained position like those poor frozen kids. It meant that soon they would be machine-like "implementors" instead of free merchants and men.

Everyone viewing the store had come to work for a company sanctified by a system of individual autonomy and local sovereignty that was predicated on the way one old man thought America was supposed to be. There wasn't even a company organizational chart or an official job description in the old days, for fear the documents might impinge on personal initiative or individual growth.

Brennan had tried hard to prepare the Field managers during the previous day of intimate corporate planning revelations and fine, flinty wine at the Chicago Club. "It's *not* control," he'd declared. "It's not control and it's not centralization. It's consistency. *Please,* be sure that your minds are open to this. This thing is you. It's you folks in the territories, and you folks in the Headquarters, all working together now. If we are wrong in this, let's be wrong together. If we are right, then, by *God,* the world is our oyster."

Bill Bass, the old soldier himself, had explained it to them like this: "The store is how you buy the goods, how it's assorted, and the manner in which it is moved to your stores. It's how goods are received, marked, and moved to the floor. It's how the goods are presented, where they're presented, how they are sold, advertised, and replenished."

The new store, in short, was everything the people used to be.

Representatives from eighty Sears sources were invited to Chicago a few weeks later to see the future. Before their tour of Vernon Hills the visitors heard an address by Joe Batogowski entitled "The Resource of the Future." There was even a banquet over at the Drake Hotel and the presentation of awards to selected suppliers for longevity, innovation, and one for being Sears' "source of the year."

Though less than 1 percent of the sources received the special treatment, the managers of a great number of the manufacturers that had survived the rough times were generally at peace in their relationship with Sears in 1983. The Merchant seemed far less predatory than it had during the early days of Joe Moran. The microeconomic plague dubbed "the Sears recession" by *The Wall Street Journal* in 1979 had lasted in its most harrowing form for over three years, altering in its persistence the nature of daily life from shoemaking villages in Maine to ill-begotten electronics assembly parts in Mexico. Suppliers tried to fill the huge gaps left by contracting orders from Sears, but years of expansion directed from buying offices in Chicago left productive capacities far beyond the levels of any other mass retailer's needs.

Ed Telling traveled out to a screwdriver factory in Colorado during the middle of the upheavals to hear the chief executive of the company complain that he'd built a new plant just to supply more screwdrivers to Sears, but Sears was suddenly ordering fewer screwdrivers. Telling observed that Sears already owned 40 percent of the screwdriver market in America, and that bumping that market share up over 50 percent was going to be a hell of a task. "It's your money," Telling said, "but I don't think I woulda built that new building if I were you."

"Your own buyers *told* me to build it," the manager said.

"Oh . . . well," Telling managed. "Now, that's another game."

During the late 1970s and the beginning of the 1980s, as plant closings eliminated some four million American manufacturing jobs, little places like Sardis, Mississippi, almost rolled over and died because someone in the Sears Tower yanked the plug. The workers who produced Sears' once-innovative injection-formed polypropylene luggage at the Sardis plant used to take their families up to the old Memphis Sears store to show how their suitcases lined Department 614 in the store. A Sears luggage-buyer gave the little factory $11.5 million worth of business in

1976, but by 1980 orders had halved. Then the suitcases suddenly disappeared from the store in Memphis, just a few months before the luggage plant and the jobs went the same way.

Since luggage was the only thing going in Sardis, men sat around in the doorways of the dusty streets during the meanest days of the more generalized recession that followed, and a lot of them took to daytime drinking. There was bad feeling among the old hands in Sardis toward Sears, Roebuck, a company many of them believed was run out of an old store in downtown Memphis.

Across the river, in the Delta town of Forrest City, Arkansas, the Sears television supplier, located in a sprawling complex just a few hundred yards from the only highway cloverleaf in the state, was now owned and operated by Japanese managers from the Sanyo Corporation. Sears televisions had been produced, from the beginning of their mass distribution, by Warwick Electronics, a company the buyers in Chicago had drawn together and eventually arranged to move to the facility in Forrest City during the mid-1970s. Few people ever knew that Warwick was one of the largest producers of televisions in the world, though owners of the Sears sets knew that the sets rarely worked. On the line in Forrest City, they used to say that five Warwick televisions came back for every four they shipped out.

The buyers had already bullied the Whirlpool Corporation into taking over Warwick (just as the Sears-dominated manufacturer Roper was "convinced" to try running the Sardis Luggage Company before it shut down). But Whirlpool's managers couldn't do a thing with Warwick, so Sears considered killing off the largest employer in eastern Arkansas.

Then they hit on the idea of "asking" the Sanyo Electric Company of Osaka, Japan, to try to turn Warwick around. After the deal was struck, twenty-four Japanese managers came in 1977 to Forrest City, led by a Japanese fellow who drove a custom-made red sports car and spoke perfect English because he'd worked his way through an American college as a houseboy for the columnist Hedda Hopper. The Sanyo team completely revivified the plant. They imported their own microchip-laden circuit boards, and sent hard-bitten Warwick line foremen to Japan to learn more sensitive management techniques. The Japanese managers were even allowed into the all-white country club, not long after the name of the street heading to the cloverleaf was changed from Warwick Road to Sanyo Road.

During 1983, Sears would do nearly $250 million worth of business with the Japanese television makers in Arkansas, and enough other business with the Sanyo plants in Japan to render Sanyo the fifth-largest supplier on the secret source list kept in a thick brown folder on the forty-fourth floor. Included among the executives invited to see the future in Chicago during the spring was the leader of Sanyo, a considerable international corporation in its own right. Mr. Kaoru Iue once described the relationship of the two companies to the executive with the red sports car during the recession times in 1981: "We must think of Sears as a god," Iue said. "Our god."

In place of the network of thousands of small suppliers, that had been built before Ed Telling's time as chairman, purchases had come to be concentrated among fewer and far more powerful suppliers. Sardis Luggage Companies fell away in favor of the Sanyos in all departments. It was rather similar to what Ed Telling dreamed might happen to the banks.

Alongside the consolidation of others, the era of Sears' ownership of manufacturers was also coming to an end. In 1954, Sears owned all or part of fifty-nine manufacturing enterprises. By 1968, the number was down to thirty-one, and by 1983 the policy of reducing factory ownership below a 50-percent interest in any company had reduced significant Sears financial interest in all but five of its suppliers.

The buyers had also been told that Sears no longer wanted all of any company's business. If this meant opening up competition among sources, that was now fine.

"Go beyond the Sears cocoon," Joe Batogowski told the buyers now. "A long-term relationship doesn't mean a company *deserves* our business. Open it up. Every order should have competition." Though the Whirlpool Corporation still sold Sears a billion dollars' worth of household machinery during the year, one third of Sears' refrigerator orders now went to White Consolidated, an arch-competitor of the company pulled together by the buyers of old.

For several months before their tour of the new store, suppliers had been hearing stories about marathon meetings in the Tower, about all-night stints out at the prototype store. Even as they were escorted out to Vernon Hills, there were disquieting rumors that a massive reshuffling of lines, purviews, job titles, and consequently phone numbers and lengthy working relationships was now in the offing. Out at Vernon Hills, executives from the big suppliers saw that some departments they serviced were gone altogether and others had been merged together. The general reaction to the new store was generally positive among the representatives from the factories, but most of them hoped that the Store of the Future marked a resting point for the company they'd once considered much too big to change.

Yet another spring evening of marbled beef, fêting, and feasting over at the Drake. This time, however, a relatively small and elite crew had been summoned to a special awards dinner: just the Merchandise Group officers, the thirty-four heads of the remaining buying departments, and the winners of the 1982 Chairman's Challenge Cup for outstanding performances by buying, Field, and international units.

On heavily textured, parchment-like stock, an eight-page combination program, list of attendees, and menu had been printed in elegant brown script and fastened together by a twisted chocolate-brown cord complete with tassle.

The awards dinner was to begin in the Grand Ballroom of the Drake at the normal feasting hour of 6:00 P.M.. A bus left from the Franklin Street side of the Tower at 5:00 P.M.; by 5:15, the consumption of liquor and fresh oysters had begun in the Walton Room. By 5:30, the required persiflage and niceties had been exchanged across the generational divide, and the room cleaved into a dichotomy between youth and experience that had become ever more evident in recent months. There was a time when the diplomatic gestures at the beginning of a Sears banquet were extended across geographical lines, departmental lines, and the gulfs between Parent and Field and staff and line, but lately you could feel everywhere that the salient difference was between the young tigers and the vets who'd made the ERIP cut by just a couple of years.

Wayne Holsinger was decompressing in the company of a small group of executives "of his vintage." "Old guys," as Wayne called them, who wore a few more pinholes and traces of old glue on their lapels from a long history of name tags. Due to consolidation, attrition, and Holsinger's own staying power, Wayne was now the vice-president of a $6-billion buying group that included cosmetics, jewelry, accessories, and all manner of apparel. He ran his buying operation from a corner office on the eleventh floor of the Tower that was so crammed with awards and mementos of a life of wandering through factories that it looked·like a pirates' den. There were handmade chests he'd picked up in Korea and numerous Oriental knickknacks he'd collected back when brass was cheap.*

This evening Wayne spoke to some of the old guys about his recent buying trip in China. "They'd never seen an order like one o' ours," he said. "You'd sit around a table with eight or nine people and you couldn't tell who the boss was. And the thing is, they don't want to make money;

---

*One tale of the previous generation of Searsmen set loose in foreign markets was about a prominent buyer who was taken to an opulent·summer palace kept by one of the large Japanese manufacturing corporations. Before a lavish feast, the chairman of the host firm bowed deeply and asked the buyer if he'd ever been to Japan before. "Thirty-five times," crowed the Searsman, "but I never landed."

they just want people to work. And they used to be the real merchants too. You know, way back, they were the originals. Then they got squished down." The circle Wayne addressed included the tall one-time apostle in charge of hardware, Bob Thompson, and the head of the television and home-electronics buyers, Danny Danhauer, a character whose father-in-law, the legendary Frank Schell, was the merchant-philosopher who taught Joe Moran.

M. E. "Burk" Burkholder, the smiling broad-faced man who ran the Midwestern Territory, was welcomed into the circle. Though he was one of the last true soldiers of the Field, Burky felt more comfortable in the corner of the Walton Room with the Headquarters veterans.

Burkholder was glad he'd decided to pass up the retirement program most of his contemporaries had accepted at the end of 1980, even though he'd been the first leader of a Sears territory to be denied a seat on the board of directors. The retail contraction in the Midwest had been particularly painful for Burkholder. After closing down just one store during his first thirty-one years with Sears, he'd closed some forty-five stores since he'd left the Far West for Chicago.

Burkholder always said that a manager has to keep negative thoughts out of his head, because a negative thought will poison you in a minute, but he still couldn't help resenting some of the sales figures that were demanded of his Field managers by Ed Brennan's vaunted merchandise-planning system. Though the Plan was supposed to be a fluid system of bargains that melded Field and Headquarters into a whole, the sales goals were in fact not open to haggling. After receiving 16-percent sales-increase goals from above during one recent review period, Burk had spent many anxious days in front of the damned computer in his office wondering how to wring a 16-percent sales increase out of places in Michigan where 22 percent of the working people were unemployed.

But, all in all, Burk wasn't one to complain—especially since you could still get together and have a drink with some of the other old guys who felt like they'd been not so much sidetracked as rerouted into a strange new town. In this new place, young tigers leapfrogged over them without the historical requisite of experience or the years of wandering across the map. The glandular power of youth seemed to have replaced the quiet wisdom of age; discipline had replaced entrepreneurialism; planning and science had replaced the legendary Searsman's instincts. Around March of 1983, the term "corporate culture" entered the company vocabulary via popular business literature and replaced the much older term "pride."

The company was young again under Ed Brennan. The older guys could be honorary members of the new via a particularly ferocious display of loyalty to the new faces and terms but ultimately, with their ponderous John Wayne verbal deliveries, the vets were still considered best suited to another time.

Many of the stories the young guys told were at the expense of the veterans. The former chairman Arthur Wood was given a tour of the Store of the Future, and at one point he asked what "feathering a rack" of clothes meant. The old patrician actually asked the meaning of a basic modern retailing term that refers to separating hangers on a rack for aesthetic effect. Some of the younger managers made fun of the way Wayne Holsinger said "to be quite frankly" and "da rag bid-nis," and everybody got a big kick out of the picture in *Sears Today* of Wayne holding the microphone suggestively in front of Miss Teenage America. It was right out of the Sears world of 1955.

Several of the younger officers in the Merchant felt that the presence of the seasoned managers was clogging up access to the better jobs. One of the top hardware men had recently left to join Bernie Brennan (and, lately, Ira Quint—as well as several other ex-Searsmen) over at Montgomery Ward. If Bob Thompson had only thrown in the towel and retired, the talented hardware man would have had Thompson's job and stayed. Since life seemed to be moving a bit too rapidly for some of the smiling Willy Lomans who still peopled corners of the organization, then maybe they ought to think about throwing in the towel.

Those who had trouble "learning the new language" quickly enough were called "cynics." "There may be a few cynics left," Brennan had said during one recent speech. "I imagine in any organization you always have a few. I don't know of any, but there may be some." Those who had trouble conforming to the new systems were occasionally called "very entrepreneurial guys," and those who bucked it openly were considered "intellectually dishonest." The company had changed, and those who wanted to come along for the ride were expected to think about change "in a very objective way." This was all part of the meaning of 1983—the Growth Year—and if it had been left up to some of the younger tigers, a large number of the veterans would already be gone. But the question of what was to be done with some of the executives saddled with images of torpor and obsolescence was one of the few things that caused Ed Brennan to exhibit ambivalence.

Brennan had personally protected more than a few of the veterans because of his deep respect for the things they knew and remembered about buying and selling. He still wanted the old guys there, for reasons connected to their hold on the company past, for their capacity for good cheer, and even for the way that they all could fall into that good old Sears, Roebuck twang after a few drinks—even if Brennan had never discovered the voice himself. Brennan wanted them near him for reasons of romance and out of respect for household gods that had been part of his life for as long as he could remember.

He would note with understanding that "discipline wasn't necessary after World War II." He would curtail critical commentary on past officers by his young managers: "Don't oversimplify the problems of Sears by looking back at specific individuals," he'd say. "It's not fair." The vets had grown up in a world of what Brennan called *perceived* autonomy—it was always more perception than reality, as far as he was concerned. It was an appropriate perception for a time when society itself was decentralized and communications had yet to link the global village. But those were the days of 10-percent margins instead of 4 percent.

An aspect of company history most lifers conveniently ignored, Brennan thought, was that time really did pass people by. There was the man who ran Department 32, farm implements, who swore up and down that horses and only horses would forever move American farmers across their fields. There was a legendary men's-clothing buyer named Whiz Williams, who ended up running the little store for the employees at the West Side Headquarters after a while. The guy was loaded down with Sears stock from the old days and he drove around in a fine La Salle automobile, but he drove to work at the employee store because the company, through no fault of old Whiz's had outgrown him.

The gleaming plan-o-grammed fixtures of the Store of the Future were just part of the general replacement of old imagery. Everything was being realigned and redesigned like the store—even the memory of Joe Moran had been recast in the image of the new.

"I don't want him to be forgotten," Ed Telling declared after the unveiling of Brennan's store. "Much of what's going on is due to Joe Moran and his courage." Claude Ireson contended often that many of the organizational concepts he'd integrated into his design for the Store of the Future came from things he'd learned from Joe Moran. When Ed Brennan spoke of Joe Moran, his voice thickened with emotion. "Joe was a paratrooper," Brennan said one day. "He was of that last generation."

During the Challenge Cup dinner, after cocktail time at the Drake, Henry Sunderland decided to say thanks to the chief organizer of the feast. Henry went to the microphone and said, "Where's Frank Tuma?"

"Everywhere!" shouted one of the veteran merchandise managers. The entire room descended into over a minute of noisy laughter and table pounding, while Tuma sat by stonily. Frank knew he still worked among his colleagues as a constant reminder of the period of terror, back when his name on a letter saying that five hundred buyers should be standing on the steps on the Wacker Drive side of the Tower for a photo meant that the next morning there would indeed be five hundred buyers standing there—no questions asked. Joe Batogowski had tried to help Tuma rehabilitate his image as spy for Joe Moran. Bato had talked Frank into dressing up as Santa Claus the previous Christmas, and that helped a bit, but in many more ways than his own personal image with his colleagues, Frank Tuma had yet to recover from the loss of his mentor.

All of the collected white papers were housed now in a large file cabinet just outside Tuma's immaculately ordered office on the forty-third floor. Tuma saved all of the written work, as Moran had once asked of him, and he was in the process of integrating the hundreds of epigrams and oaths he'd recorded in hopes of editing the work together into something that could be published at the time of the company's one hundredth anniversary in 1986. His amanuensis and hatchet man in life, Frank had become Joe's hagiographer in death. The secretaries on the forty-third floor called the locked cabinet outside Tuma's office "the memorial drawer."

In one of the 1979 epistles housed in the memorial drawer, Joe had declared himself "boy-guide, devil's advocate, keep-to-the-point moderator, and *unifier.*" He had failed at all of this, and it was acknowledged among the managers now that he had almost led the company past the point of no return. It was all right to openly remember the awful times of the late 1970s now—Batogowski brought it up regularly and told of his time running between the offices of Wurmstedt and Moran. Brennan said that he sorely missed the heady conceptual discussions he'd shared with Joe Moran, but he now harbored and expressed few illusions about Joe's failure to understand the "total standpoint" of something as futuristic as the new store.

Joe Moran hadn't turned out to be the unifier he wanted to be, and there was a powerful strain in the apocrypha of the Merchant in 1983 indicating that his lasting image would include this. Not unlike the posthumous images of Robespierre, Marat, and the other radicals of the Mountain in the hands of the Thermidorean heirs to the revolution in France, he would be remembered, it appeared, as a brilliant but demagogic pamphleteer, as an intellectual bully, and the promulgator of a purge that went too far. He was spoken of as a well-meaning representative of the lost generation, who in the end retired far away to allow the true Unifier to rise in his absence, all blameless and Galahad-white. At other times Joe would be remembered like the Gipper, a late-lamented figure for whom even harder labor was called for.

But whether or not Tuma would be allowed to publish his book of Joe for the 1986 Centennial, it seemed that Moran would be remembered despite all revisionism as a gifted writer. Like his beloved Cavaliers, he'd ended up a court poet. This part he would have liked.

Since once again the Eastern Territory dominated the Field side of the Challenge Cup awards, the dinner menu included special *Philadelphia* Bookbinder's Snapper Soup, Terrine of *Eastern New York* Seafood, and *Eastern* Sirloin Steak. As the "Action Year Key Lime Torte with Cranberry Couli" was distributed, the electronic torchlights were fired up again. The room lights went down and thirteen computerized slide projectors went into action.

On the screen in the front of the room appeared moving images of a poker game, the complex audiovisual system showing the hands above a table moving out and back as they played the game. Over the speaker system, the popular song "The Gambler," played at high volume. As Kenny Rogers told his tale of meeting a gambler on "a warm summer's evening, on a train bound for nowhere," the screen continued to coruscate with images of the game.

"Son," the singer heard the gambler claim, "I've made a life out of readin' people's faces, and knowin' what their cards were by the way they held their eyes. . . . If you're gonna play the game," the gambler warned, "Boy, you gotta learn to play it right."

When the lights went back on, Brennan walked slowly to the microphone and began to recite slowly the song's chorus—

> You got to know when to hold 'em,
> Know when to fold 'em,
> Know when to walk away,

—and now he paused to smile—

> And know when to run.
> You never count your money
> When you're sittin' at the table.
> They'll be time enough for countin'
> When the dealin' is done.

With his swirling hands and a voice slow and narcotic after the blaring sound and light, Brennan caused the song to join the other symbols, flags, phrases, and chants as an anthem. Everyone in the room that night at the Drake was perfectly capable of extending the metaphors, and afterward, in many conversations over drinks, many of them did.

You really did have to know when to fold 'em. The days of being too proud and mighty ever to back down, ever to run from a blighted store or a misbegotten line of goods or a bad decision, were over now. The days of sitting around counting up the money as of old were gone too. Once out of aces, the company had found its seat around the table again, and only the wiliest pros were welcome. "If you're gonna play the game, boy, you gotta learn to play it right."

The company had played foolishly down to its last few chips, and none of the men doubted the identity of the gambler with the brilliantly adorned scarlet linings on the backs of his vests who'd then approached the table.

Only at the upper reaches of the company were executives beginning, in the wake of the new store, to understand how specifically everything about the merchandise company now derived from Ed Brennan's hand. A buyer might still be left to wonder how to fill those plan-o-grams, waterfall racks, and Plexiglas bins, but the members of the inner circle knew that a powerful aesthetic that was once created from the input of thousands of people now sprang from the mind of one man.

This new store went beyond the reification of Brennan's philosophy of retailing. It harked backed to the Rousseauian "divine plan" that Ed Telling had once dismissed in favor of something a bit less centralized and monolithic in his 1979 address at Illinois Wesleyan. The Store of the Future in concert with the merchandise planning mechanism—the Plan—constituted an entire, enclosed system.

The Plan brilliantly harnessed the natural optimism and competitiveness of every good retailer. It began with Brennan's challenge, was passed down to the store, and then it came back up again. It girded the entire year—the merchants began the process of goal-setting in the Tower in February and the cycle ended in December. Buyers and sellers were "challenged," but that challenge was balanced by "discipline" and "accountability." Any exercise of individual power had a consequence. If you lay off too many workers in a store, the shelves will be empty.

Below was the plan-o-grammed store and above there was Brennan. The system dovetailed so seamlessly that it served to connect old and new, Field and Parent, buyer and seller, anarchy and order, freedom and control.

The Merchant now resembled a charismatic state, one in which the leader promised not just a sense of well-being but a chance to become psychologically dependent again, as one was before, as a child. All you had to do was repeat the lines, "make" the Plan, and all of that anxious political haggling and bad gambling would be done away with. There would be more for your life. If you just watched the gambler's hand, all would be revealed.

Other big companies in 1983 were responding to criticism of their managements during the early 1980s by creating "entrepreneurial venture teams" and "quality circles" so as to reinstill a sort of grass-roots populist spirit of the sort that had characterized Sears for almost a century. But Sears had never conformed to outside ideas of good business management before. Back when Alfred Sloan was breaking the powerful divisions of General Motors in the name of "good centralization," Sears was creating city-states, baronies, and kingdoms so powerful that they possessed the resources and will to wage war.

Brennan's Merchant, the believers would argue, was far more entrepreneurial than Sears had ever been. Cleansed of fractious, internal entrepreneurialism, the big store could now itself be as wily as an old riverboat gambler.

When the music stopped, Brennan handed the Challenge Cup for "outstanding retail-group sales performance" to Ralph Fiorelli, the powerful manager of the New York group of big stores.

"If somebody wrote in *The New York Times* that Ed Brennan walked across Lake Michigan," Fiorelli said, "the people of the New York group would believe that!"

There was loud applause.

Sycophancy was loose in the organization that spring, to be sure, but there was in fact a lot less of the groveling sort of brown-nosing found in a far less Hobbesian or charismatic organization than Sears. There was little doubt that much of the ritual—the entourage, the automobile caravans, the liturgical oratory, the opulent dinners, and the songs—was designed to concentrate attention on him, but most of the members of Brennan's new team would argue that this was because the human and technical systems that made up an organization like Sears appeared to Ed Brennan's mind as something close to a manageable whole.

Most of the young tigers who really understood and believed in the new ways were particularly bright young men, the sort who might have left to go out on their own in the old company rather than waiting twenty-five years for a turn at the top. All of them had considered themselves better merchants and managers than almost anyone else they'd ever worked for—but then they'd come across Ed Brennan, and in his intricate vision they'd found a leader.

Numerous executives in their fifties had indeed been "squished down" like so many of the businessmen Wayne Holsinger met in China, but a lot of the veterans had to admit that Ed Brennan was probably the greatest merchant in the history of the company. Maybe the greatest merchant in the world.

People like Wayne Holsinger, Burk Burkholder, and even Brennan's point man for the field, Bill Bass, were Sears survivors. They'd been too much a part of the bitterness and the "craziness" of recent years to be scared into line. But they were still on board, in part because they wanted to be there when the ship finally turned. They wanted to see if Eddie Brennan could make real what they knew he had in mind.

"Sears really couldn't afford the luxury of having a couple of thousand entrepreneurs anymore," Holsinger said of the changes. "The fact is, Brennan gave this company a kick in the ass and saved it."

"We couldn't afford our own entrepreneurialism," agreed the old hardware apostle, Bob Thompson.

"Eddie Brennan saved our bacon," said Burk Burkholder as he watched the Challenge Cup winners receive their silver cups. "He's the best all-around merchant I've ever seen. If you tote up general sensitivity, dedication, a love and feel for the goods, an ability to sell goods for good profit, and an ability to stand on his feet and simply light a fire in the people around him—the man is like no one I've ever seen."

Burky hadn't told the others yet, but he'd decided that the Eastern sirloin steak with Béarnaise sauce he'd just consumed would be his last piece of meat on the company. In a couple of days he was going to call up Brennan and fold his hand.

Burk Burkholder was born on the 4th of July in 1924, joined up with Sears on Flag Day in 1948, and became an officer of the company on Veterans' Day—November 11, 1979. The way Burkholder figured it, he'd experienced the last two or three years as an honored visitor from another generation, a witness to the acts of two of the company's only great builders since the General. He'd stayed long enough to help put together the gleaming new monument of a Sears store that was connected to the damned computer screen in his office. But after thirty-five years there were only so many cocktail-time rhapsodies you could share in the corner with the other vets. Burk figured he'd been short-changed a few times by Sears, but, then, he'd short-changed the company a few times too. He figured they were now "dead even," and, like the gambler says in the song, "You've got to know when to fold 'em and know when to walk away."

CHAPTER 20

The Flow

|———————————————|

By the middle of 1983 the outsider Rod Hills had effectively transcended his role as baron of the smallest business group and become Sears, Roebuck's secretary of state. Often in the company of Ed Telling, Hills had careened about the world in fee to Sears, all in an effort, he said, "to take something relentlessly Midwestern and thrust it upon the world." Hills sought to cosmopolitanize Sears both technically and conceptually. The institution was plainly too powerful and important not to be at large in the world, too deft and strong to remain encased within parochial traditions.

In an effort to open their eyes, Rod took Telling, Phil Purcell, and Stretch Gardiner to meet some powerful business and governmental contacts in the Middle East. He escorted Telling, Ed Brennan, Purcell, and each of their wives on a nine-day whirlwind tour of the Far East, to parts of the world none of the senior Searsmen had ever seen. They traveled in a late-imperial style that was in precise counterpoint to traditional Sears standards for appropriate executive opulence. The tour of Japan included all of the ceremonial trappings. In Jakarta, they were hosted by the Indonesian prime minister, and the entourage was received with similar pomp in Hong Kong and Kuala Lumpur.

Telling was a good sport about all the traveling. He'd managed to remain true to his pledge upon becoming chairman, never again to wake up in the spot in hell called a Holiday Inn, but his escapades with Rod Hills several times took him so far away from home that he had to violate his pledge always to make it home for dinner. On the way back from the Far East, Rod booked the Sears party into the sumptuous Hawaiian Resort at Mauna Kea, but Telling hated the tropical paradise and thought he heard rats in his room at night. Hills believed the regal trips abroad were essential to Sears' entrance into the international trade and other such businesses, because by their nature these enterprises involved contacts, connections, conduits, and partnerships. Consequently, he squired Telling back to the Middle East more than once and to Europe on several occasions.

Hills loved playing Ed Telling's "alter ego"—that was his own term for it. He knew from his long talks with Telling that the chairman was mesmerized by the idea of catapulting his now aggressive, now unpredictable and widely feared American corporation onto exotic beachheads. In the short time he had left, Telling had decided that he and Rod Hills—known by now as "Hot Rod" throughout the executive floors of the Tower—would assemble the basis of a *world* institution called Sears. Numerous trade experts agreed that if any American company could trade a wide enough range of goods and move with enough force to stick it to the Japanese masters of the trading arts, that company was probably Sears. All that was needed was the right deal. The task had to be accomplished quickly—"surgically quick," as Rod said—and it had to be done on a scale emblematic of Sears' size and power. Thus, lined up one after another before Ed Telling from the beginning of 1982, Rod Hills had dutifully arranged "the best-lookin' flow of deals the world has ever seen."

Hills was convinced that Sears should only consider going global in the company of partners. His strategy called not for pure world venturing but for "joint venturing" with companies big enough to add power, different enough to add more value to deals, and bold enough to help share the considerable downside risk.

The trip to Kuwait and several other petroleum-exporting nations occurred as a result of Hills' casual query to Telling during one of their discussions. Rod asked whether the chairman might be interested in joining forces with the stolid straight-shooters of Chevron, the former Standard Oil Company of California. Hills said that the combination of Chevron's oil-trading business, Sears' web of international manufacturing contacts, and the twinned expertise and financial power of the two $30-or-so-billion companies could serve to create an all-American trading entity capable of doing battle with the Japanese trading Goliaths.

"Sears-Chevron," Telling said with pleasure. Telling toyed with the physical imagery. He arranged the Sears logo so it nestled into the red, white, and blue V of the oil company's famous symbol. The combination evoked the Great American Company that had so captivated the chairman during the first three years of his tenure.

Not long after Telling delivered the anti-regulatory Economics Club speech Hills had written, Rod escorted Telling and Phil Purcell to a meeting in San Francisco with Chevron CEO George Keller. Hills' wife, Carla, was the only woman on the board of Chevron, and Rod had worked closely with the company during his dealings in the Middle East over the years. The Chevron senior executives were all old friends, and George Keller even turned out to be a card-carrying member of the franchise, a Sears, Roebuck shopper from way back. Keller was obviously quite taken with Telling's proposal of a Sears/Chevron Great American combine. With the increasing sophistication of oil-producing nations, and the preponderance of quotas and regulations being forced on oil-producing states by OPEC, the idea of bartering for oil had lately been the subject of much discussion in trading circles. The oil that companies like Chevron needed might be secured in exchange for goods, services, and factories that developing producer-nations might need. Chevron specialized in petroleum, and Sears was associated the world over with goods.

The meeting between the two chairmen set off a wave of enthusiasm in the staffs of both corporations. Numerous trips back and forth between Chicago and San Francisco led to a joint Sears/Chevron committee that produced a detailed working blueprint for the trading venture.

It was then that Hills took Telling and Purcell to the Middle East. First to the Persian Gulf oil entrepot of Bahrain, where some of Chevron's business contacts joined the Sears party at a reception hosted by the Bahrainian minister of trade, and then to Kuwait, where there was another dinner in honor of the Chicagoans. Telling mentioned to Hills that he found the Arabs he met on the trip to be strange, but the prospect of the Chevron association was still a thrilling concept.

Then the deal quite suddenly fell apart. Soon after the trip, Keller informed Sears that because of the technical proscriptions contained in a forty-six-year-old joint-venture marketing arrangement between Chevron and Texaco, a partnership called Caltex, Texaco apparently retained the right to veto Chevron's trading activity in certain regions where Caltex operated—such as the vital markets of Australia, East Africa, and all of Asia. Knowing of their chairman's passion for the concept, the Sears side continued in vain to push the deal, but since Keller believed the venture would be crippled from the start by geographical restrictions, the deal evaporated.

It was a loss that deeply upset Ed Telling. There weren't too many other corporations worthy of sharing an emblem with Sears, and the

Chevron combine struck him as the sort of monumental gesture that tends to leave a mark. But one good thing about having a fellow like Rod Hills around was that you would surely never want for a new deal to ponder.

There were still, for instance, the ongoing discussions between Hills and his old pal George Shinn, chairman of the red-hot investment-banking house First Boston Corporation. Early discussions about some form of joint venture between Rod's Sears World Trade unit and First Boston escalated quickly toward a plan by which First Boston would invest heavily in Sears World Trade, and Sears would invest heavily in First Boston. At Rod Hills' insistence, Shinn and his number-two manager flew to Chicago for talks in Telling's office. Eventually Dean Witter's entire corporate finance department would be transferred to First Boston. Dean Witter was supposed to become the wire house of the people anyway, and the trade would allow First Boston's investment bankers to become Sears' more elite financiers. The proposal was of the class of "amalgamations"—as opposed to straight acquisitions—Rod firmly believed in.

It was around the time the First Boston idea got bogged down at the interstaff discussion stage that Rod Hills made his September 1982 offer to stop being an erstwhile rainmaker for Ed Telling and join up full-time with Sears. The Sears merchant running the nascent trading wing at the time, John Waddle, was demoted and eventually left the company, and Rod soon hired Frank Carlucci, one of the most powerful bureaucrats in Washington. Carlucci had worked in the Office of Management and the Budget and the old HEW. He was ambassador to Portugal under Gerald Ford and Jimmy Carter, deputy director of the CIA under Carter, a deputy secretary of defense under Ronald Reagan, and now Frank Carlucci would be president of Sears World Trade under Rod Hills and Ed Telling.

Sears World Trade would be an export trading company that sought out new markets, took title to products, shipped goods, insured them, delivered them, and even serviced them, all in the larger world arena. Rod had his eye on a few large shipping firms he thought Telling should pick up, and there were a variety of raw-product handlers that would fit well into the flow of deals. Rod gave a breathless presentation about his plans to the board of directors, complete with slides and charts. He said the place to be in international business now was in "countertrade," ostensibly the interchange of something other than money as part of a sale. Some estimates indicated that 30 percent of all world trade would by the end of the century be done through countertrade. He explained that many less developed countries with internal economic difficulties required by law that any company importing goods there at a profit also had to create some sort of export opportunity for the nation, to ease the developing country's inevitable trade deficit and to help create new business. Hills wanted Sears to take over these large companies' obligations through Sears World Trade, to arrange the construction of factories and other facilities that might even supply the Merchant with goods.

Executives on the sixty-eighth floor noticed that Ed Telling's eyes were lit up like a young kid's after emerging from another talk with his new group chairman. "This whole world of countertrade hooks right into the fact that the world is reverting to the barter system," Telling would enthuse to his officers. "There's technical services to be supplied; there's finance. There's even consumer-driven business to explore out there."

Rod Hills told one newspaper that his quest was nothing less than to "invent a new company for Sears and for the world." By the beginning of 1983 there were Sears World Trade units in São Paulo, Brazil, and in Tokyo, and from the shuffle of smaller corporate subsidiaries between business groups, Hills had managed to extract from Allstate the small subsidiary international consulting firm called Harbridge House.

Résumés poured into the Washington office of World Trade from old trading hands stationed all over the world. Hills exhibited no interest in the original group of former merchants set up as traders in the Tower before he took over, and when he proposed that World Trade's headquarters be transferred officially and with great prominence to a landmark in the nation's capitol, he didn't even want the ex-merchants to come along.

The head of Sears' governmental affairs office in Washington, Randy Aires, had already broached the idea of Sears' buying and renovating three contiguous historical structures on Pennsylvania Avenue during the previous year. The parcel included the 123-year-old Apex Liquor buildings, and it turned out that one of the other structures had even housed the studio where in 1861 the pioneer photographer Mathew Brady had produced the image of Abraham Lincoln that appears on the $5.00 bill. Aires thought the renovation of the structure would help Sears' image in the District at a time when favorable regulation and legislation were essential to the new intergroup synergies. But Aires' proposal was rejected.

Hills resubmitted the proposal to buy the buildings to Telling. If Sears World Trade was to provide a conduit to the international arena, then what better spot could there be for its headquarters than a place that looked out on the White House? After renovations were done, "Sears House," as the beautifully colonnaded and marble-lined structures would be called, would be, if not the tallest building in Washington, D.C., then at least the grandest.

. . .

Since most international trade is serviced by a closely knit system of merchant banks, or by the international operations of other very large banks that serve as intermediaries and provide credit across national boundaries, Hills worked to strike a partnership with such a financial institution. Hills, along with a young former assistant secretary of state for economic policy named Curt Hessler, began to hold talks with the various leaders of the Bank of Boston, the Chase Manhattan Bank, First Interstate Bank, Bankers Trust, Citibank, and the First National Bank of Chicago (the First Chicago Corporation). A $35-million joint venture was eventually arranged with First Chicago. Profits gleaned from assisting American companies with their business abroad were to be split. First Chicago was to provide financial expertise and instruments such as letters of credit, and Sears was to provide the services of the world traders Hills began amassing at an ever-more-impressive pace during 1983.

Rod talked ceaselessly about further joint ventures with commodities, medical products, high-technology, and agricultural companies. He talked to the engineers of the Bechtel and the Signal Corporations about deals. But his best excitement was reserved for the idea of moving into the international financial sphere in a massive way. He and Telling talked about buying a very large foreign bank—possibly one that would cost more than Dean Witter—so as to create a billion-dollar leg for the great stool in one fell swoop. The flow continued to move out into the world like this, out and away from claw hammers and roadside evenings at the local Holiday Inn.

An old friend of Rod's, Sir James Spooner, suggested that Sears consider acquiring the venerable London banking house of Grindley's, formerly the Bank of India. The prospect of taking one of the oldest banks in the world was mulled over briefly, but the idea was overshadowed when a British consultant working for Hills was able to arrange a meeting with the mysterious Lebanese-born banker Edmond Safra. Safra had recently sold one of his operations, the Geneva-based Trade Development Bank, to American Express International Banking Corporation, but the reclusive banker still controlled the Republic National Bank of New York, which he had founded in 1966. Both of Safra's banks were filled with accumulated personal wealth entrusted to him by extremely wealthy Middle Eastern Arabs and Jews. The average deposit on accounts with the Republic National Bank was close to $500,000, and the bank had an active international wing that was of particular interest to Hills.

Telling and Hills discussed the composition of the entourage going to meet Safra in Paris, and Telling decided, in light of Safra's well-known desire for privacy, to invite only Hills and Dick Jones to accompany him to Paris on the Concorde.

When Phil Purcell heard of his exclusion from the approach to Edmond Safra, he regarded it as the drawing of a line in the dust. For one thing, it was the first major corporate fishing trip from which he'd been specifically excluded. (Phil had even been included in the more literal fishing trip Hills took with Telling in Idaho during the summer of 1982.)

Since they'd first joined forces to finally buy Telling some companies, Phil had been quite willing to grant that Rod Hills had a head full of synaptic firepower. Some of the ideas that came out of Rod Hills actually awed Purcell, stood him straight up in a way articulated thoughts seldom affected Phil. You could throw anything at Hills—ask him if he had any ideas for a new financial instrument that could be tied to agriculture in a manner that would help farmers with their problems, and in the next thirty minutes at least ten intricate conceptions would flow easily from him, as if he'd been thinking about the problem for a year. One of the ideas was usually brilliant, but as far as Phil Purcell was concerned, the ability to see that the other nine ideas were so stupid as to be laughable was something Rod Hills never managed to add to his repertoire. It was a deficiency that Purcell believed rendered Hills a terrible manager. Hills, Purcell thought, was a hot-to-trot ideas man operating way over his head as a CEO, and it galled the hell out of Phil that a noted student of human pretension like Ed Telling couldn't see it.

Worse than the blatant power-play entailed in Purcell's exclusion from the Safra journey, and from the talks about international banking leading up to it, was the fact that once again Rod Hills was moving in on his turf. Phil had only recently been moved to "Sears–New York," as Dean Witter was occasionally known, so he might have been hypersensitive, but he believed that banking fell under financial services, not international trade. Going after banks was his job, not Rod's. He'd been trying to buy Sears a bank so hard it was almost making him sick. Phil Purcell had been forced to operate with Rod Hills lodged in the corner of his eye for almost two years now, and by the summer of 1983 he thought the situation was getting out of hand.

Phil spent a great deal of his time during the first year of his mission in New York in the company of Stretch Gardiner. He sat in Gardiner's office sopping up the language, lore, and rituals of the securities sellers, just as he had once sat with members of the now departed generation of Searsmen learning the whys and wherefores of selling goods. Phil figured that there wasn't much difference between running Dean Witter and Sears and Allstate and Coldwell Banker save an element of "expertise," and he was far from the first Wall Street broker-dealer executive to note how easy it is to manage an investment company in the midst of a bull market.

Dean Witter's research staff had spotted the equities boom coming early on. Full-page newspaper ads carrying a prominent graph that augured the coming stock-market surge had successively associated the firm with the economic recovery from the beginning. By mid-1983, Dean Witter's version of the Merrill Lynch Cash Management Account, which had so intrigued Sears researchers before the acquisitions, had drawn ten thousand customers—as well as a patent-infringement suit from Merrill Lynch.

Dean Witter was packaging new financial products all the time, many of them "democratized" formerly expensive vehicles previously denied average investors. Safe and steady investment trusts backed by pools of tax-free municipal bonds and mortgage-backed securities packaged as inexpensive "units" were selling heavily. A variable-interest-rate certificate of deposit was introduced that offered rates well above those of Treasury debt, and Dean Witter even made a secondary market in the CDs that allowed customers to avoid the government-mandated penalty for selling CDs before the due date.

New stockbrokers were being hired in droves, many of them intrigued by reports from the financial-services booths deployed now in many Sears stores, where rookie brokers were apparently signing up many more new accounts than those securities sellers starting out in traditional Dean Witter offices.

Stretch Gardiner went out of his way to run interference for Phil Purcell within Dean Witter and in the Wall Street fraternity, and he tried to be unusually generous about sharing credit for company successes in his communications with Chicago. Gardiner knew that, beyond the task of showing that he could make the switch from the ultimate Sears staff adviser to a senior line manager, Purcell was under particular pressure by the middle of 1983, because once again Phil was working under a private charge from Telling. It was Purcell's job to provide the one lynchpin of the financial-services system Telling believed was needed to move in on the banks. Telling wanted his own bank.

With all of the stores and catalog outlets, all the insurance, real-estate, and brokerage agencies, there were already so many corporate conduits where the Sears network touched the paths trod by members of the franchise that the company had an ability to collect money and move it around the country on a scale not unlike the Federal Reserve system. But from the beginning of the financial-services scenario, Telling wanted to go beyond the sophisticated storage of cash to provide all services available at banks on every corner.

By the summer of 1983—the fiftieth anniversary of the Glass-Steagall

Act, which barred banks from becoming the "department stores of finance," as the bankers proclaimed during the 1920s they one day would—recent legislation had provided Sears with two loopholes through which a Sears banking network might be assembled even as banking executives and their representatives in Washington protested loudly over the "supercompany's" previous incursions. During the first two years of recession, inflation visited a plague so devastating to American savings-and-loan institutions that industry losses at the time surpassed the losses of the beleaguered steel, auto, and agricultural machinery industries combined. So many large savings-and-loans fell under protection of the government that a new law, the Garn–St Germain Depository Institutions Act of 1982, was enacted to allow the Federal Home Loan Bank Board—the agency responsible for insuring the public's savings in the savings-and-loans—to sell sick savings-and-loans by auction to companies willing to unburden the taxpayers. The law breached the legal impediments that separate banking and commercial concerns and allowed corporations to buy out-of-state savings institutions. The new loophole seemed a perfect opportunity for Sears to move into the interstate depository business and complete the financial circle at a time when most banks were either too restricted by law or too small to do anything about it.

From the earliest days of the financial-services vision, Telling knew that a business network that served all financial needs would only become possible if the same Depression-era laws that held Citibank and other would-be competitors in check were weakened or repealed. Telling said he wanted all banking and financial regulations stripped away so that Sears and the banks could go head to head. The collecting of humbled savings-and-loans, as well as superior technology and financial personnel, was all part of a stockpiling strategy designed to lead toward automated cash machines, ways to dispense many kinds of loans, a universal credit card, and all other manner of services and systems that would make the net complete.

In September 1982, Citicorp won the first auctions of a sick savings-and-loan when it secured the "right" to lose some $200 million in the process of bailing out the Oakland, California's Fidelity Federal. The next auction remained unscheduled, so Phil Purcell turned his attention to a second strategy for buying into banking, an opening called the "nonbank bank loophole."

Because Congress defined a bank as an institution that both took in deposits and initiated consumer loans, it dawned on several corporate loophole-drillers in 1983 that if either commercial lending or deposit taking was discontinued a bank would no longer be a bank under the law. Owning a "nonbank" bank would not only permit companies like

Sears to circumvent restrictions of the kinds of enterprises that can own banks, but would also obviate other restrictions on the operation of banks across state lines.

A strategy was hatched by which Sears would move to secure savings-and-loans and meanwhile try to buy at least two geographically dispersed "nonbank" banks. The twin possibilities of the end of the eight-year-old deregulatory élan in Washington, or the advent of new deregulation actions that would allow the banks into the financial-services game before Sears played its advantage, meant that Sears had to move quickly. The Garn–St Germain bill allowed banks to offer "insured money-market-rate accounts" designed to compete with those offered by the likes of Dean Witter, and the public transferred $320.5 billion into the banking industry's version of the money-market account during just three months after December 1982.

In March 1983 the comptroller of the currency declared a moratorium on new national charters for "nonbank" banks, a ruling that was successfully dodged the following month by none other than the merchants of J. C. Penney, who managed to take control of a Delaware bank and turn it into a limited-service banking facility. In May, the *nouveau laissez-faire* proponent running the Federal Home Loan Bank Board resigned and was replaced by a man known to oppose the idea of financial supercompanies. A few weeks later, Federal Reserve Board Chairman Paul Volcker called for a moratorium both on nonbank companies' buying banks and on further acquisitions by banks. Secretary of the Treasury Donald Regan weighed in during July to say that the Treasury favored a plan that would allow banks into the real-estate, insurance, and some securities activities while holding back further acquisitions by the likes of Sears, National Steel, and Regan's old employers at Merrill Lynch.

When it was announced that Sears still intended to bid against Citibank in the next Bank Board auction, of the sadly humbled First Federal Savings and Loan of Chicago, there was a great deal of public protest: "When you talk about Sears' buying a First Federal, that's intimidating," a local banker told the *Chicago Tribune*. "They, of all companies, have the ability to run a loss leader, to walk in and just buy a market for an extended period of time."

Both Citibank and Sears went ahead and entered bids for First Federal, but the new Home Loan Bank Board chairman postponed announcing the winner until July. In July he said he might make the announcement later in the year.

· · ·

Phil Purcell.
Photo © Wm. Franklin McMahon.

A meeting of the Hay Committee, 1976.
Photo courtesy M. E. Burkholder.

Charlie Wurmstedt.

C. Wesley Poulson.
Photo © Wm. Franklin McMahon.

Robert "Stretch" Gardiner, 1982.
Photo © Fred Leavitt.

Gordon Metcalf.

Rod Hills. Photo © Junebug Clark 1985.

Jack F. Kincannon.

Henry D. Sunderland.

William Bass.

"Jumpin' Joe" Moran at Challenge 82.

Sears catalog covers before (above) and after (opposite, bottom) the Challenge.

Challenge 81: Cheryl Tiegs
with "Burk" Burkholder.
Photo courtesy M. E. Burkholder.

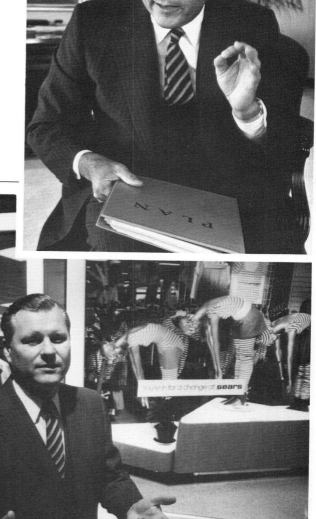

Ed Brennan, head of
Merchandising, with the
streamlined merchandising
system called "the Plan," 1982.
Photo © Fred Leavitt.

Ed Brennan in the Store of the Future, 1983.
Photo © Wm. Franklin McMahon.

Press conference announcing the purchase of Dean Witter Reynolds, Inc., 1981. From left: Robert "Stretch" Gardiner, Ed Telling, Andy Melton. Photo © Wm. Franklin McMahon.

The Store of the Future, Vernon Hills, Illinois, 1983. Photo © Wm. Franklin McMahon.

Sears corporate senior management, 1984. From left: Edward A. Brennan, president and chief operating officer; Edward R. Telling, chairman of the board and chief executive officer; and Richard M. Jones, vice chairman and chief financial officer.

Sears

Old (left) and new Sears logos.

SEARS

Phil Purcell received few phone calls from Ed Telling that summer. When they did speak, Telling would ask what was taking so long. But since you simply could not—did not—offer Ed Telling excuses, there wasn't much Phil could say. He firmly believed Sears would eventually be the number-one or -two consumer-banking entity in the country in terms of deposits, lending, and transaction accounts. Sears would be the clear number two in the investment world as well as the pre-eminent American retailer when all was said and done. It was already in the cards that the financial-services wing of Sears he'd helped construct would be as profitable as Allstate or the Merchant in less than a decade, but still the pressure from the Tower was intensifying. Though the corporate vista might reveal the brightness of new dawns, the era of Ed Telling was drawing to a close, and Phil Purcell was enough of a veteran of big-league corporate infighting not to know that, as far as his own future was concerned, this was all that really mattered.

As he considered reports of all the high-speed acquisitive globe-trotting orchestrated by Rod Hills, Phil figured the pressure he felt from the sixty-eighth floor was also Rod's doing. The double-barreled bank-buying strategy had been plotted, after all, by two banking professors Rod had scared up from Harvard and Stanford. It turned out that Rod Hills had considerable previous experience with bank loophole dodging. Of course he did. He'd even assisted the Federal Home Loan Bank Board in its early efforts to auction off depressed savings-and-loans in the first place.

Telling had finally become so impatient with the process of buying "nonbank" banks or savings-and-loans for the network that he'd asked Hills to amass the insider scuttlebutt in Washington about Purcell's progress. From sources in consulting and regulatory circles, Rod brought back reports that the Sears strategy was not "serious" enough to succeed.

Telling summoned Purcell, Gardiner, and Hills to a meeting in his office, where he voiced his suspicions that the banking initiative was stalled.

"Where did you hear that?" Purcell inquired.

Telling turned and looked at Rod Hills. "I . . . ah . . . don't think you're going fast enough," Hills said in his deep voice, though Rod wished Telling had kept his sources to himself.

Telling then said he was transferring ultimate responsibility for securing banking outlets to the corporate president, Archie Boe. Purcell was to continue his efforts, but he was to report henceforth to Archie.

The interloper Rod Hills was clearly in Phil Purcell's way. It was as if Rod had put the chairman under a spell. The year of the running of the company horses was the wrong time for Phil to lose touch with his most prominent connection to the corporation like this. The father in the "father-son" relationship that Phil pretended not to hear talk of in the halls was backing away.

Meanwhile, the task of "wiring together" the businesses Sears already owned was proving to be a matter of complex engineering. Along with Archie Boe and Dick Jones, much of the day-to-day work of creating a synthesis from the companies Sears already owned fell to Charley Moran, the "other Moran" in senior quarters at Sears, who had once served under Phil Purcell as a planner during the days of civil war.

Charley had become the corporate holding company's senior strategic planner when Phil Purcell moved out to Dean Witter. "If you weaken the entrepreneurial drive in these firms you weaken the company," Charley had proclaimed when he first got his orders to bridge inherent cultural gaps between the groups, but by mid-1983, he complained of the resistance among leaders of the five groups to "the Sears religion."

There were the petty interbusiness group incidents like the one he had to deal with in Atlanta when local Dean Witter brokers refused to move into a building run by Coldwell Banker because the structure was known in the area as the Merrill Lynch Building, but the biggest problems had arisen over operational sovereignty—specifically over issues of personnel and money. An executive from Dick Jones' staff in Chicago ordered Coldwell Banker's financial officer to provide the sixty-eighth floor with a list of the bonuses the realtor had paid its executives, and Wesley Poulson refused. Internally, Poulson faced constant queries from his hot-shot commercial-real-estate sellers as to whether they would soon be compensated on a scale similar to the big-ticket salesmen in the stores, and it wasn't helping matters that he had to tear Sears functionaries "off the backs of his people" all the time.

But the former merchants on sixty-eight like Dick Jones and Charley Moran were determined to monitor the staffing and growth of the new companies. "I refuse to watch them build up something too big and expensive," Jones said. "I've seen the kind of pain an organization experiences in the process of shrinking it back down."

On the brighter side, the product development and marketing elements of corporate synergy were moving along impressively. Some eighty-seven of the tripartite Allstate Dean Witter Coldwell Banker booths (with a savings-and-loan window attached only in California) would be in Sears stores by the end of August. Dean Witter financial products were being advertised regularly on the bangtail flaps of tens of millions of monthly Sears and Allstate bills, and Coldwell Banker home buyers were already using books of discount coupons in the retail stores.

One of the most promising developments along the lines of the "sticky money" thesis—the idea that the trick of the new ventures would be to trap all customer financial dealings within the Sears web—was in the rapidly changing business of providing, servicing, repackaging, and re-selling people's mortgages as investment vehicles. In 1983 the second-ary market in mortgages was well on its way to approaching the size of the markets in stocks or corporate bonds. From the debacle in the savings-and-loan industry had come the practice of local mortgage lend-ers' selling off their mortgage portfolios to firms willing to repackage the mortgages as debt securities for investors. The firms sold the mortgages as relatively safe (usually government-backed or collateralized) bonds and other sorts of debentures to investors more willing to shoulder the risk than trepidatious local lenders. Members of the early financial-services task force on mortgages realized that Sears was in a position to reap profits at every link along this developing "mortgage chain." The company could originate mortgages through Coldwell Banker, the Cali-fornia savings and loan, and eventually through other lending outlets, turn them into securities, and retail them through Dean Witter as unit trusts, funds, and other debt obligations. Sears would become a pipeline, pumping capital from one set of Sears customers to another. They could set up a "conduit company" to package the mortgages (it was well on the way to being organized during the summer of 1983), and even insure the mortgages through Preston Martin's PMI, the mortgage-insurance company. If something happened and PMI had to foreclose, Coldwell Banker was there to unload the property. With almost half the homes in the country carrying mortgages and some $2 trillion outstanding in mortgage loans, it was assumed that by 1990, the chain would render up $100 million in profit.

When Telling announced that Sears intended to move into the mort-gage business in a big way, smaller lending organizations reacted in panic. "What if they offer a discount on mortgages? That would just murder us," moaned one Chicago-based savings-and-loan president to *Crain's Chicago Business.*

The fearful symmetry of a Sears mortgage chain was particularly pleasing to Telling as a matter of historical justice. The savings-and-loan industry was originally chartered, in large part, to provide mortgages for new homes because local banks refused to take a risk in the name of the consumer. During the Depression, government innovators created the Federal National Mortgage Association to buy mortgages from local lenders so that Americans could pursue the national dream of owning a home. As the savings-and-loan industry went up in flames in the early

1980s, and the burden and massive need for new capital overwhelmed government capacity, Sears and other private-sector concerns were stepping in. Just as Sears had provided consumer credit for goods because the banks wouldn't respond, the mortgage chain provided an opportunity for the corporation once again to enter a business in the name of the people.

For a full year after the acquisitions, however, there was no coherent national advertising designed to inform people about the united financial-services businesses. A research study conducted during 1982 showed that only 2 percent of the population realized that both Coldwell Banker and Dean Witter were owned by Sears. During 1982, the name Sears Financial Network had been coined, but an unresolved internal debate over how to go about taking the network public had delayed the unveiling.

One school of thought held that the individual company names of Coldwell Banker and Dean Witter should be abolished in favor of the unified image of one new and multidimensional Sears. Others believed the loss of recognition would injure the two companies as well as engender internal morale problems. Some executives in "Corporate"—the term by which the sixty-eighth-floor managers were known by now—wanted to hire a tough-talking actor—George C. Scott was mentioned often—and wage an aggressive no-holds-barred anti-bank advertising campaign, in the spirit of Telling's ringing Economics Club speech. Research indicated that the general public found banks and bankers to be intimidating, distant, self-serving, and mechanical. The hard-liners argued that a Patton-like assault was in order. Others argued for public images that included mothers and babies and a slogan like "keeping faith with the future." Still other discussions centered on the meaning of the traditional Sears "money-back guarantee" when applied to a Dean Witter customer who was sold underperforming shares of stock. There were skirmishes over issues such as which new financial products should carry the Sears name and which should be named after Dean Witter.

It was eventually decided that any "savings"-related products would carry the Sears name. At Phil Purcell's insistence, the California savings and loan's name would eventually be changed from Allstate to Sears. Any financial products that seemed risky would be sold under the rubric of Dean Witter. The Tower, it was declared, would be gradually inserted as a cross-company symbol of unity, and the folksy actor Hal Holbrook was chosen as the star of the ad campaign, instead of someone either tougher- or richer-looking.

The idea of the huge introductory campaign was to hook the Sears "trust quotient" onto the other financial companies, rather as Allstate had managed to do with their famed "good hands" imagery.

The eleven billion "impressions" sent into American homes via the Holbrook campaign arrived in high contrast to the plutocratic implications conveyed by Merrill Lynch's "breed apart" theme, and the setting of PaineWebber's ads in various exclusive-looking clubs. Until July, when American Express purchased the middle-market-oriented Investors Diversified Services, and Prudential-Bache began to retrain its advertising pitches at more humble investors, it looked like whatever internal frustrations still hampered the achievement of synergy, Sears' competitors were still ceding the vast realm of the middle—the franchise—to Ed Telling.

A much less apparent but equally programmatic campaign was being conducted by Dick Jones, Charley Moran, and some of the other officers on the sixty-eighth floor that midsummer. It involved the careful insertion of roadblocks in the way of "Hot Rod" Hills. Reports were coming back to Chicago from the two Sears veterans the sixty-eighth-floor staffers had managed to plant in Washington about Hills functionaries running wild through the Far East, looking at saw mills in Borneo and negotiating to purchase bankrupt banks in Hong Kong. After all of the trauma entailed in disarming the legendary gunslinger buyers working markets for Sears, the company now had under contract its very own Milo Minderbinder. Rod Hills was littering every foreign port with Sears World Trade business cards, as F.D.R. once wished Sears would cover the Soviet Union with its catalogs.

The officers on sixty-eight tried valiantly to keep up with the flow of deals. They watched in horror as the buildup of what they considered to be high-priced government-surplus talent continued in Washington. Aside from the former CIA man Frank Carlucci, World Trade hired on a former superintendent of the Air Force, General James Allen, and several other former under- and assistant secretaries. Archie Boe got a phone call from a friend in Washington, and the friend thanked him not only for renovating a Pennsylvania Avenue landmark through World Trade, but also for assisting the federal government with its deficit problems by taking so many highly paid officials off Uncle Sam's hands. Unlikely individuals were now working for Rod, such as the foul-mouthed, hard-drinking former priest and one-time guru of the corporate Hay Committee, John Keane, who'd been hired as head of personnel for World Trade.

If it hadn't been for the style and pace of the venture, and the deeply unsettling relationship Ed Telling continued to conduct with the mercurial Hills, there would actually have been elements of the new World Trade Company's plans that made perfect sense to the minds of the former merchants who worked on sixty-eight. Moving goods from one side of a continent to another had long been a forte of Sears employees. The idea of moving wood pulp out of Java and into Italy a bit more efficiently and inexpensively than the next company made a lot of sense. The Sears merchants, after all, were the best of American traders, but Rod Hills seemed capable of doing nothing but stomping on toes, generally irritating, and even scaring the other men around Telling. It was circulated that in private conversation Hills was given to claiming that he was the mastermind not only behind the acquisition of the Dean Witter and Coldwell Banker deals but of the ERIP "golden handshake" as well.

If Rod Hills wanted to be a "Rasputin or something," as Phil Purcell put it, "let him hang out on the sixty-eighth floor and stir things up if it makes him happy. Let him make people mad, write speeches, help negotiate—but Rod shouldn't be making business decisions."

But they'd all seen how the vague expression that was almost always wrapped over their chairman's face vanished, and how his pale eyes flared, when World Trade was mentioned. Telling made no effort whatsoever to hide his special interest in the smallest and most daring of the baronies. He told an assembled group of Sears World Trade executives in Washington that there were several reasons he wished he was a younger man, but one of them was that he wished he could start a Sears, Roebuck career anew as an employee of the World Trade Company.

Telling and Hills were still making large plans together that summer, still talking of "high-risk/high-potential" forays like two buccaneers. Telling's fascination with World Trade was in some ways reminiscent of the way U.S. presidents so often focus on foreign affairs during later portions of their tenures, as if wielding great power inevitably causes leaders to seek out a way to leave a mark on the whole world before relinquishing their authority.

But the romance of taking Sears to the world was becoming ever more disconcerting to officers as rumors surfaced that summer indicating Telling's strong interest in going outside the company to find his successor. The names of the candidates in "the pool" Telling had presented to the nominating committee of the board were still a mystery. Archie Boe was sure Don Craib's name was on the list, because some of the nominating-committee members had grilled him about the Allstate chairman, but little more was known.

The coming decision made it all the more important that Rod Hills' star-lined path be blocked. Dick Jones and Phil Purcell managed to force Hills to stop conducting World Trade business with the gigantic California-based bank holding company, First Interstate Bancorp. Dean Witter had been dropped as investment banker to First Interstate, and though Hills protested that the bank's chairman, Joseph Pinola, was an old friend, Hills acquiesced to the retribution when the order was framed as a dictum from Corporate. The sixty-eighth floor asked for and received World Trade's bonus list and had successfully forced the size of various bonuses to be altered. Corporate began to issue a stream of demands concerning the design of the new headquarters in Washington—if Rod wanted an open floor plan to simulate the crowd and urgency of a *bourse,* then Corporate wanted cubicles. There were constant suggestions now that Hills take on more personnel from Tower ranks. Dick Jones insisted that a young vice-president from his tax department go to work in Washington. Hills successfully resisted the implantation, arguing that taxes were the least of the far-ranging venture's priorities.

For his part, Rod was cognizant of the suspicions his proximity to Telling aroused. His own sources had told him, after his talks with George Shinn of First Boston had broken down, that some of the problems encountered in pursuit of the deal had been caused by one Phil Purcell. Hills had also begun to think his problems with buying a foreign financial company were coming from the Sears corporate offices in Chicago and New York.

Rod had made several attempts to hold an olive branch out to Phil Purcell. If Phil felt threatened because banks were on his turf, then Rod would offer to include one of the senior Dean Witter people on the board of whatever foreign banking operation he finally bought. Hills asked Purcell to look over his strategic-planning document for World Trade, and even managed to schedule appointments with Purcell to go over the plans, but Purcell never kept them.

The bad blood between Rod and Phil particularly upset Telling. It seemed to him that Sears was big enough to harbor two high-powered mandarins and official readers of signs.

"You two have got to be friends," Telling complained to both men on several occasions when the chairman glimpsed the jockeying and bureaucratic politicking occurring outside his invariably closed office door. "Somebody has to break crockery around here, and it's a lot easier for you people from the outside."

Though he might go to some lengths to be diplomatic, the one thing Rod Hills would and could not do was compromise a deal. One never compromised a good deal; deals were above politics. As brilliant a negotiator as Hills was, there were certain kinds of compromises it was simply not in his nature to make. Rod saw the warning signs as nothing but further indications of the other officers' inability to deal in "the art of the possible." He ultimately believed his purpose within Sears was to create something capable of coming out from "under the shadow of the giant." He was there to help Sears change, and he figured that after Telling was gone the possibility for real change would decrease. When the approach to Edmond Safra had come to nothing, Hills had been warned to ease up on the throttle, but he said no. He would never compromise the integrity of the flow.

Accordingly, late during the summer of 1983, negotiations were begun under Hills' direction with a group of young trade financiers based in London, Washington, Tokyo, and New York. The talks were aimed at securing for Sears an elite international team that would serve as a sophisticated merchant bank and springboard to international financial markets, all of it to be run under Rod Hills and Sears World Trade, all of it to be constructed in the name of the new.

CHAPTER 21

The Flight of the Killer Bees

All summer long, Ed Brennan moved like a man being chased. The combination of Brennan's physical stamina and his unlimited access to the Sears air force made such paroxysms of interstate movement possible that it seemed at times almost whimsical: one day to inspect Macy's new store in Stamford, Connecticut; a quick jaunt down to Spartanburg, South Carolina, to see a manufacturer; four prototype Store of the Future visits in four states in just four days. Just moving. Racing. The aura still bristling bright but tinged now with something almost dangerous.

Brennan ordered a jet rolled out into the dawn of July 28, because there were some things that needed to be adjusted down in Florida. The pilot who got the call eased one of the seven de Havillands in the hangar out past the company's little Lear 55, past the state-of-the-art Sikorsky 76 helicopter that could make the trip from Midway—the airport a few miles southwest of the Tower—up to the helipad at Allstate headquarters in Northbrook in less than ten minutes, and under the shadow of the super-plush G-II in which Wes Poulson once had a free ride back home from France.

All the Sears pilots based at Midway anxiously awaited delivery of the $17-million plane of private planes, a new G-III that had been ordered recently. The new jet would cruise at Mach 0.85, the pilots said. The Sears G-III would be so loaded down with extras that King Fahd of Saudi Arabia was apparently irritated with Gulfstream for making Ed Telling a jet plane fancier than his. The fact that Telling really liked a fancy plane was just one of the things about him that never quite figured.

No matter how early a flight was scheduled to leave, Bill Bass always arrived at least thirty minutes earlier. Bass was naturally a punctilious sort, but the ritual of early arrival was born of his private vow never to lose touch with the real Bill Bass. Each time he climbed into one of these latter-day chariots for chairmen and kings, Bass had promised himself to recall the fact that he was just a street-fighting old peddler at heart. Each time he watched a jet fire up, he stood by in quiet reverence, in awe of his power and privilege. When Bass was dragged kicking and screaming into Brennan's service in the Tower, he had a single parting thought for his successor in the Eastern Territory. "Every damned time you tell 'em to roll out the plane, you pinch yourself," he said.

Ed Brennan and Joe Batogowski arrived four minutes before takeoff, and Brennan immediately began to pore over computer printouts containing the previous day's numbers. It was just a few months before Ed Telling was due to choose his heir and things were looking better. There was so much extra business out at the prototype Store of the Future in Vernon Hills that "you couldn't stir it with a spoon"—everyone in Brennan's circle said so in precisely that way. A legendary Sears buyer named Gene Adler journeyed out to the store. Adler had been Brennan's father's boss back in the old mens'-apparel departments and a prominent figure in Brennan's memories of his Sears childhood. "Ed," the eighty-seven-year-old gentleman said, "it's the finest retail store I have ever seen in my life." When Brennan took Ed Telling out to Vernon Hills, the chairman said: "The most exciting things about this store are the things that were least exciting about the old Sears." Brennan repeated Telling's statement often during his subsequent travels in the Field.

Summer numbers at the prototype store were up almost 40 percent over the year before, and Brennan was hoping that sales would soar up over $3.5 million when the computer toted up July. On July 25 Cheryl Tiegs cut a ribbon that spanned the entrance to the first official Store of the Future (the Vernon Hills version being more of a working scale model for the company's internal use) in a mall near Philadelphia, in King of Prussia, Pennsylvania. One industry newsletter went so far as to call the new Sears store a retailing "milestone."

During the coming months Brennan planned to replicate a single store design in every new store and in most of the best existing stores. The thing had to be completely right, and since there were things about the two prototype Stores of the Future in Miami that reports indicated were simply not right enough, Brennan and Bass and young "Bato" were heading south to do some pick-and-shovel work, and if need be to rattle a few sabers.

For a variety of reasons not unconnected to their habit of suddenly descending together from the air into a city or town like this—and the fact of the shared first letter of each of their last names—Ed Brennan, Bill Bass, and Joe Batogowski were now known throughout the midsection of the Merchandise Group as "the Killer Bees."

As soon as the men had climbed back into the long and narrow fuselage of the jet, Brennan stripped down to his vest. He fell into one of the four large, comfortable seats in the front of the cabin, his back to the cockpit, and nodded first in Bill Bass' direction and then at the seat across from his own. Bass opened his briefcase, and as the plane left the runway and headed south, the senior executive vice-president, Field took up a position opposite his boss to begin the managerial chores of the morning of July 28.

Though in many ways Bill Bass had thrived during his year at the corporate pinnacle, his day-to-day chores often made him yearn for the life in little stores. A few days before the Miami trip, he'd stomped around his big corner office, going on about how Sears, Roebuck was "too goddamned big to run," and how you couldn't "get your arms around it from a goddamned Tower in Chicago, no matter how hard you tried." The outburst was provoked by a phone call in which Bass had been asked to ascertain how many air conditioners there were in his stores. "How many *goddamned air conditioners* there are in all the stores of Sears, Roebuck?" he'd barked into the phone. "Sure thing. No problem there!" He'd find out, of course. The information would be peeled from computer disks, checked with the territorial offices, then double-checked with Claude Ireson's facilities people downstairs, and eventually a figure would find its way back to his office, but the event made Bass miss his stores and the time when he could say, "Six . . . six air conditioners," hang up the telephone, and then let life move right along from there.

It was the same thing with the misbegotten roofs over his empire of retail stores—almost all of which had sprung leaks of late. Nearly every roof laid over the top of a Sears store since the 1960s was in need of repair. The technology available to the traditionally backward roofing industry just wasn't up to the demands of the massive, flat-topped emporia of the time, and the only solace Bass could take from this sorry state of affairs was that all the other big retailers were leaking too.

"The consultants figure it'll cost $22 million to fix 'em all," Bass said to Brennan as he handed over a sheaf of authorization forms.

Brennan riffled through the papers until one caught his eye. "Four hundred thousand dollars to fix the roof on the *Port Huron* store?" He looked at Bass incredulously, his eyes narrowing. "How can you ask me to sign this? Four hundred thousand dollars for a store that makes no money? Let's close the place."

"No, sir, we shouldn't do that," Bass said, locking his unusually pale blue eyes on Brennan's. "I'm gonna turn that store for ya. Gonna be a $12-million store."

"I want to wait," Brennan said, turning his pen away from the form. "Store's gonna be a profit-maker."

"Because of the roof, no doubt," Brennan said. He looked up at the muted beige ceiling of the jet, slightly bemused. "This is being signed under protest," he said, as he scratched his signature on the document.

Brennan was imparting a form and style of management to Bill Bass that summer. For a year now, he had been consciously trying to enhance Bill Bass' sophistication and polish up his style, simultaneously broadening his exposure to various aspects of the business. Bass knew how to bulldog a store as well as anybody in the trade, but Brennan was trying to help him become a more complete general executive, a "corner-office person."

There were more documents signed rapidly. Some decreed the closing of stores and the disposal of their assets—notably the old store in Memphis, Tennessee, where the factory workers at the luggage plant in Sardis, Mississippi, used to travel with their families to see the suitcases they'd made. The Memphis store once did $27 million in a year and now it made no money at all. Bass proposed to close it down December 1.

"Do it," Brennan said.

Documents were signed concerning the sale to J. C. Penney of a huge, modern Sears store in suburban Chicago. The store at the Northbrook Court Mall had been opened in the upscale suburbs along the shore of Lake Michigan at the end of the era of drift and arrogance in 1976. A photograph of the regal facility had even graced the cover of the corporate annual report that year.

"Damn store went against the rules," Brennan said, turning his head toward the clouds below. "You never build a store next to an Indian reservation, and you never build a store against a large body of water. We *own* the whole shopping center, and we've lost millions on the store." Brennan signed the "facilities proposal" form authorizing the sale of the dog (via Coldwell Banker) to Penney's. Then he signed another that authorized the sale of twenty-five acres of prime real estate in Oklahoma City; then another for the sale of a large warehouse. By the end of the fifteen-minute signing session, Brennan had decreed the rearrangement of many more millions of dollars than pass through all but a few other business organizations in an entire year. "One thing I've learned about these approval forms," he said as he signed off on the last one. "They sometimes come back to haunt you."

"O.K.," Brennan said to Joe Batogowski, who was seated across the aisle. "Let's talk people talk."

Bass got up and Batogowski sat down in his place as Brennan lit up on of his big A and C cigars. Batogowski reported the impending retirement of yet another of the old hands in his buying organization, one of a large number of veteran managers leaving that summer. One hundred thirteen executives had retired in the wake of the Western Territory consolidations alone. Brennan said the rising stock price had something to do with it, but he knew it was largely a toll of the crushing pace. "They think it's too late in their lives to change," Brennan said once, "so they've just thrown in the towel."

Batogowski then reported the departure date of the most recent senior retiree.

"The man was the finest polyester-buyer in the whole world," Brennan said reverently.

Because the retiree had also been politically skilled and extremely powerful in the manner of the old departmental buyer-kings, many lines of goods that should have been in other departments had ended up under his control. Alternately sitting forward with great eagerness and leaning back into a more relaxed and managerial pose, Batogowski proposed to Brennan that they consolidate the retiree's department with another apparel department the fellow had dominated over the years.

But Brennan still seemed preoccupied by his own thoughts about the veteran's departure. He was puffing thoughtfully on his cigar. "You know, I only wore dress slacks as a child," he said softly. "I painted houses in rayon dress slacks, played ball in wool dress slacks, and delivered papers in dress slacks. All because Dad bought slacks for Sears. Never in my life have I even tried on a pair of blue jeans."

He eventually returned from the silence that followed to the business at hand. "I don't know about this consolidation," Brennan said in a different voice. "Tell me more about the factions you'd be merging, and why?"

Batogowski argued that the distinctions between the two departments were not perceived by the customers and were thus internal to Sears politics. "We're not strong enough in apparel to afford the luxury of internal battles," Batogowski said.

"It just scares me," Brennan replied. "If you mix Cheryl Tiegs jeans in with polyester Pants-That-Fit, the whole thing will run together and look like shit again. That's been part of the problem at this goddamned company for twenty-five years."

Brennan stood up and put his hand on Batogowski's shoulder. "I also wonder whether consolidating these two departments might do away with a healthy fight between the two factions." Brennan then strolled back toward the bathroom.

Sears, Roebuck Pants-That-Fit are material forms that closely resemble two gigantic bladders exhumed from some primitive beast, two flaccid, wrinkle-free, and ageless sacks joined at one end and ringed by a waistband of up to forty-eight inches in diameter. The pants resided prominently among the small number of "core" items that made up fully one-third of Sears' retail business. Millions upon millions of core Pants-That-Fit had been sold over the years, and, as profoundly as any element of the government's basket of economic indicators, the status at any given time of Sears core offerings like the pants defined a powerful image of the state of the American middle class. The question of "core versus fashion" had dominated internal struggles within the buying organization since the revolution in synthetic fibers had extended the concept of fashion to average consumers during the late 1950s. The eternal marriage of fashion and "core" within the context of the Store of the Future was central to the purpose of Brennan's great experiment.*

The question of merging the designer jeans and polyester factions beneath him in the Tower was clearly going to have to wait, because when Brennan returned from the bathroom he wanted to move on to the next personnel issue.

The number of "officials and managers" working for the Merchant had now contracted by almost 40 percent since 1978. Where there had been sixty-six hundred executive-level managers working in the stores in 1974, there were now just over forty-six hundred individuals, and because of a recent decision to eliminate the staff merchandise manager in each store, that number was about to fall by nine hundred. The restructuring of the buying organization in reflection of the new store began that July, and though no layoffs would come of the physical and organizational relocation of 227 of the remaining 750 merchandise lines, many buyers had been made surplus and had nothing to buy.

There were indications that summer that the massive consolidation of the Merchant was causing morale problems among the younger middle

---

*The inimitable Wayne Holsinger had recently offered his own thoughts about "core" at a "line review" that included samples of Pants-That-Fit: "See her comin'?" Wayne asked of his buyers as a piece of cyclone fencing bearing three examples of the pants was wheeled before his audience. "See the stroller and the kids grabbing at her Pants-That-Fit? She ain't outa *Vogue* magazine, and she ain't built like Cheryl Tiegs and never was. She knows she's no raving beauty, and getting things that fit is a tough issue. But what does that mean to us?" Wayne inquired, his voice rising loud in crescendo. "It means $130 million wortha polyester pants! *That's* what it means! We are Sears. Red, white, and blue and shapeless as all hell. *This*, ladies and gentlemen, is what is meant by 'core.'"

managers. Many of them were disconcerted to see jobs eliminated every time somebody moved; it was as if you were climbing a burning rope toward some point above you that was lost in the smoke. From Head-quarters to the stores, the career paths of young managers had been blocked or obscured, and many of them were looking for new jobs.

The brilliant thirty-two-year-old real-estate manager for the Western Territory, Fred Bruning, had decided to leave Sears during the summer to go to work for a California property developer. Bruning insisted that he wasn't leaving because his lobbying for an inner-city shopping center in the Crenshaw neighborhood of Los Angeles had been ignored. He had come to Sears to be a lawyer, but beneath the higher political battles that attended the submission of the once-maverick territory to forces in the Tower, Bruning had been allowed to linger in real estate so long that he actually knew too much about property and too little about other aspects of the management structure. The possibility of moving to Cold-well Banker was still several years of bridge-building away, so Bruning was lost.

Concern over the exodus of the likes of young Fred was exacerbated by the fact that the territories hadn't hired a single management recruit out of college for almost four years. Company personnel executives now feared an age gap so profound that Sears could eventually be as bur-dened by a paucity of capable representatives of a generation as they were by a surfeit of aging members of the classes of '47, '48, and '49.

But Ed Brennan scoffed at this sort of paranoid assertion when it came up and moved quickly onto other business. Whatever the source of Brennan's impatience with formal personnel procedures, he honestly believed that the only way to evaluate people was to see them in ac-tion—by which he meant that *he* had to see them in action. He spoke with such sarcastic derision about "human resource" experts that some on the forty-fourth floor thought that Brennan must have been abused somewhere along his route to the top by one of the old kingmakers who'd so imperiously run the personnel divisions in the territories.

Brennan denied that a newer, high-tech sort of cronyism existed now in the Merchant that favored a particular coterie of youthful executives trained in the Eastern and Southern territories. Though few readers of company signs were surprised when Burk Burkholder, one of the last remaining members of the "class of '48," decided to hang it up at the end of June ("The last of the dinosaurs," Phil Purcell said when he heard the news), the appointment of Eric Saunders to the top post in the Midwest sent an angry surge along the grapevine. The most repeated observation was that Eric had never run a store, and at Sears a manager from the Field just had to run a store.

Brennan was aware that the brash insertion of new people and new

systems was bound to be somewhat destabilizing. Those who were
scared probably had something to be scared about, and those who were
slow would eventually be left behind. The pace of the new appeared
lately to be overwhelming certain managers in Miami, Florida, for instance. Brennan already knew that he wasn't going to like the store he
was about to visit this day in Miami, and with so very much at stake, he
intended, along with the other Killer Bees, to find out what was wrong.

Miami had once been a source of great hope for Ed Brennan. During
the late 1970s, the rush of Latin American capital into the city brought
so many Hispanic consumers and tourists in search of all-American
goods that for a time the Miami group seemed insulated from the Sears
economic crises of those years, and insulated to some extent from the
larger international crunch that followed. When Brennan ran the South,
he viewed Miami as a nascent territorial cash machine, just as Los Angeles, Chicago, New York, and Dallas had provided wealth to their
respective Sears administrations. Brennan had just begun the process of
cleaning the cobwebs out of the Miami group of stores when Telling
called him to the Tower. But now the economy of southern Florida was
in disarray. Much of Miami resembled a vast construction site, abandoned suddenly to the humid heat and the sun.

The first official Sears Store of the Future was originally to be the one
at Miami's International Mall, a project planned during the brief regional boom. Since planning a shopping center during an economic
expansion was like leading ducks in flight with a shotgun, the DeBartolo
Development Group constructed the International Mall out in some
farmland west of the city in an anticipatory maneuver General Wood
and Sears had taught the retail industry back in the 1920s. For decades
the traditional bragging matches between Searsmen included announcing that cows and pigs had roamed the parking lot of a given store before
the community grew around it and made a store come to life. But the
housing market in Miami collapsed soon after International was begun,
and the shopping center ended up sitting absurdly in the middle of a
cow pasture—just at the time Brennan wanted to train public attention
on the mall as the site of his revolutionary new store.

When word came that construction problems would delay the April
opening of the Store of the Future at International, few on the forty-
fourth floor were resistant to the idea of making King of Prussia the
flagship.

International was finally up and running now, as was another Store of
the Future Brennan wanted to check out at the Aventura Mall, just a few
miles north of Bal Harbor, location of the abortive peace-and-planning
conference at the Cricket Club that Telling had convened back in the
spring of 1979. Aventura opened at the beginning of July, after the

venerable, rat-infested inner-city Sears store called North Court was put to rest. The old store was notable in company lore because for three years during the late 1970s it "came back from the dead"—something that happens to retail stores about as often as it happens to people in hospitals. North Court "went red" and began to expire, but the sudden cascade of Latin American money into Miami saved it at the last second and turned it into a profit-maker. But the remission had been short-lived and now it was dead and gone—"relocated and reopened in the Aventura Mall," as the press releases noted. A gleaming new Store of the Future now stood next to a 789-acre planned community replete with high-rise and mid-rise condominia, townhouses, garden apartments, pleasant landscaping, tennis courts, a golf course, and a marina.

As Ed Brennan swung his suit jacket on over his vest and strode determinedly into the store at the tip of the chevron formed by his entourage, shoppers in running clothes stood away and stared as if he was someone whose picture they must have seen. The arrangement of the moving wedge of official Sears store visitors was similar during the early hours of all Brennan's inspection tours. The manager of the store being visited usually walked within answering distance a few feet behind one of Brennan's shoulders. The territorial vice-president and Bill Bass were just behind the store manager; the group manager, joined by the other Headquarters visitors, occupied the middle of the formation; and the retail-group staffers and maybe one or two members of the store staff took up the rear.

In the long history of the company, only the infamous Gordon Metcalf had visited a store with a formal retinue similar to Ed Brennan's. "Gordo" liked to breeze through the store with his boys and get back to the lunchroom, where he would spend the rest of the time telling his inferiors about things Bob Hope had said to him during their recent golf outing ("Since none of you will probably ever get to meet Bob Hope . . ." he'd begin). The General liked to go in the back for a personal chat with the store staff, posing numerous personal questions about each manager's children, wife, and closest Sears friends—all by name. Wood had all this information carefully documented on little white cards he would bring along on his trips. For many years after his death, Sears store managers everywhere prominently displayed photographs of themselves standing next to the General, but by 1983, it was occasionally observed that those photographs had been replaced in most stores by portraits of a much younger man.

"Last store you ran was number one in the territory in luggage sales, wasn't it?" Brennan said to the manager of the Aventura store.

"Yes . . . it was," the manager said incredulously.

Brennan never used little white cards.

He moved through stores as if in slow motion, never floating past a single rack of clothing without gracefully separating each hanger so that a similar amount of space appeared between all of them. If Brennan came upon someone in a store who particularly interested him—"somebody who could teach him something," as he said—or someone who knew his mother, his father, or his uncle (as a diminishing but still amazingly large number of veterans actually had), then he or she would jump to the front of the phalanx until the group came to the edge of the next department.

An older black man at Aventura performed a fluid, easygoing pitch for the sewing machines he sold.

Brennan nodded approvingly at the end of the shtik.

"What's the *worst* thing about the machine?" Brennan asked.

"Stick you a thick ole sock in it and it breaks the bands," the man said quickly.

"Thanks for being honest," Brennan said, glancing quickly at Joe Batogowski. The glance was all that was needed to inform Bato that he was to check the validity of the statement, talk to his buyer, have his buyer talk to the machine's manufacturer, and then report back to Brennan—who would not, even weeks later, have forgotten the silent interchange.

A departmental manager or salesperson who presumed to "teach" Brennan "the business" or "tell him things" was visited swiftly with a question that indicated Brennan in fact knew more about the goods than the person feeding him lines. A look of terror often passed over the challenged employee's face that was not unlike the one seen on the faces of middle managers when they had to sit next to Brennan at a lunch or a dinner. The executive scramble before meals with Brennan usually looked like a polite dance of feigned confusion, but the fact that nobody wanted to sit next to him was never in doubt. Brennan occasionally cut short the scramble by naming two dinner partners and telling them which chair to sit in.

He often ended up sitting all by himself in the front of the jet while five or six executives crowded into the uncomfortable bench seats in the back. Ed Brennan loved more than anything to "relax" by talking about the business, and since everyone believed he knew more about the jobs they were getting paid a great deal of money to do than they did, it seemed unwise to do anything but try to stay away. In fact, Ed Brennan didn't really know "everything about everything" at Sears—as he once had been accused of believing about himself before he stormed out of a particularly tendentious Hay Committee meeting back when he was still "the kid." He knew everything about certain items, certain lines, and certain procedures, and it was these things to which his incisive questions often referred. Brennan undoubtedly did know more about Sears and the things it sold than anyone in modern memory, and he possibly knew more about merchantry for a man his age than any other merchant in the country, and as much about it as any veteran, but it only *seemed* like he knew all things. Residents of his inner circle were capable of enumerating the short list of his blind spots, but none of them had climbed up so high in the Tower by being fools.

At one point during the Aventura tour, Brennan stopped short in front of a messy arrangement of the high-tech display cubes Claude Ireson's team had designed for the Store of the Future's display of blue jeans. He looked like he'd just witnessed a horrible accident. The jeans were all folded differently, and some of them hung out of the cubes askew. "This place looks like a warehouse," he said in a loud voice. "This is the old Sears." He sprung to a nearby, overloaded rack, his pants cuffs slamming against his ankles like church bells. "And *this* is the old Sears." His fingers separated the hangers so quickly that they were hard to see. He rushed over to another cube full of dress shirts, and the tops of his ears began to take on a pinkish tint as he glared at the now quite pale store manager. The displays abutted a shelf full of heavily scented candles, scented stationery, and a smattering of Smurf greeting cards. "Joe!" Brennan yelled. Batogowski came quickly to the apex. "I want a complete study of dress shirts. The whole display. All these years of work, and it stinks. We're back where we started here!"

Ed Brennan became discernibly uncomfortable in the presence of disorder. His own preoccupation with material order clearly went back beyond his tutoring at fifteen in the proper spacing of hangers bearing men's suits at the feet of Mortie, Moe, and Eddie at Benson and Rixon.

Many of the merchants at Sears carried little amulets with them at all times. Some had lucky silver dollars marked by a year when they sold the hell out of something, and others never left home without key chains that included ornamental representations of the goods they sold, or a bit of steer horn or rock that came from a town where they'd really made a difference. Joe Batogowski carried in his wallet at all times a letter he'd once received from Joseph T. Moran, Jr., dated January 12, 1979. It was the note Moran sent in response to Bato's suggestion that Sears should get into direct-response marketing that basically called Batogowski a fool. "Mr. Batogowski," the poet of Sears wrote. "On conducting a Direct Mail program of merchandise; No. Nay. Nyet. Negativo. Nullito. Non. Ugh. You'll be fine in a day or two." Batogowski had ripped up the letter in a rage the day he received it, but Phil Purcell's secretary had salvaged the copy that now served the young merchant prince as the emperors of Rome had been served by the fellow who stood behind them while the throngs cheered to whisper, "You are only a man." Carrying the letter was for Bato a ritual not unlike Bill Bass' pre-flight reverence for the corporate jets. You needed something to keep your feet on the ground when you were spending so much of your life looking down at everything from various windows in the air.

Where Batogowski carried his humbling letter from Joe Moran, Ed Brennan carried always a tiny square photograph of a young man standing in front of a perfectly ordered display of dress shirts. The faded picture depicted a grinning, clear-faced twenty-two-year-old division manager in the men's-furnishings department at the Sears store in Madison, Wisconsin, and there behind the young Brennan appeared an ordering of white shirts that look like they were suspended in air, such was the perfection of their alignment.

Brennan hated to see square objects on table tops not sitting square to the corner, and he was forever rearranging articles around him not at right angles to one another. When he rose from a chair dressed in his billowing but wrinkle-free shirt sleeves, he would make a great ceremony of regarding the jacket hanging on the back of his chair and then picking off the tiniest piece of fuzz.

He was by no means alone in this compulsive devotion to physical order. Bill Bass and Joe Batogowski were both constantly approaching other executives to pull lint off their shoulders and straighten their ties. At home, Bill Bass' business suits were all lovingly feathered on one side of a huge walk-in closet, and his dress shirts were similarly arranged on hangers on the other side. The very cucumbers in the salads Bass made for himself in the evening were all so perfectly similar in thickness that it appeared they'd been measured with a micrometer. One of Joe Batogowski's young daughters—Bato had six children—loved to take his shoes off at night and then place them in the closet where they belonged. But Joe always had to realign the shoes in relation to the others when she was through, because she never got it quite right. Claude Ireson had actually built a little rack on which to position his shoes, so gravity would cause the heels to catch on the rack and bring the the toes into a perfect line.*

The orderliness was all built into their store. They'd built a store that

---

*For his part, Ed Telling was known to prefer a desk clean of dust, paper, or pen, and he was said to be quite particular about his bathrooms—always looking for dust balls behind the bathroom doors in hotel rooms before he unpacked—but his sartorial habits hardly fell into the realm of compulsion.

was an extension of their own closets, and now the people who worked in the stores had to learn to arrange all toes along the new line.

Many hours later, when Brennan finally finished his inspection of the Aventura store, he shook his head and sighed.

Aventura was a "retrofit" Store of the Future. The mall had already been under construction when the concept of a new store was born, so the space allotted to Sears at Aventura was comparatively limited. The logical components and adjacencies visible at Vernon Hills and King of Prussia were obscured at Aventura by the lack of space, but since others among the eleven "A" stores marked for "retrofit" by the end of the year were also smaller than the ideal, adjustments needed to be made quickly that would ensure that Brennan's store could be sustained. "Well, let's at least go check out the competition," he said in disgust.

All but the five most senior men were cut from the entourage for the reconnaissance mission into the mall. As the smaller group headed out of the store, Brennan veered over to the Allstate, Dean Witter, and Coldwell Banker booths that constituted the Sears Financial Network Center to say hello. He said after turning away from the booths that he sensed that the Dean Witter and Coldwell Banker workers were in many ways a better fit in the retail stores than the Allstate people. Telling referred to the Dean Witter and Coldwell Banker newcomers in the booths as "hucksters like us." Brennan called them "big-ticket salesmen."

Brennan raced through the contrived public squares of the mall. "It's a pretty one," he said over his shoulder after touring a Lord & Taylor store, "but a bad mix of goods on the racks." He then breezed into a new J. C. Penney store as he quoted easily from a copy of Penney's most recent strategic-planning report, which had been leaked to some retail analysts. Brennan was intrigued by Penney's recent decision to increase their apparel sales up to nearly 70 percent of their total, a move that included the abandonment of Penney's paint department, large-household-appliance departments, and even their lines of automotive products. Since Sears research indicated that Penney's was vulnerable to incursion by Sears already because of the Merchant's superior integrity rating and the fact that Penney's customers already shopped Sears for some goods, Brennan believed their decision to drop their heavy lines and go after the department stores might play into his hands with storybook timing. Penney's did almost $500 million in automotive business before the strategic move shut that sector down, and the grafting of even a portion of that figure onto the $2 billion in automotive sales the Merchant already took in would be helpful to the cause.

Penney's had humiliated Brennan on the bottom line during the second quarter of 1982, but he was running full-bore at triple their profits so far in 1983. Widening the gulf as the balance of sale in durable goods swung his way wouldn't be as much fun as surpassing the profit margins of R. H. Macy and Company, the retailer Brennan considered the best in the world next to Sears—and it wouldn't make as profound an impact on Wall Street as would shutting down K mart with a huge sales rise— but Brennan hoped to pass that latter milestone too if everything went according to plan.

That evening Brennan asked his men to congregate in a hospitality suite on the twenty-third floor of the Miami Regency Hyatt House Hotel. Only a small number of Field executives present at the store inspection had been asked to join the Killer Bees for dinner, but the huge gray tub full of ice in room 2330 at the Hyatt still contained enough beer to serve a large fraternity party.

Everyone had arrived but Brennan, and while most of the executives lingered near the bar or carved at a gigantic wheel of brie and talked about sports, Joe Batogowski sat next to Bill Bass at the far end of the suite listening to Bass snarl patriotically at the Central American revolutionaries depicted on the evening network news. "We oughta do sumpin'," Bass barked as men in khaki ran across the screen through a jungle. "Goddamn it!" Bass turned for a reaction from Batogowski, who was sitting above him on the back of the couch, his leg hooked casually over the arm. Bato decided not to react and continued to stare at the news.

The process of adapting to higher office in a manner that pleased Ed Brennan hadn't been easy for Batogowski, and in some ways it made him feel lonely. He still lived in a suburban community west of the city, along with some twenty-five other middle and upper-middle managers at Sears, several of whom were the guys he drove to work with and played golf with on the weekends. But now he sensed he was supposed to isolate himself in the name of good management practice, and it made him sad. He knew it was hard for some of his pals who were still buyers or even the heads of departments to talk shop informally in front of him lately, so he figured that once the new house he was building in a different town was done, things would be easier for everyone. The new house was being constructed high on the fairway of a former golf course. If he had to guess, Bato figured that Ed Brennan was pleased he was moving: it indicated his willingness to grow.

Though the system now called for Batogowski and Bill Bass to represent two halves of the same unified decision, it seemed on occasion that the only thing they had in common was the system and Ed Brennan.

Both men spoke of the decisions they made together behind closed doors as "unilateral" ones. They had dutifully formed a public relationship in precise counterpoint to the bickering warlords who'd preceded them both, and now, ten months after Joe Moran's death and close to three years since Charlie Wurmstedt's retirement, Bass and Bato were still in performance, still scrutinized wherever they went, as other managers tried to gauge how well they were handling the politics of corporate union.

"Know what we oughta do?" Bill Bass growled at the end of the news report. "We oughta get the Marines down there and clean the bastards out." Again he looked up at Batogowski to see where he stood, and Batogowski shrugged. Then Bato turned his face away and rolled his eyes.

The world outside of the United States was a day-to-day personal affront to Bill Bass, for reasons far more important to him than his political sensibilities. Brennan had made Bass responsible for the unholy mess that was the Sears, Roebuck international division—not the new international face of Sears revealed consistently in the press in the form of another cutting-edge trading agreement struck in some exotic capital by Rod Hills, but the one that had been created under the spell of the General's post-war belief that there was nothing wrong with a foreigner that a decent Kenmore washer couldn't fix.

The General had dreamed in particular of teaching the people of Latin America about the solid ways of the North American middle classes via exposure to Sears, Roebuck retail stores. After the first such store opened in Havana, as part of the Miami group, Wood spent a great deal of time watching local bishops bless Sears stores in Mexico, Brazil, Venezuela, and several other nations before getting back into his DC-3. By the now famous year 1955, the company was recording $75 million in pesos, cruzeiros, and bolivars on the consolidated bottom line. In 1955, the stores south of the border were known as "the sixth territory."

Other than the summary expropriation of the flagship store in Havana during the Cuban Revolution (Fidel Castro called Sears the least offensive of imperialists, while Sears internal documents referred to the nationalization of the Cuban operation as a "change in management"), the Latin American store program expanded without pause for two more decades. By 1978, there were well over a hundred stores and sales offices spread across Mexico, Brazil, Venezuela, Colombia, Peru, Costa Rica, Panama, El Salvador, Nicaragua, Honduras, Guatemala, and Puerto Rico. Though gross sales had continued to expand in most of these stores, local inflation and the concomitant currency-value adjustments made at reporting time forced the corporation to take large write-downs on the operations during the 1970s.

The smoldering of political fires in South and Central America caused a great deal of consternation in Chicago. In 1979, the Venezuelan government actually forced Sears to cough up the operation altogether. As the American empire of Sears descended into its own battles over freedom, sovereignty, and systems of governance, the old images of local soldiers holding vast and gleeful crowds away from newly opened Latin Sears stores gave way to reports of soldiers in machine-gun nests lurking on the roofs of the stores.

During 1981, Telling had flown south with Brennan and Phil Purcell to take a look at the situation. Telling and Purcell both came home from the tour intent on unloading all the operations, with the possible exception of retaining minority interests in Brazil and Mexico. But Brennan believed that Mexico—where his mother had served as one of the first Sears employees—could be completely revived under proper management; that Brazil could be turned; and that the other operations required careful monitoring.

During 1982, Brennan's determination to keep his hand in play in Latin America led to a $42-million loss. Though almost $35 million of the international division's losses in 1982 were attributable to the devaluation of the Mexican peso, the gross revenues were down nearly $200 million in the stores. After the Nicaraguan operation closed down that year, the inventories at the Managua store were donated to charity, but a subsequent investigation conducted by Sandinista authorities concluded that the Merchant had left behind a $500,000 debt, a charge Sears denied.

It was soon decided on the forty-fourth floor that it was time to cut and run. The unloading was accelerated with the closing down of Costa Rica, Honduras, Guatemala, and El Salvador. In April of 1983, Sears found a buyer for its eleven-store, thirty-six-hundred-employee operation in Brazil. After thirty-four years in residence, it was difficult to find a professional retailer working in a major store anywhere in Brazil who hadn't learned his or her trade at Sears. Sears had built the first modern stores, taught people to run them, found the goods to stock them, and helped carve new canals into the consciousness of enough people in Brazil to create the largest consumer market in Latin America.

A mood of abandonment had spread through the ranks of business people and consumers resident in many of the countries in South and Central America by 1983, because it was widely believed that Sears was leaving them partially geared and wired in a world without spare parts.

Arthur Wood had entered into a partnership called Simpson-Sears with a Canadian retailer that Ed Telling wanted to dump with the other operations until he was informed that, in the original partnership agreement, Sears had ceded the right to the Sears name and trademarks in a way that would have lasted beyond divestiture. So instead of leaving, Telling bought control of the Canadian operation for just over 211 million Canadian dollars and had lately charged Brennan—who in turn charged Bill Bass—with bringing the rejuvenative spirit of the Store of the Future north of the border under the banner of "The New Sears in Canada." The Canadian wing now held the potential of becoming the sole bright spot for the international division, but there was slight chance of its illuminating the blackness that had descended on the company's other operations in the Americas during the year.

"We are indeed backing away from many of our South and Central American ventures," Ed Brennan admitted to a Western Territory group staff he was visiting one day in the middle of 1983. "I think our future is right here. Any time you find a country that can pass an edict in one day that wipes you out with the stroke of a pen—and that's happened in several places—then you shouldn't be there anymore."

Brennan finally bounded into the suite at the Hyatt. He was wearing a gleeful smile and an astounding Astroturf-green blazer of the sort that can occasionally be found on people giving out awards on televised golf tournaments. Some of the men in the room were unaware their mouths hung agape.

Brennan paused in the middle of the room and turned for effect, then he began to inspect all of the light-gray business suits around him with obvious disdain. "Excuse me, but isn't this Miami, Florida?" he asked with a gleam in his eye. "I mean, you fellas look like a damned bunch of bankers!"

Dinners with senior executives of a local retail group—especially one like Miami, which hadn't been up to snuff—were usually just as rigidly formal and carefully staged as the great banquets Brennan held in Chicago, but the smile and the amazing jacket signaled that tonight was clearly going to be relaxed. Everyone could loosen up a bit. The vast distance between leader and led would be lessened. Brennan said the courtly formality of so many of his high-level business interactions had something to do with the residual formality of the retail business. "I've never asked any one of them to call me Mr. Brennan as they do." But, then, he never asked any of them to call him Ed.

Brennan's spirits seemed lightened this evening by the presence of his slender, sandy-haired, twenty-three-year-old son, Donny, who lived in Miami and worked as an assistant manager at a local store owned by the

Federated Department Stores chain. Donny was recognized by name in the Southern Territory as a character in several of his father's often repeated parables. Whereas Joe Moran used to take lessons from Sears home to his family, Brennan tended to bring exemplary tales about his family to Sears. During the great quandary over whether Sears should get out of the credit business in the early 1980s, the radical drain of credit costs was thought by some to be capable of destroying the company. Brennan finally rejected the idea of killing off consumer credit by declaring: "My daughter Cindy and my son Eddie are starting out in the world. They can buy a house, but they'll need a refrigerator, a washing machine, a range—and they don't have cash. I believe they have a right to borrow on the future."

Brennan often contended that the superior moral tenor that characterized a life within Sears was borne out by the fact that in thirty-one years he'd never been asked to do a single thing he couldn't go home and explain to his kids. "For me, it's the acid test of ethical conduct," he'd say. "Not whether the law of the land says something is O.K., but whether or not you can justify it to your kids."

Dinner this evening was booked into a private dining room at the Banker's Club on top of a building a few blocks from the Hyatt. Donny Brennan and his father walked out ahead of the group talking about family and home. Behind them, the rest of the entourage trudged through the fetid tropical air under a volcanic red sky and an early scrap of moon. The sidewalks along the route were as emptied of life as the partly constructed office buildings all around the center of the city. The few cars on the streets responded to the absence of pedestrians by traveling along at highway speeds, so at one corner, where it appeared that some members of the Sears group were going to attempt to cross the street at a stoplight that had been red for a while, Brennan said, "Let's wait." Unconsciously, he started to stretch his arms up from his sides like the student patrols at school crossings, before he caught himself and dropped his arms back to his sides.

When the light changed, the Brennans continued to catch up on family news. Donny's sister Linda, the youngest of the six kids, had spent the summer at home in Burr Ridge, a small suburb west of Chicago, but was about to leave for cheerleading camp and then college. Donny's brother John lived at home during the summer too, and his job managing a local McDonald's franchise kept him out until 4:30 A.M.

As with many Sears kids, when it came time to settle down several of Brennan's children chose to return to one of the many places they'd called home along the career paths that crisscross the field. Sharon Brennan had settled down in Atlanta, the headquarters of the Southern Territory, and she was doing quite well as a buyer for another division of Federated Stores. Eddie was working in the retail business in Macon, Georgia, after also living for a time in Memphis and Atlanta. A married daughter named Cindy was now in her third home in four years of marriage to a young television sportscaster. All the kids were used to moving around.

On a wall in Ed and Lois Brennan's most recent home, in Burr Ridge, there hangs a framed pen-and-ink drawing depicting some of the many Brennan family homes. A lady in a shopping mall drew the houses from photographs. The drawing includes the small house in Elmhurst, Illinois; the larger two-story colonial in Elmhurst; the colonial in Baltimore where the family moved in 1967; the New Jersey house; the Spanish-style one in Buffalo; the Philadelphia house, in which the shortest stint of all was spent in 1975; the Boston house, the first really big one; and finally the one in Atlanta.

Burr Ridge, located twenty miles outside Chicago at the far edge of the suburbs, was within the east-west suburban corridor where, from the time of the catalog men, most Sears executives tended to live. West of the city, country-style opulence was available at comparatively reasonable prices, and the commute to the old West Side Headquarters used to avoid rush-hour traffic north and south of the loop. Bass and Batogowski both lived in the western suburbs, while Telling lived near Allstate in Northbrook and played his desultory and often truncated games of golf in the restricted confines of Lake Forest, where the General and his Tall Men had separated themselves from the foot soldiers.

The Brennan house was part of a small enclosed development of the sort favored by many senior corporate executives. Managers who travel a great deal seem to appreciate the security of a manned gatehouse, and the luxury of having the grounds of their houses cared for by the community staff. Telling lived in such an enclave up in Northbrook, and Dick Jones and his wife lived a few doors away from the Brennans in Burr Ridge.

The house itself was elegant in the way of a middle-class rendition of the Petit Trianon. There was a French accent apparent in the large rooms, but it was assuredly an accent. The house revealed none of the signs of casual wealth observable at Jim Button's home or Arthur Wood's office. The rugs in the house were thick and white, and most objects rested at right angles to others. A crucifix or two hung from some of the bedroom walls, and the family always paused to say grace before sitting down to one of Lois Brennan's meals. Lois managed the large, spotless house without the assistance of a housekeeper. Ed said he couldn't stand having someone in service living in his home. "Through six kids," Brennan said at dinner before leaving for Miami, "Lois has done it all."

Lois was a singular off-the-payroll figure inside the Merchant because she was often mentioned by name. Many a Sears executive spoke with an uncommon enthusiasm not about "Ed Brennan's wife," but of "Lois."

The generic wife—"my wife" or "a man's wife" or, collectively, "the gals"—was usually brought up in company conversation only as a reflective reference to an executive's self-esteem. The rare ritual of firing a manager at Sears, for instance, revolved around "being able to go home and face your wife."

Several Sears executives noted with apparent pride that their wives didn't know much at all about their jobs or business problems. Telling said this often of Nancy, but he never went as far as some executives, who seemed to actually judge their ascent into the corporate stratosphere by how long it had been since their wives had "understood" what they did.

Bad marriages were well known but almost never discussed, and if an executive had an unusually quiet wife, a smart wife, an overly religious wife, or a wife who drank too much at the rare company functions they were asked to attend, it never seemed to reflect on her husband in the minds of his colleagues. Wives were just . . . too close to home.

Lois Brennan had managed to transcend orthodoxy through force of a strong personality and her habit of exercising the "boss's wife's" option of showing up at corporate functions where other spouses would not be welcome. Even the few female executives in the upper-middle ranks of the Merchant abjured their somewhat facetious tones about Sears wives ("the widows," as they were called for years) because they so very much liked Lois. She was a consistently warm and friendly woman with salt-and-pepper-colored hair, and eyes that were often alive with a laugh she tended to deny the rest of her handsome face. Lois was known for her "spunky" personality because she would speak her mind in public— even if it was to express her irritation with the fact that her husband's colleagues referred to her as "Lois" in front of the fellow who in the same sentence they called "Mr. Brennan." Though she would stand or sit at the back of assembly halls listening to her husband's intense, rousing speeches with a Madonna-like, impassive smile, and grow more sober when he launched a jeremiad against sloth or the waning of public civility, it seemed to many at Sears that Lois Brennan represented a looser, more relaxed side that a lot of them hoped also existed somewhere inside Ed.

From the time they were kids together, Lois had understood the paramount role work would play in a life with Ed Brennan. When they began dating in high school, Ed was working at a smoked-meat butcher in Oak Park, and no matter how hard he scrubbed himself in the shower after work, eventually the smell of his work would begin to rise from his pores. In movie theatres people would turn around sniffing. The work was ever present, and in essential ways it had dominated and defined the nature of their lives together. The Brennans were relatively isolated socially, and it seemed to both of them that each time Ed was moved up to another of the seventeen rungs on his ladder—"putting out fires for Sears and Ed Telling," as Lois saw it—they felt comfortable associating with an ever-smaller circle of Sears people.

But Lois said she saw the life as a challenge. When the family had gotten together during the past Christmas season, the six kids had sat around with Lois and Ed and reflected on their history of so many new houses, new neighborhoods, and new schools. The consensus was that for all of the tears and goodbyes, the moving was a good thing. "The kids met a lot of different people," Lois concluded, "and they learned how to be comfortable in any environment or any crowd."

After the steak arrived at the Banker's Club, Donny Brennan said, "I always figured that the reason so many Sears families were so large was because the families became like little enclosed societies that could draw together when the need arose. I know it made us very close," he said. "You didn't have many friends, because you were always new in town, so I'd get home after school and the kids would have complaining sessions together. The experience made me very outgoing, but I can see how it could just as easily have gone the other way."

Donny was in his assigned seat at the table in Miami, several chairs away from his father's side. The chairs on either side of Brennan were occupied by the vice-president of the Southern Territory and the manager of the Miami group, as was the norm.

Toward the end of dinner at the Banker's Club, Brennan suggested that each man at the table tell the story of how he had come to Sears and where he'd been since then.

"Just wasn't a job for me on the farm," said the veteran manager of the Miami group, Stu Thomas, when Brennan turned to his old colleague from the Corporate Hay Committee and asked him to begin. "So there was nowhere else to go but Sears. So I went on down to Norfolk, Virginia, and one day they told me to go around and give the people of Norfolk, Virginia, sumpin' called a credit card. Nobody I gave that card to had ever seen a credit card, and it was something pretty special. . . ."

"Well, gawd*damn* it!" crowed Bill Bass when Brennan called for his tale. "I only had one suit. Coat didn't really match the pants, but I still called it a suit—specially to anyone who wanted to argue. My first job? Well, my boss was one of your garden-variety, full-scale sons-a-bitches, a shipping-manager son-of-a-bitch at that. Worked in one of the old farm stores we used to have and we sold little chicks." There were smiles evident on all sides of the square table at the mention of the baby chicks.

"Damned things would be all alive on Saturday night, and I cleaned 'em all out dead Monday morning. I worked Boston," Bass said, invoking the East. "I've worked personnel, operating . . . lots of things. I went once to run a store in a little town called Rockland, Maine, and there . . . I had it all. I used to drive my own station wagon to deliver the people's goods. I had it all in Rockland, and it was a place where people . . . people were good." Bass clamped his mouth shut and passed on a turn to speak with his eyes.

As Claude Ireson, who'd rendezvoused with the Killer Bees in Miami, began to speak, his gentle voice fell further back into the accent of the hills of his youth. "I went to work for Sears, Roebuck 'cause I was ree-ul hungry that year," Claude said. "My daddy was a coal miner, and in 1950 the mines all went down. Day I graduated from high school was the day I went to Sears, and the first thing I had to do was pick out the dead chickens. I was eighteen years old and nobody told me they were even meant to be sold alive. I always was pretty good at art, so I started to help remodel stores. Then I met Mr. Ed Telling in Rockford, Illinois, and he put me on the staff on the Midwestern zone. . . ."

As other odysseys were revealed, the room echoed with whoops and loud laughter. Occasionally the name of a legendary difficult store or particularly hard-nosed manager would come up, and a loud groan would rise from the table.

Brennan called on the youngest man at the table, one of the staff executives working for Stu Thomas in Miami, and the fellow told a suitably terse story of himself: "There was Springfield, Missouri; Topeka, Kansas; Brownsville, Texas; Jackson, Mississippi; Beaumont, Texas; Houston, Texas; and Miami, Florida—with a detour along the way through the jungles of Vietnam."

When Brennan called on Joe Batogowski, Bato looked uncomfortable. He said that he too had shown up in a suit the first day, and that he'd never had a job outside of a factory before coming to Sears. He'd worked at a store in Torrington, Connecticut, and ran the auto center there after a while. He said he was turned down for a Headquarters job he really wanted because he was too young. Some of the people around the table chuckled at this. Then Bato raced through his perpendicular rise to the top and finished by saying, "Then I got this job," in a weak voice so absent of twang that it might have been heard on the television news.

Batogowski didn't mention that his dad was a machinist who'd worked his entire life in a factory and that his mother worked in a factory too. He'd paid some dues before coming to Sears, and done his share of motoring down rural blacktop lugging people's bags, and dodging fire in the days of Charlie and Joe, but because of a lingering sense that he'd rocketed past a few hundred thousand others too quickly by company standards, Batogowski found it hard to present his own Sears history so it sounded like a folk song.

The stories continued—short and long, happy and sad—until the circle was almost complete. All of the tales were, in a sense, about a company that had brought together the sons of miners with the sons of machinists and sons of farmers and made them all sons of the sale. There wasn't a man at the table in Miami who "didn't know how to talk English or had horns," as they used to say, and they'd all done pretty damned well by themselves and Sears, Roebuck, when all was said and done.

The circle ended with Brennan. Though the lessons of Ed Brennan's life at Sears were being told and retold in the backrooms of stores and warehouses at some time during each business day by the end of July in 1983, these moments of communal memory were not appropriate to his own tales. Brennan had consciously sacrificed the special warmth that others felt in the presence of company lore, in favor of the application of his own history to the operational rejuvenation of the company. His past was available only as lessons about merchantry, though at times the distance seemed to wear on him.

As the faces turned to him when the executive to his right was done speaking, Brennan paused before pushing his chair away from the table. "Let's go," he said. "You all know about me."

CHAPTER 22

The Gambler

A t least they knew some things.

They knew, for instance, that when the tops of Ed Brennan's ears bore even the palest stain of red—as they did when he toured the cow-pasture-bound Store of the Future west of Miami the next morning—it was best to stand clear.

Bill Bass observed the phenomenon from the cover of a rack of Cheryl Tiegs separates: "Chairman's mad," Bass mumbled.

After the tour, the visitors from Chicago joined members of the Miami-group staff and the senior territorial leadership for the South for a meeting in the training room. Brennan began the proceedings by staring intently at Tom Neal, the executive vice-president in charge of the South.

The latest "book" on Tom Neal read poorly, not only because of the precipitous decline in territorial fortunes that seemed to have commenced at the exact moment he'd succeeded Ed Brennan, but also because Neal was a weak public speaker. But, then, Neal, a long-time Telling crony, was also a particularly kind and gentle man, and whatever opinions were held about his administrative record among residents of the forty-fourth floor of the Tower, they were well compensated for by his being well liked on sixty-eight.

After formalities were exchanged between Neal and Brennan, it was time to begin the formal "Headquarters review" of the Miami group.

One of the first things Ed Brennan had done when he took over the

South in 1978 was to invade the sanctity of the Miami group. He brought in a tough cost-cutter from Greensboro, North Carolina, to help the group staff better understand the ways of goal-oriented payroll planning, and within a matter of months a turnaround occurred that propelled the group's profitability up toward 6 percent of their sales. The profit margin stayed there until 1981, when it declined radically—to below 4 percent. The slump coincided with the departure of free-spending tourists and boom-time Latin cash, but it also coincided with the promotion and sudden departure of one Ed Brennan.

There was no flashy slide show as in other group reviews, but the Miami staff had prepared a black three-ringed notebook full of statistics and maps for the meeting. On the first powder-blue page was a homemade map of Florida that showed the location of the stores in the $500-million group, as well as little symbolic waves that someone had drawn in off the shore all around the coastline.

After a section reporting the unfortunate aggregate group results, there were several pages about the Miami "Latin Market," which noted little more than the fact that there were now 750,000 Latin consumers near Sears' Miami stores. "Some evenings and Sundays, 95 percent of our shoppers are Latins," commented Stu Thomas, the veteran manager of the group.

It had been eight years since Ian Sym-Smith and the other consultants from the Hay group sought to compose a working committee from the most promising and outspoken talent then buried in the sludge of the company's middle. The Hay pickers had turned out to be remarkably prescient, in that all but two or three of the original committee members had eventually become officers. The irascible Ira Quint left Sears just weeks before Joe Moran finagled his apostles into officerships, so Ira was one who never made VP, and the jovial Stu Thomas of the Miami group—a big man with thick gray hair and an old-fashioned "looks-the-part" smile—was another.

As Brennan listened to reports on each store in the group, he peppered members of the group staff with curt questions, many of them concerning the disastrous Fort Lauderdale store—which was currently making over $1.5 million less in profit than it made during 1978. He also appeared concerned about the one in Hollywood, Florida: "You had a $2.5-million sales rise in Hollywood, but you missed the Plan in payroll. You didn't convert the sale into profit . . . and that disappoints me."

Brennan commented and asked questions, but he never once lifted his face from the matrices of numbers that covered the pages of the notebook.

A section in the back of the Miami group's report dealt with the two Stores of the Future in the area. It began with a carefully enumerated list of explanations as to why the start-up sales at both stores were so dismal. Over at Aventura there was the fact that the extension of U.S. 1 near the mall was not completed. A bridge was still under construction, the new Macy's had yet to open and draw traffic, and the seasonal shoppers dear to the region had not yet migrated south.

Brennan turned quickly through the daily sales reports from the stores until he came to a document that made his shoulders draw up and his eyebrows rise. Someone had inserted the original facilities-proposal form that decreed the construction of the International store. The last page of this 1979 proposal contained the usual list of signatures, including the autographs of Jack Kincannon, Charles Wurmstedt, Ed Telling, and the executive vice-president in charge of the Southern Territory at the time, E. A. Brennan.

Brennan stared at the document for a moment as the tops of his ears glowed a fiery-bright shade of red. Bill Bass moved his right hand up from the table, covered his eyes, and began to shake his head back and forth. Without looking up, Brennan continued to leaf through toward the end of the book, until he stopped dead once again at a page entitled "Summary Pro Forma P + L's by Years with Aventura and International Unopened, and Biscayne and Northside Open." Brennan's mouth parted slightly as his ears exploded with color.

"What . . . the . . . hell . . . is *this*?" Brennan said, grinding out each word, harsh and strained.

Stu Thomas grinned for a second before explaining the obvious fact that the sheet showed what the state of the retail group *would* have been had there not been the expense and strategic changes entailed in the relocation and building of the mandated new stores. There was also a projection through 1985 of what the numbers might look like if the stores had never been constructed. Apparently the group's computer people had whipped up the little exercise.

Brennan looked up quizzically at Stu Thomas. It was actually his gaze of utter incredulity, the one that asked, "Where do people like you come from?"

Did the Miami guys really think he was going to be fooled by this lame-brained computer-rigged excuse for a smokescreen? Did they fantasize for a moment that they could show *him* a new card trick at this stage of the game?

Several of the younger members of the Miami-group staff watched Brennan with widened eyes. The fact was, the young staffers were excited by the scene unfolding before them. The most aggressive among them were frustrated by their senior regional management's inability to fall into the new cadences. Now Brennan had seen it.

Ed Brennan was not above screaming at people at the top of his lungs.

Those closest to him had witnessed fits of ranting rage on rare occasions, when someone presumed to " 'splain the business" to him. But he was not about to raise his voice in front of so many managers.

As he began to speak, Brennan's eyes moved between Stu Thomas and Tom Neal like a metronome. "Gentlemen," he said in a soft, even voice, "we have a new Sears. The standards of the past have not been adequate. The cynics must be made to come over. They have to be gone from sight. They have to change sides."

Then Bill Bass raised his voice in a funereal chorus. "What was once acceptable no longer is."

Brennan rose and invited Bass, Tom Neal, and Stu Thomas into a small office near the training room. Then he began to scream.

Brennan detested the "lack of urgency" he occasionally saw in people. He could see it in the numbers in their books and in the deadness in their eyes. He'd seen it countless times since he'd begun to manage people's work, but it still galled him that someone could make peace with a lack of the will to succeed. Back in the days when he ran stores, he would confront people. "Why can't you think enough of yourself to really *be* here?" he'd ask. But that sort of anger didn't "fit the office," as he said, so now he had to keep it inside. Rage was certainly an available tool of leadership, but it should be displayed on rare occasions. Joe Moran had suffered for allowing himself to become far too fearsome.

"I have to remain very much aware of my role," Brennan said, slumping into the back seat of a car for the ride back to his plane. "Just as things that I suggest are quickly reacted to, if I'm not careful, they are *overreacted* to. But if five layers of management hadn't been sitting there, I would have stomped out."

Brennan hadn't come upon a screen of smoke he couldn't see through in over twenty years. The day the smoke cleared away, he was twenty-seven years old and present in a room filled with old-line Sears kingpin merchandise managers who were explaining the intricacies of their business to him. The men were filling the room with a dazzling fog of complexity and arcane lingo when it suddenly came to Brennan that they were talking a lot of crap. Beneath all the talk of fashion and the exigencies of production and marketing there were just tops, bottoms, coordinates, swimsuits, coats, dresses, and the sublines beneath them. It was just like life, which could be segmented into categories and phases and stages, given enough concentration and a strong mind. Right there and then Brennan remembered feeling the mystery drain away, and nothing much about business had seemed very mysterious ever since.

Brennan wasn't sure exactly why it was true, but during all his years moving through the management of the biggest retail system in the world, he'd only met a couple of others who really understood the mechanics of the flow. So many others had grown up in stores, as he had, but few of them had any conception of what really happened, for instance, between a customer's arrival at an aisle and the beep of the sale. Brennan had spent a lifetime studying sorting mechanisms behind people's eyes. He could look at a shopper and sense where she was in the inevitable process of decision-making: department, line, item . . . bingo. But he didn't have time to explain the architecture of a sale to an entire generation—"You can get them to church but you can't make them embrace," he said often—and that was why he had made them all one store that worked.

The Merchant's planning system was so firmly entrenched by the late summer that the expenditure of billions of dollars on the expense side of the system could be planned and controlled within a tiny error factor. The operational side of the Plan was so precise that it allowed the sort of observation of individual managerial performance that the old system was specifically designed to obscure in the name of independence. Through the planning system, Brennan drew responsibility for the promulgation of policy even further away from the territories, groups, and stores than had Ed Telling during his time of authority-gathering with Phil Purcell, but, as he'd been preaching since the time of the first Challenge Meetings, the loss had been replaced by a great number of new areas of activity that a manager needed to monitor and control. "If people don't influence their stores anymore because of centralization," he'd ask, "then why, when you take two stores with the same sort of markets, the same volume of sales, the same rent factor, and the same square footage, does one guy make money and the other lose it? Must be the manager."

But he would never understand how it came to pass that so many people "believed they were better than they really were." "So then he spoke to me as a great merchant—which he most certainly is not . . ." Brennan would often begin a story about yet another person who had tried to "tell him something." It was as if the whole company had been infected for years by some mass delusion, something the people had passed along and internalized, caught from one another like a disease.

Back in the plane, Brennan went directly to the benches in the back as Bass, Batogowski, Claude Ireson, and another store-design specialist who'd met the Headquarters group in Miami settled into the large seats near the cockpit. Someone located a deck of cards.

The Sears jet took off from the Page Aero executive airport, banked, and headed up through the heat and to the north. Within a moment after takeoff, coffee, snacks, and playing cards were flying through the cabin. The turbulence rolled the little jet from side to side in a way that caused all the seasoned air travelers on board to glance up toward the cockpit.

"Hey, George," one of the men in the front yelled up to the pilot, "find a new road."

Then the plane was lifted up abruptly from underneath, as if one of the gray-white clouds it was beginning to pierce had turned solid as snow. The gin game in front ceased and everyone pulled his seatbelt tight. Joe Batogowski turned around and looked back at Brennan, whose high facial color of an hour earlier had been replaced by the unhealthy pallor brought on by too much motion, work, or fear.

Now the nose of the de Havilland bucked up so violently that Brennan's hands flew out to grip the bench seats on either side of him.

In some senior circles within the Merchant and the senior corporate staff, the somewhat ironic comment "Let's hope Ed's plane stays up" had been made for over a year. The quip's implied criticism spoke to the sense in senior quarters that if Brennan had an Achilles' heel, it was his habit of doing it all himself. Members of Ed Telling's praetorian guard on the sixty-eighth floor observed that perhaps he'd "kept his head down" too long, that there were a few too many secrets of his grand design for the retailer's future that were not yet general company property.

A few months before Telling was to emerge from behind his constantly closed office door and choose a successor, Brennan had become aware of the criticism, and he was making efforts to back away from the potentially damaging image. He allowed that he had himself wondered what would have become of the Merchant if something had happened to him between the time he conceived of the Store of the Future and now. Even Jumpin' Joe Moran hadn't fully understood the meaning of the new store. Brennan worried at times that the project was the sort of thing that could fall into other hands at Sears—more probably a *committee* of other hands—in his absence, and just drift out slowly into the stores of the Field in some inexact general direction. It never would have been right.

Brennan considered himself "just to the right of a hands-on manager," but in truth he had to believe that the task of turning the Merchant necessitated his omnipresence—if not in person, then on video screens and reflected in slogans and careful plans. "You are out there explaining it in everyday words," he said. "You're explaining what the hell you're trying to do to people. You try to make it seem logical—and you think it is logical. But some people still have trouble with that. Some say we are trying to overmanage. 'Why don't you just let it come down through the channels?' they say. Some even say it's an ego trip, because your visibility is so high. But people *want* management—top management—to be visible."

Brennan's use of the pronoun "we" in reference to himself had first been observed back in Atlanta. At times the "we" was clearly of the imperial genre, though on other occasions it was a "we" that referred to the people who constituted his flying wedge. When not calling himself "we," he invoked "you"—a habit of usage he shared with Phil Purcell. He'd made some efforts to deflect the spotlight from himself by "personifying" business tasks. He'd taken to calling the buying organization "the Joe Batogowski organization," or the Field management structure "the Bill Bass operation," but the changes had done little to obscure the fact that just as the organizational "they" had become "we," "we" was usually him.

The de Havilland continued to be buffeted as if under attack. Though he rolled his heavy shoulders around trying to loosen up, each time the jet entered an air pocket and went into free fall for a moment, Brennan's eyes widened long enough to reveal the look of youth and innocence that he'd been trying to banish from his appearance and demeanor since he was a boy. Executives who'd worked for him in the past still talked about his insistence on appearing older than his years. One day back in the South, Brennan went out for a haircut and came back with a recent blow-dry that made him look astonishingly youthful and stylish. As soon as he got back to his desk, however, Brennan told his secretary to go out and buy some grease so he could press his hair back down into the style of responsible men of another era.

Brennan once turned to a territorial executive who was a few years younger and said, "You know, sometimes I don't get it. We're almost the same age, and it's like we're from two generations."

"Maybe because we're from different regions of the country," the other man, a Southerner, said.

"No," Brennan replied, shaking his head, "that's not it."

Except for a few veterans like Stu Thomas, hardly anybody was left who remembered how boyish and even naïve Brennan had once seemed. Since Joe Moran died, the youthful diminutive "Eddie" was rarely recalled in Brennan's presence, and after the ERIP exodus, those like Charlie Meyer—who used to remind Brennan of his former penchant for pinky-orange, polyester double-knits when he was the pickle-washer in the men's made-to-measure department—did their reminiscing about Brennan's innocence at the edge of golf courses and at tables in bars.

Brennan was forty-nine years old now, the same age the General had attained in 1929 while in the full flower of a burst of business genius that eventually marked the map of America with Sears stores. The General said he'd left a good job at Montgomery Ward a few years earlier because Sears was willing to let him exorcise his utter obsession with retail stores.

Brennan once admitted during the summer of 1983 that he too was obsessed—not with retail stores per se, but with Sears. "I probably always have been," he said. "Nothing I can really do about that. . . . Maybe it isn't terribly healthy." Later he decided that "obsession" was the wrong term for his relationship to the company. "Perhaps the right word is 'preoccupation,' " he corrected, "or . . . 'absorption.' "

Whichever term best defined his psychological connection to Sears, Brennan was intellectually preoccupied with individuals whose own fate was inextricably enlaced within the fate of great organizations. He spoke on occasion of the sense of honor he felt upon meeting François Michelin, scion of the French tire company that supplied Sears. With the rising and falling liturgical inflections Brennan usually adopted only in front of an audience, he recounted how the Michelin family had once prepared to destroy its own factories rather than allow the company to be sullied by the presence of German troops.

"Running a company like Sears isn't a job—it's a life," Brennan would say. "This is a calling, and no outsider, who hasn't grown up in the industry, could come in from the cold and try to run it—and they certainly couldn't do it in my style. Just look at the others—Finkelstein [of Macy's], Seibert [Penney], Pistner [Ward]—they all grew up in the business." Just lately, with the store unveiled and certain future events moving away from his control, Brennan had made efforts to unweld himself from the Merchant. He'd loved the vacation house down in Florida since he'd bought it, but recently he was trying to teach himself to decompress there on those weekends when he could steal away from work. There was a little bar-restaurant down in Jacksonville where he and Lois felt they'd made some extra-company friends. Among them was a conductor and a "free-spirited" couple who lived on the beach. With them, Brennan said, he never felt "on show" or required to say "something profound."

He'd always admired the way his father had been able to separate himself from work. His dad could sneak down a back stairwell known as "Brennan Pass" at the West Side plant before quitting time and drive with young Ed up to his little place in Burlington, Wisconsin. Then his father would put on an old shirt and a pair of walking shorts, stroll down to the local tavern, and shoot the breeze all weekend with a bunch of farmers.

Just two weeks before the Killer Bees headed for Miami, Brennan and his wife had actually taken a vacation to Europe together. It was their first trip there. Brennan returned more than a little proud that he'd avoided spending the whole time shopping the stores, and that his only contact with the Tower was when someone brought the sales reports to their hotel rooms. But Lois smiled when she heard him boast of the separation, because everywhere they went, at one level or another, Ed was still at work.

During their trip together through the Far East, Rod Hills was struck by Brennan's almost child-like capacity to soak up the new experiences of the journey. Like the best of the "natural" merchants of old, he had a capacity to take in sensory experience that amazed Hills, who remembered thinking at the time that, as strong and brilliant and seemingly well informed as Brennan was, he must have lived a life so limited it was deprived. The incident that Brennan brought home from the elite tour, the one he related to the merchants, was the time in Tokyo when he looked out of his hotel window and saw a Japanese window-washer swinging many stories above the ground across a façade of an office building, all the while washing windows at a breathtaking pace. "Look at him work," Brennan recalled thinking. From there the thought was broken into a thousand thoughts, ranging from the future of international competition to his own fascination with the human capacity for work. No matter how much he might have admired his father's knack for backing away from his labor, what truly thrilled and mesmerized him was a man suspended high above a sidewalk causing his life and his death to hang together in the balance, all within the span of a simple day's hard work.

Rod Hills was right about the limitations in Brennan's past. Vacations had never been a part of his life until the recent trip to Europe. There weren't even summer vacations when he was young. Before he was old enough to understand what a depression was, he was old enough to know there were money problems for the family, and since he was the eldest child the situation called for an endless array of summer jobs instead of vacations. Then there were the expensive bus trips Ed organized, when the kids would travel down to Mexico to see his mother.

The people who worked very closely with Brennan were often made uncomfortable when the subject of Brennan's family past arose. Out in Los Angeles, during a store visit in Orange County, a store manager made the mistake of having a hot lunch of Mexican food placed before the notably spice-free palates in from Chicago. As Brennan sat above his enchilladas, his eyes watering from the jalapeño fumes, he interrupted the beginnings of some derisive commentary about the cuisine. "I have a sister who's half Mexican." And a silence ensued that lasted for several minutes.

Because the Brennans were such a legend at Sears, most of the older executives of the ERIP generation had heard the story about Ed standing at a fence and watching his mother leave town. The Headquarters old-timers could well appreciate the social stigma of a mother leaving home and a subsequent divorce among poor Irish Catholics on the old West Side. It was part of the lore that Ed and his brother, Bernie, collected bottles in order to make enough money to go visit their mother at the Sears store in Mexico City after she went off to marry a Mexican military man and run merchandise over the hills for the General. Her two boys dogged her all the way to Mexico. Ed and Bernie just refused to accept the end of the family, so they tried to overcome the stark geographical indication of its demise, first through hard work and then through hard travel. For a time after Marge left and Ed ran the household, when it was just Ed and his dad together, the neighbors sometimes talked about how hard it must be for a little boy to raise a family.

His father was gone and Ed had already married Lois when he finally returned to Sears' fold, where he ascended through the swollen hierarchy at a pace his father would never have believed possible. When the merchandise company had its breakdown and fell into a state of organizational and moral decay that made its inhabitants able to concentrate their fear and hope on a hero, there he was—son, grandson, nephew, and brother of Sears, born low and risen high, like the honest-to-God heroes in books.

Brennan had arrived amid chaos and drew forth an order. His Store of the Future was more of an archetype than a prototype. The store was the final word in the unfinished debate over big versus small he'd been having with his father when Ed, the elder, suddenly died. The store was the biggest retailer in history writ small. One big store with four walls.

After he had spent just three years in control of the Merchant, the old barons of the chemical and oil and electric companies wanted to know more about him, and in some cases he'd become interested in them. The new chairman of General Electric, Jack Welch, dropped in one day, and Brennan sensed in their shared youth and general sensibility "a similarity" between them that he enjoyed.

The General used to say that no man in Chicago could run Sears. Ed Telling was on record from the beginning as saying "Nobody can run Sears." Ed Brennan had nothing at all to say on the subject.

"I am the same person I was when I was running a department in a store," he would say. "And I believe I project that. It makes people comfortable with me and I come across as believable. It's a natural quality—one of those things you can't fake." For some reason he needed to believe always that he had never changed. The month of doubt when he first came to Chicago was seldom mentioned. In retrospect it appeared that he had sprung full-born, and that everything around him had changed at his irresistible bidding.

Brennan could tell you where he was, what he was doing, and what the circumstances and forces surrounding him were at any moment during his cognitive life. He often set historical events to the calendar by employing religious holidays: "It was just before Palm Sunday," or "The day before Good Friday . . ." He could tell you about the styles of the shoes he examined that day when his father had taken him to his first store. He remembered it all with the clarity of an event in a strange dream.

"What is precious," they'd all heard at Jumpin' Joe Moran's funeral, "is never to forget."

The man was his own Homer, the powerful memory complemented by a knack for making his own experience—and even his destiny— sound to several hundred thousand people as if it was the same as theirs. If he'd elaborated a myth of himself; if he'd been accorded the sort of stomping, whooping public adulation usually reserved for rock-and-roll stars; and if he traveled to formal banquets in a style and in the company of the sort of retinue found in European courts before the Russian Revolution, then it had to be added that from the moment he stood beside the halo symbol of the first Challenge Year, he'd managed to convince the inhabitants of an apparently dying society that they had the chance to be united and young and triumphant again.

Through hard work, hard travel, and inspiration, the Merchant's spirit had indeed been reconstituted from the splinters of a shattered company that had become as physically dispersed and factioned and injured as the family of Edward Brennan's youth.

The awesome thing about the cycle of leadership in a hierarchy was that it moved inexorably toward points where events exceeded your grasp. Brennan claimed often that a business manager like him had to remind himself that you can't agonize over things you can't control. As someone once told Brennan, "Don't agonize over your neighbor's kids." The adage always made a lot of sense to him.

Interest rates can fly up without your say-so; cold winds roll off a lake and kill your prize rose; people can suddenly have heart attacks or get cancer. Your own brother can go to Montgomery Ward; and more than a few chairmen of the board have been known to choose the wrong successor.

. . .

Telling's negative reaction to Bernie Brennan's new job at Ward's surprised members of the sixty-eighth-floor coterie. The days of top retail
executives' abjuring conversation across corporate lines for fear of accusations of price fixing or anti-trust complications seemed part of the past
to most of them. But Telling's mention of the potential problems entailed in having two Brennans running the two Chicago retail giants
filtered down from sixty-eight as the strong possibility that Ed could not
move any higher in the company because of Bernie. It wasn't certain
whether Telling had actually said that Ed couldn't be chairman because
of Bernie going to Ward's, but that was the way it felt down on forty-
four.

The corporate net income for the first half of 1983 was already twice
that of the year before. The stock price had risen to almost $45 a share—
an incredible figure given the near-single-digit price of the shares so
recently. Dean Witter, Allstate, and the Merchant all contributed heavily to the general success, and whereas the merchandise company's
income was three times that of last year, 1982 had been notably weak.
The first-half rise still only made Brennan's merchants a few million
more dollars than the much smaller contenders from Allstate.

The Merchant was no longer "last among equals," but the business
had to roar now if Brennan's group was to rise up and truly stand alone.
There continued to be a disproportionate outside focus on Sears' financial businesses, and it was difficult to promote the alterations Brennan
had wrought in the merchandise company without directly juxtaposing
some of his changes to Ed Telling's early years as chairman. News of
great merchandising successes were often filtered up through Telling's
office or through Telling himself before they reached the public. The
real sense of how separately the merchandise company was being
managed was obfuscated by the pronouncements to the press and analysts from the sixty-eighth floor. A consummate retail coup, the revival
of old facilities to make them bear fruit, was being overshadowed by the
simple expansionist acquisition of things foreign and new.

Then there was the potentially damaging phenomenon of now having
two Eds worth talking about at Sears. For years Telling and Brennan
had been differentiated clearly as "Ed and Eddie," "Big Ed and Little
Ed," "the boss" and "the kid." "The chairman" at Sears for much of the
time since 1978 had been no one other than Ed Telling, but with the
dissemination of chairmen's titles throughout the new business groups
and the commencing of Ed Brennan's titanic efforts to impress his image
on the lives of several hundred thousand employees, a greater mass of
the corporate population now thought of Ed Brennan when they heard

the words "the chairman." This, from many observers' points of view, would not prove helpful to Brennan's quest at all.

To someone like Phil Purcell, the possibility of comparing the two Eds was simply beside the point: "Could Brennan have done what Telling's done to the company? Absolutely not. Could Telling have done to the Merchant what Brennan's done since he got it? No. Is one better than the other? No. Who's the better manager? Neither. They are simply totally different. Telling picks people and Brennan tells them what to do." Ed Brennan, Phil thought, was the "reasonable man" described by George Bernard Shaw. Purcell quoted the Shavian maxim that describes a reasonable man as one who adapts himself to the world, who, in Purcell's paraphrase from Shaw's *Maxims for Revolutionists*, "understands the world as it is and works within it." Ed Telling, to Phil, was what Shaw would call an unreasonable man, one who persists in trying to adapt the world to himself. "All progress," Shaw wrote, "depends on the unreasonable man."

Bill Bass, who'd served both men close at hand, was struck as much by their salient similarities as by the obvious differences. To Bass, both individuals were unlike any of the other people he had met throughout his entire life. "They're plain different from the rest of us," Bass said. "They always were—both of them. It's like they just don't come from the same place as everyone else."

Brennan's boss had been one of the least detail-oriented, least hands-on leaders of the merchandise company in its history. Telling used to say that his vision of hell was beginning a day in front of a Holiday Inn waiting for a Sears store manager. Then the local manager drives up and gives him a profit-and-loss statement. Then he is forced go to the man's retail store, where he must stand in the fellow's goddamned paint department all day, until he goes back to the awful Holiday Inn. "That's hell," Telling would say.

Though both men were obsessed with mastering the politics of human organization, two individuals could not have approached the inherent tasks in more different ways. Telling was a student of human motivation and institutional change on the grandest, most abstract levels, while Brennan wanted to know how every bolt fastened to the chassis before the thing was allowed to move. Telling was a master of timing, but so far away from the fray as to be invisible in the shadows. Brennan was everywhere.

Brennan had studied Ed Telling's style for many years. Some ten years earlier, Brennan was driving between stores in the New York group when he surprised some of the group's staff people in the car: "The problem with too many of the people who work around Mr. Telling is that you all try to emulate his style," he said. "You can't make it work like he does." So Brennan never tried.

Maybe it was because Brennan had created a persona in juxtaposition to his long-time boss—just as Telling's style was appreciated in contrast with his predecessor in office—but the Brennan men, and even the Telling men who now served Brennan, always felt slightly uncomfortable when the two Eds were together. There was something very strange about Brennan and Telling's relationship.

There was just no guessing what Ed Telling was going to do. Rumors had it that he'd told somebody on some golf course somewhere that fifteen years was much too long for one man to be a chairman of the board. Then there was Telling's strange involvement with this Rod Hills character. Bill Bass had to guess that Telling wasn't a big fan of Brennan's imperial style—not that he didn't have one of his own—but still . . . It was entirely possible that all the light shining on the young manager could burn him in the end, Bass thought. This "two chairmen" stuff wasn't going to help either.

Bass figured he could read Ed Telling as well as anyone after all the years they'd spent together, but for the life of him he couldn't figure out whether Telling even liked Brennan. They were so very strange together. If you ever thought that Ed Brennan was a man without insecurities or scars, all you had to do was see how itchy and unsettled he got in front of the man he'd worked for directly or indirectly for fifteen years now. The two of them together was something to behold: one a man of secret causes, and the other overtly driven and chased by the hounds of his own ambition.

Bass really wished Ed Telling would tip his hand, but he also knew he probably wouldn't. Telling would choose when he was ready to choose, and if he decided to pick his corporate son, the kid whom he'd sent out into the stalls of the bazaars to spread the word, then the next chairman would be Ed Brennan. But with Telling you just never could tell.

Bill Bass often looked back at Brennan during the terrible flight toward Chicago. Bass could be spotted staring at Brennan like this during a long day of work—occasionally wearing the look of fascination seen on faces in crowds gathered around accidents and fires.

Though many middle managers at Sears still believed that the thing about Brennan that was so scary was his incredible energy and knowledge, those very close to him knew that the thing about him that really unnerved you was his preoccupation with destiny. The strange holiness about the man derived from the same connection to a distant fate. There was something looming large and awesome in front of Ed Brennan that the people near him could sense but couldn't see. And behind him were very early experiences that fire an insatiable desire to surge upward and ahead. At the final turn of Ed Telling's private derby, the managers who worked at Brennan's side all knew that Ed Brennan was running a race begun a long time before he'd even heard of Ed Telling.

The way he seemed chased by his past and taunted by his future made Bass and the other members of the inner circle hurt for Ed Brennan. When he said, as he often did, "You can't be anything but what you are," all they could hear was a voice saying, "I can't be anything but what *I* have to be."

Brennan could not abide even the thought of his own failure at things. "If you truly fail at something," he said one time that summer, "then you ought to be thrown out."

But by late summer all this apparent jockeying between outsiders and the machinations of insiders on sixty-eight should by all measures of justice have been beside the point. Brennan, after all, was the gambler. He'd put out the fires and brought back the spring. The roses should be his.

"You know, I was always the youngest everything," Brennan said more than once during the late summer. He went so far as to actually articulate the idea of leaving Sears some day. The idea of growing old and unchallenged into the next century—even as the chairman of Sears—might not be enough, he said. Sometimes, he said, he thought about teaching.

The de Havilland had been bouncing through the air for two full hours when Bill Bass turned away from his hand of cards and looked out the window. The thunderheads had parted and the sun made the luminous clouds below appear as an endless, pillowy white plain. Piercing the dense, low-lying clouds in the distance there appeared a single, black-gray monolith, a familiar object adorned by two needle-thin aerials, each topped by lights like blinking eyes.

Others on the jet turned away from their game to look. Then, from the very back of the plane, a familiar voice was heard over the droning engines: "We're home," he said.

CHAPTER 23

Telling

|————————————|

Ed Telling was no more visible within the organization during the sixth year of his rule than he had been during the painful times at the beginning, when he arrived and quickly disappeared behind a closed office door on the sixty-eighth floor and into his cocoon of myth. When the chairman tired of his solitude, he would occasionally open his office door and shamble into the little alcove that connected the corner office to his private conference room.

He would loiter there beside the large and highly organized desk of Pat Jamieson, his administrative assistant and the guardian of the perpetually closed door. The chairman could have buzzed Pat from his desk when he wanted her attention, but usually he just talked in the general direction of his office door or wandered out to see her. Sometimes he arrived in front of Pat with a vague expression on his deeply lined face. He would list from heel to heel, as if he'd forgotten why he came out. Sometimes he would remember he was hungry. "Got some ice cream?" the chairman of the board would ask. Then he would go back inside while Pat—a meticulous light-haired women in her forties—rustled up something from the Sears-appointed kitchen off the executive dining room.

At least once during most days he was in residence that summer, Telling would walk a circuit around the plush and desolate halls of the sixty-eighth floor. He'd saunter out in front of Pat Jamieson, turn left between the two secretaries stationed outside Pat's breezeway, and head toward the quiet central hallway, a long beige expanse lined by rows of subdued etchings, vases full of fresh flowers, and small tables holding heavy cut-glass ashtrays that were as empty at all times as the executive corridor.

Telling would sometimes head west to say hello to Fran Brown, a pretty young woman whose blond hair was illuminated from above by a recessed spotlight. Fran was a small woman who sat at a desk in the middle of the reception area, and from the way she chirped greetings at people coming out of the elevators and fielded phone calls for the sixty-eighth-floor executive secretaries who were away from their desks, it was impossible to guess that she was a karate expert and a representative not of the Sears clerical pool but of its internal security service.

If he thought no one was looking, the chairman might pick up the copy of *The Wall Street Journal* addressed to Phil Purcell—the one that had been relegated to a table in the foyer since Phil left his office on sixty-eight and moved to New York. After checking the stock tables, Telling would continue down the hall, stopping at times to look into conference rooms and down connecting hallways to see if anybody was around. If nobody turned up to share a bag of gizzards or a joke, he would eventually end up back at his office, where he'd go inside and close the door.

So it was with Ed Telling that summer. He might have had a lot on his mind, but for all of the activity inside the business groups beneath him, it didn't appear that he had much to do. "Each unit runs itself," Telling would say, "an' it should." He wore a quality of tan now that attested to the amount of time he'd been spending in Florida with Nancy. Even the longest-term witnesses to Telling's legendary avoidance of long hours at the office had never seen him spend so much time away. Based on a forty-hour week, his remuneration during 1983 would work out to just over $2,000 an hour, but a considerable number of those hours Telling spent under the sun above North Palm Beach, barefoot and dressed in a swollen pair of Sears blue jeans that were cut off and well frayed just above the knee.

When he did come to work, Telling appeared to be more preoccupied than usual, more ethereal, and moved to wandering around and staring at walls. He said his thinking tended to be like free association. His thought train had always screeched to a halt for no apparent reason. He might fade away in the middle of a meeting or even a sentence and then resume a sentence over dinner at home with Nancy—or on a ramble through the halls, or even at assorted golf courses, ball parks, or racetracks—as if no time had passed by since he began the thought. All of his life, ideas had swirled near Ed Telling in anarchy, but now even those remaining veterans who knew enough never to try to read him had to wonder what he was thinking, because now he was nearing the end of his career.

Insiders wondered what the chairman had made of an incident at the spring annual meeting in Greensboro, North Carolina. Telling was in unusually good spirits as he presided over what would be his final meeting of shareholders as chairman of the board. He wasn't scratching himself much, and as polite questions were raised from the floor, the Southern inflections brought out his "old-hog-caller" accent in response. At one point Telling spotted the raised hand of Harry Korba, a holder of a small number of shares. Korba had become a regular attraction at Sears stockholders' meetings during Telling's tenure. Through the bad times and now the better ones, Korba had risen at each meeting to address "Mr. Tellings," on behalf of "dese here common stockholders." With his flat-top haircut, windbreaker jackets, and salt-of-the-earth speaking style, Korba seemed such a perfectly contrived testament to the good gifts of corporate democracy that many people thought he was rented by the company from a casting agency and planted in the audience each year. His photo appeared more regularly in the quarterly reports than any outside member of the board.

"As one of the three hunnert fifty thousand, two hunnert ninety-two common stockholders," Korba said after Telling called on him in Greensboro, "on behalf of these here stockholders and on behalf of the three hunnert sixteen thousand, eight hunnert employees of this here corporation as of December 31, 1982, I wanna congratulate the outstanding performance which this here corporation did for the stockholders and the employees." Korba went on to mention the rise in the price of the stock since the 1982 annual meeting (from $16 a share to around $40) and the impressive gains the employees had garnered via the profit-sharing plan. "Now," he continued, "the chairman of this here corporation, when he reaches the age of sixty-five, he has to step down, and I'm askin' the seventeen directors of this here corporation to, some kinda way, either amend the bylaws or institute some kinda withdrawal of this here law, so that this here gentleman—Mr. Edward R. Telling—is . . . extended!"

The room burst into prolonged applause and loud laughter. Telling gripped the sides of the podium and bobbed with laughter for over a minute with the crowd. Even as he called the proceedings back to order, he appeared alight with good cheer. For the rest of the meeting he was so relaxed that his strained, affectless public voice fell into the country song that he usually reserved for stories told on rare occasions to associates of many years.

Those long-time colleagues still on the payroll were thrilled to see him so happy. One of Telling's "people" (he referred to his sixty-eighth-floor coterie as "my people" more regularly than ever now) brought up Korba's audacious proposal at coffee the next morning. "Didn't hear anybody sittin' here rise to second the motion," Telling said straight-faced and clipped. He left the matter there.

Not one of the original sixty-eighth-floor officers who started out with Ed Telling in 1978 still served him in Corporate. Joe Moran was dead. The Charlies—Wurmstedt, Meyer, and more lately his long-time sidekick, Charlie Bacon—were all retired. Jack Kincannon was on his ranch near Dallas; the ever-nervous operations man, Tom Wands, was retired; and Phil Purcell was in New York learning a trade.

Telling bristled at the suggestion that the original senior officers had been replaced from the ranks of his long-time cronies, but the most casual look at the second-string cordon around the chairman revealed that old cronies, company war buddies, and former praetors of his groups and territories were exactly what most of Telling's "people" really were. Several of the senior officers in Corporate had earned their stripes in the old Eastern Territory: Dick Jones was a veteran of the East, as were Phil Knox, the corporate general counsel; Charley Moran, who had replaced Phil Purcell as the corporate planner; and Bill Sanders, Charlie Bacon's replacement as the head of corporate personnel, who had once served Telling in the East despite having hair that flowed far below his ears. Sanders had grown his hair out in order to irritate an old-school store manager who exercised his sovereign rights by refusing to hire any man not sporting a crew cut. The fact that Telling never told Sanders to cut his hair was an early indication to others in the East that Ed Telling was much more interested in people who could do the job and who exhibited a healthy contempt for the status quo than he was in appearances.

Henry Sunderland and Bill Bass resided twenty-four floors below sixty-eight, but every so often they would come up from their offices in the realm of Brennan, scare up a couple of the other Eastern Territory vets, and sit around with Telling. They would all talk in that marble-mouthed, tobacco-chaw way, and generally hee-haw together like a bunch of rural courthouse rats. Bill and Henry were the only senior merchants who could impinge on the serious-mindedness of the Brennan orbit. Sunderland told dumb jokes whenever they came to him, often with Bass as his straight man, and when Bass parried, Henry often let fly with "Fuck you." It wasn't seniority that allowed them the impunity to act outside of the forty-fourth-floor norm; it was Telling—and everyone from Ed Brennan on down knew it.

The corporate public-affairs vice-president on sixty-eight, Gene Harmon, hailed from the Midwestern Territory, but he was a particularly well-read Kentuckian with many miles of blacktop under his belt from a life in the Field, and enough grit left over to enjoy a bag of gizzards, so Harmon was in. The old bean counter Archie Boe also got a bye just for being born in a town called Estherville, Iowa. It had been five years since Telling had taken Charlie Harper's limo away and four years since the fall of the flag-draped bastion Harper inhabited as the head of the New York buying office, but Telling had mysteriously kept Harper safe since then and close at hand in his role as corporate secretary.

Harper and all the other residents of the Telling inner circle on sixty-eight saw themselves as survivors of company storms that had swept so much and so many others away. Most of them had risen from a spot so close to the humble base of the organization that they were often made uncomfortable by their elevated status and the plush, sparsely peopled quarters they occupied on the sixty-eighth floor. All the officers on the sixty-eighth floor save Archie Boe talked constantly about how much they missed the whirlwinds and the emotional highs and lows of retailing, and all but Archie believed in their hearts that they could take the elevator downstairs and take over the Merchant in a second if fate ever called them down to do so.

And of all of them, only the lawyer Phil Knox had been trained to do what he was now doing for Ed Telling and Sears. They were all merchants who'd become PR men, store jockeys who'd become financial officers, or catalog men who'd become corporate planners—and in that the modernized, souped-up new Sears was still different from other big cutting-edge corporations. Despite the presence of interlopers like Rod Hills—the shared mistrust of whom was another element that bonded the sixty-eighth-floor officers together—and the growth of elite staff apparatchiks beneath them who were trained to handle technology and systems rather than customers' goods, Sears was still run on at least one last floor by merchants and men instead of experts, M.B.A.s, or machines. And, of course, the damned robot mail-machine didn't even work on the floor because the rugs there were too thick, so a man handed them their mail, as of old.

Beyond all other things, though, what held the senior corporate staff officers both together and apart from others was their shared, usually unspoken commitment to protecting the big phlegmatic man who sometimes wandered past their offices as if in a dream. "If you so much as say a single bad word about him, we'll jump all over you," Henry Sunderland would say. The members of the coterie showed, by their constant vigilance and willingness to cast themselves in the way of any force that could injure Telling, that their devotion was something other than ordinary loyalty. Some of Telling's people shared a history of massive executive labors at his behest, of cowing maverick territories and crushing pockets of power because of nothing more than something they'd heard Telling utter in passing one day.

The men moved for him less from a pure desire to please him, or from fear of the consequences of failing him, than from a profound desire to protect the leader from disappointment. It seemed that at one time or another each one of them had glimpsed, however briefly, the great capacity to feel pain inside Ed Telling, and from that moment they'd all dedicated themselves to keeping him from being injured again. Whether they would admit it in so many words or not—because the very idea sounded so absurd—each of them knew that Ed Telling was a profoundly delicate man, and they all sought to protect him from any exploitation of his vulnerability, as parents protect a sensitive child. None of them might have known exactly who Ed Telling was much beyond Bill Bass' simple assertion that he was "different"; and they might not have been able, even after decades at his side, to call themselves his friends; but the men whom observers on other floors and in other offices considered little more than factotums to the chairman were much more than that. They were Ed Telling's votaries, all of them harboring a tragic sympathy that had dominated and in many cases enhanced their careers.

"I've been hurt so many times, you just can't hurt me anymore," Telling would say to them, but those like the now departed Charlie Bacon, or Bill Bass, or Henry Sunderland—who'd watched him drift away into silence for days on end, or had seen how slights and regrets disappeared so quickly inside him, like raindrops into sand—never believed it.

Ed Telling was a survivor who'd emerged without benefit of the survivor's protective scars. He revealed almost nothing, but all the loyalists knew he remembered almost everything in a way at times too vivid for him to bear. Each of them had seen this in reflection on those rare days when he would go yokel on them. Just as he reverted into an apparently impenetrable old hog-caller from Danville, Illinois, when things around him got too public or unpleasant, he would occasionally slip back to the same cornfields when things were particularly good—when a deal had finally been struck or an old score finally settled, or on a particularly fine summer day that touched him with its warmth and light. On those rare days, the change in his pocket would stop jangling, and he would talk, in bits and pieces, of his past. It was then that a listener might hear the echoes of his cause: "I was raised like most bo-ahs," he might begin, his accent as loose as his voice would be tight and high. "In a small town of thirty-two, thirty-three thousand. I sold magazines, carried papers. There was Boy Scouts. There was football, basketball, an' then I went off

ta college. I was lucky to grow up where I grew up, and the time and
the town were special in every way in the '20s.

"I had a good mother and good father," the story continued in the
strained and then faltering voice—"I don't mean that. I had a tremendous mother and a . . . a *good* father. He was a Boy Scout. He was *the*
Boy Scout, really, and because of that I might have been the youngest
Eagle Scout in the United States. Took me only a year to do it all. You
could start at twelve, and I was thirteen in April, and an Eagle Scout that
June. I was up and out of the Boy Scouts before most people get in."

Telling's father, Ed Senior, was the seventh of eight children, and
though young Ed's Uncle Albert stayed out on the Telling family farm
near Broadlands, the old hog-caller from Danville now running Sears,
Roebuck was the son of a small-town banker. Uncle George and Uncle
John started the bank, a small commercial trust-and-savings bank
located in the middle of Main Street. George and John named themselves president and vice-president respectively and installed Ed Senior
as an employee, but around the time Ed Junior was applying one merit
badge after another to his sash, the Great Depression began to drag the
family bank down. Uncle John died amid the financial panic, and the
bank fell into such dire straits that George decided to merge it with
the more solvent First National Bank of Danville. Then George died and
somehow saddled Ed with the outstanding family debts, a difficult situation exacerbated by Ed Senior's poor treatment by the managers of the
First National Bank. They relegated him to a job as a teller.

The newspaper paragraphs about Ed Telling's father usually referred
to him as an officer of the First National Bank of Danville, but he ended
up a teller who eventually left the banking business so burdened by
personal debts and deeply depressed by his life that he didn't work at
all for several years.

Ed's mother sold the family silver and went to work herself. He observed that as his mother found the strength to become the leader of the
family, his father receded by degrees into a state of utter inertia born
of his experience of "not being the man."

Ed Telling sensed the beginnings of a "shell" surrounding him as he
watched his father retreat. "Why risk being hurt?" he says he asked
himself at the time. "Why not just be a little more cautious, until you
know you won't be hurt? Why not just take that risk out?" He also took
away from the spectacle of his father's decline the suspicion that within
the powerful traditions that unite families were lurking betrayals and
hidden outstanding debts that can ruin your life. He realized then that
family and business were best kept apart, that businesses, like some
families, are worthy of suspicion, and he realized a few other things
worth remembering about small-town banks and bankers too.

Then came his pursuit of Nancy, and his father's decision to cut Ed loose from the family financially while he was still in school. Then there was the Navy, and after that his decision to cast his lot with the General and his company so richly endowed with a military spirit, a preoccupation with honor and epigrams, a peculiar system of programmatic levels of achievement not unlike the Boy Scouts, and a history so glorious and revered that respect for it was called a "religion." He and Nancy decided they'd go home again to Danville via the private byways of Sears, Roebuck. The Sears personnel department assured him he had a job and $50 a week to support Nancy and the two kids, but because of something called decentralization, he couldn't be guaranteed a trainee's position in Danville, because the final decision was up to the local store manager. "You go on down there," the personnel man said, "and don't feel bad if he doesn't want you and sends you away."

The Danville store manager wanted Telling, if for no other reason than to exercise his sadistic hatred of young men who'd been to college. The fellow was known as "Pop" Logan, and for much of the end of 1946, all of 1947, and the first few weeks of 1948, he dedicated himself to making Ed Telling's life miserable. "I *know* you college boys," he'd say. "Oh, you gonna want you a desk after a week or two, then you're gonna want a secretary, and then you'll be after my job—and don't you think I don't know it." Then Pop would send Telling back into the receiving room to hoist goods again. Every time a piece of large machinery arrived, Telling was singled out to put on his coveralls and move it. One day Logan called Telling out of the back and as usual made him wait outside his office for a long time. He finally called him in. "College boy," Pop Logan said. "I've got a ribbon a' inch wide and I have it clear 'round the world. It's joined. Now I cut it and add an inch. How far would that raise it off the surface of the earth?"

Telling said he didn't know offhand.

"Well, I thought you college boys knew everything," Pop said, and then he dismissed him.

Another time Logan called Telling out of the basement and, after the long wait, said, "I just thought you would like to know that I would never invite the likes of you into my home."

"Anything else?" Telling asked before going back to work. The other people in the store were consistently amazed that the big, strong kid never exploded, never even showed the slightest hint of a temper.

In early 1948, Pop Logan retired, and he asked Telling to drive him home from the store on the last day of his long career. They pulled up in front of Logan's home, and the old man turned to Telling and said, "O.K., now, you come on inside and have a drink with me."

"No," Telling replied. "Let's you and me just play the string out to the end, Mr. Logan."

"It might have hurt my feelings but it served me well," Telling would say later. He'd learned things from Pop about management, and about the vagaries of a system of sectionalist authority that everyone around him in Sears clutched close as God's writ. And he learned once again a lesson he'd learned before: that if you hold out long enough, things come back to you in the end. If you're tough enough to wait around, the girl eventually comes back from the West Coast and you marry her. If you can hold in the rage long enough, you can make a sadistic little bastard of a Sears store manager dangle a bit on the end of his own string. If you harbor and refine your hatred of bankers for much of your life, you might just end up in a position to even the score a bit.

Telling moved up from Danville to Decatur, Illinois; then to Fort Wayne, Indiana. Then, in 1951, Sears ordered him to travel the zone full-time visiting stores in the family's only automobile. Nancy was pregnant with their fourth at the time, and she had to pull the children's wagon to the store to shop for food. Meanwhile, Ed was saddled with a traveling partner so given over to his alcoholism that Telling had to nurse and cover for the fellow wherever they went. Telling was gone from Monday morning to Friday night, and the thing he would never be able to forget about those days was not the tragic man he cared for along the road, but that Sears expected him to abandon his family in his *own* car.

After that, he went on to Lexington, Kentucky; back to Danville, this time as the manager of Pop Logan's former store; then on to the Sears store in Rockford, Illinois, in 1956. The old-time Searsmen kept telling him along the way that he was being given a great deal of responsibility early on by company standards, and though Telling realized early that "Young bulls will always try to shove the old bulls off the cliff—whether it's animals or fathers and sons or companies"—he could never get it out of his head that he was being kept down by a bunch of old men who'd derived authority through vegetative persistence and a system of organizational justice resident in the mind of a single slobbering old man whose fly was always open.

He grew increasingly skeptical of the Sears "secret," as he called it, this grand system of decentralization. "No one would ever bother to define what it meant. Did it mean that you could do whatever you wished—as some said the freedom of speech in the Constitution allowed you to yell 'fire' in a crowded theatre?"

As he rode his zone and visited stores run by local warlords, his skepticism turned to smoldering resentment. He also resented his meager pay, and the constant uprooting of his family that became so torturous that Telling came to a point where, after moving Nancy and the kids to the next town, if a young couple stopped him in the street and asked who he was he'd want to say, "What the hell difference does it make who I am? I'm leaving soon."

It got so his children had no idea where they were from, so he tried to mitigate the rootlessness by planting the family in Rockford and working four subsequent jobs along his gently sloping career path from the same base. Telling knew he was born into a generation that moved across the map for reasons of work as no generation ever had, but after a while he could see the scars his children would probably always bear from the experience of their father's life, and the sight made him ache.

He tried to get a little plane to help cover his stores more efficiently, so he could spend more time at home, but Sears said he had to stop.

Still, he stuck it out. Just as he'd stuck it out through Pop Logan's abuse. He kept it all inside and just absorbed whatever came his way, waiting for the time when it would be his turn to move. Something about the journey through post-war Sears seemed to conform to things he'd already learned about a general emotional journey through life. He served the idiots and sadists with apparent loyalty, but, as with Pop Logan, he made it his private mission always to remember.

Slowly, the introverted Field soldier from Danville moved up through the organization. He eventually managed the same Midwestern zone he was once made to ride. He found himself in the decadent city-state called the New York group, and it was there, in the strangely methodical fury with which he fell upon the corruption of the group and the profligacy of powerful store jockeys, that certain individuals around him began to feel inspired by his quiet power, as if he'd touched some inverted desire in each of them to do justice at his beckoning and to even numerous scores. He was possessed of a determination to promulgate change such as none of them had ever seen before, and certain hard-bitten veterans like Bill Bass found themselves strangely moved.

By the time he rose to be the king of the Eastern Territory, he was finally in a position to deal with the arrogant baronets who ran groups and stores. He took away their stores, staffs, turfs, and titles, and gave rookies the old-soldiers' chairs. He even had access to a jet plane in Philadelphia; though few people ever understood it, there was a long-carried purpose behind Telling's ability and commitment finally to make it home for dinner with Nancy despite being hundreds of miles away in the afternoon. A certain historical balance was achieved that began, in a small way, to make up for those weeks spent in motels at the edge of cornfields while his *own car* was parked outside in the lot and Nancy was home pregnant and tugging a wagon to town.

The soldiers who worked with Telling in the East all knew of his deep disdain for Headquarters, where the myths and icons of the order were protected by people who worked nine to five. Telling detested in particular the swaggering imperial chairmanship of Gordon Metcalf during the late 1960s, and he was able to add to his own feelings the shared resentments of ever-larger numbers of Eastern Territory executives who felt discriminated against because of the General's—i.e., Parent's—prejudices. Each time the Easterners heard that Telling had said to Bill Bass, "Tell Gordo I'm home raking leaves if he calls," and then had left work at noon, those around him worked even harder in response to the sight of their leader not working much at all.

In many ways Telling's tremendous accrual of power in the East was the logical conclusion of the General's transmission of sovereignty to the localities: the power was out there away from the center, waiting to be collected. But even as Telling joined with John Lowe and the others in proclaiming the sanctity of the General's system, his "people" knew that Telling in fact loathed the Sears system of localist sway. The intimates heard of his real feelings for the remaining, self-satisfied Pop Logans of the Field, who still clung to the General's ghost. They heard him complain about the entirety of the Pacific Coast Territory, the arrogance there personified by the territory's prideful king.

Eventually, the intimates witnessed the revelation of Telling's list: there was the system of promotion through the Field that prized staying power over talent, and age over youth. There was his hatred of New York City and hatred of the decadence of the Parent organization in Chicago. He didn't like the fat cats of the buying organization or their slush fund they called "account 599." He resented the easy life the buyers granted the sources from the imperial buying outposts like the office in New York. He considered the staff kings of Parent to be dangerous petty bureaucrats. Though he sat on the board of directors, he thought it farcically loaded up with Sears insiders.

He didn't know much about Allstate Insurance, and, like all the merchants, he didn't want to know much more, but what he knew he didn't like at all. He said the bean counters were much too independent of the mother corporation. While he was on a roll, the Japanese came in for some harsh words from Telling, but they fared well compared to the derision accorded all manner of bankers. You had to watch him when bankers came up. "Goddamn it!" he'd explode. "If there's anything I don't want anything to do with, it's a bank!"

Telling didn't enumerate his prejudices all that often, but when they were articulated, they came forth with such conviction that Bass, Bacon, and the others never forgot. Sometimes, though, they were confused. Did he hate the Danvilles of the countryside or love them? Did he hate

Sears, or did he see some purer, more noble possibility for the company, something more deserving of his love and devotion? It was sometimes hard to know.

When events conspired to elevate Telling into the Tower, at first he put on a hell of a show. He gelded John Lowe out on that airstrip in Pueblo; he hired in as a senior officer Phil Purcell, not only a child, but a child not of the company blood. The elitist Jim Button fell apace, and while Joe Moran saw to the independence and presumptuousness of the buyers, to the source of their incredible power in the 599 account, to the free ride given the factories, and to the arrogant separateness of the New York office—all at the chairman's behest—Telling himself continued to usurp by degrees the sovereignty and sanctity of the territories.

But Telling arrived atop a company that had already contracted a disease of the heart, and as the stressful forces of a new order were brought to bear, it seemed for a time that the glories of Sears would be lost forever to dysfunction, failure, and fear. His loyalists ached for Telling as the company spun out of control. They watched as he suffered the taunts of retirees, analysts, and reporters, and then withdrew from sight.

But the checkoff still continued: youth was served and thrown in the face of tradition in the ascension of Eddie Brennan. A general purge of some who should have stayed was needed to be rid of those who should have gone. There was the bitter disappointment of Charlie Wurmstedt. But eventually the recalcitrants were moved aside. Allstate was reined in so very subtly that the retraining of Don Craib, their current leader, in the ways of Sears was still being interpreted in Northbrook as a process akin to grooming, and the absorption of their long-time chairman as president was seen merely as a deserved promotion. But Allstate had been just another arrogant and independent decentralized territory in Telling's mind, and now it was part of the family again.

The current board of directors could hardly be called a body characterized by its will to independent thought, but at least it was composed of a majority of outsiders. In the new epoch he'd ushered in from behind his closed door on sixty-eight, there was the possibility of Sears' stretching the ribbon of its commerce all the way around the world, possibly at the expense of Japanese traders. The hotshots of Wall Street in New York, who'd made his life so miserable with their dire analyses and injuries to the stock, now had company in their clubby little business, and only the future would reveal if a fully integrated financial-services offering to the populace by mighty Sears would do to the likes of the First National Bank of Danville, Illinois, what Sears, Rosenwald, and the General had done to America's general stores. An article on the front page of *The New York Times'* business section about the onslaught on the banks by Sears and the other financial-services giants depicted Ed Telling staring out from behind the bars of an old-fashioned teller's cage not unlike the one his father had gazed through on Main Street. "There was no fanfare," Phil Purcell said, looking back during the late summer of 1983. "He just took the things he believed were wrong with the company and corrected them."

From beneath the most bucolic sort of hayseed romance there emerged fury, methodical dedication, and grand designs. It was all a question of waiting until things came back to you.

The latter-day political analogy most applicable to Telling's sophisticated accrual of power is arguably found in the rise of Charles de Gaulle and the French Fifth Republic from the turmoil wrought by the receding of foreign empire in North Africa. With each gesture de Gaulle made as president of France, his *domaine réserve*—the realms of authority over which the president of the Republic presided—grew larger. Under the banner of "restoring the state," de Gaulle drew prerogatives to himself.

Like de Gaulle, Telling talked of decentralization as he centralized all things beneath him. He pulled the authority of individual stores into the purview of the retail groups, then the power of the groups into the territory, and then the awesome power of the territories up into the Tower—with an assist to Ed Brennan at the end. The killing off of layers of management in many large companies causes the authority to fall down as if by gravity, but Telling pulled it back up manually. Every retirement caused former authority to come up to him.

It was often said of de Gaulle that he loved France but hated Frenchmen. The great leader seemed to move as much by force of old injuries, by a restlessness and a special feeling for his own history, as he did by obedience to larger ideals.

All the while, Telling managed to convey to the outside world—the world beyond a single floor of the Sears Tower and his small home with Nancy—that he was just a country boy from Danville, a store runner who just happened atop a corporate empire because of dumb luck and the lack of someone else. But much less about it had been a matter of luck than even insiders realized.

He may have gone home to rake leaves in defiance of Gordon Metcalf, but he never did talk back to Pop Logan. When he was told to hit the road and tour the zone with Charlie Wurmstedt or someone else, he went. He was always much more aware of organizational exigencies than it seemed. It may well have been a stroke of luck, for instance, that Ian Sym-Smith of the Hay Associates was assigned to study the anthropological organization of Sears, and luck that Sym-Smith was based in

Telling's bailiwick in Philadelphia in 1974, but it certainly was not a matter of luck that Ed Telling's territorial plane with Ed Telling waiting inside was invariably present and waiting when Sym-Smith needed to fly to Chicago to help plant the seeds of change. It was more than dumb luck that his band of loyalists happened to include several supersensitive and insecure men, some deeply religious men, some obsessively ambitious men, several quite short men, and others, from secretaries to former window-dressers, who never fit into the status quo until Ed Telling discovered them and helped them flourish among his private band of irregulars. Along the way, the Eastern Territory troupe was joined by others. Whether they were bright-button kids from Utah itching to accomplish an act that truly counted on a large scale, or frustrated wordsmiths so enamored of the metaphors of power that the practice of management appeared to them in Biblical panoramas, they all had a part. All irregulars were welcome, and in his quiet way Ed Telling played them all. Telling could sense through instinct which people were willing to submit and which ones were willing to fight. Far from being unaware of his motivational skills, Telling would on occasion call Pat Jamieson into his office after one of his managers left, then convey to Pat the elliptical words he'd uttered to the manager, and predict the number of days it would take the officer to come back with the problem ironed out. He was rarely off by more than twenty-four hours. He said his management style involved giving subordinates a great deal of freedom, "the freedom," he called it, "to perform."

For all of his career he'd sent people away, not with orders, but with doubts and desires that made them able to do good jobs. He wasn't sure what he saw first in Eddie Brennan the day he stood next to him on the roof of a store admiring the view of Baltimore, and he didn't exactly know what it was that intrigued him about the lowly catalog man Henry Sunderland or the youthful consultant Phil Purcell until some time later. As with other aspects of himself, Telling's sensitivity to other people's psyches was an extremely delicate thing, and he protected it most of the time behind a thick wall of loyal men, a closed door, and his own deeply offended dignity.

His powerful management by mystery—the "peculiar alchemy," as Charlie Meyer used to call it—was certainly more reasoned and studied than it seemed, but it was also the only way Telling could bear to operate.

"Power?" he said one afternoon, his face wrinkled and quizzical. "I don't think I've ever experienced it. Don't think I ever had that much power. Never entered my mind."

Sometimes it seemed like the hurts were still unassuaged, and that, for all the lines he'd drawn through some of the injuries on the scorecard, he could still feel their sting. He grumbled often about deals that got away during the quest to assemble the Great American Company. His face still reddened at the mention of his day alone at the Dean Witter suite in New York, or the time Parent forced a white elephant of a store into White Plains, New York. His ire at hearing Pop Logan's name was such that he was moved to apologize for "dancin' on his grave" a few days later.

The annual meeting that seemed to bring Ed Telling joy in Greensboro, North Carolina, was originally slated for Seattle, Washington, but Telling vetoed Seattle because he said it was "too goddamned close to Los Angeles," where four years earlier he'd been humiliated and taunted by John Lowe loyalists and his own retirees. The event still felt like it happened yesterday.

One of the great pleasures of his invasion of new realms of enterprise was the fact that so many corporate elites—especially the money-handlers—looked down upon retailers. Now atop a "supercompany," he still had trouble seeing himself as anything but a retailer, a good-ol'-boy retailer at that.

No maids or cooks worked at the Tellings' compact little townhouse next to a fairway in Northbrook. It was just Ed and Nancy at home now. She had her love of music and books, and he had his corporation to run. Like Pop Logan during the days before he bounced on the end of his string, no colleagues had ever been invited to the Tellings' house.

Despite the small home and generally parsimonious personal habits, when he had to drive the chairman did so in a sleek Jaguar sedan. Ever since he'd begun to make a good living from Sears, he'd owned expensive cars: a Mercedes 280 SL 4.5, a few Cadillacs and Lincolns, and finally the Jag. The cars and the G-III airplane he'd ordered for the Sears air force had in common that they got him home to Nancy quickly and in high style, and that directly or indirectly they were purchased by money from Sears, Roebuck, a company once possessed of such heartlessness that they would send a man away from his young family in his own Ford motor car, like he was toting his own cross up a hill.

Though he made more money in a month now than many people make in their whole lives, the time when the Tellings needed help in the house and some more money to make their lives enjoyable was in the past. When they'd needed money there wasn't any, and that was just one other little score that Telling was constantly in the process of settling with Sears.

"I guess I'd like my kids to know their old man wasn't a failure," Telling would say when asked about the multimillion-dollar compensation package he was in the process of drawing from Sears in 1983.

Telling was a grandfather eight times over now. He remained in close touch with his five kids—including the one daughter he considered a bit "anti." He said with a somewhat sardonic smile that he'd helped his children avoid the negative influences of the 1960s and early 1970s by "sending them all out to Midwestern liberal-arts colleges where the most exciting thing they ever saw was a nude painting in art class or a streaker crossin' the quad." When his son Cole moved home after college for a while, Telling was heard to complain that Nancy was doing the boy's laundry and that the kid would probably lounge around home for the rest of his life, but he always said it with a twinkle in his eye. He was hopelessly proud of his kids, and seemed to be aware of their personal business and even their social plans on a given weekend to an unusual degree. Some said the involvement wasn't an indication of closeness as much as an indication of how, the chairman lived a part of his own retracted life through the children.

Though running into someone he liked during a tour of the sixty-eighth floor was a pleasant enough diversion, visitors to the inner sanctum made Ed Telling jumpy. He usually got up from behind his perfectly empty desk and began to lead an invader in circles around his huge office. After staring at the arrangement of easy chairs and sofas in one corner, he would move to the tables in another. But nothing ever seemed to feel right, so before settling down again behind his desk he would end up executing pirouettes in place, like a dog looking for the right spot.

Sometimes when one of the phones on the credenza behind him rang, Telling would wait until Pat Jamieson picked up the extension, then turn and pick up the phone to listen in. He would take up the telephone receiver in his massive hands and hold it away from his head as if to keep an eye on it. Then he would put the intrusive device back down on the credenza, next to the entombed dollar bill with his birthdate as a serial number that George Shultz gave him when George was the Treasury secretary, the baseball card depicting Tommy Lasorda, and that strange photograph of Nancy and their daughters looking so exhausted in front of the Houses of Parliament.

Visitors occasionally pierced the expansive armor surrounding the chairman only because Telling was so afraid to be alone. The irony of his often silent desire for companionship was observed by many who'd served him over the years, but since loyalty precluded sharing gossip about Telling, they all still assumed that Telling reserved intimacy and true friendship for others. In fact, all of Ed Telling's "friends" wondered what he really thought of them, but each would sit there with him in silence.

"There's a difference between being private and being alone," Telling would explain while admitting his hatred of physical solitude. "I'm very private, but I don't like to be alone at all. I just don't know why."

Though he invariably referred to his early years as chairman as "the lonely times," now that the company was heralded as an institution of the future instead of a dying dinosaur, Telling still seemed more surrounded by loneliness than before. "It's amazing," he said earlier in 1983, his voice high and strained. "You really end up alone." There was loneliness in winning and loneliness in losing. Loneliness in company and in solitude. Loneliness in the past and in the future.

Telling believed he could only be injured by coming out into the public with other people. He scoffed at the idea of appearing on the then Chicago-based Phil Donahue program because he believed he was no match for Donahue's verbal skills: "He'd kill me," he said. During June, the Sears government-affairs staffers convinced Telling to appear before the Senate Banking Committee to argue against the passage of legislation that would have curtailed further expansion of the financial-services industry. Sitting beside Walter Wriston of Citicorp and Roger Birk of Merrill Lynch, Telling began his statement to the committee, "After almost six years as chairman of Sears, Roebuck and Company, I had begun to think I would retire without an occasion to burden a committee of the Senate with my views."

The statement was not a rhetorical exercise in false humility. For all the big ideas that careened around in Ed Telling's head—some of which had led to monumental economic activity and others of which had reorganized a sprawling world of human activity—he had precious little faith in any of them. He believed unswervingly that a man's "feet of clay" showed quickly if he showed himself at all, and since he believed that his feet were indeed made of clay, it was best to take the risk out of the thing and just hide. He figured that only by keeping his guard up had he survived hurts that otherwise would have caused him to kill himself.

A young man from consumer-advocate Ralph Nader's office in Washington interviewed Telling one afternoon: "Mr. Telling, are there any thinkers or writers who have influenced you over the years?"

"No," Telling said.

Until the late summer of 1983, when he suddenly began quoting lengthy poems to his officers on sixty-eight, Telling had worked to keep his love and considerable knowledge of literature as secret as everything else. By hiding his fascination with the history of art and ideas, he was hiding also his deepest secret: that in an era of hardheaded, pragmatic management, he was nothing if not a hopeless romantic. He loved nothing as much as to consider symbols and nuance and metaphor. He saw in the political quandaries of a huge corporation historical parallels that harked back to the empire of Rome. He saw the entanglements of business leaders at war in the angry heads of an Eskimo sculpture. He saw a moment of structural decision for a business as a choice between the legacy of Hume and Locke on the one hand and the legacy of Rousseau on the other, but if you ever asked him about the haphazard mention of a philosopher he'd made on another day, he'd usually say, "Musta been actin' int-lect-shool that day."

Other times his voice would fill with passion, such as when he quoted the lines of his beloved eighteenth-century Scots poet, Robert Burns, a poet whose work and vision happened to have been formed by the sight of his father beaten down and ruined by financial reversals ("And he was moved too by the unkindnesses of people around him," Telling was always quick to add). Later in his life, Burns caused great controversy when he became enamored of the revolutionary dramas brewing at the time in France. Telling could unveil countless lines from "the heaven taught ploughman," Bobbie Burns.

The strong bond between Telling and Rod Hills that was so incomprehensible to some Sears executives was rooted firmly in their shared, romantic appreciation of grand actions: Hills brilliantly connected his schemes to the grandiosities of history and symmetries of high literature in a way that made Telling's eyes glaze, and Telling provided the sort of authority and indomitable will that a mercurial fellow like Rod Hills could never concentrate on long enough to accumulate. Rod was captivated by the will to exercise great power, and Telling was intrigued by great plans. To both of them deals were simply the mechanical prerequisites of grand designs. "We tilt at windmills together," as Rod put it.

Phil Purcell believed that Telling hid his reading and intellection because of a purely pragmatic realization that the people he dealt with weren't interested in that sort of stuff. Rod Hills realized that the "grand romantic" in Ed Telling was simply locked up inside him, and in that single perception the source of Rod's seeming jump on Phil could be explained. With his ability to cast the World Trade Company and other ventures as heroic quests, Rod caused Telling to spring to life.

But Hills was such a romantic himself that he was blind to traps being set for him on sixty-eight that summer. Dick Jones, Charley Moran, and some of the other members of the life guard had finally decided that Rod Hills was surely bound to hurt Telling. It was clear that the World Trade Company was losing a lot more money than Rod had said it would, and as the time for Telling to choose his successor approached, the staff leaders decided they had to move. Dick Jones had already gone so far as to try to exclude Hills from board meetings, and there were other things that could be done.

Ed Telling had accomplished so much that his "close" aides wished he could stand to accept a public role commensurate with his triumphs and pass into retirement in the public manner available to management heroes of his ilk. But Telling said he could never see himself doing things like that. In fact, Ed Telling had great difficulty seeing himself in many of the roles he'd played. His fear of public exposure was clearly connected to a tragic inability to see himself in his own romance. For all the flares and explosions, he never could pick himself out atop the parapet. "I just don't know what you'd call success," he'd manage, his eyes traveling out over Lake Michigan.

Telling once told a reporter that people who set lofty goals take a chance on having to live with never achieving them. But now that hard evidence of triumph was being offered up to him by the heads of the business groups every month, and now that most of the old scores appeared to be settled, he seemed haunted by his own achievement. As with the spirits in Dante's *Inferno,* and as with Boy Scouts who've filled up their sashes with badges for the wrong reasons, attainment can feel like punishment, if for no other reason than that it means you're done.

He claimed often that he would never look back in remorse. "What's done is done and it can't be doner" was the operative phrase. But there were exceptions to the rule, particularly where it concerned people Telling believed he'd hurt. One of the great wonders of Telling's late years as chairman was his relationship with the former head of the buying organization, Jim Button, the man who was subverted when Telling inserted Joe Moran between Button and his army of buyers. Button and Telling were playing golf together regularly by 1983, and to the wonderment of observers they even purchased Florida homes in the same development in North Palm Beach.

The two men had as little in common as any two Searsmen of the World War II generation. They were separated by backgrounds, social circles (Button having acquired one), and education. They grew up within Sears on opposite sides of the divide between Parent and Field, believing in contrapuntal ideas about the retailing of goods.

From Jim Button's wholly apolitical point of view, he had simply retired from Sears for health reasons after a good long run as the American merchant prince. From Telling's point of view, Button had lost his power, been drummed from the corps, and suffered a subsequent campaign of revisionism that included the denigration of his administration in circles occupied by academics, journalists, power-brokers, and other

members of the only fraternities Jim Button ever cared about. But unlike Pop Logan, John Lowe, or Jack Kincannon, Button had simply
gotten in the way. His name was never on Telling's list for some of the
deeper reasons for which others were visited with retribution. Button
was suddenly cut out as if his life of service had meant nothing. So now,
when Telling ordered one of the jets rolled out of the hangar and
pointed in the direction of Florida, Jim Button was occasionally inside.
When Telling rode across a golf course lost in thought, Jim Button was
quietly riding shotgun. Though he'd vowed never to turn in on himself—vowed to stare himself down in the mirror every morning—Telling never quite got over the possibility that he'd injured Jim Button,
and now, in his distant way, he was trying to be a friend.

Except for Button, Charlie Bacon, and a few others, Telling had retained little contact with Sears executives of his generation. The members of the sixty-eighth-floor life guard were certainly seasoned soldiers
by any standards, but most of them were too young to have been in the
military during World War II, so they had missed both the honor of
serving with the big wave of Searsmen and the opprobrium of being cast
off as part of the company's lost generation.

Though Telling seldom spoke of his fellow veterans, many of them
thought and spoke regularly of him.

The old Tall Man Charlie Meyer kept track of Tower events from an
office a few blocks away as Telling's day of decision approached. "When
we were in the East," Meyer said, "I sat and listened to him rail on about
the imperial chairmanship. The day he leaves, I'm going to call Ed to
tell him he was the most imperial of them all."

He was discussed at length by some of the more recently departed
officers and members of the ERIP group, who gathered for lunch in or
around Chicago five or six times a year. A few of the former apostles of
Joe Moran usually showed up, as did Charlie Meyer, Dean Swift, and the
former head of the catalog operation, Jack Kelly. Even Arthur Wood
would show up now and again.

After bailing out with the ERIP crowd, "free at last," Jack Kelly had
enjoyed three of the best years of his life. Ed Brennan's brother, Bernie,
had tried to talk Kelly into coming to work at Ward's when Kelly retired
from Sears, but Kelly had become involved instead with a small bank
that he tended to between his travels as a consultant ("A bank!" Telling
raged when he heard of his old hooky-playing buddy's venture. "A
damned bank!"). Kelly would tell the other veterans that he was consistently amazed at how utterly free he'd felt since leaving the womb of
Sears. As the time approached for Telling to show his hand, Kelly said
he only wished that Ed's departure would finally grant him a similar
sense of peace.

Charlie Wurmstedt showed up often at the lunches, appearing tanned and more relaxed than the others had ever seen him look before. He was sixty-one years old and he wore a hearing aid, but Charlie looked happy. Thoughts of what had happened to him at the end of his career at Sears haunted Wurmstedt for quite a lot longer than he would have preferred, but now it was easier to look back and see that there had also been a great deal of pleasure spaced along the thirty years of the only working life he'd ever known. Wurmy still spent the warm months in his beautiful house in Lake Forest. He wandered regularly across the street to the terrace at the Onwentsia Country Club, where six years earlier he'd cooled his heels in irritation before he listened to Ed Telling convince Art Wood to come take a trip with him to Pueblo, Colorado. Charlie liked to sit on the terrace at Onwentsia and snicker at the "little old wealthy ladies" as they navigated their walkers across the flagstones. Occasionally, as he sipped a beer on the terrace, Charlie pondered the fact that he hadn't done so badly for a poor boy after all.

Upon further reflection, Wurmy had to admit that he hadn't been very good at being a Tower person. Not very good at it at all, if the truth be known. He also had to say that Eddie Brennan had done a hell of a job on the Merchant, but the day it was suggested that Brennan be invited out to join the little luncheon group, Charlie said he might just miss that one. Wurmstedt had as much respect for the dead as the next guy, but to his own dying day he would believe that Jumpin' Joe Moran was plainly "off his rocker," just out of his goddamned mind.

As for Ed Telling, he hadn't seen or talked to the man with whom he'd ridden the backroads of the Midwestern zone in over three years.

Out next to his own golf course, in the desert east of San Diego, California, John Lowe remained full of bitterness over what Telling had done on the airstrip six years earlier, but at least he was finally out of debt for the first time in fourteen years. Lowe had finally sold off his Sears stock, an act other vets referred to as "cutting the cord," and he'd finally paid off the loans that had dragged him so far underwater as the Sears share price collapsed that he couldn't afford to tell Ed Telling to shove it up his ass that day in Pueblo.

Lowe remained utterly befuddled by whatever it was that had come over Ed Telling and caused him to change. He still didn't understand how a man who had so bitterly complained about centralization from above could have done such a thing. Lowe had to admit from afar that in Ed Brennan the Merchant had a young man who knew more about the goods than the rest of the officers put together, but Lowe would never stop believing that a centralized system destroys people.

John Lowe also said he wouldn't be surprised in the least if Ed Telling figured out some way to stay on as chairman past his sixty-fifth birthday, on April Fool's Day 1984. He was joined in this assertion by Jack Kincannon, who noted from Dallas during the summer of 1983 that he wouldn't be surprised if his old nemesis somehow stayed on either. Kincannon and Lowe both understood the pain of having to cut loose from Sears and be left so portionless of all the things that had mattered so much on the way up.

Telling was aware of the talk of the retirees. He said be could feel it. He said he was always aware that people were talking, and that a great deal more had been said "back of his back" than to his face over the years. It came with the territory and the style.

Telling said he dearly missed Charlie Bacon, the man thought to be his best friend at Sears. When Bacon came to Telling in July of 1982 and said he wanted out, Telling convinced the individual who'd shared many more silences with him than anyone else at least to retain responsibility for the endless litigation between Sears and the Equal Employment Opportunity Commission over the company's former employment practices. Bacon agreed to monitor the EEOC stuff, but he still left to live in Hilton Head, South Carolina, and he was missed.

Charlie left because he didn't want to be a details man. He said that personnel at Sears was becoming a numbers game, that there were always more scientific studies, such as the one that showed how the "mental-alertness profile" for the officer corps had jumped profoundly with the departure of the ERIP generation. Bacon had even begun to think he wasn't very good at his job on the sixty-eighth floor. There used to be personality in the life, but the life had lost its savor.

Telling especially missed Charlie, with whom he'd rearranged so many Sears chess boards, because it was now time for him to deal with the succession. He had to decide to whom he should bequeath the monstrous power he'd amassed during his tenure. But picking a successor had become a decision laden with tremendous ramifications by the end of the summer, in part because the running of the horses Telling had commenced was pulling the company into a general internal debate about the course of its future. If a merchant got the mantle as of tradition, then what did that mean for the counting house of the people, the much-ballyhooed new Sears of financial services? How could a merchant be expected to lead a company that was in the throes of hooking diversified business groups together into a technologically advanced, synergistic whole?

If the race was won by one of the outsiders from Los Angeles, New York, or Washington, what would that do to the still-healing Merchant?

Wasn't the revolution too young for the retailers to stand the shock of having their most inspirational leader in years denied?

It was like checkmate.

The grapevine was hot with rumors that Telling would have to either go outside for a successor or find a short-term caretaker—like Archie Boe—a nondecision that harked back to the sort of revolving-door chairmanships experienced after General Wood. Though he'd laughed with the audience when shareholder Harry Korba proposed that Telling be "extended," there was a cogent case to be made for not changing the guard with conditions still so unsettled, with candidates too old or too young or too uninfected with the spirit of corporate unity to carry on. The case was actually put to Telling in Greensboro at the board-of-directors meeting held at the time of the general stockholders' conclave. Some of the board members—notably Julius Rosenwald's grandson, Edgar Stern—wondered aloud whether, in light of all of the profound changes the company had gone through so recently, this was really an appropriate time to change captains.

Telling replied that there were several capable people to choose from and changed the subject. He scheduled another meeting of the nominating-and-proxy committee of the board for August.

The retirement and nonretirement of its chairmen weighed heavily in the history of Sears. The General had sought to assure the constant replenishment of fresh blood to the corporate leadership when he instituted a mandatory retirement age of sixty for officers and senior executives early during his tenure. Then, in 1939, when Wood was himself on the verge of sixty, he suddenly declared the chairmanship of Sears to be exempt from company rules. He proceeded to move aside the chairman of Sears of the time—Julius Rosenwald's son and Edgar Stern's uncle, Lessing—and to install himself as effective leader for life. The chief executive guard began to change regularly, if not quickly, with the General still pulling the strings from his "honorary" stranglehold on the board of directors. During the early 1960s, Charlie Kellstadt believed that he was going to be asked to stay on past the normal retirement age. Kellstadt even conducted a quiet campaign replete with press profiles of himself to promote the idea. But the territorial kings of the day turned thumbs down on changing the laws of Sears for Charlie Kellstadt; when his day came, Kellstadt left town the moment the board meeting broke up, so as to avoid facing the humiliation of the lame-duck months.

During luncheon reunions of retirees and at coffee in the Tower, people wondered how Telling would handle leaving. What in the world would he do with himself? He had few charitable interests, and the idea of Telling involved in a smaller company was absurd.

Other chairmen moved into public roles as members of committees and participators in causes. Telling's experience and skill, coupled with his considerable reputation, offered him access to the world of public policy. "Never!" he barked at the suggestion. "There's gotta be a chance to win in any situation, and I've never seen any winners there [in government] in my lifetime. People go in there and come back disillusioned. Some of 'em worse than disillusioned. Who needs that?"

In the past a former chairman could at least be assured the automatic respect of other Searsmen. A few of them continued to hang around the company just to be near the warm embellishments of former authority. But during the span of only five and a half years, this had changed. Former chairmen now constituted a rogues' gallery of past folly. Stories of their misdeeds and ineptitude were told far more often under the new order than were stories of their triumphs. Everyone on the executive floors of the Tower had heard a comic rendition of the sight of Gordon Metcalf trying to insinuate himself onto national television during the awarding of the winner's check on the Bob Hope Golf Classic broadcast that summer. As director of the profit-sharing plan, Arthur Wood still sat before his Monet in an office in the Tower and still had a secretary, who sat beside a large copy of the *Congressional Staff Directory* and *Who's Who*—only now the former chairman was derided on other floors of the building for his innocence of the business he'd once run.

Even the General's towering myth was reduced now—if not to negativity, then certainly to a station so far away in time that his endless reign now appeared as ancient history. Telling had seen to that.

And now Ed Telling stood at the edge of company history himself, the young bulls waiting for him to fall over into the past as he once said they would. For almost a year Telling had been proclaiming to his intimates on the sixty-eighth floor his deep desire to avoid the morning train ride. Staying on would entail a contravention of company edicts that would necessarily place him above what passed inside Sears for law and order. "You know the life span of the average male is only sixty-eight years, Gene?" Telling mused to his vice-president for corporate public affairs, Gene Harmon. "It's only fair to Nancy that I retire. What's another two and a half million if I drop dead?" The idea of someone dying in office— like the old territorial VP Cul Kennedy, who expired on his way to a catalog store, or like Joe Moran—always struck Telling as peculiarly poignant and tragic. Something about dying having "never got a chance to stop" scared the hell out of him.

But the day Telling announced his successor he was going to be a dead man anyway, and everyone at Sears knew it. There were many stories of ex-chairmen sitting in their offices after the announcement, bewildered and alone. The next day the newspaper would announce the CEO's retirement, usually in an article just a page or two away from the obituaries.

During November of 1966, when Austin Cushman announced that Gordon Metcalf would succeed him as chairman of the board, Cushman added, "I'd like to say that *I'm* still chairman until February 1." Everyone gave Cushman points for his honest try, but everyone knew he was through.

Hobbes believed that it was the combined force of men's desire for power and their fear of death that drove them to construct their vast commonwealths. The collector of great power and recaster of Sears' latter-day corporate commonwealth approached the figurative death of his retirement that summer with the same impeded passion he'd carried into all the battles behind him. Now, from ranches in Texas and restaurants near Chicago—from offices just thirty yards down the hall from his own—all the Telling-watchers wondered how powerful was his reflex to continue.

CHAPTER 24

The Tower

├─────────────────────────────────────┤

T en years after its completion, the Sears Tower remained, in 1983, paramount among all corporate citadels, the tallest building in the world. From a great distance, the Tower seemed a simple thing, an admixture of anodized field-mouse-gray aluminum and dark glass. It rose from the midsection of the Republic as a monument to the austere but awesome virtues of American industry, such as they'd been amassed and harnessed under the aegis of the world's biggest store.

Only ten years earlier, eleven thousand Sears employees and others invited in from the old neighborhood surrounding the West Side Headquarters had signed a steel beam that was subsequently hoisted almost fifteen hundred feet into the sky and then trussed into the top floor of the new company home. Bob Hope himself came to see what the wags of the time called "Metcalf's last erection" as it aspired to its apogee. Chicago's Mayor Richard J. Daley and John, Cardinal Cody, joined an emotional Chairman Metcalf when the city's premier business landmark was officially declared operative. Not unlike the Chicago city planners of the 1890s who advised the mayor of the time that the major obstacle facing the future growth of the city would be horse manure, analysts and consultants advised then Chairman Metcalf that his Tower would house nearly ten thousand Parent employees by 1983, and thirteen thousand by the end of the century. Consolidation, contraction, the possible shrinking of the Headquarters census, never crossed the planners' or builders' minds.

The Tower was the end product of the fierce sectionalist rivalries of the time it was conceived. John Lowe had built his Cube in Alhambra. The bean counters had their landscaped Northbrook campus; Ed Telling and Al Davies their respective territorial throne rooms. It stood to reason that, as chairman, Gordon Metcalf should build something terrific, just as the competing bishops of other centuries had built in competition the great cathedrals of Europe. If the St. Peter's Gordon Metcalf built was nothing but a thing of comparative utility and bland design, at least it was an honest reflection of corporate aspirations, the "B-store operator's" aesthetics of the chairman, and the residual strains of big-shoulderism still alive in the city where the Tower was constructed.

The city of Chicago was always about being big and tall. Louis Sullivan noted at the end of the last century the peculiar penchant among Chicagoans for things that were "the biggest"—the biggest lumber and food markets in the world, the biggest fire in the world. Growing up a Chicagoan for most of the twentieth century meant that you understood the virtues of being big and strong, and growing up Sears in Chicago seemed to multiply the effect.

But just as Sears was so profoundly humbled and then changed since the rise of the Tower, Chicago had changed too. Living symbols of big power like Mayor Daley and Cardinal Cody were gone, and in Mayor Harold Washington and the progressive Joseph, Cardinal Bernadin, their places were occupied by men who represented change. During the bitter economic recession, Chicago had lost its status as the American Second City and was now ranked third in population, behind Los Angeles. Within the decade since the Tower went up, the blue-collar ethic born of so much stacking of wheat, butchering of hogs, and the manufacturing of the sorts of things Sears and Ward then shipped everywhere from the material plexus, had given way to the sophisticated and occasionally ostentatious milieu of a city thriving on paper promises. A few blocks to the east and west of the Tower were the world's largest commodity and financial-futures exchanges, where, instead of real wheat and hogs, contracts were exchanged to buy and sell things that didn't yet exist and that in most cases never would. Chicago was full of capital now, and the business of moving it around at high speed was proving quite a bit more profitable than making and moving a nation's freight.

The Sears Tower still lorded over the changing city untranscended in 1983, and though few people in the company or the city liked the building, in many ways the Tower had finally come into its own. So many traditional corporate icons—notably the Sears Catalog—had receded in prominence that, when the executives assigned to create for the changed company new symbols, logos, and advertisements sat together trying to conjure an image to express the meaning of a company that was now so much more and less than it used to be, they always seemed to come back to various drawings of the Tower.

The building had been much more than a simple monolith all along, but now its carefully hidden technological wonders—small things but more powerful than the Tower-builders could have imagined—were as essential to the success of Telling's great experiment as was the control of all organizational power.

The Tower was alive with the pulsing, bleating, and blinking of machinery. Those sixteen thousand windows concealed a world enmeshed within fifteen hundred miles of live wires, a place with concealed floors between the ones with numbers that were laden with control panels and peopled by men in blue shirts with giant key chains. The skeletal girders beneath the Tower's skin were visible on these special floors, each of them covered eerily by a sprayed-on fire retardant so that the steel wouldn't melt under any circumstance.

One of the most feared places within the Tower was the twenty-eighth floor. Even the senior managers in charge of running the mysterious and highly controlled floor admitted they were uncomfortable on twenty-eight. When the computers turned off the lights in the Tower and shut down the 103 elevators, the twenty-eighth remained ablaze with light. Seven days a week, twenty-four hours a day, the tiny group of sixteen managers and 125 time-card employees of Department 764— the Headquarters Data Processing Center staff—took turns working in the strange environment, where cooled motherboards and roaring mega-modules were bolted to specially raised floors. The unusually low ceiling contained a special halogen-gas system to put out fires, because if the stuff housed on the twenty-eighth floor got wet, there was no telling what would happen.

By the standards of other computing machinery, the firepower on the twenty-eighth floor of the Tower was surpassed in strength by only one or two other installations in the world—and they were run either by the United States government or by the Sears employees working at the larger data center housed out at the West Side plant. The interconnected IBM 3084s on twenty-eight constituted several hundred "MIPs" of raw computer capability. One MIP indicates the capacity for processing one million separate "instructions" every second. When you added the MIP capacity the merchandise company controlled in the Tower with the MIPs available by virtue of the one thousand or so IBM Series I "mini" computers in the store "data centers" in the Field, you came up with 692 MIPs—or the ability within one system to record for future reference several hundred billion new things every single second of the day. "The stores," said the manager of the installation, a fellow named Norbert "Norb" Dulski, "are the ends of the tentacles."

The span of a single second in Norb Dulski's world ran on like an eternity. Where only a few years ago the "techies" on twenty-eight had spoken of the computers' executing tasks in milliseconds—thousandths of a second—they now worked in nanoseconds, or billionths of a second. Though the computer boxes themselves are humble-looking objects, much less awesome to behold than in the old days, when the machines were the size of locomotives, the peripheral equipment that helps store the information the machines process or generates the data in alternative forms has become more imaginative and other-worldly all the time. The computers on Norb's floor were surrounded by beehive-like contraptions that stored information in elongated metal octagons that were pulled in and out of a large silver honeycomb assembly by two hyperactive stainless-steel arms. A machine nearby looked like a stack of large pizzas several feet high. Each of the large disks was spinning at thirty revolutions per second as a tiny arm flowed across the surface of each plate, accurately dispensing three million characters per second onto the surface from eleven microns away. "That's like a 747 flying less than three inches off the top of Lake Michigan," Norb commented.

Another machine was able to commit 320 pages of documentation to a single playing-card-size microfiche at a rate of six hundred twenty thousand microfiches a month, and still another laser-equipped machine printed out documents at fifteen thousand lines a minute. A few laser printers threw out almost ten million pages of data a month, adding considerably to a hail of paper from the twenty-eight floor that churned forth at a rate of twelve hundred sheets per month per each employee of the company. The paper production rate was one of those figures nobody was particularly proud of at Sears. The "hubbing point," as the installation is known to Norb Dulski and his colleagues, also contained a few bits of machinery and telecommunications hardware that only a few others have even seen. The special machines were among the rewards for being, as Sears had been for years, the largest private customer of both IBM and AT&T.

One of the many miscalculations made during the late 1960s, when the Tower was in its planning stage, concerned the space allocated for the computers. As soon as the twenty-eighth floor was occupied, the "footprint," or raw space occupied by each machine, began to shrink so radically that by the summer of 1983 almost fifty thousand square feet of the floor lay empty. As the available MIP-power of the Merchant's data system multiplied exponentially each month, advances in available technology allowed a concomitant contraction in the cost and size of the computer system. During the mid-1970s, there were 143 Sears data centers around the country; by 1983, there were just seven. Between 1979 and 1983, the raw computing power available to the merchants at Headquarters tripled, while the dollar value of the processing units fell from $65 million to $56 million. The "cost per MIP" fell from $1.25 million to $277,000. Where there had been over a thousand technicians watching the blinking lights there were now seven hundred.

Norb Dulski and his team were specialists in the science of making big things very small and light. Few Sears employees—including most of the officers—were ever invited to watch the shrinking process in action on twenty-eight, but to many of those who did wander into the strange place, Dulski gave as a souvenir a tiny square of cellophane upon which was printed the entirety of the Holy Scriptures. The further shrinking of the footprints was essential to the future plans for Sears to become the lowest-cost producer of its varied futuristic wares. It all seemed a long way from the days when company officials worried that profit margins might be eroded if humidity caused the weight of the catalogs to affect postal charges.

The contraction of the Merchant's technological power plant mirrored the general contraction, rewiring, cost reducing, and updating of the entire company under Brennan's direction. The machines appeared as unwearying and consistent as their executorial master—but the near-Marxian analogy by which a concentration of capital and technology obviated the need for human labor fell apart in the face of the mystery known as Department 704.

Amid a streamlining of the merchandise company that had caused hundreds of job titles and numerous staff and line units to disappear, Department 704 had grown like Topsy. The people of 704 now occupied all of the forty-second, forty-seventh, and forty-eighth floors of the Tower. Since so few Sears people knew about the computer-hardware mavens of 764, the software specialists of 704 worked in the most shadowy and suspect department in the Tower. Among the seven hundred or so computer programmers and analysts there were large numbers of young people who wore long hair, beards, and shirt-pocket "nerd packs" laden down with fine-point pens and mechanical pencils and other paraphernalia. The 704 legions covered over four finely printed pages of the mid-1983 Headquarters phone book, and as buying departments lost personnel to attrition and long-time Sears merchants were made redundant, 704 just kept getting bigger and bigger. Hardly any of them were managers, and none of them were capable of buying or selling goods if their lives depended on it.

The programmers were there to leverage off the technological-drive train. They were responsible for turning the awesome MIP-power of the Sears system into business power through writing applications and system software such as the integrated operating, accounting, credit-checking, transaction-handling, stock-keeping, and sending-it-out-to-your-car and ordering-up-a-new-one store-based cash-register program that Eric Saunders showed off to visiting group and territorial managers during the spring internal debut of the Store of the Future.

The Department 704 people had managed to rig Brennan's entire merchandise-planning system into the computer in a way that allowed intricate profit-pattern analyses as well as historical extrapolation that generated incredibly detailed projections and estimates. The credit information system now offered everyone from the chairman to a checkout clerk detailed account information and instantaneous authorizations of cards and personal checks. By the fall, Sears' own bills would be paid to the thousands of suppliers of the company's goods and services through Automated Clearing House transfers instead of by check. The system in 1983 provided much more information about the buyers and their sources in a matter of nanoseconds than Joe Moran had extracted after three full years of effort and a campaign of intimidation between late 1978 and early 1981.

When Phil Purcell was asked if any of the buyers and suppliers that he, Ed Telling, and Joe Moran once believed were injuring Sears back in 1978 were still working for or selling to Sears in 1983, Purcell said there were indeed some. "But it's a whole different game for them now," he added. "Now they know that somebody is lookin' at what they do every day."

By late morning of each day now, Ed Brennan could pull aside the old painting of a sailing ship that covered his screen, roll up the dark wood rolltop covering over his keyboard, and survey via computer the state of every aisle in every store in the company. The only reason he had to wait until 11:00 A.M. was that that was when the Western Territory's numbers arrived via the twenty-eighth floor. He knew how to punch up accounting breakdowns, inventory reports, daily sales, comparison of those sales to last year, last week, and the store's planning goals for every single department of every store.

Brennan would swivel in his big leather chair, turn his back to the windows, and, with one finger of the hand not holding his cigar he would punch up images of the stores. One morning he noticed an unusual slide in the day-to-day sales in one department in a store, and it turned out that oil had spilled there during store hours. With the computer, the business had acquired some of the characteristics of a higher organism. Unlike in the past, the knee bone was really connected to the shin bone.

A kick in the shins registered in the Tower. An oil spill, like a burst blood vessel, stood out as a small bruise.

Sophisticated technological management arrived at the Merchant only in the wake of Brennan's revivalist regime. During the Challenge Meetings of 1982—the ones that were staged in Chicago instead of moving around to the outlying headquarters, so that all the outlander managers could finally see the Tower—each store manager was taken into Brennan's office on forty-four to see his computer screen. The store runners looked at the green-and-white matrices that glowed from the wall, and they all knew right then that the days of massaging the numbers because some idiot had spilled oil were over. A few of them commented among themselves how the old General would have loved these computers. But they guessed the old man would have used the machines to pump vast amounts of information out to the localities. This new system went the other way. The powerful computers, as with the Store of the Future, with its ergonomically rigged lights and psychologically sensitive colors, were just a logical step in a process. The gaps and diversities were all disappearing: Field and Parent, merchant and operator, now North, South, East, and West. The stores were but nodes on a grand network now, all of them controlled by the tap of a fingertip on a keyboard hidden beneath an elegant rolltop cover.

By 1983, the Merchant's data network was so powerful that the people in charge of it for the company contended with pride that it had rendered the very concept of geography obsolete. The difference between the Western Territory and the Southern one, between the "A" store in Tiffin, Ohio, and the one in Renton, Washington, was now a matter of fractional parts of a moment. The wiring had become so intricate that the only essential *place* was the floor full of motherboards and masterboards located a quarter of the way up the Tower.

The Sears retail adventure of the 1920s was also predicated on the power of a technological advance. The General was convinced that the automobile would alter fundamentally the previous limitations of geography, and he believed the business system of the time had to change accordingly. The empire that grew so gigantic in order to manage the retail stores was laid out before efficient air travel moved the cities closer together, at a time when a territorial vice-president in Los Angeles sometimes devoted an entire morning to getting various telephone operators to put a call through to Chicago. Even during the times when the will to keep Sears safe for internal democracy was strongest, new technological artifacts were arising all the time that served to tighten the cinch around the decentralized empire a little more.

Eventually, the same world war that provided the corporation with its incomparable private army of retailers and its most powerful period of expansion spawned a new machine that would be developed in civilian circles to be more powerful, less disputatious, and, in the end, longer-lasting than the men of the post-war boom. So, in important ways, the ethos of an economic organization like Sears had always been about transcending geography. What was the idea of mail order if not a way of transcending the geographic isolation of rural people and offering them the material gifts of the city? The mail-order business has persisted and prospered in the modern era because it creates a market for goods based on a common desire among a given population, rather than on the fact of their residence within shopping range of a specific store. Sears' latter-day competitor in the race to provide Americans with enhanced access to ever-more-interlocking services and opportunities, American Express, had its roots in a mid-nineteenth-century private postal service. In a sense, the two supercompanies were back where they had started in new post-industrial efforts to transcend the limitations of place.

If Sears was to prevail in competition with Amex, Prudential Insurance, Merrill Lynch, and the other companies seeking to encircle people's lives, then the machinery and authority built up in the Tower were going to have to connect with the machines and remaining authority resident at Allstate, Coldwell Banker, Dean Witter, and Sears World Trade.

A general call had gone out from the sixty-eighth floor of the Tower urging all the business groups to move beyond the internal purposes of their existing technology. The proponents of synergy argued that an electronically integrated corporate whole would constitute a consummate business war machine of the future. The integration effort was organized by the corporate planning staff working out of Charley Moran's Department 902-P, the corporate version of the old 702-P group that Phil Purcell had run before the creation of the central holding company.

For its part, Allstate had been managed with the aid of concatenated "if-then" statements for many years. Computers had been organizing the data systems needed for Allstate to sell and service its property/casualty policies since 1967. In 1983 one Allstate vice-president estimated that if it weren't for the computer power in Northbrook, the work would necessitate the employment of "every woman in America" to help service Allstate's twenty-odd million insurance policies. The bean counters' own programmers, stationed out at their private think tank in Palo Alto, California, had even designed a computerized "Top

Down Corporate Model" of the entire company that replicated every business process performed within the insurance company within the parameters of a huge spread-sheet. They also had a model of the stock market, which had successfully kept the Allstate investment portfolio a few percentage points ahead of other professional investors of capital for several years, and they even had something called a "windstorm model" in a computer, which immediately calculated the dollar effect on Allstate of a high-powered storm in any given area in the country.

Because of Wes Poulson's interest in cutting-edge techniques in general, and his background in the computer business, Coldwell Banker had an impressive data-processing plant compared with the rest of the real-estate industry. Poulson began reading about high-tech during the 1960s, and by 1967 had an on-line system for his executives that listed available properties. Dean Witter was never as computer-driven a broker-dealer as a place like Merrill Lynch, and the house's "back-office" operational tie-ups had held them back in the past, but by 1983 the corporate coordinators of technology were working hard to bring Dean Witter up to speed.

Soon after the acquisitions, an interbusiness "synergy committee" attached to the planning department began to study the possible applications of technology. One of the first discoveries made by the committee was that the total bill for all the internal communications occurring within the corporation—from computers to telephones—was over $500 million a year. The executives reasoned that if the integration and rationalization of communications systems could save just 10 percent of the astronomical cost, these savings would contribute more to the bottom line than would the entire Coldwell Banker operation.

A new corporate committee began to work under the rubric of 902-TC—for "telecommunications"—with technical personnel drafted from each of the business groups. As the word spread through the high-technology and communications industries that Sears, Roebuck was thinking of hooking its networks together, special teams assigned to work with 902-TC were formed at IBM, ITT, and AT&T.

And slowly the machines were being connected. By the time the first experimental financial-service centers "rolled out" into the stores, stock, bond, and real-estate information already flowed to the brokers and agents through the merchants' powerful computers. A customer who wouldn't want to spend the money on a long-distance call to a New York stockbroker could now call the local Sears store to the same effect. One of the Merchant's data centers in Philadelphia that had been closed down during Brennan's streamlining was reactivated as the backup installation for Dean Witter's Wall Street system.

Specialists from 902-TC concentrating on the technical aspects of "operating synergies" were amazed by the incredible power of the combined Sears network, so much of which was underutilized at any given point in time. Charley Moran and some of his technicians reported to Ed Telling that the combined capacity of the internal Sears communications network was more extensive than any other system in the world save those of the U.S. government and AT&T. The system turned out to be so big that the technical experts told Telling it could handle all existing airline-industries reservation systems and still have plenty of power available to run the Merchant's cash registers, the brokerage house's current system, the insurer's varied programs, and the systems used by Coldwell Banker and World Trade. They found that a company such as Holiday Inn, like the major airlines, maintained its own dedicated computerized reservation system at great expense, and they reasoned that Sears could conceivably run the whole system for the hotel chain, save the Holiday Inns of the nation a lot of money, and over time turn the cost-cutting 902-TC operation into a profit center. Eventually new satellite and fiber-optics systems would be added to the network, and full voice and video communications services could be incorporated into the computer data-transmission services.

At the end of July 1983, Sears publicly unveiled 902-TC when Charles Moran, as the head of the planning department, signed an agreement with the Mellon Bank that committed Sears to processing the big bank's retail remittances for a fee. A few weeks earlier, the company had announced that it planned to offer long-distance-telephone satellite communications systems to businesses as soon as the Federal Communications Commission approved the idea. There was great excitement among the technology mavens of the corporation by the end of the summer: alongside the banks and the Japanese trading corporations, the renascent retailer was going to go after the telephone company.

Since they were starting out $500 million in the hole due to existing intracorporate communications costs, most corporate executives outside the sphere of the purest techies thought it unlikely that raw computer capacity was ever going to generate black numbers. The real money derived from the synergies would come from inspired variations on good old-fashioned merchandising, or what was variously called "cross-company selling" or "intracompany cross-marketing." The big profits would come from selling existing products across business-group boundaries, and from creating new products and services that could be marketed at low cost to the enlarged universe of Sears, Allstate, Dean Witter, and Coldwell Banker customers. Telling's original strategy was to sell "more goods and services to more people," and with the assistance

of corporate-owned technology, there were very few means by which
to locate and approach more consumers anywhere that were as large
and powerful as the Sears, Roebuck list.

"The list," declared Henry Sunderland, the jack-of-all-trades executive Ed Telling assigned to organize the original task forces on potential
synergies, "is the power."

The diversification effort, in concert with the awesome technological
power at the corporation's disposal, had allowed Sears to amass one of
the most powerful data bases in the world. All those MIPs had destina-
tions. The combined master file of Sears, Allstate, Dean Witter, and
Coldwell Banker customers by itself provided a simple mailing list that
contained the home addresses of more than sixty million of the eighty-
four million families resident in the United States, but the statisticians
based at the Allstate Research Center, down the street from Stanford
University and the SRI International think tank in Menlo Park, California, were manipulating the files that summer in a way that made their
potential power seem limitless.

The manipulation of the Sears customer lists had its earliest roots in
Richard Sears' 1901 decision to designate a group of "preferred customers" who received their copy of the catalog covered by a special red
cloth binding. In 1922 a more sophisticated customer-classification system was introduced, and in 1940 efforts were made to enhance the list
with more data about the customers, such as the discovery that fully 80
percent were married and that 40 percent had telephones. But up
through the early 1980s, research experts in the Merchant expressed
continual frustration over the decided lack of sophistication with which
the customer lists were exploited during the post-war years. If the system could actually generate a list of unmarried customers, then the
company could save a lot of money by not sending them the children's-
clothing "specialog." If the files showed a customer's historical penchant
for buying only tools, then he or she could be inundated with tool
mailings instead of ones hawking apparel.

Before the mergers there was a residual high-level reticence about
pulling personal information from the customer files. Much to the chagrin of marketing executives, credit histories that at one time or another
included the buying habits and financial capacities of more than half the
families in the country were pulled regularly from the files and dis-
carded as soon as the debts were settled. The practice always seemed
to express respect for an individual's right to privacy and to maintain an
aura of general rectitude.

.   .   .

The research team out at Allstate's think tank finally received the once-guarded data tapes from other business groups and began working with a combined list in 1982. Three years' worth of account activity by the thirty-two million active credit-card customers was shipped out from the Merchant to the unassuming Menlo Park research center, and information about three hundred thousand newly signed-up accounts had been added each month since then. Forty-two million separate appliance-purchase records spanning seventeen years were entered into the system, as well as data describing thirty million catalog customers, eight million Allstate auto policyholders, four million homeowners'-insurance customers, and another five million life insurance, renters', and other sorts of Allstate insurance purchasers. After "deduping," the process of discarding duplications and discrepancies, the Sears and Allstate "master list" rendered 104 million separate data files.

The marketers at Dean Witter thrilled at the thought of access to the largest list of potential financial-service customers ever assembled. The securities sellers fantasized about drawing off the names of major-appliances customers, cross-referencing the list with a Zip Code/income analysis, and directing a marketing campaign of tax-exempt financial products at individuals with some income in need of protection.

During the summer, *Business Week* published yet another article about the fear Sears engendered now among its smaller competitors. The item noted that the jocular comments during 1982 about Sears' selling stocks next to socks was becoming a reality. Telling's "brash initiative" was reported to be predicated on an unmatched customer base and 831 stores, 2,388 catalog outlets, two thousand Allstate offices, 355 Dean Witter offices, and eighty-seven Coldwell Banker offices. The backbone of the Sears strategy, *Business Week* reported, was to use "information as a weapon."

But the file experts in California were told to be careful about sharing such cross-business-group data. The analysts found that there were various confidences revealed in their records that they couldn't afford to abuse. Underlying all of the hopes for future corporate synergies was the belief that nothing could be attempted that might undermine the hallowed "trust quotient," which made Sears different from other businesses. Individuals often revealed a great deal more about themselves in their applications for store credit, life insurance, mortgages, or brokerage accounts than they did to other large organizations. The risk of abusing that privileged information was considerable.

Because more Americans gave some wing of Sears, Roebuck their home phone number than allowed the phone company to disseminate it, for instance, the combined master files contained home numbers for

many people who had unlisted telephones. The corporation's relationship to a hypothetical customer who had just purchased a child's car seat
from the catalog was deemed too valuable to risk losing his or her future
business because of a call from an Allstate person trying to sell more life
insurance to new parents, or from a Dean Witter broker offering zero-
coupon bonds for college tuition.

The collated statistical data base within Sears might include things
that the government could never know about the citizenry. On top of
the information people divulge to obtain insurance and credit, there was
a potential available history of what people own—from the big-ticket
appliances purchased to valuables they insured, to houses and securities.
Because of the public fear and official scrutiny this unusual data base
could inspire, Phil Purcell—who was the original guru of the "list-re-
search" committee of the synergy task forces—declared that the personal information in customer files, per se, should not be shared. "Right
now, it's far more often that you hear about someone's income-tax statements' being divulged by the government than you do about people's
Sears accounts being made public," Purcell said after making the decision, "but we have to keep it that way."

The potential violation of "the trust" was debated heavily during the
early months of 1983, when Dean Witter marketers and Sears corporate
product developers worked up a plan to offer customers the opportunity
to tap into a credit line based on the equity held in their homes. If the
paid-up value of your home was $100,000, Sears would loan you $50,000
against the home as collateral. Coldwell Banker could even provide the
homes, and the savings-and-loan in California and Dean Witter could
provide the credit. An untapped pool of what Ed Telling estimated to
be $2 trillion in credit could be made available to people's Sears credit
accounts or accessible by check.

Preliminary research and product testing indicated that a tremendous
number of Americans—especially those living in parts of the Midwest—
believed that borrowing against your house was risky, bordering on
sinful. The planners eventually decided that home-equity credit was
worth the risk to the trust quotient as long as the company promoted
a sober sensibility along with the product. Efforts would be made to
dissuade people from thinking the credit—to be offered in the fall of
1983 under the name "Sears Homeowner Resource Account"—was designed to enable them to shop for goods they couldn't really afford.

The financial-services dream had to be marketed in such a way that
the dark, Orwellian possibilities of the data base never entered the
public imagination. The idea of the consummate synergy—a house
bought from Coldwell Banker, insured by Allstate, stocked by Sears
goods, financed by Sears mortgage brokers, who raised the money from

mortgage securities sold to the public by Dean Witter—with all of it
connected by a pool of personal capital, savings, and debt also enclosed
within a single system—had to be viewed publicly as nothing but a
luxurious convenience, a way of purchasing peace of mind and more
time for your life by entrusting the worrisome details to Mother Sears,
a private economic system you could trust.

Via technology, the dream of corporate synergy now included the possibility of hooking up the emerging Sears phone company to America's
phones, its growing satellite communications system to the people's
television sets. Eventually customers would be able to punch up images
from the catalog as well as pictures of houses and apartments on their
television screens. Talks were in the works with CBS and IBM to enter
into a joint venture to develop "Videotex" information-delivery systems
via television. Soon the push of the buttons on a telephone would execute orders for theatre tickets or flowers, pay bills, and move funds from
a tax-exempt money fund to an IRA.

The voluminous number of nodes already active throughout the network was multiplying all the time, and if Ed Telling's dream of providing
easy access to Sears wherever a consumer looked came true, there
would be computerized money machines connected to the network on
most streetcorners before the end of the decade. A committee was
already working on a universal credit card that would not only provide
a chassis that could connect all elements of the system inside Sears, but
could connect the corporation to services provided by other companies
as well.

Telling contended regularly that if Adam Smith had looked at the
world today, the great economist would have included services in his
definition of the sort of true production upon which economies are built.
Sears had always sold services along with its goods—whether they were
credit services, mechanical services, or installation services. But after
almost a century of *using* the mail, trains, telephones, trucks, and televisions to in some way promote the movement of goods from one place
to another, it now seemed that the process of transmission itself was
becoming a larger corporate purpose.

That summer of 1983 the intrabusiness-group grand wizards of technology were discussing the location of a new data installation to accom-
modate Dean Witter's expanding processing needs. The manager from
Sears Corporate mentioned that the Merchant just might have on inventory an unused facility that could fit the bill. After further consideration
and inspection, it was decided that, during late 1984, the Dean Witter
Financial Services Group's new state-of-the-art data-processing center

would be fitted into the abandoned former headquarters of the South-western Territory, where old Al Davies had once built himself a throne room and paneled it in rich, dark wood.

It appeared to many insiders that the whole company would eventually be stored on the twenty-eighth floor of the Tower. Department 764 would become the only appliance department that mattered. Money, images, ideas—all of it now moved in nanoseconds through space. The American company that had once contained every material object the culture found useful or beautiful or fun or new would be inscribed from start to finish on the shiny side of a silicon wafer; the central warehouse of a culture would be rendered as gaseous trails on a screen.

A great number of changes in the process of creating the great American post-industrial organization seemed to be moving Sears away from its connection to the act of collecting real goods made in places of real work and moving them into the hands of real people. As the company had transcended geography, it seemed destined now to eventually transcend things.

CHAPTER 25

The Race Extended

he members of the Sears, Roebuck board of directors were summoned to Chicago on August 9.

By mid-morning, Phil Purcell could be seen wearing his boyish grin
as he paced back and forth outside the closed doors of the board room,
a splendid chamber lined by portraits of past chairmen, located just off
the skydeck below the sixty-eighth floor. Even though he wasn't a member, Phil usually came to town on the days the board gathered.

When the meeting-room doors swung open, the members of the
board filed out toward the elevator bank. Dick Jones appeared even
whiter than usual as he read a piece of paper offered him by a member
of the public-affairs staff. Jones passed it to Ed Brennan, who read the
piece of paper without expression. "I know what it says, but I'd like to
take a look," said Don Craib, and Brennan passed it over to the contender from Allstate.

On the piece of paper was the soon-to-be-released announcement
that, at the request of the Sears board of directors, Edward R. Telling
had agreed to postpone his retirement past his sixty-fifth birthday the
following April. At the insistence of his board, Telling would stay on until
December 31, 1985.

What else could he do?

All along he'd played the whole thing by the book. He'd tried hard to ignore the nominating-and-proxy committee's early entreaties. At a meeting in July, they tried to convince him to stay through the spring annual meeting of 1986. Edgar Stern contended to Telling that he had to stay to see the company through its "time of transition." Finally, he'd acquiesced—though the board honored his preference for retirement at Christmastime 1985 rather than the following spring.

Telling shocked several of his sixty-eighth-floor associates when he began to justify the action the week after it was done. "I just don't know any other way to act," he said on several occasions. "I mean, when we were told at two in the afternoon in Decatur, Illinois, to be at work in Fort Wayne, Indiana, at eight the next morning, we'd go on home and tell our wives and kids. We'd tell 'em they'd be sent for, and we'd go. We grew up in that atmosphere, so what's so goddamned surprising about staying when the board asks you to stay?"

Telling's long-time ally Charlie Bacon was not in the least surprised at the decision, but he was quite distressed. Charlie believed that the board of directors under Telling had become one of the least animated decision-making bodies imaginable. He knew that reports to the board were all checked over by Dick Jones, and scripts were so rigidly followed that no deviation from approved texts was tolerated. Despite a certain independence of personality demonstrated by some of the outside board members, not a single tendentious discussion had occurred in the board room since Telling reconstituted the directorate after purging the terri- torial vice-presidents. The outsiders on the Sears board were by and large people who owned few shares of Sears stock and who collected $40,000 a year for attending occasional meetings. What they knew of the company came largely from the company. Bacon also knew that if Ed Telling had decided to inform his board that the corporation was stable and that he'd decided to entrust his title to another, there was no chance at all that outside members of the board would have feared chaos in Telling's absence and bullied him into staying on over and above his objections.

The board members might not have known—did not know, in most cases—why it suddenly seemed so important that they refuse to let him go. But, then, Charlie had seen people around Ed Telling respond to things they couldn't quite feel or see for over twenty years.

A few weeks after news of the extension was reported in the papers, Charlie Bacon decided to tell his long-time boss what he thought of his latest decision during a round of golf. "Think you made a mistake there, Ed," he said.

Telling contended—as he had to several other people—that he'd been asked to do a job and he'd accepted and, as everyone who'd ever come near him during his more than three decades in Sears knew, what's done is done and couldn't be doner. What he "felt" inside about it had not "one goddamned thing to do with it."

Bacon was surprised at how upset Telling became on the golf course. There were plenty of people around to tell him it was all right ("The *Queen Mary*'s sitting out there and the captain is on the bridge," Stretch Gardiner proclaimed for attribution. "Sears is a hell of a lot bigger than the *Queen Mary,* and turning the thing around takes a lot longer than five years. Another year and a half is essential to be sure that the ship is on the right course"), but Charlie's comment clearly hurt him.

By the fall, Telling was admitting his "worry" that the middle levels of the organization might not accept his decision. He'd even let it drop that he had it in mind to tip his hand long before his new departure date, but he still refused resolutely to acknowledge the potential adverse effects his decision might have on the various candidates for his title, or the effect the double report of the false-start gun so long into the race might have on the future of the corporate whole. "I just don't see it as a contest," he said. "Everybody wants to be a CEO, they tell me. That's why people leave big companies. You see these people leaving companies and sayin' they had 'style differences' with the chairman. Now, how can that happen? The guy in the chair has the privilege of having the style. The people I'm thinking of around here have excellent jobs, and if they never got another job they would have had an enviable career."

Six weeks after the track was lengthened, a rumor coursed along the Merchant's grapevine in the Field that so deeply committed was Ed Brennan to the merchants of Sears that he had *turned down* the chairmanship in order to remain with his own.

In fact, Brennan's closest aides feared that the board's sudden suspension of Telling's retirement was the old master's way of suggesting to the eager pretender that he'd gotten too big for his britches. Throughout his long career, Telling had sent messages to people through swift symbolic actions. Inside and outside of the retail wing, observers wondered if the old chairman had decided to come back for a sustained curtain call, just to remind the huge audience watching his final scenes which chairman really topped the bill—just in case the spray of events had obscured the outline of the face that was to go up there next to Sears, Rosenwald, and the General on the Mount.

But beyond the now generalized fear among the more senior merchants that some bean counter or financial-services outsider would end up with the corner office on sixty-eight, the idea that Ed Brennan might not get the job—or even the assertion that he wasn't ready for it yet—

was to many executives below the forty-fourth floor a consummate affront to merchantry itself.

Telling's decision left the senior cadres at Allstate Insurance in a state of shock that lasted well into the fall. The officers around Don Craib had talked themselves into believing there was no other possible candidate for the job, in light of the recent concentration of corporate interest and resources on financial services. Craib had to hold special meetings to address the issue of corporate succession, such was the confusion caused by Telling's move. The Allstate chairman informed his managers that Telling had said nothing to him that indicated he was out of the running.

Insiders at Allstate still considered the main contenders in the race to be Craib and Dick Jones. Ed Brennan seemed too specifically a merchant, and much too young by Sears or general corporate standards, to get the call. Brennan was a name from the past. But with the suspension of the corporate bylaws allowing Telling to stay on, the rumor swept through Allstate that Telling might be putting more time on his own tenure in order to allow Ed Brennan to study up on financial services and "grow some moss on him."

The moss factor caused odds-makers inside and outside of the company to agree that the more distant time horizon entailed in the change bode poorly for the chances of President Archie Boe, the ever-loyal CFO Dick Jones, and Dean Witter's Stretch Gardiner. Each of them was over sixty years old, and a late-1985 opening caused their chances to diminish considerably.

The dark horse, Wes Poulson, believed Telling was struck with "no logical candidate." "Nobody's right," Poulson said, "because if a merchandiser is chosen—especially a young one—the message to the financial-services and real-estate wings would be damaging." Poulson contended that personally he wouldn't like that message at all. If somebody particularly young got the job and obviated his own chance ever to be CEO (he was fifty-three now), the prospect of "coming to Chicago for the next eleven years" to report might just move Wes to jump ship.

It wasn't that he didn't like the younger runners. Poulson liked Phil Purcell quite a lot and placed himself squarely among the "Phil fans" within the company. He thought Purcell was a good thinker who occasionally got himself overextended and into a bottleneck because he hadn't quite mastered the art of delegation yet.

Though Poulson would have loved to try a turn at running Sears, Roebuck, he remained so consistently unaware of the intricate politics of Sears, and so unceasingly apolitical in his every action, that his chances of running at the front of the pack had faded considerably by the fall of 1983. Two years after the purchase of Coldwell Banker, Poulson still considered the relationship between Coldwell Banker and Sears only as a reflection of the personal relationship between himself and Ed Telling—tough guy to tough guy—and though it might have been true in part, Wes' habit of jumping issues over the corporate staff directly to Telling was viewed as a taunt by the staffers in the Tower.

Poulson couldn't seem to stop himself from referring to "the days when we were an *independent company*"—even in front of video cameras. The public expulsion of the "spy from Corporate," the controller Dick Callaghan, was still a sore subject, and Poulson's consistent comments about the inability of the merchandising mind to grasp the "people-intensive" world of real estate was never accepted with good grace on the sixty-eighth floor.

Wes' expanding army of big-ticket salesmen had sold around eighty thousand houses during the previous year, and with the addition of Sears capital, his program of adding brokers and acquiring small, independent real-estate agencies was going so well that the dream of buying up 20 percent of the market in a few years no longer seemed such a challenge. If Poulson had wanted to be a bit more politic with the Tower and ingratiate himself now and again, he certainly had been given the opportunity. Since Coldwell Banker had wrested control over the operation and business of the Tower from Corporate, and control over the Homart shopping-center developer from the Merchant, Wes was present in Chicago all the time.

Poulson was in town in September for a Homart board meeting a few blocks east of the Tower. Everyone sitting around the table in the cramped, smoky room worked in rolled-up shirt sleeves except Wes, who looked typically serious and austere in his well-fitting suit coat. A young man in charge of southern California showed the board aerial photographs of a property he wanted Homart to buy from the drug company SmithKline Beckman. Then a fellow named Wayne reported on a site in Slidell, Louisiana, where development depended on the participation of and "concessions" by Sears, the Merchant. Next, an executive Poulson had planted at Homart from Coldwell Banker spoke of the problems at a Homart shopping center located in a region where coal miners were on strike. The fellow referred to the "bargain-basement crowd" that used the center. At this, board member Claude Ireson appeared to take offense at the apparent aspersion cast toward the occupation of his father, brothers, and uncles.

Before the merger, Telling, Jones, Brennan, and several other important Sears executives had sat on the board of Homart, and all expenditures over $300,000 had to be approved by the Sears board. Now only Claude represented the Merchant, and nobody from the sixty-eighth floor oversaw Poulson's management of Homart via his board. After years of being a dumping ground for personnel from the Merchant, Poulson had laid off 20 percent of the developer's employees in 1982 ("Not only did they know nothing of shopping-center development," Poulson explained of the dismissals, "they weren't very good people to begin with").

Homart had started out with a bang back in 1961. The organization went on to construct in 1971 what was still the world's largest shopping center, at Woodfield Mall outside of Chicago, but by the mid-1970s, a new strategy was clearly needed. Along with most of the other "institutional" real-estate developers, the company suffered from the contraction of shopping-center development generally, and from the domination of the industry by more "entrepreneurial" developers like the DeBartolo Group. Homart still owned thirteen regional shopping centers alone and seventeen others jointly in 1983, but Homart was pursuing its plans to get into office-building development under Poulson. There was a twenty-two-story building in Dallas already completed, a twelve-story building in San Francisco, and about seven or eight others planned for the near future. Despite all of the bad deals Poulson contended he'd inherited at Homart, he was still rounding the bend in 1983 with an impressive 16-percent return on investment.

But much of Homart's remaining shopping-mall business was still dependent on the participation of Ed Brennan's stores. After the Homart board meeting broke, Poulson walked quickly toward the Tower for his first meeting with Ed Brennan in several months. In the company of a number of Homart executives, he strode into the conference room off of Brennan's office on the forty-fourth floor. Bill Bass was already waiting inside.

The room was decorated with paintings of New England wharfsides and old counting-house scenes. Most of the flat surfaces in the small meeting room were occupied by one sort of silver cup or another.

Brennan entered the room after keeping the visitors waiting for ten minutes. He sat down and immediately launched into a rundown of the state of the retail business, as though he'd been asked a question. "The appliance business is up 23 percent," he said jauntily. "We had some structural damage at the Houston store from that hurricane that really hurt sales. Houston and San Antonio were already our softest markets, because of the Mexican devaluation. There's also no business to speak of in Miami. Places like Laredo, Texas, are way down. . . ."

When Texas was mentioned, Wes Poulson interjected that Homart was interested in Brennan's thinking about the two proposed developments they had in the pipeline in the region, one called Humboldt near

Houston, and the other at Slidell, Louisiana. The participation of the stores was considered essential to the project by Poulson's staff, though one of the malls would probably be an "off-price" shopping center.

Brennan waited patiently until Poulson was finished, but his face tightened when Poulson appeared to be promoting "off-price" retailing.

Brennan's eyes compressed: "Humboldt is simply not going to give us what we want," Brennan said. "A new store with $16 million worth of capital in it, $5 million in inventory—we can do four Store of the Future retrofits for that. We've done some bad developmental things like this in the past, but part of that was due to . . . the industry." The Homart representatives glanced at one another as if they weren't quite sure whether they'd been insulted.

"As to the off-price market," Brennan said, "I've been studying it for five years. We considered starting up a chain without the Sears name, but we decided to go with the Store of the Future instead. Off-price is on the back burner for us. Besides, there's a lot of false advertising and manipulation of suppliers in the business, and the FTC is already subpoenaing documents. . . ."

Brennan continued to speak in machine-gun statements for some time. Poulson eventually backed off and let others from Homart attempt to disagree. Though the tone of the meeting was friendly enough, it was clear that this particular intercorporate, potentially synergistic experience was going nowhere.

Brennan was the first to get up and leave the room full of trophies. It was "interesting" to him, he said, that a bunch of real-estate guys thought they had such well-developed notions about retail stores and their strategic relationship to the consumer marketplace. Interesting if for no other reason than that just one of his refitted "A" stores was currently in the process of making more money than all of Coldwell Banker could contribute to the corporate bottom line. Just recently, Rod Hills had tried to get Brennan to go out to California to talk to Rod's old friend Saul Price, who had developed the highly profitable concept of retail "buying clubs" that were making such a hit out west. Brennan said no.

And there were others. Customers, employees, retirees—even Ed Brennan's own relatives—it seemed that people still wanted to tell him how to run the company. It was as if some collective lapse of memory had allowed the fact that just two years earlier the Merchant lost *$50 million* in the first two quarters, and that now all of that had changed without their assistance, to be ignored.

Back in his office, Brennan walked over to a chair to the side of his desk and took off his jacket. He slung it over the back of the chair so that each shoulder pad made contact with the chair at a similar spot, smoothed the back of the jacket, and finally picked specks of lint from the shoulders.

Other than the Sears Catalog, Brennan's corner office was empty of most of the Searsabilia that covered the walls and table tops of most merchants' offices. The only award not relegated to the conference room was a plaque that had been presented to him by his officers after the first Challenge Meeting in August 1980. The inscription read, "We are they. They is us."

Several times lately, Brennan had stopped meetings to say thank you to people. During the first week of September, he'd looked around at all his officers and told them that he just wanted them to know that their dedication had meant a great deal to him. For the first time he acknowledged that it must have been difficult to try to live with the pressure he generated.

"The days feel so slow to me right now," Brennan said after the meeting with Poulson. In reality he was still doing a great number of things, making decisions every few minutes. During the previous day, for instance, he'd decided to expand the Merchant's involvement with small specialty business systems and computer stores, and made another similar decision about small paint and hardware specialty stores. He'd made a decision about how to restructure the controller's organization— probably the biggest alteration of that watchdog unit since the days of the General. He'd had a long meeting with Joe Batogowski and Bill Bass about his desire to see the merchandising side of the planning system as formalized and integrated as was the operating side. He'd made decisions concerning company problems in Venezuela, Brazil, and Mexico that were mighty big deals to the people concerned—several millions of dollars were involved—but were almost meaningless to him and the larger company. He'd made some phone calls in the wake of the tragic death of some good friends of his who were killed in an accident, and he'd briefly entertained some award-winning high-school student whom, to Brennan's slightly bemused irritation, the public-affairs people had trundled into his office all wide-eyed and clean-cut and naïve.

Downstairs, the Challenge Meetings had convened to formally inaugurate 1984 as "The Year of the Store of the Future," but this year Brennan was trying to stay away from the rally. The Store of the Future was out there, and he was satisfied that it was 90-percent right. He was trying to stay in his office, trying to learn to close the door.

The computer screen aglow behind him indicated his seventh consecutive month of marking up higher sales. August had roared ahead by 20 percent over August of 1982, and September was on its way to capping a third quarter that Brennan believed would at least double the Merchant's income performance of the previous year—and that was after absorbing a heavy hit the numbers had taken on September 10 due to bad weather.

He turned away from the screen and lit a cigar—one of the good ones, the H. Upmanns, with which he treated or rewarded himself on rare occasions. "I can't say I'm bored," he said softly, slumping down in his huge leather chair, "but I'm . . . The truth is . . . I'm pushing back."

He and Lois had just gone to view the exhibition of medieval art from the Vatican's collection that was being shown at the Art Institute of Chicago. He was trying to lend a hand to his alma mater, Fenwick High School, which Brennan believed had been living off its capital for too long. Tuition didn't cover operating costs anymore at the fine old Chicago institution.

Brennan used to love to read books, but for over three years he'd barely kept up with *Forbes, Fortune,* and *The Wall Street Journal.* Now he was reading again. Some people around the company thought the best-selling how-to book *One Minute Manager* was great stuff, so Brennan read it and pronounced it "pure, unadulterated bullshit." He planned to read the popular novel *The Auerbach Will,* which was loosely based on the Rosenwald family and the early days of Sears, and he'd also picked up an old Ayn Rand novel that he'd loved as a very young man. He'd thought about rereading the Rand novels about individualists, architect-heroes, and planners of new societies when he was running the Southern Territory a bit over three years earlier, but a day after he started one of the books, Ed Telling called to ask Brennan to take over the dying merchandise business.

Now there was time to finish the book, time to smoke a few too many cigars, and time to "reflect."

Downstairs, on twenty-seven, "Mr. T" lookalikes were modeling jewelry for Department 4. "Can cosmetics replace popcorn?" a cosmetics buyer was crowing to the Field delegates. "Well, yo-u-u-u betcha! Can perfume make the markups? Can gold and diamonds give up 40 percent to 65 percent? Yes-siree!"

"I would be less than honest if I were to tell you that my ultimate goal was to come to Chicago," Bill Bass had told his former charges in from the Eastern Territory for the Challenge Meeting. "In fact, you would probably get the same response from any Sears manager who had spent his or her entire career in the Field. But that has changed for me. I didn't come here as a believer, but I am one now."

Lou Fryz, Brennan's personal assistant, slipped into his office to remind him that it was time to go down to the Wacker Room to deliver the closing speech at the Challenge Meeting.

The formidable figure of Miss Lou Fryz had guarded the gate leading to Ed Brennan since he first came north from Atlanta. Senior officers spread obsequious grins across their faces and said, "Good morning, Miss Fryz"—or, if they'd known her for a very long time, "Good morning, Lou"—whenever Lou Fryz passed them in a hall. A particularly bright woman with a deep, chainsmoker's voice and a passing sharp-featured resemblance to the late Margaret Hamilton, Lou Fryz had watched over a procession of Searsmen for thirty-seven years, realizing only lately that if she'd been born a few decades later, she would have been a corporate executive herself. But after thirty-seven years of loyal service to whoever occupied the door behind her, Lou felt she'd eventually been rewarded in full by being allowed to work with Ed Brennan, probably the only man she'd ever come across with a more powerful memory and capacity for action than her own. She worked from early in the morning to around 7:30 every night trying to be Brennan's "shadow." It was her job, Lou figured, to help Brennan manage his time just as it was "the job of the Sears wives to raise the kids." Lou said that was just the way it was at Sears.

Because of the tremendous clout that came with her control of access to Brennan, Lou was as well informed about corporate information as anyone in the organization. Lately, she'd been particularly keen on tracking down the source—and confirming the validity—of rumors that ran along the grapevine, because, more than anything else in the world, she wanted Ed Brennan to be the next chairman of the board.

Lou referred often to Brennan as "himself."

"I don't know if I have another speech in me," Brennan said rather wistfully. Like Ed Telling's, his eyes often moved toward the windows of his office as he spoke. On this day the cloudless vista was extended out to the site of the warehouses where he had begun to learn the ways of business. Brennan said that only a few weeks ago, old Moe Freeman— who, along with his much sharper brother, Eddie, and their sidekick, Mortie Marx, had taught Brennan the art of the goods—had died.

"Sure you do," Lou Fryz said with a smile.

"I'll try," he said. "You know, I played the tapes from the first Challenge Meeting the other day. I could just go down there and play them again today. It's amazing how much younger I looked back then, but I could really just play them the tapes and go out and play golf. There's nothing different to cover."

Brennan walked slowly out to the elevator. Downstairs, in the Wacker Room on twenty-seven, Dick Jones and the head of corporate personnel, the former long-hair Bill Sanders, had come down a back elevator from the sixty-eighth floor to join the territorial managers waiting to hear

Brennan's speech. Even Lois Brennan had come downtown to hear it all once again; she sat calmly in the back of the room, waiting with the rest.

Brennan entered and took his seat on the same podium from which he'd pleaded for peace and unity four Challenge Years earlier. He cocked his head and listened while he was introduced as "the architect of the Store of the Future, the man who has galvanized the entire company . . . our chairman . . . Mr. Edward Brennan."

The applause began as a deafening thunderclap, and, as so often happens with the mild hysteria loose in the most appreciative crowds, the huge noise seemed to surprise the crowd, and spurred it on to even louder clapping. Then there were cheers.

Brennan stood there waiting for a minute, his head slightly bowed. Then he said "Thank you" into the microphone, so quietly that the crowd's noise rose to drown him out. Row by row, the throng rose to its feet, as Brennan mimed "Thank you very much" into the microphone. Five more times he tried to stop it with thank-you's, but the room continued to shake with adulation.

During the last week of September, the investor-relations department conspired with Dick Jones and his financial specialists to convince Ed Telling to make a rare trip to his least favorite American city. The chairman duly agreed to appear at a function in New York hosted by the powerful Morgan Stanley & Company retail analyst Walter Loeb. Loeb was still in favor at Sears because of his early bullish reports about the Sears renaissance, so Telling decided to do Loeb the favor of allowing him to imply to his best clients that his influence was such that he could cause Ed Telling, Ed Brennan, Dick Jones, and Stretch Gardiner to appear at his beckoning. It was a part of the game Telling had never learned to enjoy.

Loeb opened the small Sears seminar on the thirty-third floor of the investment bank's midtown Manhattan headquarters by listing Ed Telling's triumphs. Telling stared down the entire time and crossed and uncrossed his giant shoes under the table. When the chairman was introduced, he tried a halfhearted Sears, Roebuck "Good morning!" but none of the assembled institutional-portfolio managers or private Morgan Stanley clients appeared to understand. Telling then read a statement describing the state of the company, running through the verbiage written for him ("Internally we have gone beyond traditional strategic planning. We have reached the conceptual attainments necessary to attain our goals . . .") with a palpable disdain.

In Don Craib's absence, Telling had to field questions about Allstate. "It's a good company," he said. "Real fine. We're up there in the top . . . well, eight or nine top insurers."

Members of the audience began to whisper. "That guy runs a $30-billion corporation?" ventured a young man who sported tortoiseshell glasses and the sort of slicked-down, young-Republican hairstyle so popular on Wall Street that season.

Most of the questions were directed at Ed Brennan, but Brennan's heart wasn't in it. He mentioned that he was refusing to talk to the press about the Store of the Future unless the reporter in question first went to see the King of Prussia store or one of the other new stores. He talked about his desire to see the Sears Catalog adopt the "rifle" approach rather than the "shotgun" approach to merchandising, in the manner of his new stores. His answers were clear but clipped—as was usually the case when he shared the podium with Telling—but this day he also seemed weary.

After the presentation ended, everyone went into another room for cocktails. Telling sought out a far corner away from the crowd, and only a few people wearing "private investor" on their name tags came up to introduce themselves. The only guest who failed to excuse himself after only a cursory exchange with the chairman was a man who appeared to know only a few words of English.

Brennan was surrounded as soon as he entered the room, but he was having unusual difficulty concentrating on the innocuous questions. Every few minutes he would lose his ray-gun eye contact with the person in front of him and look over at Telling—because Telling was staring back at him.

There wasn't an executive on the sixty-eighth or forty-fourth floor, or even a member of the unofficial alumni club of former officers that convened so regularly around the nation's golf courses, who hadn't at some point seen the "itchiness." Way back in the Eastern Territory, people talked about the charged distance between the two managers who in so many other ways appeared as father and son.

Was Telling's miserly dispensing of approbation to Brennan and his seeming refusal to grant his most gifted acolyte some of the apparent intimacy he afforded others part of a plan to get things done? Was it possible, when all was said and done, that Ed Telling's consummate stroke of managerial genius was his recognition early on of the lean and hungry look of Cassius in the eye of Ed Brennan? Was it a matter of dumb luck that during the spring of 1980, as the merchandise company seemed headed underwater for the last time, a saving grace had presented itself to Telling in the form of the driven young man from the Southern Territory?

For years Telling sat around with Charlie Bacon and talked about the fascinating relationship between work and religiosity he'd observed among his Catholic employees, about how work tasks were often perceived by them as higher missions, and how work-related reversals were taken as higher failures of the sort that characterize nightmares. It could be argued that three of the most prominent actors in the recent dramas at Sears, Roebuck were Ed Brennan, Phil Purcell, and Joe Moran. None of them were long-time cronies of Telling, and all were rather orthodox followers of the same religion. Telling could talk for hours about the mechanics of a Catholic's mind, and for years he'd been aware that the way Catholics became obsessed with "getting the hay in" blended effectively with his own habit of passing out such large and challenging work assignments that they appeared as moral quests.

Whenever a discussion of Ed Brennan's personality arose, Telling and most of his sixty-eighth-floor advisers would say, "You *know* about his personal life, don't you?" By which they meant not Ed's life with Lois and the kids, but his childhood in a broken family during a time and in a place where broken families were abject tragedies. All of Telling's intimates knew the stories about young Eddie raising his brother and sisters because his mother went off to Mexico looking for adventure. Telling called Brennan "very young/very old" long before Brennan himself began to wonder how it had happened that he seemed part of no particular generation.

Brennan was there to be touched and seen and heard and thus could be worshiped, but the query about the last duality—which Ed?—remained unbridged. Like twin Apollos charged to bring back the sunshine and to found colonies and states, they'd worked for years side by side and very far away. It appeared that Ed Telling had a profound sense of how difficult it must have been to be Ed Brennan, but over the fifteen years of their symbiotic relationship, Telling had never chosen to alleviate some of that difficulty by making Brennan his friend.

Telling led the Sears visitors into the elevator after Walter Loeb's reception ended. He went immediately to the back wall. Brennan took off his jacket and slung it over his shoulder as the stuffy elevator car made stops on several other Morgan Stanley–occupied floors. Soon the car was filled with trim young bankers, men and women in pinstripes and a profusion of silk blouses with bows. The elevator descended in silence until a booming rural voice intoned from the back, "Say there, fellas, jus' what is it this here Morgan and Stanley outfit makes, anyhow?"

Several of the young bankers' eyes rolled up to the ceiling before turning in horror toward the older fellow whose belly was sticking out from his jacket.

"Morgan an' Stanley . . . Morgan an' Stanley," Telling said with a frown. "Nah, I do bu-leeve that is a tool company . . . yes, I do. Morgan and Stanley bench and power tools," he twanged. "Why, Ed," Telling said to Brennan, who was watching the scene from the other side of the car, "seems to me, if'n ah'm not mistaken, they make a passable 'xample of a claw hammer too!"

Then, for the first time that day, Ed Brennan started to laugh.

CHAPTER 26

The Stretch

├──────────────────────────────┤

At the early November board meeting where Telling was originally due to make his choice, the board members learned instead that the corporate president, Archie Boe, had decided to throw in the towel. Boe told Telling he wanted to leave during the coming spring, and, unlike the first time Boe tried to retire, the chairman was now willing to let Archie go.

Telling had been thinking back upon the beginning of his tenure, and in retrospect, he marveled at how thoroughly unprepared he'd been to assume the chairmanship of Sears. The company would be well served, he reasoned, by a new chairman who had first been given the opportunity to consider the varied businesses of Sears as a sort of chairman-trainee. Sears had never had a chief operating officer before, but Telling thought that naming his heir as the corporate president and COO for a while might allow him to acquire a feel for the controls before sitting at them alone.

Telling had used the corporate presidency once before as a parking space for Dean Swift, and on another occasion as a symbolic means of vesting young Ed Brennan with an authority that exceeded both Parent and Field. He'd taken the title back from Brennan during the restructuring, and now—since Archie wanted to bail out—he planned to take it back as his own again, until he bestowed it upon an heir designate.

All of this Telling had decided without informing anyone else, so most observers viewed Archie's departure as a scratch from the field that would little change the contest.

Unless Telling went to the limits of corporate apostasy by hiring an unknown outsider, the remaining runners now included Dick Jones, Don Craib, Ed Brennan, Rod Hills, and, to a nominal extent, Wesley Poulson. Stretch Gardiner often contended that even if he, Stretch, had the ability or the ambition to run Sears—which he had always said he did not—he would be sixty-three years old during the December of Telling's new departure date in 1985, and that was just too old. If anyone other than Ed Telling was making the final decision, a man shy of forty years old could never have been considered in the running, but with Telling you just never could tell—so, with the extension of the current chairmanship, a sixth contender was now Phil Purcell. The mysterious fact that Phil Purcell had left his big family back in Chicago when he went to work in New York intrigued the company odds-makers. They wondered if one of the more senior men, like Dick Jones, might be paired with young Phil in an operator/planner management tandem. Others thought Jones might get the chairmanship, and Brennan would be made president and chief executive officer—thus allowing a white-haired man to occupy what was titularly the top spot. Wes Poulson's chances were never given much thought, as the volume of complaints from the sixty-eighth floor about the hard-nosed Californian's impolitic style increased that autumn.

There was no way to lay odds on a dark horse like Rod Hills, because the entire phenomenon of his presence and his free-form creation of the now sprawling World Trade operation was from start to finish a private affair between Rod and Ed Telling.

The relationship had rendered Hills blind to the traps that had been set for him on sixty-eight since the summer when Dick Jones, Charley Moran, and some of the other members of the life guard had finally decided that Rod was surely bound to hurt Telling. The Trade Company was losing a lot more money than Rod had said it would, and with the time for Telling to choose his successor approaching, the staff leaders had decided they had to move. Dick Jones had gone so far as to try to exclude Hills from board meetings, and there were other things that were soon to be done.

Because it was Telling who would declare the winner, however, there was still no chance of making an intelligent wager. Most of the entries figured the next sign from Telling would come the following spring, when Archie actually left the Tower. That would give them each two more full quarters in which to perform.

Telling was stopped in the hall after the autumn announcement of

Boe's impending departure and was asked if he'd decided yet who would succeed him when he finally bowed out.

"Oh sure," he said. Then he sauntered away.

From the perspective of the managers at Allstate headquarters in Northbrook, it would obviously have been better if Telling had retired on schedule. The current scenario let the merchants have their Christmas season, and there might also be a late burst of impressive numbers from other runners. Even if Brennan did turn in stellar results, though, it seemed utterly impossible to senior Allstaters that their man could be denied. Craib had learned the ropes on the sixty-eighth floor as vice-chairman; he was as expert in the ways of finance and investment as any insurance executive in the country; he owned the name of a great merchant of the glory years; and he happened to be in control of an organization that for three years running had blown the merchants away on the profit line.

Craib had been as gracious as could be expected about his California savings-and-loan's being appropriated by Phil Purcell for what Craib managed to call "our sister company, Dean Witter." But when Dean Witter's sales figures were quoted without noting that the source of a lot of Purcell's sales had come from a thrift operation Allstate had built, Craib became incensed. For years Allstaters had resented the way Sears reported the gains of ancillary Allstate enterprises on a separate line in the books so as to avoid a more embarrassing juxtaposition of profits between retailer and insurer. Now Dean Witter was burying Allstate gains in its results, and it made Craib mad.

Craib gave a speech at Florida A & M University that fall in which he referred to a "joint venture" Allstate was involved in with "Sears in Chicago," a quote that got back to the sixty-eighth floor and the staff guardians of corporate synergy.

During November, Craib revealed a management initiative designed to consolidate the insurer's sprawling system of regional and zone offices. The company had been divided up into four "zones" and over twenty regional offices since shortly after World War II, when the Allstate chairman of the time, Judson Branch, declared that only a program of decentralization would allow Allstate to flourish. Though this was hardly original, Branch used to tell his local office managers that they were all "presidents" as far as he was concerned.

Craib's reorganization plan—which he entitled, not coincidentally, the "Blueprint for the Future," called for the elimination of the four regional zones, and the return of administrative duties such as accounting and claims processing from the localities to the home office in Northbrook. "I emphasize that reorganization doesn't mean we're changing Allstate's culture," Craib said when he unveiled the plan.

Craib complemented his own program of modernization and streamlining with a pledge to take Allstate in a strategic direction that would address the apparent limits to growth that Phil Purcell and the strategic-planning committee had worried over during their studies between 1978 and 1981. Craib said he planned to push his faltering commercial-insurance operations, as well as the underdeveloped life and international wings. With the exception of his Florida A & M speech, the Allstate chairman went to great lengths to speak of his high hopes for the placement of Allstate agents in local Coldwell Banker offices, and when he reported proudly that Allstate had made almost $419 million from $6 billion in premiums during the first six months of 1983, he even added the Tellingesque assertion that his boys had successfully "reinvented the wheel."

But Don Craib knew that Allstate Insurance Company was already running full-bore that fall. There was simply no higher gear available. The Blueprint for the Future had a good feel for the spirit of the company times, and the results of coming quarters would certainly be good—as was now expected of Allstate. Craib would continue to try to say the right words when the opportunity arose, but he admitted he couldn't do much more. As well as he was running that fall, he had to admit that Ed Brennan and the merchants were closing fast from the outside.

Though Ed Telling rarely talked about the merchandise company, the "old Sears" was mentioned in almost every magazine or newspaper article about the boom in American consumer spending that had commenced the previous spring. The giant retailer was depicted "pacing" the sales gains or "riding the tidal wave," the phenomenon clearly induced, several stories implied, by Sears' ubiquitous young merchant and his classy-looking new stores. The retail analyst at First Boston issued a lengthy report contending that, despite all the hoopla about finance, retailing would eventually prevail at Sears. Brennan carried the research report around for days.

A few articles dredged up descriptions of the Sears of three years ago, when the company was losing its market share and ruled by viciously warring factions and ponderous men with white hair. Then "a new team of top management was elected to uproot the past strategies," as the September 19, 1983, issue of *Inside Retailing* chose to explain it. "Nothing so radical had taken place at Sears," the magazine declared, "since General Robert E. Wood transformed a mail order house into a chain of retail stores."

Readers of the periodical literature of professional buying and selling were already aware that technological innovations at Sears had allowed store transaction time to be cut fully in half. A portion of the surging volume—such as the 32-percent rise in sales being chalked up during October—was due to the rapid movement of goods, money, and customers. Several of Brennan's top managers had taken to proclaiming for quotation that the direction of the Merchant was a step in a progression. Sears was originally "the world's cheapest store"; then "the world's biggest"; and now "the most convenient store in the world." The consolidation of product lines was reported as a huge success, with a reformed grouping like fitness equipment due to pass $100 million in sales by the end of the year—this compared to just $36.5 million worth of similar merchandise retailed during the year of the great selloff in 1977.

In October, Ed Brennan's brother, Bernie, resigned from Montgomery Ward to become president of the much smaller Household International Corporation. Bernie had clashed from the beginning with Stephen Pistner, the high-priced turnaround specialist Ward's owner, Mobil Oil, had installed, and now the younger Brennan was gone from the other big retailer in Chicago.

That same October of 1983, Ed Brennan decided the time was right to concentrate the minds of the corporate directors. At the presentation of the five-year plan to his top managers back in April, the total cost of coming expansion and renovation of the retail stores was projected at just under $500 million, down from the $721.5 million set in the previous five-year plan. After taking the members of the board of directors through the King of Prussia store, Brennan planned to ask them for $1.7 billion in order to bring over six hundred stores up to Store of the Future standards. If competition for capital resources was still, as Telling had said, an arena of competition, then the request was rather significantly more then twice as large as the amount spent on Dean Witter and Coldwell Banker.

The view from Brennan's computer screen confirmed to him that, though he was asking for a lot of money, he was on his way to making a lot too. The geographical rearrangements around several of the new stores were working like a charm. The King of Prussia numbers and results from other stores indicated that one Store of the Future could more than make up for sales lost by closing two or more older stores in the same market region. Three stores were closed down and replaced by a single Store of the Future in the Richmond and Norfolk, Virginia, area. The increasingly quoted "return-on-equity" measure of performance in that market had risen from 8.17 percent to 22.91 percent.

Brennan figured that, since 1981, he'd cut more than $500 million out of the expense side, and on the sales side Sears had whipped Penney, K mart, Ward's, and Federated in percentage increases for several months in a row.

The day after Thanksgiving, the first day of the retailer's Christmas, sales in the stores were up 28 percent over the previous year.

"We've all learned some things which have made us better merchants," Brennan told *The Wall Street Journal.* Then he predicted the strongest Christmas season at Sears since the banner year of 1977.

On December 12, *Inside Retailing* came out with an update on the race for the chairmanship of Sears. The magazine picked out Dick Jones, Don Craib, and Ed Brennan as the strongest runners. ". . . we have a fourth entry," the article read. "An outsider, age 40, with a Sears tenure of little more than three years [*sic*] . . . so the bookie's odds would be long. His name is Phil Purcell."

Purcell worked now at the eastern edge of the system, with his back to a stunning view of New York Harbor and the Statue of Liberty. The windows of Sears now looked down at Liberty, the White House, freeways, junks in Hong Kong Harbor, and the tops of clouds over Chicago. As Phil noted so often, things had changed.

His office on the twenty-ninth floor of the Dean Witter Liberty Street headquarters was small by Sears "corner office" standards, so many of the tall piles of sheathed reports and red-penciled memos that inevitably surrounded Purcell often fell together in chaos. Phil's wife, Anne, wished that he could stop taking the only key to the trunk of their Jaguar to New York with him by mistake. In fact, Anne wouldn't have chosen her husband's current job for him if she'd had a choice, even though she knew he thrived on the challenge. Phil agreed that keeping the family in Wilmette while he worked in New York was hard on his boys. The right thing to do "family-wise" would have been not to take the Dean Witter job in New York, but then he would have had to leave Sears, Roebuck, because he believed that when Ed Telling offered a job, you either took it or you left. So he worked very late in his office overlooking New York Harbor, because the alternative was getting some dinner and going home to an empty hotel room.

At forty now, Phil was beginning to look his age. He appeared to have thickened considerably around the middle of late, a change probably not unconnected to his appreciation of Dean Witter's estimable private dining facility. During the period of Andy Melton's efforts to establish

Dean Witter Reynolds as "the Tiffany of the trade," the dining rooms at Liberty Street had gained a reputation in financial circles for their superb culinary offerings. The rooms where Purcell often ate his lunch were appointed with Oriental art, polished cherry-wood tables, Limoges china, fresh flowers, and dishes ranging from poached capon in cream sauce to peach crêpes. Whatever other Dean Witter employees thought of the somewhat abstract and rumpled young man the mother company in Chicago had sent in to be their president, the head chef and others who worked in the dining facility believed that the kid from points west had the best appetite on Wall Street.

Purcell sort of liked some of the account executives he'd met since coming to Dean Witter. He'd conducted a study of the backgrounds of the "AEs" and found his gut sense that they were good people—"core" people with "basic-basic" life experiences behind them—confirmed. Most of them were land-grant university grads from middle- or lower-middle-class "achievement-oriented" families.

The brokers tended to be, like he was, the first from their families to make any real money. But the amount of money some of the Dean Witter employees pulled down in a good year like 1983 was still somewhat startling to Purcell. Phil was one of those highly paid executives who believe secretly that they are getting paid a lot more than they are worth to any company. And he put Stretch Gardiner's $1.2-million base pay in the same category with his own mid-six-figure salary. But neither Phil's nor Stretch Gardiner's name appeared on the first page of the computer printout that listed gross remuneration of employees in descending order.

Phil figured that if a securities retailer with a state-university B.A. could pull down a seven-figure income through the commission-base hawking of Dean Witter products, that was O.K. with him, but he had a lot of trouble with the sums of money taken out by the people from the mergers-and-acquisitions department, and by the executives who dealt with the large corporate customers from the capital-markets division—the ones called "the bankers" inside a Wall Street firm. Purcell figured they didn't work hard enough for their huge paychecks, and he knew that Ed Telling believed precisely the same thing.

Purcell had made it clear to the investment bankers that they were expected to produce profits in proportion to their big incomes. It came back to him, after one talk about his expectations to the capital-markets division executives, that one executive had pronounced him a "real shithead" to colleagues as the meeting broke up.

Dean Witter was a company rife with internal schisms. The "bankers" opposed the brokers in most debates; operations had trouble coordinating with sales; the Reynolds people still competed with the Dean Witter

people. Purcell had to admit that in the fall of 1983 Dean Witter was a
decade away from having a sense of company.

Purcell bounded around the country at the end of the year at a
Brennan-like clip. Without the aid of a private air force, he used commercial airlines to move between New York, Los Angeles, Chicago, back
to New York, to Chicago, Washington, D.C., New York, and then Washington again, all inside a week. He raced along because he had so many
hats to wear and because that was just the way he was, but the spurs
were set hard that December: he had thus far failed to buy Ed Telling
either a new savings-and-loan institution or a "nonbank" bank, and now
it appeared as though the deregulatory aperture through which Sears
and the others had maneuvered aspects of their financial-service ag-
glomerations was closing up.

The public was suddenly hearing about the dark side of the new
industry of financial services: "The concentration of all aspects of our
financial system in financial monoliths is dangerous," railed one New
York State legislator. "It is dangerous to the country itself in that the
nation becomes dependent upon such institutions, and if that institution
is in trouble it could destabilize our entire monetary system."

The company had spent a great deal of money on advertising in
pursuit of an image as the people's counting house. Ads were designed
to break down public resistance to taking money out of the local bank,
just as Richard Sears had worked to break down the natural inclination
of people to demand to see goods before they bought them. Since 60
percent of the accounts opened at the Dean Witter booths in the stores
were set up by people who had never had a brokerage account before,
the strategy clearly had been working, but now an anti-Sears populism
was resurfacing that was reminiscent of the anti-mail-order movement
of another era.

As the most powerful mail-order house, Sears had been the object of
local merchants' organizations' campaigns of letter writing and public
catalog-burning. The mayor of one Illinois town on the banks of the
Mississippi had vowed to fire any city employee caught ordering goods
from the catalog. Between 1897 and 1935 a continuous rumor campaign
throughout the South had sought to convince would-be customers that
Richard Sears and Alvah Roebuck were black men.

The latter-day anti-Sears feeling was orchestrated in Washington by
lobbyists and congressmen connected to groups representing the sort of
independent local banks that Ed Telling loathed. Organizations like the
Independent Bankers Association of America were as fearful of big
banks in New York as they were of Sears, but stopping Sears was an
easier cause to promote, because in one form or another Sears was
indeed everywhere. When savings-and-loan executives began jumping

on the bandwagon as the decision about which corporation would own Chicago's First Federal Savings and Loan finally approached, they generally preferred that Citicorp win control of the savings-and-loan, because Sears would become too dangerously and indomitably vertical in its integration. "It would be perfect," one executive said to *Crain's Chicago Business*, "and so effective that Congress may have to step in."

It was the specter of legislative curtailment of the new industry that had pried Ed Telling out of the Tower during the summer to testify before the Senate Banking Committee. Telling and Purcell argued publicly and in private sessions with regulators and legislators that Sears was not going to become some all-powerful, all-knowing company store to the entire nation. If Sears had indeed become an institution that had transcended the boundaries of traditional definition of organizations under capitalism—in that it simply could not be allowed to fail because of the dire societal consequences of having people's mortgages, savings, and investments all go down the tubes—then it was certainly not the only one.

It was pointed out that the philosophy of capitalization under which each Sears business group operated was about as conservative as could be, and that if corporate failures began to occur, Sears, Roebuck would be among the last to go. In each of the many businesses it operated there was still plenty of competition, though rarely from the same companies. Computer printouts could prove that the same consumer was rarely buying his house, stocks, washing machines, mortgage, and insurance solely from Sears, though the possibility obviously existed. It was noted that information on the various lists Sears kept and information about Americans and their credit and purchasing history would not be integrated and shared among businesses, as a matter of strict policy.

There were a variety of bills and proposals concerning the future of financial services sitting on tables in Washington, D.C., now, and few of them boded well for Sears. The Senate Banking Committee's "Depository Institutions Deregulation Act of 1983," as well as a White House proposal and another from the Treasury Department, all sought to unleash the big banks, as was expected, but each of them also proposed to specifically limit the future activities of nonbank financial operations like Sears. During his many trips to Washington, Phil Purcell argued with legislators, Treasury officials, and other executive-branch functionaries. He learned that various congressmen had vowed to produce legislation during the coming year that would force Sears to divest itself of financial businesses like the California savings-and-loan and Dean Witter.

On top of all the other pressures and frustrations, Phil had to spend half his time in a town he hated, talking to a lot of people who he believed had come to Washington, D.C., via prep schools and elite colleges thinking they knew something about the real people who live in the United States of America. Phil had known these people at Notre Dame, the University of Chicago, and the London School of Economics, and he didn't like them any better this time around.

"The career regulator is the scariest animal I've ever met in my life," he observed one evening after returning to New York from Washington. "The regulator has never met a real person, wouldn't know one if he did. The people who built this country sweat and swear. They get drunk. They don't read Albert Camus when they come home at night—they drink beer. Most of the people down there were born wealthy—doctors' and lawyers' sons—gone to good schools, very literate and all, but they've never been out where the game's really played. They still want to tell people how to live their lives—and they think by some divine right they can do this, and do it better than if they let a guy with a lunchbox decide how to spend his money."

Purcell admitted that he'd been allowed to make his case, and he believed that he'd been heard, but they were still making him look bad in Washington just when it mattered most. In December the regulators at the Federal Reserve Board weighed in with a ruling that would limit the chartering of nonbank banks. Then Sears lost the bidding war for First Federal Savings and Loan to Citicorp. Then it was made public that Dean Witter had settled out of court the claim by Merrill Lynch that Dean Witter had stolen the Active Asset Account idea from Merrill's CMA.

Purcell also had to live with the fact that his former access to what he called "unbelievable power"—back when Ed Telling was moving so hard against the status quo according to plans and strategies they hatched together as a team—was gone. It was ironic that, after so much work at the pinnacle of the organization, he not only remained an outsider, but one whose connection to the next regime was possibly more tenuous than when he first arrived. Having outgrown his image as "wunderkind," arch-planner, and "Telling's boy," he lately seemed to be laboring in the direction of oblivion.

It was galling to watch his role in the dramatic history of recent events obscured by others. Rod Hills continued to bound prominently around the world as Telling's emissary, directing a thick flow of deals. It was as if Hills had not only arrogated the role of point man, but had managed to extend his retrospective presence at Sears back to a time when Telling and Purcell had made plans alone.

Purcell would be the last to question the brilliance or indomitable drive of Ed Brennan ("though Eddie's gonna kill himself, the way he pushes," Phil would add), but it was also hard to observe his own absence from the history of events that led up to Brennan's powerful, late sprint. From what he heard, it was as if Phil's early manipulations of structure and his effort to carve a route to the top for Ed Telling had been discounted; as if he'd been absent from the hard jobs of pulling down the kingpins of the system, killing off 599, shutting down offices, and moving out a national forest's worth of managerial dead wood. So far from the right hand of Telling now, Phil Purcell knew that what he lacked in bloodlines and continued access to his mentor, he would have to make up in hard work and the politically acute hedging of various positions. "The net of it," as he often said, came down to the fact that he had been able to get things done before inside a system so dominated by Sears lifers not because he was "any good," but because he knew whom to call on the phone.

Phil believed that things got done in a big company like Sears because of an informal network of energetic individuals aligned just below the top layer. If Purcell wanted something done at Allstate, for instance, it would never cross his mind to call Don Craib. He would call a well-positioned vice-president in Northbrook named Wayne Hedien. Wayne—invariably—would get things done: "No hassle, no memos, no nothin'."

If Phil wanted something done in the Merchant, he called Joe Batogowski. Bato had a considerable reputation up on the sixty-eighth floor as a gifted natural merchant and a first-class manager too. But few of the people who believed this of Batogowski had ever seen him in action. Bato's good rep up on sixty-eight was a gift from Phil.

During the fall, Purcell decided to bring members of this secondary network together for a weekend. He decreed that there would be "no CEOs, no old guys—just the guys who were going to end up being really important in each of their companies before it's all over." Phil said he wanted these individuals to get to know one another while there was still nothing at stake, to meet and make alliances while their bosses were still running straight ahead toward the now more distant roses.

He invited Batogowski, Bob Wood, Wayne Hedien, and another young executive from Allstate. Forrest Olson was invited from Coldwell Banker, as were two of Phil's own people from Dean Witter, one of them a big former Stanford University lineman named Steve Miller, who looked a lot like a heavier-set Phil.*

---

*Everyone except Rod Hills seemed to have a resident jock by now. Brennan had the apocryphal jock Eric Saunders; Poulson had the real-item jock in Heisman Trophy winner Gary Beban, who played football at UCLA and worked for Poulson in Chicago. Rod Hills had a former Rhodes Scholar instead—as Rod reminded listeners with regularity.

The group was asked to convene at the La Costa Hotel and Country Club, north of San Diego, California. Each participant in the unofficial gathering was supposed to work out the details and internal justification of the trip in his own way. Phil decided to try a variation on Ed Telling's old idea of mixing and matching foursomes across company lines by assigning roommates—four executives to a room.

The gathering of young Turks was billed as an informal planning meeting, but the senior vice-president for corporate planning on the sixty-eighth floor, Charley Moran, never heard about it. Though no great business decisions were made at La Costa, Purcell was pleased by the event. The important thing was that all the invitees had responded. They all showed up. Most of them were closer to forty than they were to fifty, and though it was never said during the brief meeting at La Costa, it was clear to all of the participants that Purcell was seeking to bring together intercorporate peers of the second tier—the third tier, if you considered Telling to occupy the top by himself.

Phil was pleased to be called a contender in mid-December. His numbers were tailing off a bit by the end of the year, but the wire house was on its way to chalking up $100 million in profit—a huge number by the standards of the securities brokerage industry up to that point, and almost quadruple the Dean Witter performance of 1982. For all of the media attention garnered by Brennan and his Store of the Future, the regulatory battles, in concert with the growth and performance of the financial-services wing, had kept the "socks-and-stocks" motif in public view.

At the end of the second week of December, there were some 131 Dean Witter booths in place in the financial-service centers in the stores. That would be the final number of booths running at the end of the year. There would be no further construction work done on the centers until January, because even in the new Sears, Christmas still belonged to the merchants.

Just as Brennan prophesied, the stores sold the hell out of Christmas.

At the big "A" store in Hicksville, the hottest big-ticket boys unloaded upward of $20,000 worth of goods in an afternoon. At the new Store of the Future west of Hicksville in Valley Stream, the store manager had his employees bused to work just to free up a few more spaces in the parking lot. Sales in the New York group of stores soared to nearly $10 million on just the Saturday before Christmas, and by the end of December the group had racked up almost $150 million in monthly gross sales, up 22.7 percent from the Christmas season of 1982.

In December, Sears had its first ever $3-billion month, a milestone that conjured recollections of the General's stated hope that Sears would some day have a $3-billion year. The feat was highlighted by the announcement from across town that Montgomery Ward had in December achieved monthly sales of $1 billion for the first time.

When visitors came to see Brennan during January, he would usher them quickly to his computer terminal, where he would punch up the special program the wizards in 704 had written that allowed him to compare Store of the Future results with the rest. Even the two "difficult" stores down in Miami had exceeded the Plan. The store at Aventura had more than doubled the business done by the rat-infested Miami Northside store it had replaced. Just as Stew Thomas had contended the day Brennan blew up at his excuses, the new Macy's store sharing the mall in Aventura had caused the Sears store there to go black.

"We couldn't handle some of the business it was so big," Brennan said. He lowered one finger onto the keyboard and called up the next set of figures. "Look. Look there at Yorktown up in Westchester County, New York. Gonna be a $35-million store. . . . And . . . there is Torrance, California. At $9 million, probably the best single performance ever for a Sears store." Brennan leaned back away from the screen and lit a cigar.

The gross sales for 1983 would only exceed the levels of 1977 by 8 percent—and that after six years of fulminating inflation—but the Tower was abuzz with talk of the Merchant's performance. The dollar sales increase over 1982 would turn out to be the largest in company history. The percentage increase, excluding the results of Simpson-Sears in Canada, was up 18 percent, the largest jump since they gave the store away in 1977. The profitability of the Merchant had tripled since Ed Brennan's arrival in 1980. His business group made $781 million in profit over the course of a year that began with untried leaders running both the buying organization and Field, with a planning mechanism still fitting into place, with consolidations causing the uprooting of thousands of employees, with a sick international division that still put a $17-million hit to the numbers, and with much of the available executive energy during the year being directed at experimental research on bits and pieces of what eventually became a new store. The profit figure for 1983 fell just $119 million shy of the profit goal projected for 1987 at the end of the five-year plan. Don Craib's bean counters had chalked up $660.7 million in profit—nothing to apologize for in light of the much smaller levels of Allstate's gross sales—but for the first time in several years, the Merchant produced greater profits than the insurance company.

Two weeks and two days into 1984, the Year of the Store of the

Future, Ed Brennan finally turned fifty, an age that would have barely qualified him to run a Sears retail group not so long ago. Because of the heavy emphasis on performance included in Ed Brennan's compensation package, his bonus for the year would so far exceed his base pay that he would make nearly $2 million.

But if he was denied the roses, neither the money nor the glory would mean a thing.

Brennan tried not to brood about the chairmanship, though he admitted that his plan of action in the event of one of the other aspirants' getting the job was "very well thought out."

"Nobody should ever sit in a job waiting for the phone to ring," he said. "I've preached that all my life."

Ed Telling noticed his name in the paper quite often during the early weeks of 1984. In January the *Gallagher President's Report,* which had once named him one of the ten worst executives in America, again named him one of the ten best. During the second week of February, both the *The Wall Street Journal* and *The New York Times* ran major features about Telling's Sears. The *Times* published a huge spread, replete with numerous articles by writers who'd been dispatched to the various enterprises, and the *Journal*'s piece, entitled "Prowling Giant—Sears," began in the hallowed right-hand column of the front page.

The *Journal* devoted a great deal of attention to the prospect of Telling's departure and noted that, for the first time in the company's long history, the new chairman of the board wouldn't automatically hail from the ranks of the Merchant. "Mr. Telling has told all of us that the chairman can come from any of the operations," the article quoted the outgoing corporate president, Archie Boe, as saying. "What counts now is whether you're a broad gauged businessman."

The article mentioned that there were no plans to replace Boe as president until the end of 1984, a decision that apparently irked one of the more talkative members of the executive family: "This riles C. Wesley Poulson, the chairman and chief executive officer of Coldwell Banker. Mr. Poulson wants a president named immediately. He also worries that none of the top candidates for the chairmanship is right for that job: 'There needs to be a little of the S.O.B. in some of them, and that's what I see lacking. . . . There isn't a sense of urgency in some of the candidates that I think is required if they're going to move in the financial area.' "

Telling was now certain that he would use the presidency as a grooming post for his successor, but he wasn't going to name names until "the correct time." "The correct message will be sent at the correct time," he said just before Poulson went public with his complaints. "I can tell you that often the people who run the hardest turn out to be the least successful. The job, in my mind, has to seek the guy."

During January, Telling had gone out to spend some time with Rod Hills and his staff at World Trade headquarters. Telling had become increasingly aware of what his people on sixty-eight thought of Hills and his management of the trade operation. He asked Rod if there wasn't any way he could slow things down, just enough to bring his budget back in line.

From Hills' perspective, he had to make his more audacious moves, strike his biggest deals, and hire his most expensive talent quickly. Without the shield of Telling to protect him, Hills feared that Purcell, Jones, or one of the other sycophants would cut his throat. The observation stood as a peculiarly rare though rather late example of political perspicacity on Rod's part.

So Hills was at his oratorical best when Telling came to visit. So skillfully did he adorn their dream of Sears in the world that the chairman went back to Chicago to tell his cronies on sixty-eight that "if there's such a thing as a good volcano, then that's what I've seen at World Trade." Telling said he felt "like there's going to be a tremendous explosion there."

A few weeks later, Henry Sunderland got a promotion to a job in Corporate. He would be the senior executive in charge of "administration" on sixty-eight. It was a senior factotum post that included responsibility for the corporate air force and the operation of the Tower. Phil Purcell had done these tasks and hated them back when he was the planner, and Bill Sanders held the portfolio as part of the corporate personnel job after that, but the important thing was that Henry had returned to Ed Telling's side after a long stint away from the inner circle. Ever since Telling had sent him out to pacify the Pacific Coast Territory, to "bring them back to the company," Sunderland had served Telling from a distance. By the time Henry got back to the Tower, Brennan was running the Merchant. Now, after surviving the tough assignment out west, the task of keeping up with Ed Brennan, two heart attacks, and a quadruple bypass operation, Henry was back in a position similar to the one he'd started out in back in 1977.

. . .

At the very end of February, a party was held for Archie Boe after a board-of-directors meeting in Florida. On March 1 the studious Iowan left Sears, after forty-two years of service, forty of them at the Allstate Insurance Company. Though he ended up as a custodian of corporate integration, Archie would remember with greatest fondness his time running Allstate as a separate company, charged as he'd been by Gordo Metcalf with just keeping the bean machine out of Sears' way.

The day Boe left, Telling wandered out of his office, past Pat Jamieson's desk, and then across the hall to the president's office. He asked that a pair of green chairs in the vacant office be moved to a spot near his own desk. Telling said he'd had his eye on Archie's chairs for quite a while.

In April, Telling fired Rod Hills.

At the 1984 rendition of the now annual April visit of securities analysts to the Drake Hotel, Telling rose to begin the proceeding from a shortened dais. He said he had some news to get out of the way. Pursuant to an "agreement" between Sears and Rod Hills, he announced, the chairman and CEO of Sears World Trade had resigned. Corporate Vice-Chairman and CFO Dick Jones would add World Trade to his responsibilities. When it came time for the formal business report about the state of Sears World Trade, Dick Jones read the little speech that Hills had written one week earlier and that only twenty-four hours earlier he had believed he would be delivering himself.

Rod always knew that he just didn't come equipped with any reverse gears. He'd been at war with the corporate forces on the sixty-eighth floor for over a year and had been waging a series of battles on a separate front with Phil Purcell. Up until the very last moment, when Ed Telling felt he could no longer protect him, Hills could only envisage his defeats and setbacks as temporary hitches in the endless flow of deals, momentary lapses in the never-ending quest to explore the "art of the possible." What he lacked in politesse, he sought to make up in enthusiasm and a singular capacity to describe the towering shapes of gigantic dreams.

If everyone around Ed Telling thought that buying a historic landmark building in downtown Washington, D.C., was a bad idea, Hills would personally resubmit the idea over the nay-sayers' heads, directly to Telling. Alone with the chairman, Hills would conjure up potent images of a national home for the Great American Company, right there on Pennsylvania Avenue. In Rod's hands, the acquisition of an old building became part of a romance, a great corporation taking its rightful place in the American capital and the world. When the corporate governmental-affairs department took up residence in the restored landmark, the structure would symbolize a commitment to free markets and unfettered international commerce. It would represent a company laboring in the name of the consumer to modernize the handling of money and at the same time unburden Americans from the pall of legislative restriction.

So the building was purchased. But when the refurbishing was almost completed, Hills declared the interior utterly unsuitable to his vision. The place had indeed been fitted with standard Sears, Roebuck windows on the top floors, the ceilings were built too low, and the tile was cheap. Hills wanted the future home of the corporate governmental-affairs department and Sears World Trade to have high ceilings and ornate cornices. He wanted an open layout with walls made of glass. The building was supposed to be as open and anti-bureaucratic, as freewheeling but powerful and distinguished and venerable as the version of the new Sears he was so avidly marketing around the world. But the bureaucracy was screwing the place up, and all Rod Hills knew to do when confronted by an impediment was to try to run over it.

Telling had to fly out to Washington, D.C., on two occasions before the battle over the Washington building's interior was quieted. At one point Hills simply refused to move into the building—"A trading company has to be open!" he would rail—until it conformed to the proper standards. The dullards around Telling were so unschooled in the history of international commerce that they resisted his move to call the new building Sears House, indifferent as they were to the titled headquarters of the great trading houses of old. As with the interior design, a compromise was reached; the structure was opened up as Sears House, and Rod Hills labored there under an appropriate cornice and under the illusion that he'd won.

During the late months of 1983, the flow of deals was running in torrents, and Hills, through the prate of corporate gossip, became aware that the high-priced new staff he was taking on to develop health-industry and high-technology subdivisions for the trade company was resented by the corporate staff. The former merchants on the trade-company payroll whom Hills left in Chicago ("I have no use for them") constantly fed to the sixty-eighth floor stories of mismanagement in Washington, of deals that were struck without any structural adjustments to back them up, and plans that were light-years ahead of reality. When Hills' number-two executive, Frank Carlucci, declared in late 1983 that the trade company would eventually gain "equal status with the Merchant," Carlucci added to the flow of mistakes.

Under constant pressure because of his profligate personnel policies, Hills had recently listed 130 employees who would be laid off as a cost-cutting measure. This was also a mistake, because somehow the list got around both the trade-company headquarters and the Tower, along with much attendant gossip about how heartless were the un-Sears-like policies of Rod Hills.

From the time of his late-1983 mandate from Telling and the board to take Sears in the direction of world-class "financial engineering" and merchant banking, Hills had conducted negotiations in Washington, New York, Tokyo, and London with three noted young specialists in trade finance, two of whom worked for Phibro Inc. in London and one at the Chase Manhattan Bank's international operation. The plan was to set up an integrated merchant bank and trade company, complete with global capacities and headquarters in London, New York, Tokyo, Hong Kong, and Melbourne. Once access to credit was secured via an in-house banking source, Sears' access to world markets and all manner of products and commodities would finally render World Trade fit to take on the Japanese. Rod planned to finance the new financial wing of World Trade with $25 million from Sears.

There was staff nitpicking and Tower-based resistance to the venture from the start, but Hills refused to consider the fact that merchant banking encroached on turf occupied by Dick Jones and his financial specialists—and by Phil Purcell, who as the corporate point man on banking and money-handling had stated flatly that any Sears banking operation belonged under the control of the Financial Services Group.

In early February 1984, just before the final contracts were scheduled to be signed, the corporate planner Charley Moran and Bob Gurnee, the corporate treasurer who reported to Dick Jones, flew together to London on "other business." While in town, they happened to have dinner with Doug Rice, the young banker Hills was hiring away from Phibro to run the trade-finance entity. During a sumptuous dinner at La Gavroche, the Sears executives wondered aloud if Rice realized that every move he wanted to make in the future would have to be O.K.'d by the World Trade officers in Washington. Rice replied that he was indeed unaware of this procedural aspect of the deal. Charley Moran was particularly blunt in indicating Chicago's skepticism of the venture. He mentioned that the business plan would have to be redrawn, for its scope was beyond what Ed Telling and Sears Corporate had in mind.

The next morning, Rice and the others excused themselves from further association with Sears and took the entire team they'd assembled to work for Prudential-Bache.

That same February, Ed Telling canceled a trip to Italy he and Nancy had planned to take with Rod and Carla Hills. Telling told Rod that Nancy had been ill and was too weak to make the journey. The trip was called off not long after Hills and Telling met for one of their heady dinners. The chairman told Hills over dinner that he'd agreed to give a speech in April on the occasion of his receiving the Harvard Business Club of Chicago's award as "Business Statesman of the Year." Telling asked Hills if he'd help out, and Rod promised to work on it.

During April, Hills told a reporter for *The Washington Post* that Sears World Trade would account for $5 to $10 billion of total corporate sales in just five years. The interview was given just before Hills flew off to the Far East for another meeting with his Asian advisory board. When he returned, Telling asked Hills to join him in Chicago for a cup of coffee to talk about Rod's recent resubmission of the merchant-banking idea.

"Guess ya know how everybody around here feels," Telling said.

"Yeah, Ed, I know," Hills replied, aware from Telling's tone of what was next. "Let's just call it off."

Telling said afterward that Rod had created a business without pausing to construct its working parts—"sorta like an appliance salesman without a warehouse or a delivery truck." He was like Richard Sears, who just couldn't stop himself from selling more suits than he owned or could even buy, until Julius Rosenwald came in and stopped it once and for all.

"No need to beat a dead horse if he's not able to pull," Telling said soon after he fired his rainmaker of three years' running. But Rod Hills would never forget the look of sadness on Ed Telling's face when he shook the chairman's hand and said goodbye.

Hills would return to work at his law firm in Washington, to a small office lined with framed photographs and quotations: "To Rod," said the quote from former President Jerry Ford. "To a masterful negotiator and manager of crises."

In his quest to make from the stuff of deals a reality that conformed to his own brilliant machinations, Hills never stopped to look around and see where he was. He ignored the tribal residue of the once-private and carefully ordered civilization of Sears until it finally slowed him down enough to cover him over and swallow him up. The most casual student of corporate politics such as they existed at Sears would have seen that stepping on Phil Purcell's and Dick Jones' toes at the same time—with the same audacious deal—was like asking to be put away. Hills was somewhat aware that each time he wanted to enter a joint venture with another company, some atavistic force rose up within the Sears lifers that worked against him, but for all of his political experience, he never looked at the phenomenon and traced it to its historical or psychological roots. Hills believed the entire regime of Ed Telling was something so ahistorical, so specifically designed in counterpoint to the strange, inbred ways of Sears' past, that he was free to deal. Though he was in many ways correct in this observation, he never acknowledged the multitude of old ways that remained alongside the new ones.

From the moment Hills met Wes Poulson in Paris and tried to convince his old Stanford buddy that the mysterious Ed Telling was just "old
shoe," there were aspects of Telling and his complex emotional, intellectual, and historical relationship to Sears, Roebuck that Hills never took
the time to understand. Because Telling revealed a different side of
himself when they were together, Hills never understood the protec-
tiveness most others felt toward the chairman of the board.

He would continue to believe that the great torrent of deals was
stemmed because Ed Telling had grown tired and weary of the quest.
Rod Hills' whole career had been predicated upon tilting at windmills,
and this time "the windmill won." He would return to Washington,
strike a low profile, and let the "debris" of his life clear a bit before
venturing out to deal again. He would always contend that the saddest
thing about his Sears adventure was not his own failure; it was the sight
of one of the world's last and best "grand romantics" finally slowing
down. "He's run his course," Hills said. "He's plain out of steam."

After Telling reported the departure of Hills to the April assemblage of
analysts, he went on to announce that, during the first quarter of the
year, corporate earnings had risen 34 percent, due in large part to an
unusually powerful surge by the Merchandise Group during what is
traditionally their dullest quarter. Brennan's troops made $81.6 million
during the first three months of 1984, whereas only $11.1 million had
been made during the first quarter of the previous year.

Meanwhile, the brilliant performance of Dean Witter during 1983
had fizzled out. The frenzy of equity buying that began in the summer
of 1982 actually peaked around Halloween in 1983, but the full force of
the negative wave didn't come ashore for the stock sellers until 1984.
With over $577 million in revenues during the first quarter, Dean Witter
was able to contribute only $1.5 million to the bottom line, a figure that
would just about cover Stretch Gardiner's salary for the year.

That same April, the Sears financial-services venture had been raked
over the coals during Colorado Representative Tim Wirth's public hearings, pursuant to legislation that would impose a moratorium on further
formation of financial supermarkets. During his questioning of Federal
Reserve Board Chairman Paul Volcker, Wirth implied that the impetus
behind his bill was fear of Sears. The congressman ran through a widely
reported scenario by which an unsuspecting customer enters a Sears
store in search of a hammer and walks out with a house from Coldwell
Banker, a mortgage, participation in the mortgage through a Dean
Witter security, insurance from Allstate, and a loan from the developing
savings-and-loan system.

Volcker was rather specific in his agreement with Congressman Wirth: "We don't want Sears, Roebuck in the banking business," the chairman said.

The chairman of the House Committee on Banking, Finance, and Urban Affairs, Fernand St Germain of Rhode Island, seemed to have picked up on the resurgent anti-Sears populism of the previous year and was, by the spring of 1984, insisting that the House version of the long-awaited financial-services-and-banking bill force Sears out of the business of handling consumers' money altogether.

During the first week of May, the Federal Home Loan Bank Board weighed in with a ruling that seemed not only to bar Sears from expanding its capacity to take deposits and grant loans, but also to call for the divestiture of either Dean Witter or the savings-and-loan in California. Phil Purcell immediately called a press conference to announce that Sears was filing suit against the bank board. Purcell contended that Sears had already lost business as a result of the bank board's ruling. "We've been removed from underwritings and we've had assignments withdrawn," he complained. He said Sears had tried to keep the lines of communication open with bank-board officials, but they'd been "left twisting in the wind."

The specter of specific legal proscription of the financial-services venture was far more threatening to the great experiment than any problem of internal synergy. It was the interposition of federal legislation that had doomed Richard Sears' turn-of-the-century attempt to parlay the franchise of trust into banking.

In the larger universe of lending people money, there was really no way in which Sears could be extricated from the practice. The company had moved in to do too many of the jobs the banks had left undone, but the Telling-era challenges to the banks were vulnerable. In strategic-planning committee meetings before he left, Rod Hills had vociferously questioned Phil Purcell's proposal to change the name of the Allstate Savings and Loan Association to the Sears Savings Bank. Hills thought the name change went too far in sticking it to the regulators and the banks—which, of course, was the idea. He was overruled.

Phil Purcell saw to his diplomatic chores in Washington as best he could that spring. He worked closely with the governmental-affairs specialists at Sears House. He even spent an evening at a baseball game in the company of fellow Utahan and Senate Banking Committee member Jake Garn, who, unlike Ed Telling, had come away from a childhood in a small town with warm and protective feelings toward little banks.

But Purcell was far more preoccupied that spring by the precipitous decline of Dean Witter's fortunes. The fall of Rod Hills in April did little to alleviate his depression as Dean Witter dived into the red. The company was losing money at a rate of almost $2 million a week—hand over proverbial fist. It was as if the business had simply been turned off at the spigot. Some trader in Dean Witter's mortgage-securities unit had executed a seemingly sophisticated hedge maneuver in collateralized mortgage obligation certificates that had turned into a botched speculation that cost over $20 million. Morale, especially among the high-flying investment bankers, was terrible, and many of them were on their way to new jobs.

It wasn't as if Dean Witter was the only financial-services business having trouble. Companies like Merrill Lynch and several other brokerage houses were also experiencing disastrous months. The former piano-makers turned financial-service providers at Baldwin United had recently experienced the worst quarterly loss in the history of American business when they had to write off $567 million in assets from their financial-services group.

Meanwhile, the business cycles Wes Poulson studied and tracked were beginning to turn against Wes' realtors. As interest rates nosed up, his residential-housing business was falling off—and however much money Coldwell Banker might make in commercial deals or the sale of shopping centers, the realtor's performance was based on selling lots of houses. Unlike Dean Witter, which would end up losing almost $23 million when the second quarter's devastation was toted up, Poulson would beat 1983 when the results came in, but between the quick departure of Rod Hills, the bad numbers, and the adverse publicity and potentially damaging new rules in Washington, the three-year-old star of financial services seemed suddenly less radiant. With all of the new businesses falling into a slump together, it was quite easy to see that the results were dependent on the Merchant.

After a long day, Phil Purcell would often climb into a limousine and motor through the Manhattan night while he talked business on the mobile phone. Sometimes he tried to hike uptown on foot toward one of the Italian restaurants he loved and a couple of Crown Royal perfect Manhattans, but usually Phil took the car. He'd had his slicked-down young-Republican haircut for a while now, and, more recently, he was given to a prep-school genre of sarcastic dressings-down and the nick-naming of all things, especially when in the company of Stretch Gardiner. Stretch often called him "Philsy."

One thing about line management was how deeply personal it felt, compared with advising others what to do. After so many years on staffs, Purcell never could have guessed how incredibly torn up losing money could make him feel. But most of all he hated feeling like he was failing Ed Telling. The man had asked him to come to New York City to do something, and Phil knew he just wasn't doing it.

There was still talk that Purcell might be appointed president when Telling left in order to provide a strategic balance to a more operationally oriented chairman like Craib or Brennan, but Purcell considered the idea far-fetched. He realized now that his personal time-line had lengthened considerably, and that he and the young Turks who'd come together at La Costa would have to wait—to survive—so that they were still there the next time the guard changed.

That spring, several staffers in the Tower began to notice more lines and phrases from Ed Brennan's repertoire appearing in Purcell's exhortations to his dispirited Wall Street managers and salespeople. One corporate speechwriter complimented Purcell on a specific line from one of his speeches, something to the effect that it didn't really matter if you made money in IRAs or fixed-income security sales if the branch office didn't make money at the end of the day. This was a direct transposition from Brennan's gospel of the Good Store.

"Oh yeah, I got that stuff from Brennan," Purcell said to the speechwriter. "In fact, if you come across any more of that stuff, I'd appreciate it if you'd send it out to me. Brennan says those sorts of things are good merchandising lessons, but they're not. It's just pure good business."

Life would certainly be a lot different if Brennan became the leader. It would take a while to get used to the long explanations, after years of no explanations at all; hard to wait while every piece of logic was considered, every step enumerated and enunciated and placed within a macroeconomic and historical context. Eddie Brennan was a great manager; he had considerable "executive equipment" at his disposal, in Phil's book. Just the way he'd continued to centralize the Merchant under the guise of bottom's-up management was a work of genius and art.

Even though Purcell believed great men who built things of substance invariably try to destroy what they built before they leave—witness the General's late years—he believed Sears would prevail in the end. As far as his own role in the future, he figured time was on his side. He pointed out over a huge dinner that he'd always been "the youngest everything"—the youngest McKinsey principal, the youngest managing partner, certainly the youngest officer in modern memory at Sears. He'd come to Sears as a smart kid from Utah with the curriculum vitae of an all-American achiever, a bit of a chip on his shoulder, and the nagging sense that he would never get a chance to really make a difference. What he found at Sears was the opportunity to change forever a world and a way of life that had seemed utterly immutable. At Ed Telling's side, Phil Purcell got his chance to make a mark, and no matter what happened from here, that could never be taken away.

Not long after he fired Rod Hills, Telling took a copy of the speech Hills had in a small way helped his chief speechwriter to conceive and went over to the Ritz-Carlton Hotel to get his Business Statesman Award from the Harvard Business Club of Chicago. After being so avidly contemptuous of the high-profile leaders of other companies and so careful to keep what he feared were his feet of clay far from the public eye, Telling seemed to be lowering his guard a bit in the spring of his penultimate year in office. After announcing the departure of Hills to the analysts at the Drake, Telling had proceeded to shock the audience by giving his finest public performance. He traded jocular repartee with interrogators from the floor, and even recited eight or nine lines of a Robert Burns poem—in dialect.

Telling still believed an award such as the one from the Harvard Business Club was like the kiss of death, but if the Harvard boys wanted to call him a statesman, then he figured he might as well humor them and sound like one. He arrived at the dinner toting a twenty-nine-page address entitled "The Corporate Entrepreneur: An Endangered Species?"

The rare occasion of a public address by Ed Telling caused the demand for tickets to the dinner to far exceed the capacity of the banquet hall booked by the club. Requests came from suppliers throughout the Midwest, from leaders of Chicago's banking and corporate establishment (the 1983 performance had catapulted Sears up over Standard Oil and back into its former position of pre-eminence in the city), and from hundreds of others who just wanted to take a look at the invisible man of Sears. After dispensing just under six hundred tickets, club administrators began turning people away.

Ed Brennan, Bill Bass, and most of the corporate officers were in attendance at the Ritz-Carlton when Telling informed the huge crowd that few moments in his career had meant more to him. He thanked the "four hundred and forty thousand people of Sears, Roebuck and Company." "Business executives," he said, "are only as effective as the companies they represent. For that reason, it is really Sears that is being honored tonight. The organization made everything else possible. Over the past thirty-eight years they have given me many special moments."

Telling reviewed briefly topics on which he would not dwell that evening. He touched on the issue of the federal deficit, on the vogueish interest in national industrial policy, and on his sense that nobody should honestly want people in Washington, D.C., to have the last word on who wins or loses in business. He said business people are accountable for their own destinies, and that, after allowing the public sector to supply the vision and leadership that few businessmen had been willing to offer for a long time, executives now had to face up to their crippling "fear to act."

While the total number of available jobs has increased in the United States, he continued to lecture, the leaders of the big corporations have allowed three million jobs to be lost. Brennan and Bass looked on uncomfortably as the chairman proclaimed that since "contraction—not expansion—is a far easier strategy to pursue, job elimination—rather than job creation—is fast becoming a legitimate corporate goal. . . . Big Business is no longer a viable source for job creation in this country. 'Consolidate, retrench, preserve, and hesitate' now best describe the strategies of what were once our most aggressive firms. Somewhere along the way, we lost our vision—and our nerve."

He went on in a voice less disembodied than at other times to sing the praises of the entrepreneurial creators of small business, and he urged the leaders of large corporations to seek similar sorts of innovation. He said that the public continued to vilify corporate managers as an "unduly privileged class, reaping money and benefits far beyond their worth," not because of the remuneration itself, but because short-term compensation systems obviated risk. Businesses must take risks in order to grow, and unless something changed, "preservation—not creation—will become the order of the day. . . . Executives do have within their grasp the power to release the creative forces locked deep within the heart of every major U.S. corporation. The key is to act.

"We must learn to cherish the mavericks. Differences of opinion and style will certainly occur, but you can't innovate without breaking a little crockery in the process."

Some of the guests from the Tower looked on in wonder. Wasn't the maverick executive given to the metaphorical paraphrase of Stalin's infamous "You can't have an omelet without breaking eggs"—Rod Hills—gone now? Was there really still a place at Sears for the John Lowes, the Jumpin' Joe Morans—or even for the Ed Tellings?

After the speech, Telling was asked how he would react to a young, entrepreneurial territorial executive in the Merchant who decided to conduct unilateral experimentation with the corporate planning process. "That's not an entrepreneur," he said with a smile. "That's a goddamned meddler."

Ed Telling had indeed taken a huge risk in buying new businesses and encouraging them to grow and create new jobs, but hadn't he also set in motion the veritable depopulation of numerous reaches of the old

Sears? He'd certainly released the creative forces locked deep within the corporate soul, but the creativity had been released by acts of destruction.

"A CEO must develop a thick skin, and take a stand on the issues," Telling continued at the Ritz-Carlton banquet. "In an age when business leaders get almost as much press as rock stars and professional athletes, few escape unscathed." He said that the risk-taker will suffer most at the hands of professional observers and others, because those who innovate have always been misunderstood: "One student of human nature observed more than four hundred and fifty years ago, 'There is nothing more difficult to take in hand . . . more perilous to conduct . . . or more uncertain in its outcome, than to take the lead in introducing a new order of things. The innovator has for enemies all those who did well under the old system—and lukewarm defenders in those who might do well under the new.'

". . . Some of us are associated with companies that have been part of this country for many years," the chairman of Sears, Roebuck continued. "I, for one, am not willing to accept the judgment that either size or age prevents a company from remaining a vital, productive element of society. The way to the future is not that of the secure, the comfortable, the timid, the inflexible, the indecisive, the selfish. It *is* the way of those who will put their judgment on the line and their leadership at risk. It is also the way of those who are more concerned about where their company will be in ten years, rather than where they are today.

"At Sears, we will not sit passively by and manage decline. We treasure the success of the past *only* to the extent that it lights the way of the future."

Then Ed Telling stepped back and smiled sheepishly as the crowd rose in a wave to applaud.

CHAPTER 27

The Great Works

O n August 13, 1984, a hot day in Chicago, Ed Telling summoned the chief executives of the Sears business groups to the sixty-eighth floor. The board of directors was scheduled to meet the next morning, so the group chairmen were due to come to town anyway, but Telling had telephoned each of them to request a private conference during the early afternoon of the 13th, one after another, before the rest of the board members arrived on sixty-eight for the traditional pre-meeting feast.

Somehow reporters in New York and Chicago had been alerted that something was happening in the Tower, but the public-affairs department was refusing comment. One week earlier, amid a general increase in public and internal speculation about some sort of August decision at Sears, *The Wall Street Journal* quoted a "senior executive": "Who is picked," the unnamed executive said, "depends on Ed Telling's vision of the company."

By 2:00 P.M., both Wes Poulson and Stretch Gardiner were pacing the beige corridors. The thick carpet along the main hall showed the tracks of a recent vacuuming, so Stretch's shoes left huge, clear footprints as he sauntered along with a glass of water in his hand. His face was flushed as he considered the etchings along the walls. Poulson wandered by in the opposite direction, opening several large doors along the hallway in search of a conference room where he could wait his turn in solitude.

Soon the head of the Sears board's nominating-and-proxy committee, the Colorado businessman Edgar Stern, bounded from the elevator, smiling and tanned. Everyone on sixty-eight seemed to like Julius Rosenwald's grandson, who surfaced as a figurehead each time the guard was due to change at Sears. Stern dutifully bore witness to corporate events, as if in testament to the utter inconsequentialness of a Sears-generated family fortune worth well over $300 million in comparison with the reality of corporate authority fifty years after his grandfather's death. A director since he was thirty-four years old, Stern was the only remaining member of the 1976 nominating committee that had chosen Ed Telling, a decision several board members regarded for four years afterward as a most dreadful mistake.

After exchanging pleasantries with Fran, the receptionist/karate expert, Stern noted Gardiner and Poulson at either end of the long hall, then settled back deep into one of the club chairs to Fran's left and began to watch.

Don Craib emerged from the elevator at 3:15, bulldog-faced, pale, and preoccupied. He walked slowly back to the alcove in front of Telling's suite, his eyes glassy and fixed high and far away. Craib passed by Kathy, "the den mother" of the sixty-eighth floor, whom Ed Telling had elevated from her position as a waitress back at the old West Side solely because he once saw her peel a grapefruit without leaving any rind.

Kathy allowed the Allstate chairman to pass by without a greeting. She continued down the hall to the dining room, where a long rectangular table was laid out with twenty-four place settings, each with three differently shaped glasses and gleaming china plates that were rimmed by a thin line the color of rubies. In the kitchen off the dining room that an irate stockholder had described to the crowd at the 1979 annual meeting in Los Angeles, five people were working quickly. One of them scrubbed a colander-full of those fashionable Lilliputian vegetables shrunk like so many bonsai ferns. Other workers squeezed the outer edges of leek pies into rampart patterns, stirred an essence of tomato soup, checked the home-made melba toast in the oven, and tended to the shrimp de jonghe and veal piccata.

"The board," Kathy said, "doesn't eat steak."

The ornately framed portrait of Richard Sears that hangs in the board room off the sixty-sixth-floor skydeck depicts a particularly handsome young man with the most dramatic of handlebar mustaches and hair parted just to the left of center. The look on his face and the twinkle the artist was able to capture in Sears' eyes would in other contexts have seemed appropriately roguish, given everything known about the man, but, possibly because he stares out into such an ultra-modern chamber—a softly lit beige-and-woodgrained place with a designer horseshoe-shaped table in the middle and what appears to be a judge's bench where the corporate secretary takes minutes at the side—the look on Dick Sears' face appears as one of sardonic bemusement, as if the Founder had been caught in a bewildered double-take, possibly upon being confronted by the fact of what others had made of the Cheapest Supply House on Earth.

Arrayed along the board-room wall on either side of Richard Sears were the various leaders who had succeeded him. The General appeared elderly and stiff, clutching his beloved book of statistical abstracts. The painting of the Tower-builder, Gordon Metcalf, looked nothing at all like the man in life, because Metcalf had commanded that the portrait artist give him the wrinkle-free face of a much younger man.

Two artists attempted to execute the official portrait of Ed Telling, before a Canadian painter, John Angel, produced an acceptable rendition. The first attempt was rejected because it made the chairman look something like a Soviet worker in a painting from the Socialist Realist school instead of a captain of industry. The art consultant in charge of the project also rejected the second attempt, because that one, she said, made Telling look like a "Methodist minister." Angel was apparently struck by his subject's contention that he wasn't quite sure how he got to be the chairman of the board. "I just did the best job I could and they gave me the chair," Telling had said. So now by far the brightest painting in the board room showed a relaxed, friendly-looking man with white hair: just a guy, leaning into the room with his elbows resting informally on his knees.

It was here, under the gaze of the ancestors, that the board of directors gathered the next morning—Tuesday, August 14—and elected Edward Brennan president and chief operating officer of Sears, Roebuck.

As members of the board smiled and looked over at Brennan, Telling cleared his throat and announced that their next order of business was to elect a new chairman and chief executive officer of the Sears Merchandise Group. The vote took just a few minutes. When it was over, a door next to the observation post where Charlie Harper took the minutes was opened, and Bill Bass was ushered to the far end of the horseshoe. As the other members of the board applauded, Bass took his seat in front of a printed book with his name embossed on the cover. Bass looked over at Ed Brennan, whose glow was heightened by his choice of a suit so deeply gray that it shimmered dark and silvery under the recessed spotlights. Then Bass looked at Telling, whose smile for him looked so strongly lined and marked in the expensive light that Bill Bass had to keep battening down his emotions for the rest of the meeting so he could keep them all inside.

An hour later, only the cadent undertones of a conversation between

Ed Telling and Ed Brennan were audible from Pat Jamieson's little anteroom between the chairman's office and his conference room. One voice rolled out quick and rather high-pitched, and though it was impossible to discern most of the words, the spurts of talk rose and fell in the familiar singsong of a grand vernacular tradition. The other voice arrived in the anteroom sonorous and deep, like the reverential baritone of an offer of condolences, or the low, inward whispering of someone in prayer.

The voices approached the door of Telling's office, and as it opened, the grave voice said, "Thank you, sir."

The other said just, "O.K."

Telling stood between the door and his desk after Brennan left. "I told him the news a little while back," he said. "After all, I couldn't ask the board to do sumpin' and then go back an' say, 'Eddie says no thanks.' " Telling's eyes brightened as they often did lately in the wake of a quip.

"Eddie'll work it his own way," he continued in a soft voice. "He'll be more public—I hope not at the expense of the business. We've been through that. Don't need that. He'll travel more than me. He likes to travel more than me—along with more people than I ever traveled with too. . . . He'll do all right. Bass too. Ole Bass'll give you that Lordy-I'm-not-worthy stuff, but he's got a tremendous ability to grow to the next job. They'll both do fine. Besides, as somebody once said to me, no one person can ruin Sears, because we've all tried at one time or another and all of us have failed."

Telling had clearly offered up signs before summer. During the 1984 annual meeting that spring, just before the inimitable Harry Korba called for a round of applause for Telling by saying, "I think the people should rise up!" ("Wish you'd choose another term," Telling cut in), the chairman had stated, "Clearly, retailing has been . . . is . . . and will continue to be the cornerstone of Sears, Roebuck and Company. The sustained rebound in our merchandise operations holds the key to total corporate performance." But by and large the money-handlers had failed to acknowledge the change of tack, and they continued to believe through the summer that one of their numbers had a chance.

"Just forget the personalities," Telling said as he circled his desk. "The Merchant's still the big wheel horse—probably always will be and should be. The only real judgment that counts in a decision like this comes from four hundred thousand people. And you don't get their vote as an aye or a nay—you get it through their actions. At this stage in Sears' life I really wanted to be right, and the guy who leads the Merchant should still go ahead and lead the company. If ten years from now it isn't true, fine. But right now the merchant's the guy."

As he'd decided when it first came to him the previous year, this second presidency Telling gave Ed Brennan would be much different from the first one. Each of the chairmen of the business groups and Henry Sunderland would report to Brennan, while Brennan, Dick Jones, Charlie Harper, and the head corporate lawyer on sixty-eight, Phil Knox, would report to Telling. The reporting structure during the transitional period clearly indicated that the leadership at Allstate and the other companies would be "taught to salute" the new man while Telling was still there to make sure they all did it. Telling said he'd always felt badly burned by the private agendas that were "hidden in the drawers" of people when he became chairman, and he was determined that there would be no surprises in store for his successor. "It's just a case of joining the watch on the shift, knowing the course and speed, and sailing on," he said.

Telling was traveling his circuit around the office, pausing at a variety of chairs and sofas, rejecting them after a moment, and continuing along. He finally took a small chair and placed it beside his huge desk, in the spot a visitor might sit. Then he sat in the little chair and began pointing at the huge leather-bound executive throne behind his desk. His voice took on that dreamy, whispery edge as he stared at the chair.

"I sat there alone and lonely for a long time," he said, looking at the chair, "convinced, really, that what I did was correct but hoping that the culture—the organization—would just allow it to be correct."

He folded his hands and leaned back, staring at his desk chair with a sliver of a smile on his lips.

". . . So you still don't want to say 'evolution,'" he said, his hands and feet moving but his eyes still fixed on the chair. "Sorta wish there's another word but 'revolution.' But I 'spose so. 'Spose that's just what it was. I hope I reined in the loose ends."

When Ed Telling came into authority at Sears, the organization was losing faith. As with the condition of great human systems of the past on the eve of profound change, the populace of Sears had lost confidence in what in political and historical terms was its ruling class. The new chairman proceeded to electrify the company status quo with acts that by existing standards were tantamount to regicide. He brought a petulant young outsider into the officer corps specifically to help destabilize the standing order and promote change. He recruited a brilliant Irish intellectual from the ranks to help break the inordinate power of the side of the company he knew little about.

The act of resuscitation began in hope and the spirit of moderation, but, as with so many other attempts to ring in change, events moved toward a terrible crisis that included something akin to a reign of terror and the subsequent promulgation of something not at all unlike the mass purge of an old regime. There were victims, heroes, exiles, and even martyrs, and it seemed for a time that, as with the end of great empires, the crisis caused only the most politically attuned, most mysterious, and least stable of Searsmen to rise to the top, for only they had the slightest notion of what to do.

After Telling passed the embattled merchandising system into the healing hands of another man, he directed the forces of the empire into entirely new realms. Possibly the most radical act of his tenure was his audacious decision to concentrate the might of what he believed was the Great American Company against the nation's banks, institutions that for a century had shared the local landscape with Sears stores as symbolic renderings of American order and immutability. Eventually, a company so utterly mired in the myths of its past that it was abandoned by investors and customers and publicly ridiculed was hailed as a pioneer of a new industry. In the end everything was different. The old circles of power had been broken. An entirely new form of organization was in place, and entirely new endeavors had been undertaken. The very names for things had changed. The map of the empire was different. The calendar had been altered, and some would argue that even historical facts had been changed. An apparent "new breed" of leader, full of vigor and all the promise of youth, had replaced the old guard in most quarters. In fact, not a single participant in the drama ended up in the exact same place he or she had occupied at the beginning—except for Ed Telling.

His moral justification for closing down stores and making long-time employees and the rest surplus always went beyond the standard blanket apology—that profits had to be maintained. Whether or not they might have been underscored by a psychological motive for such things, specific political expediencies were inevitably being served. Another vision of the governance of Sears was being constantly and methodically foisted upon an older order, in the name of nothing but itself.

Telling pointed at his empty chair and remembered the speech he'd delivered at Illinois Wesleyan back in 1978, the one in which he indicated his preference for a system of minimal central governance in the image of Burke and Hume over the more ordered visions of Rousseau. "Seven or eight years later, I might have reconsidered giving that speech," he admitted. Then he started to laugh.

He didn't notice when Pat Jamieson came into the room and approached him. She asked him to sign a letter.

"Everybody's always telling me what to do," Telling said. "It's done in the right way—I'm not criticizing, I'm just sayin'. Always telling me what to do."

"And *you're* always telling me that everybody tells you what to do," Pat drawled sweetly.

"They do," Telling said. "That's the thing *'bout* this job. I got it by doin' anything I wanted to do, and now I just do what I'm told."

Pat wanted Telling to sign a cover letter that was to accompany some four hundred thousand reprinted copies of that week's cover story about Sears in *Time* magazine. The company was mailing one to each employee. Telling picked up the issue of *Time* from his desk. Alongside the bold headline "SASSY SEARS," the cover of the magazine showed Cheryl Tiegs holding a copy of the catalog. The nine-page extravaganza inside—"Sears' Sizzling New Vitality"—contained photographs of Richard Sears, Alvah Roebuck, the Tower, and a sidebar accompanied by a photograph of Telling entitled "Mr. T. Rules the Tower." The worshipful ode to the company as it approached the end of its first century shocked many Sears managers—less because of its tone than because it was almost entirely about the revival of the Merchant. The vocabulary of the *Time* piece could have been lifted directly from the era of invincibility (and probably was), back when chairmen like Gordon Metcalf were pictured on the cover of national magazines next to pictures of catalogs and washing machines with headlines like "Why the No. 1 Retailer Stays on Top." Up until the last minute, the editors of *Time* considered putting Ed Telling on the cover, in the spot where the General's face had appeared some thirty year earlier.

"Somebody accused us of paying $5 million for this," Telling said as he tossed the magazine back onto his desk.

Shortly after *Gallagher President's Report* picked him as one of the ten best executives again, Telling's face did make it onto the cover of *Business Week*. An article inside contended that Telling was one of the most highly paid executives in the world during 1983, garnering some $4,221,000 through a combination of stock sales and salary. The story infuriated him, because he said some of the money was unrealized stock value accumulated via options over a decade. Worse was the article's failure to convey the important fact that money was just a means of seeing who you were and reminding you of where you are or where you've been: "After fighting your way up the ladder, there's gotta be sumpin' other than hell when you get there." Money, for Telling, was just a way of showing that you haven't failed.

But *Business Week* wasn't about to print or even understand that, so it ended up being just as wrong as the *Time* article—which was so fulsome in its praise that some Sears executives wished it had been a little bit more incisive in the name of believability. Brennan said it read as if it were scripted. Eric Saunders deemed the article "scary." But to Telling it was just more of the same: "We were never as good as we were given credit for, and we sure as hell were never as bad as we were described as being by some publications. The truth is always somewhere in between."

"You know," he said after Pat left, "I think it'll be a great feeling to be able to do what I want to do now. If it's nothin', then fine. Just being able . . . to choose. Contrary to what people think, people sitting in these chairs don't have the freedom to do what they wish—you just don't." He got up and began circling. "I might have a little trouble, though, because I do wake up at a certain time and then I come on down here. I don't know what the hell I'll do when I wake up and don't come down here. Probably gonna rattle pans . . . but I'll adjust to that. If you're up at 5:30 with time on your hands, at least you can go back to sleep."

At the door, he turned back for a moment. "You know, I owe everything to Sears, Roebuck," he said. "Sears is like a beautiful woman, and when you talk about it, talk like you're making love to a woman. We all have a secret love affair with it. That's why you see all these powerful emotions."

He smiled his big, square-toothed smile and closed the door.

After the board meeting broke up, Bill Bass went right back to his office on the forty-fourth floor. Inside he noticed a huge bunch of flowers with a card attached. It was from his kids. Bass marched over to his office door and closed it. Then he went back to his desk, sat down, and started to cry.

He slipped away from his work early and went down to get his big Lincoln Continental out of the executive garage. Bass arrived home an hour later, and immediately went to his bedroom, where he took off his coat and hung it among the carefully separated hangers in his big walk-in closet. He passed an oil painting on his bedroom wall that depicted old clothes hanging empty and wrinkled, and he went into his perfectly immaculate kitchen to exhume a steak to throw on his Sears barbecue. Then he came into the den, the one room in Bill Bass' suburban condominium that he'd filled up with memories. There were various mementos and photographs, a model of a Sherman tank, numerous copies of *Golf Digest,* and a couple of Sears Catalogs.

The new chairman and CEO of the Sears Merchandise Group shook his head back and forth. He said he was emotionally drained. "A hundred guys still stuck out there in some little forsaken place, and but for the grace of God . . . if Big Daddy hadn't come through the revolving doors back there in New York City, carrying his own luggage—" He stopped and shook his head again, as he always did when Telling's image was evoked.

Bass slumped back in a big easy chair. "It's funny that none of my friends called today. But I know why. They're scared to call. I remember not calling Telling after he got the big one." "The big one" to Bill Bass meant running the Merchant. It always would. "I'll get a little letter or a note from people, but those who would normally call me up won't, and some who never did care will start to call. It's a funny thing."

As if on cue, the phone rang. Bass' face lit up after saying hello. "Wull, yes, sir, you are indeed talkin' to the big one!" he crowed in his game-cock-of-the-wilderness, Field-man's way. "And ah do 'preciate that, sir."

"One of my golf buddies from down south," he said after returning to his easy chair.

Bass would be replaced as senior executive vice-president, Field, by Pat Galloway, the Eastern Territory VP, and Galloway would be replaced by one of the young Turks from the East who had worked with Brennan in Atlanta and then ran Brennan's old bailiwick, the Boston group. But much of the interest in a fellow's territorial bloodlines had disappeared during the last year, now that the Merchant had moved so far in the direction of one big store.

During the spring, one of the last symbols not made of brick and steel—the separate territorial newspapers—had been terminated. The move presaged a more radical one that would be announced by Chairman Bass in two years' time. In the year of Sears' one hundredth anniversary, all four territorial outposts would be closed down.

Bass began to run down his immediate agenda as the steaks hissed on the balcony. Even Brennan claimed he'd never believed that his Store of the Future was a panacea. The rollout of the rest of the stores was going to be very expensive, and there would be a great deal of business lost during the reconstruction process. Some of the stores would certainly be dogs, just because, with all the science and money in the world at your disposal, retailing was still a business predicated on weather and whim. Even if K mart did pass Sears in gross sales one of these years, the Store of the Future had to be constructed in order to provide a means of transporting the company into the modern era. Now the store was out there, and it was up to Bass and whoever came after him to see that it was sustained. The first "catalog of the future" had been published as the "spring general," and it was in dire need of adjustment. He said he planned to bear down on the distribution system to streamline further the chain of interchanges between factories and customers' homes. It took more than two weeks for goods to get into the stores after a buyer ordered them, and every day off the delivery cycle would be worth $43 million in savings. "Then the small stores," he said, growing more animated as he spoke. "We have to figure out how to make some money in small stores. I want to go after Sam Walton [chairman and owner of the Wal-Mart chain, and possibly the richest man in the United States by virtue of his retailing genius] in these small markets. He's been stealing our business."

The general retail environment in which Bill Bass was becoming a leader was entirely "on sale." Huge price cuts were apparent throughout the industry as the off-price discounters waged their war on the department stores. J. C. Penney was keeping pressure on Sears and the other big stores in its effort to buy into the lucrative apparel business, but because of the huge cost of financing, Penney had made only $50 million during the second quarter, in which the Sears merchants made $215 million.

Inventory control was going to be an issue for the Bass administration, but first he had to address the morale problem. The Merchant was exhausted. There were large numbers of managers who had been made "surplus" by streamlining, and many of them deeply resented the water-walkers, boy wonders, and young tigers who were catapulted over their heads. But the main source of the demoralization was the pace.

Bass had heard rumors from other retailers of résumés from Sears buyers circulating outside the family. The buyers had passed instantaneously from the period of Joe Moran's Draconian rule into the monumental labors of taking the store apart on paper and reconstructing something new. There had been no break. The old kings of the system reigned full of power; then they were cowed; then the buyers and sellers divided into two camps; then Brennan arrived with his inspired call to the barricades.

So now, when the grapevine carried word that Joe Batogowski—"the Polish prince," as so many buyers now called him—intended to send buyers from departments exhibiting erratic track records out of the Tower to work in a catalog order plants, the resentment was considerable. "It's not punishment," Bato said in defense of the new program. "All I want them to know is that it inflicts pain on people when a customer orders goods and we don't have them." Each buyer would soon be required to work in a store for a week. "They'll come back stronger," Batogowski said.

Bill Bass was hardly the student of politics, history, and psychology that Telling was, nor was he the student of merchantry in a league with Ed Brennan, but he just knew by gut instinct that people cannot endure for long the high tenor of spiritually resonant tasks. Even the heartiest of revolutionary fervors has to die away, and as the sociologist Max

Weber wrote of the end of the reign of a charismatic leader, as the society "flows back into the channels of workaday routes," people lose their desire and tolerance for the former religiosity they embraced under the spell of the great leader.

The company Bill Bass had just inherited was exhausted from trying to keep up with Ed Brennan and his fiery dreams. In the old days, when Bass joined up with the General's boys, you worked like a dog and moved across the map for the thrill of a cold sellout or a great promotional week you'd plotted yourself. You worked for a wall-full of trophies or the sight of half the crowd at a little-league game wearing clothes from your rack; or you worked because a factory you controlled or had even erected had made those clothes or mixed the paint. There was glory in the old way of free merchants and men, and there had been glory in the act of pulling the company back from the abyss according to Brennan's plan. But Brennan had transcended that now. He'd left behind systems and plans and protégés. The demoralization was nothing like the terror and pain of the late 1970s—the time of "the excesses," as they now were known. There was much less danger in the working life at Sears, but less glory too. And people were tired.

"We've just been workin' 'em too hard," Bass said as he dragged the steak off the grill. "The people will be able to talk freely with me, and they'll know they have the freedom to talk. It's not how hard you work people that's the problem, really—it's the lack of recognition. I understand this kind of stuff, because I *have* morale—just like them."

. . . By which Bill Bass was saying what those who'd formed the chevron behind Ed Brennan day after day knew was the truth. Brennan didn't have morale. Where other people had morale, Ed Brennan had his destiny.

"Do I want to follow him?" Bass said, the color returning now to his pale, pinched face for the first time since all those people began to applaud for him when he sat down at the end of the horseshoe in front of the fancy book with his name on it. "You think I like the idea of followin' him? He's the last guy in the world I'd like to follow into the chair."

Bass did have to wonder on occasion why such a brilliant, gifted man as Ed Brennan acted so uptight sometimes, and why he seemed to need to be stroked like he did, but there was no question that Brennan was "a cut above." Bass told everyone who asked. Brennan was quite simply the best.

After Telling gave Brennan advance warning that the presidential grooming post would be his, Bass was also warned that he would be asked to run the Merchant. So, for a period of several weeks, only the two of them knew that the long race was over. "Aren't you excited,

Bill?" Ed Brennan would enthuse to Bass during those weeks. But Bass was in fact more excited by the fact that his son, Billy, had asked him to be the best man at his wedding in October. The thought of the honor of standing up for Billy brought tears to his eyes as he cleaned up the kitchen after dinner.

The fact of the matter was that he was scared as all hell about running the retail empire that had encompassed his whole life—just as he'd been scared each and every one of the thirteen times over the last thirty-three years that Sears had moved him into a new peg. The fact of the matter was that he'd never really wanted another job.

But still the question had been posed. "Aren't you *excited*, Bill?"

"Yes, sir, Mr. Brennan," Bill Bass said, all Sears and formal, "I sure as hell am."

The next morning there was a flurry of movement around the new president's office, as Brennan's files and trophies were transported up from the forty-fourth floor. The operation was supervised by an ecstatic Lou Fryz. "Am I happy?" Lou boomed in her deep, smoky voice. "Am I pleased to work for a genius, the star of the future?" Within hours of the announcement of Brennan's new job on sixty-eight, the secretarial ranks of the Tower were abuzz with speculation about the coming struggle between the company's two most powerful executive secretaries, Lou and the formidable Pat Jamieson, who had already been told by Telling that she would remain on sixty-eight after he was gone.

Dick Jones appeared to be resting at one of the secretary's desks outside of Brennan's office door, his face in his white hands. Instead of the presidency, Telling had given Jones the unruly mess of Sears World Trade. Since it was Jones and his financial people who'd been at the forefront of the final campaign to make Ed Telling see the profligacy of Rod Hills' experimentations, Telling's decision to make Jones the trade company's chief rectifier was a clear example of the sort of justice Telling enjoyed. A plan of consolidation and force reduction had already been drawn up for Rod Hills' creation that would relieve the organization of 150 employees. "We can't be all things to all people," Telling had stated publicly, "we know that. Sears World Trade, through too much posturing, caused expectations to be too high."

After Brennan had said thank you to Ed Telling the previous day, he'd gone back to his office on forty-four to make some phone calls. He talked to Stretch Gardiner and then to Phil Purcell. Brennan decided to believe Phil's contention over the phone that he was only "delighted" by Telling's choice. "Phil said his people in New York came in to see him yesterday, to ask what my approach would be," Brennan said. "He said he told them what he thought it would be like, and he says they're very enthusiastic. . . . I don't think it's a show."

Outside the office door on sixty-eight, Lou Fryz could be seen putting down armfuls of files in order, pleasantly but firmly, to inform one representative of a major news organization after another that Brennan would have no further comment on his new job. Telling told the press through a spokesman that he considered the turnaround of the Sears merchandising fortunes "engineered by Mr. Brennan" to be the most significant accomplishment of his term, and Brennan returned the powerful endorsement by paying Telling the high compliment of noting the chairman's managerial *consistency.* Brennan told Steve Weiner, *The Wall Street Journal* reporter assigned to Sears, that as far as he was concerned things weren't being done any differently at Sears from the way they had been back in the Eastern Territory during the early 1970s. But Brennan had decided to curtail further public comment for the time being. Few had forgotten Arthur Wood's assertion of six years earlier that "nothing would change" at Sears under his successor. Lou Fryz came into the office. "Don't you have some place to go? I've got an office to assemble in here."

"Yes," Brennan said. "We're goin' out to look for ghosts."

When Brennan entered the elevator on the skydeck below the sixty-eighth floor, all conversation in the crowded car suddenly ceased. Some shorter women in the back of the stainless-steel chamber stood on their toes to look at Brennan, who positioned himself next to the button panel. The elevator was on one of the lines that went directly to street level, but out of habit, Brennan mistakenly pressed the button for the thirty-third-floor skydeck, where Tower travelers must transfer in order to get from sixty-eight back up to the forty-fourth floor. Brennan blushed when he realized his error. As the doors opened on thirty-three, he regarded the startled crowd looking in at the packed car. "We just needed some air," he said.

There was a great deal of activity around the lobby levels of the Tower that August 15. For several months, construction crews had been working on Ed Telling's addition to the building. Telling said the airy postmodern, greenhouse-like entranceway would cost around $25 million. It would actually end up costing $40 million—three times the cost of the Cube John Lowe had built during his reign in the West, and one-third the cost of the original construction of the tallest building in the world.

Nothing would remain unaltered.

Brennan strolled into the small executive garage beneath the lobby, nodding warmly at the congratulatory stares and smiles of men in work clothes who were simply too junior to say anything out loud. Then Brennan noticed that the cement floor of the garage was littered with pieces of paper. "What's going on here?" he demanded of one of the attendants. He bent down and began to collect large handfuls of garbage until his car and driver arrived.

Before he got into the car, he slowly took off his jacket, folded it carefully into quadrants, and put the coat in the middle of the back seat. It was the one with the scarlet saloon-gambler lining. After he climbed inside, Brennan said something about looking older lately, and as the car pulled out onto Franklin Street, the light falling between the office towers suggested it was true.

The sedan moved quickly through the wet heat of a Chicago August, out toward the Great Works, the mammoth catalog plant where in the name of the common people, according to Richard Sears, "Miles of railroad tracks run lengthwise through, in, and round this building, for the receiving, moving and forwarding of merchandise; elevators, mechanical conveyers, endless chains, moving sidewalks, gravity chutes, apparatus and conveyers, pneumatic tubes and every known mechanical appliance for reducing labor, for the working out of economy and dispatch."

The streets near the old West Side plants were empty of almost everything. Empty lots had surrounded the Great Works over time, just as the suburbs came to surround the General's stores. The row house where Brennan's grandfather had lived a few blocks from the plant was gone; Silverstein's delicatessen, where Joe Moran used to hold forth upon the works of Euripides and Aeschylus—and with the same passion upon the deeds of the boys from Notre Dame—was gone. Even the General's first Sears retail store, the one where Ed Brennan's mother took him to see Santa Claus, was empty now. After years of hesitation, Brennan had ordered the closing of the big West Side store a few months earlier. The store that had begun the epoch of stores was losing over a million dollars a year, so it had joined the list.

"The place still has a certain smell," Brennan said as he walked past plaques bearing the names of Sears, Rosenwald, and Wood in the lobby of the old administration building.

He greeted an elderly man who sat near the entrance. The fellow had worked as a guard back in the days when guards at Sears were called "ushers." Even the guards in the stores were called "ushers," because there was nothing to guard against but the possibility of too many people's converging on the goods.

The administration building's famous long hallway, which the employees of the horizontal years used to fill with the noise and movement of an urban thoroughfare, was still covered with the same linoleum that had lined the floors of all the Sears stores before the era of maroon rugs and strike zones. "Here's the old chairman's and president's office," Brennan said as he turned off the hall into a suite of small, modest rooms. "We try to keep people moving through here now, because the mice took over after we left."

Brennan moved through the series of old buildings quickly, stopping at various spots where his relatives had worked. He pointed out the small office on the second floor where the General had continued to pull the strings from the sham of his retirement. He stopped at the old Club Seraco. The name of the old officer's smoking room was written ornately on an old-fashioned pane of frosted glass that protruded into the hallway.

Brennan said that many of the offices looked exactly the same as they had when he first came to work for the Parent, just after Christmas in 1959. He strolled along quickly into a steamy, overheated warehouse building with the sort of exposed brick walls that had lately become a popular design touch in upmarket dwellings and office developments. Since the interior brick was simply the other side of the building's outer wall, during the winter it used to get quite cold in the little ceilingless cubicles that were the haunts of the buyers. Later, when the neighborhood changed, kids throwing balls against the wall made it sound like the place was under aerial bombardment—but the fact that the most powerful purchasers of man-made things ever assembled had worked here under such spartan conditions was all part of the idea back then, part of the thing that made them different and better.

The partitions between the old buyers' lairs were mostly gone, but Brennan moved through the open space and pointed into invisible offices as if they were still occupied. "Here's Vlad Kay, the suit buyer. Here's his assistant, Irv Heller. Ted Morgan . . . Woody Woods . . . Jim Zalusky, the sportswear buyer, and his assistant, Dick Hassler. And here was Cliff Joy. Cliff Joy of 641," Brennan said, his voice thickening slightly at the thought of a man whom both he and his father had worked for. A man who'd taught him things. "What a great, great guy. I rode to work with him."

The official chronicler of the deeds of Cliff Joy was none other than Jumpin' Joe Moran. Joe could tell stories about Joy for hours on end. Listeners would cry from laughing.

Good old Joe—so much better an evangelist than he could ever manage to be a dictator. "I really miss him," Brennan said as he continued along. Back in January, Brennan had had lunch with Margie Lou Moran who was doing pretty well. A few weeks before the lunch, *Time* magazine had run a feature about Sears that was much shorter than t summer cover story. The piece centered on the flashy new Stores of

Future, and in it Brennan had paid anonymous homage to the poet of Sears. "We're really changing the face of the store," he was quoted as saying, "not the soul."

Before heading back out into the misty heat, Brennan stuck his head in a room where a very old woman sat at a long table laden with boxes of dusty files. He smiled at her, but she frowned back in irritation. "Help ya?" she barked.

"*That,*" Brennan said as he went back out into the sun, "is the old."

As security men watched him protectively from doorways and from around the corners of walls, Brennan strolled through the parched formal gardens—the curiously named "hanging gardens" of the old days—where the employees used to eat lunch, and where they would cheer the executive who climbed up on a wall and read the profit-sharing tally several times each year. At the side of one of the massive buildings in the complex, Brennan pointed up at a huge polyurethane prototype of the new Sears logo hanging against on an expanse of brick. "*That,*" he said with pride, "is the new."

The familiar old Sears logo had been enclosed within its rectangular box for twenty years when Ed Brennan decided it was time for a change. The industrial designer hired to reimagine the logo told *Industrial Design* magazine that the old logo was "schoolmarmish and obedient." He said the bland character of the logo he was bound to replace was "the result of it being handed down without being questioned." The designer proclaimed his determination to design Sears a symbol that would "inject vigor and excitement into a conservative company while retaining enough of the past to avoid alienating its loyal followers." Privately, the designer, who was to be paid a million dollars for his rendition of the five letters, said the assignment was "like redesigning the American flag."

The first version of the logo was rendered in italics with the letters slanting forward, as if leaning into the wind of the future. A broad stripe was to snake through each of the letters, but when the logo was presented to Brennan, he sent the artists away with instructions to make what he called "the racing stripe" much thinner. He thought it distorted the clarity of the characters. Brennan didn't pretend to have a deep knowledge of industrial design, but he knew a lot now about the power of logos, symbols, and flags.

The final version of the logo would soon be imprinted immutably upon the national consciousness, because the Merchant had decided to purchase $20 million worth of advertising time during the coming 1984 Summer Olympics. Brennan squinted up at the prototype. "If you think about it, there aren't more than two or three other companies in the world that do enough business to establish a new logo and the 'More for

Your Life at Sears' theme by simply projecting it to every man, woman, and child in this country—in two weeks."

For all of the huge changes he'd decreed, all of the movement of people and money, Brennan said he was only stopped in his tracks by the breadth of his own control over such a pervasive and powerful business mechanism on a single occasion. It was right after the day he had decided that the tens of thousands of Sears trucks in America should all be painted white. He happened to pass by a freight terminal a few days later, and there, lined up in neat rows, were six service trucks, six delivery trucks, and six Sears semis—"six, six, six, and all of them painted white," as neat as a cube of dress shirts, all in a row. "I thought, 'Geez!'"

For the coming occasion of the hundredth anniversary of the day in 1886 when a kid named Sears moved to Minneapolis and began selling watches out of a room that contained only a table, a few books, and a fifty-cent chair, the merchants on the forty-fourth floor had decided to add to the side of every truck, to every sign in a store, and to every badge on every employee the same simple statement: *"I am Sears."*

Barring disaster or some consummately perverse change of Ed Telling's mind, Brennan would eventually take over the company as it passed $40 billion in sales, a figure that would place Sears behind Exxon, General Motors, Mobil, Ford, Texaco, and just a bit behind IBM, as the seventh-largest corporation in the country. Sears was number seven in 1977 and number seven in 1984.

But Sears was now a vast network of businesses held together at this point by paper plans, technological devices, and an underlying well-spring of public trust. New ways of leveraging off the franchise so as to enlarge and reinforce the web were being discussed all the time now. For some months, company planners had discussed moving into the business of medical care. Why not Sears, Roebuck clinics and hospitals? Telling in particular liked the idea of going at the hospitals, because he figured that hospitals were examples of fat and arrogant institutions that had been given a free lunch through the indulgence of big insurance companies, and at the ultimate expense of the American people.

The work of 902-TC with intercompany technology was proving so successful that the network had already been made available to people who wanted to pay their telephone bills through Sears, and the capacity was enlarging all the time. If the idea of Sears hospitals didn't strongly underscore the capacity of a private institution to be seen as a provider of the common welfare, then the state of New Jersey was about to make a controversial decision to allow citizens there to get their driver's licenses at Sears.

The network was getting geared up for the integration of a universal Sears card designed as the physical medium by which consumers would be connected to all nodes on the network. Since the planning task-force work in 1983, the idea of a card had been promoted as a way of tying together credit, purchases, savings accounts, securities, insurance, real estate, and a system of machines in which to plunge the card at any time so that people could access their little piece of the system. The card would not only prove a technical means of drawing the business groups closer together, but it could well be the best means of circumventing the moribund legislation that was holding back the eternal flow of money. Extant regulatory laws were all written before computers and cards.

The responsibility for the introduction of the card would fall to Ed Brennan. The fact that the twelve separate corporate entities were gearing up to provide mortgages, most of them unaware of the others, would be Brennan's problem to work out. The management of further institutional synthesis would be his challenge, and the disconnected pieces of the empire were now spread out before him like five separate pyramids, each offering a unique view of the world. The cycle of breaking down historical impediments, of reviving, restructuring, and reimbuing with direction and spirit, was about to start again. Once again Brennan was going to have to figure out how to create a sum from the parts, and this time without the assistance of the crisis that he'd always admitted was essential to his ability to turn the Merchant back from the edge.

From afar, witnesses to the early days of Ed Telling's rise looked on. "Telling was the transitional ruler," said Jack Cardwell, who assisted the early planning of the fall of the old order as the director of the McKinsey team. "This next man is going to have to cement in place the parts of Telling's revolution that are fit to survive. The story won't end for four or five years. That's when we'll see how Brennan does."

Another student of the secret world of Sears, Ian Sym-Smith of Hay Associates, who had formed a committee of angry young men and stood before a felt board lecturing Ed Telling about his early executive gestures, agreed that the story hadn't ended. "Brennan's next task will fit his personality well. Now he must create a philosophy of unification for the whole network."

So now he was supposed to run the whole thing like a store. There was little question about his ability to master all the technical nuances of the task. As with everything else, once you got inside a thing its mystery would fall away. If anyone had the ability to create the requisite technical, methodological, and emotional atmosphere in which to draw the new Sears into a whole, it was him.

But there was an irony in the ascension of Ed Brennan to the chairmanship that many of those who'd served him considered a tragedy. In some important ways, Ed Brennan was a throwback to the old Sears. In his heart he still felt that no one in the world could teach him a thing about merchandising. Like the departed generation of mid-century Searsmen, he believed that the love and knowledge of real goods made an understanding limited to money and numbers a form of fakery.

Ed Brennan was one of the most brilliant American merchants of his generation, but in his startling success, he was now faced with having to leave the world of goods for the first time in his life and be a merchant no longer. After all of that work amid the landscape of stores, Ed Telling pulled a chair up to the table and raised the stakes on him—and because of the way he was, Brennan had to play out the hand, as other men had to breathe air. Suddenly he was the consolidator again, the preserver— the son still unproved. In the end, his fervent lifelong climb had one too many steps, and somehow it made his achievement fragile, as if it wasn't quite enough.

Brennan threw his coat over his shoulder now and turned away from the old red brick warehouse to look at the Tower. The Sears, Roebuck stock certificate still depicted the old West Side warehouse sitting next to the gray Tower, the two icons abutting as incongruously as old Indian burial mounds beneath a shopping mall. A famed architectural historian wrote of the Sears Tower, "Up close it's a faceless screen. You can't read it in any way. I think it's an architecture that is dehumanized." But the Tower was also a unity, and it was still the tallest thing on earth built by human beings, even if the human component didn't show at first glance.

Sprawling behind the heir apparent was a relic of an erratic system, and in the distance the center of a streamlined, cleanly notched, and finely ruled empire. A system once dedicated to a proposition was now a dedicated system. The Merchant was just a portion of something else now, and many of the things about the company that had held such a spell over most of Ed Brennan's life were gone. Where there were good old boys and thousands of soldiers who'd never lost a war—where there were once kings—there now were managers. A place that once offered a life now offered only a job.

But the company in which the Eds, Brennan and Telling, had grown up as others grow up in a family had been bound for failure not so very long ago. It would certainly have been a proud and noble and all-American failure. It would have been the sort of romantic fall that makes the glory of the rise all the more brilliant in the retelling.

But there was too much at stake, so they decided to try to change it. It was still Sears, and all the world could see that it was certainly different. But it had been sustained.

Brennan's voice was far away when he spoke. "All right . . ." He lifted his arm in the air without looking to call for his car. "I gotta get back to work."

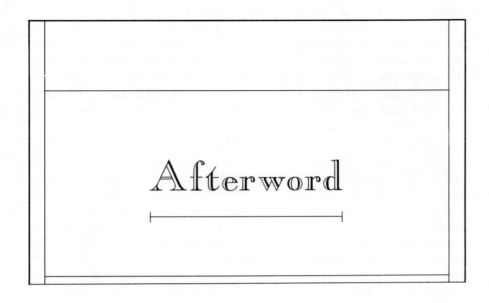

Afterword

I was never quite sure why Ed Telling allowed an observer to come inside Sears to study these years of change. I was reminded of my confusion about Telling's motives often during my time among the managers of the company, because at some point during every single day I was asked to explain how the invitation had come about. Employees would take me aside after meetings, or beckon me from elevators before the doors closed, or they'd say, "Now I have a question for you," at the end of an interview or before hanging up the phone. In different ways, each would then ask me to tell how it had happened that a man who loathed public observation in general—and individuals who observe and record events for a living in particular—had decided to throw open the doors of an institution that was famed for its distrust of outsiders to someone in fee to a publishing company in New York City (of all places), and who had made no prior agreement to show anyone at Sears his final work.

"You must be a hell of a salesman," several scores of Sears employees said over time. "How'd you work it? How'd you get him to say yes?"

At first I flattered myself in thinking it had only to do with the "Sears, Roebuck snap-decision-from-the-guts" tradition, that long-held, old-culture belief that a good person of Sears blood could take a quick look at someone and know whether there was value there without asking a single question. Telling was famous for trusting his earliest knee-jerk reaction to a person's eyes or a smile. The habit seemed to be part of the

Sears swagger, another behavioral quirk born of so many years of so much unquestioned power and success. After a while, though, I saw that the instantaneous decision was also a utilitarian if somewhat sub-conscious acknowledgment that, for all the manipulation of numbers and hardheaded analysis available to a modern manager, business rela-tionships are mainly predicated on faith and hope.

As pleased as I was by the thought that the mysterious chairman of Sears simply liked what he saw and heard, I knew that several members of the chairman's protective inner circle were quite upset when Telling apparently followed his instincts and decided to allow a chronicle of the years of turmoil and change to be assembled. Bill Bass was particularly upset about an outsider's being let loose within the company, and his predecessor in the East, the eventual chief financial officer Dick Jones, was at first said to be extremely skeptical of the project. Phil Purcell pointedly demanded that I spend some time alone with him before I began my first series of interviews with Telling. But at the end of my period of research, after offering a great deal of valued assistance, Phil announced, "I'm never going to read your book. Even if it's completely accurate, it won't ever seem right to me."

Almost every single formal contact between Sears as a corporation and the outside world is made by people who are either being paid directly by Sears or are beholden to the company because they want to sell something. The purpose of any outsider vis-à-vis the corporation is, if not utterly under control, at least well defined. During the days of a decentralization so complete that local store runners made "off-the-reservation" deals with manufacturers, local territorial and group public-relations men were still proscribed from having any dealings with a national publication or television network without permission from Headquarters.

An outsider with a tape recorder and a notebook was deeply unset-tling to the majority of employees who'd grown up in Sears. Retirees who'd left the company long ago—even those who believed they'd been purged so heartlessly from their corporate family that they would never be the same—often refused to talk about Sears until they'd checked with the public-affairs department or the corporate office. After a year of research I heard that several employees referred to me sardonically as "our Gibbon," but I heard too that to others I was "walking early retire-ment."

Middle-level managers sometimes refused to present reports at a meeting until they knew what I was doing there, and the first time I was seated next to Ed Brennan at a meeting, there was an audible gasp when he leaned over during the proceeding to whisper an explanation. Some-times Brennan would say, "Oh, we work together," or "I'm just teaching him the business," in response to the astonished looks the presence of an outsider evoked. At other times he would say nothing at all, as if the suspension of a wariness of outsiders that had been taught to Sears people for all of their careers was part of the respect Brennan demanded and believed he deserved.

After a while—quite a long while—my movements became more casual. I was allowed to move past security cordons and protective secretaries with some impunity. I had the strange experience of watching a press conference or two from the other side of the table. Files were opened and endless piles of little pocket-size appointment books were drawn from the bottoms of desk drawers and unwrapped with care, like prized mementos from a war.

By this time I had taken on some of the physical characteristics of the lifers, such as the permanent gummy rectangle that so many Hello-My-Name-Is tags had left on the lapel of all my suit coats, and a blood serum cholesterol level of 285 from all of that steak.

The opportunity to move from side to side along a corporate structure highlights the utter verticality of a big company, even one like Sears that so prized a history of organizational "flatness." The lack of horizontal personal communications made it easier to understand how factions within the same company could have actually gone to war. Technical boundaries were buttressed everywhere by emotional ones. Even the senior executives, allowed considerable latitude within the greater corporation, seemed to have little real knowledge of what their colleagues did or really thought. If a passing compliment paid to one senior executive by another was transmitted, a profound reaction could be observed. Sometimes the person admired across the gulf seemed visibly moved by the news. "Well, will you please tell him that I . . . feel the same way," was said on more than one occasion.

Since such a small number of the sprawling corporation's managers had the luxury of traveling its routes or observing the vista from above, people were forever saying, "How *is* it out there? What's it like?" At least ten senior managers in the Tower asked of each of his *own* purviews, "How's morale?"

The famous Sears grapevine carried a great deal of news and gossip to all corners of the empire, but, as with a wire service, the information arrived without embellishment or commentary. The lack of a generalized sense of the state of things explained how an outsider like Phil Purcell, who circumambulated the troubled company as a McKinsey-man—moving from office to office with the mandate to ask questions and the will to plant seeds of doubt and change—ended up with both the idea that the promulgation of a specific series of actions could take the place apart and then the power to go ahead and do it.

But Phil's study of Sears coincided perfectly with the rise of Ed Telling and his decision to act upon his long list of things that needed to be addressed. I remained as confused about why Ed Telling invited scrutiny again at the end as I was at the beginning.

Some executives believed that it had to do with the ritualistic politics of corporate succession. In August of 1983, just before Telling announced that he would not announce a successor for a time, Coldwell Banker's straight-talking CEO, Wesley Poulson, contended that he'd thought all along that I was collecting information about the candidates for Telling. "Now, I don't think it's wrong," Poulson said, "and it may even be good. But I think that you're the guy asking his questions." After I assured Poulson this was far from the case, Wes smiled. "You sit and talk with him, don't you? You might not even know you're doing it for him."

During the most heated times of the race to succeed Telling, I did receive calls from executives at Allstate in which they inquired as to Don Craib's chances. Several of those in the Brennan camp began to worry, in light of the unusual relationship between the two Eds, that if it appeared that the book might turn out to be too favorable to Brennan, Telling might pass him over out of spite, rather as Lyndon Johnson made J. Edgar Hoover director of the FBI for life simply because the press leaked news of the President's determination to fire the aging director.

Everyone I met at Sears believed that my presence was indicative of some secret purpose in Ed Telling's mind. "I don't know what it is, and this isn't meant to flatter you," a note that attended some photocopied documents sent by a middle manager read, "but 'ERT' has a remarkable knack for picking the right person for the job he wants done."

Several retirees believed that by giving me access to a sense of how painful, dark, and terrifying were Telling's first few years, and by letting me study the heated prose of Joe Moran, the chairman had in mind the creation of a sophisticated piece of political propaganda. "It will be very much like de-Stalinization in Russia," one of the ERIP retirees stated. "Just as Khrushchev benefited from publicizing the crimes of the past, whatever you write about that awful period of time will play into Telling and Brennan's hands."

Perhaps it was about a place in history—that the mere chance that Telling had managed to change something so apparently unchangeable should be written about. "Around here," one of Telling's sixty-eighth-floor confidants declared one day, "history began on February 1, 1977."

Maybe he invited me in because that first day we met I said I thought something far more compelling had occurred at Sears, Roebuck during his tenure than was implied by the available nomenclature of "corporate turnaround." Perhaps Telling the romantic, Telling the reader of books,

Telling the man utterly contemptuous of the existing vocabulary of business life as a means of describing what it's really about, had opened the long-sealed doors on the odd chance that something could emerge about his tenure that sounded true.

The CEO of a corporate leviathan looks down upon an enterprise, and only the leader has the vantage point or even the right to gaze down upon the sprawling economic mechanism and draw abstractions and conclusions from what can be seen. One of Telling's long-protected secrets was how constantly stimulated and intellectually intrigued he was, how fascinating he found the whole thing. The fact that such a special and enclosed civilization could still have existed into the fourth quarter of the century amazed him.

Certainly an element of the decision to let me in came from Telling's love of books. A part of it may well have involved intricate corporate politics I failed to understand. If it was a connection to history he had in mind, then I sensed it was in lieu of other connections he might have missed along the way. Some of it clearly had to do with old-fashioned Sears-style gut instinct, but I think, in retrospect, that it had a lot to do with a man who'd decided to cast out into the water in the hope of reeling in a part of himself that had somehow gotten away.

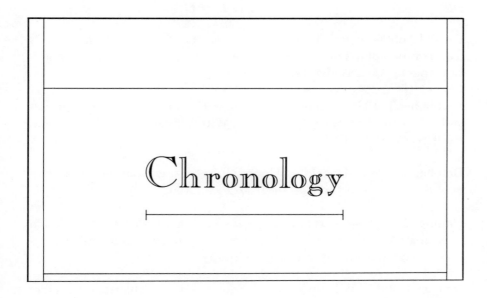

Chronology

September 17, 1984—The complex of historic structures called "Sears House" opens officially in Washington, D.C.

April 24, 1985—The "Discover Card," a new combination credit- and financial-services card, is unveiled in Atlanta by Sears President Edward A. Brennan.

May 6, 1985—Bernard F. Brennan leaves Household International Inc. to become the president and chief executive officer of Montgomery Ward.

August 31, 1985—C. Wesley Poulson, fifty-five, retires as chairman and chief executive officer of the Coldwell Banker Real Estate Group.

January 1, 1986—After thirty-nine years of service, Edward R. Telling retires as chairman and chief executive officer of Sears, Roebuck. He is replaced by Edward A. Brennan, fifty-one.

February 3, 1986—Sears wins its seven-year legal battle with the Equal Employment Opportunity Commission.

June 30, 1986—All four territorial headquarters are closed. The Field will henceforth be administered from the Sears Tower in Chicago. As the old Southwestern Territory headquarters became Dean Witter's data center, John Lowe's headquarters in California would become a Los Angeles County detention center.

September 1, 1986—Robert M. "Stretch" Gardiner retires as chairman and chief executive officer of the Dean Witter Financial Services Group. He is replaced by Phillip J. Purcell.

October 7, 1986—Donald F. Craib, Jr., retires as chairman and chief executive officer of the Allstate Insurance Group.

October 29, 1986—Sears announces it will close the domestic operation of its Sears World Trade unit. The remaining international units will be folded back into the Merchandise Group.

January 1, 1987—William I. Bass, sixty-one, retires as chairman and chief executive officer of the Sears Merchandise Group. He is replaced by forty-five-year-old Mike Bozic, one of the "young tigers" during the years of great change.

Author's Note

A lmost every one of the active and former Sears executives mentioned in *The Big Store* contributed generously of their time in order to document and reflect upon their long and productive careers, offering thoughtful answers to questions sometimes repeated to them several times over the course of several years. Those current and former members of the Sears officer corps who were of particular assistance in the creation of this book include Ed Telling, Ed Brennan, Phil Purcell, Dick Jones, Arthur Wood, Jack Kincannon, Jack Kelly, Jim Button, Charlie Bacon, Charlie Wurmstedt, Bob Anderson, Dean Swift, Bill Sanders, Bob Wood, Burk Burkholder, Joe Batogowski, John Lowe, Archie Boe, Wes Poulson, Al Goldstein, Ira Quint, Claude Ireson, Ray Kennedy, Con Massey, Woody Haselton, Henry Sunderland, Bill Bass, Danny Danhauer, Bob Johnson, Charley Moran, Charlie Harper, Don Craib, Mike Bozic, Don Deutsch, Wayne Holsinger, Eric Saunders, Jack Wirth, Bob Thompson, John Easter, Al Davies, Jim Worthy, Rod Hills, Stretch Gardiner, Andy Melton, and Chuck Carlson.

Even after Ed Telling sanctioned my access to the corporate and personal record of his tenure, I don't think I could have drawn a tale from the welter of material I found without the help of Ed Brennan, who took me under his wing to "teach me the business," and of Gene Harmon, Vice President, Corporate Public Affairs at Sears throughout the course of my research. Gene is a learned friend, a deep reader and sensitive student of literature, and a Sears soldier of the post-war years who understood that the singular way of company life he'd chosen was worthy of a chronicling.

I was an eyewitness to many of the events and discussions described at the end of Part II and in all of Part III of *The Big Store.* I used a tape recorder to make a record of what was said along with a notebook in which I wrote down how the scenes looked and felt. I was an employee of Sears at the Hicksville store during the Christmas rush of 1981 described in Chapter 15, "A Christmas at Hicksville," and I would like to thank my supervisor, Milly Morrison, for teaching me a few of her moves and a few lines from the song of the sale.

After Ed Telling decided to cooperate with my research activities in January of 1983, I accumulated over ten thousand pages of single-spaced notes and transcripts drawn from just over three hundred hours of tape recordings and a large cardboard box filled with over a hundred reporter's notebooks. I also collected or was allowed to see many thousands of pages of official documentation provided by Sears.

At Sears, as with most other large companies in recent years, a tremendous amount of corporate activity has been committed to videotape. I was able to view tapes of both large and small meetings that occurred before I arrived on the scene, and for obvious reasons, I found this access to such a vivid historical record an invaluable tool when I reconstructed events such as the Challenge Meetings described in Chapter 10. I also had access to Sears audiotapes, verbatim minutes from meetings, drafts of speeches, interoffice memoranda, internal research documents and surveys, and photographs, and I was able to present long lists of queries to Sears department heads that were invariably answered with a speed and a clarity that was dizzying to a writer used to conducting research from outside the walls of public and private institutions.

Frank Tuma provided me with voluminous written and technological documentation of the career of Joe Moran, the only major figure in this story I never had the opportunity to meet. Aside from the famous White Papers and Frank's notes from Joe's lengthy orations, I studied several hours of videotape in order to glean a sense of the way Joe talked both in large public gatherings and among his intimate associates. Joe's son, Larry Moran, was also very helpful in conveying a loving picture of his father at home.

When I wasn't an eyewitness to an important incident and didn't have access to a video- or audiotape account of it, I relied on interviews with witnesses. One of the advantages of spending over five years on a book was that I could schedule interviews over such long periods of time and thus was able to compare a subject's answers for consistency. I relied heavily on certain key sources, especially the ones whose memories appeared most accurate when compared with written and mechanical records, and the ones who appeared least affected by the bitterness and urgency that characterized the period the book covers.

For all of this, I am sure that some bits of dialogue, physical descriptions, and maybe even some bald facts are not precise in the way I would have wanted them to be.

This is certainly not the fault of the Sears archivist, Lenore Swioskin, who made tireless efforts in my behalf of my quest for accuracy. Donna Peterman, Lew Smith, Ernie Arms, Doug Fairweather, Philo Holland, Vicki Cwiok, Manny Bonayo, Debbie Dowley, and many other public-affairs specialists within the company also helped point me in the direction of the best information.

Other Sears people who assisted me greatly include Lou Fryz, Pat Jamieson, Helen Chisholm, Howard Lasky, Fred Bruning, Steve Thorpe, Bob Greer, Bob Brothers, Forrest Olson, Ed Homer, John Jerrard, Dave Williams, Jim Keller, John Gragnola, Curt Hessler, Don Hughes, Robert Dickson, Prep Lane, Harry Anderson, Bill Grant, John O'Reilly, George Ross, Empson Walker, Dick Strauss, and Ray Ewing. Sears outside directors Julius Rosenwald II, Edgar B. Stern, Jr., Donald H. Rumsfeld, Nancy Clark Reynolds, and Luther H. Foster all spoke with me at various times.

Several current and former CEOs found time to be interviewed. George Keller of Chevron, Bill Hewitt of John Deere, Walter Wriston of Citicorp, George Shinn of First Boston, and Jeffrey C. Kiel, president of Republic Bank of New York, were all gracious in answering questions.

I relied on many outside students of Sears, including Ian Sym-Smith, Jack Cardwell, Jim Goodrich, Andrew Kahr, Walter Loeb, Maggie Gilliam, Helene Maslow, Geoff Boisi, Doug Rice, Frank Richardson, Steve Yahn, Carol Loomis, Bruce Nussbaum, Peter Kaplan, Andy Moore, Perrin Long, and Senator Jake Garn.

This book would have taken many more years to complete if not for the assistance of my researchers: Lisa Decker, Mark Padnos, and Patti Katz; of my ace fact-checker, Linda Williams; and my tireless transcribers and typists, Margaret Schutz and Carolyn Anthony.

Several trusted readers—David Blum, Anita Leclerc, Fred Smoler, and Gene Stone—tackled the first, much longer draft of the manuscript and offered valuable comments. My friend Peter Petre of *Fortune* offered not only a line-by-line analysis of the manuscript, but throughout the years of my work on the book he was always available to provide ideas and encouragement.

My patient editor at Viking, Amanda Vaill, and my literary agent for the past eleven years, Elizabeth McKee, were from the start supportive of the idea of writing something big and (I hope) something dramatic about our business civilization. My dear friends Paul Ringel and Michele

Lorand kept a room in their Chicago home for me for several years, though I told them at first I would be staying only a few weeks.

But no one has been more a part of this book than my wife, Leslie Larson, who day by day and year by year came to know the people in this book as if they were members of our family. Leslie's acute reading of my prose, her energetic charm, her beauty, and, most of all, her love, made all of the work worth it—as did the arrival of our sweet daughter, Chloe, who had the good sense to wait until twelve hours after I finished the first draft of *The Big Store* to come into the world.

Index

├─────────────────────────┤

Advertising Age, 275–76, 375
A. E. Le Page, 277–79, 283
Aeschylus, 75
affirmative action, 138–41
Allen, James, 437
Allstate Insurance Company, x, 26, 71, 131, 147, 196, 197, 210
Allstate Insurance Group, 223, 228–29, 230–32, 240–41, 243, 247, 384–86, 489
Allstate Life Company, 131
American Can Company, 125
American Express Company, 250, 272, 302, 394, 437
American Motors Corporation, 232
American Security Council, 93
Anderson, Bob, 322
Angel, John, 561
Anne Klein, 195
anti-Semitism, 92–95, 363
Atari, 330
AT&T, 139, 140, 233, 507
Audit Transfer Memoranda (ATM) system, 55, 71
Auerbach Will, The, 527

Bacall, Lauren, 194
Bache, Halsey, Stuart, 250

Bacon, Charlie, 56–59, 133–34, 142–43, 147, 166, 171, 208, 216, 313–14, 397, 482, 500, 520–21
"bait-and-switch" selling, 24, 312
Baldwin United, 554
Barrie, James, 199
Bass, William Irwin, 365–69
  as chairman and CEO, Merchant, 566–70
  Eastern Territory run by, 176, 346, 347
  Sears career of, 366–68, 421–22, 442–45, 461–62, 482
  as senior executive vice-president, Field, 346, 347, 352, 357, 397, 399–400, 410–11, 452, 454–55, 476–78
Batogowski, Joe "Bato," 346–47, 411, 413, 418, 442–43, 450–55, 543, 568
  family of, 452
  as planning group member, 100–101, 156, 253–54
  Sears career of, 462–63
Baxter, Bill, 296
Beban, Gary, 543*n*
Bell system, 139
Benson and Rixon, 165, 178
Berle, Adolf, 136

Bernadin, Joseph, Cardinal, 505
Birk, Roger, 269–71, 274, 495
Black and Decker, 53
Boe, Archie, 227, 230–33, 235,
    383–84, 391, 433, 434, 437, 483,
    501, 522, 533, 535, 546, 548
Boisi, Geoff, 282–83, 288, 290–93,
    296
Bombeck, Erma, 101, 346
Booz, Allen & Hamilton, 26, 29
Bozic, Mike, 400
Bradley, Tom, 356–57
Brady, Mathew, 427
Brennan, Bernard F., 164–65, 170,
    369, 473
  Montgomery Ward joined by,
    338–39, 416, 474–75, 498, 537
Brennan, Cindy, 458, 459
Brennan, Donny, 457–58, 461
Brennan, Edward (Edward A.'s
    father), 163, 164, 165, 369,
    471–73
Brennan, Edward A., 160–92,
    213–18, 253–64, 324–59, 401–10
  centralization directed by, 189,
    262
  as chairman and CEO, Merchant,
    223, 253–57, 302–305, 315–16,
    367–70, 383, 395–97, 401–403,
    407–10, 415–22, 441–78, 509–10,
    521–22, 525–38, 544–46
  Challenge Meetings and, 183–205,
    213–17, 263–64, 337, 526–27
  characteristics of, 37, 477, 531
  Courtesy Campaign of, 327–28
  early life of, 163–66, 311, 369,
    473–74, 531
  executive reorganization by, 216,
    253, 255, 343–44, 367–68
  family of, 370, 457–61, 531
  personnel cuts by, 105, 148, 169,
    207–208, 349, 351–54
  as president, 167–92, 213–18, 223,
    561–63, 569–78
  principles enunciated by, 261–62,
    326, 329, 416–17
  promotional programs of, 177–78,
    183, 189, 330
  reading tastes of, 527
  Sears jobs of, 165–66, 201–202

Southern Territory run by, 105,
    148, 339
  store design and, 256–59, 442–43
  Store of the Future campaign of,
    399–422, 451, 526, 529–30,
    573–74
  stores closed by, 354–57, 444
Brennan, Edward J. (Edward A.'s
    son), 458, 459
Brennan, John, 458
Brennan, Katy, 358
Brennan, Linda, 458
Brennan, Lois, 459–60, 473
Brennan, Luke, 164–66, 358
Brennan, Marge, 164–65, 473
Brennan, Sharon, 458–59
Briggs, Rod, 292, 294
Brigham Young University, 226
Brooks, Wiley, 102*n*
Brothers, Bob, 407
Brown, Fran, 480
Brown, Harry, 17, 121
Brown, Paul, 28
Browning, Robert, 128
Bruning, Fred, 357–58, 363–64, 447
Burgess, Bob, 297
Burkholder, M. E. "Burk," 37, 115,
    151, 354, 415, 421–22, 447
Burns, Robert, 496, 556
Burroughs, Edgar Rice, 78
Bushnell, Nolan, 330
"Business Leaders Hall of Fame,"
    142
Business Week, 21, 25, 324–25, 332,
    374, 515, 565
Button, James W., 77, 194, 333
  background of, 35–36, 497
  customers studied by, 35, 325–26
  illness of, 86, 261
  retirement of, 86–87, 216, 403,
    490
  as senior executive vice-president,
    merchandising, 20, 34–36, 38,
    40, 46, 51, 54–56, 60, 71–75, 99,
    401
  Telling's relationship with, 391,
    497–98

Calder, Alexander, 258
California Club, 4, 5, 279

California Savings and Loan, 392
Callaghan, Dick, 382, 523
Caltex, 425
capitalism, 10, 13–14, 93
Cardwell, Jack, 29, 40, 41, 59, 81, 576
Cargill, 234, 236
Carlucci, Frank, 426, 437, 549
Carnegie, Andrew, 142
Carter, Jimmy, 141, 172–73, 174, 426
"Casey at the Bat," 77
Castro, Fidel, 455
Catalogues and Counters (Jeuck), 110, 385n
Chain Store Age, 60, 135, 149, 156, 264, 348
Chairman's Challenge Cup, 414, 417, 419, 422
Challenge Meetings, 183–205, 213–17, 245, 259, 263–64, 337, 510, 526–27
Chandler, Alfred, 16
Château Louise, 85–86, 104
Chevron, 233, 424–26
Chicago Economics Club, 375–76, 389–90, 425
Chicago Sun Times, 65, 70
Chicago Tribune, 13, 134, 432
Christmas selling season, 70, 98, 102, 146–47, 264, 303–23, 544–45
Chrysler Corporation, 121, 141
Citicorp, 394
Civil Rights Act (1964), 139
Cody, John, Cardinal, 504, 505
Coldwell Banker, 277–85, 292–97, 381–83, 434–36
  Sears' acquisition of, 297, 299–300, 302, 324, 374, 381
Commission on Money and Credit, 376
COMSAT General, 236–38
Consolidated Foods, 59
Control Data Corporation, 231
Corning Glass, 265
Coulter, Tom, 65
Council on Wages and Price Stability, 141
Craib, Donald, Sr., 20, 22, 197, 385

Craib, Donald F., Jr., 197, 212, 241, 245, 252, 277, 384–86, 438, 490, 522, 534–36
Crain Communications, 275
Crain's Chicago Business, 101, 102n, 119, 435, 541
Crawford, Joan, 194
Credit Control Act (1969), 173
Cressap, McCormick and Paget, 29
Cricket Club, 103–104, 110, 122, 144, 175, 216
Cunningham, Harry, 23
Cushman, Austin "Joe," 15, 306, 503
Customs Bureau (U.S.), 265

Daley, Richard J., 504, 505
Danhauer, Danny, 415
Davies, Al, 16, 18, 50, 215, 410, 518
Davis, Bruce, 313–14
Dayton Hudson, 256
Dean Witter Financial Services Group, 379–81, 392, 429–30, 434–36, 511–17, 538–41, 553–54
Dean Witter Reynolds, 272–77, 285–92, 295–300, 302, 374
DeBartolo Development Group, 448, 524
Deere, John, 234
Deere & Company, 233–36, 265, 271
de Gaulle, Charles, 491
Depository Institutions Deregulation Act (1980), 376
Derek, Bo, 194
DieHard batteries, 229, 320, 405–406
Dillon, Read, 250
Dimma, William, 277, 279
"Discover Card," 585
Disney, Walt, 234
"Dixie Progress," 33
Doering, Otto, 360n
Donough, Stan, 30
Drucker, Peter, 13, 41–42
Duggan, "Hollywood Joe," 343, 344, 345, 351, 357
Dulski, Norbert "Norb," 507–508

Early Retirement Incentive Plan (ERIP), 206–19, 246, 362–63

economic recession (1973–74),
    24–25, 46
E. F. Hutton, 271–72
Eisenhower, Dwight D., 13
Encyclopædia Britannica, 230
Equal Employment Opportunity
    Commission, 138–40, 362, 500,
    585

Fahd, King of Saudi Arabia, 441–42
Federal Express, 231
Federal Home Loan Bank Board,
    431, 432, 553
Federal Home Loan Mortgage
    Corporation (Freddie MACS),
    246
Federal National Mortgage
    Association, 435
Federal Reserve, 173, 301
Federal Trade Commission:
    "bait-and-switch" tactics charged
        by, 24
    deceptive advertising charged by,
        141
Fed Marts, 359
Ferris, Dakin, 270
Financial Services Advisory
    Committee, 393–94
Financial Services Group, 299
financial-services industry, 239–50
Financial Services Planning
    Committee, 380
Financial Times (London), 375
Fiorelli, Ralph, 194, 421
First Boston Corporation, 426
First Boston Securities, 396
First Chicago Corporation, 428
First Interstate Bancorp, 439
Fitzgerald, Greg, 270
599 funds, *see* Parent slush fund
Flom, Joseph, 235
Forbes, 72–73, 136
Ford, Gerald, 267, 426
Ford, Henry, 142, 360*n*
Fortrell, 53
Fortune, 13, 15, 32, 35–36, 135–37,
    174, 196, 348
Fraunces Tavern, 90, 117, 133, 251,
    299, 374

Freeman, Moe, 165–66
Freud, Sigmund, 195
Fryz, Lou, 527–28, 570, 571

Gallagher President's Report, 112,
    375, 546, 565
Galloway, Pat, 567
"Garden of Persephone, The"
    (Swinburne), 77
Gardiner, Elizabeth, 285
Gardiner, Robert M. "Stretch," 388,
    429–30, 559–60, 570
    as CEO, Financial Services Group,
        379–81, 522
    as Dean Witter officer, 273–75,
        284–87, 292–93, 296–97,
        299–300
Garn, Jake, 553
Garn–St Germain Depository
    Institutions Act (1982), 431–32
General Electric, 139
General Motors, 139, 421
Getting Acquainted, 319
G.I. Bill, 140
Glass–Steagall Banking Reform Act
    (1933), 242, 249, 377, 431–32
Goebbels, Joseph, 93
Goethals, George, 12
Goldman, Henry, 249
Goldman, Sachs, 249, 265, 282–83,
    292, 380
Goldstein, Al, 107, 124–25, 156
Gorter, Jim, 249
Graham, Vince, 218
Gray, Gordon, 279, 294
Great Depression, 4, 34, 41, 167,
    173*n*, 175, 228, 240, 435
Grindley's, 428
Gross National Product, vii, 15
Gudeman, Eddie, 93–95, 97
Gurnee, Bob, 550

Harmon, Gene, 139, 171, 403, 483,
    502
Harper, Charlie, 483, 561, 563
Harvard Business Club of Chicago,
    556–58
Harvard Business School, 17, 82, 83,
    262, 279

Harvard University, 93, 126
Haselton, Forrest R. "Woody,"
    343–44, 350–52, 362, 365–66,
    370
Hassler, Dick, 573
Hawkins, Gertrude, 269
Hawkins, Johnny, 358
Hay Associates, 25–29, 37–41, 60
Hay Committee, Corporate, 28–29,
    37–40, 54, 60, 73–74, 79, 81,
    91–92, 105, 160, 170–71, 180,
    263
Haystacks (Monet), 6, 333
Hayward, Susan, 194
"Headquarters Merchandising Plan,"
    87–88, 95–96, 101, 107, 147, 275
Hecht, Fred, 193
Hedien, Wayne, 543
"Heidelberg Belt," 10
Heller, Irv, 573
Hessler, Curt, 428
Hewitt, William, 235–36
Hiden, Bob, 298
Hills, Carla, 267, 278, 279, 389, 425,
    550
Hills, Roderick Maltman, 472, 474,
    547–52
  acquisitions sought by, 268,
    269–70, 271–72, 273, 276–79,
    280–99, 390, 424–28, 433–34,
    437–40
  as chairman of Sears World Trade,
    391, 423–29, 496–97, 547
  firing of, 548, 551
  Telling's relationship with, 265–68,
    276–77, 389–90, 392, 423–24,
    438, 496–97, 534, 550–52
Hitler, Adolf, 92–93
Holbrook, Hal, 436
Holsinger, Wayne, 95–96, 106,
    123–24, 193–95, 414–15, 416,
    421–22, 446n
Homart, 47, 247, 523–24
Hope, Bob, 449, 504
Hopper, Hedda, 412
Household International
    Corporation, 537
Houser, Ted, 94–95
Howard, Bob, 198

Hudson River School, 333–34
Hyatt Regency O'Hare Hotel, 150

IBM, 82, 208, 233, 336, 408, 507
Illinois Wesleyan, 44, 111–12
Independent Bankers Association of
    America, 540
Individual Retirement Account
    (IRA), 208
Industrial Design, 574
inflation, 172–73, 210, 229, 305
Ingraham, Garland, 187, 191,
    198–201, 204, 208, 218, 403
Inside Retailing, 158, 536–37,
    538
Institutional Investor, 131
International Brotherhood of
    Teamsters, 361
International Harvester, 121, 141,
    234
Investors Diversified Services, 437
Ireson, Claude, 259, 262, 331, 336,
    344, 345–46, 347, 406–407, 417,
    443, 451, 452, 462, 523
ITT, 141
Iue, Kaoru, 413

Jackson, Jesse, 140
Jackson, Kate, 194
Jamieson, Pat, 143, 295–96, 479,
    564–65
J. C. Penney, 67, 230, 444
  catalog of, 156
  financial services of, 432
  Sears vs., 23, 72, 124, 191, 253,
    260, 302, 326, 335, 453–54,
    538
Jefferson, Thomas, 244
Jeuck, John, 385n–86n
Johnson, Bob, 363
Johnson, Lady Bird, 308
Johnson, Lyndon, 152
Jones, Richard, 134, 176, 212, 270,
    296, 367, 386–88, 434, 437,
    438–39, 482, 496–97, 522, 534,
    563
Joy, Cliff, 96, 573
Junior Achievement, 141–42
Justice Department (U.S.), 296

Index

Kahr, Andrew, 242, 248, 249, 269
Kay, Vlad, 573
Keane, John, 37, 38–39, 437
Keller, George, 425
Keller, Jim, 272, 274
Kellstadt, Charlie, 21, 33, 56, 501
Kellwood Corporation, 33, 124
Kelly, Jack, 151–57, 198–99, 213–15,
    218–19, 333, 403, 498
Kenmore products, 239, 311, 455
Kennedy, Cul, 22, 50, 369, 502
Kennedy, Edward M., 375
Kennedy, John F., 152
Kennedy, Robert F., 366n
Keynes, John Maynard, 35, 240
Kincannon, Jack, 60, 89, 91, 130–35,
    144, 160, 176, 208, 212–13, 216,
    218, 227, 230–32, 234–35, 237,
    243, 245–46, 382, 482
King, Martin Luther, Jr., 306, 364
K mart, 23, 32, 55, 67, 358
    credit card dropped by, 173
    growth rate of, 210, 326
    Sears vs., 72, 124, 191, 227, 253,
        260, 302, 335, 407, 538
Knowlton, Hugh, 293
Knox, Phil, 482, 483, 563
Korba, Harry, 481–82, 501, 562
Korvettes, 159, 321–23
Kresge chain, 23, 264

Labor Department (U.S.), 140, 207
Ladd, Cheryl, 194
L'Ami du Peuple, 129
Lasky, Howard, 354–57, 367
Lasorda, Tommy, 110, 494
Latham, Wadkins, and Hills, 267,
    390
Lee, Helen, 170
Lehman Brothers, 95
Leighton, George N., 137–38
Lewis, Sandy, 268
Lifetime Income for the Years
    Ahead, 117
Lincoln, Abraham, 11, 427
Lincoln National, 232
Lindbergh, Charles, 93
Lives of American Merchants, 109
Lochmoeller, Bill, 215, 254–55,
    343–44

Lockheed, 141
Loeb, Walter, 260, 396, 529, 531
Logan, "Pop," 486–87, 488, 493
Loomis, Carol, 136–37
Lord & Taylor, 453
Los Angeles Times, 121
Lovelace, Richard, 77
Lowe, John, 50, 58, 72, 108, 115,
    117, 254
    company rise of, 3–4, 13, 20, 66
    Far Western Territory run by,
        4–8, 16, 18, 22, 51, 63, 67, 92,
        115, 313, 355, 360
    Midwest Territory run by, 148,
        354
    personal style of, 5, 60, 63
    retirement of, 148, 212, 216
    Telling's transfer of, 7–8, 62–63,
        65, 213, 324, 490, 499

McCarthy, Joseph R., 93
McCue, John, 119
McDonald's, 401–402
McKinsey & Company, 29–32,
    40–42, 47, 50–51, 56, 59, 67–69,
    82, 99, 196, 226, 327
McLellan, Lloyd, 218
Marat, Jean Paul, 129, 418
Marin, Don, 271
Marquette University, 165
Martin, Preston, 196, 246–48, 277,
    281, 300–301, 435
Marx, Mortie, 165–66, 528
Maslow, Helene, 334
Maxims for Revolution (Shaw), 476
May Company, 13
Mead, Margaret, 209
Means, Gardiner, 136
Melton, Andrew, Jr., 273–76,
    284–300, 379–80, 538–39
Merchandise Policy Committee
    (MPC), 156
Merrill, Charlie, 268, 286
Merrill Lynch, 242, 249, 268–72,
    276, 394, 430, 437
Metcalf, Gordon, 17–18, 22–23, 27,
    47, 135, 139, 231, 449, 489, 502,
    503, 504–505
Meyer, Charles, 19–20, 29, 32, 47,
    55, 60, 94n, 134, 143, 203, 211,

218, 227, 232, 236, 243, 246,
    470–71, 482, 498
Meyer, Martin, 241
Michelin, François, 471
Miller, Johnny, 195
Miller, Steve, 543
Miller-Tydings Act, 406
Missouri, U.S.S., 136
MITI (Japan), 266
Mitsubishi, 390
Mitsui, 390
Monet, Claude, 6, 61, 333
Montgomery Ward, 230, 545
    ex-Sears employees at, 95, 97,
        338–39, 416, 474, 498, 537
    Sears vs., 23, 67, 72, 210, 302, 326,
        335, 538
Moody's Investor Services, 210–211,
    302
Moran, Charley, 81, 83, 434, 437,
    482, 496, 513, 550
Moran, Joseph T., Jr. "Jumpin' Joe,"
    37–39, 73–92, 252–54, 261–63,
    326, 330–41, 451–52
    advertising cuts by, 149, 175–76
    catalog criticized by, 151–56
    characteristics of, 75–78, 96, 100,
        125–26, 143, 147, 150–51, 154
    family of, 75, 125–26, 334–35,
        340–41
    "Four Myths of Management"
        outlined by, 122, 137
    heart attack of, 154
    illness and death of, 332–35,
        337–38, 340–41, 345, 346, 455
    "Medicare visits" of, 77, 149–50
    memos by, 78–79, 80, 83–84, 97,
        100–101, 122, 127, 129, 137,
        143, 157, 183
    prose style of, 78–79, 80, 83–84,
        87–88, 97, 101, 127
    reading tastes of, 75, 76–77
    terror campaign of, 122–29,
        153–54, 169
    as vice president, merchandise
        groups, 79, 83–88, 92, 95–98,
        108–109, 110–11, 122–30
    vice-presidents under, 99,
        104–106, 108–109, 122, 127–28
Moran, Larry, 334–35

Moran, Margie Lou, 125–26, 334–35,
    341, 573
Moran, Peggy Lou, 340–41
Morgan, Charles, 140
Morgan, Jack, 311–12
Morgan, Ted, 573
Morgan Stanley & Company, 260,
    396, 529, 531–32
Murtaugh, Tom, 290–91
Museum of Science and Industry
    (Chicago), 164

National Image Survey, 325, 327
National Organization for Women,
    114, 211
NCR, 82, 408
Neal, Tom, 464, 467
Needham, Harper, Steers, 401
New Deal, 240
Newsweek, 245, 375
New York Society of Financial
    Analysts, 90
New York Times, 65, 78, 116, 211,
    253, 307, 324, 421, 491, 546
Nixon, Richard, 246
Notre Dame University, 126

Office of the Chairman, The
    (sculpture), 110
Officer Friendly Program, 141
Oliver, Lou, 17
Olson, Forrest E., 282–84, 292, 294,
    382, 388, 543
One Minute Manager, 527
OPEC, 425
Organization Man, The (Whyte), 13
"overbilling," 53–54, 71

PaineWebber, 248, 271, 395
Palmer, Potter, 5
Panama Canal, 12
"Parent slush fund (599)," 53–54,
    70–71, 72, 79–80, 84–85, 88, 90,
    97, 99, 153
Peabody Coal, 267
Peale, Norman Vincent, 183
Pearce, Harold, 120
People's Choice, The, 230
Perma-Prest, 53
Peter Pan (Barrie), 199

Pinola, Joseph, 439
Pistner, Stephen, 338
Plato, 333
PMI, 246–47, 435
Poulson, C. Wesley, 278–86, 292–95,
    381–83, 388, 434, 512, 522–25,
    559–60
Power of Positive Thinking (Peale),
    183
"Power Plus 80" program, 176–77
Practice of Management, The
    (Drucker), 13
Price, Saul, 525
Price, Vincent, 195
Priest, Dick, 187
Procter & Gamble, 175
Proposition 13 (California), 115
Prudential-Bache, 272, 302, 437
Prudential Insurance Company,
    250
Purcell, Anne McNamara, 69, 225,
    392
Purcell, Evan, 225–26
Purcell, Phillip, 92, 123, 162, 177,
    180, 254, 262, 270, 330, 376–77,
    468, 476, 570–71
  acquisitions and, 271, 274–79,
    281–83, 288, 289
  background of, 69, 126, 225
  family of, 148, 538
  as managing director, McKinsey,
    29–32, 34, 36–37, 38, 40–42, 66,
    100–101, 121, 124
  as president and COO, Dean
    Witter, 392–93, 429–31, 433–34,
    438–39, 482, 538–44, 553–56
  Sears' position accepted by, 67–69,
    490
  Telling's relationship with, 50, 59,
    63, 112, 132, 136, 143, 148–49,
    166, 224, 248, 346, 376, 434
  as vice-president for planning, 68,
    73, 79, 81–87, 149–50, 179, 181,
    223–29, 232–39, 241, 243–44,
    246–49, 251, 268, 354

Queen Mary, 136, 521
Quint, Ira, 38–39, 54, 73, 80, 86, 97,
    100, 102*n*, 156, 170, 311, 333,
    339, 416, 465

Rand, Ayn, 527
Reader's Digest, 15
Reagan, Ronald, 246, 301, 347, 426
recession of 1981, 264, 303, 335, 374
Regan, Donald, 268, 271, 273, 375,
    432
Retail Furniture Association, 260
Reynolds Securities, 380
R. H. Macy and Company, 453, 466
Rice, Doug, 550
Richardson, Frank, 290–91
Riesman, David, 5
Roadhandler tires, 53
Robbins, Stu, 395
Roberts, Peter M., 137–38, 140, 374
Rockefeller, John D., 142
Roebuck, Alvah Curtis, 9–10, 565
Rogers, Ginger, 194
Rogers, Mister, 141
Roosevelt, Franklin Delano, 13–14
Roosevelt, Theodore, 194
Roper Reports, 238–39, 374
Rosenwald, Julius "J. R.", 12, 22, 23,
    57, 65, 93–94, 121, 240, 243,
    261, 360*n*
  organizational structure designed
    by, 10, 33, 41, 182
  philanthropy of, 10–11, 164
  policies of, 116, 175, 268, 281
Rosenwald, Lessing, 93, 501
Royko, Mike, 101
Rumsfeld, Donald, 249
Rural Free Delivery, 243

Sadat, Anwar, 295
Safra, Edmond, 428–29, 440
St Germain, Fernand, 553
Sanders, Bill, 482
Sane Sex Life, 195
Sanyo Corporation, 275, 359
Sanyo Electric Company, 412–13
Sardis Luggage Company, 411–12,
    444
Saunders, Eric, 179–81, 189, 336,
    345, 347, 400, 408–409, 447
Save-A-Stop, 339
Schell, Frank, 152, 156, 157, 415
Schreyer, Bill, 270
Schumpeter, Joseph, 159
Schwadron, Jack, 322

Schwinn, Arnold, 33
Scott, George C., 436
Sears, Richard Warren, 21–22, 33,
  57, 84, 175, 243, 268, 316
  banking department established
    by, 239–40, 553
  catalog developed by, 9–10, 514,
    540
  company founded by, xii, 9–10,
    182, 304
  death of, 10
Sears, Roebuck Acceptance
  Corporation, 131–32, 172
Sears, Roebuck and Company:
  accounting system of, 16, 53–54,
    63, 71, 72, 84–85, 348n
  acquisitions considered by,
    232–38, 250, 265, 268–303,
    428–29
  advertising by, 107, 108–109, 141,
    149, 175–76, 243, 286, 401–402,
    436–37
  allegiance to small manufacturers
    by, 91
  annual meetings of, 114–21, 363n
  annual reports of, 262
  anti-Semitism in, 92–95, 363
  anti-union efforts at, 366
  autonomy of management in, x,
    6–7, 12–13, 16, 28, 29, 36, 41,
    45–47, 66
  Bal Harbor conference of,
    102–109
  beginnings of, xi, 9–13
  borrowing by, 132, 240
  budgets of, 82
  business campaigns against,
    540–41
  businesses affiliated with, x–xi, 10,
    16, 26, 33–34, 53, 90–91, 412
  capitalism embodied by, 10, 13–14
  centralization in, 51, 66, 189, 262,
    555
  Christmas selling season at, 70, 98,
    102, 146–47, 264, 303–23,
    544–45
  Coldwell Banker acquired by, 297,
    299–300, 302, 324, 374, 381
  competitors of, 13, 23, 26, 32, 50,
    55, 67, 72, 87, 90, 210, 227

computer technology used by, 28,
    305, 336, 506–10
  consulting firms hired by, 25–32,
    37–41, 50–51, 74
  controversy and dissent
    discouraged by, 28, 40,
    79
  corporate customers of, 82
  corporate size of, vii–viii, 15–16,
    22, 135, 149, 575
  costs vs. profit of, 105
  credit-card system of, vii, 28,
    131–32, 172–74, 201, 248,
    302–303, 314–15
  as cultural warehouse, vii–viii, 11,
    31, 32–33
  customer figures of, vii, 15, 32,
    238, 325
  customer letters to, 121
  customer lists of, 514–16
  customer loyalty to, vii, 12, 32,
    238–39
  customer profile by, 87
  customer surveys by, 35, 87,
    325
  Dean Witter Reynolds acquired
    by, 298–99
  decentralization of authority in,
    12–13, 16–17, 25, 39, 45–47, 92,
    104–105, 120, 253
  decision-making matrix of, 82
  decline of, 23–25, 29, 42, 45, 54,
    59, 69–73, 87, 88, 90, 96, 102,
    121, 157–59, 250–51, 323
  demographics vs. sales at, 228–29
  discrimination charged to, 24, 114,
    138–41, 362–63, 500
  Eastern Territory of, 22, 43–50,
    91–92, 115, 224, 305–306, 344,
    351, 419
  economy affected by, 33
  employees of, *see* Sears employees
  entrepreneurs sought by, 33
  executive business meetings of,
    102–109
  executive privileges at, 99, 103
  executive salaries at, 119, 120
  Far Western Territory of, 4, 5–8,
    13, 16, 20, 63, 67, 115–17,
    342–45, 354–61

Sears, Roebuck (*cont.*)
 Field vs. Parent in, 4, 16, 25, 41,
  51–53, 66, 73, 102–109, 112,
  117, 137, 147–48, 203, 314
 financial services of, 239–41,
  244–50, 490–91, 511–13
 first retail stores of, x, 11
 five territories of, x, 13, 16–17, 25,
  27, 37, 40, 51, 103
 foreign stores of, 455–57
 free market system within, 16
 grapevine within, 65, 69, 143, 213,
  259, 396, 581
 Great American Company
  concept of, 223–51, 268, 493,
  548–49, 564
 "hard" vs. "soft" products of,
  310–11
 Hicksville store of, 304–23, 544
 interior store design of, 256–59
 as "Jewish family firm," 93
 layoffs at, viii, 24, 46, 105, 169,
  349, 351–54
 litigation involving, 121, 137–41,
  265–66, 362, 500
 logo of, 574
 losses incurred by, 34, 80, 81–82,
  303
 management selection in, 55–69
 market saturation experienced by,
  23
 middle-class image of, 87
 Midwestern Territory of, 7–8, 17,
  50–51, 63, 65, 105
 as model of progressive
  management, 13–14
 "Modern Homes" division of,
  230
 motto of, 399
 non-firing policy of, 7, 14, 37
 old-fashioned style of, 27, 30–31,
  36–37, 40–41, 42, 65–66
 organizational study commissioned
  by, 25–42, 50, 56, 74
 "People's Book Club" of, 230
 personnel department of, 138,
  139, 141, 313
 planning department of, 81–83,
  97–98, 100, 228, 231–32,
  245–46, 468

 pocket watch first product sold by,
  xi, 9, 304
 press coverage of, 101, 133–38
 pricing systems of, 84, 85, 88, 98,
  154, 228, 336n
 private brands of, 229, 239, 311,
  320, 405–406, 455
 product development by, 33–34,
  124, 137–38
 product range sold by, vii, 9–10,
  23, 32–33, 82–83, 106, 151, 186,
  263
 profit margins vs. sales volume at,
  228
 profit-sharing plan of, viii, 14,
  39–40, 113, 116–18
 promotion from within policy of,
  x, 14–15, 34, 67–68
 public image of, 135, 137
 public purpose of, vii, 13, 36–37,
  87, 121, 190, 240
 research department of, 35, 70,
  229, 325–26
 retail stores growth in, 11–12,
  34
 retirement program at, 115–18,
  206–19, 246, 362–63
 Roman Catholic Church compared
  with, 39, 531
 rumors as communication in, 122,
  157–58
 rural vs. urban customers of, 11,
  135
 sales figures of, 4, 16, 24, 29, 52,
  54, 59, 70–72, 87, 90, 102, 141,
  147, 255–56, 260, 335
 sales promotions of, 55, 59, 69–71,
  80, 84, 85, 87, 88, 108–109,
  176–77, 183–85, 189, 260, 316
 secrecy in, xi–xii, 26, 27, 102n,
  325
 selloff debacle of 1977–78 at,
  69–72, 80
 shoplifting at, 316–17
 shopping malls anchored by, 23,
  159, 307
 slush fund of, 53–54, 70–71, 72,
  79–80, 84–85, 88, 97, 99, 153
 small stores vs., 23, 227
 Southern Territory of, 17, 105

Southwest Territory of, 16, 216, 254–55
stock prices and dividends of, viii, 7, 15, 29, 69–70, 90, 113, 116–18, 214, 349
structure of, x–xii, 11, 12–13, 16–17, 25, 27, 29–30
suburban growth around stores of, 11, 15
war veterans attracted to, 12–13, 44, 76, 81, 140
washing-machine business at, 83
wearing apparel from, 163, 166, 445–46
Sears Catalog, 151–56
cities associated with, 114
competitors of, 156
cultural importance of, 9, 11, 13–14, 152
decline of, 11, 123, 198
experiments with, 252
Kelly's management of, 151–57, 198–99
models featured in, 194
plants and outlets for, viii, 4, 11, 47, 115, 153, 302, 360–61
retail stores sales vs., 11, 153
Richard Sears development of, 9–10, 514, 540
Rosenwald's use of, 10–11, 68
sales generated by, 153, 198
writing of, 9–10, 78, 151, 152
Sears employees, 97–98, 304–23
blacks as, 138–41, 363, 364
bonuses of, 30, 85
buyers creativity at, 32–34
buyers importance as, 73, 76–77, 85, 122–29, 153
catalog-staff, 151–54
characteristics of, 30–31
company communication with, 327–28
earnings of, 13, 30, 313–14
employment figures on, x, 4, 15, 17, 23, 25, 105
esprit de corps of, 12, 13–15
hiring of, 318–19
layoffs of, viii, 24, 46, 105, 169, 349, 351–54

loyalty of, 13–14, 42, 62, 122, 128–29
merchants vs. operators as, 31–32, 47–48
mobility of, 14–15, 62, 78, 369–70
morale of, 27, 169, 260, 581
part-time, 319–20, 328
pensions of, 113
profit-sharing of, viii, 14, 39–40, 113, 116–18
retired, 114–21
salesmen vs. buyers as, 25, 27, 31
small town image of, 5, 28
surveys taken of, 27, 49
war veterans as, 12–13, 44, 76, 81, 140
women as, 24, 139, 319, 362–63
Sears Headquarters (West Side), ix, x, 16, 19, 52, 164
Sears Investment Management, 231
Sears Merchandise Group, 223, 253, 255–56, 260, 262, 335–36, 389, 400, 421, 468, 474–75, 566, 577
Sears Pension Fund, 231
Sears Today, 219, 328, 416
Sears Tower, 504–18
building of, vii, 21–22, 24, 50, 135
corporate suite in, 109–10, 255
employees' reaction to, 257–59
symbolic effect of, 135–36, 255, 348
Sears U.S. Government Money Market Trust, 275
Sears World Trade Company, 390–91, 426–27, 437–40, 496–97, 548, 551
Securities and Exchange Commission, 265, 267, 275
Seeger Corporation, 33
Sellers, Wallace, 270–71
Senate Banking Committee, 541, 553
Seraco Real Estate Group, 223, 240, 246–47, 294, 300–301
702-P (planning group), 81–83, 85, 87, 100, 154
Sharp, Dick, 277, 279
Shaw, George Bernard, 476
Shearer, Norma, 194
Shearson, Loeb, Rhoades, 250, 272

Shefferman, Nathan, 366*n*
Shinn, George, 426, 439
Shultz, George, 110, 494
Simpson-Sears Limited, 277, 456
Singer Company, 90, 275
Sloane, Alfred, 142, 421
Smith, Art, 165–66
Smith Barney, 286–87
Social Security, 116
Sogo Shosha, 390–91
Spender, Stephen, 340
Spooner, James, 428
Sports Illustrated, 194
SRI International, 241–44, 248, 272,
    301
Standard & Poor's Corporation, 174,
    210–11, 396
Standard Oil of California, 233, 424
Standard Oil of Indiana, 167
State Farm Mutual Insurance
    Company, 229
Stearns, Russell, 94
Stein, Clem, 340–41
Stern, Edgar, 121, 158, 237–38, 501,
    520, 559–60
"Store of the Future" campaign,
    399–422, 451, 526, 529–30,
    573–74
Struthers, George, 20, 261
Sullivan and Cromwell, 297–98
Sunderland, Henry, 66–67, 114–15,
    117, 118, 135, 143, 166, 254,
    336, 343–44, 345, 347, 361, 362,
    397, 400, 482, 483, 514, 547,
    563
Swanson, Gloria, 194
Swift, Dean, 22, 40, 49, 56–60,
    64–65, 107, 160–61, 168, 403
Swinburne, Algernon, 77
Swing, Joseph, 75
Sylvan, Yvonne, 119
Sym-Smith, Ian, 27–29, 30, 32,
    37–39, 40, 60, 73–74, 465,
    491–92

Telling, Albert, 485
Telling, Cole, 494
Telling, Edward, Sr., 485–86
Telling, Edward Riggs, 3–4, 18, 22,
    43–52, 373–98, 479–503

board chairman appointment of,
    ix, 6, 58–66, 74, 76, 79–80, 88,
    95, 99–101, 227
business relationships of, 142–45,
    219, 265–70, 273–75, 288–89,
    389–90, 423–26, 483–84, 494–98,
    547–48
Chicago Economics Club speech
    of, 375–76, 389–90, 425
criticism of, 112–13, 136, 212–13
early life of, 484–88
earnings of, 119, 120, 493–94, 565
Eastern Territory run by, 22, 43,
    45–50, 60, 80, 488–89
education of, 43–44, 111, 484–85
expansion and diversification led
    by, 223–24, 233–35, 244–51,
    276–78, 303, 324, 378, 393
family of, 110, 142, 488
Harvard Business Club speech of,
    556–58
honors awarded to, 111–12,
    556–60
Lowe transferred by, 7–8, 62–63,
    65, 213, 324, 490, 499
Midwestern Territory run by, 7–8,
    50–51, 62–63, 65, 105, 148, 151,
    324, 490
personal style of, xi, 5, 43, 47–49,
    52, 56–59, 68, 80, 89, 92, 108,
    109–10, 112–13, 144–45, 224,
    373–75, 377–78, 476–77, 480,
    491–92, 552
reading tastes of, 110, 111, 113,
    495–96
restructuring policies of, 45–48,
    50–51, 55, 58, 65, 67–70, 72–73,
    75, 83, 85, 90–91, 102–104, 117,
    223–24, 226–27, 491
retirement of, 559–66
retirement plan approved by,
    207–13
retirement postponed by, 519–23
as senior executive vice-president,
    Field, 51–52, 55–63, 66, 104
74th annual meeting and, 117–21
shareholder criticism of, 119–21
stores closed by, 45, 46
Telling, George, 485
Telling, John, 485

Telling, Nancy Hawkins, 43–44, 110, 143, 289, 375, 460, 486, 488, 493, 550
Texaco, 425
Texas Instruments Corporation, 82
Thomas, Stu, 37, 461, 466–67, 470, 554
Thomas Aquinas, Saint, 75
Thompson, Bob, 95–96, 415, 422
Thorpe, Steve, 352
Thurstone, L. L., 318
Tiegs, Cheryl, 193–95, 260, 307–308, 318, 445, 446n, 565
Time, 13, 22, 308, 565–66, 573–74
Tinker, Grant, 236
Tippet, Bob, 37
Toughskins blue jeans, 53
Toys-R-Us, 124
Treasury Department (U.S.), 265, 541
Tudor, Wally, 27–28, 48, 58, 60, 138, 361
Tuma, Frank, 96–97, 122–25, 127–28, 155, 171, 176, 334, 337, 417–18

Urban League, 138

Veblen, Thorstein, 394
Volcker, Paul, 432, 552
von Furstenberg, Diane, 184–85, 195

Wachtell, Lipton, Rosen & Katz, 297
Waddle, John, 390, 426
Wall Street Journal, 49, 143, 207, 212, 245–46, 295, 347, 411, 480, 538, 546, 559, 571
Wal-Mart, 568
Walt Disney Productions, 233, 234–36, 238
Walton, Sam, 568
Wands, Tom, 103, 108, 482
Warwick Electronics, 412
Washington, Booker T., 11
Washington, Harold, 505
Washington Post, 137–38, 551
Weber, Max, 568–69
Weinberg, Sidney, 93
Weiner, Steve, 571

Welch, Jack, 473
Wendy's, 232
Wharton School of Business, 27
Wheeler, Linden, 28, 218
Whirlpool Corporation, 33, 39, 90, 275, 413
White Consolidated, 413
Whitman, Walt, 304, 317, 323
Whyte, William, 13
Williams, David, 231–32, 241, 249
Williams, Ted, 31, 195
Winski, Joseph, 341
Winters, George, 119–20
Witter, Dean, 273
WLS radio station, 230
Wood, Arthur, 70, 71, 94, 207, 333
    affirmative action espoused by, 139, 183
    ascension through the ranks of, 20–21, 385
    background of, 5–6, 21
    board chairmanship of, 4, 5–6, 21–22, 55–65, 68, 101, 223
    consulting firms hired by, 25–32, 37–41, 50–51, 74
    leadership of, 26, 27–30, 40, 41, 49–51
    personal style of, 21, 25, 35, 36, 51, 57, 61
    policies of, 22, 24, 139
Wood, Robert E., II, 81, 100, 151, 346
Wood, Robert E. "General," 15, 33
    background of, 12
    characteristics of, 76, 93–95, 110
    death of, 18, 20, 115
    Eastern Territory neglected by, 44–45
    economic principles of, 130, 132, 240
    honors awarded, 141–42
    leadership of, 4, 11–13, 18–20, 25, 34, 39, 41, 61, 65–66, 90, 148, 209–10, 471, 537
    mergers considered by, 230
    "On to Chicago" campaign of, 182–83, 209–10, 213–14
    policies of, 7, 12–13, 16, 18, 22, 25, 28, 29, 47, 55, 58, 66, 93–94, 112, 116–17, 120, 148, 455

Wood, Robert E. (*cont.*)
  retirement of, 17–18, 19, 94
  tall executives preferred by, 4–5,
    19–20, 21, 27, 32, 61
Woods, Woody, 573
Woolco, 359
World War II, 41, 44, 76
  store growth after, 12, 33, 70, 93,
    147
Wriston, Walter, 240–41, 301–302,
  495
W. T. Grant, 159, 322
Wurmstedt, Charles Christian, 37,
  61–63, 65, 72, 74, 90, 98–100,

  103–108, 110–11, 113, 131, 133,
  137, 143, 147–50, 153–54, 162,
  171, 175–76, 181, 187–88,
  191–92, 199–200, 204–206, 208,
  210, 215–19, 254–55, 354, 387,
  397, 482, 490, 499
Wyeth, Andrew, 195

"yellow book," 87–88, 95–96, 101,
  107, 147, 275

Zalusky, Jim, 573
Zenith Corporation,
  265